RENAISSANCE ARCHITECTURE

Classic Architecture
Volume 2

Gene Waddell

Printed on demand by CreateSpace.com

2017

CONTENTS

Volume 2: Renaissance Architecture

Preface, 5

15. Early Renaissance Architecture, 10
    Renaissance Art History, 12
    Renaissance Men, 15
    Renaissance Design Principles, 23
    Architectural Problems, 29
    Why the Renaissance Began in Florence, 30
    Florence's Cathedrals, 39
    Brunelleschi, 46
        Dome of the Duomo, Florence (1420-1436), 46
        San Lorenzo, Florence (1421-1460), 54
        Other Buildings, 57
    Ghiberti, 62
    Alberti, 77
        Writings, 77
        Documented Churches, 86-90
            Sant'Andrea, Mantua (1465-1494), 90-91
            Santissima Annunziata, Florence (1470-1473), 92-93
            San Francisco, Rimini (1450-1461),
            San |Sebastiano, Mantua (1470-1472),
            Santa Maria Novella, Florence (dated 1470), 90
        Undocumented Buildings in Rome (attributions), 95
        Development of the Unaisled Church, 102
        Choir of St. Peter's Basilica (c. 1451-1455), 104

16. Renaissance Palaces and Villas, 105
    Palaces, 108
        Palazzo Medici, Florence (1445-1460), 108
            Renaissance Libraries, 114
            Cosimo de' Medici's Patronage, 116
        Palazzo Strozzi, Florence (1489-1538), 127
        Pitti Palace, Florence (begun 1458), 129
        Palazzo Rucellai, Florence (1446-1451), 132
        Ducal Palace, Urbino (1465-1482), 133
        Cancelleria, Rome (1486-1498), 141
        Palazzo Venezia, Rome (1455-1471), 144
        Attributions Based on Classical Details, 146
        Palazzo Caprini (House of Raphael), Rome (begun 1509), 148
        Palazzo Massimo, Rome (1532-c. 1536), 151
        Palazzo Farnese, Rome (1530-1589), 155

Villas, 164
- Lorenzo de' Medici's Villas, 164
- Villa Farnesina (Chigi), Rome (1505-1511), 176
- Villa Madama, Rome (begun 1518), 181
- Villa d'Este, Tivoli (1549-1572), 185
- Palazzo Farnese, Caprarola (begun 1558), 187
- Villa Giulia, Rome (1551-1555), 188

Sansovino, 190
Summary, 192

17. Palladio, 197

Four Books on Architecture (1570), 203

Villas, 205
- Villa Foscari, Gambarare (1558-1561), 205
- Villa Rotunda, Vicenza (1566-1567), 210
- Villa Pisani, Montagnana (1552-1554), 212
- Villa Cornaro, Piombino Dese (1552-1554), 214
- Villa Saraceno, Finale di Agugliaro (1545), 216

Palaces, 219
- Palazzo Porto, Vicenza (1547-1552), 219
- Palazzo Valmarana, Vicenza (1565), 222
- Palazzo Thiene, Vicenza (1542-1546), 224
- Palazzo Chiericati, Vicenza (1550), 226

Churches and Related Buildings, 227
- Carità, Venice (begun c 1561), 227
- San Giorgio Maggiore, Venice (1560-c. 1610), 230
- Il Redentore, Venice (1577-1592), 234

Other Building Types, 239
- Basilica, Vicenza (1546-1549), 239
- Teatro Olympico, Vicenza (1580), 240

18. Bramante and Michelangelo Before St. Peter's, 241

Bramante, 242
- Bramante's Early Life, 243
- Bramante in Rome, 250
- Courtyard of Santa Maria della Pace, Rome (1500-c. 1504), 251
- Tempietto, Rome (c. 1502-c. 1506), 255
- Belvedere Courtyard, Rome (begun 1505), 257
- Vatican Palace, 261
- Santa Maria della Consolazione, Todi (begun c. 1508), 264

Michelangelo, 266
- Tomb of Julius II, Rome (1505-1545), 268
- Sistine Chapel Ceiling, Rome (1508-1512), 278
- Designs for the Front of San Lorenzo, Florence (1517-1520), 292
- Michelangelo's Study of Ancient Roman Architecture, 303
- Medici Chapel, Florence (1522-1534), 307
- Laurentian Library, Florence (1524-1534), 323
- Patronage of Leo X and Clement VII, 334
- Capitol, Rome (1537-1654), 336
- Michelangelo's Working Methods, 345

Secular Renaissance, 353
　　　Athens, Rome, and Florence, 369

19. Michelangelo's Design for St. Peter's, 371
　　　Bramante's Designs for St. Peter's (from 1505-1514), 376
　　　Stages of Construction for St. Peter's (from c. 1532-c. 1569), 383
　　　Bramante's Intended Dome, 389
　　　Bramante's Apprentices, (from 1514-1546), 391
　　　　　Raphael (from 1514-1520), 393
　　　　　Peruzzi (from 1520-1527), 398
　　　　　Sangallo (from 1520-1546), 400
　　　Michelangelo's Designs for St. Peter's (from 1547-1564), 403
　　　　　Michelangelo's Plans, 406
　　　　　Michelangelo's Dome, 410
　　　　　Michelangelo's Intentions, 424
　　　　　Designs for San Giovanni de' Fiorentini, Rome (1550-1559), 428
　　　　　Cupolas for St. Peter's, 435
　　　　　Michelangelo's Designs for the Front of St. Peter's, 437
　　　　　Attic Story Intended for St. Peter's, 443
　　　　　Summary on the Design of St. Peter's, 447

Conclusion, 449

Appendices, 451
　　　I. Outline of Italian Architecture from Julius II to Alexander VII, 451
　　　II. Vasari's Prefaces, 453
　　　III. Latin Literature and the Latin Church: the Survival of Knowledge During the Medieval Period, 473
　　　IV. Greek and Latin Classics Printed by Aldus Manutius, 500
　　　V. Chronological List of Principal Buildings, 516
　　　VI. Locations of Principal Buildings, 519
　　　VII. Glossary, 522

Bibliography, 533

Topical Index, 553

Preface

During most of the history of architecture, architects had to be artists, engineers, and scholars. This three-volume series of books is about what architects needed to know to create the most important buildings in Western Architecture from 600 B. C.-A. D. 1943.

This first volume is about Greek and Roman architecture and the architectural traditions that diverged from the Classic Tradition. The second volume is about the revival of classic architecture during the Renaissance. The third volume is about academic architecture since the Renaissance.

Greek architecture was the first type that continued to be influential indefinitely and beyond the limits of its civilization. Most of the subsequent architecture of Europe was influenced by Greek architecture, but indirectly through Roman architecture.

Rome owed a great debt to many aspects of Greek civilization including language, philosophy, and history as well as architecture and art. Roman art was essentially Greek art, but Roman architecture eventually became fundamentally different in the materials that were used and in its approach to design. The Greeks created the classical Orders and used them to plan and design the exterior of their buildings; the Roman developed the arch and concrete, which enabled spans and spaces of unprecedented size to be created. Greek architecture was more sculptural in its emphasis on exterior form and finish, and Roman architecture was more like engineering in its emphasis on spans and interior space. In general, Greek architecture was designed from the outside in, and Roman architecture from the inside out, but Greek design elements continued to embellish both the interiors and exteriors of Roman buildings.

More specifically, the first volume of this series is about the development of Greek architecture, the influence of Greece on Rome, and the early influence of Rome on other architectural traditions outside the Roman Empire. The second volume is about the revival of Roman architecture and secular thought. The third volume is about the revival of all styles of architecture, their scholarly study by archaeologists and architects, and an increasingly eclectic used of design elements within the framework of the design principles of Classic Architecture.

The greater amount of information that is available on individual Renaissance architects, buildings and patrons enables more detailed consideration to be given to documentation, and less reconstruction is necessary than for Greek and Roman buildings. In particular, Vasari provides an unprecedented amount of biographical information for every major architect and artists in Italy for the two centuries of the Reniassance. The architects whose work is considered in most detail are Brunelleschi, Bramante, Palladio, and Michelangelo. Palladio produced the first major treatise on architecture since Vitruvius, and his *Four Books* had an equivalent influence for centuries together with Vitruvius's *Ten Books.* Two new buildings types developed during the Renaissance, the palazzo and the villa; and the design of both types was profoundly influenced by Palladio. The building site for St. Peter's Basilica was a school for the training several generations of architects, and it became one of the most influential buildings of all time. How its design developed and changed is dealt with in the greatest detail of all. Taken together, the revival of Roman architecture and the new building types of the Renaissance formed the basis for the later and more academic architecture of the Neoclassical and Beaux Arts periods, which are considered in the third volume.

The classic tradition in architecture has determined the overall appearance of most buildings worldwide, and it has done so through the use of a versatile architectural vocabulary, a flexible set of rules, changing building types. Regardless of style, most buildings continue to be characterized by regularly proportioned and spaced design elements that were established through the use of the classical orders.

This series of books discusses how a consistently high standard of excellence was achieved in design and construction over a period of 2,500 years. It includes the following periods of architecture: Greek, Roman, Renaissance, Baroque, Neoclassical, Greek Revival, Italianate, and Beaux Arts. Regardless of the style chosen, architects were in agreement about what constituted excellence. This book considers what all periods and styles have in common and what is most distinctive about each period, style, and major example.

The primary emphasis is on how buildings were designed and constructed. Design processes, materials, and methods of construction are considered in detail. Everything an architect had to consider is discussed for each period and each building type. Every type of knowledge required to create buildings is considered. The ideas of the most influential architects are summarized, particularly those that were widely influential through the publications of Vitruvius, Palladio, Adam, Ledoux, and Schinkel.

Most of the buildings included are standard selections found in books such as Henry A. Millon and Alfred Frazer's *Key Monuments of the History of Architecture*. These buildings are ones that most students who have taken a course in architectural history should recognize. I have tried to include what is most important and most worth remembering about each major building and each major architect, and I have included information about patrons when it is relevant to the design. I have also tried to show how each building is outstanding and is characteristic for its time and place. About one hundred buildings are considered most fully, and many others are mentioned for comparison. By concentrating on a relatively small number of the best designed buildings, it is possible to determine the most important sources of design, to trace major influences, and to understand why buildings within the Classical Tradition look as they do.

Great architectural designs were created in the same way Shakespeare wrote plays: he adapted the best stories and characters created by other writers. His greatness was largely achieved by improving upon the works of other writers such as Plutarch and Holinshed; no one can accuse him of copying them. Similarly, designing great building requires great insight, learning, and skill. The Classic Tradition demonstrates how an architectural vocabulary can be used as creatively and continuously as the vocabulary of any language. Buildings that are structurally sound and adaptable are necessarily similar in many respects, but can always be improved upon in ways that the same story can be retold and made better in at least some respects.

The Classic Tradition in architecture can be readily identified by two different types of characteristics: design elements and building types. The principal design elements are columns, entablatures, and pediments. The proportions of these elements depended largely on the strengths of the materials that were used to construct them, but since there was no way to test their strengths except by trial and error, buildings were generally overbuilt, and this helped to provide for their permanence. For example, the Athenians considered the thicker columns of the Doric Order more suitable for the Parthenon (a temple with a peristyle or columns all the way around), but soon afterwards used thinner columns of the Ionic Order for the nearby Erechtheum. Proportions varied substantially when relatively weak shellstone was replaced by much stronger marble, but even in two buildings that were both constructed of marble at about the same time and place, the thickness of the columns continued to vary substantially depending on which Order was preferred and what looked right.

The Greek Orders gradually became standardized during the period from around 600-400 B. C. The Roman orders were largely standardized by the time Vitruvius wrote around 20 B. C., but the Composite Order was added around 70 A. D.

Since buildings were designed and constructed using numbers, it is necessary to consider the extent to which architects used mathematics. Proportions were usually applied through the use of ratios. Greek and Roman buildings were often planned and laid out by counting modules. Since architects design and communicate their designs through the use of numbers, it is sometimes necessary to reconstruct the numbers they used and the sequence in which they used them to understand their intentions fully and particularly for buildings that are poorly documented.

The Greeks used mainly wood, adobe, and stone, and the Romans added concrete. The two great structural systems were post-and-lintel and vaulting. The Greeks used almost exclusively post-and-lintel (trabeation) until the Hellenistic Period. The Romans used both structural systems, but constructed their greatest vaulted spaces through the use of concrete. Although the Romans were greatly indebted to the Greeks, they went beyond them by using concrete to create increasingly large spaces for new building types. The Greeks usually started their designs with a conception of what the exterior would look like, and the interior was residual space. The Romans started with generously sized spaces, and their exteriors reflect well proportioned interiors.

The building types that were most influential after the end of Antiquity were largely Roman: basilicas (law courts and exchanges, which were adapted for churches); temples (with pedimented porticoes, which were adapted for houses largely through the influence of Palladio's *Four Books*); palaces (with plans and decoration for houses adapted particularly through the Adam Brothers' *Works*); apartment blocks (insula, which developed into palazzos, which in turn were the basis for the Italianate Style and which continued to be used for the design of apartments and condominiums), and baths (with great spaces that were adapted for railroad stations, museums, and other building tyupes, through the influence of the École des Beaux Arts).

The three main places where the Classic Tradition developed from the 15th Century through the first half of the 20th Century were Rome, Paris, and London. These cities attracted the most talented architects by offering the best education and the best commissions. The most architecturally significant buildings constructed in these cities were widely influential through their high standards of excellence and through being most often seen, studied, and published. The invention of printing coincided with the revival of the Classical Tradition during the Renaissance and greatly facilitated its spread worldwide.

Why does a space have a given length, depth, and height? Why does a building have a particular form? These are questions architects continually asked themselves and that architectural historians also need to answer. Questions such as these will need to be answered as well as possible in numerous monographs on individual buildings and architects, but some valid generalizations can be made by carefully considering what architects wrote about their work and particularly what Vitruvius, Palladio, and Adam wrote. They designed buildings intended to be useful indefinitely. As an adjective, the main meaning of "classic" is "of the first class, of the highest rank or importance; approved as a model; standard, leading" (*Oxford English Dictionary*, 1933). It is not a passing style; it is essentially the same style that has been derived from structural principles worldwide depending partly on materials and construction methods that were locally available, but following the same basic principles of design.

When concrete allowed for buildings to be designed without regard to the spacing required for the use of less strong material, architects continued to design in much the same way and for the same reason that writers continue to use the same words, but in different arrangements. Architects continued to adapt an architectural vocabulary equivalent to a linguistic vocabulary as a useful means of creating more of the same kinds of things they admired most. Moreover, what survives in architecture and evolution is what works best and looks best to those most concerned.

My approach has been to focus on the development of building types and to credit the architects who created the most influential examples of each major type. Until all aspects of the past were increasingly rejected following World Wars I, there was general agreement when an architect had surpassed his predecessors, and his work became another model to be adapted further. Usually, the buildings most admired were the best designed, and better designed buildings continued to be produced by using similar means.

When relatively little information is available on the architects of Greek and Roman buildings, I have focused on the long periods of development that were required before buildings such as the Parthenon and Pantheon could be created. For later periods, as information becomes increasing available about the intentions of architects, I have focused more on the development of the individuals themselves. In both ways, I have tried to determine what was required to produce great buildings.

The principle goals of this book are thus to show how excellence was achieved over such long periods of time in so many places, to provide an outline of the development of the Classic Tradition with an emphasis on what its periods have in common; to indicate what is most distinctive about each period and style; to introduce the principal design approaches, materials, construction techniques, building types, and design elements; to enable readers to recognize the most influential examples of the Classical Orders; to indicate the significance of the key buildings of each period; to show the influence of periods, styles, and specific buildings and architects on one another; to provide the basic vocabulary needed to describe and discuss buildings of the Classic Tradition; and to demonstrate how an architectural vocabulary can be adapted continually and creatively.

Acknowledgements

This book is based on a course I taught on the Classic Tradition at the College of Charleston as a series of lectures in 2003 and 2004, and I rewrote the text on the basis of handouts I prepared for seminars in 2006 and 2009. Although the intended audience was undergraduates who had taken at least one course in architectural history, I have attempted to make the text intelligible for anyone seriously interested in architecture.

I have visited nearly every building I discuss and taken photographs of the great majority of them, but instead of preferring my own photographs, I have usually selected the best illustrations I could find that were out of copyright. I have reproduced albumens in particular because they were made with large format cameras that provided high resolution and perspective correction and because the process ceased to be used around 1920. If I have inadvertently used an illustration that is still in copyright, please provide proof of copyright with an invoice for appropriate compensation.

I am grateful most of all to Randolph Martz and John Poindexter for numerous suggestion for improving all aspects of this study.

15. Early Renaissance Architecture

Main doors by Ghiberti for the Baptistery, Florence (albumen)

The next five chapters are devoted to the Italian Renaissance, which can be considered to have begun in 1400 with the competition for the doors of the Florentine Baptistery. The Renaissance ended in 1580 with the death of Palladio.

During this period of nearly two centuries, the Ancient World and the New World were rediscovered, making this world seem more worthy of consideration than the possibility of an afterlife. Classical architecture, art, and knowledge began resumed having a greater impact on daily life than religious beliefs. The Renaissance was a period of increasing secularism until it was abruptly repressed in Italy by the Inquisition and censorship, but its revival in Italy continued in northern Europe, where efforts to suppress it were less successful.

By 1400 architects were far enough along that they could hope to equal the achievement of the Ancient World. Artists began again to observe, depict, select from, and recombine various parts of Nature in an attempt to surpass it rather than continuing to emulate the highly stylized masterpieces of Medieval art. The Renaissance broke with the recent past that focused on religion to return to the worldly concerns of a more distance past, and although religion continued to influence Renaissance thought, it rapidly came to have little influence on Renaissance architecture and art.

Filippo Brunelleschi (1377-1446) began as a sculptor, but after losing the competition for the doors of the Florentine Baptistery, he taught himself to be an architect. Michelangelo (1475-1564) had no formal training as an architect. Andrea Palladio (1508-1580) began as a stone mason and applied practical consideration to the design of houses. From Brunelleschi to Palladio, Italian architects were largely self-taught, and they learned primarily by studying ancient buildings. In Italy there was no guild of architects equivalent to the guilds that produced the great Gothic cathedrals of northern Europe. Italian architects studied ancient buildings with the same care that Italian artists studied Nature rather than Gothic painting. This different approach to design enabled the crucially important break to be made with the Medieval tradition.

Although many Greek and Roman architects wrote about their work, none of the treatises cited by Vitruvius survived. Only Vitruvius's own *Ten Books* survived, and although it was widely copied during the Medieval Period, copies of copies produced numerous errors, and without his illustrations, his work was not well understood. With the Renaissance, Italian architects began the scholarly study of Roman buildings and to augment Vitruvius with an increasing knowledge of architecture that was created after Vitruvius wrote. Renaissance artists and architects also began again to write about their own research and designs, and printing enabled illustrations to be inexpensively obtained and widely distributed. Numerous drawings have survived, and innumrable buildings were well enough constructed to have survived. intact. Consequently, a great deal more is known about how buildings were designed and constructed during the two centuries from 1400 to 1580 than for earlier architecture, and it is possible to reconstruct the development of Renaissance architecture more accurately than for earlier periods.

In this initial chapter, Italian architecture of the 1400s (the Quattrocento) is discussed through the designs and writing of the two architects who did most to achieve the rebirth of the Classical Tradition: Brunelleschi attempted to equal the greatest achievements of Roman architecture. In his treatise *On the Art of Building in Ten Books*, Alberti attempted to go beyond Vitruvius. They taught their successors to learn from Ancient architecture and to try to surpass it rather than to continue to emulate Medieval architecture. Throughout most of Italy, architects and artists abruptly ceased to study Medieval architecture and art and began to learn from the Ancient World and from Nature.

The next chapter, Chapter 16, is about early examples of the palazzo and villa as building types. The Classic tradition was first revived in Florence, and the Renaissance palazzo developed there into a distinctive building type. It quickly spread to Rome, where the principal examples were constructed during the 16th Century. The Roman villa was revived as a country retreat in much the same way that it had been during the Roman period.

Chapter 17 is about Palladio, who deserves a chapter by himself because his own buildings are among the most influential ever designed, because he studied ancient architecture more comprehensively and incisively than any previous architect, and because his *Four Books* was one of the two most influential ever published on architecture. Palladio established a parallel design tradition that developed into Neoclassicism, including English and American Palladianism. The Renaissance style of architecture began with Brunelleschi, was developed further by Bramante, and culminated with Palladio. The Renaissance Style was characterised by restraint rather than the exuberence of the Baroque Style that began with Michelangelo. Both styles persisted, but the Renaissance Style had the most influence during the Neoclassical Period, and the Baroque Style was revived during the Beaux Arts Period.

Palladio was a fully professional architect by 1540, and Michelangelo began to devote himself fully to architecture in 1547. Although Bramante had begun to design St. Peter's in 1505, Michelangelo entirely redesigned it in the second half of the 16th Century, and it continued to be redesigned until early in the 17th Century. In order to considere the design development of the most important building of the Renaissance, I have considered Palladio before Bramanate and Michelangelo and followed Michelangelo with a chapter on the Baroque that includes the completion of St. Peter's in the third volume of this series (Chapter 20).. In this way, it has been possible to consider the design and construction of St. Peter's sequentially and coherently as the principal subject of three successive chapters.

Chapters 18 and 19 are devoted to Bramante and Michelangelo and their training and their designs for St. Peter's. Like Renaissance architects, both of them began as artists and trained themselves to become architects, but Bramanate began also to train numerous apprentices who became archtiects and who in turn trained other archtiects. Bramante and his apprentices were restrained,

Michelangelo used restraint in his decoration, but sculptural forms, and Bernini used both sculptural forms and lavish decoration that were uncharacteristic of the Renaissance. The Renaissance lasted two centuries, and it was followed in Italy by repression that lasted for three centuries. When the Renaissance ended with the Counter-Reformation, its influence continued to increase in northern Europe, but largely in terms of the Baroque and Neoclassical styles and local developments. The impact of the Renaissance beyond Italy is the principal subject of the volume on *Academic Architecture*.

Renaissance Art History

Giorgio Vasari (1511-1574) wrote the first history of the development of art and architecture since Vitruvius and Pliny, and he considered the period in between Antiquity and the Renaissance to have been degenerate. To resume the creation of art and architecture as good as had been done by the ancient Greeks and Romans and to prevent another period of deterioration of standards, it was necessary to start over from the point that the Ancient World had ended. In his first preface, Vasari wrote that his subject was "...the rise of the arts to perfection, their decline and their restoration or rather renaissance..." (Vasari 1568: I, 6). As Vasari demonstrated, this revival of ancient art took place entirely in Italy before spreading to the rest of Europe and the world. It was regaining the highest levels that had been previously achieved rather than starting over, but some highly important and influential innovations were also introduced in Italy during the three centuries from c. 1260 to c. 1560.

Vasari dated the beginning of the end of ancient architecture from the reign of Constantine, and he used the examples of the Arch of Constantine and of Old St. Peter's. In both cases, Constantine appropriated architectural elements from pagan buildings and reused them for his own purposes.

> Clear testimony to this is afforded by the works in sculpture and architecture produced in Rome in the time of Constantine, notably in the triumphal arch made for him by the Roman people

at the Colosseum, where we see, that for lack of good masters not only did they make use of marble reliefs carved in the time of Trajan, but also of spoils brought to Rome from various places. Those who recognise the excellence of these bas-reliefs, statues, the columns, the cornices and other ornaments which belong to another epoch will perceive how rude are the portions done to fill up gaps by sculptors of the day. Very rude also are some scenes of small figures in marble below the reliefs and the pediment, representing victories, while between these side arches there are some rivers, also very crude, and so poor that they leave one firmly under the impression that the art of sculpture had begun to decline even before the coming of the Goths and other barbarous foreign nations who combined to destroy all the superior arts as well as Italy [Vasari 1568: I, 7].

"Architecture, as I have said, maintained its excellence at a higher though not at the highest level. Nor is this a matter for surprise, since large buildings were almost entirely constructed of spoils. ... A good illustration of the truth of this statement is afforded by the church of the chief of the apostles in the Vatican, which is rich in columns, baes, capitals, architraves, cornices, doors and other incrustations and ornaments which were all taken from various places and buildings, erected before that time in very magnificent style" (7-8). He provided numerous other examples.

But the most harmful and destructive force which operated against these fine arts was the fervent zeal of the new Christian religion, which, after long and sanguinary strife, had at length vanquished and abolished the old faith of the heathen, by means of a number of miracles and by the sincerity of is acts. Every effort was put forth to remove and utter extirpate the smallest things from which errors might arise, and thus not only were the marvellous statues, sculptures, paintings, mosaics and ornament of the false pagan gods destroyed and thrown down, but also the memorials and honour of countless excellent persons, to whose distinguished merits statues and other memorials had been set up in public by a most virtuous antiquity [10].

To create the capitol city of Constantinople at Byzantium, Constantine took with him the best architects and artists of Rome :..[;] the best of them had all gone to Constantinople with the emperor Constantine, and those left behind were dissolute and abandoned" (10). "...the masters of that day produced nothing but shapeless and clumsy things which may still be seen to-day. It was the form and good methods where lost by the death of good artists and the destruction of good buildings, those who devoted themselves to this profession built erections devoid of order or measure, and totally deficient in grace, proportion or principle" (12).

Although there were exceptions such as the architecture of Byzantine Ravenna, the thieving precedents set by Constantine were largely followed for a thousand years. For example, the cathedral at Pisa was constructed using

...an endless quantity of spoils brought by sea from various distant parts, as the [mismatched] columns, bases, capitals, cornices and other stones there of every description, amply demonstrate. Now since all these things were of all sizes, great, medium, and small, [the Greek architect] Buschetto displayed great judgment and skill in adapting them to their places, so that the whole building is excellently devised in every part, both within and without. Amongst other things he devised the façade very cleverly, which is made up of a series of stages, gradually diminishing toward the top and consisting of a great number of columns, adorning it with other carved columns and antique statues [15].

"As the men of the age were not accustomed to see any excellence or greater perfection than the things thus produced, they admired them, and considered them to be the type of perfection, barbarous as they were. ... Those who came after were able to distinguish the good from the bad, and abandoning the old style they began to copy the ancients with all ardour and industry" (17).

Vasari ended his preface by indicating his purposes and theme:

> I wish to be of service to the artists of our day, by showing them how small beginning lead to the highest elevation, and how from so noble a situation it is possible to fall to utterest ruin, and consequently, how these arts resemble nature as shown in our human bodies; and have their birth, growth, age and death, and I hope by these means they will be enabled more easily to recognise the progress of the renaissance of the arts, and the perfection to which they have attained in our own time. And again, if ever it happens, which God forbid, that the arts should once more fall to a like ruin and disorder, through the negligence of man, the malignity of the age, or the decrees of Heaven, which does not appear to wish that he things of this world should remain stationary, these labours of mine..., by means of the things discussed before, and by those which may remain to be said, may maintain the arts in life, or, at any rate, encourage the better spirits to provide them with every assistance... [18].

Previously, in the report to Leo X on ancient Rome almost certainly by Raphael, the author wrote that

> the cruel and atrocious storm of war and destruction broke not only over Italy but spread also over Greece, where once the inventors and perfect masters of all the arts had prevailed, and there also the worst and most worthless style of painting and sculpture came into being. Next, in almost every country, the German style of architecture appeared— a style which as one can see by its ornament is far removed from the good manner of the Roman and the antique [Holt 1981: 294-295].

Thus, from the point of view of these and many other Renaissance writers who could be quoted, the Renaissance was not viewed historically as a continuation of the Medieval Period, but as a rejection of the Medieval approach and a return as quickly and fully as possible to earlier and better ways of designing architecture and art. While crediting individual artists of the 13th and 14th Centuries with progress towards this goal, Vasari continually pointed out how much they were still limited by the Medieval point of view. The theme of his biographies is that only by using nature as models as ancient artists did could their work be equalled if not surpassed, and only by adapting ancient methods could equally great spaces be created permanently.

Much Medieval art and architecture is worthy of study for the same reasons that primitive art worldwide is worthy of study. However, this was not the point of view of Renaissance artists and architects, and an entirely different point of view enabled them to surpass all Medieval art and architecture. Even when the subject matter was the same, the approaches were different and the results bear little resemblance to one another.

Art history consists of images rather than words, and the same thing is true of architecture. What is most important to consider is how architecture and art looked, and what is most important to understand is what was required to achieve the excellence of its appearance. Form is of primary importance architecture and art, and meaning is much less important, and a work is not worth considering unless it is worth looking at. Overall, Vasari is the best guide for what the Renaissance was attempting to accomplish and for how well it had succeeded at any given time and in any given place. What the deluded thought is irrelevant. The way in which architecture and art came to be seen was one of the most fundamental differences between the Medieval Period and the Renaissance.

When Vasari states that an architect designed a building, it is not an attribution, but the best available evidence unless better evidence can be produced. What he wrote was often based on primary sources, but sometimes no more than local traditions were available. He made mistakes, but he was generally unbiased and fair. What he wrote does not need to be confirmed; the burden of proof is on anyone who disagrees. He was a mediocre artist, a better architect, and a great art historian.

All three of Vasari's prefaces to the three parts of his Lives have been quoted in full in Appendix 1 herein. They provide an excellent introduction to Renaissance thought, art, and architecture.

Renaissance Men

The ideal of the Renaissance man had been accepted at least by the beginning of the 1400s when men who like Brunelleschi were sculptors as well as architects; similarly, Alberti and Bramante were artists a well as architects. In his *Lives of the Most Excellent Sculptors, Painters and Architects*, Vasari demonstrated that Italians and especially Tuscan artists and architects since the time of Giotto had been attempting "...to reflect in their work the glories of nature and to attain, as far as possible perfect artistic discernment or understanding" and how their efforts in all three fields culminated with Michelangelo" (Vasari 1568: I, 17). Giotto is the earliest known Renaissance painter who achieved fame also as a sculptor and architect and so merits the designation of a Renaissance man. Some earlier artists must have been highly skilled in art, sculpture, and architecture, but only during the Renaissance did it become usual for individuals to be highly accomplished in all three fields.

Prior to the Renaissance, most artists belonged to guilds, and each guild practiced a single art (in the sense of anything that is man-made). The separation of the arts into guilds, the attempts by each guild to monopolize its particular art, the legal apprenticeship that was required to become a member of a guild, and the high level of accomplishment that was required to be accepted as a master by a guild, and the general secrecy about technical skills were all impediments to working in more than one field of art. In addition, during the late Medieval period, architecture had no guild in Italy, and the leading Gothic architects were all or nearly all Germans who had been trained through apprenticeships with members of guilds in northern Europe. There was almost no way that an Italian artist could become accomplished in all the arts until around 1400, but a few early exceptions are mentioned by Vasari.

The most important considerations were that Renaissance artists began to break away from the guild system by drawing from life rather than by copying the work of an individual master or locally available examples. Cimabue (1240-1302) is the earliest Italian artist known to have drawn "...from nature to the best of his power, although it was a novelty to do so in those days. ... The painters of those times had taught one another that rough, awkward and commonplace style for a great number of years, not by means of study but as a matter of custom, without ever dreaming of improving their designs by beauty of colouring or by any invention of worth" (I, 22-23). Cimabue was the teacher of Giotto, who became an architect as well as a painter and sculptor, and Cimabue was also the teacher of Arnolfo Lapi, the architect of the Florentine Duomo (26, 34-35)

Italian artists had the great advantage over northern artists in the accessibility of art and architecture in ancient styles rather than only in the Gothic style, and they had the advantage of being part of the increasing discovery of ancient literature as well as art and architecture and of the increasing acceptance of the superiority of the Ancient World in every respect to the Medieval World. They were part of the attempt to get beyond the Dark Ages and to put the secular considerations of this life ahead of concerns about the possibility of a next life. "As the men of the age were not accustomed to see any excellence or greater perfection than the things thus produced, they greatly admired them, and considered them to be the type of perfection, barbarous as they were" (I, 17). "Those little things of Cimabue are done like miniatures, and although they may appear rather crude than otherwise to modern eyes, yet they serve to show to what extent the art of design profited by his labours" (28).

Ancient art and architecture Italian, and everything Italian was again being preferred to everything foreign, and those who could do similar things to what was Italian were increasingly preferred to better trained artists and architects from other "nations" (including all of independent republics and principalities of Italy). Although there was no Italy around 1400 and many Italian dialects, the influence of Dante in spreading the Tuscan dialect in the 1300s

helped to prepare the way for Tuscan artists and architects to do the same:
One part of the country after another came to adopt the classical dialect offically. Venice, Milan, and Naples did so at the noontime of Italian literature, and partly through its influence. It was not until the present [19th] century that Piedmont became of its own free will a genuine Italian province by sharing in this chief treasure of the people—pure speech..." [Burckhardt 1944: 229].

Also of great importance was the growing conviction during the Renaissance of the unity of the visual arts. This gradual process was well documented by Vasari, who wrote that "invention has been, and always will be, considered the true mother of architecture, painting and poetry, as well as all the superior arts and of all the marvels produced by man. It affords great delight and displays for them the fantasies and caprices of those imaginative minds which discover the infinite variety of things, while the abundant praise bestowed on such novelties acts as an incentive upon all those who are engaged upon noble works, who impart extraordinary beauty to the things they produce..." (I, 186-187). No matter how different art and architecture were in some respects, they were all based on the ability to select subject well, to draw well, and to organize elements into well unified compositions whether the elements were figures, patterns, or words.

Cimabue designed in the Byzantine style, but went beyond his immediate predecessors in the greater realism of his figures and draperies. Arnolfo di Lapo was an architect whose father was from Germany, but although he himself was born in Florence, he never entirely abandoned the Romanesque style. He was influenced to some extent by its buildings, but apprenticed under his father. About Gothic architecture, Vasari wrote, "...although the buildings are neither beautiful nor in good style, but only very large and magnificent, yet they are none the less worthy of some consideration" (28). Arnolfo might qualify as the first Renaissance man if any of his painting or sculpture had survived, but Vasari mentions no painting or sculpture by him (35). Like Giotto, he "...had studied design under Cimabue in order to make use of it in sculpture, so that he was reputed the best architect in Tuscany," but this could also mean only that he sculpted the models of buildings. In any case, Vasari makes the point that Arnolfo's training under a painter was useful to him as an architect, but he continued to design buildings in the Gothic style (35).

The same thing is true of Niccola Pisani (c. 1205-1278) and his son Giovanni Pisani (1250-1328) in that they were both sculptors and architects, but as early Renaissance sculptors and late Gothic architects. As with painting, sculpture advanced more quickly than architecture. As a sculptor, Niccola Pisano

> ...was originally associated with some Greek sculptors who were engaged upon the figures and other ornaments in relief for the Duomo at Pisa and the church of S. Giovanni there. Among the marble remains brought home by the Pisan fleet were some ancient sarcophagi now in the Campo Santo of that city, including a very fine one which was an admirable representation of the chase of Meleager, hunting the Calydonian boar.... Both the nude and the draped figures of this composition are executed with much skill, while the design is perfect. This sarcophagus, on account of its beauty, was afterwards placed by the Pisans on the façade of the Duomo opposite S. Rocco, against the principal door on that side.... Niccola, considering the excellence of this work, which greatly delighted him, applied such diligence in imitating that style, and other excellent sculptures on the other antique sarcophagi, that before long he was considered the best sculptor of his time [I, 40]

"...not only in Tuscany, but throughout Italy, where the number of buildings and other things erected without method and without design betray the poverty of their minds no less than the bountiful riches wasted on them by the men of their day; because there were no masters capable of executing in good style anything which they did for them" (43). However,

> In Niccola's day there were many moved by a laudable spirit of emulation, who applied themselves more diligently

to sculpture than they had done before, especially in Milan, where many Lombards and Germans were gathered for the building of the Duomo. These were afterwards scattered throughout Italy by the dissentions which arose between the Milanese and the Emperor Frederick. They then began to compete among themselves, both in carving marble and in erecting buildings, and attained to some measure of excellence. The same thing happened in Florence after the works of Arnolfo and Niccola had appeared [I, 43].

"...Giovanni, who was always with his father, and under his care learned both sculpture and architecture, so that in the course of a few years he became not only the equal of his father, but his superior in some things" (46). In Arezzo, Giovanni "...designed the church of S. Maria dei Servi, which has been destroyed in our day, together with many palaces of the noblest families of the city..." (48). He designed, restored, or augmented other buildings elsewhere in Italy, but all presumably in the Gothic style (49-51). "When he had completed his labours in Perugia, Giovanni wished to go to Rome to learn from the few antique things there, as his father had done, but sufficient reasons prevented him from ever realizing his desire, the main one being that he heard that the court had just gone to Avignon..." (51). The lack of patronage in Rome until the Papacy returned prevented other artists from studying there for most of the 14th Century.

"Cimabue was, as it were, the first cause of the revival of the art of painting, yet Giotto, his disciple, moved by praiseworthy ambition, and aided by Heaven and by Nature, penetrated deeper in thought, and threw open the gates of truth to those who afterwards brought art to that perfection and grandeur which we see in our own age" (I, 27).

> The works of these masters obtained credit for some time, but when the productions of Andrea, Cimabue and the rest had to bear comparison with those of Giotto..., people came to recognise to some extent where perfection in art lay, for they saw how great a difference there was between the early manner of Cimabue and that of Giotto and the delineation of figures, a difference equally strongly marked in the case of their pupils and imitators. From this time others gradually sought to follow in the footsteps of the better master, surpassing each other more and more every day, so that art rose from these humble beginnings to the summit of perfection to which it has attained to-day [I, 56]..

"...the manner of the painters of those days cannot be of great assistance to artists; and I shall dwell at greater length upon the lives of those who may be of some help because they introduced improvements into the arts" (60).

In his *Lives*, Vasari demonstrated that Italians and especially Tuscan artists and architects since the time of Giotto (1266-1337) had been attempting "...to reflect in their work the glories of nature and to attain, as far as possible perfect artistic discernment or understanding" and how their efforts in all three fields culminated with Michelangelo.

Vasari also credited Giotto with the invention of foreshortening: "...it is from these works that the origin of foreshortening is derived..." (I, 77). This is an exaggeration, but it was probably true that Giotto was the first artist since Antiquity who used foreshortening consistently to create figures that appeared to be three-dimensional rather than two-dimensional views either from the front or side, and he did this by drawing exactly what he saw rather than by imitating Medieval painters. As a child and a shepherd, Giotto was constantly drawing how things looked rather than using existing conventions for how to depict anything because he taught himself to draw before receiving any instruction, and this was also the case with Michelangelo. Vasari wrote that

> ...he was always drawing something from Nature or representing the fancies which came into his head, on flat stones on the ground or on sand, so much was he attracted to the art of design by his natural inclination. Thus, one day, when Cimabue was going on some business from Florence to Vespignano, he came upon Giotto, who, while his sheep were grazing, was drawing one of them from

life with roughly pointed piece of stone upon a smooth surface of rock, although he had never had any master but nature. Cimabue stopped in amazement and asked to boy if he would like to come and stay with him. Giotto replied he would go willingly if his father would consent. Accordingly, Cimabue asked Bondone, who gladly consented, and allowed him to take his son with him to Florence. After his arrival there, assisted by his natural talent and taught by Cimabue, the boy not only equalled his mater's style in a short time, but became such a good imitator of Nature that he entirely abandoned the rude Byzantine manner and revived the modern and good style of painting, introducing the practice of making good portraits of living persons, a thing which had not been in use for more than two hundred years. And although some had made the attempt, as has been said above, yet they had not been very successful, nor were their efforts so well executed as those of Giotto. Among other portraits which he made, the chapel of the Podestà place at Florence still containing that of Dante Aligheri, his close companion and friend, no less famous as a poet than Giotto then was as a painter [I, 66].

In the *Divine Comedy*, Dante wrote, "Cimabue thought to hold the field in painting, and now Giotto has the cry, so that the fame of him is obscured" (Purgatory, XI, 92; Norton tr.).

Vasari wrote that "the debt owed by painters to Nature, which serves them continually as an example, that from her they may select the best and finest parts for reproduction and imitation, is does also, in my opinion, to the Florentine painter Giotto; because, when the methods and outlines of good painting had been buried for so many years under the ruins caused by war, he alone, although born in the midst of unskilled artists, through God's gift in him, revived what had fallen into such an evil plight and raised it to a condition which one might call good. Certainly it was nothing short of a miracle, in so gross and unskillful an age, that Giotto should have worked to such purpose that design of which the men of the time had little or no conception, was revived to vigorous life by his means" (65-66).

In addition to depicting individual figures with great accuracy even for poses in suspended motion, Giotto depicted entire compositions with realistic backgrounds rather than backgrounds of gold leaf. In this way, initially through ignorance of the conventions of his time, Giotto taught himself and his successors how to depict what they saw rather than how they imagined the Biblical past might have been or how an Afterlife might be. Without any knowledge of ancient art initially, he drew as ancient artists had taught themselves how to draw. Although he was indebted to Cimabue for teaching him how to see and for learning the techniques of tempera and fresco, he surpassed him in all other respects. Michelangelo's own artistic development followed very nearly the same course as Giotto's in that initially he drew whatever attracted his attention as accurately as he could without any artistic training until after he had mastered the art of drawing on his own.

Giotto represented the turning point in painting though still not in architecture. He continued to design in the Gothic tradition for his bell tower, and nearly all of the architecture he represented in his paintings were either Gothic or Romanesque. One of his frescoes does include an early attempt to design a classical building, but with quatrefoil windows.

A classically inspired building in a fresco by Giotto of St. Francis (Bardi Chapel of S. Croce, Florence; c. 1330)

Vasari provided for the Renaissance what Plutarch and Pliny provided for ancient Greece and Rome. He nonetheless produced the "all-important work" on the art and architecture of the Renaissance (Burckhardt 1944: 201). Some of what Vasari wrote has been superseded by the discovery of better evidence than was available to him, but most of what he wrote has been confirmed, and much evidence he recorded has been lost since he wrote.

Vasari deserves to be considered correct unless he can be shown to be wrong by better evidence. His conscientiousness cannot be doubted for he often corrected his own mistakes in the second edition of his *Lives*. Overall, Renaissance architects and artists were fortunate to have had Vasari to identify their best works and to credit every imrovement and innovation. Although he was a second-rate artist and a somewhat better architect, he knew hsi subject first-hand, and he personally knew many of the architects and artists of his own time. He had biases, and he sometimes slighted individuals who deserved more praise, but he was generally impartial, and his judgments and attributions have largely withstood much biased criticism.

Vasari divided his study of into three parts of unequal size. He devoted 62 percent of his study to the late Renaissance (starting with Leonardo da Vinci); he devoted 23 percent to the early Renaissance (starting with Jacopo della Quercia); and he devoted 15 percent to the precursors of the Renaissance (starting with Cimabue). Thus, he devoted 85 percent to the Renaissance and 15 percent to the precursors of the Renaissance rather than the reverse yet many books written about the Renaissance and many courses taught on the Renaissance devote a far greater amount of time to the precursors and far less to the Renaissance itself.

Vasari is explicit that although he greatly admired the innovations of the precursors of the Renaissance, "...if there had been no improvement to follow, the advances they made would have been of little service, and would not have been worthy of much esteem" (I, 206). He equated the first period he considered with the "childhood" of the Renaissance and the early Renaissance with its "youth" (207, 209). According to Vasari, the first Renaissance architect was Bramante (1444-1514); the first Renaissance sculptor was Della Quercia (c. 1371-1438); and the first Renaissance painter was Masaccio (1401-1428; Vasari 1568: II, 183; I, 210; I, 263).

In Vasari's opinion, the precursors of Bramante, Della Quercia, and Masaccio merit consideration for one or more innovations, but cannot be considered Renaissance artists because Renaissance artists soon ceased to learn directly from them or to emulate their work. Although they were important for the development of Renaissance architecture and art, they were superceded rather than continuing to be influential. Instead, it was the artists of the Renaissance who increasingly imitated Nature and Ancient art, which in turn had also imitated Nature rather than earlier Greek and Roman art. As Vasari pointed out, the imitation of a master even as significant as Giotto usually produces only more of the same rather than further improvements:

> When artists have no other aim in their works but to imitate the style of their master or some other excellent man, whose methods of work, posture of figures, carriage of the heads or folds of the draperies please them, and if they seek no more than this then, although they may produce similar works by dint of time and study, yet they will never attain to the perfection of art by this means alone, and it is naturally a most rare thing for one who is always following to get in front, because the imitation of Nature is arrested in the style of the artist with whom long practice has developed a set manner. Imitating is the art of reproducing things, exactly taking the most beautiful things Nature affords in their purity, without adopting the master's style or that of others, who infuse their personality into the things which they take from Nature. For although the works of excellent artists appear natural and real, yet no one can display such diligence as to make his things like Nature itself, nor even by selecting the best can a composition be made so perfect that art will surpass nature. It therefore follows that the things taken from Nature constitute perfect paintings and sculptures, and whoever closely studies the methods and habits of artists alone, and not natural bodies and objects, produces works inferior to those of Nature and also of the artists from whom he borrows his style. Thus, it may be observed that many of our artists have studied nothing but the works of their masters, neglecting Nature, from which they have learned nothing whatever, while they have not surpassed their masters, but have done the greatest injury to their talents. If they had studied both his style and Nature as well they would have produced better works [II, 35-36].

Notably, Lorenzo the Magnificent had an inscription placed on Filippo Lippi's tomb "which concludes: 'Nature herself by my expressive figures stilled/ Confesses me the equal of her arts'" (Kent 2000: 337; 262).

The pre-eminent need to study Nature directly does not mean masters had nothing to teach of value about the use of materials, about means for making two-dimensional art seem three-dimensional, or about how to select and combine elements into a coherent whole. Incoherent architecture is like incoherent speech.

> In the first place, by means of the study and diligence of the great Filippo Brunelleschi, architecture once again discovered the measurements and proportions of the ancients, as well in the round columns as in the square pilasters and in the rough and polished corners; order is distinguished from order, the difference between them being made apparent, matters are arranged to proceed according to rule with more order, things are partitioned out by measure, design shows increased power and method, gracefulness pervades everything and exhibits the excellence of the art, the beauty and variety of capitals and cornices are rediscovered, so that the plans of churches and other buildings are well conceived, the buildings themselves being ornate, magnificent, and in proportion [I, 207].

Since there was no earlier Renaissance rchitect, what deserves most to be studied are the ancient sources he himself studied, how well he applied what he learned, and to what extent he went beyond them. Nearly every Renaissance architect after him had to go to Rome to study how ancient buildings were designed and constructed.

Ancient sculpture had been more accessible than ancient Roman architecture. For example,

> among the marble remains brought home by the Pisan fleet were some ancient sarcophagi now in the Campo Santo of that city, including a very fine one on which was an admirable representation of the chase of Meleager, hunting the Calydonian boar.... Both the nude and the draped figures of this composition are executed with much skill, while the design is perfect. ... Nicola [Piano], considering the excellence of this work, which greatly delighted him, applied such diligence in imitating that style, and other excellent sculptures on the other antique sarcophagi, that before long he was considered the best sculptor of his time [I, 40].

Again, it was by using ancient examples instead of medieval examples that great progress began to be made. However, despite having the more widespread advantage of good examples of sculpture to learn from, Della Quercia "...was the first sculptor after Andrea Pisano, Orcagna, and the others named above, who, by applying himself with greater study and diligence to sculpture, began to show that it was possible to approach Nature, and was also the first to inspire others with courage and the belief that it would be possible to equal her in some sort" (210). He began by teaching himself by imitating Nature as closely as possible, but improved his style by studying the work of Florentine sculptors who had been to Rome to study (211-213); "...besides is natural desire to do well, the rivalry... proved an even greater stimulus" (213).

In the case of painting, "...Masaccio entirely freed himself from Giotto's style, his heads, draperies, buildings, nudes, colouring and foreshortening being in a new manner, introducing that modern style which has been adopted by all our artists from that time to our own day, embellished and enriched from time to time with additional graces, invention and ornaments" (I, 209). Giotto was thus entirely superseded despite having had great influence; like the students of Medieval masters, all his students painted like him rather than trying to be more realistic than him. He was as much a medieval artist as Arnolfo was a Gothic architect. By contrast,

> ...the [sculpted] figures of Jacopo della Quercia of Siena possess more movement, grace, design and diligence; those of [painted by Frà] Filippo better knowledge of the muscles, better proportions and more judgment; and those of their pupils exhibit the same qualities. But Lorenzo Ghiberti added yet more in his production of the doors of S. Giovanni, in which he displayed his invention, order, style and design so that his figures seem to move and breathe. Although Donato [Donatello] lived at the same time, I was uncertain whether I ought not to place him in the third period, since his works are up to the level of the good antiques... [I, 208-209].

From explicit statements such as these and from the small part of the *Lives* that is devoted to the precursors of the Renaissance, Vasari considered the Renaissance to have begun with Brunelleschi, Jacopo della Quercia, and Masaccio. As Vasari wrote, "...the eye is a considerably better guide and judge than the ear" (I, 204).

Although sometimes mistaken, Vasari was generally unbiased and has rarely been proven wrong. Since many sources were available to him that are no longer available and since many early accounts are vague about who deserves credit for designing a work of art or architecture, the only legitimate approach for using Vasari and other early secondary sources is to accept them unless an earlier and better primary source can be found. To "question" the best available information that "cannot be confirmed" is a lawyer's trick to discredit inconvenient evidence rather than a sound historical approach.

In addition to having extracted portions of his first preface, I have reproduced Vasari's second and third preface as appendices. He made highly important observations about the parallel developments between Ancient architecture and art and Renaissance architecture and art, both of which began as provincial imitations of Egyptian and Roman architecture and art respectively. In both cases, local developments were widely adopted and continually improved upon until the end products became so difficult to surpass that younger artists claimed that being different was more important than being better.

Vasari designated Leonardo as the first artists to have developed another distinctive style that influenced an entire period of development. Nonetheless, he praised Raphael for being superior in grace and Michelangelo for being superior in vigor. It is always possible to do the same thing differently and better in at least some respects if not to a large extent. Michelangelo and Shakespeare provided sufficient proof.

Vasari made three main points in his prefaces: (1) that Ancient and Renaissance art had parallel developments by becoming increasingly realistic, (2) that by studying Nature the artists of both traditions had achieved perfection, and (3) that by studying both Ancient art and Nature, it was possible to surpass even Ancient art. Although Ancient art showed methods for depicting nature more realistically, it was not a substitute for Nature, which was the ultimate guide for achieving realistic depictions. Essentially the same thing was true for architecture in that Ancient buildings showed how to utilize materials and methods of construction better than they had been used during the Medieval Period and so to achieve wider spans more permanently, but by also trying additional ways of doing the same things as Brunelleschi did, it was possible to equal and eventually if not surpass the Ancients, which Brunelleschi did by discovering and systematizing the principles of perspective. The ancients had used perspective, but not systematically. By contrast, Medieval artists had allowed themselves to be confined to one tradition whether it was Byzantine, Romanesque, or Gothic at any given time and place. Vasari pointed out the importance of learning from multiple traditions the best of what each had to offer, but he thought the Renaissance had gone so far beyond Medieval art that to study it was no longer necessary or desirable. He did not recommend doing the same thing in the same way indefinitely, but always trying to improve art and architecture, and he had good reason to believe that continual progress was possible.

Moreover, Medieval artists had been limited almost entirely by the Bible for subject matter. In turning to Nature for models, Renaissance artists considered themselves to be using another source for the same purpose in that they were trying better to understand why God had created Nature as He did including the anatomy of the human body. By depicting Nature more realistically, they were showing the greatness of God more correctly. By studying anatomy, Renaissance artists had already gone beyond the Ancients. By using oil paints rather than tempera, Renaissance artists had already surpassed the Ancients in the subtlety with which colors could be depicted.

Nonetheless, frescoes could be more permanent, and Vasari did not reject the use of mosaics or stained glass. Vasari appreciated the advances of late Medieval artists enough to credit them in his writings, but he emphasized that they had been superseded and that still further advances were possible so long as artists were not content to do the same things in the same ways. No one need study Byzantine art or architecture any longer, and everyone needed to study Nature most of all.

Vasari did not suggest that further advances were impossible and that everyone should sculpt, paint, or design buildings like Michelangelo depicting only the subjects that he depicted and designing only the building types that he designed, but he recommended that everyone should continue to try as Michelangelo had done to surpass the best that had been previously achieved in art and architecture by returning to the study of Nature and by solving the practical problems in architecture to enable larger and more permanent buildings to be built.

Since Vasari's second edition of the *Lives* was published in 1568 or about five years after its final decrees, he was careful to conform to them. In 1563 the Council of Trent had been explicit about "the legitimate use of images":

> ...great profit is derived from all holy images not only because the people are thereby reminded of the benefits and gifts bestowed on them by Christ, but

also because through the saints the miracles of God and salutary examples are set before the eyes of the faithful, so that they may give God thanks for those things, may fashion their own life and conduct in imitation of the saints and be moved to adore and live God and cultivate piety. But if anyone should teach or maintain anything contrary to these decrees, let him be anathema [quoted in Holt 1982: 63-64].

The Council of Trent cited the Second Council of Nicaea and other councils as rejecting iconoclasm, but stipulated that nothing heretical or lascivious was to be depicted, and the illiterate were to be cautioned not to pray to images, but to learn from the examples they depicted. In churches, nothing "profane" was to be depicted. Elsewhere, they did not attempt officially to stop the growing demand for the depiction of classical subject matter. Instead of objecting to the realistic depiction of religious subjects, they insisted upon accuracy in depictions, and art continued to achieve continually greater realism as through the perfection of the use of light and shade by Caravaggio and subsequently through the use of the camera obscura. The Catholic Church was in no way opposed to increasing realism or increasingly dramatic representations so long as they were not in any way irreligious, and the Inquisition began to censor art as well as publications and preaching to ensure that "...no representation of false doctrines [teachings] and such as might be the occasion of grave error to the uneducated be exhibited" (64). In brief, the Church was not at all opposed to better ways to represent what it approved of, but it insisted that pagan subject matter and pagan architecture were not to be used for churches. This was a purposeful refutation to any Protestants who insisted that no images at all should be used in churches and that Catholic as well as pagan images should be destroyed. The Council of Trent decreed nothing specific about architecture, but it was covered by rejecting all that was profane from anything to do with churches. Since the temple form and the portico were pagan, they were not to be used for churches.

Most Renaissance men were self-taught in one or more of the fields of art and particularly in architecture since there was no guild of architecture in Florence to teach them. Self-taught men like Brunelleschi learned by seeing rather than be being told how things should look.

Painting is drawing with a brush; sculpting is drawing with chisel; painting, sculpture, and architecture are drawing with a pen. The principles of design are the same regardless of the materials or methods.

Since Brunelleschi designed the first fully Renaissance building and was also a Renaissance sculptor of the highest rank, he was the first Renaissance man. There were many to follow including Alberti during the lifetime of Brunelleschi; there were more and greater Renaissance men during the 16th Century culminating in Michelangelo, but the tradition continued in the 17th Century with Bernini. Subsequently, the Beaux Arts method of training architects included mastering the principles and techniques of drawing, painting, and sculpture, and no better method has been found for teaching artists and architects how to see, design, and create lasting work of permanent value.

Renaissance Design Principle

Italian editions of Giorgio Vasari's *Lives* begin with his "Introductory Essay" on the techniques that Renaissance architects and artists used to create works of architecture, sculpture, and painting. Although this information is indespinsible for for understanding Renaissance design principles and workmanship, it was many omitted from most English editions during the 20th Century. The parts that are most relevant to the design of buildings are quoted in the remained of this section:

(1) *Of Painting* (Vasari 1907: 205-211; completely transcribed below except that footnotes have been omitted and paragraphing has been augmented):

The Nature and Materials of Design or Drawing

[*Proportion:*] Seeing that Design, the parent of our three arts, Architecture, Sculpture, and Painting, have its origin in the intellect, draws out from many single things a general judgement, it is like a form or idea of all the objects in nature, most marvelous in what it compasses, for not only in the bodies of men and of animals but also in plants, in buildings, in sculpture and in painting, design is cognizant of the proportion of the whole to the parts and of the parts to each other and to the whole. Seeing too that from this knowledge there arises a certain conception and judgement, so that there is formed in the mind that something which afterwards, when expressed by the hands, is called design, we may conclude that design is not other than a visible expression and declaration of our inner conception and of that which others have imagined and given form to in their idea. And from this, perhaps, arose the proverb among the ancients 'ex ungue leonem' when a certain clever person, seeing carved in a stone block the claw only of a lion, apprehended in his mind [p. 206] from its size and form all the parts of the animal and then the whole together, just as if he had it present before his eyes. [Similarly, an entire classical temple can often be reconstructed from a single surviving part.]

[*Practice:*] Some believe that accident was the father of design and of the arts, and that the use and experience as foster-mother and schoolmaster, nourished it with the help of knowledge and of reasoning, but I think that, with more truth, accident may be said rather to have given the occasion for design, than to be its father. But be this as it may, what design needs, when it has derived from the judgement the mental image of anything, is that the hand, through the study and practice of many years, may be free and apt to draw and to express correctly, with the pen, the silver-point, the charcoal, the chalk, or other instrument, whatever nature has created. For when the intellect puts forth refined and judicious conceptions, the hand which has practiced design for many years, exhibits the perfection and excellence of the arts as well as the knowledge of the artist. And seeing that there are certain sculptors who have not much practice in strokes and outlines, and consequently cannot draw on paper, these works instead in clay or wax, fashioning men, animals, and other things in relief, with beautiful proportion and balance. Thus, they effect the same thing as does he who draws well on paper or other flat surface.

The masters who practice these arts have named or distinguished the various kinds of design according to the description of the drawing which they make. Those which are touched lightly and just indicated with the pen or other instruments are called sketches, as shall be explained in another place. Those, again, that have the first lines encircling an object are called profiles or outlines.

Use of Design (or Drawing) in the Various Arts
[*Unity of the Arts*] All these, whether we call them profiles or otherwise, are as useful to architecture and sculpture as to painting. Their chief use indeed is in Architecture, because its designs are composed only of lines, which so far as the [207] architect is concerned, are nothing else than the beginning and the end of his art, for all the rest, which is carried out with the aid of models of wood, formed from the said lines, is merely the work of carvers and masons.

In Sculpture, drawing is of service in the case of all the profiles, because in going round from view to view the sculptor uses it when he wishes to delineate the forms which please him best, or which he intends to bring out in every dimension, whether in wax, or clay, or marble, or wood, or other material.

In Painting, the lines are of service in many ways, but especially in outlining every figure, because when they are well drawn, and made correct and in proportion, the shadows and lights that are then added give the strongest relief to the lines of the figure and the result is all excellence and perfection. Hence it happens, that whosoever understands and manages these lines well, will, with the help of practice and judgement, excel in each one of these arts.

[*Attaining Proficiency:*] Therefore, he who would learn thoroughly to express in drawing the conceptions of the mind and anything else that pleases him, must after he has in some degree trained his hand to make it more skillful in the arts, exercise it in copying figures in relief either in marble or stone, or else plaster casts taken from the life, or from [208] some beautiful antique statue, or even from models in relief of clay, which may either be nude or clad in rags covered with clay to serve for clothing and drapery. All these objects being motionless and without feeling, greatly facilitate the work of the artist, because they stand still, which does not happen in the case of live things that have movement. When he has trained his hand by steady practice in drawing such objects, let him begin to copy from nature and make a good and certain practice herein, with all possible labour and diligence, for the things studied from nature are really those which do honour to them who strives to master them, since they have in themselves, besides a certain grace and liveliness, that simple and easy sweetness which is nature's own, and which can only be learned perfectly from her, and never to a sufficient degree from the things of art. Hold it more over for certain, that the practice that is acquired by many years of study in drawing, as has been said above, is the true light of design and that which makes men really proficient. Now, having discoursed long enough on this subject, let us go on to see what painting is.

Of the Nature of Painting

A painting, then, is a plane covered with patches of colour on the surface of wood, wall, or canvas filling up the outlines spoken of above, which by virtue of a good design of encompassing lines, surround the figure.

[*Depicting Relief:*] If [209] the painter treats his flat surface with the right judgement, keeping the center light and the edges and the background dark and medium colour between the light and dark in the intermediate spaces, the result of the combination of these three fields of colour will be that everything between the one outline and the other stands out and appears round and in relief. It is indeed true that these three shades cannot suffice for every object treated in detail, therefore it is necessary to divide every shade at least into two half shades, making of the light two half tints, and of the dark two lighter, and of the medium two other half tints which incline one to the lighter and the other to the darker side. When these tints, being of one colour only whatever it may be, are gradated, we see a transition beginning with the light, and then the less light, and then a little darker, so that little by little we find the pure black. Having then made the mixtures, that is, these colours mixed together, and wishing to work with oil or tempera or in fresco, we proceed to fill in the outlines putting in their proper place the lights and darks, the half tints and the lowered tones of the half tints and the lights. I mean those tints mixed from the three first, light, medium and dark, which lights and medium tints and dark and lower tones are copied from the cartoon or other design which is made for any work before we begin to put it into execution.

[*Negative Space:*] It is necessary that the design be carried out with good arrangement, firm drawing, and judgment and invention, seeing that the composition in a picture is not other than the parceling out of the places where the figures come, so that the spaces be not unshapely but in accordance with the judgement of the eye, while the field is in one place well covered and in another void. All this is the result of drawing [210] and of having copied figures from the life, and from models of figures made to represent anything one wished to make.

[*Anatomy:*] Design cannot have a good origin if it has not come from continual practice in copying natural objects, and from the study of pictures by excellent masters and of ancient statues in relief, as has been said many times. But above all, the best thing is to draw men and women from the nude and thus fix in the memory by constant exercise the muscles of the torso, back, legs, arms, and knees, with the bones underneath. Then one may be sure that through much study attitudes in any position can be drawing by help from the imagination without one's having the living forms in view. Again, having seen the human bodies dissected, one knows how the bones lie, and the muscles and sinews, and all the order and conditions of anatomy so that it is possible with greater security and more correctness to place the limbs and arrange the muscles of the body in the figures we draw. And those who have this knowledge will certainly draw the outline of the figures perfectly, and these, when drawn as they ought to be, show a pleasing grace and beautiful style.

[*Interrelated Parts:*] He who studies good painting and sculpture, and at the same time sees and understands the [natural] life, must necessarily have acquired a good method in art. Hence springs the invention which groups figures in fours, sixes, tens, twenties, in such a manner as to represent battles and other great subjects of art. This invention demands an innate propriety springing out of harmony and obedience; thus, if a figure move to greet another, the figure saluted having to respond should not turn away. As with this example, so it is with all the rest. The subject may offer many varied motives different one from another, but the motives chosen must always bear relation to the work in hand, and to what the artist is in process of representing. He ought to distinguish between different movements and characteristics, making the women with a sweet and beautiful air and also the youths, but the old always [211] grave of aspect, and especially the priests and persons in authority.

[Unity:] He must always take care however, that everything is in relation to the work as a whole; so that when the picture is looked at, one can recognize in it a harmonious unity, wherein the passions strike terror and the pleasing effects shed sweetness, representing directly the intentions of the painter, and not the things he had no thought of. It is requisite therefore, for this purpose, that he form the figures which have to be spirited with movement and vigour, and that he make those which are distant to retire from the principal figures by means of shade and colour that gradually and softly become lower in tone.

[Virtuosity:] Thus, art will always be associated with the grace of naturalness and of delicate charm of colour, and the work be brought to perfection not with the stress of cruel suffering, so that men who look at it have to endure pain on account of the suffering which they see has been borne by the artists in his work, but rather with rejoicing at his good fortune in that his hand has received from heaven the lightness of movement which shows his painting to be worked out with study and toil certainly, but not with drudgery; so will it be that the figures, everyone in its place, will not appear dead to him who observes them, but alive and true. Let painters avoid crudities, let it be their endeavor that the things they are always producing shall not seem painted, but show themselves alive and starting out of the canvas. This is the secret of sound design and the true method recognized by him who has painted as belonging to the pictures that are known and judged to be good.

(2) *Of Sculpture* (Vasari 1907: 145-147; completely transcribed except that footnotes have been omitted)

The Nature of Sculpture

Sculpture is an art which by removing all that is superfluous from the material under treatment reduces it to that form designed in the artist's mind.

Qualities Necessary for Work in the Round

Now seeing that all figures of whatever sort, whether carved in marble, cast in bronze, or wrought in plaster or wood, must be in salient work in the round, and seeing too that as we walk round them they are looked at from every side, it is clear that if we want to call them perfect they must have many qualities. The most obvious is that when such a figure is presented to our eyes, it should show at the first glance the expression intended, whether pride or humility, caprice, gaiety or melancholy—according to the person portrayed. It must also be balanced in all its members: that is, it must not have long legs, a thick head, and short and deformed arms; but be well proportioned, and from head to foot have each part conforming with the others. In the same way, if the figure has the face of an old man, let it have the arms, body, [146] legs, hands, and feet of an old man, the skeleton symmetrically ordered throughout, the muscles and sinews and veins all in their proper places. If it has the face of a youth, it must in like manner be round, soft and sweet in expression, harmonious in every part. If it is not to be nude, do not let the drapery that is to cover it be so meagre as to look thin, nor clumsy like lumps of stone, but let the flow of the folds be so turned that they reveal the nude beneath—and with art and grace now show, now hide it without any harshness that may detract from the figure. Let the hair and beard be worked with a certain delicacy, arranged and curled to show they have been combed, having the greatest softness and grace given to them that the chisel can convey; and because the sculptors cannot in this part actually counterfeit nature, they make the locks of hair solid and curled, working from manner rather than in imitation of nature. Even though the figure is in the round, it is essential that in front, in profile, and at the back, it be of equal proportions, having at every turn and view to show itself happily disposed throughout. Indeed, the whole work must be harmonious, and exhibit pose, drawing and unity, grace and finish; these qualities taken together show the natural talent and capacity of the artists.

Works of Sculpture Should Be Treated with a View to Their Destined Position

Figures in relief as well as in painting ought to be produced with judgement rather than in a mechanical way, especially when they are to be placed on a height, at a great distance. In this position the finish of the last touches is lost, though the beautiful form of the arms and legs, and the good taste displayed in the cast of drapery, with folds, not to numerous, may easily be recognized; in this simplicity and reserve is shown the refinement of the talent. Figures whether of marble or of bronze that stand somewhat high, must be boldly undercut in order that the marble which is white and the bronze which tends towards black may receive some shading from the atmosphere, and thus, the work at a distance appear to be finished, though from near it is seen to be left only in the rough. This was a point to which the ancients paid great attention, as we see in their figures in the round and in half relief, in the arches and the columns in Rome, which still testify to the great judgement they possessed. Among the moderns, the same quality is notably exhibited in his works by Donatello (or Donato; 1386-1466). Again, it is to be remembered, that when statues are to be in a high position, and there is not much space below to enable one to go far enough off to view them at a distance, but one is forced to stand almost under them, they must be made one head or two taller. This is done because those figures which are placed high up lose in the foreshortening, when viewed by one standing beneath and looking upwards. Therefore, that which is added in height comes to be consumed in the foreshortening, and they turn out when looked at to be really in proportion, correct and not dwarfed, nay rather full of grace. And if the artist should not desire to do this he can keep the members of the figure rather slender and refined, this gives almost the same effect.

The Proportions of the Human Figure

It is the custom of many artists to make the figure nine heads high; dividing it in the following manner; the throat, the neck, and the height of the foot (from the instep to the sole) are equal to one head and the rest of the body to eight; of these, the shinbone measures two heads, from the knee to the organs of generation two more, while the body up to the pit of the throat is equal to three, with another from the chin to the top of the forehead, so that there are nine in all. As to the measurements across [breadth], from the pit of the throat to the shoulder on each side of the length of a head, and each arm to the wrist is three heads. Thus, the man with his arms stretched out measures exactly as much as his height.

Artists Must Depend on Their Judgment Rather Than on the Measuring Rule

After all, the eye must give the final judgement, for, even though an object be most carefully measured, if the eye remain offended it will not cease on that account to censure it. [147]

Let me repeat that although measurement exercises a just control in enlarging the figure so that the height and breadth, kept according to rule, may make the work well proportioned and beautiful, the eye nevertheless must decide where to take away and where to add as it sees defect in the work, till the due proportion, grace, design and perfection are attained, so that the work may be praised in all its parts by every competent authority. And that statue or figure which shall have these qualities will be perfect in beauty, in design and in grace. Such figures we call 'in the round,' provided that all the parts appear finished, just as one sees them in a man, when walking round him; the same holds good of all the details which depend on the whole. But it seems to me high time to come to the particulars of the subject.

(3) *Of Architecture* (Vasari 1907: 95-98; fully transcribed except that footnoted have been omitted and paragraphing has been augmented)

The Principles of Planning and Design

But since talking of particular things would make me turn aside too much from my purpose, I leave this minute consideration to the writers on architecture, and shall only say in general how good buildings can be recognized, and what is requisite to their form to secure both utility and beauty. Suppose then one comes to an edifice and wished to see whether it has been planned by an excellent architect and how much ability he has shown, also whether the architect has known how to accommodate himself to the site, as well as to the wishes of him who ordered the structure to be built, one must consider the following questions. First, whether he who has raised it from the foundation has thought if the spot were a suitable one and capable of receiving buildings of that style and extent, and (granted that the site is suitable) how the buildings should be divided into rooms, and how the enrichment on the walls be disposed in view of the nature of the site, which may be extensive or confined, elevated or low-lying. One must consider also whether the edifice has been tastefully arranged and in convenient proportions, and whether there has been furnished and distributed the proper kind and number of columns, windows, doors, and junctions of wall-faces, both within and without, in the given height and thickness of the walls; in short whether every detail is suitable in and for its own place. It is necessary that [96] there should be distributed throughout the buildings, rooms which have their proper arrangement of doors, windows, passages, secret staircases, anterooms, lavatories, cabinets, and that no mistakes be apparent therein. For example there should be a large hall, a small portico or lesser apartments, which being members of the edifice, must necessarily, even as members of the human body, be equally arranged and distributed according to the style and complexity of the building; just as there are temples round, or octagonal, or six sided, or square, or in the form of a cross, and also various Orders, according to the position and rank of the person who has the buildings constructed for when designed by a skillful hand these exhibit very happily the excellence of the workman and the spirit of the author of the fabric.

An Ideal Palace

To make the matter clearer, let us here imagine a palace, and this will give us light on other buildings, so that we may be able to recognize, when we see them, whether they are well fashioned or no. First, then, if we consider the principal front, we shall see it raised from the ground either above a range of outside stairs or basement walls, so that standing thus freely the building should seem to rise with grandeur from the ground, while the kitchens and cellars under ground are more clearly lighted and of greater elevation. This also greatly protects the edifice from earthquakes and other accidents of fortune. Then it must represent the body of a man in the whole and similarly in the parts; and as it has to fear wind, water, and other natural forces, it should be drained with sewers, that must be all in connection with a central conduit that carries away all the filth and smells that might generate sickness.

In its first aspect the façade demands beauty and grandeur, and should be divided as is the face of a man. The door must be low down and [97] in the middle, as in the head the mouth of the man, through which passes every sort of food; the windows for the eyes, one on this side, one on that, observing always parity, that there be as much ornament, and as many arches, columns, pilasters, niches, jutting windows, or any other sort of enrichment, on this side as on that; regard being had to the proportions and Orders already explained, whether Doric, Ionic, Corinthian, or Tuscan. The cornice which supports the roof must be made proportionate to the façade according to its size, that rainwater may not drench the façade and him who is seated at the street front. The projection must be in proportion to the height and breadth of the façade.

Entering within, let the first vestibule have a greater amplitude, and let it be arranged to join fittingly with the entrance corridor, so that the press of horses or of crowds on foot, that often congregate there, shall not do themselves any hurt in the entrance on fête days or other brilliant occasions. The court-yard, representing the trunk, should be square and equal, or else a square and a half, like all the parts of the body, and within there should be doors and well-arranged apartments with beautiful decoration.

The public staircase needs to be convenient and easy to ascend, of spacious width and ample height, but only in accordance with the proportion of the other parts. Besides all this, the staircases should be adorned or copiously furnished with lights, and, at least over every landing-placed where there are turns, should have windows or other apertures. In short, the staircases demand an air of magnificence in every part, seeing that many people see the stairs and not the rest of the house. It may be said that they are the arms and legs of the body, therefore as the arms are at the sides of a man so ought the stairs to be in the wings of the edifice. Nor shall I omit to say that the height of the risers ought to be one fifth of a braccio at least ["That is, about 4 ½ inches."], and every tread two-third's wide ["About 15 ½ inches."], that is, as has [98] been said, in the stairs of public buildings and in others in proportion; because when they are steep neither children nor old people can go up them, and they make the legs ache. This feature is most difficult to place in buildings, and notwithstanding that it is the most frequented and most common, it often happens that in order to save the rooms the stairs are spoiled.

It is also necessary that the reception rooms and other apartments downstairs should form one common hall for the summer, with chambers to accommodate many persons, while upstairs the parlours and saloons and the various apartments should all open into the largest one. In the same manner should be arranged the kitchens and other places, because if there were not this order and if the whole composition were broken up, one thing high, another low, this great and that small, it would represent lame men, halt, distorted, and maimed. Such works would merit only blame, and no praise whatever.

When there are decorated wall-faces either external or internal, the composition must follow the rules of the Orders in the matter of the columns, so that the shafts of the columns be not too long nor slender, nor over thick nor short, but that the dignity of the several Orders be always observed. Nor should a heavy capital or base be connected with a slender column, but in proportion to the body must be the members, that they may have an elegant and beautiful appearance and design. All these things are best appreciated by a correct eye, which, if it have discrimination, can hold the true compasses and estimate exact measurements, because by it alone shall be awarded praise or blame. And this is enough to have said in a general sense of architecture, because to speak of it in any other way is not matter for this place.

Architectural Problems

The architects of the Renaissance had one main problem to solve for two building types: how to unify the fronts of churches and of palaces. These two aspects of one problem had been solved to the satisfaction of the Greeks by the adoption of the temple form and the courtyard house. The Romans adapted the Greek temple and adapted the courtyard house for both villas and apartment blocks. For their houses and other building types such as basilicas (law courts) and termae (public baths), the Romans had paid less attention to exteriors than to interiors and had allowed the interiors to be reflected in the exteriors rather than imposing a form on its contents. Renaissance architects were obsessed with the idea of creating coherent designs for at least the fronts of their buildings of all types, but they almost consistently rejected the pagan temple form and never found an equally coherent solution.

The problem of how to unify the front of a Christian church was not a new one. Throughout the Medieval period, attempts had been made to give the ancient Roman basilica into a more coherent front. By the late Middle Ages, the standard solution in northern Europe had been to place two towers on the front to conceal the disunity between the clearstory and the aisles. The ancient Romans had provided multiple entrances to their law courts so that they could also serve as exchanges, but Christians insisted on using one main entrance and retained aisles for funerary chapels with separate altars for masses to be said for the dead.

Christians turned their churches into cemeteries rather than like the ancient Romans requiring burials to be outside the walls of a city. In republican cities like Florence and Venice, there was the additional problem of how to fund a church for every neighborhood, and the solution was generally to line the interior with privately funded funerary chapels for each family that could afford one.

Renaissance architects tried every solution they could think of to unify the fronts of basilican churches except using a temple form or at least adding a free-standing portico to the front of a church. For example, Michelangelo attempted to add a triumphal arch block in front of San Lorenzo in Florence, but it was not built, and he attempted to add a portico to the front of St. Peter's in Rome that was also not built. Palladio succeeded in placing houses on podiums and in adding free-standing porticoes to villas and adding the sides of temples to palaces, but his church fronts were compromises that indicated the basilican form without entirely unifying their fronts.

Renaissance architects also had the problem of unifying the interiors of basilican churches. Aisles divided the interiors into at least three parts, and Alberti finally solved this problem by turning the aisles into alcoves that opened into the central space. In his Sant'Andrea in Mantua, he largely solved the problem of concealing the discrepancy between the two-storied clearstory and one-storied chapels by concealing the front with a compromise between a triumphal arch and a temple front that was neither one, but he spoiled the coherence by adding a large dormer on top of the pediment. His interior was later disunified by adopting a cruciform plan.

Successively, Brunelleschi, Bramante, and Michelangelo tried to equal the span and unity of the interior of the Pantheon. For the new St. Peter's in Rome, Bramante attempted to get away from the cruciform plan by adopting the Greek cross, but that too was a compromise in that all of the interior was still not visible from anywhere within the church. Michelangelo eventually produced the best solution with a centralized plan for San Giovanni dei Fiorentini in Rome that included funerary chapels around its perimeter much as Brunelleschi had proposed for a chapel and as Michelozzo (1396-1472) had created for a choir in Florence, but Michelangelo's church was not built because neither the reigning pope, the reigning duke of Florence, nor the wealthiest Florentine merchants in Rome wanted to bear the main part of the expense or to share the glory of having done so. Michelangelo's ideal solution for a church went unheeded until Protestants decided that the ancient temple was a good way to distinguish their churches from Catholic churches and still later to identify with Greek democracy as opposed to the absolutism of the Catholic hierarchy.

The problem of how to unify the fronts of houses also produced many compromises, none of which was as satisfactory as those finally adopted by Palladio. Earlier Renaissance architects had used graded rustication in place of the orders to create at least the semblance of a podium, had superimposed one-storied colonnades as for ancient Roman theatres and basilicas, or had used little temple fronts to enframe each window in a repeated pattern. They added stringcourses between floor levels or to connect window sills; they hid roofs with widely projecting cornices; and so forth, but no solution was entirely satisfactory as long as they refused to use porticoes or two-storied columns or pilasters. As in classic archtiecture, the elements of the orders were used to enframe and organize planes and spaces into coherent wholes.

Although Michelangelo provided the best solution of a clearstoried church and although Palladio provided the best solution for houses, their solutions were largely ignored until centuries later. Nonetheless, many different solutions were tried that were more or less successful, and better solutions did finally emerge to be put to better use eventually. The Renaissance was a period of continual attempts to improve the appearance of buildings inside and out, and many of its partial solutions continued to be put to good use.

Why the Renaissance Began in Florence

Florence was not one of the principal powers in Italy. "The four great Powers, Naples,

Milan, the Papacy, and Venice, formed among themselves a political equilibrium which refused to allow of any disturbance" (Burckhardt 1944: 16). Why did the rebirth of Antiquity start in Florence rather than in one of these cities?

After being the principal city of Italy for six centuries, Rome was reduced to a city of the second rank in the Empire when the capitol was relocated to Constantinople in 330. It was captured and sacked in 410 by the Visigoths for the first time in eight centuries since 390 BC, when it had been sacked by the Gauls. In 455 it was attacked by Vandals, in 546 by Ostrogoths, in 846 by Saracens, and in 1084 by Normans (https://en.wikipedia.org/wiki/Timeline_of_the_city_of_Rome).

In the first jubilee year of 1300, approximately 200,000 persons came to Rome to take advantage of the indulgences that were being offered to pilgrims, and they enriched the Vatican further (Burckhardt 1944: 48). With the greatest remains of Antiquity including the Pantheon, the Colosseum, Diocletian's Baths, and other evidence of the greatness of the Roman Empire, it might have been expected to become the birthplace of the Renaissance, but it mainly quarried its ancient buildings to construct neighborhood churches and houses in the Romanesque style, and like other Italian cities in the middle of the 1300s, it was overbuilt when the Black Death killed a large part of its population. Within two centuries, it did become the place offering the greatest opportunities to architects and artists from throughout Italy, but during most of the 1300s, it offered very little opportunity. In 1309 the Papacy was forced to relocate to Avignon, and it remained there until 1377. In the meanwhile, anti-popes were elected, and the Great Schism in the Catholic Church was not resolved until the Papacy to Rome under Martin V. Consequently, during the critical period of the late 1300s when Florence was building its cathedral and putting the first set of bronze doors on its Baptistry, Rome was dormant, and its principle families fought one another more or less continually even though 140 fortified houses had been demolished in 1257 in an attempt to stop the fighting (Burckhardt 1944: 109). Moreover, it already had more churches than were needed by its decreasing population, and its swamps made it increasingly unhealthy through malaria. Florence got a head start on Rome, and when it later surpassed Florence, it relied on artists who had been attracted from elsewhere, and the uneven competition largely prevented local talent from developing.

Venice

Venice was founded in 413 as an island retreat for Paduan emigrants during the period of barbarian invasions (Burckhardt 1944: 40). In 764 the power of its doges began to be limited by the election of two tribunes annually, and its republican began and lasted until 1797, when Napoleon added the city to his conquests. Venice had become the most prosperous city in Italy during the Medieval Period by being inaccessible to invaders and by monopolizing the trade between the Byzantine Empire and northern Europe, and its prosperity an an international center of trade increased during the Crusades from 1095-1291. Venice even managed briefly to maintain trading relations with the Ottoman Empire after 1453, but later fought seven wars with the Turks over disputed territories in the eastern Mediterranean (https://en.wikipedia.org/wiki/Timeline_of_the_Republic_of_Venice).

Like Florence, Venice was controlled by its great families of merchants, but directly rather than indirectly. "In Venice, the 'nobili,' the ruling caste, were all merchants..." (Burckhardt 1944: 219). In 1498, Aldus Manutius contrasted the men who governed Venice with all other places he knew of:

> They are skilled not only in governing the state and ruling its subjects—in this respect to which they are so much to be admired that without any argument they must be judged superior to all rulers of states, both past and present—but also in rhetoric and in every possible branch of learning [Manutius 2017: 183].

The political system of Venice was more stable than Florence by electing doges for life through a voting process that defied corruption. "The Council of Ten, which had a hand in everything, was eyarly chosen afresh from the whole governing body, the Gran Consiglio, and was consequently the most direct expression of its will. It is not probably that seriour intrigues occurred at these elections, as the short duration of the office and the accountabiity which followed rendered it an object of no great desire" (Burckhardt 1944: 43). The isolation and defenses of Venice enabled it to ignore most threats including those from the Papacy. Its government "... reserved to itself the appoint of all important ecclesiastical offices, and ... one time after another dared to defy the court of Rome..." (47).

The close connections of Venice with the East and the example of nearby Ravenna had enabled it to construct buildings in the Byzantine style, and by the 1400s, it available building space was largely filled. More recent buildings were superficially Gothic in ornament. Venice had no classical architecture to influence its architectural development, and it was too isolated from classical influences to have been the place where the rebirth of Antiquity could begin, but after the fall of Constantinople in 1453 and the invention of printing, it became the center for the transmission of classical Greek texts and of pivotal importance for the transfer of Greeks knowledge to northern Europe as well as to the rest of Italy.

When Venice eventually began to construct buildings with classical elements, they were designed by architects from elsewhere until Palladio went from the Veneto to Rome, made the most through study of its ancient architecture, created the style that became most popular throughout Europe and its colonies, and returned to the Veneto to start his career as an architect and to publish his work, and it was the superb presention of his work in print even more than the buildings themselves that made him one of the most influential architects of all time. Although Venice got a late start compared to Florence, through Palladio and the excellence of its publications, it eventually had a permanent influence on architectural design worldwide as well as on the transmission of Ancient knowledge.

Within decades of the invention of printing, Venice because the center of publishing in Italy, and Manutius published most of the Greek classics for the first time and ensured their survival (Appendix IV herein). "...Venice can now be called a second Athens on account of Greek literature..." (Manutius 2016: 229).

During the Renaissance, no one made a more careful of ancient architecture than Andrea Palladio or published a more useful and better illustrated book on architecture. Late in the 16th Century while the rest of Italy began to be censored by the Inquistion, Venice continued to be a great center of learning and architecture. The twilight of the Renaissance was in Venice.

Through the machinations of the Congress of Vienna in 1815-1816, the Austrian Empire acquired Venice along with much of northern Italy. In 1866 Venice finally joined the rest of Italy.

Naples

Naples (Neopolis) was founded as a Greek colony in the 6th Century BC. After being briefly ruled by the Samnites in the 5h Century, Naples became an integral part of the Roman Empire from the 4th Century BC until AD 536 (https://en.wikipedia.org/wiki/Timeline_of_Naples). During the Medieval Period, the city was attacked successively from 536-902 by Byzantines, Goths, and Saracens. The foreign occupation of southern Italy for seven centuries began in 1139 with Normans from Sicily; it continued with kings of French origin from 1309-1442, and its Gothic cathedral was begun in 1313. From 1442 to 1861 a nearly continuous succession of Spanish kings and viceroys ruled southern Italy with or without Sicily, which was sometimes ruled separately. Even though there are major architectural remains built by the ancient Romans at Baia, they had little if any influence during the Renaissance. Herculaneum was discovered in 1738 and along with Pompeii had a great impact on the Neoclassical Style, but was centuries too late to influence the Renaissance. Even though Naples is as close to Rome as Florence is to Rome, Spanish conservatism and absolutism largely prevented any major new developments for centuries: "...the Spanish rule over Naples and Milan, and indirectly over almost the whole peninsula, withered the best flowers of the Italian spirit" and especially "...in the neighbourhood of the

Holy Inquisition at Rome..." (Burckhardt 1944: 191).

Milan

Milan had been a prosperous city during the ancient Roman Empire. It was conquered by the Romans in 222 BC, and in AD 286 it served briefly as the capitol of the Western Empire (https://en.wikipedia.org/wiki/Timeline_of_Milan). During the Medieval Period, as a wealthy city on the path of invasions into Italy from 402-772 Milan was attacked successively by Visigoths, Huns, Ostrogoths, Lombards, and Franks. In 1162 the city was largely destroyed by Frederick Barbarossa. From 1183-1500, it was ruled by Italian tyrants; from 1500-1512 and 1514-1522, it was ruled by the French; and from 1535-1848 it was ruled successively by the Spanish Hapsburgs and as part of the Australian Empire except during the Napoleonic occupation of the city (Burckhardt 1944: 230, n. 89). Like Rome, Milan also built many Romanesque churches during the late Empire and Medieval Period, but being close to northern Europe, in 1386 it chose to build its new cathedral in the Gothic style (which Florence had also chosen for its cathedral, but had redesigned its exterior during construction). Milan's politics and aesthetic preferences were dominated successively by authoritarian rulers from 1183 to 1848. As with Naples, Milan also got a late start, and its great promise did not begin to be realized fully until it became part of the Kingdom of Italy in 1861.

Thus, foreign influences largely determined the fate of architecture and art in Rome, Venice, Naples, and Milan. By contrast, the less powerful city of Florence was better able to develop on its own. Its relative remoteness from foreign influence during the 1300s and 1400s was greatly to its advantage by enabling it to develop uniquely in ways that eventually influenced all of Europe and much of the World.

Florence

Florence became a Roman colony around 59 BC, but very little has survived from the period while it was an integral part of the Roman Empire. During the Medieval Period, it was occasionally attacked, but never occupied for long. The Republic of Florence was created in 1115-1116, and the Florentine Baptistery is believed to have been built in 1128 as the city's cathedral (https://en.wikipedia.org/wiki/Timeline_of_Naples). The city is said to have been named for the Roman Consul Fiorinus, who was killed at Fisole and who death was avenged by Julius Caesar (Staley 1906: 4).

"Charlemagne was a key figure in Florentine history and civic tradition, being credited with the second founding of the city and the rebuildings of the walls..." (Kent 2000: 472, n. 225). Later in the Medieval Period,

The struggle between the Popes and the Hohenstaufen left Italy in a political condition which differed essentially from that of other countries of the West. While in France, Spain, and England the feudal system was so organized that, at the close of its existence, it was naturally transformed into a unified monarchy, and while in German it helped to maintain, at least outwardly, the unity of the empire, Italy had shaken it off almost entirely. The Emperors of the fourteenth century, even in the most favourable case, were no longer eeceived and respected as feudal lords, but as possible leaders and supporters of powers already in existence; while the Papacy, with its creatures and allies, was strong enough to hinder national unity in the future, not strong enough itself to bring about that unity. Between the two lay a multitude of political units—republics and despots—in part of long standing, in part of recent origin, whose existence was founded simply on their power to maintain it... [Burckhardt 1944: 2].

Except where feudalism was imposed in southern Italy "...and in a few other districts, a direct tenure of land prevailed, and no hereditary powers were permitted by the law" (22). "The Italian princes were not, like their countemporaries in the North, dependent on the society of an aristocracy which held itself to be the only class worth consideration, and which infected the monarch with the same conceit" (32). "The feudal state of the Middle Ages know of nothing more than catalogues of signorial rights and possessions (Urbaria); it looked on production as a fixed quantity, which it approximately is so long as we have to do with landed property only. The towns, on the other hand, throughout the West must from very early times hae treated production, which with them depended on industry and commerce, as exceedingly variable..." (45). Feudalism was an "artificial scheme of rights" intended to transfer authority and property to descendants irrespective of their ability, and states were treated as property that could be transferred by marriage or bequest (60).

The usurper was forthcoming when long conflicts between the nobility and the people and between the different factions of the nobility had awakened the desire for a strong government and when bands of mercenaries ready and willing to sell their air to the highest bidder had superceded the general levy of the citizens which party leaders now found unsuited to their purposes. The tyrants destroyed the freedom of most of the cities, here and there they were expelled, but not thoroughly, or only for a short time; and they were always restored, since the inward conditions were favourable to them, and the opposing forces were exhausted. Among the cities which maintained their independence are two of deep significance for the history of the human race: Florence, the city of incessant movement, which has left us a record of the thoughts and aspirations of each and all who, for three centuries, took part in this movement, and Venice, the city of apparent stagnation and of political secrecy. No contrast can be imagined stronger than that which is offered by these two, and neither can be compared to anything else which the world has hitherto produced [39-40]. Burckhardt contrasted Florence with despotic states, compared Florence to Venice, and concluded that

> the most elevated political thought and the most varied forms of human development are found united in the history of Florence, which in this sense deserves the name of the first modern State in the world. Here the whole people are busied with what in the despotic cities is the affair of a single family. The wondrous Florentine spirit, at once keenly critical and artistically creative, was incesantly transforming the social and political condition of the State, and as incessantly describing and judging the change. Florence thus became the home of political doctrines and theories, of experiments and sudden changes, but also, like Venice the home of statistical science, and alone and above all other states in the world, the home of historical representation in the modern sense of the phrase [in the sense of unbiased history based as fully as possible on primary sources; 48].

"At length Machiavelli in his Florentine history (down to 1492) represents his native city as a living organism and its development as a natural and individual process; he is the first of the moderns who has risen to such a conception" (53). His *Prince* was a warning of what could happen and soon did. His recommendation for Forence was, though, to adopt a constitution to ensure the continued existence of a "...republic in the form of a moderate democracy..." (55). Aside from Venice and Florence, nearly all other states in Italy "...were the result of recent usurpations..." (57).

Florence flourished as a republic for several centuries, but Venice had flourished as a republic centuries earlier and continued to be a republic centuries longer than Florence. The Renaissance started in Florence, but had largelhy ceased to exist there before it eventually reached Venice and northern Europe largely through the influence of expatriates of Florence.

During the Renaissance, the city of Florence's prosperity developed largely through commerce and industry that were controlled by its 21 secular guilds. Through appointments, guilds indirectly controlled most aspects of the city's life. During the medieval period, guild membership required demonstrating mastery at the creation of a particular art (in the sense of the art of making anything). During the Renaissance, an artisan or artist could belong to as many guilds as he could master, and the employers of artisans could also become members. Although neither artisans nor artists, the Medici achieved much of their influence through their membership in guilds.

By at least 1182 the guilds of the city of Florence were beginning to flourish, and the cloth guild is known to have existed then, and the banking guild existed by 1202. From 1355-1436 the cloth guild was given charge of supervising the construction of the Duomo or new cathedral. By 1338 the bankers Bardi and Peruzzi were able to lend a king of England 1,365,000 gold florins (with the purchasing power of a florin at about $2.50 in 1944; Burckhardt 1944: 50, 53 n. 21).

In a monograph on *the Guilds of Florence*, Edgcumbe Staley identified the main functions of the city's 21 guilds. There were seven greater guilds (judges and notaries, importers and exporters [calimala], wool, bankers and money changers, silk, doctors and apothecaries, and furriers and skinners); five intermediate guilds (butchers, blacksmiths, shoemakers, masters of stone and wood, and retail cloth dealers and linen manufacturers); and nine minor guilds (wine merchants, inn keepers, tanners, oil merchants and genral provision dealers, sadlers, locksmiths, armourers, carpenters, and bakers; Staley 1906).

Education was secular and was controlled by guilds. Their schools taught mainly reading, writing, and math and used relatively simple prose as examples of Italian and Latin. In 1338, approximately 6,000 children were baptised each year; at the time, "...8,000 to 10,000 learned reading, 1,000 to 1,200 in six schools [later learned] arithmetic; and besides these, 600 [advanced] scholars who were taught Latin grammar and logic in four schools" (Burckhardt 1944: 50). Numerous surviving commonplace books of artisans indicate the masters of Tuscan literature were widely read and copied by adults despite being little used as textbooks. Thus, most Florentines got enough of an education to be able to continue to educate themselves and did so.

In addition, Florence had a university by 1349, and by 1421 its "Studio" had 42 professors (Stayley 1906: 15-16). The university later relocated to Pisa, which was a possession of Florence.

As in Venice, the appointment of leading clerics of Tuscany was controlled by a secular government whose head was chosen by lot for short terms of service. Florence was well organized into parishes, and each major church had lay groups of performers and flagelators or penitants (in about equal numbers; Kent 2000: 57). Religion continued its hold on the hopes and fears of most of people, and the fear of Hell had a more persistent influence than the hope of Heaven.

To an unusual extent, Florentines controlled their own lives, and they also controlled the lives of most Tuscans. "Although Florence posed, and even persisted in seeing herself in the image of David, the beleaguered little defender of liberty against the tyrannical princely Goliaths, in fact throughout the fifteenth century the Florentine state pursued an aggressive imperialistic policy dedicated to the domination of Tuscany" (Kent 2000: 272). Like republican Athens and Rome, it started out defending itself before taking the offensive.

Early in the 1400s the Strozzi were richer than the Medici, but so much of their wealth was tied up in land that Palla Strozzi could not pay his taxes in 1423 (Kent 2000: 454, n. 187). After the Strozzi conspired to get the Medici exiled in 1433, the Medici returned a year later and took their place.

According to the meticulous chronicles of the Villani, the population of the city was estimated at 90,000 in 1338, but so many people died during the Black Death in 1348 that the population was reduced to about 37,000 when taxes began to be collected systematically in 1427, and it rose to about 45,000 in 1480 (405, n 10; Burckhardt 1944: 50).

Until the 1400s Italy had numerous relatively small republics that had survived the Medieval Period, but to maintain their independence and to enlarge their territories at one another's' expense, they generally hired mercenaries to fight their wars, and the result was that the successful condottiere often took over the places they were hired to attack or defend, and numerous small tyrannies came into being in place of republics until the only two principal republics were Venice and Florence.

The greatest threats to the freedom of Florence as a republic in the 1400s were from the despotic governments of Naples and Milan with "...Florence, Venice, and [the condottiero Francesco] Sforza on one side, and the Visconti [duke of Milan], Naples and the pope on the other. [The condottiero] Sigismondo [Malatesta] himself had secured the victory for the Florentines and their allies by switching sides and defeating Alfonso of Aragon at Piombino in 1447" (Kent 2000: 353). In 1450 Sforza replaced the Visconti, who had been dukes of Milan since 1354 (Burckhardt 1944: 7). Cosimo de' Medici negotiated an alliance with Sforza that ended the threat of Milan until it was successively captured by the French and Spanish in the 1500s.

Throughout his life, Cosimo was strongly attracted to pagan philosophy. "…all the evidence suggests that his political education derived… from the large number of classical republican works, particularly those of Cicero, which he owned and annotated" (Kent 2000: 447, n. 152). In 1433-1434 while in exile, the Duke of Milan offered to reinstate Cosimo in Florence, and he refused. "In March 1448 Cosimo supported the imposition of a tax to finance war with Alfonso, Kingle of Naples, asserting that 'if this is a bitter drink, it has to be swallowed in the defence of liberty'" (411, n. 86). "…Pius II enjoined Cosimo to see that Florence contributed to the proposed crusade against the Turks, his response [was], 'I am not a prince and cannot dispose of these things as if I were…'" (348). Regardless of what his descendants wanted to do and the Medici later did, "both public and private erecords show that he was obliged to pursue these ends with the aid of his partisans in a roundabout way, respecting the constitution and the opinions of the *principes civitatis* (the leading citizens)" (350). "Machiavelli… averred that he did not recognize in the Medici 'any ambition … contrary… to the benefit of the commune…'" (367).

With Lorenzo de' Medici, "…his death was seen as unleashing the great turblence that soon followed, for example in Francesco Guicciardini's *Storia d'Italia* 1.1, who credits Lorenzo with maintaining the peace through a balance of power" (Wilson in Manutius 2016: 359, n. 464). Manutius himself wrote "…that in Lorenzo's lifetime Florence was, and was acknowledged to be, a second Athens" (243).

Despite continual manipulation behing the scenes by Cosimo and Lorenzo, Florence was a republic until 1532, when it lost it through the machinations of Clement VII. Although Rome had been invaded by the Emperor Charles V in 1527, Clement invited Charles to invade Florence in 1529. After the siege of Florence in 1529-1530, the Republic of Florence ended, and a Medici duke was imposed. When the first Medici duke was assassinated by another member of the family, another Medici duke was installed, and he married the daughter of the Spanish viceroy of Naples. During the siege of Florence, Michelangelo had sided with the Republic of Florence and against the Medici, and he had designed fortifications in an attempt to prevent the Republic from being destroyed.

The Renaissance ended in Florence when Michelangelo moved to Rome, and it ended in Rome when Michelangelo died in 1564 and in the Venito when Palladio died in 1580. It was almost wholly during the 1400s and almost wholly in Florence that the Renaissance developed to the point that it survived the destruction of the Florentine republic, but only by being adopted elsewhere.

It was not by default that the Renaissance started in Florence but it was by default that it was able to develop and flourish in Florence. As Vasari documented, the greatest architects of the Renaissance starting with the Florentine Brunelleschi and ending with the Florentine Michelangelo were largely self-taught, and they learned architecture primarily by studying the ancient remains of Rome; Palladio was also largely self-taught, and the remains of ancient Rome were also his principle teacher, but he made in addition a throughout study of Vitruvius, and he has mastered construction before becoming an architect. Brunelleschi and Michelangelo never apprenticed to an architect or builder. Both Giotto and Michelangelo taught themselves how to draw by studying nature closely before they apprenticed to artists who worked in contemporary styles, and they were consequently able to surpass their masters.

This is not to imply that a few architects and artists deserve all the credit for the revival of Antiquity, but that they deserve the most credit. These individuals also had to master the aesthetic conventions that were in use to surpass them, and they had to learn how to use materials and methods before making better use of them. They also had to have opportunities to create works that were more classically inspired than Byzantine or Gothic, and during the 1400s, Florence provided the best opportunities for the best architects and artists to develop further.

The needed opportunities were provided by wealthy and sophisticated patrons who were largely merchants and particularly bankers. Florence flourished economically in large part because of its wool industry, trade, and banking. It was located too far north for grapes and olives to do as well as in places farther south, but its location was ideal for raising sheep and other livestock. Giotto was discovered drawing while he minded a herd of sheep. Florence also had suitable building stone nearby, and large numbers of Tuscans were stone masons. Michelangelo facetiously credited his interest in sculpture to having been placed with a wet nurse among stone masons, but when he needed sandstone for building, he relied on the stone masons he had been raised among. Although most Florentines made their livings thorough agriculture or craftsmanship, the wealthiest Florentines were bankers including the Strozzi, Medici, Pitti, and Rucellai, all of whom built palaces in the classical styles and all of whom furnished their palaces with realistic works of art rather than stylized representations of other-worldly beings.

Self-taught Artists

The reasons why the Renaissance began in Florence can best be sought in the biographies of its greatest artists and architects. Vasari was right to write about the individuals who made the most difference, and the information he recorded needs to be compared for valid generalizations to be found rather than used selectively to support theories deductively. An inductive approach will provide the best answer.

Vasari's chronological account of the progress of Tuscan art seemed to him to confirm this explanation for how good design could be revived and could continually improve. The untrained shepherd Giotto took the first step by drawing what he observed, and the untutored Michelangelo took the last step by teaching himself to draw in the same way, and their initial approach enabled the two main turning points in Renaissance art: the break with Medieval conventions and the perfection of new conventions. Michelangelo said that Donatello "…in instructing his pupils used merely to bid them to draw and would sum up all his teaching in the phrase: 'My pupils, when I bid you draw I give you the whole art of sculpture'" (Michelangelo quoted by Francisco de Hollanda, *Dialogues*; Goldscheider 1949: 22, n. 1).

In the preface for his *Lives*, Vasari stated that for art to improve continually, artists need to train themselves by drawing naturally occurring objects. In this way, they develop the ability to observe correctly, to select what is most worth representing, and to develop facility at drawing. Much can also be learned through an apprenticeship about the use of materials and artistic conventions, but there is the danger that an apprentice will be taught to paint like his master rather than like nature and end up painting like a Byzantine rather than a Renaissance artist. It is always necessary to refer to nature to develop the ability to achieve life-like results (Vasari 1568: I, 1-19).

Vasari accepted the Biblical account that the "Divine Architect" created man in his own image, and that as a sculptor "...God fashioned the human form out of clay...." (1, 5).

> ...I think that anyone who will take the trouble to consider the matter carefully will arrive at the same conclusions as I have, that art owes it origin to Nature herself, that this beautiful creation the world supplied the first model, while the original teacher was that divine intelligence which has not only made us superior to the other animals, but like god Himself, if I may venture to say it. In or own time it has been seen, as I hope to show quite shortly, that simple children, roughly brought up in the wilderness, have begun to draw by themselves, impelled by their own natural genius instructed solely by the example of these beautiful paintings and sculptures of Nature. ...I know that our art consists entirely of imitation, first of Nature, and then, as it cannot rise so high of itself, of those things which are produced from the masters with the greatest reputation [5-6].

The Byzantines could draw skillfully, but preferred to draw as their masters had drawn. They preferred to imagine what Heaven must be like rather than seeing any reason to draw what this World was like. In both cases, though, attempts were made to produce art as carefully as possible to resemble previously made art despite different objectives. Nonetheless, Vasari was correct that to create life-like representations, it is necessary to learn to draw initially and primarily from life and secondarily to master conventions and techniques and to improve upon them by making gradual refinements. The principal value of his history of several centuries of Italian art is that he demonstrates this conclusively.

What was true of drawing and painting was equally true of sculpture and architecture. To surpass the Ancients, it was necessary to study anatomy more fully than they had and to learn how they had designed and constructed buildings. Vasari stated repeatedly that the best architects all made careful studies of the ancient architecture of Rome. After learning how to draw, it was then necessary to learn what was most worth drawing and how to create equally good or better examples. Drawing could be self-taught and had to be mastered by individuals through long practice, but to improve upon what had already been accomplished, it was necessary to study the works that had long been most highly regarded over a wide area to prevent developing as a provincial artist or architect.

Equaling the Ancients

No one even in Florence knew how the ancient Romans had been able to span such wide spaces permanently, and it was necessary to go to Rome to try to determine how such accomplishments were achieved. With good reason, this continued to be the final stage in the training of the best architects from the 15th through the 19th centuries. Brunelleschi and Donatello "...left no place unvisited, either in Rome or its neighbourhood, and took measurement of everything when they had the opportunity..."; Brunelleschi's "...only concern being architecture, which had been corrupted, studying the good ancient orders and not the barbarous Gothic style then in general use. Two great ideas possessed him: the one to bring back to light the true architecture, whereby he believed he should make a name for himself not inferior to that of Giotto and Cimabue, the other was to find a method, if possible, of vaulting the cupola of S. Maria del Fiore..." (Vasari 1568: I, 274-275). Similarly, Bramante "...set about this task ["to measure all the ancient buildings of Rome"] alone and wrapped in thought. In a little while he had measured all the buildings there and in the neighbourhood, going even as far as Naples, and wherever he knew antiquities to be" (II, 184). Likewise, Peruzzi made many measured drawings of ancient buildings that were used by Serlio for his publications; Giulio and Antonio da Sangallo made an enormous number of drawings that have been preserved and recently published; and Palladio began to publish his unequalled drawings of ancient buildings. Michelangelo also made careful studies of ancient architecture to be able to adapt design elements and to combine them in new ways. Ancient buildings and sculptures provided for Renaissance architects and sculptors the exemplars that Nature and the best Renaissance artists provided for Renaissance painters providing they were able to observe, select, recombine, and depict what they admired with increasingly good judgment based on increasingly broader range of knowledge. This was the only way to go beyond what was being done in isolation in any one place.

Vasari also emphasized the great importance of competition. Renaissance artists competed to surpass one another as well as the greatest art and architecture of the ancient world. With the great monuments of the past accessible to them, Renaissance artists and architects were obsessed by the desire to at least equal if not surpass them, and they were able to do partly by continually competing with one another. Competition were often held, for example, for the doors of the Baptistery of Florence and for ways to create a dome for the Duomo in Florence. Competition were implicit in employing Leonardo and Michelangelo to create large paintings for the same hall on the same subject. Michelangelo competed with Raphael while working at the same time on frescoes for

Julius II. The architects for St. Peter's competed successively with one another.

As noted, Alberti wrote that Brunelleschi, Donatello, Ghiberti, Luca della Robia, and Masaccio "…should not be slighted in favour of anyone famous in antiquity in these arts" (of architecture, sculpture, and painting; Alberti 1436: 39). Vasari considered Ghiberti's "…nude Sampson embracing a column and holding a jaw-bone in his hand, [as] displaying the highest degree of perfection attained by the ancients in their figures of Hercules, whether of bronze or of marble…" (Vasari 1568; quoted in Goldscheider 1949: 25, paragraph 19).

Patronage

The opportunities for such great accomplishments had to be provided, and patronage was an essential requirement as it had always been, but before the Renaissance, patronage had for a thousand years produced largely the same results. Patronage was not the principal requirement for the creation of increasingly better works of art and architecture, but a necessary requirement. Patrons were generally less well informed than artists, often had different objectives, and often changed their minds or were unable to afford what they commissioned. A great part of Michelangelo's life was wasted by being forced to switch from one project to another. He alone was equally able to achieve greatness in everything he attempted, but only by having developed his talents and through persistent effort. Even near the end of his life when he was the most famous artist and architect in Europe, he could not secure the patronage necessary to build the church he had designed for the Florentines in Rome, the building by which he hoped to surpass the Ancients.

In considering the role of patrons, it needs to be kept in mind that there were as many or more good patrons as good artists, and that artists could accept or reject commissions as readily as patrons could select or fire artists. Most artists were not dependent on the whims of any one patron unless they chose to be, and the better artists like Michelangelo, Verrocchio, and Donatello fired clients who treated them badly.

Individuality was far more characteristic of the Renaissance than it had been of the Medieval Period, and "…Florence was then the scene of the richest development of human individuality…" (Burckhardt 1944: 7).

Florence's Cathedrals

The Renaissance began in Florence to a large extent in order to complete its two cathedrals. Its earliest known cathedral, San Giovanni (St. John the Baptist) is its present Baptistery. Its second and present cathedral, Santa Maria del Fiore (Holy Mary of the Flower [a symbol of the Annunciation]), which is usually referred to as *the* Duomo (though every city with a bishop had a cathedral). A single separate bell tower (campanili) was added to one side of the Duomo. To facilitate discussion, I will refer simply to the Baptistery, Duomo, and bell tower.

Baptistery: The Baptistery is an octagonal building that was constructed during the Romanesque period, and its walls probably date from around the 11thth Century for it was "blessed" by Pope Nicholas II in 1059 (Conant 1973: 230). It reused some ancient Roman columns, and it was believed to be an ancient Roman building. This is one reason it was widely emulated; "…the good architecture in use to-day is derived from that building..." (Vasari 1568: I, 55; n. 1 by Gaunt).

The main importance of the Baptistery for the Renaissance was that the shape of its octagonal dome was adapted for the dome of the Duomo. In addition, two of its bronze doors have the earliest examples of Renaissance sculpture, and they depict some of the earliest examples of buildings designed in the style of the Renaissance.

The Baptistery must originally have had a timber roof because in order to support the present dome, another building was literally constructed inside the walls. Vasari noted that "...to judge by appearances, the vaulting is of a later date" (I, 55). Since the dome rests on the separate wall that was added to the interior of the building, it cannot be as old as the original walls, but when the inner wall was added to provide support for the dome is uncertain. White noted that "already in 1293 the Guild of the Calimala had provided funds for new marble piers for the nearby baptistery. Arnolfo himself may have carried out this work..." (White 1993: 52). The dome was thus definitely added, and the question is: was it added before or after the design of the dome of the Duomo? It was definitely constructed prior to 1294, when Andrea Tafi died because Vasari is explicit that "...Andrea made the Christ, 7 braccia high, for the vaulting..." (Vasari 1568: I, 56). Vasari stated that the foundation stone of the Duomo was laid in 1298 (56). The dome of the Baptistery was thus undoubtedly completed and decorated before the Duomo began to be constructed. Vasari also stated that Arnolfo, the architect of the Duomo, "...proceeded to incrust al the eight sides of the exterior of the church [of San Giovanni, the Baptistery] with black Prato marble, moving the rough stone which was originally used along with the antique marbles ["sarcophagi and tombs of marble and stone which were there"]" (35). Since Arnolfo redesigned the exterior of the Baptistery and since he based the design of the dome for the Duomo on the dome of the Baptistery, it seems likely that he also redesigned the interior of the Baptistery and added its dome, and the likelihood becomes still greater when it is considered that he cannot have received permission to begin a new cathedral with a dome with a span nearly twice as wide without having done so.

The earliest known view of Florence shows that in 1342 the Baptistery closely resembled its present appearance ("the Madonna of the Misercordia" in the Muse del Bigallo). Throughout the 1300s in central Italy, two colors of stone had been used only as a pattern of alternating bands (White 1993). The motif of a plain rectangle of marble outlined in a contrasting color does not appear in the fresco of Arnolfo's model of the Duomo, but suddenly appeared as the new cathedral was being constructed. Since this motif had been used for the facing of the interior of the Pantheon, it seems to me most likely that Brunelleschi introduced it to Florence after having studied how the dome of the Pantheon was constructed, and locally available colors of marble were necessarily substituted. He was influenced by the earlier use of banded stones, but he probably got the motif from Rome.

There are now no visible traces of Gothic architecture in the Baptistery with the crucially important exceptions of its pointed dome and its Medieval mosaics. Neither of these features dates from the Romanesque Period that is generally assigned for the entire building. Some windows depicted as round-headed in the fresco have been made square headed and were later given classical enframements; this type of window enframement was introduced by Baccio d'Agnolo (1462-1543; Vasari 1568: 56).

Further evidence that Arnolfo added the inner wall and dome is that Vasari recorded that his father had "...raised the level of the piazza S. Giovanni.... It was he who invented the useful method of paving the streets with stone, when they had previously been paved only with bricks" (34). Excavations beneath the Baptistery have revealed another floor level (visible through grates about 2 m. below the present level). Raising the level of the piazza in which the Baptistery was located required raising the floor of the Baptistery to the same level, and the new interior walls start at the level of this new floor level; the ancient Roman columns that were reused *in antis* rest on the present floor level. Taking these facts into consideration, I think the decision to build a new cathedral with a Gothic dome of unprecedented size depended on Arnolfo's demonstration that he could span the Baptistery with an octagonal dome of masonry.

Even though the interior with the inner wall added has a span of 25.5 m., Conant was convinced, though, that the vault dates from about a century earlier (Conant 1973: 231). He noted that the Baptistery (then the cathedral) was "blessed" by Nicholas II in 1059 and that a lantern was added in 1150. However, the existence of a lantern does not imply the existence of a dome or the absence of internal supports, and so wide a span is more likely to have required a wooden roof structure. In any case, it is not credible that the addition of the inner wall "...was made possible by the extra width within the foundation of 1059 (as already mentioned), and the wall, thus thickened and strengthened, was perfectly positioned to sustain the remarkable existing masonry vault" (231). More than adequate foundations were regularly provided, but if a masonry vault had been planned, the original wall would surely have been designed to support it, and the vault would rest on the original wall rather than on the added inner wall.

The dome itself is thin and was reinforced by making the stone roof an integral part of the dome (with cement in between (cf. Pietramellara 1973 drawing in Bruschi 2007: 40). Arnolfo apparently took advantage of the compressive strength of the intact outer wall to buttress the newly added inner wall, but when the designed the Duomo, he constructed walls more than thick enough for a masonry dome without requiring any thickening of the piers. If a dome had been planned from the start, encircling aisles or extremely thick walls would probably have been built initially as for the baptisteries at Pisa and Parma (234).

As Conant noted, the city of Florence "...was illustrious in Roman, Early Christian, and Byzantine times, and throughout the Middle Ages.... Florence was relatively peaceful and well governed during this long epoch, which saw the cathedral of this Early Christian see progressively rebuilt and augmented during a period of eleven hundred years (c. 350?-1456)" Consequently, the archaeological remains in the center of the city "...are difficult to understand..." for the Baptistery as well as for the Duomo (Conant 1973: 230). As White noted about the Duomo, "...unfortunately many of the key problems remain unsolved...," but "...recent excavations... seem to show that the east end was indeed planned like the existing structure, as a triconch, centered on an octagonal crossing which was almost certainly to be covered by a cupola" (White 1993: 495, 52).

Eighty feet was an immense distance to be spanned during the entire Medieval Period.

The Byzantine dome of San Vitale in Ravenna is only 50 feet in diameter, and the central dome of the Byzantine cathedral St. Marks in Venice is only 42 feet. The dome of the Carolingian cathedral of Aix la Chapelle is only 47 ½-feet across. The nave of the Gothic cathedral in Cologne is only 41 ½-feet across, and the nave of the Duomo is only 55-feet across (Fletcher 1905). The nave of the Florentine Duomo is only about 35 feet wide, and the nave of Milan's cathedral is about 50-feet wide (White 1993: 496, 519). According to Vasari, the Baptistery originally had a "pillar" in the middle in order to reduce the width to be spanned to about 40 feet, and to create a dome for the Duomo, a number of architects suggested that the best would be "...to make a pillar in the middle and construct it in the manner of a tent, like that of S. Giovanni at Florence..." (Vasari 1568: 278). This must originally have been the case.

When it is considered that the nave of old St. Peter's was about 80-feet across and was spanned with wooden trusses reinforced with iron and that the nave for new St. Peter's is also about 80-feet across and is spanned in masonry, spanning even the Baptistery in Florence eventually with masonry was a major accomplishment during the Medieval Period. Spanning a width greater than both the nave and aisles of the Duomo was considered almost impossible, yet it had been possible for the ancient Romans and so could somehow be done. Surely, Arnolfo's plan for a dome of 137 ½-feet for the Duomo would not have been accepted and he would not have been allowed to create foundations deep and wide enough for so large a dome without a demonstration that at least the 80-foot width of the Baptistery could be spanned in masonry, and this is why another wall needed to be added within the original walls of the Baptistery.

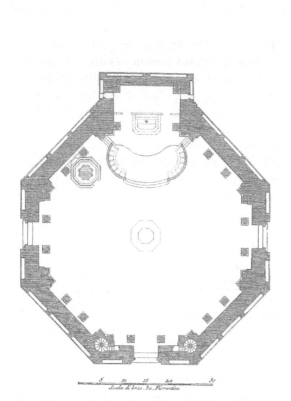 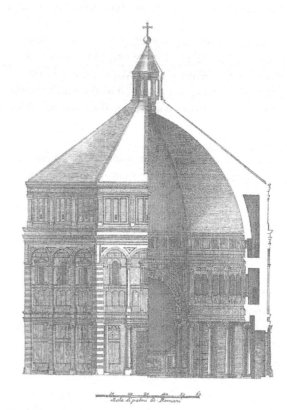

Florentine Baptistery (Sgrillius)

Baptistery, Florence, in 1342 (2017)

Duomo: The Duomo or present cathedral was designed by Arnolfo di Lapo (or Cambio; 1232-1302) in the Gothic Style. Arnolfo was the son of the famous German architect, Jacopo (Lapo), who had been invited to design the cathedral in Assisi and who afterwards settled in Florence (Vasari 1568: I, 33). The vaulting of the Duomo is Gothic, and the lower part of its exterior still has Gothic windows. A fresco in Santa Maria Novella depicting Arnolfo's model for the Duomo shows that its clearstory was also to have had Gothic windows and that the dome was not intended to have a drum. During the long period of construction, various changes were made during the 1300s that have been discussed in detail by John White (White 1993: 495-502). It suffices to note here his conclusion: "this documentary evidence that the main lines of the commission's project were never altered is confirmed by Andrea da Firenze's fresco of the mid sixties in the chapter house of S. Maria Novella..." (498; 347).

Arnolfo "...caused the exterior of the building to be incrusted with marble of various colours, and the interior with hard stone, making even the most unobtrusive corner of the building of the same stone. But, in order that everyone may know the proportions of this marvellous edifice, I will add that from the doorway to the far end of the chapel of St. Zanobius, the length is 260 braccia, the breadth at the transept is 166 braccia, that of the nave and aisles 66. The nave is 72 braccia high, and the aisles 48. The external circumference of the entire church is 1280 braccia..." (37; a Florentine braccio is nearly 2 English feet [0.586 m. or 23 ¼ inches; Frommel 2007: 218]). The proportions of 166 to 260 and of 48 to 72 are very nearly 2:3 (both being 64 percent of one another); the proportion of 66 to 166 is 2:5 (40 percent). Thus, simple proportions were used as in ancient Roman architecture.

Arnolfo was a skilled engineer as well as an architect: "...besides the broad foundations of fifteen braccia deep, buttresses were, with great foresight, placed at each angle of the eight sides [of the transept of the Duomo], and it was the presence of these which encouraged Brunellesco to impose a much greater weight there than Arnolfo is likely to have contemplated" (Vasari 1568: I, 36-37). Considering that the Baptistery has a span of about 80-feet and that Arnolfo was allowed to design the Duomo to have a dome with a span of about 130-feet, there is good reason to believe he created the dome of the Baptistery specifically to prove the feasibility of creating a dome for the Duomo. In any case, he had vaulted the three apsidal arms of the transept before his death and so had demonstrated that the dome was feasible: "...he left S. Maria del Fiore not only with its foundations laid, but saw three principal apses under the cupola vaulted in, to his great praise..." (38). The painting of his model at Santa Maria Novella makes it

> ...clear that Arnolfo proposed to begin to vault his space, starting immediately above the first cornice, whilst Filippo di Ser Brunellesco, desired to lighten the weidht and make the appearance of the structure more graceful, added above this the whole of the space [in the drum,] which contains the round windows before he began his vaulting. This matter would be even more obvious than it is had not thenegligence and carelessness of those who had charge of the works of S. Maria del Fiore in past ears allowed Arnolfo's own model, as well as those of Brunellesco and others, tobe lost [39].

After Arnolfo's death, its clearstory and the drum of the dome were completed with round windows (oculi), and its exterior walls were faced using a rectilinear motif for the marble facing. It was thus begun as a Gothic building, but was completed as a Renaissance building.

As completed, the interior of the Florentine Duomo appears to have influenced the design of Brunelleschi's churches in several respects: in the openness of the interior, in the use of blocks on top of the columns as a base for the arches, and in the white walls of the interior. Whether or not these features were part of Arnolfo's design is uncertain, but they had been adopted by 1368, when "...a formal declaration was drawn up to bind all future capomaestri under oath to do no work of any kind except in absolute conformity to the commission's model..." (White 1993: 498). Previously, one or more previous supervisors of construction had attempted to persuade changing groups of officials to alter the design. White concluded that a fourth bay was added to Arnolfo's model, but he also stated that the fresco showing what the church was painted in "the mid sixties" (498) rather than later, and it shows the nave already had four bays. Most importantly, Vasari is explicit that this fresco "...was taken from the actual model of wood which Arnolfo made" (Vasari 1568: I, 39). Without better evidence such as an undisputed interpretation of the foundations, the only changes that are certain to have been made in the exterior were the ones White mentions: "In it [the fresco] the 'Arnolfan' first bays of the nave and all the external marbling are ignored. Pointed window are shown in the clearstory instead of oculi, and there is a simplified and fully gothic treatment of the flanking chapels. ...the main distribution is fundamentally that of the existing building" (498).

In my opinion, the interior is also likely to represent Arnolfo's intentions for the most part because the interior of S. Croce, which was begun at about the same time (both being begun around 1294) and which Vasari also states was designed by Arnolfo, has tall pointed arches on low columns, no gallery above the aisles, and white walls (31). All of these features had also been previously used for S. Maria Novella, which was begun in c. 1279 (28). Considering that three of Florence's principal Gothic churches were completed in the same style, the largely open and unornamented interiors for Florentine churches was a well established practice more than a century before Brunelleschi designed his churches. Similar features had been used still earlier in S. Francesco, Bologna (1236-1250; p, 26), and although it also omits a gallery, its interior is much less open and well unified, and it has a French Gothic chevet. There may be still earlier examples, but in any case, even the elaborately decorated Romanesque naves of the cathedrals of Siena (largely completed by 1260) and Orvieto (begun c. 1290) omitted a gallery over the aisles and used tall piers to create a more unified interior (46, 50). The omission of a gallery was an important difference between Italian churches and those of northern Europe of the Medieval period.

There are some significant differences. In S. Maria Novella, the arches of the nave are supported on tall colonettes, and the arches of the aisles are supported on more classically proportioned columns (forming a square pier faced with Gothic half-columns). The arches have alternating bands of white and green marble. In S. Croce, the columns are still more classically proportioned, but octagonal, and the nave was not vaulted. In the Duomo, square piers are faced with classical pilasters on pedestals with pedestal-like blocks above the capitals. The four pedestals of each pier conform to the pattern of arches and pilasters between arches in the nave, and they seem to be the earliest use of four pilasters facing a square pier with the corners of the pier left visible. Brunelleschi preferred the less structurally sound arrangement of resting three arches on one column, and he preferred semi-circular arches to pointed arches, but since the overall visual effect of his interiors is much the same as for these three Gothic churches, he was undoubtedly influenced by them in terms of spacial effect and ornamentation limited mainly to grey architectural elements against a white background.

Whether or not more elaborate interiors were planned for the Gothic churches of Florence, Brunelleschi consistently preferred plain interiors with architectural elements as the principal ornament. Sculpture in his churches and chapels was usually limited to a few reliefs within rondels, and it was his work with classical architectural elements that had the greatest influence for the adoption of the restrained Florentine style throughout Italy.

The still greater importance of the Duomo for the Renaissance is that in order to construct its dome, Brunelleschi had to make an intensive study of ancient Roman buildings and to adapt what he learned to create an entirely new type of dome, and he invented the double-shelled dome to lighten and strengthen the dome enough to span the largest space to be spanned since Antiquity. He also raised the dome on a clearstory to provide most of the light for the crossing. The clearstoried dome influenced Bramante's design for the Tempietto, and the tri-lobed plan influenced Bramante's plan for St. Peter's. The double-shelled, ribbed, and pointed dome with a lantern that influenced Michelangelo's design for St. Peter's.

Arnolfo also designed Santa Croce and "...began the palace of the Signori..." (the Palazzo Vecchio), which incorporated an existing tower and which was subsequently enlarged by Michelozzo and by Vasari). Although Arnolfo's "works do not nearly approach the perfection of those of the present time, ye he none the less deserves to be remembered with affection, since, in the midst of so great darkness, he pointed out the road to perfection to those who came after him (Vasari 1586: I, 38-39).

Bell Tower: The artist Giotto (1266-1337) designed the entirely separate bell tower in the Gothic style with pointed arches and pier buttressed, and he intended for it to have a steeple. Giotto was the first Renaissance man by being a painter, sculptor and architect even though he predated the Renaissance. In 1334

> ...he began work on the campanile of S. Maria del Fiore, the foundations of which were laid on a surface of large stones, after the ground had been dug out to a depth of 20 breccia, the materials excavated being water and gravel. On the surface he laid 12 braccia of concrete, the remaining 8 braccia being filled up with masonry. ... While the work was proceeding on its original plan, which was in the German style in use at the time, Giotto designed all he subjects comprised in the ornamentation, and marked out with great care the distribution of the black, white and red colours in the arrangement of the stones and friezes. The circuit of the tower at the base was 100 braccia, or 25 braccia on each side, and the height 144 braccia [85 meters]. If what Lorenzo di Cione Ghiberti has written be true, and I most firmly believe it, Giotto not only made the model of this campanile, but also executed some of the marble sculptures in relief, which represent the origin of all the arts. Lorenzo asserts that he had seen models in relief by the hand of Giotto, and particularly those of these works, and this may be readily credited, since design and invention are the father and mother of all the fire arts, and not of one only. According to Giotto's model, the campanile should have received a pointed top or quadrangular pyramid over the existing structure, 50 braccia in height, but because it was a German thing, and in an old-fashioned style, modern architects have always discountenanced its construction, considering the building to be better as it is. ... He was also appointed director of the work, which was carried on after him by Taddeo Gaddi ["his godson"], as he did not live long enough to see its completion [in 1359. Vasari 1568: I, 80]

Giotto evidently learned how to create more than adequate foundations directly from Arnolfo, as Brunelleschi did indirectly and as Bramante never learned how to do.

The importance of this bell tower for the Renaissance are its pier buttresses and polychrome facing. Brunelleschi later used pier buttresses for the clearstory of the Duomo and omitted Arnolfo's planned flying buttresses, and Brunelleschi also used pier buttresses for the drum of the Duomo.

BRUNELLESCHI

Dome of the Duomo, Florence (1420-1436)

Model by Arnolfo for the Duomo as painted in c. 1367 (Bruschi)

Brunelleschi's dome for the Duomo (albumen)

Filippo de ser Brunelleschi (1377-1446) was the first architect known to have made a careful study of ancient Roman buildings to determine how they were designed and constructed. He initially did so in order to be able to design a dome for the Florentine Duomo, which had been ready for a dome to be added by 1421, but no one before Brunelleschi was able to propose a credible way to span its octagonal crossing of about 130 English feet (somewhat less than the Pantheon's 144 English feet). Cathedral officials had a competition for ideas, and none was considered feasible and affordable.

While still a sculptor, Brunelleschi had competed to design a pair of bronze doors for the Florentine Baptistery, but failing to win the competition, he and the sculptor Donatello decided to go to Rome, where Brunelleschi lived for about six years from c. 1401-1407 and made a thorough study of its architecture. Vasari wrote that

> after the doors had been allotted to Lorenzo Ghiberti, Filippo and Donato [called Donatello by his friends] met, and determined to leave Florence and go to Rome for a year or so, the one to study architecture and the other sculpture. Filippo did this because he wished to be superior to Lorenzo and Donato since architecture is much more useful to men than either painting or sculpture. ...they left Florence and proceeded to Rome, where at the sight of the grandeur of the buildings, and the perfection of the churches, Filippo was lost in wonder, so that he looked like one demented. He set to work to measure the cornices and take the plans of these buildings. He and Donato were constantly going about and spared neither time nor money. They left no place unvisited, either in Rome or its neighbourhood, and took measurements of everything when they had the opportunity. As Filippo was free from the cares of a family, he abandoned himself to his studies, neglecting to sleep and to eat, his only concern being architecture, which had been corrupted, studying the good ancient orders and not the barbarous Gothic style then in general use [in central and northern Italy]. Two great ideas possessed him: to bring back to light the true architecture, whereby he believed he should make a name for himself not inferior to that of Giotto and Cimabue, the other was to find a method, if possible of vaulting the cupola of S. Maria del Fiore at Florence, the difficulty of which had deterred anyone, after the death of Arnolfo Lapi, from wishing to attempt it, except by incurring a great expense for a wooden covering. However, he did not communicate this purpose of his to Donato or to any living soul, but in Rome he attentively observed all the difficulties of vaulting of the Rotonda [the Pantheon]. He had noted and drawn all the vaulting in the antique, and he was continually studying the subject, and if pieces of capitals, columns, cornices and based of buildings were found buried he and Donato set to work and dug them out to find the foundations. ... He then studied the Doric, Ionic and Corinthian orders, one after the other, and to such purpose that he was able to reconstruct in his mind's eye the aspect of Rome as it stood before its fall [Vasari 1568: I, 274-275].

Brunelleschi's first biographer, Antonio Manetti, wrote, "...he lived in my time, and I knew him and talked with him":

> ...he saw the way the ancients built and their proportions. As if he were enlightened concerning great things by God, he seemed to recognize quite clearly certain order in their members and structural parts. This he noticed especially, for it looked very different from what was usual in those times. He proposed, while he was looking at the statues of the ancients, to devote no less attention to the order and methods of buildings. And so he observed closely the supports and thrusts of the buildings, their forms, arches and inventions, according to the function they had to

serve, as also their ornamental detail. In these he saw many wonders and beauties, for the buildings were made at various times and for the most part by good masters who became great because of their experience in building and because the rewards of the princes made it possible for them to study, and also because they were not uneducated men. Brunellesco proposed to rediscover the excellent and highly ingenious building methods of the ancients and their harmonious proportion and where such proportions could be used with ease and economy without detriment to the building. Having perceived the great and difficult problems that had been solved in the Roman buildings, he was filled with no small desire to understand the methods they had adopted and with what tools ["they had worked"]. ... Because of his genius, by experimenting and familiarizing himself with those methods, he secretly and with much effort, time and diligent thought, under the pretense of doing other than he did, achieved complete mastery of them, as he afterwards proved in our city and elsewhere... [translated in Holt 1981: 167, 176-178]

Vasari wrote that soon after Brunelleschi returned to Florence in 1407,

...there took place a gathering of architects and engineers of the district upon the method of vaulting the cupola, at the instance of the wardens of S. Maria del Fiore and the consuls of the art of wool. In this Filippo took part, giving his advice that it was necessary to take away the roof of the building and not to follow Arnolfo's design, but to raise the walls fifteen braccia [to create a drum about 30-feet tall at nearly 2-feet per braccia] and make a large eye in the middle of each face, for this would both lessen the weight on the piers beneath and the cupola could be vaulted more easily. Models accordingly were prepared and the work started [Vasari 1568: I, 275-276].

The taller drum added extra weight, but enabled the drum to have a clearstory of eight large oculi rather than four windows.

Bruneleschi made another trip to Rome and stayed there until he was recalled to reveal how he intended to construct an affordable dome. When he returned to Florence, he refused to reveal specifically how he would solve the problem, but stated that if the crossing "had been circular, it would have been possible to follow the method observed by the Romans in vaulting the Pantheon or Rotonda at Rome, but here it was necessary to follow the eight sides, and to dovetail and chain the stones together..." (277). Vasari noted that he was aware "...that there was a stone chain in the vaulting of S. Giovanni [the Baptistery of John the Baptist] from which he might derive hints for part if not the whole of the work" (286).

Instead of presenting drawings or a model, Brunelleschi recommended that the most experienced architects of Italy, Germany, France, England, and Spain be paid to come to Florence to propose how best to construct the dome (277-278). In the meanwhile he returned yet again to Rome from 1417 to 1420, and thus, from 1401 to 1420, he spent at least eight years studying architecture in Rome and considering how best to deal with every aspect of the problem of creating a dome for the Duomo. In addition, he also became "...the first, and for many years the only, architect who systematically banished the Gothic vocabulary from his buildings. Only under Brunelleschi's direct influence did other masters of his time do so..." (Frommel 2007: 14).

When many of the most experienced architects of Europe had assembled in Florence, they offered

...curious and varied opinions upon the subject, for some said that they would build pillars from the ground level to bear arches to carry the beams which should support the weight; others thought it would be good to vault it with pumice stone, not that the weight might be lighter; and many agreed to make a pillar in the middle and construct it in the manner of a tent, like that of S. Giovanni at Florence; and there were not wanting those who said that it would be a good thing to fill the space with earth mixed with small coin and vault it, giving the people license to go and take the earth so that it should be removed without cost. Filippo alone said that he could easily vault it without so many beams and pillars or earth, at less expense than would be involved by a quantity of arches, and without a framework [without centering, but with scaffolding]. ...

[He said,] "according to the method I have thought out it is necessary to employ the ogive shape, and to make two vaults, an outer and an inner, with sufficient space to walk between them, and that the structure must be bound together at the angles of the eight sides by dove-tailing the stones, and by oak ties over the front of it. Moreover, it is necessary to consider the lights [windows], the ladders, and the channels for carrying of the rain-water...." He might have shown a small model which he had by him, but he did not wish to, because he saw how little the consuls understood and realized the envy of the artists and the instability of the citizens, who favoured now one and now another, according to the caprice of the moment [Vasari 1568: I, 278-279].

Brunelleschi was ridiculed, but he persisted and pointed out defects in all of the models that had been presented. In his favor, he had previously constructed the vault of a chapel in S. Jacopo sopr' Arno without centering and had helped a builder do the same for a chapel in S. Felicita, "...and these things inspired more confidence than his arguments" (282).

Brunelleschi continued to refuse to show his own model, but

...proposed to the masters assembled that whoever should make an egg stand upright on flat marble surface, should make the cupola, as this would be as test of their ability. He produced an egg and all the masters endeavoured to make it stand, but no one succeeded. Then they passed it to Filippo, who lightly took it, broke the end with a blow on the marble and made it stand. All the artists cried out that they could have done as much themselves, but Filippo answered laughingly that they would also know how to vault the cupola after they had seen his model and design. And so it was resolved that he should have the conduct of the work [280].

Being required to state specifically what he planned to do, he wrote a detailed description of how he intended to solve all of the major problems that needed to be dealt with. Since this is one of the earliest surviving explanation by an architect of his design since Vitruvius, it is worth considering in full:

Sirs, in taking into consideration the difficulties of this structure, I find that it is impossible for anyone to make it perfectly round [hemispherical], seeing that the space over which the lantern is to go would be so great that, when any weight was put there, the whole would [thrust outward and] speedily fall down. Yet it appears to me that those architects who have not an eye to the eternity of their buildings, have no care for their memory or do not know what they are about. I accordingly resolved to make the inside of the vault in sections, corresponding with the outside, adapting the manner of the pointed arch, as that tends most upward, and when the weight of the lantern is imposed the whole will be made durable [with a compression ring that could make it function like a keystone in an arch at least until the masonry cured thoroughly]. The thickness of the mass at the base is to be 3 ¾ braccia, and it will diminish pyramidically as it rises to the point where the junction with the lantern is to be made, where it will be 1 ½ braccia thick. Then another vault is to be made outside the first one, 2 ½ braccia thick at the base, to preserve the inside one from the weather. This will also diminish in thickness towards the top, so that at the point of its junction with the lantern it will be only 2/3 of a braccia in width. At every angle there will be a buttress, eight in all, and two for each front including on in the middle and making sixteen in all. On the inside and outside in the middle of the angles at each front there will be two buttresses, each one 4 braccia thick at the base. The two vaults will rise pyramidically in due relation to each other to the top of the circle which is closed by the lantern. Thus 24 buttresses in all will be made about the vaulting and six long arches of hard stone, well braced with iron, and covered over, the stonework and buttresses being all bound together with an iron chain. The masonry must be solid without a break to a height of 5 ¼ braccia, and then come the buttresses and the springs of the vaulting. The first and second circles will be strengthened at the base with long blocks of macigno stone set horizontally, so that both vaults of the cupola shall rest upon these stones. At every 9 braccia in the vaulting there will be small arches between the buttresses with ties of thick oak to bind the buttresses which support the inside vaulting. These oak ties will be covered with iron plates for the sake of the ascents. The masonry of the buttresses is to be entirely of macigno, as are the sides of the cupola, the walls to be tied to the buttresses to the height of 24 braccia and then built of bricks or pumice stone, as those who make it may decide, to obtain the utmost possible lightness. Outside a promenade will be made above a round window with a terrace below and open parapets 2 braccia high, similar to the galleries below, forming two promenades one above the other on a decorated cornice, the upper one being open to the sky. The water will be carried off the cupola in a marble channel, 1/3 braccia wide, and will throw the water to a part made of strong stone below the channel of the outside of the cupola there will be eight marble ribs at the angles, as large as is necessary, 1 braccia high, above the cupola, corniced at the head, 2 braccia wide, so that there may be eves and gutters everywhere. These must have a pyramidal form from the base to the top.

> The cupola will be built as aforesaid without a framework, to the height of 20 braccia, and the rest in the manner preferred by the masters who are charged with the work, as practice will show the best method [Vasari 1568: I, 280-281].

"The consuls and the wardens being thus reassured by the document and the work which they had seen, allotted the cupola to him, making him head master by a majority of votes. But they would not allow him to build higher than twelve braccia, saying that they wished to see how the work succeeded, and that if everything prospered in the manner described by him, they would not fail to allow him to complete the rest" (282).

Some influential men persuaded the others

> ...to give Filippo a colleague in order to bridle his ardour. Lorenzo Ghiberti had proved his genius in the doors of S. Giovanni, and ...they contrived that Ghiberti should be associated with him in the work, under the pretext of their love and affection for the building. Filippo was rendered so desperate and bitter when he heard what the wardens had done, that the proposed to flee from Florence, and had it not been for the consolations of Donato and Luca della Robbia he might have lost his reason. ... However, he took courage in the assurance that this condition would not last for long... [282-283].

Ghiberti knew far less about architecture than Brunelleschi, but he had submitted two designs for the dome that were considered to be competent though not preferred, and he had included original designs for buildings in the panels he designed for bronze doors of the Baptistery. He respected Brunelleschi's superior knowledge and deferred to him in everything that had to do with structure. Brunelleschi had helped with the finishing of the doors and probably taught one-point perspective to Ghiberti as he is known to have done for Masaccio (272), but Brunelleschi never designed anything quite like the buildings depicted on the Baptistery doors. Moreover, Ghiberti too had "...the transferabled esign skills typical of the city's goldsmiths and woodworkers" (Kent 2004: 51)

By 1426, "Filippo had carried the double vaulting of the cupola to a height of 12 braccia, and now the chains of stone and timber were to be put up" (284). He pretended to be sick, and Ghiberti had no idea what to do next. The wardens told Brunelleschi that Ghiberti "...will do nothing without you...," and he replied," I could manage very well without him..." (285). Even by 1423 (three years before the expiration of Ghiberti's contract), Brunelleschi was awarded a lifetime annuity of 100 florins (286). When Ghiberti's contract as a supervisor expired in 1426, only Brunelleschi's contract was renewed.

Brunelleschi added a chain "…above the 12 braccia [level], to bind together the eight sides of the cupola in order that the whole of the superimposed weight may be so distributed that it will not push or spread but rest equally upon the entire edifice" (286). He created scaffolding for the safety of the workmen and to enable heavy stones to be more readily raised.

The murmurers had now been silenced, and the genius of Filippo had so far triumphed in the smooth progress of the building, that all who were not blinded by passion considered that he had displayed more ability in this structure than almost any other artist, ancient or modern. This feeling was caused by his producing his model, by which he showed with what care he had considered every detail: the ladders, the lights within and without, so that no one could injure himself in the darkness, and various iron staples for the purpose of mounting where it was steep, and similar considerations. Besides this, he had devised the iron staples to bear the scaffolding inside if it was ever to be adorned with mosaics or painting, and had put in the least dangerous places the channels to carry off the water, showing where they should be covered, and where uncovered, arranging spaces and apertures to break the force of the winds, and to provide that tempests and earthquakes should not injure the structure, in all which things he proved how much he had profited by the long years he spent in Rome [288].

"He did not live to see the completion of the lantern, but he left directions in his will that it should be built as the model showed, and as he had directed in writing. If done otherwise, he declared that the structure would fall, as it was vaulted in ogive and needed a counterpoising weight to render it more strong" (290). His model shows that he intended for a large band to be constructed around the base of the dome.

Baccio [D'Agnolo] was appointed architect of S. Maria del Fiore, and designed the balcony encircling the cupola, which Filippo Brunelleschi had been prevented by death from doing, though he had prepared designs, lost by the negligence of the ministers of the building. Baccio, after designing the whole, carried out the part on the Bischeri side, but Michelagnolo [Michelangelo] on returning from Rome, seeing that in carrying out the work they were cutting away the projections purposely left by Filippo, made such a disturbance that the work was stopped. He said that Baccio seemed to him to have made a cage for crickets, whereas such a great monument required something larger, possessing design, art and grace, such as were entirely lacking in Baccio's plan, and that he would show them what to do. Accordingly he made a model, and the matter remained a long time in discussion between expert artists and citizens before cardinal Giulio de' Medici, and ultimately neither model was put into execution [Vasari 1568: III, 57].

More than two models have survived for the facing of the drum.

Despite this structural deficiency and incompleteness,

> the extraordinary beauty of the structure is self-evident. Its height from the ground-level to the lantern is 154 braccia, the lantern itself being 36 braccia, the copper ball 4 braccia, and the cross 8 braccia, making 202 braccia in all [approximately 400-feet tall]. It

may be safely asserted that the ancients never raised their building so high or incurred such great risks in contending with the skies as this building appears to... since it is continually being struck by lightning [290].

The Great Pyramid of Cheops is about 482-feet tall and was somewhat taller, but the maximum span of its burial chamber is about 35-feet. Upon its completion in 1436, Alberti considered Brunelleschi's dome to be "...the first great achievement of the new art, equaling or even surpassing antiquity" (Heydenreich and Lotz 1974: 3).

(Fletcher)

Brunelleschi's models for the dome of the Duomo (Baguzzi in Millon and Lampugnani)

San Lorenzo, Florence (1421-1460)

Around 1419 "…by order of the parishioners, who had made the prior chief director of the works, he being a person who professed to understand such things, and who amused himself with architecture as a pastime. The building had already been started with brick pillars when Giovanni de Bicci de' Medici, who had promised the parishoners and the prior that he would make the sacristy and a chapel at his own cost invited Filippo [Brunelleschi] to breakfast one morning…" (Vasari 1568: 291-292). Thus, the initial design for a church was provided by its prior, and brick piers for its transept were being built before Brunelleschi became involved in its design. In 1421 Giovanni de' Medici (the father of Cosimo) asked Brunelleschi

> …if he could devise anything better and finer, to which the later replied, "Without doubt, and I wonder that you, as head, do not spend several thousand crowns and make a church with all the requisites for the place and for the numerous family tombs of nobles, who, when they see a start made, will follow with their chapels to the utmost of their power, especially as we leave no other memory but the walls which bear witness to their authors for hundreds and thousands of years." Stirred by these words of Filippo, Giovanni determined to make the sacristy and principal chapel together with the body of the church, although no more than seven other houses would join him, the others not having the means, these seven being the Rondinelli, Ginori, della Stufa, Neroni, Ciai, Marignoli, Martelli and Marco di Luca, and these chapels were to be made in the cross. The sacristy was the first thing to be put in hand, and the church was afterwards built by degrees. And in the nave of the church chapels were granted one by one to notable citizens. The roofing in of the sacristy was no sooner completed than Giovanni de' Medici passed to the other life ["in 1429"], leaving his son Cosimo. The latter being more enterprising than his father, and loving to cherish his memory, caused this building to be carried on. It was the first thing that he [Cosimo] built, and he took such delight in it that up to the time of his death he was always erecting something there. Cosimo prosecuted this work with more ardour, and while one thing was under deliberation had another one completed. Having taken up this work as a pastime, he was almost continually at it, and his care provided that Filippo should finish the sacristy whilst Donato [Donatello] made the stucco as well as the stone ornament above and the bronze doors of the porch [292].

Brunelleschi made the church and an adjacent cloister both 144 braccia long (approximately 280 feet). The model he made was followed after his death in in 1446, and construction continued intermittently until the 1460s (Frommel 2007: 18-19). Brunelleschi's model probably included a design for a façade, and presumably a miniature of c. 1492-1517 that includes the church and the Medici Palace is based on his design (Kent 2000: 229, fig. 98; 238); if so, it would have been similar to the front Alberti designed for Santa Maria Novella.

Although the front has never been completed, the interior set highly influential precedents for Renaissance buildings. San Lorenzo has an aisled plan that is basically similar to early Christian churches such as San Apollinare in Classe in that their clearstoried naves and aisles are separated from one another by arcades supported by columns. This form had persisted in Italy, where with the major exception of Milan Cathedral, most nominally Gothic have little more that is Gothic about them except pointed arches. Rome has one Medieval Gothic church, and its exterior is plain. Although the Duomo in Florence has Gothic cross-vaults in its nave, there are only three about 60 feet square, and the space and lighting more closely resembles a Roman bath than a Gothic church. Its interior is largely white with contrasting gray stone trim, and Brunelleschi adapted the restraint of most Italian Gothic as part of his style, and Palladio later used white and gray for the interiors of his major churches. "It may be safely said that from the time of the ancient Greeks and Romans until now there has been no man more rare or more excellent than he, and he deserves the greater praise because in his time the Gothic style was admired in all Italy and practised by the old artists, as we see in a countless number of buildings" (299-300). Although San Lorenzo has the plan and some features of an early Christian church, it also has numerous domes in place of pointed cross-vaults. He placed a dome on pendentives over the square crossing of the church; he placed small domes over each bay of the aisles; and he used an umbrella dome in the sacristy similar to those at Hadrian's Villa (adding Gothic ribs). His columns have the proportions, capitals, and entablatures of the Roman Corinthian order, and by adding entablature blocks to his columns, he raised the arches higher than usual to make the nave and aisles seem more nearly a single space. His creative use of impost blocks with the form of a Roman entablature was widely emulated. What is most striking about his interiors are their simplicity. There were no mosaics, no stained glass, no frescoes, no figural capitals, and little color. His white walls are strikingly different from Roman architecture and most later Christian architecture except in northern Italy.

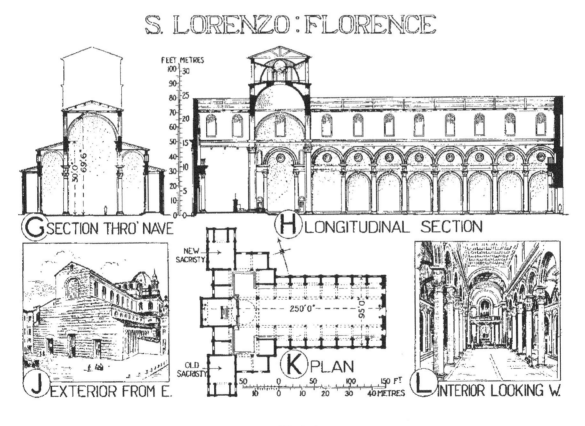

(Fletcher)

San. Lorenzo (Anderson in Millon and Lampugnani)

Old Sacristy in San Lorenzo by Brunelleschi with sculpture added by Donatello from 1434-1443 (Brogi)

Other Buildings by Brunelleschi

Foundling Hospital (begun 1419)

Brunelleschi's Foundling Hospital is an orphanage commissioned in 1419, and it was his first major building. "In the Spedale degli Innocenti the Florentines could... for the first time admire a genuine revival of architecture in the antique style" (Frommel 2007: 16).

The front of the building has a loggia with a design similar to one side of his churches, and the loggia makes a highly effective portico. The story above the portico resembles a clearstory seen from the inside.

The glazed terracotta roundels are by Andrea della Robbia, the nephew of Luca della Robbia. "By dint of many experiment he [Luca] discovered a method of protecting it [clay sculpture] from the injury of time, for he found that he could render such works practically imperishable, by covering the clay with glaze made of tin, litharge, antimony and other materials, baked in the fire in a specially constructed furnace" (Vasari 1568: I, 227).

Foundling Hospital by Brunelleschi, Florence (Alinari in Millon and Lampugnini)

Rondel by Andrea della Robbia for the Foundling Hospital (2017)

Pazzi Chapel (1442-1461)

Of all of Brunelleschi's architectural work, his 1421 design for the Old Sacristy of San Lorenzo was most influential. He used largely the same design for the interior of the Pazzi Chapel, which was commissioned in 1429, which began to be constructed at Santa Croce in 1442 while the Pazzi were still on good terms with the Medici (Heydenreich and Lotz 1974: 12; Kent 2000: 488, n. 59). Brunelleschi also adapted his design for San Lorenzo for the church of San Spirito.

"In the interior Brunelleschi could now project the system of the altar walls onto the other three walls" (Frommel 2007: 21). The rondels with Apostles in the pendentives are by Luca della Robbia (Vasari 1568: I, 226-229).

The plan and domed space of the Old Sacristy determined the basic design for Michelangelo's Medici Chapel in terms of plan, form, scale, and the use of pietra serena to enframe the space. The overall restraint is also essentially the same.

Pazzi Chapel by Brunelleschi with rondels by Luca della Robbia (Anderson)

San Spirito (begun 1432)

Brunelleschi's later buildings have similarly restrained interiors including the cruciform Church of S. Spirito (1432-1482), which was similar in most respects to San Lorenzo including its scale. It is 171 braccia long (about 330 feet) rather than 144 braccia, but the extra length mainly consists of an aisle with chapels behind the choir (creating an ambulatory that San Lorenzo lacks; Vasari 1568: I, 299). Its chapels are semi-circular rather than rectangular, and they projected individually beyond the aisles (creating what appeared to be row of small apses along the sides, but they were later concealed a flat wall that was added to the exterior). Vasari wrote that

> ...it is so well arranged that no building could be richer, finer or more spacious in the disposition of its columns and other ornaments. Indeed, had it not been for the cure of those who, from lack of understanding more than anything else, spoil things beautifully begun, this would be the most perfect church in Christendom, as in some respects its is, being more beautiful and better divided than any other, although the model has not been followed, as is shown by some things begun outside which have not followed the disposition as of the interior for the doors and window decoration as shown in the model [299].

In addition to the concealment of the chapels on the outside, the front was only stuccoed, and Brunelleschi's plan for a piazza to the Arno was not carried out.

The impact Brunelleschi was almost immediate and was widespread throughout Italy. For example, "...as early as 1432 Cardinal Branda Castiglioni ordered the parish church in his hometown of Castiglione d'Olona to be erected on the model of Brunelleschi's Old Sacristy. Yet eleven years previously he had held firm to the Lombard late Gothic style in the Collegiata in the same town where he is buried next to the choir" (Frommel 2007: 77). Giuliano da Sangallo (Giuliano di Francesco di Giamberti [1445-1516] called Sangallo [Vasari 1568: II, 213) based the cruciform church of Santa Maria delle Carceri in Prato on the Pazzi Chapel. Francesco di Giorgio Martini (1438-1502) based the interior of his church of the Osservanza in Siena on Brunelleschi's interiors. Alberti was directly influenced by Brunelleschi himself and helped greatly to spread his ideals about an architecture based on ancient Roman buildings through his *Ten Books of Architecture*.

Brunelleschi single handedly introduced a more classical version of Romanesque architecture in place of Gothic architecture that had become prevalent throughout much of Italy. Although the interior of Florentine Duomo had been constructed with Romanesque restraint, it was designed to be a Gothic cathedral. The baldachino of San Spirito dates was added from 1599-1608. Brunelleschi created a Florentine style that was prevalent in Italian architecture from around 1430 to 1510 and in some parts of Italy much longer. As usual, Venice was always an exception, but eventually Palladio introduced even there a closely similar style that spread to northern Europe as a Protestant alternative to the architecture of the Catholic Baroque period.

San Spirito, Florence (Anderson)

GHIBERTI

Ghiberti's competition model for the Baptistry doors (Goldscheider)

Brunelleschi's competition model for the Baptistery doors (Goldscheider)

In studying the Renaissance, the relationship of architecture and sculpture needs to be kept in mind. The first major architect of the Renaissance who started out as a sculptor was Brunelleschi and the last was Michelangelo, and the same was true of Bernini following the Renaissance. The importance of sculpture to Michelangelo's architecture and painting is manifest, and although the importance of sculpture for earlier architecture may be less obvious, it is significant that although primarily a painter, Giotto was also an architect and sculptor (Vasari 1568: I, 80). Although primarily a sculptor, Andrea Pisano was also an architect (105). As during Antiquity and during the Medieval period, sculpture was often created to be an integral part of architecture, and this was as true of the door of the Florentine Baptistery as of the sculptures of the Parthenon, of the friezes of Roman triumphal arches, and of the facades of Gothic cathedrals. So many of the same skills required for drawing, painting, sculpture, and architecture were the same that during the Renaissance, all the arts advanced together at the same time, at much the same rate, and often as accomplishments of the same individuals.

In most cases, any given individual was best at one profession. However, many of the greatest works of the Renaissance were created by individuals who were good at more than one thing. Even Michelangelo had to work equally hard to master architecture as Brunelleschi did. Alberti was equally knowledgable about painting and architecture, but so much more interested in developing his abilities as an architect that he produced little as a painter or sculptor. Ghiberti was primarily a sculptor, but knew much more about architecture than Vasari gave him credit for knowing, and his contribution to Renaissance architecture was largely ignored until Richard Krautheimer gave him due credit.

Lorenzo di Bartoluccio Ghiberti (1378-1455) was another of the earliest Renaissance men in the sense that he excelled in many fields. He intended to be a painter, but he had apprenticed with the goldsmith Cione. In addition to creating reliefs with minute details, he created three bronze statues in the round that were larger than life, and he was associated with Brunelleschi as the architect of the dome of the Florentine Duomo. Successively, "in 1409 Ghiberti joined the guild of the goldsmiths, in 1423 that of the painters, and in 1427 that of the stonemasons" (Goldscheider 1949: 15). He was also a writer, and in c. 1445 he wrote the earliest autobiographical sketch of any Renaissance artist or architect as part of a treatise on art entitled *I Commentarii*. He is best known for having created two pairs of bronze doors for the Florentine Baptistery.

In his autobiography, Ghiberti wrote, "...I have ever striven to observe her [Art's] fundamental laws, to examine the ways of nature, to discover how pictures are conceived, how the sense of sight works and in what manner the canons of painting and sculpture can be determined" (Ghiberti c. 1445: paragraph 1). He wrote that in 1400 "...it was my intention to devote myself solely to the art of Painting...," but when the competition was announced for a second set of bonze doors for the Baptistery, he decided to enter. Upon presenting a sample of his work, he was one of seven artists who were given sheets of bronze and paid a salary for a year to create a small quatrefoil panel the same size as the panels on the first bronze doors created for the Baptistery by Andrea Pisano (da Pontedera) from 1329-1338; these doors have 28 scenes from the life of John the Baptist, and they show the influence of figures Pisano had studied on classical sarcophagi in Pisa. The competitors for a second set of doors were required to represent the Sacrifice of Isaac (a subject chosen as prefiguring God's sacrifice of His Son). Ghiberti's entry was chosen unanimously by 34 judges over entries of six other artists, who included Brunelleschi and Jacopo della Quercia (Goldscheider 1949: pls. 2-3).

After winning the competition, Ghiberti worked intermittently from 1403-1424 to create 28 panels nearly 1 ½-feet square. His subjects are from the New Testament except for eight panels at the bottom of the doors that represent the four Evangelists and four Doctors of the Church. The quatrefoil centers of the panels are mostly filled by a few figures. Together with an enframement, the doors are about 18-feet tall and 12-feet wide, and the total weight of the bronze is about 34,000 pounds (par. 4).

After completing the first set of doors, Ghiberti was asked to prepare another set of doors for the Baptistery to go opposite the front of the Duomo (where Pisano's doors had initially been placed). Ghiberti's second set of doors are the same size overall as the two earlier sets for the Baptistery, but they have 10 panels about 2 ½-feet square. With the aid of numerous assistants, he worked on them intermittently from 1425-1452:

> At long last I was commissioned to produce the other, i. e. third door of the Baptistery and received a free hand to carry out this work as I thought fit, which meant that it would be conceived perfectly and executed with splendour and a wealth of ornament. So I began working out the panels measuring one and a third cubits which were to illustrate, with a multitude of figures, stories from the Old Testament. I took great pains to observe all the rules of proportion and, as far as lay in my power, to imitate nature in just relationships and countours. In some stories I introduced nigh a hundred figures, and in some less, and in others more. Truly I worked with the greatest diligence and love. There were ten stories altogether and all the architectural settings introduced were in perspective, and so true to life that they looked like sculpture in the round seen from the right distance. They are carried out in very low relief and the figures visible on the nearer planes are bigger than those on the distant ones, just as they appear in real life. The whole work was executed with these proportions kept well in mind. ...
>
> The friezes framing the stories contain twenty-four figures, and the same number of heads [in rondels] appear between one frieze and another. This is the most outstanding of my works and I laboured at it with the utmost ardour and technical attainment, completing it with all possible artistry, sense of proportion and knowledge of art. In the outermost borders on the door case and cornice a decorative pattern of foliage, birds and all sorts of small creatures are introduced in a manner fitting for such types of ornamentation. In addition, the inside of the door-case is adorned with bas-relief decorations in bronze shaped with greatest art, and even the threshold is likewise ornamented [autobiography; paragraphs 17-18, in Goldscheider 1949: 22-25; notes omitted].

Vasari provided additional details. As a youth, he had "...continued to pursue his study of design, and to work in relief in wax, stucco, and other like things, knowing that such small reliefs are a sculptor's method of drawing, and that without them it is impossible to attain to perfection" (Vasari 1568: 239-245). As Ghiberti noted, San Giovanni had been "...the ancient and principal church of the city..." before being converted into a baptistery for the Cathedral (paragraph 3).

For the competition from 1400-1401, the sacrifice of Isaac "...was considered to be a good subject in which the masters could grapple with the difficulties of the art, because it comprises a landscape, figures both nude and draped, and animals, while the figures in the foreground might be made in full relief, those in the middle distance in half-relief, and those in the background in bas-relief" (par. 4). Even on the first set of doors, "the limbs of the nude figures are most beautiful in every part.... He was the first to begin to imitate the masterpieces of the ancient Romans, studying them very carefully, as everyone should who wants to become a good craftsman" (par. 8). When Ghiberti was commissioned to make the main doors, the consuls of the guild of Merchants "...left the whole matter in his hands, saying that they give him full liberty to do as he pleased and that he should make it as ornamental, rich, perfect and beautiful as he possibly could, or as could be imagined, without regard to time or expense and that as he has surpassed all the other figure-makers up to that time, he should in this work surpass himself" (par. 18)

Ghiberti's Isaac (Brogi in Krautheimer)

Ghiberti's Joseph (Brogi in Krautheimer)

Ghiberti's Solomon (Brogi in Krautheimer)

Primitive huts depicted on Ghiberti second set of doors (Alinari and Brogi in Krautheimer)

Architectural designs from the second set of Ghiberti's doors f (Anderson in Krautheimer)

Design by Ghiberti for an octagonal dome and drum with a peristyle (Krautheimer)

In 1436, when the main doors of the Baptistery had been partially completed in the dome of the Duomo had been nearly completed, Alberti wrote in the prologue to his book *On Painting*, "...especially in you, Filippo [Brunelleschi], and in our close friend Donato [Donatello] the sculptor and in others like Nencio [the diminutive for Lorenzo (Ghiberti)], Luca [della Robbia] and Masaccio..., there is genius for ["accomplishing"] every praiseworthy thing" (Alberti 1436 [1966]: 39; 99, n. 3).

Benvenuto Cellini later wrote, "Lorenzo Ghiberti! He was a goldsmith indeed! ... no man can rival him!" (Cellini c. 1566 [1923]: 17). Michelangelo said about the main doors, "they are so fine that they might fittingly stand at the entrance of Paradise..." (Vasari 1568: paragraph 22). Vasari gave Ghiberti the supreme complement of having equalled the ancients in sculpture with his "...nude Sampson embracing a column holding a jaw-bone in his hand, displaying the highest degree of perfection attainted by the ancients in their figures of Hercules, whether of bronze or of marble..." (Vasari 1568 quoted in Goldscheider 1944: 25).

Despite praising Ghiberti for having equalled the ancients in sculpture, Vasari consistently underrated his contribution to the dome of the Duomo (Vasari 1568: I, 239-254 and 269-301). Without question, Brunelleschi could have done without Ghiberti altogether if he had been trusted by the commissioner, but he would probably not have been given the commission without associating him with someone they had more confidence in, and he never had the unlimited authority to do as he thought best that was given to Ghiberti for the second set of the Baptistery's doors. Even for the lantern of the dome, a separate competition was eventually held before accepting Brunelleschi's design.

Ghiberti was paid only for the time he spent supervising construction, particularly while Brunelleschi was away working on other projects or ill (as when he pretended to be). Brunelleschi was the designing architect, and Ghiberti was a superintending architect for the first six years in order to supervise the workmen when necessary and to report on Brunelleschi, whose secrecy and apparent overconfidence caused a great deal of mistrust. Ghiberti made sure the workmen were doing what Brunelleschi had instructed them to do, and when Brunelleschi was not available to solve problems that arose, work stopped. Rather than attempting to undermine Brunelleschi in any way, Ghiberti helped to ensure that Brunelleschi's designs were followed and that high standards of construction were maintained.

Ghiberti's Sampson (Goldscheider)

Richard Krautheimer presented convincing evidence that Ghiberti was a pivotal figure in the architecture of the Renaissance as well as in its sculpture, and he gave the following reasons: (1) Ghiberti had a greater role in the creation of the dome of the Duomo than Vasari's life of Brunelleschi indicated, but a lesser role than Ghiberti's autobiography implied. (2) Ghiberti was involved in a number of other architectural projects. (3) He analyzed the use of architectural backgrounds in all of Ghiberti's work and showed that they represent the development of a unique architectural style rather than having been created by Brunelleschi or Michelozzo, both of whom assisted Ghiberti. (4) He presented evidence that Ghiberti probably had a substantial impact on the writing of Alberti and through Alberti on the work on others. This evidence takes away nothing from the entirely separate and distinct accomplishments of Brunelleschi, Michelozzo, and Alberti, but it adds considerably to the impact that Ghiberti definitely had and is also likely to have had. (5) Ghiberti had been to Rome at least once and probably twice and that he created the finest private collection of classical sculpture known to have existed in the 15th Century. Consequently, Ghiberti's knowledge of ancient architecture and art went far beyond what he learned from his contemporaries. Krautheimer provided detailed evidence to support each of his five conclusions.

(1) *Dome of the Duomo:* Krautheimer summarized the evidence for Ghiberti's involvement in the design and construction of the dome of the Duomo:

Ghiberti's part in preparing and supervising the construction of the dome of the Cathedral is hard to define. The report given in the *Vita di Brunellesco* is twisted and the documents of the Opera of the cathedral are open to interpretation. This much seems clear, that in the preparatory stages, three phases stand out. ["Sanpaolesi (bibl. 468) has given careful study to these documents with regard to the preliminary stage of work, 1417-1420, and I gratefully refer to his analysis. But I fear that throughout he is inclined to overestimate the importance of Ghiberti's contribution to the building of the dome."] In a first exploratory period, May 1417 through August 1418, preliminary models were designed, seemingly under Brunelleschi's supervision, both for the dome and for a centering; in the second period of implementation, Ghiberti and Brunelleschi, in the fall of 1419, competed with one another and with a large group of other contestants each designing a model and executing it in masonry (Digs. [Digests of Documents] 60ff). Apparently, Ghiberti planned to vault the dome over a centering while Brunelleschi intended to do without one, and this, indeed, would have been a fundamental difference.... Possibly a second contest limited to Brunelleschi and Ghiberti, took place in the summer of 1419.... In the winter of 1419-1420, after receiving further direction from a committee of four, constituted by the *Opera*, Brunelleschi and Ghiberti appear to have worked jointly on a definitive model (Digs. 74, 75). Finally, in the spring of 1420, both were appointed supervisors of construction together with the reliable master mason of the Cathedral, Battista d'Antonio, and two substitutes (Dig. 76), all three working at a salary of three florins monthly. Except for two intermissions, one lasting from June 1425 through January or possibly March 1426 (Digs. 120, 123ff), the other through the first half of 1431 (digs. 160, 163) Ghiberti was regularly appointed at more or less fixed intervals, together with his two colleagues and maintained this position through 1436 (Dig. 192). During this entire period, however, his name was specifically mentioned only three times: once in 1426 when he jointly signed with his colleagues and one of the substitutes a report to be followed in building the upper portions of the dome (Dig. 123); again in 1429, when he and Brunelleschi received the commission to have execute a model of the entire cathedral (Dig. 156); finally in 1432 when he collaborated with Brunelleschi and Battista d'Antonio in designing a wooden model for the terminating key ring of the dome (Dig. 171), a model which was changed at Brunelleschi's insistence six months later. As a freelance he entered the competition for the lantern of the dome in 1436 but his project was rejected as were those of three other contestants in favor of Brunelleschi's winning design (digs. 193, 196). ... The documents, then, cast serious doubt on Ghiberti's assertions regarding his contribution to the building of the *cupolone* [Krautheimer 1956: 254-255].

Moreover, starting in 1426, "...the *Opera* retained Brunelleschi's full-time services, but Ghiberti's only part time. He could draw pay only for those days when he reported at least for one hour's work. Brunelleschi's salary was raised to 100 florins yearly, Ghiberti's remained the same 36 florins (Dig. 124). ... True enough, both suspensions were undoubtedly linked to his having both hands full with other tasks. Yet at the same time Brunelleschi's salary was seemingly never suspended, despite an otherwise crowded outside schedule" (255). "The real responsibility for the construction obviously rested from the outset with Brunelleschi and his importance grew as the work progressed" (256).

Krautheimer illustrated, but did not discuss a large octagonal dome in a cityscape by Ghiberti that could well represent how he would have designed the dome of the Duomo (pl. 111b). In any case, it represents a more classical approach by adding a peristyle around the drum for the dome. This relief was executed by Ghiberti more than a half century before Bramante added a peristyle to his Tempietto and his design for the drum of St. Peter's and about a century before Michelangelo added a peristyle to the drum of St. Peter's.

(2) *Other Architectural Commissions:* Ghiberti was also involved in a number of architectural projects independently of the Duomo though minor projects compared to those of Brunelleschi. Although he is not known to have designed an entirely separate building, he was commissioned to make changes in the architecture of other buildings or to supervise other architectural work. His intelligence, expertise, and trustworthiness made him someone who was relied upon to supervise workmen on other projects as well and to at least some extent to provide designs (as his architectural designs for the Baptistery doors prove he was also competent to do).

Documentary evidence is altogether scant regarding Ghiberti's activities as an architect. In May 1419, he designed a stairway for the papal apartment, then in preparation in the convent of S. Maria Novella (Dig. 65; Docs. 127f), but neither a trace nor a description are left.... Beginning January 1420 together with one Cola di Niccola (Spinelli), a goldsmith, Ghiberti supervised work on the choir stalls and other furnishings of the sacristy and Strozzi tomb chapel adjoining S. Trinità (Dig. 73a). ...He made a late bid, in competition with Brunelleschi and one Angel d'Arezzo, for the choir of the Cathedral, submitting a project for it in 1435 (Dig. 191). Evidently in conformity with his competitors, Ghiberti designed an octagonal choir screen with the altar in the very center underneath the lantern of the dome; ...but the jury rejected his project on the grounds that it did not provide sufficient space for the singers and officiating clergy. This criticism proves, if nothing else, how inconsequential were questions of practicability in Ghiberti's architectural thinking.... [256-257].

Brunelleschi's design was considered to be better overall and particularly for having anticipated the need for enclosing a larger area. Nonetheless, it is certain even from the small amounts of documentary evidence that from time to time Ghiberti submitted architectural designs for various projects, but like every other competitor, he was consistently less successful as an architect than Brunelleschi though more successful as a sculptor. His failure to win architectural competitions is less a reflection on Ghiberti than an admission that Brunelleschi was by far the pre-eminent architect of his time. Krautheimer argued persuasively that even though "as a practicing architect Ghiberti may have been a failure, but even so his importance to architecture might still be supreme" (257).

Ghiberti was unusually well informed about the history of architecture during the first half of the 1400s. He was even aware, for example, that the earliest designs for buildings were like two different types of primitive huts. In a relief of Cain and Able, he depicted a domoid hut covered with bark (88a), and in a relief of the nakedness of Noah, the hut has post-and-lintel construction and a low gable (fig. 89) that is much like the archetypal primitive hut from which Laugier derived his principles of architecture. Thus, Ghiberti distinguished at least five distinct styles and successive periods of architecture: primitive, Roman, Romanesque, Gothic, and Renaissance. He also distinguished two stages of primitive architecture: a hut of bent saplings and the post-and-lintel system that was adapted for stone construction successively in Egyptian and Greek architecture. This is not to argue that he knew enough about engineering to create a permanent dome for the Duomo, but that he knew enough about architecture to develop a distinctive style of his own even though it was consistently less successful than the distinctive style that Brunelleschi created.

(3) *Unique Style:* Krautheimer showed that the architectural backgrounds of the panels for Ghiberti's doors and for other reliefs have characteristics that are not represented in the work on Brunelleschi and Michelozzo, both of whom assisted him at various times in the finishing of the doors (Krautheimer 1956: 265, n. 21). He also showed that the design elements and principles characteristic of Brunelleschi and Michelozzo do not occur on the doors. It needs to be kept in mind that Ghiberti apprenticed informally, but over a long period under Brunelleschi, he undoubtedly learned a great deal about architecture at least by observing what he did. He had the best training then available in architecture.

By the time Ghiberti began to design the main doors of the Florentine baptistery, he had "...fully absorbed the new vocabulary and the outstanding principles of Brunelleschi's style of the twenties. ... None of the settings of the Gates of Paradise, however, are completely Brunelleschian. ... The architectural settings of the Gates of Paradise convey an impression of monumental grandeur and of a fully antique flavor that Brunelleschi never achieved: palaces with two upper [super]imposed orders, Renaissance church façades, the round structure in the Joseph panel..." (265-266). The palazzi flanking his basilican church are particularly striking early examples of features that later became characteristic of the Renaissance palazzo.

"In the Solomon [panel]... the architectural setting for the first time creates an ideal plaza of the Renaissance" (258). For the Zenobius Shrine, Ghiberti created ...the first church façade of the Renaissance" (258). "The vocabulary and the design are consistent, and form evidently part and parcel of the newly developing concepts of classical architecture. The architectural skeleton, conversely, is anything but classical. The buildings lack body, they are cardboard-thin. Their plans, their structural framework, and their individual parts stand in no clear relationship to another, either in whole or in detail" (259).

Whether they are temples, round or octagonal buildings, or palaces, all are well defined in every part.... Pilasters are integrated with the entablature into fully developed orders. A smaller order on the top floor takes up and continues the larger order on the ground floor, intercolumniations on arches are repeated by a corresponding series above, at times in double rhythm.... Arcades on piers and entablatures resting on pilasters form arch-and-lintel combinations... Bays are clearly marked off, windows or doors are set in the very center of the bays. The corners of buildings are stressed by strong double-faced piers. The capitals are of a simple sketchy Corinthian type, the entablatures have their three clearly distinct members.... Columns appear to be avoided throughout. Arches, except for the Temple of Solomon, are invariably round. They are carried by piers, either square or cross-shaped. In the Zenobius Shrine, a series of square spires carries the architrave of a portico.... Windows are set either into plain rectangular frames or into aediculas with flanking pilasters and triangular gables...; oculi when they occur are surrounded by beautifully strong, clearly shaped moldings.... Doors are flanked as a rule by pilasters and surmounted by precisely deigned wide architraves with dentil friezes. Departures from this uniform vocabulary are rare and limited.... The entire membering is unencumbered by ornament. ... If Ghiberti himself, prior to 1437 designed them, then indeed, he holds an important place in the history of Renaissance architecture [259-260].

Krautheimer's conclusion that Ghiberti designed the buildings in the backgrounds of his sculptural reliefs is well supported. The architectural designs for the earlier bronze doors indicate that Ghiberti's knew of Brunelleschi's discovery of one-point perspective, but this was something that Brunelleschi widely publicized. He made some mistakes that cannot not be attributed to Brunelleschi such as using polygonal bases for columns rather than circular bases (261). The unusually correct versions for the capitals for the columns may well have been given their final form by Michelozzo rather than by either Ghiberti or Brunelleschi.

Ghiberti's most unusual design was a pair of concentric rings of arcades in the Joseph panel, and Krautheimer concluded that he was most likely influenced by the ruins of San Stefano Rotunda in Rome. The central roof of this building had collapsed and turned the center into an atrium. This building dates from the late Roman or early Byzantine period, but was assumed to have been constructed earlier. Some of its external arches are obviously infilled and were originally open (266-268, n. 23). Most importantly, this building was not in any respect Gothic or foreign.

(4) *Impact on Alberti*: The architectural backgrounds for the main doors were cast by April 1437 and completed around 1439, and they show that at least by then Ghiberti had developed an architectural style of his own (257), and this was around the time that Alberti was in Florence and still primarily interested in painting.

"The architectural settings of the Gates of Paradise were designed fifteen or more years before Alberti set down on paper his architectural concepts, and they date roughly forty years before the Baltimore and Urbino panels [of ideal cities] were painted. Yet they call to mind the principles and particular vocabulary employed in Alberti's architectural treatise and in related paintings" (269).

Like Alberti, Ghiberti left a substantial body of writing about his work and ideas. He wrote more about his accomplishments and less about principles of design. Also like Alberti, he wanted to influence thinking about design rather than keeping everything secret and anonymous like earlier guild members. Unlike Alberti, Ghiberti had been an apprentice, and he belonged to several guilds rather than being limited by membership to a single guild. Alberti did not have the important practical experience about the use of materials and methods of construction that the guild system provided, but like Brunelleschi, he taught himself architectural design by studying ancient Roman architecture.

Krautheimer discussed the development of Alberti's ideas about architecture in detail and concluded Vasari was undoubtedly correct that Alberti's *Ten Books* had been completed by 1452 despite evidence that minor changes continued to be made (268-270, n. 28; 273-274). Alberti had been interested to some extent in architecture at least by 1434 when he published *Della Famiglia*, but it had been a minor interest until he returned to Florence around that time and saw what was being accomplished there (274). It seems more likely that Ghiberti influenced Alberti than the other way around, but much less than Brunelleschi influenced both of them (274).

(5) *Knowledge of Ancient Architecture and Art*: Ghiberti had been to Rome at least once by 1430, and while there he undoubtedly saw depictions of ancient Roman buildings in sculpted reliefs on triumphal arches and columns as well as ruins that were then more nearly intact (275, 278). Although ancient buildings had been quarried to build churches during the Medieval

Period, they did not begin to be quarried systematically until the Renaissance. From influences that are evident in Ghiberti's reliefs, Krautheimer was convinced that "...prior to 1416 [he] must have visited both Pisa and Rome" (284).

As a sculptor, Ghiberti assembled a major collection of ancient Greek and Roman sculpture. He "...bequeathed to his heirs many antiques of marble and of bronze, such as the bed of Polycletus, which was a rare treasure, a bronze leg of life-size, and some heads of women and men, with a quantity of vases, for which he had sent to Greece at great expense. He also left some torsos and many other things, which were dissipated like his property, some being sold..." (Vasari in Goldscheider 1949: 25). In addition, in his writings, Ghiberti referred to the works of Pliny the Elder on sculpture. He was easily one of the best informed artists of the early Renaissance on ancient art and architecture. Vasari wrote that Ghiberti began "...to imitate the masterpieces of the ancient Romans, studying them very carefully, as everyone should who wishes to become a good craftsman,"; and in his opinion, Ghiberti was the first Reniassance sculptor who equaled the ancients: "...a nude Samson embracing a column and holding a jaw-bone in his hand, displaying the highest degree of perfection attained by the ancients in their figures of Hercules, whether of bronze or of marble..." (Vasari 1568: I, 246, 249).

The available evidence and particularly buildings Ghiberti himself designed for the backgrounds of his relievs indicate that he made independent designs of his own and that he created a distinctive architectiral style of his own. He was neither an architect nor an engineer, much less a great architect like Brunelleschi or a highly influential writer on architecture like Alberti, but he was not dependent on other architects for his architectural designs. The evidence Krautheimer presented indicates that Ghiberti had a significant impact of architectural thought and on the creation of a Renaissance style of architecture during the early decades of the Renaissance in addition to a great impact on Renaissance art. As a sculptor, architect, and writer, he was one of the first Renaissance men.

ALBERTI

Leone Battista Alberti (1404-1472) also was an artist before becoming an architect. Like Michelangelo, he began as a painter and only late in life became an architect.

In 1436 Alberti summarized what he had learned as a painter in a treatise. His earliest known architectural commission was about a decade later around 1447. By 1452 he had written a book on architecture, and again like Michelangelo, the last two decades of his life were devoted largely to architecture.

Most of Alberti's documented buildings are in central and northern Italy. However, from 1431 to 1472, Alberti earned his living as a member of the Papal Curia and spent most of the last three decades of his life in Rome (Frommel 2007: 47). From 1434-1443, he followed the papacy to Florence and elsewhere, and from time to time, he travelled widely on papal business (Borsi 1989: 27). Several of his buildings were influential, particularly the Palazzo Rucellai in Florence, Sant'Andrea in Mantua, and a new front for Santa Maria Novella in Florence, but since his influence was primarily as a writer, his writings will be considered first.

Writings

Ten Books of Architecture

Alberti was the first person to write a book about the principles of architecture since Vitruvius. He was strongly indebted to Vitruvius and often praised his recommendations, but was able to go beyond him to some extent by studying buildings constructed after Vitruvius wrote. The Latin text of Alberti's *Ten Books* (*De re œdificatoria*) had been completed by 1452, when he presented a copy to Pope Nicholas V. When it was first printed in Latin in 1485, it became the first book on architecture to be printed (Vasari 1568: I, 346).

Although Vitruvius had continued to be copied for its practical application during the Medieval Period, copies of copies had become increasingly inaccurate and were unillustrated. Surviving copies had to be relocated and compared as with all other classical writers. As Burckhardt noted,

> we may mention, in conclusion, the analogy between Ciceronianism in literature and the revival of Vitruvius by the architects in the sphere of art. And here, too, the law holds good which prevails elsewhere in the history of the Renaissance, that each artistic morvement is preceeded by a corresponding movement in the general culture of the age. In this case, the interval is not more than about twenty years, if we reckon from Cardinal Andrian of Corneto (1505?) to the firs avowed Vitruvians [Burckhardt 1944: 152].

Alberti's treatise was more exclusively about architecture, but he agreed with Vitruvius that an architect needed to master drawing and engineering to design good buildings. Both books were written in Latin; both remained in manuscript until 1485 (Kent 2004: 37). Neither edition was illustrated when it was initially printed (Vitruvius' illustrations having been lost and Alberti text being without illustrations). Alberti's book would have had greater immediate impact if he had written it in Italian rather than Latin or had translated his book on architecture as he did his book on painting. Even Leonardo da Vinci could not read Latin. The first Italian translation was published in 1546 and the second in 1550, but these translations became available about a century after the Latin version was initially published in manuscript and almost a century after Johannes Guttenberg had invented printing in 1457 (Vasari 1568: I, 347). Although the principles Alberti insisted upon continued to be influential, by that time his work had been to a large extent superseded for practical application by Serlio's illustrated treatise with Italian texts, and within a few decades, Serlio had been almost wholly superseded by Palladio. Vitruvius was not translated into Italian until 1556, when it appeared with illustrations by Palladio. A French translation of Alberti's *Ten Books* was published in 1553 and an English translation only in 1726. Because Alberti was unavailable to most practicing architects in their native languages until the mid-16th Century, its influence was more limited than it deserved to be, but in the meanwhile it had much indirect influence.

Alberti set out to produce a more comprehensive treatise than Vitruvius' *Ten Books,* and by studying later ruins carefully, he was able to make significant additions, but he augmented Vitruvius rather than superseding him. The topics covered in each of their books indicates what was most emphasized by each of them.

Alberti's serious interest in architecture began around the time that he returned to Florence from exile and saw the great advances that Brunelleschi had initiated, but he had previously been in Rome and had seen the ruins of ancient Rome. By 1436 he no doubt was already as much aware of the potential for ancient Roman architecture to revive architecture as for the potential of nature to revive painting, and the parallels are made explicit in his 1452 book on architecture.

In his preface, he outlined what his approach would be for dealing with all aspects of architecture:

> ...we shall observe this Method: we consider that an Edifice is a King od Body consisting, like all other Bodies, of Design and of Matter; the first is produced by the Thought, the other by Nature; so that the one is to be provided by the application and Contrivance of the Mind, and the other by due Preparation and choice. And we further reflected, that neither the one nor the other of itself was sufficient, without the Hand of an experienced Artificer, that knew how to form his Materials after a just Design. And the Use of Edifices being various, it was necessary to enquire whether one and the same Kind of Design was fit for all Sorts of Buildings; upon which Account we have distinguished the several Kinds of Buildings: Wherein perceiving that the main Point was the just Composition and Relation of the Lines among themselves, from which arises the height of Beauty, I therefore begin to examine what Beauty really was, and what Sort of Beauty was proper to each Edifice. And as we often meet with Faults in all these Respects, I considered how they might be altered or amended. Every Book therefore has its Title prefixed to it, according tot he Variety of the Subject: The First treats of [the functional requirements for] Designs; the Second, of Materials; the Third, of the [methods of] work; the Fourth, of [the types of buildings and engineering] Works in general; the Fifth, of [the parts of] Works in particular; the Sixth or Ornaments in general; the Seventh, of the Ornaments proper for sacred Edifices; the Eighth, of those for publick and profane ones; the Ninth, of those for the Houses of private Persons; the Tenth, of Amendments and Alterations in Buildings [to correct defects]; To which is added, various History of Waters, and how they are found, and what Use is to be made of the Architect in all these Works; As also Four other Books, Three of which treat of the Art of Painting; and the Fourth, of Sculpture [as integral embellishments for architecture; Alberti 1755: a].

He fulfilled his intentions by discussing in detail functional requirements, design procedures, materials, and methods of construction. To show the similarities in the ways that paintings and buildings were designed and to reveal further the unity of art and architecture during the Renaissance, it will suffice to mention some of the more important principles of design for architecture.

Vitruvius 10 bks.	Alberti 10 bks.
1. Education, city, sites	1. Site, geometry, roofs, fenestration
2. Materials	2. Materials
3. Proportion, foundations, Ionic proportions	3. Construction
4. Doric, Ionic, and Corinthian details	4. Public works: buildings, bridges
5. Forum, basilica, theatres, baths	5. Works of Individuals
6. Climate, room proportions	6. Ornament
7. Floors, stucco, colors	7. Ornament for sacred buildings: temples, churches, orders
8. Water, aqueducts	8. Ornament for public secular buildings (ancient)
9. Astronomy, astrology, sundials	9. Ornament for private buildings (proportion)
10. Machines, defense	10. Restoration of buildings

In a chapter entitled "the Business and duty of a good Architect, and wherein the excellence of the ornament consists," Alberti summarizes what he has previously stated:

> A Prudent Architect will proceed in the Method which we have been just laying down. He will never set about his Work without proper Caution and Advice. He will study the Nature and Strength of the soil where he is to build, and observe, as well from a Survey of Structures in the Neighbourhood, as from the Practice and Use of the Inhabitants, what Materials, what Sort of Stone, Sand, Lime, or Timber, whether found on the Place or brought from other Parts, will best stand against the Injuries of the weather. He will set out the exact Breadth and Depth of the Foundation, and of the Basement of the whole Wall, and take an Account of every Thing that is necessary for the Building, whether for the outward Cost or the filling up, for the Ligatures, the Ribs, or the apertures, the Roof, the Incrustation, for Pavements abroad, or Floors within; he will direct which way, and by what Method every thing superfluous, noxious or offensive shall be carried off by Drains for conveying away the rain Water, and keeping the Foundations dry, and by proper Defences against any moist Vapours, or even against any unexpected Flood or Violence from Winds or Storms. In a word, he will give Directions for every single Part, and not suffer any thing to escape his Notice and Decree. And tho' all these Particulars seem chiefly to related to Convenience and Stability, yet they carry this along with them, that if neglected they destroy all the Beauty and Ornament of the Edifice.
>
> Now the Rules which give the Ornaments themselves their main Excellence, are as follows. First all your Ornaments must be exactly regular, and perfectly distinct, and without Confusion: Your Embellishments must not be too much crowded together or scattered as it were under Foot, or thrown on in Heaps, but so aptly and neatly distributed, that whoever should go about to alter their Situation, should be sensible that he destroyed the whole Beauty and Delicacy of the Work [that is, that nothing can be added or subtracted without detriment to the design as a whole]. There is no Part whatsoever but what the artist ought to adorn; but there is an Occasion that all should be adorned equally, or that everything should be enriched with equal Expense; for indeed I would not have the Merit of the Work consist so much in Plenty as in Variety. Let the Builder fix his richest Ornaments in the principal Places; those of a middling Sort, in Places of less Note, and the meanest in the meanest. And here he should be particularly careful, not to mix what is rich with any thing trifling, nothing little with what is great, nor to set any thing too large or high in narrow or close Places; tho' things which are not equal to each other in Dignity, nor alike even in Species, may very well be placed together, so it be done artfully and ingeniously, and in such a Manner, that as the one appears solemn and majestick, the other may shew chearful and pleasant, and that they may not only unite their different Beauties for the Embellishment of the Structure, but also seem as if the one without the other had been imperfect; nor may it be amiss in some certain Places to intermix some what even and a coarse Sort, that what is noble may receive a yet further Addition from the Companion:
>
> Always be sure never to make a Confusion of the Orders, which will happen if you mix the *Doric* member with the *Corinthian* as I observed before, or the *Corinthian* with the *Ionic*, or the like. Let ever Order have its own regular Members, and those all in their proper Places, that nothing may appear perplexed or broken. Let such Ornaments as are proper to the Middle be placed in the Middle, and let those

which are [paced symmetrically] at equal Distances on each side, be proportioned exactly alike. In short, let every thing be measured and put together with the greatest Exactness of Lines and Angles, that the Beholder's Eye may have a clear and distinct View long the Cornices, between the Columns on the Inside and without, receiving every Moment fresh Delight from the Variety he meets with insomuch, that after the most careful and even repeated Views, he shall not be able to depart without once more turning back to take another Look, nor, upon the most critical Examination, be able in any part of the whole Structure to find one Thing unequal, incongruous, out of Proportion, or not conducive to the general Beauty of the whole.

All these Particulars you must provide for by means of your Model; and from thence too you should before-hand consider not only what the Building is that you are to erect, but also get together all the materials you shall want for the Execution, that when you have begun your work you may not be at a Loss, or change or supersede your Design: but having before-hand made provision of every thing that you shall want, you may be able to keep your workmen constantly supplied with all their Materials. These are the Things which an Architect is to take care of with the greatest diligence and Judgment. The Errors which may happen in the manual Execution of the work, need not be repeated here; but only the Workmen should be well looked after to see that they work exactly by their Square, Level and Plumb-line; that they do their Business at the proper Seasons, take proper Season to let their work rest, and at proper Seasons go to it again; that they use good Stuff, found, unmixed, solid, strong, and suitable to the Work, and that they use it in proper Places, and finish every Thing according to their Model [Alberti 1755: 204-204; book IX, chap. IX].

In order to prepare himself to practice architecture successfully, Alberti stipulated that he ought to be a Man of fine Genius, of a great Application, of the best Education, of thorough Experience, and especially of strong Sense and sound judgment, that presumes to declare himself an architect. It is the Business of Architecture and indeed its highest Praise, to judge rightly what is fit and decent: For though Building is a matter of Necessity, yet convenient Building is both of Necessity and Utility too....to raise a edifice which is to be compleat in every Part, and to consider and provide before-hand every thing necessary for such a work, is the Business only of that extensive Genius which I have described above: For indeed his Invention must be owing to his Wit, his Knowledge, to Experience, his Choice to Judgment, his Composition to Study, and the Completion of his Work to his Perfection in his Art; of all which Qualification I take the Foundation to be Prudence and mature Deliberation. ...

Lastly, in the Study of his Art I would have him follow the Example of those that apply themselves to letters: For no Man thinks himself sufficiently learned in any Science, unless he has read and examined all the Authors, as well bad as good that have wrote in the Science which he is pursuing. In the same Manner I would have the Architect diligently consider all the Buildings that have any tolerable Reputation; and not only so, but to take down in Lines and Numbers, nay make Designs and Models of them, and by means of them, consider and examine the Order, Situation, Sort and Number of every Part which others have employed, especially such s have done any thing very great and excellent, whom we may reasonably suppose to have been Men of very grate Note, when they were intrusted with the Direction of so great an Expense. Not that I would have him admire a Structure merely for being huge, and imagine that to be a sufficient Beauty; but let him principally enquire in every Building what there is particularly artful and excellent for Contrivance or Invention, and gain a Habit of being pleased with nothing but what is really elegant and praise-worthy for the Design: And where-ever he finds any thing noble, let him make use of it, or imitate it in his own Performances; and when he sees any thing well done, that is capable of being still further improved and made delicate, let him study to bring it to Perfection in his own Works....

...Painting and ["practical"] mathematicks are what he can no more be without, than a Poet can be without the Knowledge of Feet [meter] and Syllables; neither do I now whether it be enough for him to be only moderately tinctured with them. This I can say of myself, that I have often started in my Mind Ideas of Buildings, which have given me wonderful Delight: Wherein when I have come to reduce them into Lines, I have found in those very parts which most pleased me, many gross Errors that required great Correction; and upon a second review of such a Draft, and measuring very Part by Numbers, I have been sensible and ashamed of my own Inaccuracy. Lastly, when I have made my Draught into a Model, and then proceeded to examine the several Parts over again, I have sometimes found myself mistake, even in my Numbers [Alberti 1755: 205-207; book IX, chap. X].

Beauty: "...there is hardly any Man so melancholy or stupid, so rough or unpolished, but what is very much pleased with what is beautiful.... We should therefore consult Beauty as one of the main and principal requisites in any Thing which we have a Mind should please others. ...we see that Nature consults Beauty in a Manner to excess, in every Thing she does, even in painting the Flowers of the Field. If Beauty therefore is necessary in any Thing, it is so particularly in Building, which can never be without it, without giving Offence both to the Skilful and the Ignorant" (112).

"We may often observe that base Materials managed with Art, make a handsomer Shew than the Noblest heaped together in Confusion" (119). "I shall define Beauty to be a Harmony of all the Parts, in whatsoever subject it appears, fitting together with such Proportion and Connection, that nothing could be added, diminished or altered, but for the Worse" (113; book VI, chap. II).

Alberti On Painting

Alberti began as a painter, and by 1436 he had written the earliest surviving treatise on painting (Alberti 1436: 98). Since many Renaissance architects including Alberti, Brunelleschi, and Michelangelo began as artists and applied the principles of art to architecture, it is relevant to consider the principles that Alberti considered most important (as opposed to technical considerations such as the preparation and use of materials and which he did not consider in his treatise).

Alberti wrote that "...the function of the painter is this: to describe with lines and to tint with colour on whatever panel or wall is given him similar observed planes of any body so that at a certain distance and in certain position from the centre they appear in relief, seem to have mass and to be lifelike" (89). In brief, to depict anything successfully, it must seem lifelike.

Alberti's book is divided into three parts in which he first discusses how to achieve one-point perspective, then considers how to imitate Nature successfully, and finally how to achieve mastery. "Never doubt that the head and principle of this art, and thus every one of its degrees in becoming a master, ought to be taken from nature. Perfection in the art will be found with diligence, application and study" (91). "Nothing is ever so difficult that study and application cannot conquer it" (93). His purpose in writing was primarily to introduce all painters to the potential of perspective and to make perspective easier to grasp within the context of geometry. Thus, to succeed he advised all artists to "...always take from nature that which you wish to paint, and always choose the most beautiful" (94). This was a different approach from that of late medieval painters such as Cennino Cennini, who was a contemporary of Alberti and who also wrote on art, but who advocated working in the style of a single master painter (134, n. 12).

"They say that Phidias made in Aulis a god Jove [the Zeus of Olympia] so beautiful that it considerably strengthened the religion then current" (63). "Trismegistus, an ancient writer, judged that painting and sculpture were born at the same time as religion, *for thus he answered Aesclepius: mankind portrays the gods in his own image from his memories of nature and his own origins*" (65). As Protagoras and others wrote, "...man is the mode and measure of all things" (55). Nonetheless, it is necessary to learn to paint everything in nature well to be able to make effective compositions (95).

To make anything "seem lifelike," he wrote in his second part that it was necessary to learn how to imitate nature to achieve mastery in the five distinct aspects: (1) Proportion, (2) Anatomy, (3) Movements, (4) Emotions, (5) Light and Shade. I will extract what he concluded on each of these components. I have omitted footnotes except for those quoted in brackets. The passages in italics occur only in the original version in Latin (and not in the Italian translation made by Alberti himself).

(1) *Proportion:* " A thing to remember: to measure an animate body take one of its members by which the others can be measured [a module]. Vitruvius, the architect, measured the height of man by the feet. It seems a moreworthy thing to me for the other members to have reference to the head, because I have noticed as common to all man that the foot is as long as from the chin to the crown of the head. Thus, one member is taken which corresponds to all the other members in such a way that none of them is non-proportional to the others in length and width" (73).

"A small man is proportional to a larger one, because the same proportions between the palm to the foot, the foot and the other art of the body were in Evander as in Hercules whom Aulus Gellius considered to be the largest of men. There was no difference in the proportions of the bodies of Hercules and Antaeus the giant, for both continued the same ration and arrangement of hand to forearm, forearm to head and thus through all members. ... Things which are proportional to each other correspond in every part, but where they are different and the parts do not correspond they are certainly not proportional" (53). Vitruvius wrote that

> if we take the height of the face itself, the distance from the bottom of the chin to the under side of the nostrils is one third of it; the nose from the under side of the nostrils to a line between the eyebrows is the same; from there to the lowest root of the hair is also a third comprising the forehead. The length of the foot is one-sixth of the height of the body of the forearm, one fourth; and the breadth of the breast is also one fourth. The other members, too, have their own symmetrical proportions, and it was by employing them that the famous painters and sculptors of antiquity attained to great and endless renown [Vitruvius III.I.1; Morgan tr.].

Since the features of men, women, children, and the elderly are distinct, it is necessary to select features that are consistently appropriate to each figure depending of sex and age and proportioned in relation to one another. "First of all, take care that all the members are suitable. They are suitable when size, function, kind, colour and other things correspond to a single beauty. If in a painting the head should be very large and the breast small, the hand ample and the foot swollen, and the body puffed up, this composition would certainly be ugly to see. Therefore, we ought to have a certain rule for the size of the members" (72-73).

Developing good judgment is also essential. "...it is useful to take from every beautiful body each one of the praised parts and always strive by your diligence and study to understand and express much loveliness. This is very difficult, because complete beauties are never found in a single body, but are rare and dispersed in many bodies. Therefore, we ought to give our every care to discovering and learning beauty" (92). Only by using good judgment is it possible to select and combine the best parts of individuals, to equal nature, and even to surpass nature as the ancients did. For example, "in order to make painting which the citizens placed in the temple of Lucina near Croton, Zeuxis, the most excellent and most skilled painter of all, did not rely rashly on his own skills as every painter does today. He thought that he would not be able to find so much beauty as he was looking for in a single body, since it was not given to a single one by nature. He chose, therefore, the five most beautiful young girls from the youth of that land in order to draw from them whatever beauty is praised in a woman" (93).

Alberti refers to Homer three times and to Castor and Pollux as examples of how to depict things well, but does not note that Homer provided a rule for perfect proportions in his description of Castor and Pollux in the Iliad.

(2) *Anatomy:* "Before dressing a man we first draw him nude, then we enfold him in draperies. So in painting the nude we place first those bones and muscles which we then cover with flesh so that it is not difficult to understand where each muscle is beneath. Since nature has here carried the measurements to men, there is not a little utility in recognizing them" (73). John R. Spencer noted that "as the first to advocate the practice of building the human figure from the bones to the skin, Alberti already prefigures the anatomical researches carried on by Florentine painters in the latter half of the fifteenth century" (124, n. 41).

(3) *Movement:* "...I should like to recount here some things about pose and movement which I have collected from nature. From this we shall clearly understand that they should be used with moderation. Remember how man in all his poses uses the entire body to support the head, heaviest member of all. When he is resting on one foot, this foot always stands perpendicularly under the head like the base of a column, and almost always in one who stands erect the face is turned in the same direction as the feet. ... We see that when a weight is held in an extended arm with the feet together like the needle of a balance, all the other parts of the body will displace to counter-balance the weight. I have noticed that in raising the head no one turns his face higher than he would in looking at the zenith; horizontally no one can turn his face past a point where the chin touches the shoulder; the waist is never twisted so much that the point of the shoulder is perpendicular above the navel" (79).

"The painting ought to have pleasant and graceful movements, suitable to what is happening there. The movements and poses of virgins are airy, full of simplicity with sweetness of quiet rather than strength; even though to Homer, whom Zeuxis followed, robust forms were pleasing even in women. The movements of youths are light, gay, with a certain emonstrations of great soul and good force. In men, the movements are more adorned with firmness, with beautiful and artful poses. In the old the movements and poses are fatigued; the feet no longer support the body, and they even cling with their hands" (80).

(4) *Emotions:* " Who could ever believe how difficult it is to attempt to paint a laughing face only to have it elude you so that you make it more weeping than happy? Who could ever without the greatest study express faces in which mouth, chin eyes, cheeks, forehead and eyebrows all were in harmony with laughter or weeping? For this reason it is best to learn from nature...." (77-78). Depicting emotion as well as movement successfully were important for achieving a convincing impression of vitality.

(5) *Light and Shade:* "It is worth all your study and diligence to know how to use these two well, because light and shade make things appear in relief. ... With this balancing of white and black the amount of relief in objects is clearly recognized" (82-83).

Once these five basic components of paintings have been systematically and thoroughly mastered through the most careful study of nature, the elements of design can then be combined into compositions in which the overriding principles moderation, harmony, and coherence are so much taken for granted that they are mentioned only in passing. Most importantly, each element must be selected as appropriate to the scene that has been chosen in order to create a coherent whole regardless of what materials can be afforded.

One-point Perspective: After learning how to create individual figures, a student is ready to learn how to combine them into compositions. To create compositions with sense of depth, it is necessary to understand the use of perspective. As a sculptor and architect, Brunelleschi had demonstrated the principles of one-point perspective through the use of models. He had done so in more than one way because viewers sometimes looked through a peephole into a box and at other times looked into a mirror held at arm's length (obviously not through a peephole). In any case, Brunelleschi did not write about his discovery, and it was Alberti who wrote about its application for painting.

Most importantly, it is necessary to learn how to imitate nature, but to create an effective composition, it is also necessary to understand the use of perspective. Alberti gave precedence to perspective even over the imitation of nature because it was a recent discovery by his friend Brunelleschi that enabled Renaissance painters to go beyond anything ancient painters could have accomplished (consequently dedicating his treatise to him).

"How difficult this is can be seen in the works of antique sculptors and painters; perhaps because it was so obscure, it was hidden and unknown to them" (58). Alberti wrote that "the first great care of one who seeks to obtain eminence in painting is to acquire the fame and renown of the ancients" (67), and the discovery of one-point perspective was another way the Renaissance had surpassed Antiquity.

Alberti recommended viewing a scene through a grid of strings from a single point of view to a single point in the center of the grid and then drawing both a grid and radiating lines from the central point on a page. In this way, each part of each object to be depicted could be accurately outlined on the page to correspond to the squares of the grid of strings. He did not illustrate his manuscript, but in 1525 Albrecht Dürer drew such a grid in use and published it as a woodblock print to show how all parts of a three-dimensional figure could be foreshortened correctly in two dimensions.

Use of a gridded screen and page (Dürer)

Alberti wrote, "I do not believe that infinite pins should be demanded of the painter, but paintings which appear in good relief and good likeness of the subject should be expected. This I do not believe can ever be done without the use of the veil [grid]" (69).

In addition to being used to reduce and draw outlines correctly and to foreshorten figures correctly, this device could be used to draw distant scenes in perspective. For example, if a painter wanted to represent a scene with a foreground, middle ground, and background, all three vertical planes would automatically be reduced proportionate to their distance from one antoher and every object in each plane would be in correct to proportion to every object in the same plane. Thus, the device produced results equivalent to those later produced by a camera obscura, but without a lens (106). After having sketched the outlines of an actual scent, the composition could be improved upon, and other objects could be substituted of similar size in any given plane.

Composition: "I say composition is that rule in painting by which the parts fit together in the painted work" (70). In other words, the parts need to be selected that can be combined into a coherent whole for a composition to be successful. Just as the parts of a human body or lower animal need to be interrelated, the parts of a composition need to be appropriate for inclusion, need to be arranged coherently, and need to be made proportionate to one another. "It seems to me that there is no more certain and fitting way for one who wishes to pursue this than to take them from nature, keeping in mind in what way nature, marvellous artificer of thigs, has composed the planes in beautiful bodies. ... First of all, take care that the members are suitable. They are suitable when size, function, kind, colour and similar things correspond to a single beauty" (72).

Moderation: In all things including variety, the number of objects depicted, and the number of colors used, moderation should be observed:

> ...copiousness and variety please in painting. I say that *istoria* is most copious in which their places are mixed old, young, maidens, women, youths, young boys, owls, small dogs, birds, horses, sheep, buildings, landscapes and all similar things. ... However, I prefer this copious to be embellished with a certain variety, yet moderate and grave with dignity and truth. I blame those painters who, where they wish to appear copious, have nothing vacant. It is not composition but dissolute confusion which they disseminate. ...
>
> *I strongly approve in an istoria that which I see observed by tragic and comic poets. They tell a story with as few characters as possible. ...*
>
> A painting in which there are bodies in many dissimilar poses is always especially pleasing. ... If it is allowed here, there ought to be some nude and others part nude and part clothed in the painting; but always make use of shame and modesty [75-76; *istoria* as used by Alberti to refer to the use of gestures to indicate meaning (24)].

Color: "I prefer a good drawing with a good composition to be well colored" (82) Although color was also important to master, Alberti noted that some of the most famous Greek artists used only four colors and that the ability to draw and to use white and black to indicate relief were more important than what colors were chosen. Colors should not be so conspicuous as to disunify a composition, and for this reason, white and black should only be mixed to produce lighter or darker colors, and gold should not be used at all (49-50, 84-85; cf. 104, n. 23).

Avarice: "It is useful to remember that avarice is always the enemy of virtue. Rarely can anyone given to acquisition of wealth acquire renown. I have seen many in the first flower of learning suddenly sink to money-making. As a result they acquire neither riches nor praise. However, if they had increased their talent with study, they would have easily soared into great renown. Then they would have acquired much riches and pleasure" (67).

Alberti's Documented Churches

Among Alberti's most influential buildings were two façades, one for a palace and the other for a church. The Palazzo Rucellai in Florence, was primarily important for using pilasters to unify its front, and it will be discussed in the next chapter on Palaces and Villas. Only his churches will be considered in this section.

San Francisco, Rimini (Alinari)

San Francisco, Rimini (1450-1461)

Alberti designed a new exterior for the large Gothic church of San Francisco in Rimini. He partly redesigned the spacious interior, which has an open-timbered roof. The most significant feature of the Gothic interior is that its chapels (with pointed arches) open directly into the central space, and Alberti probably adapted this feature for the plan of Sant'Andrea in Mantua.

Alberti was able to put into effect many of the recommendations included in his *Ten Books* such as using piers to support the arches along the sides of his building. The design of the front was based on the triumphal arch of Augustus in Rimini. He planned to put a large dome at the back of the church. as was eventually done for Sant'Andrea in Mantua.

Alberti's patron was Sigismondo Pandolfo Malatesta, who was employed Piero della Francesca. Malatesta was a condottiero second only to Federico da Montefeltro, a fellow patron of the arts. Malatesta was so uniquely vilified by the Church as a devil incarnate that the accusations have as much credibility as legends about medieval saints.

Alberti's design for San Francisco, Rimini; foundation medal by Matteo de' Pasti (1450; Heydenreich and Lotz)

San Sabastiano, Mantua (begun 1460)

San Sebastiano, Mantua (Biblioteca Hertziana; Frommel)

Other churches Alberti designed or redesigned in northern Italy had significant influence though less than his writings, and he was often unable to follow his own recommendations. He completed no major building during his lifetime. Also before designing Sant'Andrea, he designed the entirely new Church of San Sebastiano in Mantua in 1460. It has a cubical central block with four arms that give it a Greek-cross plan. The front is an attached temple with a pediment supported by monumental pilasters above a podium. Neither its interior nor exterior were completed, and the crossing has a cross-vault rather than a planned dome. The ground floor is a mausoleum with arches in front to provide access, and in place of a broad flight of steps are a pair of flanking steps.

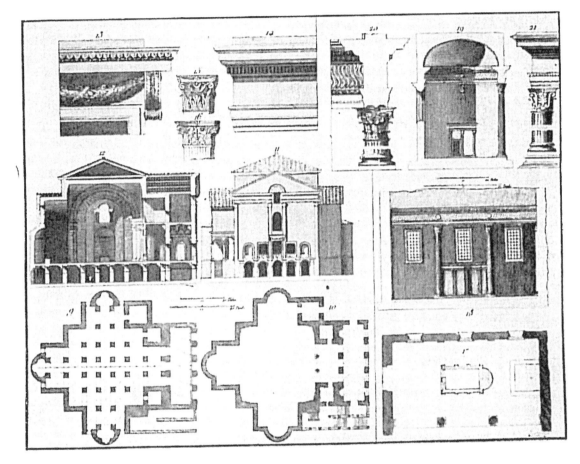

Record drawings of San Sebastiano, Mantua (Seroux d'Againcourt; Heydenreich and Lotz)

Santa Maria Novella (1458-1477)

Alberti's most influential church design was the front for Santa Maria Novella in Florence from 1458-1477 rather than his more important church commissions that were relatively remote from the centers of early Renaissance design. For the front, he added engaged columns to the main story and pilasters and a pediment to the clearstory, and to connect the clearstory to the main story, he added scrolled brackets to either side of the clearstory that closely resemble the form of the buttresses Brunelleschi used for the lantern of the Duomo. Most of the front for the lower story was pre-existing.

Alberti's design for the front of Santa Maria Novella is dated 1470, but is said to have been completed in 1477 (Vasari 1586: I, 347-348). In any case, most subsequent fronts for Renaissance churches with a basilican plan added scrolls in an attempt to create more unified designs. His design directly influenced Michelangelo's design for the front of San Lorenzo, and it became the standard front for Italian Baroque churches. Giovanni di Paolo Rucellai funded the front of Santa Maria Novella after having commissioned Alberti to design his equally influential palazzo.

Vasari praised Alberti highly, but with reservations as a Renaissance man who

...studied the Latin tongue, and practised architecture, perspective and painting, [and who] has left works to which modern artists can add nothing, although number of them have surpassed him in practical skill. His writings possess such force that is it commonly supposed that he surpassed all those who were actually his superiors in art. Thus, it is clear from experience that, with respect to fame and name, writings enjoy the greatest power and vitality, for books easily penetrate everywhere and inspire confidence if they are true and lie not. It is no marvel, then, if the famous Leon Battista is better known by his writings than by the works of his hands. ...he endeavoured not only to explore the world and measure antiquities, but also paid much more attention to writing than to his other work, following his inclination [Vasari 1568: I, 346].

Santa Maria Novella, Florence (Alinari)

Sant'Andrea, Mantua

Sant'Andrea, Mantua (above, Borsi in Frommel; below, McKenna in Millon)

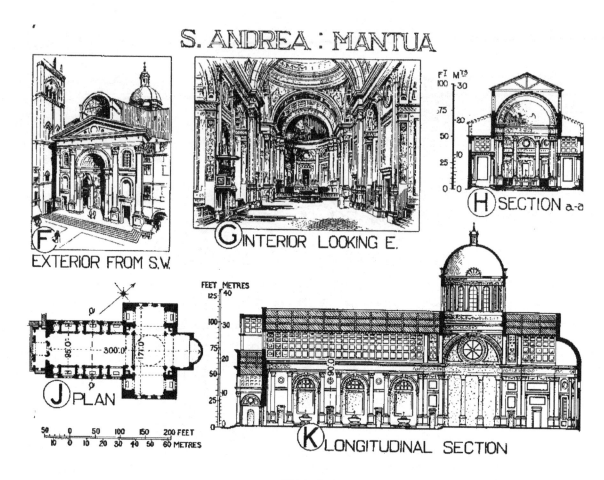

(Fletcher)

Instead of being aisled like nearly all large churches, Alberti's Sant'Andrea in Mantua has side chapels that open directly into the nave and that become an integral part of it. Its plan is most similar to the Basilica Nova though its central space had cross-vaults. As noted, conceptually, the Gothic interior of San Francisco, Rimini, is likely to have been the most direct influence since its chapels also opened into its central space.

Sant'Andrea was begun in 1470. the year of Alberti's death and only the nave was constructed to his design; it was completed in 1494. The cruciform plan and dome are said to have been intended, but no drawing or model survives by Alberti for this building or for any of his other architectural projects.

Santissima Annunziata, Florence

Santissima Annunziata (2017)

Vasari is explicit that the tribune added to Santissima Annunziata was designed by Alberti, and he was so sure that this was the case that he criticized him in detail for a defect in its design and attributed the defect to Alberti's inexperience:

> At this same time [when Alberti designed Rucellai's tomb], Ludovico Gonzago, Marquis of Mantua, wished to make the tribune and princpal chapel in the Nunziata of the Servites at Florence, from designs by Leon Battista. Accordingly he pulled down an old square chapel there of no great size, painted in the old style and made the beautiful and difficult tribune in the shape of a round temple surrounded by nine chapels forming an arc and constructed like niches [|"in 1476"; note by Gaunt]. The arches of the chapel being born by the pilaster in front the stone ornamentation of the arches inclining towards the wall, tend to lean backward in order to meet the wall, thus turning away from the tribune. Accordingly, when the arches of the chapels are looked at from the side, they have an ugly appearance, as they fall backwards, although the measurements are correct and the method of construction difficult. Indeed, it would have been better had Leon Battista avoided this method, because, besides being awkward to carry out, it cannot be done successfully, being ugly as a whole and in every detail. Thus we see that, though the great front arch is very fine when looked at from the outside at the entrance of the tribune, it is extremely ugly on the inside, because it has to be turned in conformity with the round chapel, and this gives it the appearance

of falling backwards. Possibly Leon Battista would not have done this if he had possessed practical knowledge and experience in addition to his learning and theories, for any other man would have avoided such difficulties, and striven rather to render the building as graceful and beautiful as possible. In other respects this work is entirely beautiful, ingenious and difficult, and the courage of Leon Battista must have great to make the vaulting of the tribune in such a manner in that age [Vasari 1568: I, 349].

Although this building has been repeatedly attributed to Michelozzo, Vasari's statement must be accepted as more than an attribution unless better evidence can be provided.

There is no question that Michelozzo was involved in this project, and Heydenrich considered it his "chief religious work" and noted that the project began in 1444. However, Heydenreich also noted that "Michelozzo left the building unfinished when he retired from work on it in 1455; in 1460 operations were temporarily resumed by Manetti, but only completed in 1470-3 under Albderti's superintendence." (Heydenreich and Lotz 1974: 20).

Since SS. Annunziata was the principal pilgrimage site in Florence, objections were made to the involvement of an outsider even though he had been a condotierro in the service of the Florentines and was owed money by them. In 1471 Lorenzo de' Medici intervened and told Gonzaga he was free to complete the project as he saw fit. According to F. W. Kent,

Lorenzo's contribution in early 1471 to the public debate concerning the suitibility of Leon Battista Alberti's model for the tribune of the Servite church of the Annunziata, under Gonzaga patronage, was also curiously muted, given that he was an *opeaio* of the church and the son of a major benefactor. According to one contemporary source, Lorenzo may have shared the majority Florentine view that Ludovico Gonzaga's project begun at the site should be utterly demolished, allowing the Florentines to proceed "in a different manner and with another model...". Or it might be that he expressed public opposition because he did not wish to be seen as dissenting from the critical view of the project held by envious older men with whom he was struggling to cooperate politically; there is some evidence that Lorenzo, who would becaome an avid reader of Alberti, in fact thought the architect's central-plan solution a "beautiful thing," or so the well-informed Mantuan agent in Florence, Piero del Tovaglia, informed his master.... Whatever the case, when Ludovico Gonzaga, annoyed by what he described as the "swarm" of Florenctine objections, threatened to withdraw from this dynastic commitment to a foreign church and spend his money in Mantua, Lorenzo, diplomatically professing ignorance of such aesthetic matters, hastened to advise the marquis on 21 May 1471 to proceed "precisely according to your own taste and desire...." [Kent 2004: 48].

Moreover, "during the last twelve years of his life he [Alberti] was given the opportunity by Lodovico Gonzaga, lord of the little margravate of Mantua, to design his two most original buildings and those most prescriptive for the further devewlopment of architecture" (Frommel 2007: 40). Considering that Albert was from Florence and had previously designed two major commissions in Florence, he seems likely to have been entrusted, as Vasari stated, with the redesign of SS. Annunziata.

Alberti's Undocumented Buildings in Rome

Vasari implies that Alberti was responsible for the design of many buildings that were constructed during the reign of Pope Nicolas V, and considering that Alberti designed major buildings elsewhere, he must also have designed major buildings in Rome for this pope and other popes:

> Leon Battista happened to arrive in Rome at the time when Nicolas V ["1447-55"], by his manner of building had turned the city upside down, and by the offices of his close friend, Biondo da Forli, he [Alberti] became intimate with the Pope, who had hitherto been advised in architectural matters by Bernardo Rossellino, sculptor and architect of Florence, as will be said in the life of his brother Antonio. This man [Rossellino] having begun to restore the Pope's Palace and to do some things in S. Maria Maggiore in conformity with the Pope's wishes, always previously took the advice of Leon Battista. Thus the Pope, by following the advice of one of them and the execution of the other, carried out many useful and praiseworthy things… [Vasari 1568: I, 347].

I interpret this to mean that Alberti designed everything Rossellino constructed including the additions Rossellino constructed for St. Peter's.

The buildings that Vasari specifies Alberti designed in Florence, Rimini, and Mantua have little in common with one another in terms of their forms, but they frequently used the same clusters of design elements regardless of building type. As he stated in his *Ten Books*, Alberti designed buildings in the same ways ancient Roman architects had designed. When he realized that existing ancient buildings differed greatly from one another in the handling of elements, he accepted Vitruvius's advice that the best architects needed to adapt rules to suit specific situations rather than to make entirely new rules or to ignore rules.

Alberti's most influential adaptations were the ways in which he handled fornices and pedestals. Like ancient Roman architects, he often used arches between piers with half-columns to create wider intercolumniations. Consequently, he insisted that for structural reasons arches needed to rest on piers or walls as when arches were used for aqueducts. He insisted that free-standing colums be used to support horizontal entablatures rather than arches, but when arches and columns were used together, they could be combined in any way that made structural and visual sense. When designing arcades of stone for aqueducts or using arches within fornices as for the Colosseum or for triumphal arches such as the Arch of Titus, ancient architects had inserted cornices at the base of the arched element to serve as impost blocks during construction. In other words, they had treated the supports as if they were piers with capitals. Alberti went a step further and inserted pilasters within arches and used shorter columns within taller columns, but with similar proportions as for the front of Sant'Andrea in Mantua. These immensely influential innovations were immediately and widely copied. Raphael and Michelangelo went a step further in putting smaller columns with entablatures in between taller columns. Moreover, Alberti turned fornices into rows of deep niches for his Malatesta temple and into alcoves for his Sant'Andrea, and this was also a highly influential adaptation of a classical combination of elements.

Another immensely influential innovation was the adaptation of an extended pedestal block as on the upper floors of the Colosseum, where the moldings of podiums were adapted for what amounted to an external wainscoting to conceal the barrel vaults of the passages behind them. Alberti extended pedestals similarly to provide apparent support for the widely spaced pilasters on the ground floor of his Palazzo Rucellai in Florence, and running pedestals soon began to be used as organizing elements to connect window enframements as on the Cancelleria and Palazzo Farnese in Rome. In the case of the Palazzo Rucellai, his running pedestal breaks forward beneath each pilaster as on the Colosseum and in way similar to how entablature blocks break forward in the entablature for the door surround he added to the entrance of Santa Maria Novella in Florence.

Primarily on the basis of his reintroduction of the use of fornices and running pedestals, I have attributed a number of early Renaissance projects to Alberti. The details of these projects differ greatly from one another as do the details in all of his documented projects. The fact that there is no documentation to support the attribution of any of these projects individually is irrelevant considering that Alberti is known to have produced at least a first edition of his *Ten Books* by 1452 and is documented as having been employed by the Vatican during from 1444 To 1472. In my opinion, there is no reason to expect him to have been paid separately for supplying designs and still less reason to assume that documented builders must have been architects. Builders often designed minor buildings, but rarely like Palladio taught themselves to become architects. Skill in the execution of a design is a different skill than is needed to produce a successful design, and to assume consistently that an otherwise undocumented building must have been designed by a builder is a mistake in principle. By knowing how to draw and design, an artist could more readily become an architect than a builder could. For example, Arnoldo Bruschi discusses the insufficiency of abundant primary sources for determining who designed Santa Maria della Consolazione at Todi (as will be discussed in the section on Bramante). Unless a builder is documented as having produced designs, it is less likely that a major building was designed by a builder than by an architect.

Some Renaissance architects were more innovative even than Alberti, Michelangelo, and Palladio, but architects such as Giulio Romano (c. 1499-1546) used design elements freakishly to amaze and amuse. Showmanship and self-indulgence were dead ends rather than the beginning of new possibilities. The most influential architects did similar things in ways that expanded the range of alternatives rather than creating more dead ends. Ancient architects had also created numerous dead ends when they tried more to be different than better than their predecessors. It needs to be kept in mind that the controlling theme of the Renaissance was to equal if not surpass Antiquity in every respect and that many ways to be different had proven to be worth adapting further. This is what it meant to design like an ancient architect.

As noted in the chapter on Roman temples and orders (Chapter 5), the earliest known use of fornices was for the Tabularium in 78 B. C., and they were later widely used for the facings of theatres and amphitheaters including the Theatre of Marcellus and the Colosseum. Anyone could have copied these surviving examples of fornices, but no one seems to have done so until Alberti called attention to the usefulness of this design motif in his *Ten Books*, and no one used them more consistently than he did in during the last three decades of his life. I have used them as a basis for attributing four Roman projects to him. Bearing in mind that there are three distinct types of fornices will help to determine sources: an arch between a pair of columns without pedestals (the Tabularium); an arch between a pair of columns with pedestals (the Colosseum); and an arch flanked by two pairs of columns with pedestals (the Arch of Titus).

The principal advantage of putting an arch in between a pair of columns was that the columns could be more widely spaced, and the entablature could consist of flat arches. In other words, the width of an intercolumniation was no longer limited by the strength of a lintel, and the columns became more ornamental than necessary for support, but engaged columns did function as pier buttresses and so enabled walls in between them to be thinner; this was particularly important when fornices were used on the curved facings of theatres in that an arch with a curved plan cannot function as securely as an arch with a straight plan.

Free-standing columns could be more widely spaced by putting arches on top of columns rather than in between them, and this was the arrangement most often used during the Medieval Period and during the early Renaissance. As noted in the chapter on diverging tradition (Chapter 14), arches on columns were used for the aisles and atrium of Old St. Peter's and throughout Old St. Paul's, and they continued to be preferred as late as by Brunelleschi. This arrangement has the advantage of opening adjacent spaces visually as between a nave and aisles and of allowing light to better penetrate into all parts of a building, but it is an inherently unstable method of building. Iron rods have usually needed to be added between the arches on columns and nearby walls to prevent collapse and have sometimes needed to be added in between the arches themselves.

Alberti had begun to spend most of his time in Rome in 1444, when he became a member of the Papal Curia, and after he had studied ancient Roman architecture for six or more years, by 1452 he had completed the first edition of his *Ten Books*. In this treatise he specifically recommended the use of fornices or piers rather than arches on columns.

In his architectural designs, Alberti did not place arches on top of columns (not withstanding the courtyard of the Palazzo Rucellai that was not designed by him as Frommel noted [2007: 32]). Also notably, the ground floor of the front of Santa Maria Novella has arches on columns, but the only part of the ground floor that Alberti designed is the entrance, which has an arch between columns (36-37). Alberti later placed arches in between columns in his Sant'Andrea in Mantua and his Malatesta Temple in Rimini (the interior of which had been built with Gothic arches on top of columns). In his Ten Books, Alberti insisted that for structural reasons arches should either rest on piers or should be placed between columns as on ancient Roman triumphal arches and theaters. For the Malatestino, he used both: arches between columns on the front and arches on piers along the sides.

Alberti certainly popularized the use of fornices even if others had used them previously, and in any case, he almost certainly at least suggested their use on a number of buildings constructed during the second half of the 15th Century in Rome, and this becomes a matter of some importance when it is considered how often arches on columns continued to be used even as late as for the courtyard of the Cancelleria but began suddenly to be superseded in the courtyard of the Palazzo. The relationship of the Palazzo Venezia and the Cancelleria and the attributions of additions to them will be discussed in the following chapter on palaces and villas (Chapter 16).

Benediction loggia and Vatican Palace of Old St. Peter's in c. 1532 (left half of drawing; Heemskerck in Dunbar)

Santa Maria del Popolo, Rome (Frommel)

Benediction loggia and Vatican Palace of Old St. Peter's in c. 1532 (right half of drawing; Heemskerck in Dunbar)

Santa Maria del Popolo in c. 1532 (Heemskerck in Dunbar)

Alberti's direct influence can be suspected yet Frommel wrote, "from 1444 right down to his death in 1472 Alberti mainly lived in Rome as an employee of the curia. He was personally attached to Popes Nicholas V and Pius II. Yet he left not one building in Rome" (Frommel 2007: 47). Frommel attributed nearly all buildings constructed in Rome from 1444 to 1472 to the workmen who constructed them on the basis of financial records that document their participation and that do not mention Alberti, but since Alberti was a salaried member of the Curia, it is not to be expected that he would have been paid extra for architectural designs or the supervision of architectural projects. In my opinion, the circumstantial evidence is very strong that at least some if not all of the buildings attributed to various workmen during this period were designed by Alberti. It seems implausible to me that Alberti designed at least a half-dozen buildings elsewhere and that he designed none for his principal employers. It seems more likely that the buildings with fornices attributed to Antonio da Firenze and Francesco del Borgo (c. 1420-1468) are more likely to have been designed by Alberti and executed by them.

Primarily on the basis of the use of fornices, but also taking into consideration how carefully the designs were detailed, I attribute the following buildings and additions in Rome to Alberti:

(1) the earliest part of the Vatican Palace built for Nicholas V from 1450-1454 and constructed by Antonio da Firenze;
(2) at least the ground floor of the Benediction Loggia for Paul II begun in c. 1458;
(3) the front of the church and the courtyard for the Palazzo Venezia, which was enlarged when Paul II was pope from 1464-1471; and
(4) Santa Maria del Popolo, begun in 1471 for Sixtus IV and constructed by Francesco del Borgo.

All four of these projects used well-proportioned fornices as their principal design motifs, and as Frommel noted, the front of Santa Maria del Popolo is similar to Alberti's design for the front of Santa Maria Novella. Del Borgo probably designed the hospital of Santo Spirito in Rome (completed in 1475), and its design with fornices is more indebted to Alberti than to Brunelleschi's hospital in Florence that has arches on columns. These designs seem too well informed and consistent to have been created by three different architects rather than one. Individually, they were less influential than as a group, and taken together, they provided recent and prominent examples of the use of fornices and so were more directly influential on the revival of fornices than Alberti's unillustrated treatise.

Of these four projects, the Benediction Logia was the most conspicuous and influential and is most directly paralleled by the entrance surround he designed for Santa Maria Novella in that the columns are on pedestals like the ground floor of the Benediction Loggia and the adjacent entrance to the atrium of Old St Peter's. This loggia was planned to be two-storied and to extend entirely across the front of the atrium, but only four bays of one-story were built initially. "Under Paul II and Alexander VI, it was continued to include the second story. Under Julius II and Bramante, it was even given a third story, before being demolished entirely by the remodelling of the piazza by Paul V" (Frommel 2007: 51; the three stories were 105 feet high [Heydenreich and Lotz 1974: 340, n. 32]). Julius II planned to have all three stories extend across the atrium, which would have blocked the view of the fronts of Old St. Peter's and of the new St. Peter's. While it existed, the Benediction Loggia influenced successively the design of Bramante's Belvedere Corridors, the courtyard of the Palazzo Farnese, and of the front of the Palazzo Barberini (Waddy 1990).

The Papal Palace was repeatedly enlarged, but initially its front consisted of two stories of fornices and an uppermost story with a colonnade. "It contained three apartments, each for a different season in the year: the Appartamento Borgia [of Alexander VI on the lower floor], the set of rooms we now know as the Stanze [on the middle floor]; and the rooms in the story above it; they faced onto an extensive garden to the back, the later Cortile del Belvedere. ... The programme for the Papal Palace remained binding for the following century" (Frommel 2007: 47). The stanze face north towards the Belvedere, and Raphael's loggia is at a right angle to them facing east like St. Peter's. The large block that is now the main residence of popes was later built adjacent to the east corner of the palace of Nicholas V. The Sistine Chapel was built by Sixtus IV adjacent on the west side of the Papal Palace.

Back of the Vatican Palace (with Bramante's courtyard and Michelangelo's drum for St. Peter's; Lafreri, 1565)

As Vasari noted, the impact of Alberti was primarily through his writings rather than the few buildings he is definitely known to have designed in Florence, Rimini, and Mantua. His palazzo in Florence will be discussed in the next chapter.

Alberti did not equal or supersede Vitruvius, but he augmented him greatly by dealing with Roman architecture that was created after the time of Vitruvius. Alberti's buildings were influential, but less so than his solutions for how to deal with the fronts of palaces and churches and the interiors of churches. His ideas were his greatest contribution to Renaissance architecture.

Alberti surely must have had influenced the decisions made about many of the buildings constructed in Rome during the three decades he was employed by the Papacy, and his indirect influence probably continued after his death.

In addition to advising several popes, he advised Federico da Montefeltro, later Duke of Urbino, and is likely to have influenced the design of the ducal palace at Urbino at least to some extent. In turn, the scale of the palace at Urbino undoubtedly influenced the plans of Julius II to enlarge the Vatican Palace, and one of the principal supervisors of the work at Urbino designed the Sistine Chapel. Moreover, a daughter of Sixtus IV married Federico's son, who was consequently a nephew of Julius II. The palace at Urbino will also be discussed in the next chapter.

Development of the Unaisled Church

Medieval churches that were small enough to be spanned by wooden beams generally lacked aisles and side chapels, but larger Medieval churches nearly always has aisles for structural reasons whether or not they had chapels. An exception was the cathedral at Assisi, which has a nave without aisles or side chapels, but it is unusual also in having been built above a lower church on the sides of which chapels were later added.

Alberti had an important role in the development of unaisled churches by large chapels open directly into a large nave. His Sant'Andrea was the prototype for the unified interior that gradually developed to become the standard Renaissance plan for a church.

Early Christian churches usually had the aisled plan of an ancient Roman basilica primarily because the size of their naves was limited by the ability to span a space wider than about 40-feet during the Medieval Period, and the addition of aisles of about 20-feet on each side doubled the amount of floor space to accommodate a congregation. In general, neighborhood churches did not need to be as large as Christian basilicas, which were often pilgrimage sites and consequently needed to be as large as possible.

The use of aisles in churches divided their interiors into three or more spaces and made sight and sound more difficult for most people in the aisles and made interiors more difficult to light. Music was initially more of a consideration than preaching. These problems were dealt with at the beginning of the Medieval Period by supporting clearstories on an arcade and by supporting the arches on columns. Monolithic columns of stone had enough compressive strength to support the weight of masonry walls and enabled the interiors of basilicas to be more unified, and early Renaissance architects, most notably Brunelleschi, continued to use the same basic plan.

As Alberti pointed out, walls were better supported by piers than columns. However, piers blocked sight, sound, and light more than columns. He dealt with these problems by subdividing the aisles into alcoves that could be used as funerary chapels and that could also be used to buttress a wider nave covered with a barrel vault. His source for this solution was almost certainly the Basilica Nova, which had been built as a law court with large barrel-vaulted alcoves like those of the frigidarium of an imperial Roman bath. With a wider nave, everyone got to be in the central space, and the entire interior was better unified and lighted and more structurally sound. This plan was widely adopted by many later architects including Palladio for the Redentore, but it did not supplant the aisled plan, which was had been used for the Old St. Peter's and which was invariably part of plans for the New St. Peter's.

Small churches or chapels in rural areas generally had unified spaces even early on, but until wider spaces could be spanned, they had little if any impact on the development of large aisle-less churches. A more important factor was the introduction of preaching as a regular and important part of a services. Preaching became a major factor for the design of churches with the Reformation and Counter-Reformation. After preaching had become the main part of Protestant services, Catholic churches and particularly Jesuit churches were increasingly designed to deal with the problem of better acoustics, and aisle-less church that had been created for other reasons came to be more widely preferred for most types of churches. Indoctrination became a competitive and life-long process.

Some monks had earlier specialized in preaching and supported themselves as they travelled from place to place. Since "...preachers were generally monks...," they had an immense influence on lay ideas about the advantages of poverty, chastity, and obedience as ways to obtain forgiveness for sins (Burckhardt 1944: 141). They impoverished way of life influenced architecture beyond thier monasteries.

Most monks had served primarily to say masses in family chapels for the souls of contributors to the construction of the church or for those able to pay for special masses for the dead. Monks in orders that emphasized contemplation and silence needed a separate area within a church, and this was usually provided in a choir, but was sometimes placed in the center of the church. With the abolition of monasteries by Protestants and with the increasing concern of Catholics to counter the influence of Protestantism, the interiors of churches of all denominations were increasingly built or renovated more to serve congregations rather than monks, and funerary chapels were replaced by wall tombs and cemeteries.

Withdrawal from this world to prepare for an afterlife appealed less and less to most members of congregations, and the emphasis of preaching had more to do with this world than the next. As Protestant churches became less and less elaborate, Catholic churches appealed more and more to the senses. Protestant churches became lecture halls, and Catholic churches became theatres. Palaces began to be as large as churches.

St. Peter's Basilica

During the reign of Pope Nicholas V (1447-1455), Alberti presented a report confirming that Old St. Peter's was in danger of collapse. He found that the long wall on the south side was leaning outward by six feet and that it had pulled the roof trusses and north wall with it; the north wall was leaning inward by six feet; in a report to Nicholas V, he wrote, "'I am convinced that very soon some slight shock or movement will cause it ["the south wall"] to fall. The rafters of the roof have dragged the north wall inwards to a corresponding degree'" (Lees-Milne 1967: 124). Nicholas gave very serious consideration to replacing the ancient church, "...which he wished to make so large, so rich and so ornate that I shall do better to keep silent than to attempt to depict that which is utterly indescribable, especially as the model was afterwards destroyed..." (Vasari 1568: II, 33). Nicholas lived long enough only to build the lower part of the walls for a large choir, which began to change the T-shaped plan of Old St. Peter's into a fully cruciform plan.

Alberti had been a member of the papal court since 1431.

In 1434 he went to Florence in the suite of Eugenius IV and remained there for two and a half years.... In 1444 he was back in Rome. With the elevation of Nicholas V he began his collaboration as adviser in the Pope's great projects for the restoration of Rome (1447-55). At the same time he also became architectural adviser to Sigismondo Malatesta (from 1450 on). THe beginnings of his owrk *De re aedificatoria* may also be place in the forties; it was practically finished in 1452 [Heydenreich and Lotz 1974: 28].

As Alberti wrote in the preface to his book on painting, he was most impressed of all in Florence by the achievement of Brunelleschi's dome:

> Who could ever be hard or envoius enough to fail to praise Pippo [Filippo] on seeing here such a large structure, rising above the skies, ample to cover with its shadow all the Tuscan people, and constructed without the aid of centering or great quantity of wood? ...if I judge rightly, it was probably unknown and unthought of among the Ancients [Alberti 1436 (1966): 40.

Brunelleschi's dome proved the Renaissance could equal if not surpass the Ancients and could do so in different ways. I do not think it was a coincidence that Alberti's 1450 foundation metal for the renovation of the Gothic church in Rimini proposed adding a dome and that in c. 1450 a dome was being planned for an enlarged crossing in Old St. Peter's; I do not think it was a coincidence that Alberti presented a copy of his *Ten Books on Architecture* to Nicholas V in 1452, and it included some specific suggestions for dealing with the structral problems of Old St. Peter's (I, 10, and X, 17; Alberti 1755: 15, 240).. Most significantly, in 1448 Nicholas V had granted Alberti income from "...the priory of Borgo a S. Lorenzo, which Mancini consideres quite out of proportion to the importance of Alberti's position..." (Borsi 1989: 26; citing G. Mancini's 1967 *Vita di Leon Battisti Alberti*).

Bernardo Rossellino joined the papal court in 1451 or nearly two decades after Alberti had began to work for the papacy. Around 1451, Rossellino began to construct the large choir that ceased to be built in 1455 or for about four years, and the walls of "his" choir got no higher than about 25 feet above ground (Frommel 2007: 48). Although no payments for work on St. Peter's has been found for Alberti, "...there is no mention of Rossellino in the treasury accounts...." (Borsi 1989: 42).

The "Rossellino choir" was later redesigned and completed by Bramante, who completed most of the walls, added the vault, and applied Doric pilasters to the exterior (Vasari 1568: I, 347; II, 32-33). "The entire Constantinian basilica was to e preserved, but supported by new strong exterior walls. Towards the last, the building was to be enlarged by vast transepts and a monumental choir—an ingenious conceit in that it made the claim of a true 'ristauratio' of the most venerable monument of Christianity..." (Heydenreich and Lotz 1974: 29-30, 54; fig. 12 [as described by Gianozzo Manetti and reconstructed by Günter Urban).

Rossellino constructed a great deal, but there is no definite evidence that he designed a building. Particularly during the 1400s, the word "architect" was used loosely, and unless a workman is explicitly said to have provided a design, it should not be assumed he must also have produced the design for a major building. In northern Europe, master builders were generally architects, but this was not generally the case in Italy where there were few if any guilds of builders. As noted, the church of San Francisco at Assisi was designed by a German architect, ant the Duomo in Florence was designed by his son Arnolfo; and when proposals were sought to construct the dome of the Duomo early in the 1400s, many architects were invited to come to Florence from northern Europe.

The apsidal plan of the choir was important for influencing both Bramante's and Michelangelo's plans for the shape of three arms of the present St. Peter's, but ultimately the three apsidal arms owe more to Arnolfo's design for the Florentine Duomo. My conclusion is that the credit for the design of the new choir and for its influence on the design for the new basilica belongs to Alberti, who like Brunelleschi taught himself to be an architect by studying ancient Roman buildings.

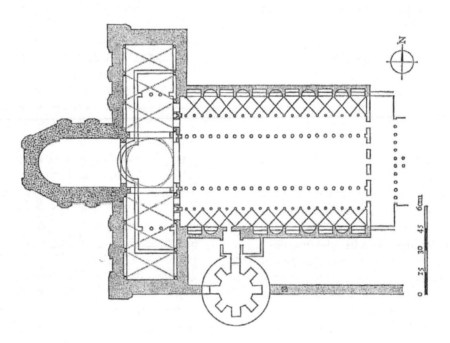

Reconstruction of the plan to enlarge Old St. Peter's (Urban in Heydenreich and Lotz)

16. Renaissance Palaces and Villas

Palazzo Medici by Michelozzo, Florence (albumen by Alinari)

During the 15th Century, the palazzo developed as a new building type, and during the 16th it reached a fully developed form that had great impact on subsequent architecture. Also during the 15th Century, the villa was revived as a place for recreation and entertainment in the countryside as it had been during the Roman Period. The earliest examples of palaces and villas will be considered in this chapter, and the culmination of their development will be considered in the following chapter on Palladio.

By 1450 Florence had developed primarily as a center for banking and the wool trade. Its wealth was based to a large extent on providing funds at high rates of interest to tyrants to hire mercenaries. Bankers and merchants built most of its palaces and provided much of the funding for its churches. It was a small city surrounded by defensive walls that generally sufficed to keep out intruders, but a greater danger was the factions that existed within the city itself.

Florentine factions were increasingly dominated by members of the Medici family, which was bankers for the Vatican. The banker Cosimo de Medici (1389-1464) was followed by his grandson Lorenzo the Magnificent (1449-1492), who diversified his investments. The family's influence in central Italy increased with the popes Leo X (Giovanni; 1476-1521; reigned 1513-1521) and Clement VII (Giulio; 1478-1534; reigned 1523-1534). Its influence culminated with the dynasty begun by Duke Cosimo I (1519-1574; reigned 1537-1574 and as Grand Duke from 1569).

The elder Cosimo built the first major palace in Florence, and Duke Cosimo later turned the medieval city hall (the Palazzo Vecchio) into his palace and connected it to an enlarged Palazzo Pitti. The palaces of Florence generally had or were given a defensive character to protect them against internal tumults. Its early palaces and villas were intentionally kept relatively small and compact to prevent envy until the republic ended. In the meanwhile, trade with northern Europe was increasingly disrupted by wars between expanding nation-states in Italy and elsewhere and by religious differences of opinion.

By 1450 Venice has reached the zenith of its wealth and influence by controlling trade between the eastern Mediterranean and western Europe. Being located on islands that were protected by its navy, Venice had no need of defensive walls, and with a method of electing doges that defied corruption, its government lasted longer and was more stable than any other city in Europe. The restricted space available resulted in the creation of palaces that were more often taller than they were wide, and like the city itself, the palaces were not fortified. The prosperity of Venice declined with the rise of the Ottoman Empire and greatly decreased with the fall of Constantinople in 1453, but many families inherited wealth and continued to build palaces. Some Venetian aristocrats took up agriculture and built villas on the mainland, and the influence of Venice on Europe was late was largely through Palladio.

By 1450 Rome was well on its way to reviving. While the Papacy was at Avignon from 1305 to 1377, Rome was left to rival aristocrats who continued to build mainly fortified castles, and after cardinals began to build palaces for themselves and their relations, the palaces continued to have strong walls with small windows and sometimes even crenellations, but mostly for decorative effect. Rome had built innumerable churches during the Medieval period, and many of them either had courtyards to house monks or more elaborate buildings to house cardinals, and both churches and existing buildings were frequently renovated, redesigned, and augmented until Rome became prosperous enough to construct great buildings that were entirely new. Initially, cardinals had no restrictions on how they spent their sources of income to enhance their chances of becoming pope or after becoming pope on enriching their families. Some of the finest buildings in Rome were created by its aristocratic families, but most were created with funds from the Church, and at one time or another many of Rome's most prominent families produced popes. Where individual popes were from, what their personal interests were, and how much money was available to them at any given time had a great impact on what was built in Rome and also in their places of origin.

Unlike Florence and Venice, Rome has an immense area to expand into, and as soon as its system of aqueducts began to be restored around 1450 and its increasing prosperity attracted immigrants and craftsmen from throughout Italy, it expanded far more rapidly and continued to prosper longer than Florence or Venice. However, its city walls were largely useless except for gathering taxes; parts were restored, but they were too extensive to be manned, and each palace or villa generally needed to be individually defended. The city continued to be largely defenseless against invasion until after 1527.

The principal influences on the architecture of Rome were, though, the papal state, the influence of ancient Roman ruins, and the availability of building materials from its ruins. Florence and Venice had none of these advantages and disadvantages. Florence needed continually to resist the expansion of the Papal States and of the Medici, who had largely funded the Renaissance and who helped greatly to make Florence what it was, but who were determined to control the city for their own benefit.

Thus, to a large extent, the types of palaces and villas that developed in Florence, Venice, and Rome depended on how secure the cities were against invasion and tumults. This changed over time as the walls of Florence covered a larger area and the walls of the Vatican were better fortified, but the introduction of artillery and the use of mercenaries made walls obsolete. Entangling alliances became the main means of providing for defence, and as often as not, these alliances were as likely to cause invasion as to prevent them.

These were the overriding considerations that had the most impact on the development of the most influential centers of architecture in Italy. There were exceptions to the rule that nearly all major developments took place in one of these three places. Naples and southern Italy were dominated largely by kings of foreign origin, and Milan and northwestern Italy were often invaded by France. Tyrants controlled most of the smaller places throughout Italy and in a few cases such as Urbino and Mantua made major contributions to architectural development, but these were relatively uninfluential exceptions. Urbino was an importance center of culture for only two generations, and its palace was grand, but never completed. Its greatest architect and artist, Bramante and Raphael, had to go elsewhere to find work and to Rome to learn how to design. Both of them remained in Rome; neither returned to Urbino. Mantua was influential chiefly because Alberti and Giulio Romano went there from Rome.

Overall, the wealth that the Church brought to Rome that attracted the largest number of artists from throughout Italy, and although they brought their preconceptions with them, they were usually overwhelmed by the influence of the buildings and sculpture that had survived from ancient Rome. Although the Renaissance started in Florence, the Renaissance style of architecture developed largely in Rome and spread from there to the rest of Italy and beyond, and for centuries Rome continued to be where every architect and artist had to complete his education.

PALACES

Palazzo Medici, Florence

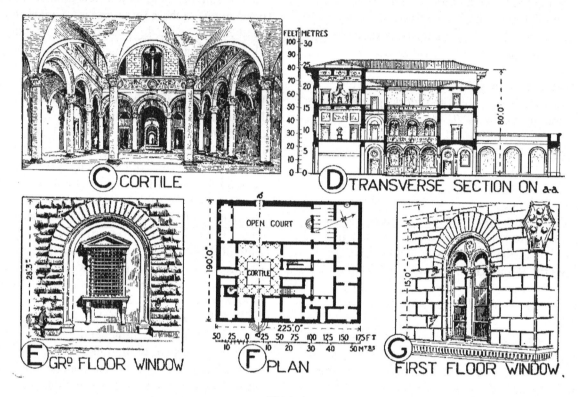

(Fletcher)

In 1445 Cosimo de' Medici commissioned Michelozzo di Bartolomeo Michelozzi (1396-1472) to design a palazzo, and it was completed between 1456 and 1459 (Kent 2000: 218, 220, 240). The frescoes of the chapel of the palace had been completed by December 1459 (309).

A large number of pieces of property in the area had been acquired earlier by Cosimo's father: "In 1427 Giovanni di Bicci owned seventeen houses, as did his sons in 1433. Between 1443 and 1446 eight new houses were purchased or traded to the Medici expressly to be demolished to build the palace, altogether twenty-one or twenty-two houses were torn down to accommodate it" (446, n. 73). Even so, the original front of the building was only 10-bays wide. Minor additions were made by 1468 (465, n. 5), and in the 17th Century seven additional bays were added by the Riccardi following the original design and almost doubling the size of the building.

Michelozzo's use of a regular pattern for the fenestration made his design extendable in either direction, and such patterns were generally used for later palazzi and for their enlargement. The more or less cubical form and the use of a large cornice proportioned to the entire height of the building also became usual characteristics of the new building type, and its blockish form gave palaces an immediately recognizable shape and profile. The cornice was closely adapted from an ancient Roman example, and being scaled to the building as a whole indicates that Michelozzo Michelozzi had studied the proportions of Roman buildings such as the Colosseum.

By having a cubical form, regular fenestration, and a courtyard, the Palazzo Medici most closely resembles the Roman insula or apartment block, and surviving examples in

Rome were undoubtedly also influential and had continued to be to some extent throughout the Medieval Period on the design of castles, but the palace is distinct from a fortified castle, and it developed independently. Some design elements of the palace are, though, ones that were more medieval than ancient including narrow pairs of vertical windows and arcades resting directly on columns. The rectangular windows with pediments on the ground floor are later additions by Michelangelo after the ground floor was enclosed; it had been originally designed as an open loggia.

Rustication had been used by the ancient Romans, for example, for the back wall of the Forum of Augustus with equivalent stringcourses, and it has often been used by the Emperor Claudius as for the Porta Majjore. It continued to be used during the Medieval Period though primarily for fortifications, and it was used by Arnolfo di Cambio for Florence's Palazzo Vecchio, which was begun in 1299. "In the last quarter of the fourteenth century a *provvisione* of the Signoria prescribed that the ground floor facades of all the buildings lining the Via Calzaiuoli were to be rusticated in cornformity with the appearance of the Palazzo Vecchio" (Kent 2000: 218). By c. 1426, the Da Uzzano Palace (or Palazzo Capponi alle Rovinate) in Florence had a rusticated ground floor (171), but by 1510 it was believed that Cosimo had been "...the first to use the example of Trajan's forum—that is, the Augustan wall—in the decoration of his palace" (463, n. 53). Rustication came to be more widely used during the Renaissance than it had been in ancient Rome.

The Medici palace was begun in 1445, at the first possible opportunity offered by an improvement in the city's economic and political conditions. Following this example, in the course of the next two decades construction began on at least ten major palaces. By 1470 Benedetto Dei, enumerating the assets of his native city, counted thirty important patrician palaces contributing to the glory of Florence... [Kent 2000: 218; pp. 236-237 lists palaces created during Cosimo's lifetime].
"At the new Medici palace, along with most others built in the fifteenth century, the traditional practice of renting the ground floor space to accommodate shops was abandoned" (234). The local branch of the Medici Bank was at the manager's house, but some banking had been done in the house of Cosimo's father. The open loggias of the Medici Palace were to enable friends and clients to use the courtyard and garden, but the openings were closed in 1517 (235).

The interior of the palace was furnished with innumerable works of ancient sculpture and Renaissance painting and sculpture that are mentioned by Vasari in the lives of artists including Donatello, and some of these works became the property of the city when the Medici were overthrown in 1527 and the palace was looted (Vasari 1568: II, 22,38, 96, 98, 152, 208; III, 192; IV, 11, 29). A 1459 description of the interior was recorded by Niccolò de' Carissimi da Parma, who accompanied Galeazzo Maria Sforza:

> ...on a tour of the palace, and especially of its noblest parts, such as some studies, little chapels, living rooms, bedchambers and gardens, all of which are constructed and decorated with admirable skill, embellished on every side with gold and fine marbles, with carvings and sculptures in relief, with pictures and inlays done in perspective by the most accomplished and perfect of masters, down to the benches and all the floors of the house; tapestries and household ornaments of gold and silk; silverware and bookcases that are endless and innumerable; the the vaults or rather ceilings of the chambers and salons, which are for the most part done in fine gold with diverse and various forms; then a garden all created of the most beautiful polished marbles with varous plants, which seems a thing not natural but painted... [Kent 2000" 239].

The original interior is now best represented by Benozzo Gozzoli's frescoes in the chapel with portraits of Cosimo de Medici and his household as participants in the procession of the Magi. Benozzo was "...a man of fertile invention and prolific in animals, perspective, landscapes and ornaments" (Vasari 1568: II, 23).

Chapel of the Medici Palace (Toesca)

Chapel of the Medici Palace (Toesca)

"The Medici household, consisting primarily of Cosimo, his sons, and their wies and chidren, was a large but close domestic unit that expressed the continuity and cohesion of the line over three generations" (Kent 2000: 240). It also included employes such as a tutor of his sons and servants. How many people lived in the palace is unknown, but in 1458 Cosimo stated in his tax return, "'there are fifty mouths to feed in our family, including the villas and Florence, and we also employ forty-one retainers...'" (319). For comparison, Federigo, Duke of Urbino, "...had 500 persons in his service; the arrangements of the court were as complete as in the capitals of the greatest monarchs..." (Burckhardt 1944: 29).

Michelozzo Michelozzi began as a sculptor and created a number of outstanding works before becoming primarily an architect. Vasari wrote,

> In his youth Michelozzo studied sculpture and design with Donatello, and whenever a difficulty presented itself, whether in clay or wax, or with marble, he worked so hard that his productions always displayed genius and great talent. But in one thing he surpassed many and even himself, for after Brunellesco he was considered the most skillful architect of his time, the one most skilled in devising and planning palaces, convents and houses, showing the best judgment in their arrangements.... Michelozzo was so friendly with Cosimo de Medici that the latter, recognising his genius, employed him to make the model of the house and palace which is on the side of the via Larga next to S. Giovannino, when he concluded that the one prepared for him by Filippo de ser Brunellesco was too sumptuous and magnificent, as has been said, and because it would have excited envy among the citizens which would more than counterbalance the gain to the city by its beauty and convenience or the advantage for himself. Accordingly the one deigned by Michelozzo pleased him, and he caused it to be completed in its present form so conveniently and with so much beauty that there are majesty and grandeur in its very simplicity. Michelozzo deserves the more praise because this building was the first to be erected in the city after the modern order, containing a useful and beautiful division into apartments. The cellars are dug out to a depth of four braccia, with three above ground for he sake of the light, and comprise the buttery and larders. On the ground-floor their are two courtyards with magnificent loggia, communicating with salons, chambers, anti-chambers, studies, lavatories, kitchens, wells, secret and public staircases, and upon each floor there are the dwellings and apartments for a family [of three generations], with every convenience not only for a private citizen as Cosimo then was, but for a king, however renowned and great, so that in our own day kings, emperors, popes and all the illustrious princes of Europe have been comfortably entertained there to the equal glory of the magnificence of Cosimo and of Michelozzo's excellence as an architect [Vasari 1568: I, 314-315].

Michelozzo had not been Cosimo's first choice to design the Palazzo Medici. Brunelleschi prepared an earlier design, but as Vasari noted, "Filippo had given such free rein to his art that Cosimo thought the [model he constructed for the] building too sumptuous and grand, and more to escape envy than expense, he refrained from putting the work in hand," and Brunelleschi "...wrathfully broke the design into thousand pieces" (Vasari 1568: I, 293).

Michelozzo designed much else including the monastery of San Marco. He also substantially rebuilt the Palazzo Vecchio that had been designed by Arnolfo and that was subsequently redesigned by Vasari to serve as a palace for Duke Cosimo (Vasari 1568: I, 316-319). Michelozzo was the most influential architect after Brunelleschi until Alberti.

Medici Palace (above, Alinari in Millon and Lampugnini; below, antique gem and rondel by Donatello in Giuliano)

113

Renaissance Libraries

Among Michelozzo's other major works was the monastery of San Marco, which included a vaulted library 18 braccia wide and 80 long (about 36 by 160-feet; Vasari 1568: I, 320). The library was built primarily to house the bequest of manuscripts collected by Niccolò Niccoli, who stipulated that it be open to the public. Cosimo provided the funds for its construction and added part of his own collection of mansucripts (Kent 2000: 35). "The library, designed by Michelozzo, was opened to the public in 1444, but damaged by an earthquake in 1457. A new building, probably a replica of the original, was at once erected. It has lost its books and furniture but survives otherwise unchanged, the most beautiful library-room of the early Renaissance" (Hobson 1970: 88).

San Lorenzo's library was the first public library since Antiquity, and it served as a model for many others including the Biblioteca Malatestiana in Cesena by "...the architect, Matteo Nuti, who had worked for the Malatesti in Fano and Rimini..." (Hobson 1970: 66).

Building probably started in 1447 and was completed in 1452. It took another two years to furnish the interior and supply the elaborately carved wooden doors.

The new wing of the convent was on two stories with a refetory on the ground floor, a dormitory and the library above. The latter follows Michelozzo's design for the library of San Marco in Florence, constructed about 1440...: a rectangular room with a vaulted ceiling carried on two rows of columns. Each aisle is occupied by twenty-nine benches and desks, three to a bay. The light (now partly obscured by new buildings) enters by a rosace [round window] in the end wall and a line of [segmental] arched windows on either side, falling conveniently at right angles to the reader's position [Hobson 1970: 66-68; cf. 88].

Similarly, Pope Clement VII de' Medici later required Michelangelo to place the Laurentian Library within a monastery on an upper floor, and Michelangelo's design for a long rectangular room lighted from both sides was also based on Michelozzo's design for San Marco's library, but without aisles and with a coffered wooden ceiling.

From his youth, Cosimo collected copies of ancient manuscripts on a wide variety of subjects including Roman history, Greek philosophy, Patristic writings, and Italian literature, and he carried his books with him when he planned to be away for long periods. He also collected antique gems and sculpture and commissioned contemporary artists to create primarily religious works. His sons Piero and Giovanni and his grandson Lorenzo the Magnificent were also major collectors of manuscripts, and the Medici family's collection formed the basis for the Laurentian Library. Their books and art collections continued to be housed largely in the Medici Palace until the Medici were exiled in 1495, and they were largely reassembled there when the Medici returned to Florence in 1512 (Kent 2000: 266).

Pope Eugenius IV became interested in creating a library for the Vatican while he was in Florence attending the Council that Cosimo had relocated there to try to unify all Christian denominations. Earlier papal libraries had been left behind when papal courts relocated, particularly when leaving Avignon. Eugenius IV collected 340 manuscript volumes that became the nucleus for a largely if not entirely new library (Hobson 1970: 77-78). Nicholas V increased the number of volumes to 1,200 and made them available to the public. Sixtus IV employed Bartolomeo Platina, who increased the number of manuscript volumes from 2,500 to 3,600, but many of the volumes collected by Nicholas and Sixtus were destroyed during the Sack of Rome in 1527 (78-80). From the 17th through the 19th Century, the library continued to grow including the presentation copy of Henry VIII's pamphlet against Luther, but following the Council of Trent, the library was largely unavailable for research and became primarily "...an arsenal of intellectual weapons against heresy" (79, 81).

Michelozzi's Library in the Monastery of San Marco, Florence (2014)

Cosimo de' Medici's Patronage

To understand how Cosimo became a great patron, it is important to bear in mind that he "…in his youth had spent a great deal of time in Rome, studying Roman ruins under the tutelage of Poggio Bracciolini and [Niccolò] Niccoli…," two of the greatest humanists of the early Renaissance (Kent 2000: 225). Cosimo's father had founded the first branch of the Medici bank in Rome even before founding a branch in Florence, and there had been even earlier bankers in the family (465, n. 26). However, it was primarily by gaining control of papal finances that Cosimo was able to become the greatest private patron of the Renaissance.

From 1386-1397, Cosimo's father, Giovanni di Bicci de' Medici, "…was in Rome establishing the Medici bank" (Kent 2000: 164). Cosimo himself was born during this period in 1389. How much time Cosimo himself spent in Rome as a youth is unknown, but it must have been considerable. In any case, in 1421 Cosimo persuaded Pope Martin V (who had returned the papacy to Rome) to continue to appoint

> …the manager of the Medici bank at the papal Curia depositary of the apostolic chamber. Thereafter, for the best part of four decades, the Medici were the pope's exclusive bankers, handling most of the enormous financial resources of the church. Their business with the papal court was the basis of the family's wealth, as their wealth was the basis of their political influence in Florence [164; cf. 448, n. 18 for minor exceptions].

Thus, it was Cosimo's ties to Rome that enabled him to accomplish so much more in Florence than its other bankers; the Medici bank rose with the improving finances for the Papacy and declined with Cosimo's death.

Although the Rome branch of the bank had a manager, being the banker of the Catholic Church necessitated frequent trips by Cosimo to Rome, and he took advantage of being there to study its antiquities. For example, in 1427 he and Poggio Bracciolini went to Ostia Antica together to copy ancient inscriptions (Kent 2000: 25). Previously, they had no doubt studied inscriptions in Rome before seeking them in Ostia, and while doing so Cosimo had the opportunity to personally examine a great deal of ancient Roman architecture and art. Although the early part of Cosimo's life is poorly documented, he cannot have neglected the principal source of his income. Although the Medici Bank eventually had branches in 18 other European cities, none of these branches was of comparable importance or even all of them put together: "…Venice, Naples, Milan, Pisa, Genoa, Perugia, Siena, Bologna, Ferrara, Geneva, Lyons, Avignon, Montpellier, Bruges, London, Barcelona, Cologne, and Rhodes…. Cosimo kept in close personal contact with most of them" (369). Although Cosimo did not have the in-depth knowledge that Brunelleschi and Donatello acquired of Roman antiquities by making systematic studies of them for years, he was highly knowledgeable about both ancient Rome and contemporary Florence and about much of the rest of Europe. As the contemporary chronicler Gregorio Dati wrote, "'a Florentine who is not a merchant and who has not traveled through the world, seeing foreign nations and peoples and then returned to Florence with some wealth is a man who enjoys no esteem whatsoever'" (491, n. 10). Cosimo's knowledge of Europe was probably unparalleled for his time. His wide knowledge enabled him to become the most influential man in Florence and one of the most influential in Europe and to become a good judge of architects and artists and a great patron.

As a patron, Cosimo deserves great credit for his *oeuvre* (in the sense of his "life's work" as a patron), and Dale Kent has brought together all of the relevant evidence known to exist (Kent 2000: 331).

> Patrons' oeuvres, like those of artists, were unified and distinguished by particular problems and themes. At the same time, this comparison demonstrated that Medici patronage, however special, was not unique, even with the city of Florence. In terms of his choices of artists, subjects, and forms, Cosimo's patronage oeuvre was closely related to the bodies of work commissioned by other citizens with whom he shared a common culture [366].

Cosimo deserves most credit for having accepted Brunelleschi's design for the church of San Lorenzo and for paying most of the cost for constructing the church. He deserves great credit for having accepted Michelozzo's design for the innovative and influential Medici Palace and for frequently employing Donatello. However, it should also be taken into consideration, that before Cosimo hired him, Brunelleschi was already famous for having found a way to create a dome for the Florentine Duomo and that Cosimo rejected his design for the Medici Palace even though he could have asked him to scale it down. Cosimo's father was the one who initially Brunelleschi as an architect to design the old sacristy and a major chapel for San Lorenzo, and Cosimo greatly expanded the scope of the commission rather than initiating it. Moreover, Cosimo hired Donatello to decorate the old Sacristy even though Brunelleschi himself was a great sculptor; these two rejections caused Brunelleschi to destroy the model of a palazzo he had made for Cosimo and to break off relations with his close friend Donatello, who had been trained by Brunelleschi to become a sculptor. Even though Brunelleschi lived until 1446, Cosimo continued to employ him only for San Lorenzo and, instead, employed Michelozzo for San Marco even though Brunelleschi's family tomb was in San Marco, and Cosimo employed Michelozzo all other architectural commissions (Vasari 1568: I, 299). Michelozzo worked under Brunelleschi in the disastrous siege of Lucca, but escaped blame. Regardless of what his reasons were, Cosimo must be given credit for having recognized what Brunelleschi and Michelozzo could do best. On the other hand, Donatello was better at sculpture in the round, but Brunelleschi was better at reliefs. Eventually, Brunelleschi was buried in the Duomo; even though burials there were ordinarily prohibited, there was no place else he could be buried. Donatello was buried in Cosimo's tomb in Brunelleschi's church (312). Michelozzo was buried in San Marco along with Brunelleschi's ancestors (324). "...Cosimo's character remains opaque; similarly, one of the most plausible comments about Donatello is that he was 'molto intricato'" (343). An enigmatic painting by Giorgio Vasari depicts *Brunelleschi and Ghiberti Presenting a Model of San Lorenzo to Cosimo*" while "...Donatello and Michelozzo look on..." (344-345, fig. 171). The relationships of Brunelleschi, Donatello, and Michelozzo with Cosimo and with one another varied over time and were complex, but they all did some of their best work for Cosimo.

Brunelleschi had lost a great deal of credit when at great expense he diverted the river Serchio during the siege of Lucca and inadvertently flooded the Florentine encampment instead of causing the capitulation of the city. After this debacle, he "...ceased to be entrusted with important communal offices. However, Michelozzo [who was assisting Brunelleschi in the siege] continued to enjoy close relations with the Medici" (Kent 2000: 176; 275). Cosimo has opposed the war, but had continued to serve as a member of the commission that directed the war. Florence generally hired condottiere to do its fighting and borrowed money to pay them, and Cosimo was one of the principal lenders "at high interest" (276).

Overall, Cosimo was a great patron for having enabled two great buildings to be created and for having a great impact on the development of a great sculptor. However, his patronage must be viewed in perspective. Before he became a major patron, the Renaissance was well advanced; the dome of the Duomo and the doors of the Baptistery were well along. It is true and important that his patronage helped to make Michelozzo a major architect and Donatello a major artist, but it is also true, as Dale Kent pointed out, that Cosimo was following precedents that had already be set by others:

> Cosimo's was not the first monumental palace of the early Renaissance; that was constructed for a political opponent, Niccolo da Uzzano and his brother around 1417. Giovanni di Bicci [de' Medici]'s was not the first sacristy to double as a family burial chapel; that was built by Palla Strozzi at the behest of his father Nofri in their neighborhood church of Santa Trinita. Nor was it the first self-contained chapel within a church, which was made by Brunelleschi for the Barbadori at Santa

Felicita. Cosimo's decoration of the old sacristy was not the first decorative program for a family chapel in the innovative style of the early Renaissance; that was created by Masaccio and Masolino for the Brancacci family at Santa Maria del Carmine. Cosimo's building patronage of the Dominican convent of San Marco had precedents in that of the degli Agli at Fiesole, and the Acciauolo at the Certosa outside the city. It was not Cosimo who commissioned the first major Florentine image of the Magi; this was the altarpiece painted for Palla Strozzi by Gentile da Fabriano. Most of these patrons were men of wealth, influence, education, and originality, from whom more might have been expected—until the political confrontations of 1433/4 resulted in an overwhelming Medicean victory, and they were exiled or ruined.

> Beyond these immediate precedents there was a long tradition in Florence of wealthy and powerful families financing great patronage projects, both secular and ecclesiastical… [Kent 2000: 355].

In other words, the Medici were major patrons, but they followed more precedents than they set. They were not why the Renaissance began in Florence. It is also important to bear in mind that the later impact of the Medici was mainly through the misuse of the papacy by Leo X and Clement VII, who like Cosimo and Lorenzo de' Medici were great patrons, but there is no evidence that Cosimo foresaw or intended anything of the kind to take place. There is no evidence that Cosimo planned to create a hereditary dukedom that was begun by his distant relation Cosimo I. After a comprehensive study of all available evidence, Dale Kent concluded,

> Florence needed leadership in moments of crisis; Cosimo took charge of the republic's affairs because he could, and because he believed that he could handle them better than anyone else. Clearly he took pleasure in his power and predominance, on occasion rather unpleasantly it would seem. But that is about all that we can say. If he secretly schemed to become first Caesar and then Augustus in Florence as some of his encomiasts envisioned him in the very last decade of his long life, he left no clear legible trace of this ambition.
> …
> Of all the communes that flourished in the twelfth and thirteenth centuries, Florence in the fifteenth century was one of the few remaining republics. Until overcome by the external force of foreign invasions, Florentines resisted the drift to one-man government to which other important cities had long since succumbed. The blueprint for an intermediate solution lay close at hand in the example of Venice, Florence's oldest ally and for much of the quattrocento, her citizens' most admired political ideal. Under the Medici, a numerically expanded but in substance increasingly static Florentine *reggimento* came more and more to resemble the Venetian hereditary patriciate. After the expulsion of the Medici, the city experimented with a Gonfalonier for life who resembled the Venetian doge [Kent 2000: 367].

While in exile in Venice, Cosimo was offered help by Milan to take over the government of Florence, and he refused. When he returned to Florence, he was briefly made gonfalonier (administrative head of the government ruled by the Signoria, which included eight elected "priors," two of which were elected from each of the four quarters of the city, but only for two months. The first gonfalonier elected for life served from 1494 through 1512, when the Medici were again required to live in exile. Cosimo's grandson Lorenzo was more open about using his influence, but was short-lived, and in 1485 he wrote, "…I am resolving not to want everything my way and to live what time I have left as peacefully as possible…" (Kent 2004: 80); he died of ill health in 1492 at age 43; and despite ill health, Cosimo had lived to be 75. Cosimo himself never tired of giving good advice, of helping out his family and friends, and of calling in favors.

Cosimo was well qualified to give advice on many subjects. He knew less about most subjects than professionals, but he had wide interests; he was well read; and he accumulated an immense deal of useful experience. He was greatly respected for his wisdom. He acknowledged that he was no expert in any field except banking, but that he knew enough to be a good judge of competence:

> "Although we do not have the expertise in feats of war of those who practice it continually, nevertheless, seeing what others do, we are able to judge who does it better. I believe that although you [his cousin Averardo de' Medici] are not a great painter, nevertheless you would judge the figures of Giotto to be better than those of Balzanello…" [Kent 2000: 279].

One of the ways he exerted influence was to wait until someone else had propose what he wanted to recommend so that they got the credit, but he got his way. The main way was to get his supported elected or appointed to positions and to call in favors. Corruption was not required to exercise great influence. He chose men well and delegated responsibility to those more knowledgeable and skillful than he was in their various professions.

Although not an artist, Cosimo was a good judge of art. Although not a scholar, he created a great library. Although not a soldier, he lent his support to military leaders who were well qualified and who produced results.

How much influence Cosimo exerted as a patron is the principal subject of Dale Kent's *Cosimo de' Medici and the Florentine Renaissance: the Patron's Oeuvre* (2000). By "patron's oeuvre," she means the body of work that Cosimo commissioned and collected, and she discusses what the body of work as a whole reflects about his interest and influence. She acknowledges that it is often difficult or impossible to determine how much Cosimo influence the design of any given work of art, but that the works he collected rather than commissioned indicate an interest in similar themes. He obviously indicated in some detail what he wanted to be represented in commissioned works, and he selected the best artists of his time to carry out his commissions.

Cosimo preferred a combination of restraint for architecture and opulence for ornamentation. Generally, he preferred restraint, and the interior of San Lorenzo is as restrained as the exterior of the Palazzo Medici. However, the interior of the Palazzo Medici was lavishly decorated, and Cosimo collected works of art as much or more for their rarity and the inherent qualities of their materials as for their content and excellence. He was widely read, but he wanted his books to have superb calligraphy and beautiful illustrations. He was a good judge of artistic merit, but he tended to be influenced as much or more by execution as by design. His selection of Benozzo Gozzoli to paint the chapel of the palace, its centerpiece, is somewhat surprising, but despite the unrealistic landscape, Gozzoli turned a small space into a magnificent room and created a large number of convincingly realistic portraits (Kent 2000: 339).

It was not to be expected that the monasteries Cosimo paid for would be lavishly decorated for that would have been inappropriate for their purpose. San Marco was the first major building he commissioned, and it is plain except for the large number of relatively primitive, but effective paintings by its resident artist, Fra Angelico. The only large space is its library, which was also plain, but well designed for its purpose. Cosimo should not be blamed for having done differently in this case, but neither should this commission and his other religious commissions be taken as proof of deeply religious convictions. More importantly, they are examples of his gratitude to this and other monasteries for having safeguarded funds during his exile that would otherwise have been confiscated or stolen. He made no major contributions to any religious institution except the ones that had helped him in his time of greatest need and to the church in which his father had been buried and in which he himself expected to be buried. He turned the entire church of San Lorenzo into a Medici funerary chapel and agreed to fund its completion only on the condition that no one but Medici be buried there, and later Medici added more Medici funerary chapels. He made contributions to religious organizations that had or would provide direct benefits to the Medici. As Kent noted,

> Cosimo approaching fifty, and driven by an urgent desire to expiate in charitable patronage the sins of a lifetime, turned to Pope Eugenius IV for advice.
> Vespasiano [the close friend and supplier of books who wrote Cosimo's biography] in his account of Cosimo's decision to rebuilt San Marco, stressed that in the conduct of his business as a banker and politician, Cosimo had "accumulated quite a bit on his conscience, as most men do who govern states and want to be ahead of the rest."
> … When the renovation of the convent was complete, Eugenius issued a bull testifying to the expiatory effect of Cosimo's charity… [Kent 2000: 172].

In other words, it was more from not having led a religious life that the commission resulted than in always having acted like a Christian was expected to. San Marco was singled out for what it had done for Cosimo in the recent past.

Although the religious paintings that Cosimo commissioned were exclusively religious in subject matter, but they often included SS. Cosmas and Damian, who were *medici* (doctors) martyred during the reign of Diocletian. It was well known that Cosimo and his deceased twin brother had been named for these two saints and that they were the patron saints of the Medici family. By contrast, the main subject of the frescoes of the Medici Chapel is his family and employees rather than the visit of the Magi to the baby Jesus. The books and works of art he collected were largely pagan rather than religious, but many were religious. Cosimo was by no means simply a product of the Middle Ages. He did not depend on the next life being better than this one, but kept his options open. He became more interested in religion and patronage as he got older and was often reminded of the pain he might endure in an afterlife by the chronic gout he suffered as an old man. This is not to imply that he was insincere, but that he was never motivated solely by religion in anything that he did. Notably, "Dante had identified Scrovegni's father among several Florentine usurers 'on whom the dolorous fire falls' in the seventh circle of hell, a pouch around the neck of each…" (132-133).

"As early as 1408, when Cosimo was nineteen, Poggio Bracciolini copied a codex of Cicero's Letter to Atticus for him…" (Kent 2000: 34). These letters alone fill two printed volumes, and they were written by Cicero to his publisher. "The letters of Cicero, Pliny, and others were at this time diligently studied as models" for writing Latin (Burckhardt 1944: 138).

> From the fourteenth century Cicero was recognized universally as the purest model of prose. This was by no means due solely to a dispasionate opinon in favour of his choice of language, of the structure of his sentences, and of his style of composition, but rather to the fact that the Italian spirit responded fully and instictively to the amiability of the letter-writer, to the brilliancy of the orator, and to the lucid exposition of the philosophical thinker [151].

Cicero was early on Cosimo's favorite author, and this expensive commission was from admiration of Cicero as a philosoper and politician. By 1417/18, his library contained 70 handwritten volumes, and "classical texts, especially historians and the works of Cicero predominated…. Cosimo owned most of the classical works in general currency in the early years of the quattrocento…." (35). In c. 1435, he had the biographies of Greek philosophers by Diogenes Laertius translated for him (35). Towards the end of his life, he had large parts of Plato translated to be able to read him. "Cosimo was increasingly fascinated by Neoplatonic ideas, and Ficino's famous translations of Plato for Cosimo were completed in 1463-4" (286). Facino stated a number of times "…his conviction that without Plato, it would be hard to be a good |Christian or a good citizen" (Burckhardt 1944: 131).

Plato was not a new interest for Cosimo. James Hawkins "…pointed out that the philosophy in which Cosimo was most interested was not in fact mid-century Neoplatonism…, but the moral philosophy of Aristotle and Plato transmitted via Cicero, the stuff of Bruni's translations in the early decades of the fifteenth century…" (Kent 2000: 398, n.

9). Towards the end of his life, he looked to Platonic and Neoplatonic philosophy for consolation

> ...when he was taking an increasing interest in Neoplatonic philosophy, with its strong otherworldly orientation. It was during the mid-fifties that Argyropoulos and other Greek scholars arrived in Florence [following the fall of Constantinople in 1453] bringing with them their manuscripts, which they translated for Cosimo's benefit. ... This was the period of the foundation of the Platonic Academy, whatever its precise form may have been, and of Cosimo's patronage of the philosophical studies of Marsilio Ficino. Cosimo's letter summoning Ficino to Careggi to tell him the way to happiness was written in 1463, the year preceding his death... [212].

"A copy of Ambrose's treatise *On the Trinity*, containing notes by Niccoli and one perhaps by Cosimo, and coupled with ten dialogues of Plato translated into Latin by Ficino for Cosimo was included among his gifts to San Marco's library" (325). Cosimo had personally paid the expenses to relocate from Ferrara to Florence the Council that attempted to unify the divisions of Christianity, but "the Trinity was the chief point of theological dispute between East and West at the Council of Florence in 1439 and a preoccupation of many ordinary Florentines...," and the attempt failed (325), and its failure made many Italians aware of unbridgeable disagreement about some of the most fundamental doctrines of Christianity.

> The fourteenth century was chiefly stimulated by the writings of Cicero, who though in fact an eclectic, yet, by his habit of setting forth the opinions of different schools, without coming to a decision between them, exercised the influence of a sceptic. Next in importance came Seneca, and the few works of Aristotle which had been translated into Latin. The immediate fruit of these studies was the capacity to reflect on great subjects, if not in dirct opposition to the authoeity of the Chruch, at all events independently of it.

> In the course of the fifteenth century the works of antiquity were discovered and diffused with extraordinary rapidity. All the writings of the Greek philosophers which we ourselves possess were now, at least in the form of Latin translations, in everybody's hands. It is a curious fact that some of the most zealous apostles of this new culture were men of the strictest piety, or even aesceticss. Fra Ambrogio Camaldolese... at the request of Cosimo de' Medici, undertook to translate Diogenes Laertius into Latin [Burckhardt 1944: 309]

If Cosimo had been any less fluent in Latin, he would almost certainly have had Camaldolese translate the biographies of Greek philosophers into Italian rather than Latin. "Cosimo however spent three formative adolescent ears attending lectures in Latin and Greek and disucssing philosophy in the 'academy' of Roberto di' Rossi and emerged with fully developed humanist tastes" (Hobson 1970: 85).

Although only the simplest texts in Italian and Latin were used in schools, education was widespread and sufficed for most Florentines to become largely laself-taught. In the middle of the 1300s, the chronicler Giovanni Villani estimated "...that well over two-thirds of the male population attended schools where they were taught to read..." (42). This may be an exaggeration, but it seems not to be. By 1427 when tax returns began to be required and have survived, "...it seems that a high proportion of the 10,000 or so heads of households representing a population of approximately 37,000 wrote their tax reports in their own hands, and the remainder usually managed at least to sign them" (42).

Florence's educational system probably embraced a higher proportion of the city's inhabitants than that of any other community in Europe. Reading and writing were skills essential to the prosperity of a town primarily engaged in banking, trade, and manufacturing; and commerce fostered a commitment to reading and writing, and to literature, that clearly occupied a good deal of citizens' leisure time…. A major component of this literature was the product of Florence's brilliant vernacular culture built upon Dante, Petrarch, and Boccaccio [Kent 2000: 42].

Although the secular schools controlled by the guilds taught mainly reading, writing, and math and used relatively simple prose as examples of Italian and Latin, numerous surviving commonplace books of artisans indicate the masters of Tuscan literature were widely read and copied by adults.

Cosimo himself and his descendants were tutored privately and mastered Latin as well as Tuscan literature. Florence let Italy in literature and in education as well as in art.

Among the books many Florentines owned, read, or borrowed was Giovanni Villani's *Cronica*, a history of Florence which incorporated the essential elements of the Florentine civic ethos…. Fundamental to this ethos was the legend of the Roman foundation of Florence, which was the basis of communal ideology in the thirteenth and fourteenth centuries, and became a cornerstone of humanist history in the fifteenth…. This legend was a powerful impetus to the incorporation of classical ideas, themes, and personalities into popular vernacular literature and art. Precedents from the Roman republic supported the communal ideal of broad citizen participation in government, and the primacy of public affairs over private loyalties… [Kent 2000: 50].

Florence had been a Roman city regardless of when it was founded, and the continued use of Latin by the Catholic Church facilitated its use in education, which was controlled by the guilds rather than by the Church. Although the Church continued to be influential in the daily lives of Florentines, it did not have the monopoly on thought in Florence that it did in many other European cities. Nonetheless, for whatever combination of reasons, Cosimo was the principal contributor to the Church in Florence, and as the Papal banker, he could well afford to be. Cosimo and his brother Lorenzo "…spent extensive periods of time in Rome, where Giovanni di Bicci di' Medici [their father] began his banking business before Cosimo's birth, and members of the family made frequent journeys to deal with the financial and diplomatic business of the branch of the bank attached to the papal court" (142). As noted, from 1421 for nearly four decades "…the Medici were the pope's exclusive bankers, handling most of the enormous financial resources of the Church. Their business with the papal court was the basis of the family's wealth, as their wealth was the basis of their political influence in Florence…" (164). "Shortly before his exile [in 1433] Cosimo, anticipating a move against him, entrusted his money to the safekeeping of the Church" including the monasteries of San Miniato al Monte and San Marco (166). As the most influential person in the political life of Florence, Cosimo needed to be grateful and to create obligations.

Between the late 1430s and his death in 1464 Cosimo was responsible for rebuilding or redecorating three major religious foundations—the convent and church of the Dominican monastery of San Marco, his parish church of San Lorenzo, one of the city's oldest and largest centers of worship, and the Augustinian church and convent of the Badia in Fiesole. He built also a chapel for the novices at the chief Franciscan foundation in Florence of Santa Croce, and renovated the Franciscan convent of Bosco ai Frati, adjacent to the Medici estates in the countryside north of the city. He had a magnificent chapel made for the Medici palace in Florence, and there were chapels in all the family's country villas. He contributed to the refurbishing of a host of smaller churches and chapels in Florence, Tuscany, and places as far away as Friuli. He commissioned a reliquary from Ghiberti for the Camaldolensian convent of Santa Maria degli Angeli, and altarpieces for the churches of San Marco, Santa Croce, and Bosco ai Frati…, as well as for the Medici domestic chapels in Florence and at the villas of Cafaggiolo and

> Careggi…. The commissions made him the major Florentine patron of the Church in his time. [Kent 2000: 131].

Cosimo spent 70,000 florins at Badia, 60,000 at San Lorenzo, 40,000 at San Marco, and 15,000 at Bosco ai Frati for a total of 185,000 florins (457, n. 251). This was nearly half of the total amount he contributed to the city of Florence through construction, by giving alms, and by paying taxes (Burckhardt 1944: 52). The sum spent on these four religious buildings was about twice what he spent on constructing the Palazzo Medici.

> Modern historians speculating on the motives for Cosimo's extensive patronage of churches have tended to be skeptical about the role of religious feeling, and concerned to distinguish and quantify pious and political impulses, civic and dynastic interests. To Renaissance patrons, as observed, these were not alternatives. Their patronage simultaneously served "the honor of God, and the honor of the city, and the commemoration of me" [Kent 2000: 131-132; quoting Giovanni Rucellai, 357].

In any case, Cosimo's choices for patronage generally reflected his personal interests and followed precedents his father had set most notably at San Lorenzo and that his descendants were to follow in their turn. "Cosimo's eventual assumption of sole responsibility for the major rebuilding at his extremely large parish church, one of the four great 'quarter' churches of Florence, and the oldest in the city after the baptistery, was a unique even in the history of private patronage in Florence, unprecedented in its sheer scale…. Cosimo turned to San Lorenzo in the early 1440s, after the building he had commissioned at San Marco was substantially completed…." (183). As noted, he had himself buried beneath the center of the dome.

"San Marco was not simply a forum for Medici patronage; it was also the family's refuge—spiritual, financial, and even physical. In 1433, on the eve of their exile, Cosimo and [his brother] Lorenzo had stored a large quantity of their assets in the convent, where they would be safe from confiscation by a hostile government" (Kent 2000: 178). For the church of San Marco,

> only the *tribuna* was rebuilt and enlarged. … Cosimo's main building work at San Marco consisted of the reconstruction of the living quarters of the monks—their individual dormitories, corporate spaces such as the refectory and the chapter room; and cloisters for recreation. Rebuilding of the convent began in 1437…. In his chronicle [the administrator of the monastery] Lapaccini enumerated the benefits of the Medici interventions at San Marco, 'among which the library takes price of place'; he also listed the monks' quarters including forty-four cells; the pictures painted by Fra Giovanni di Piero de Mugello [Fra Angelico], 'the greatest master of painting in Italy…'. It was in the library, completed in 1444, that the architect's [Michelozzo's] talents and Cosimo's style of patronage most effectively converged…. The library—cool, classical, spare, and graceful, in harmony with Angelico's painting and his strongly articulated sense of space—is the architectural masterpiece of San Marco [Kent 2000: 177-178].

Cosimo had a double cell created there for his own occasional use, but with frescoes attributed to Gozzoli. The library contained about 400 handwritten manuscripts, and although most were contributed by Niccolò Niccoli, Cosimo himself substantially augmented them and ensured Niccoli's stipulation that "…his books were to be freely available to all Florentine laymen…" (178).

Hobson noted that the total number of manuscript volumes in the San Marco library was considered to have been between 600 and 800, but that the final total provided by was uncertain.since Cosimo himself added some books and subtracted others (Hobson 1970: 87-88). Niccoli

> …had earlier intended them to go to [Ambrogio] Transversari's convent [of Santa Maria degli Angeli] "for the use of both the monks serving God there and of all citizens develoted to learning," …

But Cosimo, as the estate's largest creditor, was in a position to block other claims. ...Cosimo succeeded in persuading the trustees to considgn the books to him, some ofr his own collection (though the record of this part of the transaction has disappeared), the remainder for the projected library in San Marco. In return he accepted responsibility for Niccoli's debts to a limit of seven hundred florins... [88].

Regardless of the final total, Niccoli's library was at the time of his bequest "...the largest library in Florence... with unrivalled weatlth in classical texts" and the first public library since antiquity (87). In 1494 when the Medici were exiled,

> ...1,019 volumes... [of the family's collection] were transferred to San Marco. ..one-third of the collection was bought by the Salviati family of Florence and two-thrids by the Dominicans of San Marco, who resold their share in 1508 to Lorenzo's younger son, Cardinal Giovanni de' Medici, later Pope Leo X. Cardinal Giovanni removed the colleciton to Rome.... Pope Clement VII [de' Medici] returned the books to Florence... [91]

When monasteries were eventually suppressed, all of Niccoli's books in the San Marco library were transferred to the Laurentian Library.

Both Niccoli and Cosimo de' Medici attempted to acquire the old and rare copies of manuscript books and succeeded partly by buying them from monasteries in widely scattered locations throughout Europe. For example, Cosimo's collection

> ...included Seneca's *Tragedies* from the abbey of Pomposa; Ammianus Marcellinus's history of the later Roman Empire from Fulda; Apuleius's *Metamorphoses*, Tacitus's *Histories*, books 1-5, and *Annals*, books 11-16, and Varro's *On the Latin Language*, all bought from Monte Cassino by Boccaccio; Celsus's on Medicine from Sant'Ambrogio in Milan...; Cicero's orations, found by Poggio in France,; and *Familiar Epistles* from Vercelli Cathedral, and Quintilian's *Institutio Oratoria* from Strasbourg [Hobson 1970: 89].

When Niccoli could not afford an early copy, he sometimes borrowed money from Cosimo to buy it or persuaded Cosimo to buy it: "We find him recommending Cosimo to accept a Sicilian friar's offer for his Boethius (in gothic script)... [and] reporting the discovery in a Dominican convent in Lűbeck of a mnauscript of the Elder Pliny's *Natural History* which Cosimo succeeded in buying..." (87). In additiion to indicating how some of the most valuable acquistions were made, this evidence is important for reflecting how rare and widely scattered pagan literature in Latin had become and how willing monasteries were to sell copies.

Before relocating to the Medici Palace at least by 1459, Cosimo had continued to live in his father' house near Santissima Annunziata, which is located diagonally opposite Brunelleschi's Foundling Hospital, and Cosimo and his son Piero took a personal interest in the church, which contained a painting of the Virgin that was believed to cause miracles and which had become the principal pilgrimage site in Florence. In 1444 Michelozzi was commissioned by the city to added a domed tribune with seven chapels, and "...during Cosimo's term as Gonfalonier of Justice in September-October 1445, a Commission of Eight was appointed to review communal legislation in the interests of the regime. As the Signorial edict declared, the cult at Santissima Annunziata was a matter of great concern to the state, for the sake of the devotion of the city and her people to the Virgin, and for the sake of her reputation in the eyes of the world" (204). Piero was one of the first commissioners to oversee the project, and he personally commissioned Michelozzo to construct a marble tabernacle at the entrance to the chapel with the painting in 1448 (202, 207-208); the marble for the tabernacle cost 4,000 florins (458, n. 282). "Piero was the patron of [Luca] della Robbia's first major commissions in painted terracotta: the vaults of the tabernacles for San Miniato and Santissima Annunziata" (297). A substantial part of the cost of the new tribute was paid "...by Francesco Gonzaga, marque of Mantua, who was captain of the Florentine army for some time at mid-century, and also Cosimo's close friend and political ally. Cosimo wrote to Gonzaga and persuaded him to divert some of his salary to financing the reconstruction at Santissima Annunziata...." (207).

At Fiesole, near one of Cosimo's villas, he renovated the church and monastery. "Cosimo's patronage at the Badia was part of his life-long interest in the monastic way of life. His reading in his twenties and thirties of Cassian and Chrysostom indicates that he admired a cloistered virtue.... The Badia was the only major building omission conceived in the last decade of Cosimo's life..." (212), and it was a relatively minor commission, but one that was again given to Michelozzo.

As noted, Cosimo began the Palazzo Medici after having spent a great deal on the Church and having committed to spend a great deal more on San Lorenzo. He chose a cite diagonally opposite San Lorenzo for his palace, but fronted it on a street a block away on the via Larga. He could have afforded to build the much larger palazzo that Brunelleschi had designed for him, but preferred the smaller, but by no means small palazzo designed by Michelozzo that was grander than any other palazzo that had been built in Florence for a private individual. The cost of construction was estimated to be 100,000 florins (Kent 2000: 295. In 1944, a florin was worth about $2.50 [Burckhardt 1944: 53, n. 21]; the total cost to construct the original portion of the palace in 2017 would be roughly $ 3.5 million [http://www.usinflationcalculator.com/]). Vespasiano estimated that the palace cost 60,000 ducats (465, n. 4; possibly including artwork. A Roman ducat was worth about $50 in 1976 or about $5 million [Bull in Condivi 1553 [1976]: 147).

Over his lifetime, Cosimo paid more than 400,000 florins or roughly four times as much to the city of Florence for religious buildings, alms, and taxes as for the construction of his palace (Burckhardt 1944: 51-52).

Dante had popularized Aristotle's dictum that "man is naturally a political animal," referring to his membership of the polis or city as necessary to humankind; "just as a man need a family, a family needs a neighborhood, a neighborhood needs a city...."

Cicero in his *De Officiis*, the most commonly read, summarized, and quoted of the Roman orator's works in Renaissance Florence, invoked the authority of Plato to spell out the responsibilities created by this interaction: "as Plato has admirably expressed it, we are not born for ourselves alone, but our country claims a share of our being, and our friends a share...." Debating the question of "what sort of a house a man or rank and station should... have," he concluded that "as in everything else a man must have regard not for himself alone but for others also, so in the home of a distinguished man, in which numerous guests must be entertained and crowds of every sort of people received, care must be taken to have it spacious"; conversely, "one must be careful too, not to go beyond proper bounds in expense and display..." The competing claims on the citizen of magnificent and moderation, frugality and honorable hospitality, had to be carefully balanced in accordance with the classical view, eagerly embraced by medieval Christian scholars and teachers, that moderation in all things was a shining virtue, excess the darkest vice [Kent 2000: 220].

"Cosimo had *De Officiis* in his library by 1418 and knew it well..." (221). The same advice from the source was cited by Giovanni Rucellai in a letter to his son (221-222). Howard Burns considered Flavio Biondo to be most knowledgeable about the topography of Rome of anyone except possibly Alberti, and Biondo considered the Palazzo Medici to be finer than any ruin in Rome: "'Whatever private houses had recently been built on the Via Larga must be compared to the work of former Roman princes and certainly to distinguished ones; indeed I myself, who have achieved some measure of fame from my writings, do not hesitate to state that there are no remains of private princely residences in Rome which display any greater splendor than these'" (225). In his opinion, the ancient Romans had been surpassed. This was despite the fact that Cosimo had used restraint about the size and exterior finish of his palace so that it would not resemble the palaces of princes. When asked by Pope Pius II to get the city of Florence to contribute to a crusade, Cosimo responded, "I am not a prince and cannot dispose of these things as if I were….a republic cannot be run in the same way as a despotic regime…" (348). He ran Florence, but through the use of persuasion and example rather than force. He preferred that others get credit for what he wanted done (350-351).

"…as Alberti pointed out, "citing the views of Plato, Aristotle, Thucydides, and Cicero, even in the eyes of the Greeks magnificence, arguably a personal vice, was justified as a social virtue. … Alberti stressed that whatever was done must be *decens*—fitting. Pleasing proportions in a building were those proportionate to the builder's dignity as well as to the dignity of the building…" (220-221). As was well known from classical writings, on one front of the Temple of Apollo at Delphi was inscribed, "nothing too much" and on the other "know thyself." Bearing such principles in mind, Cosimo made his palace and his family church grand without the excess that later characterized Duke Cosimo when he greatly enlarged the Palazzo Pitti and added an immense funerary chapel to the back of San Lorenzo in between the modestly scaled and far better designed Old Sacristy and Medici Chapel.

Irrespective of his motivations, Cosimo was one of the great patrons of the Renaissance and at the critical moment of its beginnings in Florence. It says a great deal that the best designed church and place in Florence were by two different architects for one patron. Nothing is known about the influence Cosimo may have had on the design of either building, but there can be no doubt about the excellence of his judgment, which is further confirmed by his choice of the best artists of his time. Although he was generally vague about his intentions, there can be no doubt that he was grateful to the religious organizations that helped him most in his time of greatest need and the he revered the example of his father. However, to overemphasize his religious convictions is contrary to his interest in preserving classical writings, and the subject matter even of the religious art he commissioned was not purely religious.

Donatello's David manifestly has little to do with the Old Testament, but there is as much disagreement on this point as on everything else to do with the Renaissance (Kent 2000: 473-474, notes 242-270). Gozzoli's procession of the Magi has little to do with the New Testament despite numerous attempts to prove the contrary. Instead, the frescoes are more equivalent to the decorative margins of prayer books that provided something to look at during monotonous rituals. Similarly, most depictions of the nearly nude St. Sebastian have little to do with the saint himself, and many paintings of clothed saints are fashion plates "…appropriate to cloth merchants from a cloth manufacturing town" (Kent 2000: 476, n. 301). "…nowhere was so much importance attached to dress as in Italy" (Burckhardt 1944: 224). Thus, the subject matter chosen for a work of art was often considered less important than how much it was embellished and how superbly the folds of cloth were depicted. Although the skill that was required was admirable, it was sometimes misapplied to conceal rather than enhance form as it invariably did with Michelangelo. Until the Council of Trent, what any given figure symbolized became less significant than how they looked. Artists were selected on the basis of how well they painted rather than on their knowledge of religion or on how religious they were. The largely religious subject matter of the works of art Cosimo commissioned needs to be contrasted with his greater interest in politics than religion and with his greater interest in classical literature than in contemporary art.

Cosimo was a great patron because he could see who most deserved to be hired, and he was able to do so primarily because he had a good knowledge of ancient architecture, art, and literature. Anyone who considers the Renaissance to be anything other than a revival of ancient learning purposely ignores aesthetics as being what was considered most important by Renaissance architects, artists, and patrons.

Palazzo Strozzi

Palazzo Strozzi (albumen by Brogi)

A number of other palazzi in Florence adapted the design of the Palazzo Medici including the Palazzo Strozzi. Although the Strozzi and Medici eventually intermarried, their truce came only after an exile of six decades. The Palazzo Strozzi was begun by Filippos Strozzi the Elder in 1489; and when he died in 1491, he left funds to complete it and named Lorenzo de'Medici as his executor, but Lorenzo died in 1492. The palace was finally completed by Filippo Strozzi the Younger in 1538, the year of his death.

The Strozzi Palace was designed with graded rustication on all three floors, and it eventually filled an entire block. "It is said that when Filippo Strozzi the elder was about to build his palace he desired the opinion of Benedetto [da Maiano], who made him a model, in conformity with which the building was begun although after Benedetto's death it was continued and completed by Cronaca," Simone del Pollaiuolo called "il Cronaca" for his eloquence in describing the marvels of Rome (c. 1457-1508;Vasari 1568: II, 92):

> Accordingly Benedetto da Maiano was called in by him [Strozzi] and made a model, standing alone, which was afterwards carried out, though not entirely, as will be said below because some neighbours would not oblige him with their houses. Benedetto therefore had to begin ["in 1489"] the palace as best he could, the front shell being nearly completed before Filippo's death. It is in the rustic order, and graduated, as may be seen. The bocks of the first floor, from the first windows downwards, and the door are large rustic-work, the second floor is lesser rustic-work. At the very moment when Benedetto left Florence, Cronaca returned from Rome [where he had studied "...the fine antiquities of the city, measuring them with great diligence"]. Obtaining an introduction to Filippo, he pleased him so much by his model of the court[yard] and the great cornice round the outside of the palace, that Filippo entrusted the entire work to him and continued to employ him ever afterwards. In addition to the beautiful exterior [of the courtyard] in the Tuscan order, Cronaca made a magnificent Corinthian cornice round the exterior at the end of the roof, half of which may now be seen, finished with such singular grace that it would be impossible to add to it or to desire better. This cornice was borrowed by Cronaca from an antique measured by him at Rome at Spogliacristo, which is ranked among the finest in the city. It is true that Cronaca increased it in proportion to his palace, an added the roof, thus his genius appropriated the works of others, transforming them into his own, a thing in which few succeed. The difficulty is not only to borrow beautiful designs, but to know how to adapt them to the purpose they are to serve, with grace, measure, proportion and convenience [257].

Pitti Palace

Another major example of the influence of the Palazzo Medici was the Palazzo Pitti, which is sometimes attributed to Brunelleschi despite Vasari's statement to the contrary:

> Filippo also planned a rich and magnificent palace for M. Lucca Pitti outside the S. Niccolo gate at Florence in a place called Ruciano, but not at all like that which was begun by the same man in Florence, and carried as far as the second story, with such grandeur and magnificence that no finer piece of Tuscan work has yet been seen. The doors of this later palace are double, 16 braccia by 8 [with the proportions of 1:2 and the same size as those of the Medici Palace], the windows of the first and second stories resembling the doors in every respect. The vaulting is double, and the entire edifice [as it was then being enlarge] so artistic that nothing finer and more magnificent could possibly be desired. The one who carried out this work was Luca Fancelli, architect of Florence, who did many buildings for Filippo; and for Leon Battista Alberti he did the principal chapel of the Nunziata at Florence, for Ludovico Gonzaga, who took him to Mantua, where he did a goodly number of works... [Vasari 1568: I, 294].

This does not necessarily mean that Fancelli designed the Palazzo Pitti, but it does mean that Brunelleschi's design for a Pitti palace was not constructed. Cosimo de' Medici had rejected "...more to escape envy than expense..." and which Brunelleschi "...wrathfully broke the design [model] into a thousand pieces" (I, 293). The front of the Pitti Palace originally had seven bays (Kent 2000: 238, fig. 108).

Vasari becomes less explicit as he tries to flatter his patron Duke Cosimo, who bought the Pitti Palace and allowed his extravagant wife, Leonora di Toledo, to enlarge it greatly:

> Duke Cosimo could not possibly have undertaken anything more worthy of the power and greatness of his spirit than this palace, which really seems to have been built expressly for his Illustrious Excellency by M. Luca Pitti from Brunellesco's design. ... Filippo' model being lost, her Excellency caused another to be made by Bartolommeo Ammannati, and excellent sculptor and architect, and the work was carried on in accordance with that, and a great part of the courtyard has been made of rustic work, like the exterior [I, 294-295].

In other words, neither the front nor the back were designed by Brunelleschi, but that the palace as it was enlarged was eventually completed on a scale that Vasari considered to be worthy of Brunelleschi as well as the Duke. How much Pitti had earlier built behind the seven-bay front is uncertain, but it is certain that the Duke greately expanded the front and that he had Bartolommeo Ammannati redesign the garden front with three levels of rusticated and superimposed columns.

Vasari went so far as to call the Pitti Palace "the finest in Europe" (III, 181). It is one of the biggest, and its extended version set a precedent for using patterns with little or no attempt to unify designs. The part Pitti completed was on a much smaller scale and better designed. Its design was most directly influenced by Michelozzo's Palazzo Medici and by Benedetto da Maiano's front for the Palazzo Strozzi, and it originally had a seven-bay front with a recessed bay to either side.

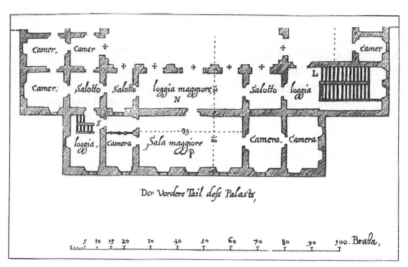
Initial plan of the Pitti Palace (Millon and Lampugnani)

Palazzo Pitti, Florence (Alinari in Frommel)

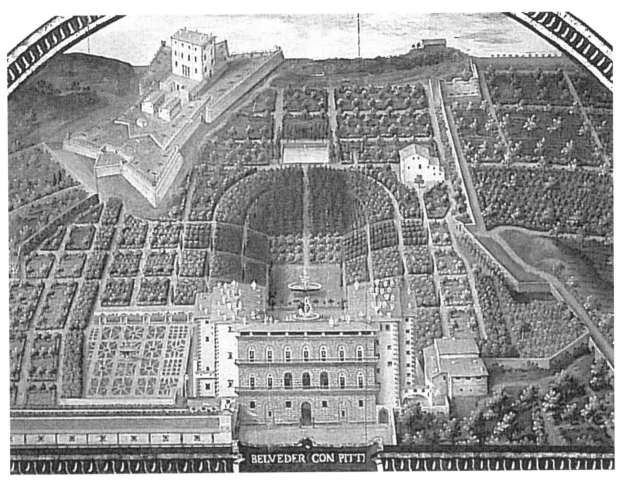

Pitti Palace and gardens painted by Giusto Utens (Museo di Firenze; Kent 2000)

Palazzo Rucellai, Florence

Palazzo Rucellai, Florence (Anderson in Millon)

Alberti's Palazzo Rucellai was begun around 1455, and it differs fundamentally by using pilasters on each of its three floors in much the same way that engaged columns had been used by the Romans for theatres and amphitheaters. Alberti a employed ashlar on all three floor rather than using the more conspicuous rustication. His design reflects the greater knowledge of Roman architecture he gained while residing in Rome and preparing his *Ten Books*.

Alberti's design for the Palazzo Rucellai had much greater influence in Rome than in Florence, where rustication (without pilasters) was generally preferred. "In the Palazzo Rucellai..., Alberti established the prototype of the pilaster façade..." (Heydenreich and Lotz 1974: 33).

For the courtyards of this palace, he supported its arches on piers rather than columns. "This method is the true one, and was observed by the ancients because the architraves which are laid upon the capitals of the columns make things level, while a square thing such as arches are, which turn, cannot rest upon a round column, without throwing the corners out; the true method of construction therefore required that the architraves shall be placed upon the column and that when arches are made they should be borne by pilasters [piers] and not by columns" (Vasari 1568: I, 348).

Ducal Palace, Urbino (1465-1482)

Ducal Palace, Urbino (west front; Baldi in Frommel)

The significance of the Ducal Palace at Urbino was primarily in terms of it scale and decoration rather than in its architectural design. It was built for Federico da Montefeltro, who became head of the duchy of Urbino in 1444, when he was 18 years old, and who was confirmed with the hereditary title of duke in 1474 (Frommel 2007: 68, 70). He was so successful as a condottiero that he amassed great wealth and did not need to spend it on city walls. Instead, he spent it on the creation and embellishment of a palace for himself and his descendants.

Federico was deeply interested in architecture as well as the arts and humanistic scholarship. He almost certainly decided his palace would center on a courtyard that would be the width of an existing medieval building on the hillside above the valley of Urbino (Heydenreich and Lotz 1974: 73, fig 28).

"There was a sincere friendship between him [Federico] and Alberti, whom Baldi mentions as one of his advisers. For many years Alberti visited Federico at Urbino" (Heydenreich and Lotz 1974: 72). Alberti's "...close friendship with Federico finds eloquent testimony in the letters of both" (343, n. 18; cf. 342, n. 8). Nonetheless, since no earlier palaces were equivalent, Heydenreich concluded that "the conception of the palazzo must therefore be attributed to Federico; who advised him we do not know."

In any case, Federico decided to incorporate three existing, but relatively small buildings into a largely new palace that he commissioned to be built between a cathedral and a small palace about two hundred meters away. In this space he had a new palace built that is about 200 meters long and 150 meters wide.

Three of the four sides of the large courtyard of the new palace were added along with a smaller courtyard, a number of wings, and new façades to face the town and the cathedral. In between the two new courtyards, the largest space by far is the throne room, and it is a barrel vault with curved ends that resembles a coved ceiling, but is continuously curved and has lunette-like openings around the perimeter; this type of ceiling widely used during the early Renaissance as, for example, in the earlier Palazzo Medici and the later Sistine Chapel.

Even the throne room was designed with as much restraint as the rest of the palace except for the use throughout of well designed window and door enframements and fireplaces. Furnishing such as tapestries, easel paintings, and painted chests provided additional embellishment of the interior. Little further work was done on the palace after Federico's death in 1482.

Construction for the new palace was begun around 1460 by Maso di Bartolommeo, who had studied architecture with Michelozzo and who seems to have worked chiefly on renovating the two existing buildings that were adapted to serve as the east side of the courtyard and as part of an east wing and possibly also renovating a surviving tower (castellare) of the former city walls that eventually served for the apartments of the Duchess.

The new portions of the Ducal Palace at Urbino were created primarily by Luciano Laurana from 1468-1474 and secondarily by Francesco di Giorgio Martini from 1474-1482 (Frommel 2007: 69). In both cases, their designs were particularly influenced by the restraint that Brunelleschi had introduced into Florentine architecture and that continued to be the main influence on Italian architectural design from around 1420 to 1510.

Most of the palace was probably constructed by Laurana (1420-1479), including the vaulted room leading to the throne room, the exceptionally wide main staircase, and the main front that faces the town and that is flanked by circular towers that contain spiral staircases. However, "the Palazzo Ducale at Urbino is his only certain work [in architecture]. Laurana owed his reputation mainly to his skill in building technique" (Heydenreich and Lotz 2007: 343). He was from Dalmatia, and he had gone to Venice for training, and he had worked for the Sforza (in-laws of Federico. "...Laurana had prepared a model of the palace s early as 1465; ...though often absent he was in charge of building operations till 1472," and in 1468 Federico gave him full authority to make decisions in his own absence (76; 344, n. 20). Nonetheless, Federico and Alberti are also likely to have been involved in the design of the palace. In any case, according to Heydenreich, Laurana and the supervisors he sometimes left in charge of construction completed the first two stories of the palace "...except for the square tower on the west front and the loggia of the Cortile del Pasquino on the south side... the decoration and the continuation into the upper storey like the facing of the façade, dragged on into the next period" (344 n. 26). Presumably he was discharged for being frequently absent despite what had been achieved.

Frommel concluded that Laurana "...showed himself to be one of the great pioneers of the renewal of secular architecture" (Frommel 2007: 70). Laurana constructed a palace larger than the new cathedral that was built nearby, and the difference in scale between palaces and churches began to be characteristic of the Renaissance. "By reducing the cathedral to an unassuming brick building and concentrating all the magnificence on the Palazzo Ducale, Francesco [di Giorgio Martini] and his patron [Federico] reversed the hierarchy of the piazza of Pienza.." (73).

How much of the structure of the palace was added by Martini (1438-1502) is uncertain, but he was definitely responsible for much of the interior work of the palace and for the design of the adjacent cathedral. He was definitely a great architect, and he was also a painter, an engineer, and a writer. He and he had previously designed the church of the Osservanza in Siena in c. 1467 (Frommel 2007: 71), and Laurana was fired and replaced by Martini. However, Vasari explicitly credited Martini with the design of the palace and cathedral at Urbino and in additon the design of to new core for the town of Pienza: "...he made all of the designs and models of the palace and Vescovando of Pienza, the Pope's native place, originally called Corsagnano ["Barnardo Rossellino was the architect" (note by Gaunt)]. These were of the utmost possible magnificence and nobility for that place. He also devised the form and fortification of the city, as well as the palace and loggia for the same Pope" (Vasari 1568: II, 27). Whenever there is not better evidence to the contrary, Vasari deserves to be credited rather than rejected as lacking confirmation.

In architecture his [Matini's] judgment was excellent, showing a thorough grasp of the profession. This is amply displayed in the pace which he built at Urbino for the Duke Federigo Feltro..., the distributions being made in a beautiful and convenient manner, while the staircases are remarkable and more pleasing than any erected before that time. The halls are large and magnificent, and the apartments useful and exceptionally noble. To sum up in a word, the entire palace is as fine and well built as any other that has been erected to the present [26].

"This Francesco [di Giorgio Martini] deserves our regard because he smoothed the difficulties of architecture and did more for that art than anyone from the days of Filippo di ser Brunellescho to his own time" (27). Martini's design for the Church of the Osservanza in Siena provides strong support for Vasari's conclusion.

Vasari made no mention of Laurana in his *Lives* as having worked on the palace or having designed any other building, and he is more likely to have been the superintendant in charge of construction or the master builder. In any case, since Federico was made a duke in 1474 and since Martini was hired around the same time, all parts of the building marked "FD" (for *Fredricus Dux*) rather than by "FC" (*Fredericus Comes*) are notable for a much better knowledge of classical design than earlier details (Frommel 2007).

Although remote, the palace at Urbino was well known and influential. "Lorenzo de' Medici and Francesco Gonzaga had detailed drawings made for them of the palace..." (Heydenreich and Lotz 1974: 342, n. 11). Leonardo da Vinci noted the unusually generous size of the staircase, but the staircase of the Palazzo Piccolomini had previously been given exceptional prominence for a Renaissance palace, and Venice, where Laurana had studied, had unusually wide staircases earlier than central Italy (343, n. 17; cf. p. 44). The courtyard was especially admired, but like the staircase and throne room was more exceptional for its size than for its design. Among the most admired spaces were the smallest and particularly Federico's studiolo or private study, which though only 11 ½-feet square is lined with book cabinets with outstanding examples of inlay (*tarsia* or *marqueterie,* a specialty of Martini; 77).

What was most remarkable about Federico's court was the number of first rate artists and architects he attracted to work in Urbino and the number of individuals from Urbino and its vicinity who as a consequence became first rate. In addition to employing Martini, he employed Piero della Francesco, whose "...'Flagellation of Christ,' painted for Federico looks like prototypes for the decorative apparatus of the Palazzo Ducale..." (Heydenreich and Lotz 1974: 72). Bramante was born near Urbino in 1444 and his distant relation Raphael was born there in 1483; both had to go elsewhere to find additional training and challenging employment. Baccio Pontelli worked under Martini at Urbino from 1479-1482 before going to Rome to construct most of the buildings commissioned by Sixtus IV including the Sistine Chapel (with a ceiling similar to that of the throne room at Urbino; Heydenreich and Lotz 1974: 345, n. 43; Frommel 2007: 91-96, and Frommel attributes the Cancelleria to Pontelli). Martini was the mentor of Balthasar Peruzzi (1481-1536), whose palazzo will be discussed in this section and whose Roman villa and palazzo will be considered in the next section.

Florence was by far the most important center for the development of Renaissance art and architecture, and Rome became and remained the most important center for Renaissance art and architecture, but before Rome began to make unparalleled advances, Urbino was an important center for all aspects of Renaissance culture.

Unfinished main entrance to the Ducal Palace, Urbino (Alinari in Frommel)

Main courtyard of the Ducal Palace, Urbino (Alinari in Frommel)

Ducal palace, Urbino; throne room (Luce in Heydenreich and Lotz)

Painting of an idea city attributed to Giuliano da Sangallo (from Urbino; Frommel)

Flagellation of Christ by Piero della Francesca (detail; Millon and Lampugnani)

Ducal palace, Urbino; characteristic door enframement by Martini

Federico married a Sforza; his only son married a Della Rovere; and a grandson married a D'Este. By marrying a niece of Sixtus IV, his son and heir became a nephew of Julius II and eventually became the principal executor in dealing with Michelangelo for the completion of the tomb of Julius II. His grandson Guidobaldo da Montefeltro and Isabella d'Este created the model court that was idealized by Baldassare Castiglione in *the Courtier*. About Federico himself, Castiglione wrote, "in the rugged place of Urbino he built a palace which is, in the opinion of many, the most beautiful that can be found in all Italy; and he furnished it so well with everything fitting thing that it appeared to be, not a palace, but a city in palace form" (Heydenreich and Lotz 1974: 74).

The influence of Federico's palace was chiefly in terms of its scale and court life and the example he himself set by bringing together the best architects and artists working in Italy during his time. Frederick undoubted influenced the ambition of Julius II to construct a still larger palace and to become as much of a condottiero as a pope (particularly considering Federico's son was Julius's nephew). Since Federico married a Sforza, and Francesco Sforza, who began to construct Castello Sforzesco in 1452, had "detailed drawings" made of the palace at Urbino (Heydenreich and Lotz 1974: 342-343, n. 11). Ludovico Sforza began enlarging the castello in 1494, and he was undoubtedly mindful of the patronage of Federico and Julius when he employed Leonardo and other artists and architects. Like the villa in Tivoli, the castello in Milan is not comparable architecturally to the palace in Urbino, but the motives were comparable and considering the connections of these families and Bramante's childhood in Urbino before he went to Milan, there was clearly substantial influence on the architecture of Rome and Milan from remote Urbino. The influence of Florence on Italy was far greater, but the influence of Urbino was also important during the 1400s.

Martini's Church of the Osservanza, Siena (Alinari in Frommel)

Cancelleria, Rome (1486-1498)

Cancelleria, Rome (albumen by Anderson)

By far the most important 15th Century example of a palazzo is the Palazzo della Cancelleria in Rome, and as noted, Bramante was involved in its construction and probably designed at least the front, but Antonio Montecavallo was in charge of the project (Vasari 1568: II, 185). It was built for Cardinal Raffaello Riario from 1486-1498, and it incorporated the existing early Christian basilica of S. Lorenzo in Damaso. The first story has an ashlar facing, and the two upper stories have pairs of pilasters like those of the attic of the Pantheon, but on pedestals and a running base like the pilasters of the attic of the Colosseum.

The exceptionally large and impressive courtyard with arches on columns resembles early Christian basilicas and bears no resemblance to Bramante's courtyard at Santa Maria della Pace or the Cortile del Belvedere. Moreover, the front of the Cancelleria closely resembles the contemporary front of the Palazzo Giraud (Torlonia), which Lanciani found was also at least partly constructed by Bramante and was presumably also designed by him.

The travertine used for the front was also taken from the Colosseum. The large courtyard or cortile (about 60 by 100 feet) has two tiers of Roman Doric columns with granite shafts stolen from the Baths of Caracalla. The main entrance was added by Fontana in 1585.

Cancelleria, Rome (albumen by Alexandri)

When the Palazzo Venezia began to be constructed in 1455, it was also intended to be the residence of a cardinal, and by incorporating a church and a cloister, it too was given a plan more like that of a monastery than a palazzo. The ground floor still has small round-headed windows, and Letarouilly concluded that the main front would have had round headed windows on all three floors. When the cardinal, Pietro Barbo, became Pope Paul III in 1464, he began to enlarge his palazzo and continued to use it as his residence (prior to the construction of the Vatican Palace by Nicholas V). Paul III added a two-storied façade or loggia to the church on the side of his palazzo from which to give papal benedictions (similar in design to the nearly contemporary three-storied Benediction Loggia that was added to the atrium of Old St. Peter's). He began to embellish the courtyard with basically the same design as these loggia consisting of two stories of arcades flanked by engaged columns, but only a portion of the courtyard was faced, and work stopped abruptly when Paul III died in 1471 (Heydenreich and Lotz. 1974: 66-67). Pius IV (1559-1565) permitted the Venetian Republic (which did not recognize the Papacy as head of its church) to use the palazzo as its embassy, but the Papacy continued to retain control of the property until 1797, when by treaty it became the Austrian Embassy. Italy took the building over in 1917, and Mussolini used it as his headquarters (Macadam 2000: 133). Although this building continued cannot be considered characteristic of a Renaissance palazzo, its barrel-vaulted entrance with coffers, its courtyard, its enormous reception room, and its plain front influenced the Palazzo Farnese more than the Cancelleria.

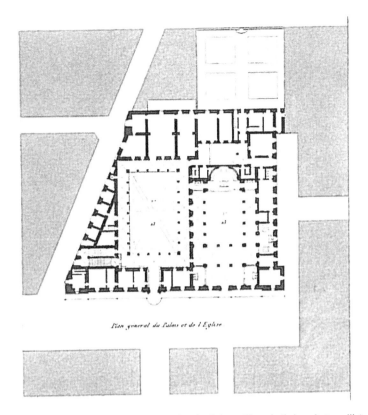

Plans of the Cancelleria (above) compared to the Palazzo Venezia (below; Letarouilly)

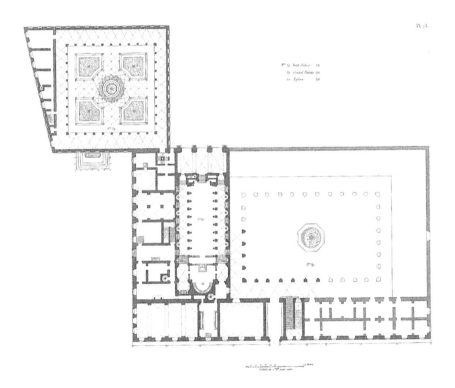

143

Palazzo Venezia (1455-1471)

Palazzo Venezia as enlarged with the front of San Marco on the left side (Von Matt in Millon)

Benediction logia of San Marco (albumen)

Courtyard of the Palazzo Venezia (Anderson)

Attributions Based on Classical Details

I have considered the Cancelleria and Palazzo Venezia together because they were atypical in incorporating churches. I think they also deserve to be considered together to help determine how much credit should go to Alberti and to Bramante for their respective contributions. Both palazzi were started by earlier architects, but their best and most influential features are more likely to have been added later.

Since Renaissance architects often adapted features from the same ancient buildings and since they often learned from one another, it is often difficult to assign priority and credit for the use of any given feature. As I have noted, I find it impossible to believe that Alberti designed nothing in Rome even though he spent most of his time in Rome for the last three decades of his life, and I find it impossible to believe that Bramante never visited Rome before 1500. I will point out some classical details that I think only they could have designed at the time the Palazzo Venezia was enlarged and the Cancelleria was being completed.

In chronological order rather than in importance, I will discuss the Palazzo Venezia's additions first. I consider the front of San Marco earlier than the courtyard because the orders are incorrectly superimposed on the front, but correct in the courtyard and because pedestals and half-columns were used on both stories in the courtyard, but pilasters on the upper story and no pedestals were used on the front. Both designs use fornices and look similar, but are distinctly different, but almost certainly by the same architect. For example, in both cases, the entablatures project above the half-columns of the lower floor, but do not on the upper floor. Most surprisingly, on the church front, Corinthian is superimposed over Composite while on the courtyard Corinthian is superimposed over Roman Doric.

This structural mistake in superimposition is significant, and in my opinion it was probably intentional even though it might seem to be against an attribution to Alberti. In a courtyard Alberti designed for Pietro Lunense in Viterbo, he intentionally used thicker Composite column to support an entablature and thinner Ionic columns to support arches; he considered structural considerations more significant than the standard proportions for the orders, and he turned the Ionic capitals to their sides rather than have half of an Ionic capital over a half-column to support an arch at each end bay (Burns 2007: 119). Departures from Vitruvius and from Alberti's published recommendations were justified by the casual way in which the classical orders were often used on ancient Roman buildings.

The front for the church of San Marco is unusual in having a Corinthian order above a Composite order rather than the other way around. Ordinarily, both stories would have been of equal height, and the Composite order would have been made proportionately thinner and so been place above the Corinthian order for structural as well as visual reasons. In my opinion, the architect decided instead to use Composite half-columns on the lower floor where they would be visually more impressive and to put Corinthian pilasters on the upper floor so that he could incorporate the coat of arms of Pope Paolo II (1464-1471). He also decided to break the entablature and bring it forward above the half columns, but to run it straight across the pilasters, and he did this in the courtyard as well. Alberti used Composite half-columns for the lower order of San Francisco in Rimini with pilasters above. I see these choices as reflecting careful consideration for the overall visual effect rather than as examples of ignorance about classical precedents. Alberti was well aware that Roman architects broke rules where there was a good reason to do so.

In the courtyard of Piazza Venezia, the handling of the orders is more conventional in most respects including the use of pedestals on both stories (as in the Colosseum), but the corner solution is unprecedented. On both stories, the architect chose to put one-fourth of a column between the corner piers to be consistent with the pattern of the fornices and to be less noticeably different from the rest of the overall pattern. Moreover, the capitals are Renaissance capitals rather than copies or adaptations of ancient capitals, and Alberti preferred Renaissance capitals even for his temple for

Malatesta. In my opinion, the use of fornices, piers, and pedestals, and the corner solution in around 1468 makes Alberti the most likely architect for the additions to Palazzo Venezia even though the front for the church is unconventional.

The Cancelleria itself was begun in 1489, and its courtyard was begun in 1496. Frommel attributes the initial work on the building to Baccio Pontelli and the courtyard "possibly" to Antonia da San Gallo (Frommel 2007: 95). Vasari wrote that Bramante "...was one of the eminent artists consulted about the palace of S. Giorgio, and the church of S. Lorenzo in Damaso, near the Campo di Fiore put in hand by Raffaello Riario, cardinal of S. Giorgio, which, though improved after, was and still is considered a convenient and magnificent bode for its size. The director of this building was one Antonio Montecavallo" (Vasari 1586: II, 185). He does not state when it was "improved" or who improved it, but clearly it was designed in more than one phase, and a number of architects were at least "consulted."

The courtyard of the Cancelleria has arches on columns like the interiors of Brunelleschi's churches rather than more structurally sound fornices as for the additions to the Palazzo Venezia. The reason Roman Doric columns were chosen for two stories is undoubtedly because they could be readily taken from Diocletian's Baths. They happened to be Doric, and the shafts happened to be granite. Less heavy Corinthian pilasters of travertine were placed above them to support an entablature rather than arches. The thinner columns of granite had more than enough compressive strength to support the loads placed on them, but the use of arches on columns was so structurally unsound that iron rods had to be used to tie the base of the arches to the walls behind them. Since about half of the available columns were smaller in height and diameter than the other half, the smaller ones of the same order were placed above the larger ones, but had to be raised on pedestals to give the the upper story of the arcade the same height as the lower story, which does not have pedestals. The corner solution is a cluster of piers, a favorite solution of Giuliano da Sangallo. He is credited with having created the first mezzanines during the Renaissance, and the upper story of the Cancelleria has mezzanines (Frommel 2007: 58). Since he was the personal architect for the Della Rovere family, I attribute this courtyard to him.

Giuliano da Sangallo had been castellan at Ostia when Giuliano della Rovere (the future Julius II) was Bishop of Ostia, and in my opinion, he probably designed the exemplary temple-form church there. He designed a palace for San Pietro in Vincoli when the future pope became a cardinal and relocated there. He designed a family palace for the Della Rovere at Savona, and he accompanied the future pope in exile. When Giuliano della Rovere became Pope, he initially continued to favor Giuliano da San Gallo as his architect until Bramante proved to be a much superior architect (Vasari 1568: II, 215-216). Giuliano da Sangallo undoubtedly knew more about engineering than Bramante, and he probably knew as much or more ancient Roman, but his initial design for St. Peter's was passed over in favor of Bramante's. Julius also selected Bramante's designs for the Belvedere Courtyard as well, but made Sangallo second in charge more of St. Peter's, the design of which he later influenced (Chapter 19 herein).

Palazzo Caprini (House of Raphael), Rome (begun 1509)

Palazzo Caprini (House of Raphael) by Bramante, Rome (Lafreri)

Bramante "...erected the palace for Raphael of Urbino in the Borgo, built of bricks and blocks of concrete the columns and the bosses being of Doric and rustic work of great beauty, and the concrete blocks a new invention" (Vasari 1568: II, 188). Although better known as the House of Raphael, it was designed for the Caprini family in 1509; Raphael acquired it in 1517 and lived there until his death in 1520. It "...was as important for the development of the palazzo as St Peter's was for religious architecture" (Heydenreich and Lotz 1974. 163)

The Palazzo Caprini had pairs of engaged columns rather than pilasters like Alberti's Palazzo Rucellai and the Cancelleria, and the ground floor is arcaded and has rustication rather than an ashlar facing (combining facings that had been used separately in earlier palazzi). Small shops with mezzanines were placed across the ground floor to produce rental income (as for Roman insula). The arcade and columns give this building a more classical appearance than any palazzo that had preceded it. Palladio was much influenced.

Raphael is fairly certain to have adapted the design of the Palazzo Caprini for the Palazzo Vidoni on the Via del Sudario in Rome (c. 1515-1520). It has pairs of engaged columns on single pedestals on its piano nobile, and his ground floor has windows with pedimented surrounds alternating with arches. Horizontal rustication connects the tops of its voussoirs. It was originally five or seven bays long, but was later lengthened, and an attic story was added.

Bramante's Palazzo Caprini (House of Raphael), Rome (sketch by Palladio)

Reconstruction of Raphael's Palazzo Vidoni (Hofmann in Frommel *et al.*)

Palazzo Vidoni-Caffarelli (Piranesi)

Palazzo Massimo, Rome (1532-c. 1536)

Palazzo Massimo, Rome (2017)

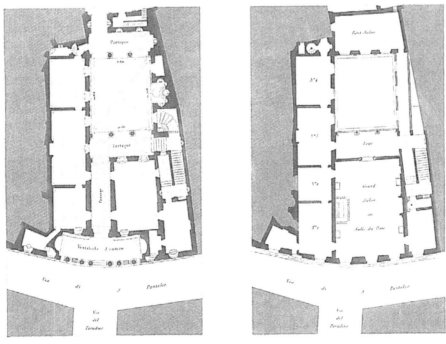

Palazzo Massimo (Letarouilly)

Baldassare Peruzzi created the Palazzo Pietro Massimo, one of the finest palazzi ever created for its spaces and ornamentation even though it is one of the most eccentric. Peruzzi was commissioned to rebuilt within the ruins of a residence that had been burned during the Sack of Rome in 1527, and he was able to conceal irregularities required mainly by the reuse of the foundations of an ancient Roman theatre.

The site itself presented serious problems in that a narrow street curved around the front, and the existing entrance was off-center. Peruzzi persuade his client to acquire enough of the front of an adjacent lot, which belonged to another member of the Massimo family, to be able to create a symmetrical front. He placed a colonnade across much of the ground floor in front of a deep loggia, and by adding an attic above the entablature of this colonnade, he gave by far the strongest emphasis to the ground floor. The upper two stories of the front are unlike those of any other palazzo in that the design appears to represent a double attic, but the lower set of attic windows provide clearstory lighting for the rooms of the piano nobile (principal floor), and the upper attic windows are for a true attic story of lower height. The overall height of the front is 70 feet, and the travertine facing of the lower story is 30 feet tall, leaving 40 feet for the stuccoes stories above it (3:4).

The main entrance to the house is on the second story and is reached through the courtyard. A long, open vestibule runs back to one side of a courtyard (rather than to the center), and it appears to continue on axis through to the back of the property. The near side of the courtyard provides a covered passage to an outside staircase that leads to another loggia on the upper story and to the entrance. Thus, from the street to the principal room of the piano nobile, the path is entirely outdoors, but this was also the case for the Palazzo Medici, the Cancelleria, and many other palazzi.

The main room or salone is centered on the courtyard and off-center in relation to the front of the building, but there is no indication of this asymmetry from the front. This room is somewhat trapezoidal, but it appears to be a perfect rectangle of 45 by 60 piedi (feet equal to 0.298 m.) and so has nearly the proportions of 3:4, but it tapers to 40 feet wide at the entrance. Since it is 45 feet high, the proportions of the height to width are 1:1 and for height to length are 3:4. Although the front wall curves on the outside, it was made straight across on the inside by varying the thickness of the wall. A side wall tapers dramatically to gain as much extra width as possible for the entrance end of the room.

When the doors of the salone are closed, the only light enters from the south side, but three large windows below and three clearstory windows provide more than ample light. The large room is prevented from seeming empty by having its walls subdivided by pilasters and an attic story, by the use of a coffered ceiling, and by the addition of a sculptural mantle and classical sculpture on pedestals. The combination of the space, light, detailing, and decoration is uniformly successful.

As an example of the refinement of details, Wilson Jones noted in his study of the design of the palazzo that Peruzzi used five different sizes of doors, but in each case the width to height of the opening is 1:2, and the height of the opening to the height of the door enframement is 3:4. All five sizes of doors are enframed by essentially the same architrave moulding except that the largest has lateral extensions at its top corners like Greek door enframements. All have a similar cornice except that the largest is embellished. The smallest door has a plain bolection moulding for a frieze, the next two sizes flat friezes, the forth largest a flat frieze within brackets, and the largest a bolection with embellishment. Each one has been scaled to the space it is part of and has been embellished to corresponding to the relative size and importance of the space.

Palazzo Massimo (Letarouilly)

Salone and plans of the Palazzo Massimo by Peruzzi (Letarouilly)

Palazzo Massimo loggia (albumin by Alinari)

Palazzo Farnese, Rome (1530-1589)

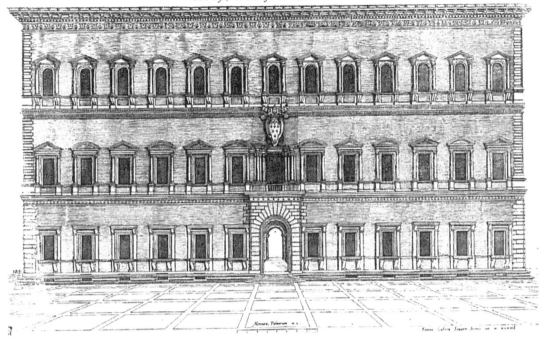

Farnese Palace as it was to be completed in 1549 (Betrizet; Argan and Contardi)

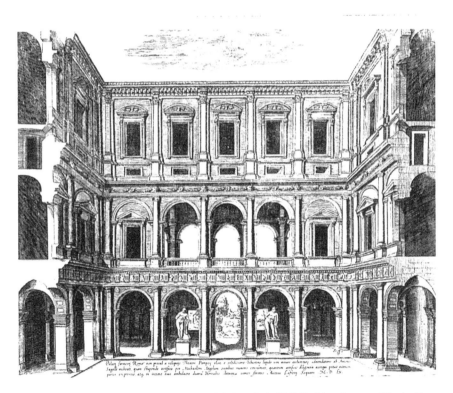

Farnese Palace courtyard as intended by Michelangelo in 1560 (Lafréry; Argan and Contardi)

PALAZZO FARNESE: ROME

A CROWNING CORNICE
B FACADE TO PIAZZA
C ENTRANCE
D BAY OF FACADE
E THE CORTILE FROM ARCADE
F BAY OF CORTILE
G GROUND PLAN
H ENTRANCE VESTIBULE
J FIRST FLOOR PLAN

(Fletcher)

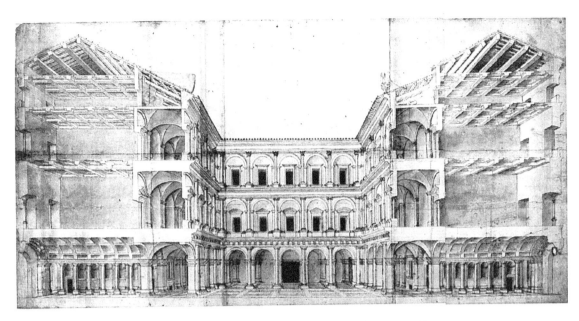

Palazzo Farnese as planned in c. 1546 (Millon and Lampugnani)

Antonio da Sangallo the Younger (1485-1546) designed most of the Palazzo Farnese for the family of the cardinal who became Pope Paul III and reigned from 1534-1555. Construction began around 1515, and the project was greatly enlarged upon his elevation to the papacy. It was the first major palace constructed by a pope to ennoble his family, a precedent that was followed most conspicuously by the Borghese, Barberini, and Pamphili families and that did not end until the Counter-Reformation (Ackerman 1986: 171-192; Heydenreich and Lotz 1974: 200).

The site was occupied by a relatively small house when Cardinal Alessandro Farnese acquired it in 1495. He renovated the house in 1517 and began to enlarge it in 1530 for an extended family that included five children of his own and a staff that eventually numbered about 300 persons. Upon becoming pope in 1534, he had Sangallo prepare a new plan on a grander scale. The Palazzo Farnese's front is nearly 200 feet long and 100 feet high, and the building surrounds a courtyard about 80 feet square and a walled garden in back. It occupies a block of its own and takes up one side of one of Rome's largest piazzas, and the piazza was created to be the width of the palace and was intended to hold a large number of carriages (Waddy 1990).

Although trained as a painter, Sangallo came to Rome to work with his uncles Giuliano da Sangallo (1445-1516) and Antonio da Sangallo the Elder (c. 1460-1534). Since the younger Sangallo

> ...was much inclined to architecture, he gave promise of future eminence, displayed in later years in so many things all over Italy. When Giuliano, suffering from the stone, was forced to return to Florence, Antonio became known to Bramante, the architect, helping the paralytic old man with his drawings, as he could not use his hands. Antonio did these with such finish that Bramante, finding the measurements correct, gave him the care of many things supplying his with the necessary inventions and compositions. Antonio showed such judgment, quickness and diligence that, in 1512, Bramante gave him the charge of the corridor leading to the moat of the Castle of St. Angelo, which he began with provision of 10 crowns a month, but the work was interrupted by the death of Julius II [in 1513]. Antonio, however, had already acquired the reputation of being a skillful architect, and his excellent walls led Alessandro Farnese, the first

cardinal of the house, afterwards Pope Paul III, to think of restoring his old palace in the Campo di Fiore, where he lived with his family. Antonio, being anxious to win a position by his work, made various designs, one of which, arranged in two apartments, was adopted by the cardinal after consulting his sons Pier Luigi and Ranuccio, whom he expected to accommodate in this structure. The work was therefore begun and advanced steadily every year [Vasari 1568: 87-88].

Vasari later indicated how much had been accomplished by the 1546, when Sangallo died:

When a cardinal, Paul III had advanced the place to good state, and had begun the front windows, the inside hall, and cleared part of the court, though it was not sufficiently advanced to show its perfections. After the Pope's election Antonio entirely changed the design for something befitting a pope and not a cardinal. Pulling down some houses and the old staircases, he made new and more pleasant ones, enlarging the court in every sense and the whole of the palace, making larger salons, more numerous rooms, and finer ceilings, with beautiful carvings and other decorations. He completed the second [floor] windows, and it only remained to set up the surrounding cornice. The Pope, being a man of spirit and of good judgment, wished to have a finer cornice, the richest possible, and better than that of any other palace, so in addition to the plans prepared by Antonio all the best architects in Rome made theirs through Antonio was to superintend the work. ... The Pope examined the designs carefully, and praising all as being ingenious and beautiful, but especially that of Michelagnolo [Michelangelo]. Antonio did not like all this, as he wished to be the chief... [Vasari 1567: 96].

Sangallo had designed a cornice for the top of the building about the same size as the cornices for the ground and first floors, but with rafters projecting somewhat farther projecting farther with the exposed rafters farther (Millon and Lampugnani 1994: 194-195; Ackerman 1986: 188, fig. 85).

Sangallo was one of the finest draftsmen during the Renaissance, one of its most prolific architects, and an architect with an unusually good knowledge of structural requirements, but for the Palazzo Farnese, he used relatively small design elements on an immense front in a way similar to his later design for St. Peter's. He adapted Raphael's c. 1520 design for the smaller and incomplete Palazzo Pandolfini in Florence without using proportionately larger elements. Sangallo was employed by Raphael from 1515-1520 (Heydenreich and Lotz 1974: 186-187, pl. 189).

Uncompleted Palazzo Pandolfini, Florence; designed by Raphael in c. 1518 (Brogi)

Neither Sangallo nor Raphael used rustication extensively as Michelozzo had done for the Palazzo Medici or ashlar pilasters as Alberti had done for the Palazzo Rucellai. Instead, they used rustication only around the entrance, and the orders were used on the fronts only as inconspicuous parts of the window enframements. Relatively thin stringcourses do not suffice to made up for disproportionately large amounts of blank space between the floors. Overall, the composition lacks coherence even with the improvements Michelangelo was able to make after the building had been largely constructed. The vestibule and courtyard were far more successful.

Sangallo's barrel-vaulted vestibule achieves a sense of monumentality in a small space. It has only six pair of free-standing columns set within a space surrounded on all sides with engaged columns and so appears to be four rows of columns.

Pope Paul III had told Sangallo, while he was alive, to carry forward the palace of the Farnese family, but the great upper cornice, competing the outer edge of the roof, had still to be constructed, and his holiness wanted Michelangelo to undertake this and to use his own designs. Unable to refuse the Pope who so greatly esteemed and favoured him, Michelangelo made a full-scale wood model, twelve feet long, and he caused this to be placed on one of the corners of the palace to show the effect of the finished work. His holiness and everyone else in Rome being please by the result, the part which can be seen now was carried to completion, producing the most beautiful and varied cornice that has ever been known in ancient or modern times. Consequently, after Sangallo died the Pope wanted Michelangelo to take charge of the whole building as well; and so Michelangelo made the great marble window with the beautiful columns of variegated stone which is above the principle door of the palace, surmounted by a large marble coat-of-arms, of great beauty and originality belonging to Pope Paul III, the founder of the palace. Within the palace over the first story of the courtyard Michelangelo continued the two other stories, with their incomparably beautiful, graceful, and varied windows, ornamentation and crowning cornice. Hence, through the labours and genius of that man, the courtyard has been transformed into the most beautiful in Europe. He widened and enlarged the great hall and reconstructed the front corridor [of the courtyard], making the vaulting with a new and ingenious kind of arch in the form of a half oval [Vasari 1568 (1971): 83-84].

Michelozzo Michelozzi had used a cornice on a similar scale been placed on the Medici Palace in Florence, but with a different design. The concept of using an upper corniced to an entire front was ancient and well known through examples such as the Colosseum, which Michelangelo had studied with care and used similar proportions. The ten-foot cornice is the principal embellishment of the exterior. Michelangelo also designed the large window and coat of arms above the entrance to give greater emphasis to the center and greater unity to the patterned front. Michelangelo was criticized for using Corinthian brackets together with Ionic dentils in his cornice, but Raphael had done the same for the Palazzo Pandolfini.

Inside, Michelangelo enlarged the enormous reception room (salone), which is located at the front left corner of the piano nobile and which extends through two floors with upper windows serving as its clearstory. It occupies three by five bays, and seems incomplete. Only its ceiling and floor were designed by Michelangelo (Heydenreich and Lotz 1974: 253). The magnificent section Sangallo drew in perspective shows that Michelangelo inserted the mezzanine in between the two upper floors of the courtyard, and it accounts to some extent for the use of a U-shaped vault in the corridors of the piano nobile and the omission of the arches in the upper story and the addition of pedestals, but not for the designs of the window surrounds and the pilasters (Millon and Lampugnani 1994: 194-195; Ackerman 1986: 180, fig. 77).

The interior has numerous rooms with walls and ceilings covered by frescoes. A central room of the piano nobile facing the garden and river was planned by Michelangelo, but is attributed to Vignola. This room was later embellished with superb frescoes by Annibale Carracci.

The window surrounds by Michelangelo are major examples of his highly individualistic and influential style. The two lower stories of the courtyard by Sangallo have engaged columns of the Doric and Ionic orders on the top floor. Michelangelo superimposed the Corinthian order as usual, but used pilasters rather than engaged columns (as on the uppermost story of the Colosseum). He gave emphasis and distinction to his pilasters by placing half-pilasters alongside them, an arrangement similar to the Doric pilasters that Bramante had used in the courtyard of Santa Maria della Pace to complete "Rossellino's choir" for old St. Peter's (Vasari 1568: II, 188-189). At the upper corners of the Palazzo Farnese's courtyard, nearly adjacent pilasters have projecting corners that are also similar to Bramante's corners, but that have a much more complex and continuous resolution of the details. Michelangelo's window surrounds have segmental arched pediments above uniformly triangular pediments of the second story windows. The brackets and ornamentation are uniquely his in their design and sculptural quality.

Michelangelo also designed the spacious and well lighted corridor with an elliptical vault. The vault is similar in shape to the bridge design he recommended to Bartolomeo Ammannati for the Ponte San Trinità in Florence (Heydenreich and Lotz 1974: 321). Michelangelo planned to build a bridge across the Tiber to connect the

Palazzo Farnese with the Villa Farnesina, which the Pope acquired.

While pope, Paul III has extensive excavations made in the Baths of Caracalla primarily for building materials, but also recovered large quantities of sculpture including the Farnese Bull. This large collection of sculpture decorated the courtyard of the Palazzo Farnese, but is now in the Archeological Museum in Naples.

Palazzo Farnese vestibule designed by Antonio Sangallo the Younger in c. 1517 (albumen by Alinari)

Palazzo Farnese courtyard; third story windows enframements by Michelangelo (albumen by Anderson)

Michelangelo's drawing for the window enframement of the Palazzo Farnese (De Tolnay, *Corpus* no. 589r)

VILLAS

Lorenzo de' Medici's Villas

Lorenzo de' Medici examining a model for his villa at Poggio a Caiano (Baggio n. d: cover)

Villa Medici at Poggio a Caiano in 1801 (Fontani in Belluzzi, Elam, and Fiore)

Villa Medici at Poggio a Caiano (Heydenreich and Lotz)

"The most precious document on this subject ["domestic life"] is the treatise on the management of the home by Agnolo Pandolfini (actually written by L. B. Alberti, in 1472" (a separate, but complimentary treatise to the *Ten Books*; Burckhardt 1944: 244):

One feature of this book must be referred to, which is by no means peculiar to it, but which it treats with special warmth—the love of the educated Italian for country life. In northern countries the nobles lived in the country in their castles, and the monks of the higher orders in their well-guarded monasteries, while the wealthiest burgers dwelt from one year's end to another in the cities. But in Italy, so far as the neighbourhood of certain towns at all events was concerned, the security of life and property was so great and the passion for country residence was so strong, that men were willing to risk a loss in time of war. Thus arose the villa, the country-house of the well-to do citizen. This precious inheritance of the old Roman world was thus revived, as soon as the wealth and culture of the people was sufficiently advanced.

Pandolfini finds at his villa a peace and happiness, for an account of which the reader must hear him speak himself. The economical side of the matter is that one and the same property, must, if possible contain everything—corn, wine, oil, pasture-land and woods, and that in such cases the property was paid for well, since nothing needed then to be got from the market. But the higher enjoyment derived from the villa is shown by some words of the introduction: "Round about Florence lie many villas in a transparent atmosphere, amid cheerful scenery, and with a splendid view; there is little fog, and no injurious winds; all is good, and the water pure and healthy. Of the numerous buildings many are like palaces, many like castles costly and beautiful to behold." He is speaking of those unrivalled villas, of which the greater number were sacrificed, though vainly, by the Florentines themselves in the defence of their city in the year 1529 [Burckhardt 1944: 244-245].

"Most Florentine families, patrician and otherwise, sought pleasure and a renewal of their roots by regularly visiting the farms and villages of the countryside whence their ancestors had come to the City. These pilgrims went at Christmas and at Easter and stayed for weeks at a time during the intolerably hot Tuscan summer and early autumn. ...These rural resorts were also productive working farms..." (Kent 2004: 112-113). For example, Cosimo de' Medici continued to visit "...the beautiful and isolated upland valley of the Mugello, in the Apennines north of Florence, and they maintained extensive rural properties there, and control of much ecclesial patronage, throughout the Renaissance period. Lorenzo de' Medici (1449-1492) spent long months of his youth at Cosimo's great fortified house, Cafaggiolo..." and particularly enjoyed going there with his brother Giuliano to hunt, but in 1486 had to turn it and its 67 farms over to Medici cousin (112, 118).

Lorenzo built relatively little compared to his grandfather Cosimo, but he lived only 43 years while Cosimo lived nearly 75 years; both of them and Lorenzo's father Piero suffered greatly from gout (uricaemia), and in old age all three were crippled; the disease had also been the cause of Piero's death when he was about 53 years old (Kent 2000: 244). In his early thirties, Lorenzo began to acquire vast amounts or rural property, completed a small villa, began a large villa, and planned to construct additional villas as agriculture became one of his principal investments. "The Medici were among the Tuscan leaders expanding the commercial cultivation of olives.... Lorenzo himself was responsible for planting thousands of olive trees on his estates in the Pisano, including Agnano... He also established mulberry plantations for the propagation of silkworms..." at Poggio a Caiano in addition the thousands of mulberry trees that had been planted there earlier by Giovanni Rucellai. (120-121). He acquired pasturage and large herds of sheep and cows. He had bottom lands drained and uplands irrigated.

Together with land he had inherited, Lorenzo acquired additional estates that gave him rural property in almost every direction from Florence and throughout much of Tuscany:

> Just outside of Florence, to the west, was Cosimo's villa of Careggi, which Lorenzo often visited and showed off to visitors. In the environs of the city there was another retreat, of which we know little, at Grassina.... Farther

south lay Montepaldi, which was near the important fortified town of San Casciano. To the southwest, in the almost lunar landscape of lower Tuscany, was the villa and hunting lodge of Spedaletto [chiefly a hunting lodge, but much embellished with frescoes]. …

Aross from Spedaletto, toward Pisa…, Lorenzo developed extensively the agricultural interests of which his and other Florentine families had been investing for most of the century. Lorenzo had several estates around Vico Pisano, Buti, Calci, and Fucecchio, and he owned an iron mine, as well as substantial houses, in the area. … In 1486 he acquired Agnano, which commanded a view of Pisa and the Tyrrhenian Sea from its position in the foothills above the Pisan plain. …Poliziano pictured Lorenzo reading at leisure there and enjoying the sea view from the pine woods his master had ordered planted at Agnano…. The views from Poggio a Caino, which stands between Pisa and Florence on the highway to the subject town of Pistoia, were almost as fine. …

It is striking that all of Lorenzo's new villas, including Montepaldi, which still offers astonishingly long southern views of hills and valleys…, conformed to Alberti's prescription that a gentleman's country house should not only be clearly visible to passersby but also "have a View of some City, Towns, the Sea, an open Plain, and the Tops of some know Hills and Mountains" [Kent 2004: 124-125].

If Lorenzo had done nothing else, he would deserve great credit for recognizing the potential of Michelangelo and having him trained as a sculptor and treated him as a member of his family. "Michelangelo was between fifteen and sixteen years old when he went to live in the house of the Magnificent, and he stayed there until the latter's death, which was in 1492, about two years" (Condivi 1553: 13). Michelangelo was living with him while Lorenzo was working closely with Giuliano da Sangallo on the creation of a major villa at Poggio a Caiano, which is about 10 miles from Florence, and Michelangelo undoubtedly then began to learn the basics of architecture and became friends with Sangallo, who later helped him when they both worked for Julius II. Considering that Michelangelo's earliest knowledge of sculpture, architecture, and fortifications date from the years he spent in the Medici household and considering that Lorenzo's villa building is unusually well documented, it is worth considered his projects in some detail even though only one of his villas fully represents his intentions.

Lorenzo's son Giovanni was nearly Michelangelo's age, and they were raise together for several years. When Giovanni served as Pope Leo X from 1513-1521, he was a major patron of Michelangelo. In 1520 the painter Sebastiano del Piombo wrote Michelangelo that "'I know the pope's regard for you, and he speaks of you as if you were his brother, almost with tears in his eyes, because he has told me you were brought up [*nutriti*] together, and he makes it clear he know and loves you, though everyone's afraid of you, even popes'" (Kent 2004: 9; note omitted). Leo X died young at age 46 like his father and grandfather. From indecision and lack of funds, his patronage of Michelangelo produced little results. It was only with the election of Leo's cousin as Clement VII (1523-1534) that the Medici Chapel and Laurentian Library were commissioned and that Medici patronage enabled Michelangelo to achieve some of his principal accomplishments.

Cosimo de' Medici, Lorenzo's grandfather, had been unofficial head of the government of Florence from 1434 until his death in 1464. Piero de' Medici, Lorenzo's father, inherited Cosimo's influence, but not his judgment and was assassinated by a Medici cousin in 1469. Consequently, when 20 years old, Lorenzo inherited immense wealth and became head of one of the most prominent families in Europe, but "as Lorenzo was later to lament, he spent the rest of his life reading and wring letters and giving audiences to clients" (Kent 2004: 15). By 1485 he was so fed up that he wrote, "get these petitioners off my back… because I have more letters from would-be

Priors than there are days in the year and I am resolving not to want everything my way and to live what time I have left as peacefully as possible..." (80). From 1469 to 1485 Lorenzo continued to attempt to have "everything my way," but "when Louis XI offered him aid in the war against Ferrante of Naples and Sixtus IV, he replied, 'I cannot set my own advantage above the safety of all Italy...'" (58).

Before moving to the Palazzo Medici, Cosimo had lived three blocks northeast of the Duomo near the church of Santissima Annunziata, which is adjacent to Brunelleschi's Spedale degli Innocenti, the orphan asylum. SS. Annunziata is a block from the church and convent of San Marco, which Cosimo had paid most of the costs to build. When about 10 years old, Lorenzo moved with his family into the newly completed Palazzo Medici, which is one block north of the Duomo and diagonally opposite the church of San Lorenzo, which Cosimo also largely paid to build.

The northern part of Florence was where most of the Medici faction lived, and following Cosimo's example, one of Lorenzo's earliest independent actions was to pay most of the cost to build a monastery for 100 friars at the San Gallo gate, the main northern entrance to Florence. It has been nearly completed at the time of his death in 1492, but was destroyed in 1530 during the siege of Florence and is poorly documented (Kent 2004: 62,142; Vasari 1568: II, 213). Lorenzo hired Giuliano di Francesco Giamberti to design it and was so pleased with the work that he nicknamed him Sangallo (Vasari 1568: II. 211, 213). Around 1485 he had him designing the church of Santa Maria della Carceri at Prato and the villa at Poggio a Caiano (Kent 2004: 86-87). Lorenzo also contributed substantially towards the completion of San Lorenzo, and he later built rental housing along a newly created street in Florence.

Otherwise Lorenzo built little in Florence, but was indirectly involved in the design and construction of the city's architecture by serving on various public works committees ("opera") including the opera of the Duomo. One of the numerous committees on which he served in order to extend his influence was the opera of SS. Annunziata, and his four-year term began there in 1468 (Kent 2004: 22). Cosimo had previously hired Michelozzo (the architect of the Palazzo Medici) to add a vestibule and atrium to SS. Annunziata, and while Lorenzo was serving on its opera, Ludovico Gonzaga of Mantua commissioned Michelozzo to add a large domed tribune (choir) with seven chapels. Since Gonzaga was an outsider, there was much opposition to this major addition to one of the principal shrines in the city (a pilgrimage site famous for miracles that were believed to be performed by a painting of the Mother of God; "Lorenzo shared his own mother Lucrezia's special devotion to the mother of God," and the Annunziata and the Church of Santa Maria delle Carceri at Prato were both visited by multitudes to implore her to intervene [87]). Michelozzo was a close personal friend of Cosimo, and at his request, Lorenzo allowed him to be buried in Cosimo's tomb in San Lorenzo when he died in 1472. "...when Ludovico Gonzaga, annoyed by what he described as the 'swarm' of Florentine objections, threatened to withdraw from this dynastic commitment to a foreign church and spend his money in Mantua, Lorenzo, diplomatically professing ignorance of such aesthetic matters, hastened to advise the marquis on 21 May 1471 to proceed 'precisely according to your own taste and desire...'" (48).

Since Lorenzo inherited the Palazzo Medici, he had no need to build another house in Florence. He had no need to build a villa since he had inherited some if not all of the villas that his grandfather Cosimo built at Badia Fiesolana, Careggi, Caffagiolo, and Trebbio and the villa that his uncle Giovanni had built at Fiesole (Frommel 2007: 42-44). He is known as early as 1468, when he was about 18 years old, to have considered Caffagiolo to be his property, and its factor wrote to his father, "'...Lorenzo has the urge to level the piazza here in front of the villa. We will do what he says, and keep you informed'" (Kent 2004: 21.

Passionately fond of both rural pleasures and profit, patently desirous of relieving, if not curing, his physical ailments by spending time in the fresh air, in his building campaigns in the country Lorenzo was seeking to express still other feelings and desires, to achieve still other objectives. There was, one suspects, the urge to refashion himself and his immediate family, transform himself and his descendant from Florentine citizen-bankers—cim—Mugello countrymen into learned landed gentlemen who like ancient Roman patricians, from their villas molded and domesticated their vast estates as they wrought to shape and control the republican politics of the city [122]. Despite his influence and great wealth, Lorenzo was concerned about the relative status of his family, and in 1473 he noted that the great amount it had provided for public projects since 1434 had been money "…well spent… having greatly enhanced our status…" (Kent 2004: 78). In 1472 he lamented, "'how long it has been our family's desire to have a cardinal in its ranks.' … Many years later, after much effort and expense, an extremely youthful Giovanni di Lorenzo attained the purple causing his father to call it 'the greatest achievement ever our house…'" (72). The pope at the time was Innocent VIII, and "in 1487 he married his elder son Franceschetto Cybo (d. 1519) to Maddalena de' Medici (1473–1528), the daughter of Lorenzo di'Medici, who in return obtained the cardinal's hat for his thirteen-year-old son Giovanni, later Pope Leo X" (Pope Leo X. https://en.wikipedia.org/wiki/Pope_Innocent_VIII; Burckhardt 1944: 68). Giovanni was initially a cardinal-deacon and was admitted to full membership in the College of Cardinals three years later. Although great land holding enhanced the status of the family, royal connections required access to the influence and funds of the Papacy.

Leo X greatly increased the prestige of the family, but the extravagance of the Vatican and Leo's abuse of the existing practice of indulgences (forgiveness of sins upon sufficient payment) so outraged Martin Luther as to be among the principal causes of the Protestant Reformation. As Machivelli wrote, "we Italians are irreligious and corrupt above all others... because the Church and her representatives set us the worst example" (Burckhardt 1944: 202). The historian Guicciardini, who was for many years in the service of the Medicean Popes, says (1529) in his "Aphorisms": "no man is more disgusted than I am with the ambition, the averice, and the profligacy of the priests.... Nevertheless, my position at the Court of several Popes forced me to desire their greatness for the sake of my own interest. But, had it not been for this, I should have loved Martin Luther as myself... [Burckhardt 1944: 285-286].

After a brief interval, Leo X was followed in the papacy by Clement VII, a Medici cousin whose duplicity resulted in the Sack of Rome in 1527. Pope Clement arranged for Lorenzo's eldest grandson to marry into the French royal family, and that marriage produced Catherine de' Medici, who in turn married the prince who later became a second son of Francis I who unexpectedly became King Henry II of France; and Catherine children included three French kings and a Spanish queen. After the Sack of Rome by troops hired by Charles V, Clement VII formed an alliance with him to besiege Florence, destroy its republic, and install Cosimo I de' Medici as the first Duke of Florence, and Cosimo I founded the dynasty of the Grand Dukes of Tuscany. A daughter of Catherine married Henry IV of France, but produced no heir, and being in debt to a later grand duke of Florence, Henry married Marie de' Medici, a descendant of Lorenzo through a female line, and she became the mother of Louis XIII and the grandmother of Louis XIV of France and of Charles II of England. In these ways, the Medici went from being the first citizens of a republic to becoming ancestors of numerous kings and queens. Thus, among the disasters that resulted from Lorenzo's intrigues to elevate his family, the most direct ones were the Reformation, the Sack of Rome, and the siege of Florence and destruction of its republican government.

Having noted some of the consequences of Lorenzo's actions, it is only fair to credit him with having set good examples by helping to train promising artists, by collecting rare manuscripts to preserve and make available knowledge, by commissioning major works of art, by improving the urban fabric of Florence, and by increasing appreciation for classical literature, art, and architecture. As Kent pointed out in *Lorenzo de' Medici & the Art of Magnificence*, what Lorenzo was able to achieve was limited by a short life, but nonetheless has been minimized rather than dealt with fairly by revisionist historians. Although some writers have attributed accomplishments to him without any evidence, some historians have gone so far as to try to discount good evidence by Condivi, Vasari, and other contemporary writers about the beneficial influence Lorenzo had even on Michelangelo. As Kent concluded, "yet by 1492 Lorenzo had begun several major architectural projects that expressed an innovatory, modern taste informed by a studious appreciation of the antique. As [the contemporary Florentine historian] Guiccardini also remarked, in a passage that is neglected by scholars, Lorenzo 'delighted' not only in fine books and music but also in 'sculpture, painting, and architecture, rewarding and supporting all the men excellent in those arts,' a view endorsed by Raffaele Maffei, a hostile contemporary witness...." (Kent 2004: 5-6). He was without question so fluent in Latin that he wrote a large and highly respected body of Latin as well as Tuscan poetry. "As for that quintessential 'myth,' the sculpture garden presided over by the sculptor Bertoldo di Giovanni, where the young Leonardo da Vinci and Michelangelo Buonarotti learnt their trade under Lorenzo's benign eye, research by Carolina Elam has quite literally put the Medici garden firmly back on the Florentine map, from which our academic fathers had almost erased it..." (7; 155-157, notes 27 and 35). Lorenzo acquired the property for the garden between 1472 and 1474 and built a garden pavilion (*casino*) there (75). Leo X's statement that he and Michelangelo were "brought up [*nutriti*] together" and much equally well supported evidence cannot be simply dismissed by those who specialize in belittling others. Anyone who dismisses the best available evidence is no more a scholar than those who make assertions without any evidence to back them up.

As the political situation in northern Europe made trade and banking less profitable and his agents more independent, Lorenzo decided to invest instead in agricultural land in Tuscany. As a contemporary noted,

> "foreign trade having been interrupted, ["Lorenzo"] began to concentrate upon landed estates. ...In his *History of Florence* Niccolò Machiavelli was more explicit, anticipating modern scholarship in his emphasis on how poorly managed the Medici bank was in Lorenzo's time: "In his commercial affairs, ["Lorenzo"] was very unfortunate, from the improper conduct of his agents.... To avoid similar inconvenience, he withdrew from mercantile pursuits, and invested his property in land and houses, as being less liable to vicissitude." ... Close to this account is the biographer Niccolò Valori's, which asserts that Lorenzo "came to hate the mercantile life" and to recognize "how useful and delightful is agriculture, and not unworthy of some prince... [Kent 2004: 119].

During most of the last decade of his life, he devoted much of his time to creating a series of estates that were intended to be income producing and that would also provide needed food for his large household, opportunities for hunting, for making his influence felt throughout Tuscany, the chance to get away from the importunities and unhealthiness of the city, and places to build as he pleased without the limitations of urban sites.

Principally, his villas were investments rather than farms on which to live or vacation houses for occasional visits. Although they served multiple functions, there would have been no need to have so many of them if there had been better ways to invent available funds. At the time Lorenzo began to acquire vast amounts of agricultural land, the income provided by the Medici banks throughout Europe was declining and becoming unreliable. He also invested in portable objects of great value such as hundreds of ancient gems and about 4,000 rare coins and large numbers of illuminated manuscripts. He did not cease to lend money, but he increasingly diversified his investments.

As noted, Cosimo had refused to build the large palazzo that Brunelleschi designed for him and that he could well have afforded and instead built a smaller palazzo. Bankers were looked down upon and resented as usurers, and they tended to marry one another (including the Medici, Strozzi, and Rucellai, all three of whom built major palaces in Florence during the 1400s). Although Cosimo encouraged other families to contribute to the cost of the construction of San Lorenzo, after his death the church was turned into a mausoleum in his honor; he was buried in front of the altar; none of the families that had contributed were allowed to bury their dead there; and those who had previously been buried in the church had their bones removed. Such abuse of influence made his descendants increasingly unpopular and resulted in their being exiled from 1494-1512 and again from 1527-1530 (66-67).

Lorenzo often read a manuscript copy of Alberti's *Ten Books* that he had acquired in 1480, and he arranged for the first edition to be printed in Florence in 1485 (Kent 2004: 88). Architecture was one of his main avocations, and he indulged himself as often as circumstances permitted. As a youth, he knew Alberti personally, and Alberti dedicated his *Trivia* to him in 1459 and showed him Rome's ancient architecture in 1471. He had travelled extensively as a young man from Milan to Naples including Mantua, where he saw Alberti's churches under construction, and in 1485 he asked for a model of San Sebastiano in Mantua to be sent to him. (30, 36-37). He was well informed about construction, but he is not known to have prepared drawings from which a building could be constructed. "Lorenzo was a genuine intellectual with brad yet educated and discriminating tastes" (42).

Lorenzo often visited his estates to ensure that construction was progressing according to plans, to give instructions for drainage and other improvements to the land, to ensure that planting and herds were being well cared for and were beginning to produce profits, and for his health, which was slowly deteriorating with gout and other ailments (129, 137). When he had to be in Florence, he was kept well informed about everything that was being done on each estate, and he often issued detailed instructions for what he wanted done. He looked forward to leaving town and was reluctant to return "'...and have all Florence in my house to no end...'" (136). As he became more ill, he became less interested in always having his way with others and found greater satisfaction in having his ideas put into practice by architects and artists.

Lorenzo's favorite villa was under construction at Poggio, which is 10 miles west of Florence (Kent 2004: 72). At the time of Lorenzo's death, only about one-third of the villa at Poggio had been completed, but an earlier building was usable in the meanwhile, and eventually Leo X completed this villa according to the model that his father had approved

"The Laurentian villa-building campaign dates from about 1486 on but was long and carefully prepared. The site at Poggio a Caiano had been acquired when Lorenzo was a very young man, in 1474" and about 25 years old (126). Lorenzo had acquired Poggio from Giovanni Rucellai (who had commissioned Alberti to design the Palazzo Rucellai, but afterwards got into financial difficulties).

The earlier building at Poggio had been constructed by Palla Strozzi, Rucellai's father-in-law, and it was Palla Strozzi and Rinaldo degli Albizzi who had Cosimo de' Medici exiled in 1433, but Cosimo was exonerated and recalled in 1434, he had the Stozzi and Albizzi families exiled and became the richest and most influential man in Florence until his death in 1464. Filippo Strozzi the elder went to Naples and did so well in banking there that when he returned to Florence, he began building the Palazzo Strozzi to a similar design, but on a grander scale than the Palazzo Medici. Upon his death in 1491, he made Lorenzo his executor with the request that he complete the Palazzo Strozzi with funds provided for that purpose, but Lorenzo died the following year (140). Palla Strozzi's grandson Filippo the younger married Clarice de' Medici, a granddaughter of Lorenzo, and completed the Palazzo Strozzi in 1538 (Ramsden in Michelangelo 1963: I, appendix 2). Giovanni Rucellai was extremely pleased to have arranged for his son Bernardo to marry Nannina de' Medici, Lorenzo's sister, but Bernardo was extremely displeased that Lorenzo used legal maneuvers to acquire Poggio and opposed him in court for five years (Kent 2004: 78, 135-136). This was a reason for the delay in the construction of a villa at Poggio. Lorenzo did not gain full possession of the property until 1479. In addition, the late 1470s was a period of economic depression with high unemployment and shortages of food (79). In the meanwhile, Lorenzo planted large numbers of mulberry trees to raise silkworms, acquired a large herd of cows to create a dairy farm, and had increased the size of the estate by pressuring the government of Prato to transfer the rights to Church property to him.

"Having commissioned 'several models from Francione and others,' Lorenzo 'had Giuliano [da Sangallo] make a model of what he himself had in mind, which was in form so very different and diverse from the others, and so close to Lorenzo's fancy [*capriccio*] that he had work started on it at once as the best of all…'" (Vasari quoted in Kent 2004: 141). It was more like a mansion or town house than a villa in being detached and in having its main floor raised a story above ground (a piano nobile), and it was atypical in having a terrace raised on arches around the perimeter of the main floor and in having a pair of steps leading up to the entrance. Although some Roman villas had an upper story, their main floor was at ground level, and a podium was reserved for a temple.

As built, the entrance is unusual by having an external alcove fronted by columns that support an applied pediment rather than a projecting portico, and the pediment is disproportionately tall in relation to the thin and widely spaced columns. The front is symmetrical, but its design elements are not well interrelated to one another. The main room of the interior is unusually in extending from side to size across the middle of the house and also having a barrel vault.

Unfortunately, after Lorenzo's death, his son Piero "…sent a model of Poggio a Caiano made by Giuliano da Sangallo to Lodovico il Moro in October 1492…" in Milan and stated that "'from the master himself Your Excellency will understand still better the mind and intention of Lorenzo'" (91). The model must have ceased to be available when Leo X tried to complete the villa as he though his father would have wished.

In the Uffizi is a tapestry that shows Lorenzo considering a model of the villa at Poggio with the building under construction in the background. The model is large enough to need two men to support it, and beside it is a man who must be Sangallo, the architect. What is most extraordinary about this image is that neither the model nor the building under construction are like one another or like the villa as it was completed. The implication seems to be that Lorenzo is considering Sangallo's model and making changes during construction that were intended, but not carried out. The villa under construction is depicted in more detail than the model, and it is clear that it was to have had a monumental applied portico supported by six pilasters or engaged columns and a front door with a pedimented enframement flush with the front. In other words, the portico was to have been two storied rather than one as it was built, and there is no indication of a loggia behind the portico either on the model or on the building under construction. The building was also evidently being constructed or intended to be constructed with a pair of straight rather than curving steps (shown on both the model and the building itself, and on the building, the steps turn inward before reaching the terrace rather than going straight up to the terrace; moreover, in the Museum of Florence is a fresco showing the villa with straight steps). The model shows a cornice in between the main floor and the upper floor entirely around the building with the upper windows resting on the cornice and with the pediment of the entrance below this mid-level cornice; the building under construction shows no mid-level cornice and has pairs of windows flanking the monumental portico rather than extending across the entire front as on the model and on the villa as it was completed. On the building under construction, there are four upper and four lower windows on the main floors of the front; on the model, there are five upper windows and apparently three pairs of lower windows flanking the entrance; and on the building as completed, there are six upper widows and two pairs of lower windows. The building as completed also has a roof ornament in the center of the front that is not on the model. Considering that so many significant differences between the model, the building under construction, and the building as completed, my conclusions is that both Lorenzo's final intentions were for a villa that would have been be more monumental rather than with the more usual design Sangallo initially made, and either design would have been more classical, more coherent, and less provincial than what was finally constructed.

So unusual a design with a podium and pair of staircases is likely to have been suggested by an unusual source, and it is probably no coincidence that in 1485 while the villa for Poggio was being designed, "…Lorenzo asked [the Florentine architect Luca] Fancelli to send him 'a model of San Sebastian in Mantua,' an unusual Albertian creation…," and in the same year Lorenzo was reading proofs for the first edition of Alberti's *Ten Books* as it was being published in Florence (Kent 2004: 37). . Lorenzo is known to have seen Alberti's church and the classically inspired house with a circular courtyard designed for himself by the artist Andrea Mantegna that was also under construction when Lorenzo visited Mantua in 1483. Alberti's influence on the siting of all of Lorenzo's villas has been noted. As unlikely as it is that Lorenzo would have adapted a church for a villa, the strongly expressed central block of this church has a hipped room despite its temple front, and being raised on a podium, it is more like a classical temple and a house than a Renaissance church; in fact, while it was being built, Federigo Gonzaga objected that it did not look like a church (85). It flanking pair of straight steps leading up to a loggia with an arcade in between them was highly unusual if not unique at the time, and these features appear to have inspired Lorenzo's design for the ground floor of his villa; the monumental portico with engaged pilaster would well also have suggested the monumental portico shown in the tapestry and the stunted version and atrium that were eventually built. In addition to wanting a model of San Sebastian to consider some of its features for his villa, Lorenzo is also likely to have wanted the model for Sangallo to make use of while designing the cruciform church of Santa Maria in Carceri that was being designed in 1485 for Prato even though it owes more to Brunelleschi than Alberti.

No earlier villa is known to have had a podium, piano nobile, monumental portico, or pair of front steps, but Palladio later used these features in combination. It is unlikely that Palladio saw Sangallo's model in Milan even though he often used some of the same clusters of features. More likely, Lorenzo and Pallaio had a common source in Alberti's St. Sebastian. The influence of Alberti's Sant'Andrea in Mantua on Palladio's Il Redentore in Venice is manifest.

The overall form of the villa and its main floor a story above ground bore some resemblance to the villa that Giovanni de' Medici (1421-1463; Lorenzo's uncle), built at Fiesole several decades earlier near Cosimo's villa at Badia Fiesolana (Kent 2004: 18; fig. 4; Frommel 2007: 43-44). This much smaller villa initially had a square plan and a vaulted loggia across its front (but with arches on columns) and with lower story that was partly a ground floor and partly a basement on a terraced hillside. However, its design is asymmetrical, and it has arches resting on columns rather than piers as Alberti stipulated and as Lorenzo used for the arches of the ground floor at Poggio. Since Giovanni's villa was unfortified, Frommel considered it to be "…the first true villa since antiquity…" (44), and he attributed it to Alberti. There is reason, though, to believe that the design was by Rossellino, who designed the choir of Old St. Peter's. In 1456 Giovanni recommended Rossellino to Francesco Sforza, who was planning to build a hospital and had asked for advice on how to proceed. Giovanni wrote, "'…one should see many designs by different masters and should choose the best after careful scrutiny. And because here [in Florence] there are many extremely able masters, I have commissioned each of them to make a number of different models.' Giovanni judged Bernardo Rossellino's model to be the best and said that 'these days he is without equal'…" (Kent 2004: 19). In any case, it too looks more like a town house set against the side of a hill than a villa, and aside possibly from its overall blockish form with a hipped roof, it otherwise bears little resemblance to the villa at Poggio.

Although appearing to be cubical from the front, the Poggio villa is actually H-shaped, and in the middle of the H is a two-storied, barrel-vaulted room less wide than the rest of the plan with windows at each end. The other rooms on the main floor and on the ground floor have ovoid vault with. The construction is more like that of the palace at Urbino than the Palazzo Medici in Florence, and in 1481 Baccio Pontelli "…had sent detail measurement 'so that Your Magnificence should now have everything and will see room by room what has been done and what it will take to finish the said house'" (85).

Neither Guilaino da Sangallo nor Lorenzo de'Medici's designs was closely followed for the front of the Villa Medici at Poggio a Caino. If either had been followed, the front would have had a more coherent design.

> …with three sons in 1486 and possessed, one suspects, of a confident sense of the virility of his lie, [Lorenzo] also began almost at once to improve Spedaletto and then to build Agnano as if they would belong to the Medici race forever. He visited Spedaletto very soon after its acquisition, no doubt to take the waters of Bagno a Morbi but very likely also to discuss the building works, which despite some difficulties were well under way by 1487 [Kent 2004: 127].

"…if any of his villas was a genuine retreat, it was this hunting lodge near Volterra" (128). By 1490

> …among the villa's delights for Lorenzo must have been the now lost fresco cycle including 'The Forge of Vulcan,' which he had commissioned there presumably in late 1487-88 after building had been completed and the house had been made habitable. Unlike a suburban villa such as Careggi, Spedaletto had almost no portable devotional images or works of art…. Instead Lorenzo chose to have the *sala grande* and the external loggia frescoed, setting to work what has been described as "almost an official team" of artists, most of whom had earlier painted in the Sistine Chapel in Rome, probably at Lorenzo's suggestion, and later in Florence's Palazzo Vecchio: Sandro Botticelli, Filippo Lippi, Domenico Ghirlandaio, and Perugino [129].

"The Spedaletto paintings by Filippino and others, which according to Giorgio Vasari constituted a great mythological cycle that included "the story of Vulcan, in which many nude figures are at work with hammers making thunderbolts for Jove…," demonstrated the secular taste shared by the Medici and their Lanfredini friends, who found it both appropriate and delightful to decorate a private house in the country with classical and mythological, often erotic scenes despite the more conservative and pious taste displayed in country housed by most contemporaries…" (130-131).

Santa Maria delle Carceri, Prato (1485)

Santa Maria della Carceri, Prato (Alinari; Frommel)

Santa Maria delle Carceri, Prato (Frommel)

In 1485, Lorenzo de' Medici commissioned Giuliano da Sangallo to design Santa Maria delle Carcere in Prato, and it was under construction at the same time as the villa at Poggio a Caiano. "In the interior Giuliano combined the system of the Pazzi Chapel with that of the crossing of Santo Spirito. He remained faithful to Brunelleschi right down to the ribbed cupola...," but the exterior shows more the influence of Alberti's San Sabastiano in Mantua, a drawing of which was sent to him (Frommel 2007: 60). The cruciform church that was built seems likely to have been a prototype for the others that followed within the next two decades.

Villa Farnesina (Chigi), Rome (1505-1515)

Villa Farnesina (Luce)

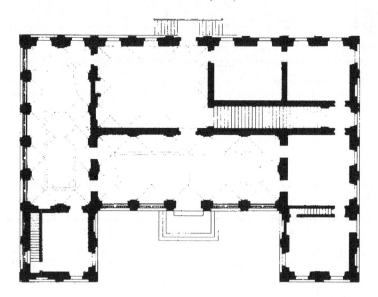

Villa Chigi ground floor (Letrouilly)

Villa Chigi (Farnesina); main entrance (Kent 1925)

Across the Tiber from the Palazzo Farnese, the Villa Farnesina bears the Farnese surname of a later owner. The villa was designed by Peruzzi in 1505 for the banker Agostino Chigi, and it was the first great villa of the Renaissance. The Farnesina sits within a garden that was initially even larger and is still large for what is now an urban setting.

The building itself is U-shaped, and its exterior is symmetrical. The regular pattern of pilasters and windows on the present street front and sides is similar to that used for the Cancelleria, but on a smaller scale with a better unified design. Chigi was a banker who could have afforded a much larger villa, but built one that could be competed to perfection. It is, though, larger than it seems, and nearby he built a palatial stable. Small, square windows were inserted for a partial mezzanine between the two main stories and for an attic story, and the building has a basement and a belvedere (altogether six levels). In the center of the garden front is a loggia with five arches that was initially open to the outside and that contains a vaulted ceiling with frescoes designed by Raphael: "Raphael did all the cartoons of this work, and coloured many figures in fresco with his own hand" (Vasari 1568: II, 241-242). Without exception, the numerous paintings in the villa have pagan subjects; none has a Biblical subject. It is a fully Renaissance villa.

The proportions used for the building were simple, but became complex as they interrelated and overlapped one another. A cross section through the center of the building forms a square (to the centers of end columns); the street front is a double square twice the size of the thickness of the central square; and the sides of the building are rectangles with the proportions of 1:1.414 (the square root of 2). As Wilson Jones has pointed out in his study of Peruzzi, the fronts include orders with the complex relationships recommended for stories of a Roman theater by Vitruvius: "...the lower story should have pedestals and an entablature respectively 1/3 and 1/5 of the height of its columns, and the upper story should have pedestals ½ as tall, and columns and an entablature ¾ as tall as their counterparts below." These proportions were probably chosen because the garden front of the villa was often used as the setting for theatrical performances.

The plan of the building features large and long rooms on each of the main floors, rooms about the same size and with proportions similar to Raphael's loggia. The loggia and the large room on the river side of the first floor are somewhat less than 1:3. The large room upstairs is somewhat less than 1:2. Within the controlling proportions of the exterior, Peruzzi found it necessary to use rooms with widths divisible by 10 feet (either 30 or 40 feet wide for the principal rooms) rather than using standard proportions, but the proportions used are within the standard range for interior spaces. The smaller rooms of the main floors are approximately square and large enough to be usable for multiple purposes.

Loggia beside the Tiber with frescoes by Raphael, Peruzzi, and Sebastiano del Piombo (Hermanin)

Garden loggia with frescoes by Raphael and his assistants (Gabinetto Fotografico Nacionale, Rome, in Heydenreich and Lotz)

Room with perspective views by Peruzzi and Giulio Romano (Hermanin)

The wedding of Alexander and Roxanne by Giovanni Antonio Bazzi, il Sodoma (Hermanin)

Villa Madama, Rome (begun 1518)

Villa Madama (Vasi, 1761)

The Medici family controlled the Papacy from 1513-1534 except during 1522-1523 when Adrian VI reigned for about a year. Leo X was pope from 1513-1522, and Clement VII reigned from 1523-1534. In 1518, Clement was a cardinal, and with family money, he commissioned Raphael to design this major villa. Raphael had studied with Bramante, and after Bramante's death, he was one of his principal successors at St. Peter's.

The Villa Madama is located on a hillside north of the Tiber River on the same side as the Vatican, but several miles to the east, and it is within sight of the Milvian Bridge, where it is visible to all visitors who enter Rome from the north and pass over this partly Roman bridge that connects to the Via Flaminia and its extension, the Corso.

The Villa Madama was planned to resemble Roman villas, and it could well have been inspired by the remains of a Roman villa near Tivoli that includes a small theatre on axis with the villa itself and that had extensive formal gardens (a villa once believed to have belonged to Brutus or Cassius; Neuerburg 1964: fig. 4).

Vasari attributed the design of this villa to Giulio Romano, but as with his painting, Raphael delegated much of the execution of his designs for architecture to his large staff of artists and artisans; he allowed them to contribute to designs, but did not turn major projects over to his assistants and particularly not a project for a client who was a Medici, a cardinal, and an influential member of the papal court (Vasari 1568: II, 240-241; III, 98). There is good evidence this was the case with this project as it was also with the Vatican projects and for the pagan paintings for the Villa Farnesina. Antonio da Sangallo the Younger superintended the project, and Romano, Udini, and a number of other staff members again contributed importantly to the success of the parts of Raphael's designs (Heydenreich and Lotz 1974: 171-173; 366, n. 7).

Villa Madama loggia by Raphael (Anderson)

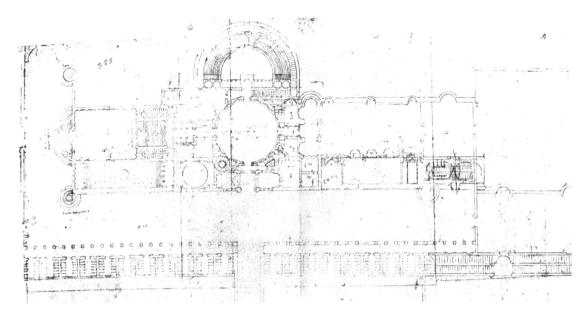

Villa Madama as designed by Raphael (copy of plan by Antonio da Sangallo)

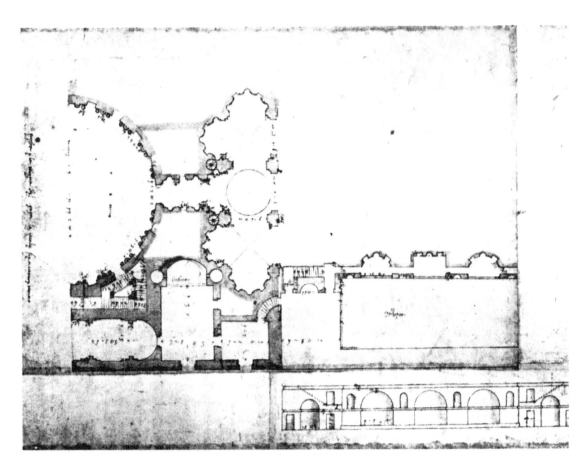

Villa Madama by Raphael (plan by Palladio)

Raphael's plan was centered on a large circular courtyard with a theatre to the north, a rectangular forecourt to the west, formal gardens to the east, and stables to the south at a lower level. The forecourt was to have had a huge semicircular stair leading to the entrance to the rectangular courtyard, at the end of which was to be a wide flight of straight stairs leading up to a vestibule and passage to the circular courtyard. The plan of the villa itself is symmetrical, and the separate, but adjacent theatre was placed to one side so it could be built into a hillside.

Only about half of the plan was executed, but that half is nonetheless as large as many palazzi. The part built was the eastern half, which consists of half the courtyard, adjacent rooms, a palatial loggia, and various other rooms on two floors (with a tall podium on the south side). A garden on two levels was also completed and has a large pool on its lower level. A description by Raphael explains why he planned the villa as he did:

> To have the villa face the most salutary winds I have disposed it lengthwise on a South-West/North-East axis minding that there should be no windows nor any accommodations facing South-East except where warmth is required.... The main characteristic of the entrance is that it is set between two large circular towers which make it both handsome and forbidding while permitting some defence in case of need. In the center is a very fine Doric portal leading into a court, measuring 22 by 11 *canne* [1:2].... At the opposite end, on the dwelling side, is a portico facing South-East and South, made for winter use. It is through it that one enters the dwelling. ...at the foot of the loggia lies the hippodrome [the Greek prototype of the circus]...,.a reception room, 4 *canne* wide and a long as the diagonal of a square formed by its width [4:5.66].... The first two [rooms] have a sesquitertial length to width relationship [4:3]. ...the fishpond is reached from the Xystus [Greek stadium].... In the hemicycle formed by the twin upper ramps is a fine theatre... [and there were] stables for 400 horses... a Cryptoporticus [a largely underground passage with clearstory lighting]... a warm bath... tepid and a cold baths, the latter being large enough to swim in if one desires [Dewez 1993: 21-31].

The principal room is the loggia, which as on Peruzzi's villa for Chigi (the Farnesina) was originally open and was decorated with sculptural enframements and paintings designed by Raphael. After his death in 1520, the decoration of this space was skillfully completed by his assistants Guilio Romano and Giovanni da Udine. The space itself resembles the frigidarium of a Roman bath in consisting of three vaults and in having very nearly the proportions of 1:3, but the central vault has a saucer dome supported on pendentives. Pendentives had been used in late Roman vaulting as for the Temple of Minerva Medica (which was probably a nymphaeum for a villa). They were widely used to support Byzantine domes including the saucer dome of Hagia Sophia, but had been little used in Western Europe until the Renaissance. Brunelleschi had made good use of pendentives for San Lorenzo and other buildings, and Bramante had planned to support his dome for St. Peter's on pendentives.

The way in which Raphael used these elements was exemplary and was widely influential. Later architects including Serlio and Palladio assumed the loggia was intended to be symmetrical rather than as it was built (Serlio 1611: III, iv, 69v). Among the features that most impressed later architects were that an entablature was omitted, and its place was taken visually by turning the capitals of pilasters into a running band of moldings. The cross vaults rest on the projecting corner of a pier as in Bramante's courtyard for Santa Maria della Pace, and the base of the pendentives rest on a diagonally placed fragment of a pilaster. Following Roman precedents such as Trajan's Arch at Beneventum, the pilasters have recessed panels that enframe decorative detail in low relief.

Villa d'Este, Tivoli (1549-1572)

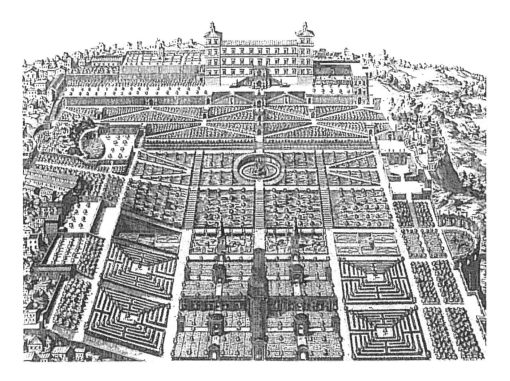

Villa d'Este in 1641 (Lauro in Frommel)

Villa d'Este (2016)

In c. 1550 Pierro Ligorio (1513/14-1583) terraced a hillside to create a garden in Tivoli for Cardinal Ippolito d'Este in a way that was similar to Bramante's courtyard between the Vatican Palace and the Belvedere. Fountains, plantings, and statues were added by members of the D'Este family for generations.

By contrast to the formal layout of this garden, nearby in the 19th Century Pope Gregory XVI (1831-1846) preserved a natural area as a park on hillsides where waterfalls are created by the Aniene River (the Villa Gregoriana).

Tivoli was also the site of Roman villas. The remains of a villa are part of the Villa Gregoriana, and a concrete platform for a villa is visible across the valley. The round temple of Tivoli, one of the earliest surviving Roman buildings, is adjacent to and visible from the Villa Gregoriana.

Villa D'Este (2017)

Palazzo Farnese, Caprarola (beguin 1558)

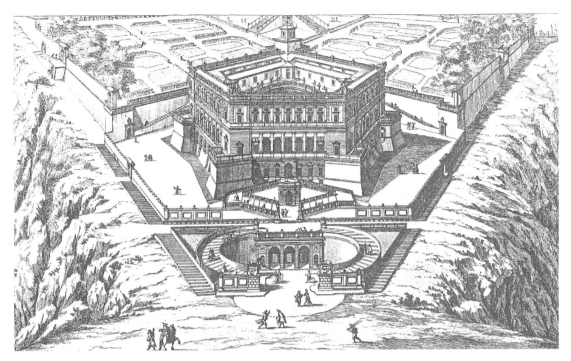

Castello Farnese (above, Specchi; below, Falda)

One of the grandest of all country houses was the Palazzo Farnese that was commissioned in 1556 and begun in 1558 in Caprarola by Jacomo Barozzi da Vignola (1507-1573; Frommel 2007: 189). It is a country villa built on a hillside and dominating a small community; it is also a palazzo, a castle, and a fortress.

Villa Giulia, Rome (1551-1555)

In 1551, Vignola began the Villa Giulia in Rome for Pope Julius III, who continually changed his mind about what he wanted and enlisted Michelangelo and Vasari to help him decide. Vasari wrote that he persuaded Julius III "...to plan nothing without asking Michelangelo's advice. The Pope kept to his promise, for neither at the Villa Giulia did not do anything without finding out Michelangelo's opinion, nor in the Belvedere..." (Vasari 1568: 87). On at least one occasion, Pope Julius "...ordered him and Vasari to go to the Villa Giulia, where they had many discussions together, which brought that work almost to its present beauty: nor was any aspect of the design planned or carried out without Michelangelo's advice and judgement" (91-92). The building was compelted by Bartolommeo Ammannati (Vasari 1568: 91-92; Heydenreich and Lotz 1974: 268-270).

Vasari did not indicate what impact Michelangelo and he had on the design of the Villa Giulia, but he did state that

> his holiness commissioned Michelangelo to make a model for the façades of a palace he wanted to build alongside San Rocco, with the idea of using the mausoleum of Augustus for the remainder of the walls. So Michelangelo produced a design of incomparable richness, variety, and originality, for in everything he did he was in no need of architectural rules, either ancient or modern, being an artist with the power to invent varied and original things as beautiful as those of the past. This model now belongs to Duke Cosimo de' Medici, to whom, when he went to Rome, it was given by Pope Pius IV, and who keeps it among his most precious belongings [92].

Nothing is known about this design except that its front and one side-bay are represented in a model in a painting in the Casa Buonoroti. The model shown is three storied with a tall ground floor two much shorter upper stories like the Medici Palace, and the windows sit on string courses. The model bears no resemblance to the VIlla Giulia. and what influence Michelangelo had on its design is unknown.

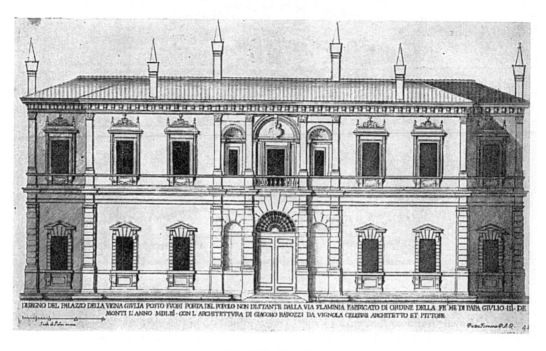

Villa Giulia (Ferrerio)

Villa Giulia, Rome; courtyard (Letarouilly)

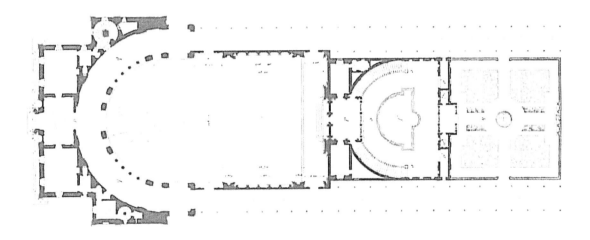

Plan and section of the Villa Giulia (Letarouilly)

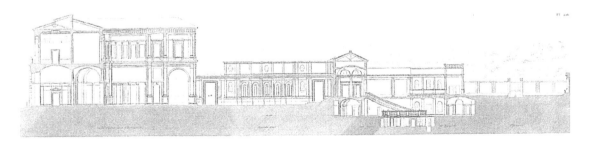

Sansovino

During the late Medieval Period, Venice flourished as a stable republic that controlled the lucrative trade between the eastern Mediterranean and western Europe, and many of its merchants were able to build palaces in the Gothic style, and most had asymmetrical fronts. Since land is at a premium, most of its houses are row houses. Since Venice is subject to flooding, its palaces were built with largely open ground floors. The upper stories generally had large rooms lighted by numerous windows.

When Constantinople was captured by the Turks in 1457, the prosperity of Venice declined substantially, but it already had numerous buildings that were well constructed and that did not need to be replaced. Vasari wrote that "...to chastise the pride of Rome God permitted Bourbon and his army to sack it on the six days of May 1527. In this disaster, when so many men of genius suffered, Sansovino was forced to fly to Venice, to the great loss of Rome" (Vasari 1568: IV, 221).

As an engineer, architect, and sculptor, Jacopo Sansovino (Jacopo Tatti; 1486-1570) gained immediate trust by replacing the foundation under the principal dome of San Marco that "...from bad foundations, age and faulty construction was cracking and threatening to tall" (221). He did most to introduce classic architecture into the Byzantine and Gothic city of Venice.

Sansovino designed four major palaces, and the "most beautiful of all is the palace of M. Giorgio Cornaro on the Grand Canal ["Palazzo Corner Cà Grande; now the Prefettura, erected in 1532"], undoubtedly surpassing the others in convenience, majesty and grandeur, and reputed the finest in Italy" (223). In 1537, he was commissioned to design the library of S. Marco and the adjacent Zecca (Mint). The library "...has led to all houses and palaces in the city... being erected with new designs and better order, following Vitruvius." "...the finest, richest and strongest of Jacopo's buildings is the mint of Venice..." (222-223). On the mainland near Venice in c. 1537, he designed the Villa Garzoni around a large courtyard, adapting the plan of a palazzo for a villa.

Sansovino took the name of his mentor, the architect Andrea Sansovino, and he was also influenced by Giovanni Maria Falconetto (1468-1535) and by Michele Sanmicheli (1484-1559), architects who worked early on in the classic tradition in northern Italy and who also influenced Palladio.

Villa Garzoni; near Venice (Courtauld Institute of Art; Frommel)

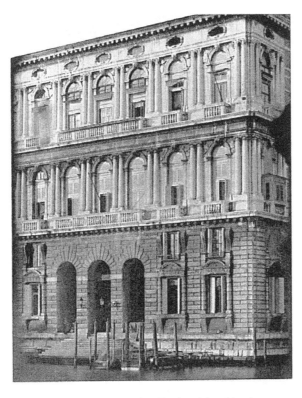

Palazzo Corner, Venice (Heydenreich and Lotz)

Library of St. Mark's, Venice (2017)

Summary on Villas and Palaces

Types of Palaces

Six types of palaces developed during the 16th and 17th centuries and continued to provide the basis for the designs of palaces and large public buildings until the middle of the 20th Century. All six types used design elements that had been used in similar ways for Roman temples, baths, and basilicas. All five types included a courtyard characteristic of Greek and Roman houses.

The design elements used include columns and pilasters with structurally related proportions, pediments, porticoes, architrave moldings, cornices, podiums and pedestals, rustication, ashlar, stringcourses, hemispherical domes, and attic stories. Of these, little use had been made other than of cornices and attenuated columns. In addition, the design elements and proportions of triumphal arches were often used in combination including a rectangular profile, an enlarged central element, an attic story, paired columns, and extended pedestals.

During the Medieval period, Romanesque windows were usually holes in a wall without enframements. Gothic cathedrals often had colonettes flanking windows supporting tall pointed arches, but without proportions and without an entablature. Cornices were used, but used decoratively rather than structurally or with structural proportions. Side aisles and clearstories had continued to be used since ancient Egypt and were adapted by both Romans and Christians.

Although the Christian basilica was based on a Roman building type, its entrance was usually at a narrow end, and it was generally T-shaped or given the shape of a Latin cross rather than rectangular. The ancient Romans and the Renaissance preferred more compact and coherent designs.

Although cathedrals had to be symmetrical to support vaulting and heavy roofs, secular buildings were often asymmetrical to start with and became more so with additions. Symmetry as well as proportion largely ceased to be architectural requirements until the Renaissance.

In the discussion of the five main types of palaces that follows, I have listed several of the earliest and most influential examples. One of more of the design elements may have been used earlier, and after used in combination sequentially, all of the types continued to be used simultaneously, but at various times some types were used more often than others:

(1) *Rusticated Fronts:* In 1444, Michelozzo introduced rustication for the design of palaces with the Palazzo Medici in Florence, but he reserved rustication for the ground floor and used ashlar for the middle story and a plain surface for the upper story. In 1458 the designer of the Palazzo Pitti used essentially the same design for the ground floor of the Palazzo Medici for rustication on all three of its floors. In 1490 Giuliano da Sangallo and others used rustication for the design of all three floors of the Palazzo Strozzi. The main source of rustication for Renaissance palace fronts was probably the back wall of the Forum of Augustus in Rome, but rustication had continued to be used during the Medieval Period for fortifications and for fortified buildings such as the Palazzo Vecchio in Florence (Kent 2000: 218; 463, n. 53).

(2) *One-storied Pilasters:* In c. 1456-1460 Albert used one-storied pilasters and ashlar on all three floors of the Palazzo Rucellai in Florence (superimposing two levels of Corinthian over Tuscan pilasters). He also used architraves to completely enframe the square window of his ground floor. Shortly afterwards, in 1460-1462 a closely similar design was used for the front of the Palazzo Piccolomini in Pienza, but even made the pilasters of his ground floor of ashlar. In or around 1485, Bramante can be credited with having added pairs of pilasters to the two upper stories of the Cancelleria (with ashlar on all three stories, but treating the ground floor as a podium by omitting pilasters). He also added a stringcourse of pedestals beneath his pilasters in imitation of a podium, and he enframed his windows with moldings supporting a classical lintel. In c. 1512 Peruzzi used a similar design for the main front of the Villa

Farnesina, but with single pilasters rather than pairs of pilasters, but on the garden front, he added a tall arcade in place of a mezzanine between floors, and he flanked each arch with pilasters and flanked the five-bays of arches with two bay projecting wings. He also added a mezzanine in a frieze and cornice scaled to the entire building.

(3) *Engaged Columns on a Podium:* In c. 1510 Bramante used engaged columns on a rusticated podium for the Palazzo Caprini (the House of Raphael) in Rome. For its upper floor, he also used paired columns on pedestals, and pediments above each window. On its ground floor, he inserted a mezzanine above shop fronts (using the typical arrangement for ancient Roman apartment blocks). In c. 1515 Raphael made a similar design for the Palazzo Vidoni-Caffarelli in Rome.

(4) *Stringcourses Without Pilasters:* In c 1518 Raphael used stringcourses and running pedestals to create a broad band across the upper story of his Palazzo Pandolfini in Florence. He used stringcourses to separate the two floors, to connect the entablatures of his upper windows, and to connect the balconies and pedestals of his windows. His design for the ground floor was simpler, having a pedestal beneath each window rather than a running pedestal. Both floors have plain walls except for rustication around the central entrance of what was intended to be a nine-bay front. Each window has columns supporting an entablature with pediments alternately angular and curved. In c. 1518 Antonio da Sangallo the Younger adapted this design for the front of the Palazzo Farnese, but simplified it by omitting the band of entablature across the upper story and by using relatively small and closely spaced. In 1586 Domenico Fontana adapted the design of the Palazzo Farnese for the Lateran Palace with similar results. Its main fronts have 15 bays rather than the 9 planned for the Palazzo Pandolfini or the 13 executed for the Palazzo Farnese. On a relatively small scale, this pattern works well and was reintroduced and much used in the 19th Century through the influence of Charles Barry.

When stories are made larger, at least some design elements such as windows, pilasters, and arches have to be fewer and larger (as in the Villa Farnesina, the Palazzo Barberini, and Palazzo Pitti) or the front has to be divided into parts with a projecting center and/or ends to be a coherent design rather than an extended pattern. An unbroken front cannot be extended indefinitely. In general, something needs to be done to enframe a building to give it a coherent design.

(5) *Two-storied Pilasters:* In c. 1516 Raphael used two-storied pilasters on the back of his Villa Madama (with the three arches of his loggia in between pilasters and with two-storied piers at the corners of the shorter side of his main block. In 1525 Giulio Romano used two-storied pilasters on his Palazzo del Te in Mantua, but with a mezzanine (like the ground floor of the Villa Farnesina). In c. 1535 Michelangelo used two-storied pilasters on [oers for the fronts of the flanking buildings of the Capitol in Rome, and he used two-storied columns on a podium for his Senate building. His designs more than any of the earlier ones influenced Palladio's extensive use of two-storied pilasters as for his c. 1565 design for the Palazzo Valmarana in Vicenza. A century later, Bernini's design for the front of the Palazzo Chigi-Odescalchi was also influential. The use of two-storied columns was characteristic of Roman triumphal arches.

(6) *Porticoes:* Palladio first applied temple-fronts to houses on the grounds that temples must initially have been houses (Chapter 17). He used two-storied columns to support pediments on podiums, and he treated his entire ground floors as podiums. The best known example is his c. 1566 design for the four porticoes of the Villa Rotonda. Palladio also used relatively large and few windows (partly for structural reasons), and he frequently used attic stories as well as podiums to enframe his building and stringcourses and entablatures to add coherence to his designs. Although enframed windows and stringcourses continued to be widely used in Italy, Palladio's designs were more widely used elsewhere.

Types of Villas

During the Renaissance, there were three basic types of villas: the country house, the Roman villa, and the working farm.

(1) *Country House:* The earliest Renaissance villas were "detached" palaces built in the country. They differed little from palaces built in the city except in not having common walls with adjacent dwellings. Being entirely separate, they could have better light with windows on the sides as well as on the front and back. They sometimes had front steps leading directly to the piano nobile in addition to internal stairs between floors. Examples are the two Medici villas near Florence, the Villa d'Este in Tivoli, the Palazzo Farnese at Caprarola, and the Villa Mondragone and Villa Aldobrandini at Frascati. These country houses were palaces in the country in the scale, and they were lived in for extended periods if not all year round rather than visited from time to time.

(2) *Roman Villa:* The ancient Roman villa was best known to the Renaissance through the ruins of Hadrian's Villa and the writings of Pliny the Younger. These examples in particular influenced the design of the Villa Madama and the Villa Giulia, which were integral parts of their gardens. To some extent this was also true of the Villa Farnesina and Villa Borghese in Rome and the Villa d'Este, but they overlook gardens rather than being parts of gardens with pools, fountains, and outdoor statuary. The Roman villa was more of a retreat and a place to entertain guests in the country than a place to live even part of the year.

(3) *Estates:* In ancient Rome, the difference between a farm house and a villa that serves as the headquarters for an estate were chiefly in terms of scale and who did the work. Farm houses were small and added to as families grew generation by generation, and everyone in the family did farm work. An estate generally had employees or slaves and overseers to do the work, and the house was on a larger scale, more likely to be built at one time, more likely to be built to a coherent design, and more likely to be lived in year round. Some Roman villas were the headquarters of estates, and some had palatial buildings (particularly the villas of emperors such as Nero and Hadrian).

Although there is some overlap in most respects for these three types of villas, they served basically different purposes. It was Andrea Palladio who combined the functions and produced symmetrical country houses with porticoes and flanking wings for services to serve as the headquarters of estates. These villas were often lived in year round; they were sometimes palatial, but always exceptionally well designed; and they were a coherent group of architectural buildings rather than less formal arrangements of buildings that were integrated parts of their gardens. They were more often located where there was good agricultural land rather than good views, and they were intended to produce income rather than consuming it. They combined work and leisure rather than being largely or entirely for leisure, and they set a pattern for gentile life in the country worldwide.

Comparison of Villas and Palaces

Peruzzi's archetypal villa and palace in Rome make an excellent comparison. His Villa Farnesina is a detached house within a garden in a suburban part of Rome, and its plan and exterior are almost entirely symmetrical. His Palazzo Massimo is a row house with other houses on both sides of it, and it has a small courtyard rather than being within a garden. The villa and the palazzo are within a few blocks of one another, but one is a country house on the other side of the Tiber, and the other is a town house built in the heart of medieval Rome. Both are among the finest buildings designed during the Renaissance even though their functions were largely different.

Alberti's contrasted the advantages and disadvantages of the villa and palace succinctly: "The Country House and town House for the Rich differ in this Circumstance; that they use their Country House chiefly for a habitation in the Summer, and their Town House as a convenient Place of shelter in the winter. In their Country House therefore they enjoy the Pleasures of Light, Air, spacious Walks and fine prospects; in town, there are but few Pleasures, but hose of Luxury and the Night" (Alberti 1755: 108-109)." "In building a House in Town, your Neighbour's Wall, a common Gutter, a publick Square or Street, and the like, shall all hinder you from contriving it just to your own Mind; which is not so in the Country, where you have as much Freedom as you have Obstruction in Town. For this, and other Reasons, therefore, I shall distinguish the Matter thus: That the Habitation for a private Person must be different in town from what it is in the Country" (100).

    The villa as a building type was thus primarily a place to vacation during the summer to get away from the heat, noise, and unhealthiness of a town during the part of the year when it was most likely to be uncomfortable and unhealthy. A villa was entirely distinct from farm house ordinarily, but an agricultural estate could include a villa with a resident overseer in charge. It was also distinct from a cottage in which to spend a weekend or a holiday, but more nearly equivalent in that both the villa and a vacation house were intended for part-time use rather than year-round use like most farm houses. Two distinctly different types of villas had existed since ancient times, and one was a large villa built a considerable distance from a city and occupied for part of each year, and the other was a relatively small house close enough to a town that it could be visited frequently for short periods throughout the year. "A Country House ought to stand in such a Place as may be most convenient for the owners House in Town. Xenophon would have a Man go to his Country House on Foot, for the Sake of Exercise, and return on Horseback. It ought not therefore to lie far from the city, and the Way to it should be both good and clear, so as he may go it either in Summer or Winter, either in a Coach, or on Foot, and if possible by Water" (100-101). The Villa Farnesina was so eminently well situated just across the Tiber that the Farnese planned to build a bridge to enable them to go directly from their palazzo on one side of the river to their villa on the other side and to have the advantages of either type of house as often as they liked.

    Alberti noted that a remotely located villa could be on a grander scale than a palazzo in town with less likelihood of causing envy or resentment. "Between a House in Town and a House in the country, there is this further Difference, besides what we took notice of in the last Book, that the Ornaments, for that in Town ought to be much more grave than those for a House in the Country, where the gayest and most licentious Embellishments are allowable" (188).

    There is certainly a vast deal of satisfaction in convenient Retreat near the Town, where a man is at Liberty to do just what he pleases. The great Beauties of such a Retreat, are being near the City, upon an open airy Road, and on a pleasant Spot of Ground The greatest Commendation of the House itself is its making a chearful Appearance to those that go a little Way out of Town to take the Air, as if it seemed to invite very Beholder: And for this reason I would have it stand pretty high, but upon so easy an Ascent, that it should hardly be perceptible to those that go to it, till they find themselves ta the Top, and a large Prospect opens itself to their View. Nor should there be any Want of pleasant Landskips, flowery Meads, open Champains, shady Groves, or limpid Brooks, or clear Streams and lakes for swimming, with all other Delights of the same Sort which we before observed to be necessary in a Country Retreat, both for Convenience and Pleasure. Lastly, what I have already said conduces extremely to the Pleasantness of all Buildings., I would have the Front and whole Body of the House perfectly well lighted, and that it be open to receive a great deal of Light and Sun, and a sufficient Quantity of wholesome Air. Let nothing be within View that can offend the Eye with a melancholy Shade. Let all things smile and seem to welcome the Arrival of your Guests. Let those who are already entered to be in Doubt whether they shall for Pleasure continue where they are or pass on further to those other Beauties which tempt them on. Let them be led from square Rooms into round ones, and again from round into square, and so into others of mixed Lines, neither all round nor all square; and let the Passage into the very innermost Apartments be, if possible, without the least Ascent or Decent, but all be upon one even Floor, or at least let the scents be as easy as may be [189-190].

In "a free City" (a republic such as Florence) the only exceptionally large palazzo should be "the House of the Senator or Chief Magistrate" (187), but a "Royal Palace" could also be so large as to be considered a public rather than a private building. Cosimo de' Medici the Elder considered it wise to reject Brunelleschi's design for a palazzo that would have been resented by his fellow citizens and to build a number of small villas a considerable distance from the city rather than a conspicuously large one nearby. About a century later, Duke Cosimo had the Palazzo Vecchio, the former city hall, renovated to become his town house, greatly enlarged the Pitti Palace as his country house, and connected the two by a private viaduct that crossed the Arno in the way that the Farnese later planned to do to connect their palace and villa. Duke Cosimo and his ambitious wife (the daughter of the Viceroy of Naples) turned a relatively small palazzo into the grandest and most palatial villa in Europe until Versailles was created.

Alberti was unimpressed by large buildings and by expensive buildings whether they were palaces or villas, and he recommended competing in terms of refinement rather than expense. "I, for my Part, hate every thing that favours of Luxury or Profusion, and am best pleased with those Ornaments which arise principally from the Ingenuity of Beauty or the Contrivance" (192).

> I think no prudent Man in building his private House should willing differ too much from his Neighbours, or raise their Envy by his too great Expense and Ostentation; neither, on the other Hand, should he suffer himself to be out-done by any one whatsoever in the Ingenuity or Contrivance or Elegance of Taste, to which the whole Beauty of the Composition, and harmony of the several Members must be owing, which is indeed the highest and principal Ornament in all Building [187].

"I cannot be pleased with those who make Towers and Battlements to a private House, which being of right entirely to a Fortification, or to the Castle of Tyrant, and are altogether inconsistent with the peaceable aspect of a well-governed City or Commonwealth, as they show either a Distrust of our Countrymen, or Design to use Violence against them" (194).

17. Palladio

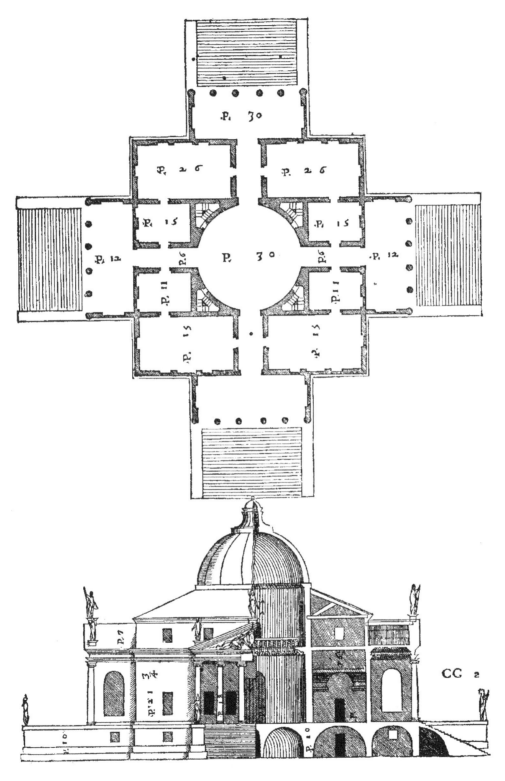

Villa Rotunda, Vicenza (Palladio, 1570)

Andrea Palladio's realization that temples must have been derived from houses rather than the other way around justified adding a portico to the front of a villas and turning its ground floor into a podium. Palladio also emulated the cubical massing of triumphal arches and treated upper floors as an attic story. The Villa Rotunda has all three: portico, podium and attic. His Villa Pisani shows how triumphal arches influenced his designs and explains why the largest cornices are sometimes in the middle of his buildings rather than at the top. The practical knowledge he gained as a stone mason enabled him to design and construct buildings that were sound and economical. His knowledge of ancient architecture was unparalleled and more effectively represented in his publications than by those of any previous writer or illustrator.

I have included a chapter on Palladio before chapters on Bramante and Michelangelo because his work follows stylistically the architecture of the Early Renaissance and because Michelangelo's architectural career began around the same time as Palladio's, but led directly to the Baroque style. To have considered Michelangelo first and Bernini after Palladio would have made less sense, particularly considering that the Palladian tradition continued to be highly influential in Neoclassical and Greek Revival architecture while the Baroque turned into Rococo was revived mainly through Beaux Arts training in the mid-19th Century. As the greatest building of the Renaissance, St. Peter's needs separate consideration for the long period that was required for its design and construction and to consider the contributions of the many architects who were involved, and it was being most fully redesigned by Michelangelo at the same time Palladio was creating his finest buildings. Thus, Palladio represents the continuation and culmination of a design tradition that began with Brunelleschi, and Michelangelo represents the beginning of a diverging tradition in which he was never equaled and that was largely replaced by Neoclassicism. Bramante would have been much less of a pivotal figure without Michelangelo and Palladio, and if Antonio da Sangallo's St. Peter's had been built, it would not have been one of the world's greatest buildings.

During the mid-16th century, Palladio (Andrea di Pietro; 1508-1580) made the most careful and comprehensive study of major Roman ruins shortly before many of them were destroyed. While measuring and drawing ancient buildings, he also sought and rediscovered the underlying basis for many Roman designs:

> ...I proposed to myself VITRUVIUS for my master and guide...and set myself to search into the reliques of all the antient edifices, that...yet remain; and...I began very minutely with the utmost diligence to measure every one of their parts...(not finding any thing which was not done with[out] reason and beautiful proportion)...that I might entirely, from them, comprehend what the whole had been, and reduce it into design.

Palladio was most impressed by buildings that postdated Vitruvius and, particularly, by the Pantheon and Roman baths such as Diocletian's.

Nearly two centuries before the discovery of Herculaneum, little more was known about Roman domestic architecture that what could be inferred from Vitruvius, and Palladio inferred about as much as anyone could while preparing illustrations for Daniele Barbaro's 1567 edition of Vitruvius' *Ten Books*. From careful study of texts and buildings, Palladio concluded that "private houses...first gave rise to public edifices."

> I have made the frontispiece [pedimented portico] in the fore-front in all the fabricks for villa's, and also in some for the city, in which are the principal gates; because such frontispieces shew the entrance to the house, and add very much to the grandeur and magnificence of the work.... The antients also made use of them in their fabricks, as is seen in the remains of the temples, and other public edifices; for which, as I have said...it is very likely that they took the invention, and the reasons for private edifices or houses.

Because he assumed that early Roman houses were raised on podiums or platforms like Roman temples, he gave his houses ground floors.

Although influenced by the symmetry of Roman architecture, Palladio adopted symmetry more for practical reasons. As a former stone mason, he knew that symmetrical buildings settled more evenly and supported their roofs better.

Practical considerations extended, for example, to the placement of windows:

> The windows on the right hand ought to correspond to those on the left, and those above directly over them that are below; and the doors likewise ought to be directly over one another, that the void may be over the void, and the solid upon the solid, and all face one another, so that standing at one end of the house one may see to the other, which affords both beauty and cool air in summer, besides other conveniences [including good circulation].

He was careful to position his windows some distance from the corners of his buildings so as not to weaken the corners. His symmetry was functional, and ancient architects had undoubtedly reached many of the same conclusions he did. Similarly, he wrote that windows should be large enough to provide adequate light to the walls opposite them. He used relatively few windows, but sufficiently large windows, and the reason he gave was that for permanence, the corners of a building strong; windows should not be close to the corners of a building.

Palladio's plans for his villas and palazzi usually have the same basic features: the largest room is in the center and to each side were smaller rooms and a flanking pair of staircases. Nearly all room are rectangular, but the largest rooms were sometimes circular, cruciform, or T-shaped. His plans have much in common with the plans of the Romans baths he studied, and on a reduced scale, he can be said to have put a temple front on a bath. Almost every room is a generously sized, well lighted, and well proportioned. Only a simple plan can accommodate consistently well-designed rooms within a compact exterior, and by using simple plans, he was able to achieve uniformly well portioned interiors and exteriors. His houses with a podium usually have their principal room on the piano nobile, but his villas without a podium usually have corresponding spaces in their lower story. The plans and vaulting of both types of houses could be closely similar, but the courtyard of a palazzo might well be replaced by a large two-strories room in a villa.

Palladio solved practical problems in exemplary ways. His plans and spaces, interiors and exteriors, and walls and vaults are more consistently compact and integral parts of a whole than in the work of any previous architect.

There is nothing mysterious about such practical considerations. A tree will fall if its roots do not suffice to remain standing. A biped needs larger feet than a quadruped to remain upright. A biped, quadruped, or millipede need a symmetrical number of feet to walk. Buildings need to be symmetrical and proportionate for equivalent functional reasons and most of all for permanence.

A building without an intelligible plan is as incoherent as an unorganized group of words. Similar principles of design are needed for functional reasons, and they also provide visual coherence. Clarity facilitates comprehension, and comprehension augments usefulness. The best organized arrangements are the most creative, and the most clearly organized plans and most adaptable spaces are the most useful.

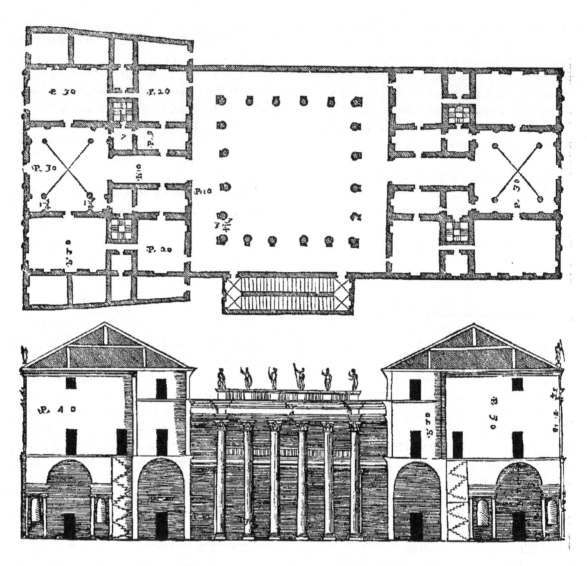

Palazzo Porto section with planned courtyard (Palladio, 1570)

Many Renaissance palaces designed before Palladio had symmetrical façades, but usually had asymmetrical plans. Palladio's plans could be completely symmetrical partly because he was minimally concerned with the problem of adjacencies—the difficulty of fitting together rooms of minimal sizes and odd shapes to accommodate specialized and temporary functions. Instead of designing a building to serve a highly specific purpose at the time of its completion, he designed buildings with versatile plans. His rooms were almost uniformly generous in size, and they were readily adaptable for almost any function that might later be required. Any given room opened into two or more other rooms, enabling circulation to be flexible.

The usual design for the front of a Renaissance house consisted of a pattern of elements that could be repeated almost indefinitely. Palladio adapted the same design elements, but usually gave his designs a composition with a strong central emphasis and bi-lateral symmetry both horizontally and vertically. He gave emphasis horizontally by placing a portico or projection in the center of his façades. He emphasized the center vertically by giving the main floor greater height and larger windows, producing a characteristic piano nobile in a three-story building. Since his most important rooms were centrally located, he was expressing his plans on the outside of his buildings in the same way his symmetrical façades expressed symmetrical plans. Thus, his plans, the vertical proportions of his fronts, and the horizontal proportions of his fronts all have a strong central emphasis.

Palladio considered proportions as guidelines to be observed unless practical considerations made it desirable to do otherwise. He felt that proportions were worth observing carefully for the orders, and he created a set of the five orders that was considered a principal standard for centuries. He was not overly concerned, though, about proportion when it came to the shapes of rooms, and he recommended seven different proportions for the plans of rooms. He provided three methods for determining the relative height of a vault for any plan, and any one of them could produce essentially the same results.

It was a functional requirement to have the principal rooms on the main floor, service spaces below, and bedrooms above, and consequently the ceilings of the middle story were taller than those above and below. The rooms on each floor were mostly similar in size so that load-bearing walls would align with one another and so that most rooms would be large enough to be adaptable to serve a variety of purposes in the future.

Ideally, square rooms should be as tall as wide and long. Rectangular rooms should be at least as tall as wide, and ideally they should have a height that is the average of their width and length. It was, of course, not possible to have rooms with ideal height on lower and upper floors, and it was not possible for large and small rooms on the main floor to have the same heights. Two-storied rooms were flanked by one-storied rooms and a partial mezzinine.

The proportions of rooms were usually the simple ones recommended by Vitruvius. The dimensions Palladio gave for the sizes of rooms in the *Four Books* indicate that almost one-third of all rooms have the proportions of 1:1, and they were generally square in plan, though sometimes round (29 percent altogether). Nearly one-third more has the proportions of 1:2 (another 29 percent). Nearly one-third has the proportions of 2:3 or 3:4 (14 percent each for a total of 28 percent). Thus, 86 percent of the rooms he dimensioned have one of four simple proportions: 1:1, 1:2, 2:3, or 3:4. Rooms that are 1:1 and 3:4 are square or nearly so, and rooms that and 1:2 and 2:3 are double cubes or less. He rarely made rooms more than twice as long as wide, and he preferred compact spaces as well as compact exterior forms.

Palladio added variety by using different types of vaulting. He listed six types of vaults: cross vaults, barrel vaults, segmental vaults, domes, lunette vaults (with small semicircular vaults around the edge of a ceiling), and coved ceilings. He also refers to domes over square spaces needing to be supported on pendentives (such as he had seen in the Baths of "Titus" that were actually in the adjacent Baths of Trajan).

The combination of the new way that elements were applied and the practicality of their application made Palladio's designs extremely influential. Other architects had used the same elements and concepts, but had not combined them in ways that were reasonable, distinctive, and visually satisfying. Palladio succeeded to an unparalleled extent because his concepts were useful for his own and later times and because, in addition to being a great architect, he was a great illustrator and a great writer. Most of his buildings were widely scattered in rural areas and had less direct influence than his illustrations and his explanations. His ideas were primarily influential through his *Four Books* and through the innumerable books that were based on it, especially manuals produced in large numbers, numerous editions, and immense quantities, particularly by the English.

In the 1540s Palladio made five trips to Rome to study its ancient architecture, and while there he made hundreds of measured drawings and reconstructions. He studied numerous ruins that were subsequently destroyed in whole or part, and his drawings are by far the most accurate and comprehensive visual record ever made of ancient Roman buildings. He also studied some modern buildings carefully and made drawings of buildings by Bramante and Raphael. He was also influenced by Michelangelo's architecture.

Palladio mentioned Alberti as one of the "excellent writers" who had preceded him by making an in-depth study of ancient Roman architecture, but it was Serlio's *Five Books* that he specifically set out to surpass and did surpass. Alberti's treatise was unillustrated, and Serlio's treatise had illustrations that were less accurate and detailed than Palladio's.

Sebastiano Serlio (c. 1475-c. 1554) had produced more of a manual for architects and builders, and the first two of his five books deal mainly with geometry, perspective, and similar subjects, but the rest of the treatise is about ancient Roman buildings with some of his own designs. Serlio's numerous measured plans, elevations, perspective views, and details of the classical orders and his Italian text made his work highly useful, and his representations of the classical orders, the first to be printed, contributed to standard versions of them. Although the format he used was larger, less visual information was provided, and his own designs were influenced by French architecture and were much inferior to those buildings by Palladio.

Vasari noted that Baldassare Peruzzi had planned to produce a book on architecture and that Serlio made substantial use of his work. Peruzzi

> ...began a book on the antiquities of Rome, and a commentary on Vitruvius which he illustrated, some of his designs for this being still in the possession of Francesco da Siena, his pupil, containing drawings of antiquities and modern methods of building. ... Sebastiano Serlio of Bologna inherited many of Baldassarre's things, and he did the third book of architecture and the fourth book on the survey of the antiquities of Rome, being greatly aided by the studies of Baldassarre some of which were put in the margin. The writings of Baldassarre were mostly left to Jacopo Melighino of Ferrara, who was appointed architect to Pope Paul [III; Vasari 1568: 299].

Palladio made the measurements and did the drawings for his *Four Books*, which was also published in a two-volume edition (Vasari 1568: IV, 235; Palladio 1570 [1997]: xv).

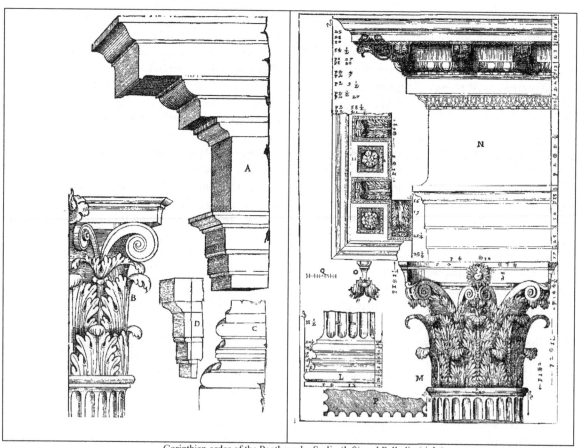

Corinthian order of the Pantheon by Serlio (left) and Palladio (right)

When Palladio's *Four Books* was published 1570, it included most of the buildings that Sebastiano Serlio had published in his *Five Books* in 1551, but in greater detail, with greater accuracy, with a more informative text, and with a better overall design. Serlio had set a new standard for architectural illustrations, but it was quickly surpassed by Palladio as is shown, for example, by a comparison of their depictions of the Corinthian order of the Pantheon.

Serlio's *Five Books* is one volume with five parts, and the first two parts deal with types of information that Palladio did not include (geometry and perspective), but the last three parts were treated by Palladio: antiquities, the orders, and temples. His version of the Roman orders was the first treatise on the orders to be published, and it appeared separately in 1537 and was reprinted as the fourth of his *Five Books*. Before publishing all five books together in 1551, Serlio also published his antiquities in 1540, geometry and perspective in 1545, and temples in 1547. His plans for Roman baths, the Colosseum, and other major buildings that were well preserved were exemplary for their time, but his elevations were partially perspective views, and his details were generally inadequate for a practicing architect to utilize. Serlio prepared a separate book on his house designs, and although it was not published in his lifetime, some copies circulated in manuscript.

The standard edition of Palladio's *Four Books* is one volume with four parts: Part one is about materials, foundations, and the five orders. Part two is about his own palazzi and villas and about ancient housing. Part three is about roads, bridges, piazzas, basilicas, and xisti (covered tracks or gymnasiums). Part four is about ancient Roman temples. Palladio noted in his preface that he hoped to prepare additional books on ancient theatres and palaces. Another edition was published in two volumes in 1570.

Although Palladio does not mention a book on Roman baths, he had prepared enough drawings that they were published in the 18th Century as a separate book by the Earl of Burlington, and he surely would have published them himself if he had not died in 1580. He would undoubtedly have published at least another part on the churches he created in Venice.

Palladio combined the principles of Vitruvius and Alberti with even better illustrations than those by Serlio, and he added numerous designs of his own. He brought to his work the training of a mason, the scholarship of a classicist, and the design ability of a great architect. No architecture book except Vitruvius has had equivalent impact to Palladio's *Four Books*.

Altogether, about three dozen buildings are certain to have been designed by Palladio, and all are located in the Veneto within a radius of about fifty miles of Vicenza. He designed at least 18 villas in this area and at least 14 buildings in the city of Vicenza (including six palazzi and one villa on the edge of the city). In Venice, he designed four buildings including two major churches.

Vasari wrote, "the one who merits the highest praise among the Vicentines as a man of wit and judgment is Andrea Palladio, the architect. This is proved by his numerous works at his native place and elsewhere..." (Vasari 1568: IV, 233). "In short, Palladio has erected so many fine buildings in and about Vicenza that they would by themselves suffice to constitute a noble city with its district" (234).

Vitruvius 10 bks. (1486)	**Alberti 10 bks.** (1485)	**Serlio 5 bks.** (1551)	**Palladio 4 bks.** (1570)
1. Education, city, sites	1. Site, geometry, roofs, fenestration	1. Geometry (1545)	1. Materials, foundations, five orders
2. Materials (1545) villas, ancient houses	2. Materials palazzi,	2. Perspective	2. Palladio's
3. Proportion, foundations, Ionic proportions	3. Construction	3. Antiquities (1540)	3. Roads, bridges, piazzas, basilicas, and xisti
4. Doric, Ionic, and Corinthian details	4. Public works: buildings, bridges	4. Five Orders (1537)	4. Ancient Roman temples
5. Forum, basilica, theatres, baths	5. Works of Individuals	5. Temples (1547)	5. Baths (published later)
6. Climate, room proportions later)	6. Ornament (unpublished)	6. Dwellings (published	6. Palladio's churches
7. Floors, stucco, colors orders	7. Ornament for sacred buildings: temples, churches,	7. Irregular sites (1575)	7. Theatres (planned)
8. Water, aqueducts buildings (ancient)	8. Ornament for public secular		8. Roman palaces (planned)
9. Astronomy, astrology, sundials	9. Ornament for private buildings (proportion)		9. Details of Roman orders and cornices (planned?)
10. Machines, defense	10. Restoration of buildings		
Illustrations: Lost	Unillustrated	Woodcuts in text	Woodcuts in text

VILLAS

Villa Foscari, Gambarare (Malcontenta; 1558-1561)

The Villa Foscari is in many respects the most characteristic of Palladio's villas. Its overall form is essentially cubical, which gives it a massive appearance, and the relatively small number of windows make it seem still more massive. The more compact the building, the more economical it is to construct.

Villa Foscari (Zorzi)

The front is divided vertically and horizontally using his characteristic central emphasis. The center of the middle story has a pedimented portico like a temple front, and each side of the house is much narrower than the center. The Roman portico on a podium has the same maximum width as the main room of the piano nobile.

The rooms of the Villa Foscari also exemplify Palladio's usual proportions: the side rooms are 16 feet square and so 1:1. The front rooms on either side are 16 by 24 feet and so 2:3. The back rooms on either side are 12:16 and so 3:4. The cruciform room in the center is 16 feet wide at each end and 32 feet wide overall and so 1:2.

Villa Foscari (2008)

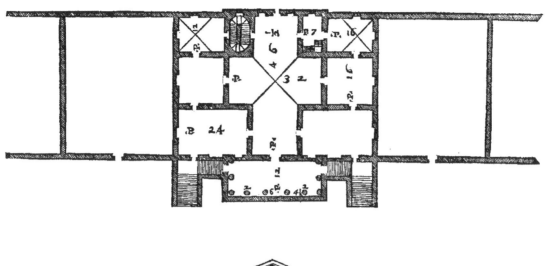

Villa Foscari (Palladio, 1570)

The Villa Foscari's principle room is cruciform in shape, and it has a cross vault in the center and barrel vaults in each end. It can be conceived of as two intersecting barrel vaults, but the cross vaulted section functions differently from a barrel vault by containing its thrusts. The two lower floors were also vaulted, and most rooms in the house are fireproof.

The back of the Villa Foscari is idiosyncratic, but distinctively Palladian in having a strong center created by its pavilion in place of a portico and in having a thermal window in the center (serving as a clearstory window for the two-storied space). The open gable is also characteristic of Roman baths.

Back of the Villa Foscari by Palladio (above, Puppi; below, 2008)

Main room of the Villa Foscari with frescoes by G. B. Zelotti (Phyllis Dearborn Massar in Cevese)

Villa Rotunda, Vicenza (1566-1567)

The design of the Villa Rotunda is very similar in its proportions to the Villa Foscari. Each of its four sides has porticoes on podiums and attics with central emphasis both vertically and horizontally. As Palladio noted, it has four porticoes to take advantage of the excellent views from a promontory, and it also shows to advantage when seen from any direction. Its porticoes are even more temple-like in having broad steps within corner blocks rather than the baroque arrangement of steps to each side as for the Villa Foscari.

In the center of the Villa Rotunda is also a two-storied space, but a circular room that is domed rather than a cruciform one. Circulation between the upper rooms is provided partly by a balcony around the domed space. In 1570, when the Villa Rotunda was published in the *Four Books*, Palladio planned for the dome to be hemispherical on the exterior. It was constructed differently and better.

The Villa Rotunda has walls constructed of fist-sized field stones embedded in thick mortar, and the combination resembles Roman concrete, but lacking pozzolana or an equivalent substance, the walls are of rubble rather than concrete. Brick was used to surround the fenestration, but otherwise, this extremely sophisticated design was constructed using the simplest of material that were then given a protective and finishing layer of stucco.

Villa Rotunda (albumen by Alinari, 12801)

Villa Rotunda (2008)

Villa Pisani, Montagnana (1552-1554)

Palladio's Villa Pisani has a two-storied portico with a pediment, but instead of a podium, the walls rest on a low foundation. Palladio's two-storied porticoes usually have loggias on one or both fronts, and in this case, the loggias are on the garden side. The street front has an engaged portico. This type has stories of nearly equal height with the principle cornice in between them. Since Palladio planned triumphal arches as connectors between the main building and its wings, the cornice across the middle of the building would have run continuously from side to side and helped to unify a complex and horizontal composition, but neither the arches nor wings were built.

The principal room in this type of villa is on the first story, and the smaller rooms of the first story have a partial mezzanine. The entire upper story has a mezzanine, and the fenestration of the garden front resembles Peruzzi's Villa Farnesina.

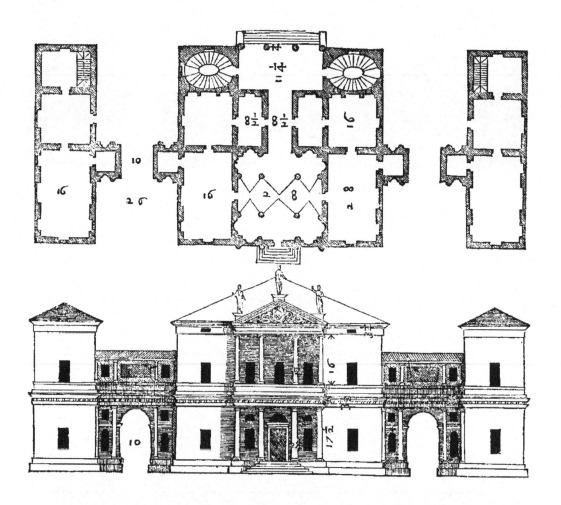

Villa Pisani as designed by Palladio (1570)

Villa Pisani (Puppi)

Villa Cornaro at Piombino Dese (1552-1554)

The Villa Cornaro has similar facades and flanking two-storied wings (similar to the wings planned for the Villa Pisani). The main space has four columns and faces the garden (as for the Villa Foscari). The columns create the effect of being in antis.

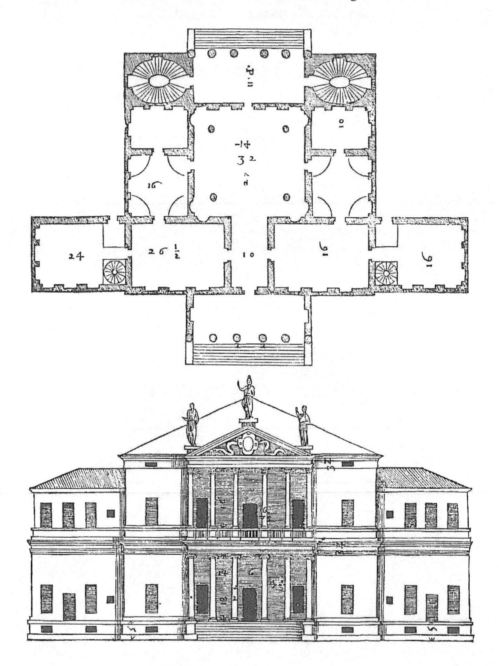

Villa Cornaro, Piombino (Palladio, 1570)

Garden front of the Villa Cornaro (2008)

Villa Cornaro salone (Puppi)

Villa Saraceno, Finale di Agugliaro (1545)

Palladio designed a number of smaller villas with pedimented arcades rather than columns. One has triple arches beneath a pediment, and another has a Palladian motif beneath an open gable. These smaller villas are two-storied with two-storied spaces in the center and partial mezzanine stories.

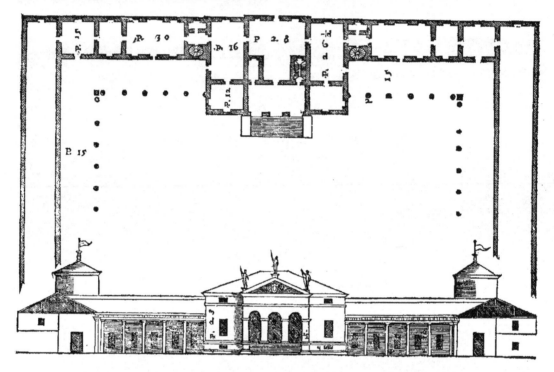

Villa Seraceno, Finale di Agugliaro (Palladio, 1570)

Whether large or small, many of his villas were intended to be both retreats and the centers of estates that included working farms. Palladio brought together the numerous smaller buildings required for farm use and arranged them in flanking wings with colonnades and a forecourt. There were unlike most villas in having symmetrical wings connected to or flanking the main house rather than scattered outbuildings and more like Michelangelo's Capitol, the wings of which influenced Palladio's palazzo designs. This coordinated arrangement enhanced the impressiveness of the main building as well as the group of buildings as a whole, and it was one of his most influential concepts.

Although no large than most American double houses, the Villa Saraceno has frescoes as well as a two-storied space. The finest series of frescoes created for any of Palladio's buildings was the set painted by Veronese for the Villa Barbaro in Maser. The Villa Barbaro has a nearly temple-form center with flanking wings that have the profiles of a baroque church and arcaded connectors. It is uncharacteristic of Palladio's work as a whole, but a nearby funerary chapel based on the Pantheon is more characteristic.

Villa Seraceno, Finale di Agugliaro (2008)

Villa Poiana; Vicentino (2008)

Frescoe by Veronese in Palladio's Villa Barbaro at Maser (Puppi)

PALACES

Villa Porto, Vicenza (1547-1552

Palladio designed several palazzi with a piano nobile only fronted by an order one-story tall and with the ground floor serving as a tall podium, and in the case of the Palazzo Giuseppe Porto, he added an attic story (above the main cornice as for the Palazzo Valmarana). He used an ashlar pattern for the ground floor with relieving arches and reveals above the windows. The *Four Books* shows a flat arch above the windows, and this would have sufficed beneath the semi-circular arch (which was to have a sculpted keystone), but the space was better filled in execution with an oversized set of different sized keystones.

Palazzo Porto, Vicenza (albumen by Alinari)

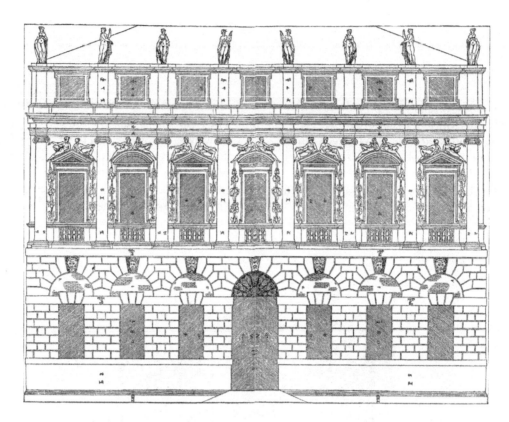

Palazzo Porto (merged images of front [above] and courtyard [below]; Palladio 2008)

Alternative designs drawn by Palladio for the Palazzo Porto

The influence of Bramante's Palazzo Caprini (the house of Raphael) on Palladio has already been mentioned (Chapter 16). Among the significant differences are that Palladio used the ground floor as a podium rather than a tall ground floor for shops with a mezzanine as Bramante had followed the ancient Roman precedent of insulas. Although Palladio often used attic stories, he had offered his client an alternative design with and without, and the version preferred was the one with an attic rather than an upper mezzanine floor and a taller order. In another drawing, Palladio offered an additional variant, proposing an arcaded ground floor with winds set in reveals between piers. The variant chosen was most like Bramante's and the most effective design, but all of the alternatives would have made good choices.

Palladio's palazzi usually have courtyards in between the main building and subsidiary buildings (like the Greek House) and often had open vestibules (like the Roman domus), and this makes their plans resemble the early Roman type of urban house (rather than the insula). By contrast, the courtyards of his villas are in front rather than in back of the house (in between flanking outbuildings and U-shaped with a front wall forming one side of the courtyard). What in a villa might be an interior vestibule with four columns was in this case an open space with the same plan.

Palazzo Valmarana, Vicenza (1565)

One of Palladio's most influential urban houses was the Palazzo Valmarana. It owes its use of monumental pilasters to Michelangelo's designs for the Campidoglio and for St. Peter's, but it is Palladian in its proportions and details. Palladio used monumental pilasters on a podium as on the city hall of Rome, and he used pilasters as a colonnade to be viewed along a narrow street rather than for a portico. He used one-storied half-pilasters alongside his monumental pilasters like the arrangement Michelangelo used for the flanking buildings of the Campidoglio. The overall design differs through the addition of an attic that gives the composition central emphasis vertically, and the substitution of caryatids at each end give the composition central emphasis horizontally.

Although the plan of the Palazzo Valmarana in the *Four Books* shows a front that is perpendicular to the side walls, the street cuts through at an angle, making the front rooms irregular in shape, but the front itself appears regular. This is but one of many indications that the *Four Books* was what Palladio would have designed if a site or client had made it possible. He planned an impressive courtyard, but only a portion was built.

Palazzo Valmarana (Palladio, 1570)

Palazzo Valmarana (albumen)

Palazzo Thiene, Vicenza (1542, 1546)

Palazzo Thiene (Puppi)

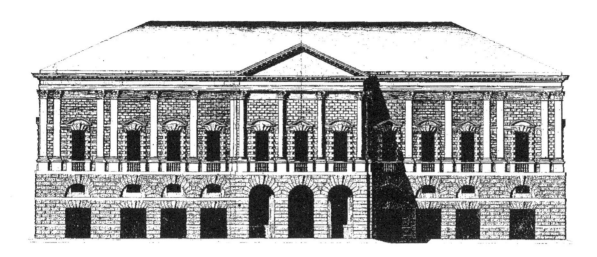

Palazzo Thiene (Scamozzi)

One of Palladio's earliest designs was for the Palazzo Thiene, a building with rustication that gives it a resemblance to Guilio Romano's Palazzo del Te in Mantua, but Palladio was familiar with the same ancient Roman sources of rustication (including the Porta Maggiore and the wall of the Forum of Augustus, both of which he measured and drew). It has less in common with it than with its sources: ancient architecture and Bramante.

Palazzo del Te, Mantua, by Romano (Heydenreich and Lotz)

The final design for the main front of the Palazzo Thiene owes more to Bramante's Palazzo Caprini in its use of an arcaded ground floor with shop fronts and mezzanine windows, but even so the main floor is much taller than the ground floor rather than about the same height. Since every other building in Palladio's second book was designed by him and since it includes his characteristic podium and pedimented portico, this one also is surely his.

The Palazzo Thiene was intended to have 11X12 massive bays with a 1X3-bay portico projecting from the main block. Only seven bays of one side was built, but it is

225

nonetheless imposing. It has two floors of more nearly the same height, but the upper floor is taller and more embellished (including an order, balustrade, and pediments over the windows as in Bramante's palazzo). Columns with blocks between drums had been used at the Temple of Claudius, which was probably a common source for Romano and Palladio. Undoubtedly, Palladio had seen the Palazzo del Te, a major building in its own right, but Palladio's buildings have better proportions, details, and spaces without the exaggerations that Romano delighted in creating such as immense keystones

Palazzo Chiericati, Vicenza (1550)

The Palazzo Chiericati shows what Palladio was capable of designing early in his career, and it too shows indebtedness, but is also distinctively Palladian and one of his best designs. It resembles the wings of Michelangelo's Capitoline group, but instead of having a giant order, Palladio used superimposed Roman Doric and Ionic. Instead of having an entirely closed upper floor, Palladio created his usual strong center and flanked it with loggias. He made the entire ground floor a loggia, and the city council of Vicenza was so pleased with his design that they granted permission for the building to be larger than it would ordinarily have been permitted to be. It provides a striking and memorable entrance to the city, and the colonnade of the ground floor is a public space.

Palazzo Chiericati (albumen)i

The plan is U-shaped with a courtyard in back. There are few rooms, but most of them are major spaces. The oval room in the center of the first story is 16 by 54 Venetian feet and the flanking rooms 18 by 30, and the main room is on the piano nobile. The building now serves as the City Museum.

CHURCHES AND RELATED BUILDINGS

Carità, Venice (begun c. 1561)

Palladio designed a monastery for the 15the Century brick church of Santa Maria della Carità, and in 1561 he was paid for a model. The portion completed consists primarily of one side of a three-storied courtyard with superimposed orders and with an influential elliptical staircase.

Since the publication of Palladio's works was in progress, Vasari simply listed most of Palladio's existing buildings, but he particularly admired his building and described it in detail:

> At Venice he has begun several buildings, but the monastery of la Carita, in imitation of the ancients, is more marvellous than the rest. The atrium is 40 feet by 54, it wings being half as long again as the breadth. The columns are Corinthian, 3 ½ feet thick and 35 feet high. From the atrium one enters the peristyle or cloister as the friars call it, divided into five parts towards the atrium and even at the sides. It has three rows of columns, one above the other, Doric, Ionic and Corinthian. Opposite the atrium is the refectory, two bays long and reaching to the level of the peristyle, with its offices conveniently disposed about it. The staircases are spiral and oval in shape. There is no well or column in the middle to support the steps, which are 15 feet broad and ar fitted into the wall, resting on each other. The building is entirely of brick except the base of the columns, the capitals, the imposts of the arches, the steps, the face of the cornice and all the windows and doors [Vasari 1568: IV, 234].

In the 18th Century, Goethe greatly admired the staircase and wrote in his Italian journal that it was the most beautiful staircase ever created (http://yearofpalladio.classicist.org). In the 19th Century, Robert Mills designed similar staircases with open centers and cantilevered stone steps.

The former church and monastery are now integral parts of the Academia del Belle Arti, the principal museum of Venice.

Carità (Palladio)

Carità (2017)

Main courtyard of the Carità (2017)

San Giorgio Maggiore, Venice (c. 1560-1610)

Palladio's Monastery of San Giorgio Maggiore was his largest and most prominent commission in Venice, and it is located on a small island directly across from the Ducal Palace. A refectory for monks of Santa Giustina was begun in 1560. The church was designed in c. 1565 and completed in c. 1610. Its façade with half-pediments fronting side aisles resembles the front that Palladio added San Francesco della Vigna in Venice in 1564 (brochure). Neither design is as coherent as the more integral design of Il Redentore, which was Palladio's last major commission.

The interior of San Giorgio Maggiore is larger and more elaborately ornamented than Il Redentore, but less well unified in that it is an aisled church rather than a nave with chapels opening directly into it. The complex arrangement of monumental columns and pilasters is the principal decoration.

As monastic churches, the interiors of San Giorgio Maggiore and Il Redentore are both restrained by Venetian standards. San Giorgio Maggiore has a larger and more ornamented choir than Il Redentore. The elliptical vault of the naves in both churches are similar, but since San Giorgio Maggiore faces west-northwest, it is better lighted in the morning and is poorly lighted in the evening unless its front doors are open and sunlight is reflected off the water. Since Il Redentore has an open plan and faces north, its clearstoried interior is better lighted during all daylight hours even though the naves of both churches have clearstories with termae windows.

San Giorgio Maggiore (Compagnia Rotografica, 3113)

San Giorgia Maggiore (Anderson in Heydenreich and Lotz)

San Giorgio Maggiore (2017)

San Giorgio Maggiore (2017)

San Giorgio Maggiore (2017)

Il Redentore, Venice (1577-1592)

Il Redentore (2017)

Il Redentore (above, Alinari in Heydenreich and Lotz; below, 2017)

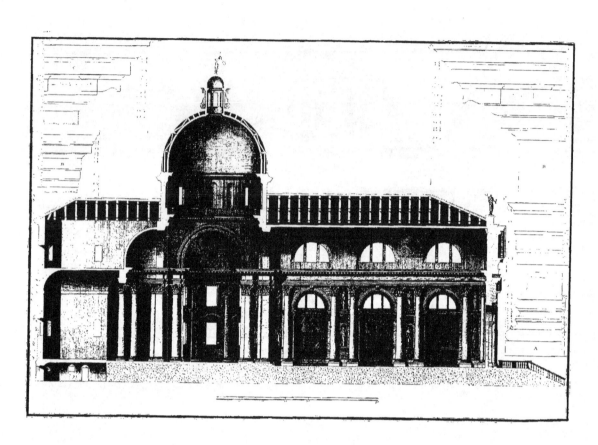

Il Redentore (Bertotti Scamozzi)

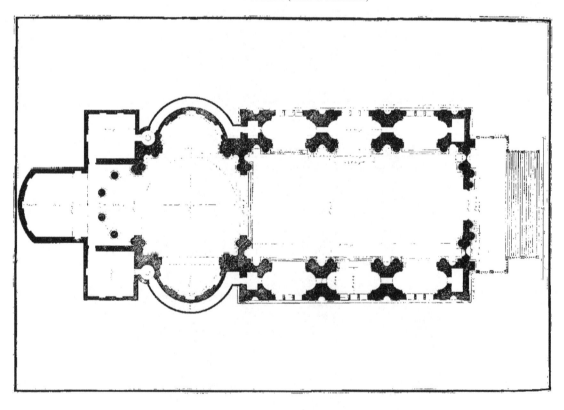

Il Redentore (Church of the Redeemer) was one of Palladio's last commissions. The church was vowed to end a plague from 1475-1476 that killed more than 50,000 persons. Construction began in 1577, and the church was consecrated in 1592. This building best represents one of the most influential architects of all time at the height of his creative power.

The nave of Il Redentore is similar in plan the nave of Alberti's Church of Sant'Andrea at Mantua, which also has a series of three chapels on each side that are fully open to the central space and which, in turn, was based on the plan of the Basilica Nova (Chapter 6). Palladio could have gotten his plan directly from the Basilica Nova (which he reconstructed), but since his church and Alberti's are both cruciform and domed and since Mantua is not far from Venice, Sant'Andrea is also likely to have been directly influential. Palladio's plan has more parts and was differently shaped to serve the purposes of a monastery as well as a congregation. Like Sant'Andrea, Il Redentore is unified visually by allowing all spaces to the nave to be perceived as a unified space and by proportionally by the pervasive use of the ratio of 1:2 in the plan of the nave, crossing, and choir.

The nave and screen behind the altar use a monumental Corinthian order, but in a less complex arrangement than for San Giorgio Maggiore, and the choir is purposely plain. Palladio wrote that since "...this church is to be officiated by the Capuchin order, I have devised that the chorus behind in the rear should be of humble structure" (brochure). The side apses of the cruciform plan were intended primarily for the seating of Venetian officials during the annual commemorations of the end of the plague, and they consequently lack altars.

The front of the church is exceptionally complex with multiple enframements that resemble Michelangelo's late designs. Palladio added an attic and buttresses to the top of the front to give it a more nearly cubical design. The flanking half-pediment front the chapels rather than aisles the marble faced buttresses are otherwise like the brick buttressed along the sides of the nave.

The interior is unusually open and light. The white walls and vaulting reflect light so well that the interior resembles more Protestant than Catholic churches, but similar interiors had been created in numerous churches and chapels in Florence (including the Gothic interior of the Duomo, Brunelleschi's two churches and two chapels, and Michelangelo's Medici Chapel).

The front of Il Redentore is unique, and the 1:1 proportions of its central block were probably based on the Pantheon's intermediate block and portico. Palladio give the Venetian Senate a choice between a rectangular plan and a square plan with a square front. They preferred the rectangular plan and possibly it had a square front, but the front of the centralized plan seems to have been adapted and aisles added. Huge buttresses similar to ones used for S. Augustino in Rome were needed for the elliptical ceiling, and Palladio took advantage of them to give his front a more regular outline as well as to conceal the projecting arms (that are broader and distracting in the case of his San Georgio). His unusual combination of features seems to have accumulated, and he managed to interrelate all of them so that none distracts attention from the design as a whole, but the interior is more successful than the excessively elaborated front.

Il Redentore (Bertotti Scamozzi)

OTHER BUILDING TYPES

Palladio primarily designed houses, but in addition to his two principal churches, at the beginning of his career he redesigned the exterior of a town hall, and at the end of his career he designed a major theatre.

Basilica, Vicenza (1546, 1549)

Vicenza had a pre-existing town hall that had been constructed during the late Medieval Period, and a previous attempt to add a portico had failed. Palladio won a competition to design another portico by repeating the pattern of fornices that were used for Roman basilicas, and he adapted the pattern to include semicircular arches similar to those that Jacopo Sansovino designed for the Library of St. Marks (begun in 1536). Other architects also used this motif, including the architect of Diocletian's Palace, Bramante, and Serlio, but Palladio made it his own and did most to cause others to adopt it, and it deserves to be called the Palladian motif.

Basilica, Vicenza (portico by Palladio; Alinari)

Theatre Olympico, Vicenza (1580)

Palladio provided a full set of designs for the Theatre Olympico, and the Olympic Academy of Vicenza constructed it in 1580. Its is based on most respects on the Roman theatre as described by Vitruvius, but has an oval plan. The scene building reconstructs a Roman palace (with an elaborate program of sculpture), and above the seats is a colonnade.

The most street visible through the opening in the scene building provide great apparent depth by being constructed using one-point perspective. The buildings along these streets were designed by Scamozzi (Frommel 2007: 213)

Theatre Olympico, Vicenza (albumen by Alinari 12794)

18. Bramante and Michelangelo Before St. Peter's

Tempietto by Bramante, Rome (Richter, 334)

Brunelleschi, Bramante, and Michelangelo were all artists before becoming archtiects. None of the three of them is known to have apprenticed under an architect. I have dealt with the development of Bramante and Michelangelo as architects in this chapter and considered what they achieved on St. Peter's in the next chapter.

Bramante set the parameters for a new St. Peter's from 1505-1514, and Michelangelo did most to determine the final form of the building from 1547-1564. Although their work on St. Peter's was separated by several decades, Michelangelo largely adapted Bramante' initial plan, but created entirely different elevations.

Donato Bramante (1444-1514) was born about three decades before Michelangelo Buonarotti (1474-1564), who outlived him by a half century. Their combined lifetimes spanned about 120 years, and their combined work on St. Peter's spanned about 60 years. I have dealt summarily with their early architectural work and in detail with their work on St. Peter's.

Michelangelo is the first architect whose life was well documented, and St. Peter's is the first building with a well documented design process. Considering the importance of Michelangelo and of St. Peter's, they both deserve to be considered in detail.

BRAMANTE

In 1547 Michelangelo wrote that "one cannot deny that Bramante was as skilled in architecture as anyone since the time of the ancients" (Michelangelo 1963: I, 69). In 1570 Palladio called Bramante "a supremely talented man and observer of ancient structures" and wrote that he "was the first to make known that good and beautiful architecture which had been hidden from the time of the ancients till now..." (Palladio 1570 [1997]: 276). In 1568 Vasari had compared Bramante's contribution to the revival of ancient architecture with Brunelleschi's:

> The modern methods of Filippo Brunelleschi proved of great assistance to architecture, as he had copied and brought to light after long ages the excellent production of the most learned and distinguished ancients. But Bramante has been no less useful to our own century, for he followed in the footsteps of Filippo, and paved a safe way for those who succeeded, his spirit, courage, genius and knowledge of the art being displayed not only in theory but in practice. Nature could not have formed a mind better adapted than his to put into practice the works of his art with invention and proportion and on so firm a basis. But it was necessary that she should create at the same time a pope like Julius II., ambitious of leaving a great memory. It was most fortunate that this prince should have afforded Bramante such unrivalled opportunities of displaying his abilities and of showing the full force of his genius, for such a thing rarely happens. Bramante took full advantage of this chance, the moldings of his cornices, the shafts of his columns, the grace of his capitals, his bases, corbels, angles, vault, steps, projections and every other detail of architecture being marvellously modelled with the best judgment, and men of ability seem to me to be under as great a debt to him as to the ancients. Because, while the Greeks invented architecture and the Romans imitated them, Bramante not only added new inventions, but greatly increased the beauty and difficulty of the art, to an extent we may now perceive [Vasari 1568 (1927): I, 183].

This great praise cannot refer to Bramante's additions to Santa Maria della Grazie or to the Chiesa di Santa Maria Presso di San Satiro in Milan, but only to the work Bramante was able to accomplish only after he had studied ancient architecture in Rome.

Bramante's transept in relation to the earlier nave of Santa Maria della Grazia (albumen in Frassineti)

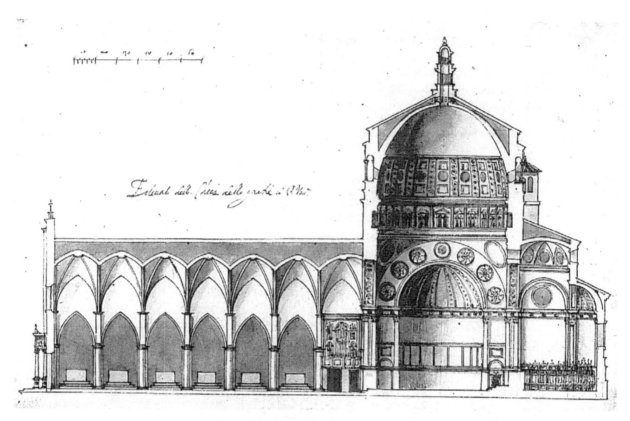

Section showing the orignal nave with Bramante's transept in the 16th Century (Franssineti)

Bramante's addition to Santa Maria della Grazie (as restored; 2016)

Santa Maria presso San Satiro, Milan (Aragozzini in Frommel)

Bramante's Early Life

By everyone's estimation, Bramante was a pivotal figure in Renaissance architecture. A succession of brilliant buildings in Rome leave no doubt about his excellence as an architect and the immense impact he had on subsequent design: the cloister of Santa Maria della Pace, the Tempietto, the spiral stair of the Belvedere, the Palazzo Caprini (the House of Raphael), and St. Peter's were all greatly admired by his contemporaries and were immensely influential. All of these projects date from the last 15 or so years of his life, and he had done nothing previously that equaled any of them. This requires some explanation, and a great deal has been written to try to explain his development as a architect, but what has been written has been based largely on assumptions and speculation.

The main assumption has been that Bramante was profoundly influenced by developments in the city of Urbino. He was generally referred to as Bramante da Urbino, but there is no evidence that he ever saw Urbino much less that he worked there, and his work in Milan shows little if any influence of the principal architects who worked at Urbino. Moreover, his later work shows little if any influence of his buildings he designed in Milan that consisted mainly of two additions to existing churches. He suddenly appears as undeniably one of the greatest architects of the Renaissance without any definite information on how he became a great architect or any earlier work that relates directly to his later accomplishments.

Very little is known about the first 56 or so years of Bramante's life, and what little is recorded by Vasari is significant mainly for indicating how little was known in 1568. Vasari wrote that "he was born at Castello Durante, in the state of Urbino, of a poor man of good condition" (Vasari 1568: II, 183). Castello Durante is about 10 miles west of the city of Urbino and has been renamed Urbania. In 1510 Bramante stated that he was "a native of Monte Asdrualdo" (Bruschi 1977: 15). Bruschi explained that Bramante's father Angelo"...went to live in his father-in-law's house, became his heir and took his surname, handing it on to his children" (15; 190, n. 4). Since Bramante considered himself to be from Monte Asdrualdo, he evidently grew up there rather than at Castello Durante, and Monte Asdrualdo is about 4 miles southwest of the town of Urbino.

In any case, Bramante was born and raised near the town of Urbino around 1444, but aside from what Vasari wrote, there is no other documentation about where he was or what he was doing until 1477, when he was about 33 years old and in Bergamo and in 1481 when he was in Milan (27). Vasari continued,

> In his childhood besides reading and writing, he was continually doing the abacus. But as it was necessary that he should learn some trade, his father, perceiving his great fondness for design, apprenticed him while still a child to the art of painting. Here he carefully studied the production of Frà Bartolommeo, otherwise Frà Carnovale da Urbino, who did the picture of S. Maria della Bella at Urbino. But as he always delighted in architecture and perspective, he left Castel Durante, and passing to Lombardy, worked as best he could in on city after another, not producing things of great cost or value because as yet he had neither fame nor credit [Vasari 1568: II, 183-184].

Vasari provides no more information about Carnovale, and this is all we know about Bramante from 1444 until 1447, when he was in Bergamo on his way to Milan.

Vasari implies that Bramante went to Urbino "while still a child" to study with Frà Bartolommeo, but soon returned to Castel Durante and later went to Lombardy to study architecture. What he does not indicate is as important as what he does indicate in that there is not the slightest suggestion that being in Urbino while a child provided any training in architecture or that Bramante ever returned to Urbino. This seems incredible until a statement about Bramante by Cesariano is considered: "Though he could not write, he had a wonderful memory and spoke with ease and eloquence" (quoted in Heydenreich and Lotz 1974: 149). Evidently, Bramante's formal education was limited to his childhood, and he was largely illiterate though Cesariano noted that "he was also familiar with the work of the Italian poets... [and] had a wonderful memory and spoke with ease and eloquence. Originally court architect to Duke Ludovico Sforza, he later restored many papal buildings, especially under Julius II. And he became the pre-eminent architect, rebuilder, and recreator of the basilica of St Peter..." (149). Both Vasari and Cesariano are unlikely to be incorrect that Bramante had very little formal education, and most of Bramante's early life must have been spent working on his grandfather's farm rather than in the city of Urbino.

Moreover, there is little if any indication of influence by Laurana, Martini, or Della Francesca on what Bramante did while in Milan. From around 1481 to the late 1490s, his style was almost completely different from theirs, and judging by a ruined temple he drew that was engraved by Právedari in 1481, Bramante knew much about painting, but little about architecture. For example, he included a dome that is separated entirely from the pendentives beneath it (Bruschi 1977: 32, fig. 26); if this were a mistake by the engraver, it could easily have been corrected.

What Vasari wrote about Bramante's years in Milan was limited to this statement:

> Determined to see at least one notable thing, he proceeded to Milan to visit the Duomo, where there happened to be one Cesare Cesariano, reputed a good geometrician and architect, who had written a commentary on Vitruvius. Enraged at not having received the reward which he had expected, Cesare refused to work any more, and becoming eccentric, he died more like a beast than a man. There was also Bernardino da Trevio, a Milanese engineer and architect of the Duomo, and a great draughtsman. He was considered a rare master by Leonardo da Vinci, even though his manner in painting was crude and somewhat dry. There is a Resurrection of his with some fine foreshortening at the top of the cloister of the Grazie, and a Death of SS. Peter and Paul in fresco in a chapel of S. Francesco. He painted many other works in Milan and did several others in the neighbourhood, which were valued, and our book contains a very meritorious woman's head in charcoal and white lead, a good example of his style.
>
> But to return to Bramante. After an examination of the Duomo, and having met these masters, he determined to devote himself entirely to architecture. Accordingly he left Milan, and arrived in Rome before the Holy Year 1500 [Vasari 1568: II, 184; footnotes omitted].

This is all Vasari initially wrote about Bramante's life before c. 1500, and it contains a number of errors.

Vasari implies that Bramante visited Milan briefly before going to Rome and that he was influenced there only by Cesariano and Da Trevio and by the impressiveness of the cathedral. He implies that Cesariano influenced Bramante, but Cesariano himself later wrote, "my teacher, Bramante, was an artist of the first order" (quoted in Heydenreich and Lotz 1974: 149). However, in some miscellaneous notes about Milanese artists, Vasari later added that the artist Bramantino

> ...was the first painter in the good style there, and led to Bramante's excellence in architecture by the good style of his buildings in perspective; for the first things studied by Bramante were these of Bramantino, and under that influence S. Satiro was erected, which pleases me as a very rich work, ornate within and without with columns, double corridors and other ornaments, including a handsome sacristy full of statues. But it chiefly merits praise for the middle tribune, the beauty of which, as related in Bramante's Life, led Bernardino da Trevio ["Bernadino Zenale"]to follow the same method in the duomo of Milan, and to study architecture although painting was his first profession; and he had done four scenes of the Passion in the cloister of the monastery of le Grazie, and some others in grisaille [Vasari 1586: III, 324].

This Bramantino has been conflated with the pupil of Bramante called Bramantino, and the two cannot be the same person. Vasari discusses the work of this earlier Bramantino in some detail and mentions him by name repeatedly (322-324). His works included ...painting some chambers in Rome for Pope Nicholas...," who died in 1455 and a sketchbook "containing the antiquities of Lombardy drawn and measured by Bramantino..." (323). This cannot refer to Bartolommeo Suardi (the later Bramantino), who was born the year Nicolas V died (322, n. 2). According to Vasari, Bramante learned perspective from someone called Bramantino (rather than from Piero della Francesco as has often been stated).

In passing, Vasari referred to Bramante's work at San Satiro, and he noted about San Ambrogio that "this church was restored by Bramante, who made a stone portico at one side, with columns resembling clipped trees, both novel and varied" (Vasari 1568: III, 323-324). He also corrected what he had written about Bernadino da Trevio, who he acknowledged was influenced by Bramante rather than having influenced him. Thus, Vasari later learned that Bramante did architectural work in Milan rather than simply having visit it as he implied in Bramante's biography, and he corrected some of his earlier mistakes, but without correcting the biography. Also in his miscellaneous notes on Lombard Artists, Vasari added about the cathedra at Parma, "the design of the church is due to Bramante" (315).

Frommel summarized the available evidence for Bramante's architectural work during the period of his residence in northern Italy. In 1487/88 Bramante was commmissioned to design the cathedral at Pavia: "The Pavians wanted a building modelled on Hagia Sophia in Istanbul, and indeed some of the elements of the cathedral executed under Bramante, such as the vault of the crypt or the two-storied pillars of the octagonal crossing under the dome, come extraordinarily close to that of the model [Hagia Sophia]. ... In 1495, when the crypt was finished and the area of the dome and choir had barely risen above the entablatyure of the lower order, Bramante was supplanted by [Giovanatonio] Amadeo" (Frommel 2007: 83). Similarly, in c. 1492 Bramante was commissioned to enlarge Santa Maria della Grazie in Milan "...but the building was soon removed from Bramante's control and transferred by the duke to Amadeo..." (83-84).

How much of either of these buildings was designed by Bramante is uncertain. Although Bruschi considered the interior of Bramante's adition to Santa Maria delle Grazie likely to have been influenced by Leonardo (whose painting of the "Last Supper" is adjacent), he acknowledged that its exterior does not provide a good reflection of its interior: "Very little that is truly Bramantesue is now visible on the exterior, with its often labored piling up of parts and superficial combination of disperate elements" (Bruschi 1977: 57; cf. his figs. 41-43); the exterior is characteristic of Amadeo's work (Frommel 2007: 78, fig. 100).

Vasari stated that Bramante "...arrived in Rome before the Holy Year 1500" (Vasari 1586: II, 184). How much earlier he arrived in Rome is not indicated, but

> Bramante had earned money in Lombardy and at Rome, and on this he hoped to live by dint of severe economy, and to be able to measure all the ancient buildings of Rome without it being necessary to work. He set about this task, going alone and wrapped in thought. In a little while he had measured all the buildings there and in the neighbourhood, going even as far as Naples, and wherever he knew antiquities to be. He measured what there was at Tivoli and the villa of Hadrian, and made considerable use of this, as I shall have occasion to relate [184].

His intensive study of ancient architecture soon after arriving in Rome suffices to account for the dramatic change in his style from what he had designed in Milan.

What Vasari wrote casts serious doubt on much that has been assumed about the influence of Urbino on Bramante's development as an architect. If he had worked on the palace at Urbino, his work in Milan would probably have been different and better. In my opinion, Bramante, like Michelangelo, did not begin to become a great architect until late in life. Prior to that, they both had been primarily artists, but that was good training to become a great architect.

The only early indication that Bramante is likely to have been even briefly at the court of Federigo da Montefeltro does not state that he worked there. Writing in 1549, Saba da Castiglione stated that Bramante "...was a good painter, as a follower of Mantegna, and a great perspectivist, as a pupil of Piero dal Borgo (Piero della Francesca)" (Bruschi 1977: 15-16). A "follower" and an "pupil" is not equivalent to being an apprentice. Considering the obvious influence of Mantegna and Della Francesca on the few paintings believed to be by Bramante, he was certainly influenced by both of these masters, but he was only a "good" painter and not a great one (41; figs. 37-39). The use of perspective to create the appearance of an apse in S. Satiro is the work of a "great perspectivist," but the illusion that an apse exists on a flat wall is effective only from one point in the church, and it is so unsuccessful from any other point of view that it was not influential.

Unless better documentation becomes available, what can be written about Bramante's early life will necessarily be based on assumptions and will continue to consist largely of speculation. In my opinion, it is best to accept the fact that Bramante's early work is largely unrelated to his later work and that it is more worthwhile to deal with his later work, which was consistently great and influential while his earlier work was neither great nor influential.

Much has been written on the possible influence of Leonardo on Bramante and vice versa. For example, Heydenreich stated that
> ...for seventeen years Leonardo and Bramante worked side by side in Milan as court architects, exchanging ideas and practical experience. No drawing of Bramante's has come down to us which could explain the metamorphosis of his style between his early Renaissance work in Milan and his 'Roman style' of after 1500. This gap is closed by Leonardo's ntoes, and for that reason, if for no other, as evidence of teh architectural ideas of teh period, they are of supreme importance for there is no other whether in writing or drawing [Heydenreich and Lotz 1974: 144].

However, "there is no building which we can confidently regard as Leonardo's own work..." (143), and "the total neglect of the classical repertory of form... set him [Leonardo] apart from the important practical architects of his generation, although he was in constant touch with them" (145).

Although one of the world's greatest artists, Leonardo is not definitely known to have designed a building or to have made any attempt to teach himself how to be an architect. His interest in architecture was primarily in solving structural problems, in the potential of proportion and geometry for dealing with design problems, and in methods of construction. He was more interested in engineering than architecture (Pedretti 2007). Notably, Leonardo is not among the 33 architects that Frommel discussed in *the Architecture of the Italian Renaissance* (2007).

It is true that Bramantae's Tempietto is conceptually similar to Leonardo's designs for centralized churches, yet Leonardo's superb permutations of coherent forms resemble Michelangelo's designs for St. Peter's more than Bramante's. There may thus have been some indirect influence by Leonardo on the design of St. Peter's. In my opinion, these similarities reflect the impact of the apsidal ends and dome of the Florentine Duomo on all three architects.

The only probable reference to Bramante (as "donnjno") in Leonardo's notes refers to a drawbridge (71). Leonardo's interest in architecture was largely theoretical like his other interests, and he planned to write a treatise on architecture that might well have been as valuable as his treatise on painting:
> While the first main section of the treatise was to have covered the theory of architectural types and forms, of sacred and secular buildings and of architectural proportions and ornament, the second was planned as a theory of architectural constructions. Leonardo made extensive preliminary studies for this part two, and one or two chapters, e. g. *The Causes of Dilapidation in Buildings* and *The Theory of the Arch* (Plate 148F), were far advanced. ... In

one respect Leonardo's treatise differs fundamentally from its predecessors. It was planned in the first instance as a classified collection of technical drawings which were merely explained by an accompanying text [Heydenreich and Lotz 1974: 144-145].

Bramante in Rome

Very few of Bramante's drawings survive, but one shows that he made a careful study of the Baths of Diocletian. This is significant because his later design for St. Peter's owed much to the grandeur of ancient Roman baths.

The formal repertory of the building pilasters and niches, arches and domes, was not new, but Bramante was the first to invest these forms with the monumentality they were to have from that time on. There was no work of architecture in antiquity or the Quattrocento from which this repertory could be derived in its entirety, but Bramante had become familiar with the clarity of the proportional relations, the simplicity of great spacial organizations in the Pantheon and the Basilica of Maxentius, and it was in these ancient buildings that posts and lintels expressed the forces at work in the mass of the building with the same power and clarity as in Bramante's crossing. ... Benvenuto Cellini wrote of Bramante: "He began the great church of St Peter entirely in the beautiful manner of the ancients. He had the power to do so because he was an artist, and because he was able to see and to understand the beautiful buildings of antiquity that still remain to us, though they are in ruins" [Heydenreich and Lotz1974: 162].

"Self-taught, his [Bramante's] education was necessarily unsystemicic, casual and fragmentary, even if critically selective" (Bruschi 1977: 182). However, he continued his education when he got to Rome, and his work greatly changed and dramatically improved.

Bramante's Tempietto indicates that he also made a careful study of the relatively small round temples in and near Rome. The study of ancient architecture prepared Bramante to develop a style of his own that was based on ancient design, but that incorporated Renaissance ideas such as placing domes on clearstoried drums, but surrounded by a classical colonnade and surmounted by a hemispherical dome.

Bramante's additions to two churches in Milan were provincial in nearly all respects, and if he had not left Milan, he would be a minor architect. His early work consists largely of attempts to adapt Brunelleschi's designs for medieval building types. As far as Vasari was concerned, Bramante's career as an architect began in Rome.

Courtyard of S. Maria della Pace, Rome (1500-1504)

Bramante's Courtyard (Anderson in Millon)

Bramante's first major commission in Rome was to redesign an existing cloister:

> Bramante's spirit being thus disclosed, the cardinal of Naples ["Oliviero Caraffa"] happened to observe him, and took him into favour. Thus Bramante pursued his studies and was charged to restore in travertine the cloister of the friars of the Pace which the cardinal wished to have done. Being anxious to make a name and to please the cardinal, Bramante displayed the utmost industry and diligence, and speedily completed the work. Although it was not of perfect beauty, it brought him a great reputation, as there were not many in Rome who devoted so much love study and activity to architecture as he [184-185].

The Roman design elements that were used for this monastic cloister include fornices and columns on pedestals (both elements having been used for triumphal arches and for the Colosseum). The orders used were Corinthian superimposed over Ionic. Plain modillions similar to those of the Pantheon and Forum of Augustus occur in pairs above each pier and more widely spaced in between.

Bramante designed by aligning the interaxials of columns (the distance between the centers of columns regardless of the thickness of the columns) to the lines on grid paper. This is a method that had not been used by the Greeks and Romans or by Palladio, who used incolumniations (the distance between columns based on whatever diameter was chosen for the column). As I noted previously, contracted corners prevented Greek Doric temples from conforming to a grid, and wider central intercolumniations prevented Ionic temples from conforming to a grid. By contrast, Gothic architects generally designed using bays that were based on interaxials, and Gothic plans can conform to a regular grid. Bramante adapted the Gothic method for designing plans on the basis of interaxials rather than the method of using intercolumniations recommended by Vitruvius and adopted by Palladio.

Arnaldo Bruschi demonstrated that Bramante used a regular grid to work out the plan and elevations for the courtyard of Santa Maria della Pace (Bruschi 1977: 76-77). Since Bramante later used graph paper to work out the plan for St. Peter's, no doubt Bruschi was correct (154; fig. 157).

Since Bramante's courtyard is square, it has the proportions of 1:2; this is true both of the courtyard itself and of the courtyard with its aisles. For a grid, Bramante used one of the cross-vaulted bays of the aisles (1:6), and he aligned the interaxials of the four principal piers of the courtyard with this grid. As Bruschi's diagrams show, the courtyard is thus four times as wide as the aisles (1:4). Since the aisles continue all the way around the courtyard, the courtyard is twice as wide as the combined with of the aisles (1:2); in other words, the overall space in which Bramante built the courtyard is six bays wide, and four of the six was used for the courtyard itself (2:3).

I am not suggesting that Bramante set out to achieve all of these proportions for his plan, but that such simple proportions as these were the consequence of his adoption of a grid of six bays. The main consequence of the adoption of this approach for designing the courtyard was that the piers and pilasters align with the grid. Otherwise, the two-storied elevations of the central space do not align with the grid, and Bramante had to adjust the classical design elements to fit the spaces available for them.

Both stories of Bramante's aisles have nearly the same height though the upper story is slightly less tall than the lower story. However, rather than having two stories of roughly equal height and piers of equal width for the courtyard itself, Bramante made the lower story much taller than the upper story and added four much smaller Corinthian columns above the centers of the arches of the lower story in order to make the interaxials on each level appear to be proportionately about the same. This was not a classical solution, but an excellent compromise that helps to make the courtyard seem larger and taller than it would otherwise. The central space is somewhat less than 50 feet across, but with the aisles, the entire space is nearly 80 feet across, the wide openings of the ground floor enable the aisles to become visually part of the space. However, because the Ionic order conforms to the grid of the floor, there was room in the corners only for a fragment of a pilaster. This minor flaw is inconspicuous, and overall the design for the courtyard is as eminently successful as his design of the Tempietto and his design for St. Peter's, but his designs and his structural solutions were sometimes deeply flawed.

Bramante used classical design elements, but a Gothic design method to create one of the most visually effective spaces of the Renaissance. Later, when he designed St. Peter's, he also ignored the proportions Vitruvius recommended for the classical orders and used disproportionately tall orders. Eventually, the floor of St. Peter's was raised to make St. Peter's more classical than Gothic, as its interior and exterior would have been if Bramante's corner towers had been constructed. It is true that Bramante's style changed dramatically for the better once he was able to study ancient Roman architecture, but his design for St. Peter's was less successful than his design for the Tempietto, which Palladio considered to be the first great building since antiquity and which Michelangelo adapted for the dome of St. Peter's even though Bramante had not.

Bramante's Courtyard (Letarouilly)

Bramante's Courtyard at Santa Maria della Pace

Tempietto, Rome (c. 1502-c. 1506)

Bramante's Tempietto at San Pietro in Montorio bears such a close resemblance to the Dome of St. Peter's Basilica that it was manifestly the principal influence on Michelangelo's design. It bears no resemblance to Bramante's earlier work, and being circular its design could not be based on a grid.

The circular plan and colonnade of the Tempietto are based on the ancient Temple on the Tiber and to the Temple of Sybil in Tivoli, but they were Corinthian, and neither had a dome. They were generally assumed to have had domes, but no doubt had conical roofs with timber frames like the Greek tholos. As with the Tiber temple, Bramante used three steps, but he added a podium as for the Tivoli temple, thus combining the Greek krepis and the Roman podium. The upper drum is where a clearstory would ordinarily have been placed in a church, and the balustrade is a feature he invented. The combination is new, and even though most of the elements are old, this is unmistakably a Renaissance building and a turning point in the Renaissance and in Bramante's career.

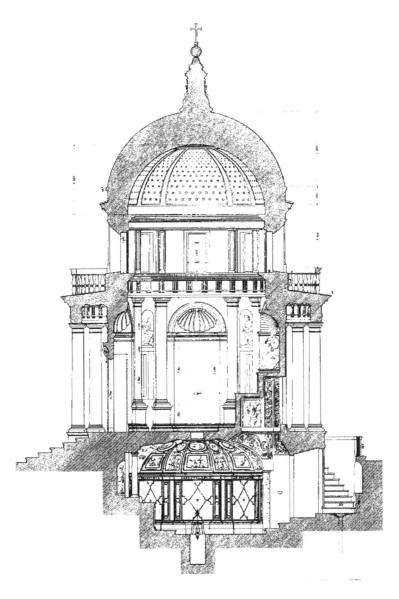

Tempietto (Letarouilly)

Serlio devoted four pages to the Bramante's Tempietto, which is located on the site that was believed to have been where the Apostle Peter was martyred and beside the Church of S. Pietro in Montorio. Serlio provides the very important information that "...the sayd Temple is to bee measured by the old Romane foote, which foot is sixteen fingers...: whereof also you shall finde the measure by the Romane Palme, augmenting the said foure fingers." Wilson Jones measured the Tempietto to determine how the Roman foot (0.296 m.) and palm (0.222 m.) were used in the building's design, and he noted that the foot is 4/3 of a palm, which is 1/2 of a cubit. He found that that "...by giving the inside of the cella a radius of 10 palmi, the outside one of 10 piedi and the colonnade one of 10 column modules, Bramante was distilling the perfect number...." The module was the column diameter, and the measurement was to the center of the column. Since these measurements are for radii, the measurements for diameters would have been 20 palms, feet, and modules. Mark Wilson Jones also noted that the entire height for the order for the exterior is 20 palms. The column height 16 palmi and so relates to the order height as 4:5. Since the height of the Roman Doric columns are 9 modules, they have the proportions of 1:9.

Bruschi had previously analyzed the plan in terms of column diameters (modules), and he found that the diameter of the interior is equal to 6 modules, and the diameter of the exterior of the cella is 10 modules (with the walls two modules thick). Since the number of columns for the Tempietto and for its courtyard are 16, he proposed that Bramante intentionally used all three of the numbers Vitruvius considered to be perfect: 6, 10, and 16. Bruschi also found that the height to width of the drum and the height to width of the Doric peristyle relate in both cases as 3:5. The exterior width of the cella apparently relates to the overall height of the Tempietto (including its steps) as 1:2, but its dome was to some extent redesigned during construction. The width of the peristyle to the overall height seems to relate as 3:4. While not all of the proportions proposed by Bruschi and Wilson Jones may have been intended, many seem to have been.

Bramante designed a circular courtyard to surround the Tempietto, but it has not been constructed. It was to have been about 100 palmi in diameter.

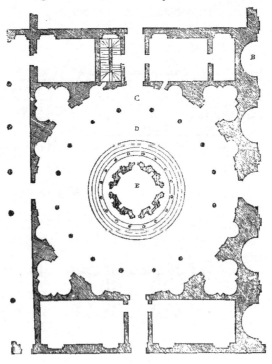

Courtyard designed for the Tempietto (Serlio)

Belvedere Courtyard, Rome (begun 1505)

Bramante had previously been hired by Cardinal Giuliano della Rovere to work on his titular church of San Pietro in Vincoli (Condivi 1563 [1976]: 30). After Della Rovere became Julius II in 1503, he commissioned Bramante to construct two corridors to connect the Vatican Palace with the Villa Belvedere a thousand feet away and to provide a great courtyard in between the corridors. Utilizing existing city walls on two sides of the Vatican, Bramante created an immense quadrangle. He terraced the rising ground in between the palace and villa and constructed a spiral ramp adjacent to the Belvedere large enough for horses. Vasari wrote,

> that Pope had a fancy to cover the space between the Belvedere and the palace, and that it should take the form of a square theatre, embracing depression between the old papal palace and the buildings erected there for the pope's dwelling by Innocent VIII [1484-1492], and that there should be a passage by two corridors on either side of the depression leading from the Belvedere to the palace covered by loggias, and so from the palace to the Belvedere, the level of which should be reached from the valley by flights of steps, variously arranged. Bramante, who possessed a good judgment and a fanciful genius in such matters, divided the bottom part into two stories, first a fine Doric loggia like the Coliseum of the Savelli ["i.e. the theatre of Marcellus."], but instead of half-columns, he put pilasters, building the whole of travertine. The second stage was of the Ionic order and with windows, rising to the level of the first apartments of the papal palace and of those of the Belvedere, to form subsequently a loggia more than four hundred paces on the side towards Rome and another towards the wood, with the valley between, so that it was necessary to bring all the water of the Belvedere and to erect a beautiful fountain. Of this design Bramante completed the first corridor rising from the palace and leading to the Belvedere on the Roman side, except the last loggia, which was to go above. Of the part towards the wood he laid the fountains, but could not finish it, owing to the death of Julius, followed by his own. It was considered such a fine idea that it was believed that Rome had never seen better since the time of the ancients. But, as I have said, nothing but the foundations of the other corridor were laid, and it has barely been completed even in our own day, Pius IV putting the finishing touches. Bramante also did the antique gallery on the Belvedere for the ancient statues with the arrangement of niches. Here in his own lifetime Laocoon was put, a very rare and ancient statue, and the Apollo [Belvedere] and Venus, and others later on by Leo X, such as the Tiber, the Nile and the Cleopatra some others by Clement VII, and a number of important improvements were carried out at great expense in the time of Paul III and Julius III.
>
> But to return to Bramante, if those who supplied him were not sparing [in providing funds] he was very expeditious and he understood the art of construction thoroughly. The building of the Belvedere was carried out with great rapidity, his own energy being equalled by the fever of the Pope, who wanted his structures not to be built but to grow up as by magic. Thus the builders carried away by night the sand and earth excavated by day in the presence of Bramante, so that he directed the lying of the foundations without taking further precautions. This carelessness has occasioned the cracking of his works, so that they are in danger of falling. Of the corridor in question eighty braccia fell down in the time of Pope Clement VII, and it was rebuilt by Pope Paul II., who caused it to be restored and enlarged. There are many other flights of steps of Bramante in the

palace, high or low according to the situation, in the Corinthian, Ionic and Doric orders, very beautiful, and executed with the utmost grace. His model is said to have be of marvellous beauty, as we may judge by the part actually constructed. In addition to this, he made a spiral staircase on rising columns, which a horse may go up, the Doric merging into the Ionic and the Ionic into the Corinthian all carried out with the utmost grace and art, doing him no less honour than his other works at the same palace. This idea was borrowed by Bramante from Niccolo of Pisa, as has been said in the Life of Giovanni and Niccolo Pisani [Vasari 1568: 185-187].

Although Bramante prepared designs for the façades of this enormous courtyard (the Cortile del Belvedere), they were changed significantly during subsequent construction, and the courtyard was subdivided successively by the insertion of transverse wings for the Vatican Library and later for the Braccio Nuovo.

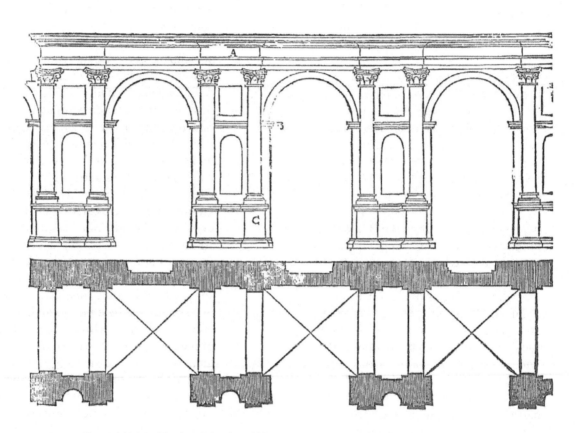

Bramante's use of the riumphal arch motif for the lower story of the Belvedere Courtyard (Serlio)

Pre-existing walls and Belvedere in c. 1532 (Heemskerck in Dunbar)

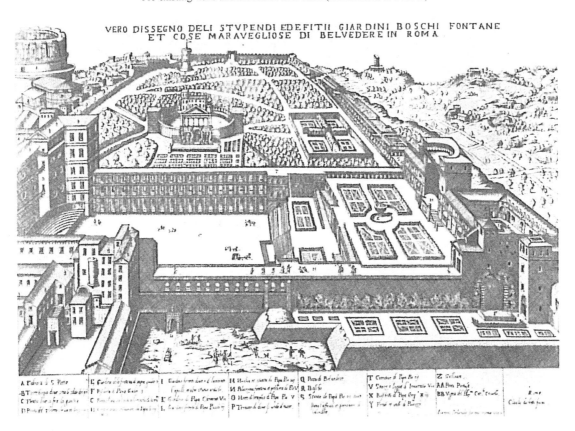

Vatican Corridors in 1579 (Lees-Milne)

James Ackerman wrote about Bramante's Cortile del Belvedere that
> here his raw material was the entire mountain side; his design had to impose the authority of intellect upon nature. Inspired by antique precedents, he devised a sequence of rectangular courts on ascending levels, bound by stairways and ramps of varying form and framed by loggias. His principles of organization were: first, emphasis on the central axis (marked by a centralized monumental fountain in the lowest court, a central stairway and niche in the central court, and a focal one-story exedra in the garden at the upper level, the last [set of steps] already destroyed by Michelangelo...; second, the symmetrical design of the lateral façades; and third, a perspective construction in three dimensions devised for an observer in a fixed position within the Papal *stanze*, and reinforced by the diminishing heights of the loggias as they recede towards the vanishing point" at the rear... [Ackerman 1986: 140; citing his *Cortile del Belvedere* (1954: 121 ff.)].

Initially, the courtyard was subdivided only by the varying levels of the terraced hillside. When the Vatican Library and the Braccio Nuovo (1817-1822) were built across the courtyard, they concealed the difference in levels except for the stairs that were required in the corridors on the ground floor.

The stanzas of the Vatican Palace, a series of large vaulted rooms in the palace, had been built during the reign of Nicholas V (1447-1455). The Belvedere was initially designed by Antonio Pollaiuolo mainly as a viewing pavilion that was one room wide and on the top of part of a wall around the Vatican (Lees-Milne 1967: 132). Julius II acquired the Apollo Belvedere in 1506 and the Laocoön in 1511 (141). Pius V (1559-1565) "...wanted to dispose of the collection of pagan sculpture in the Belvedere Court, but on being dissuaded merely stripped the walls of the reliefs and closed the court to the public. He did however present to the Roman Senate... the sculpture on the stairs leading to the Belvedere. ... He erected the Library cross the great courtyard, thus cutting it in half—in order to destroy the open-air theatre as much as to encourage learning" (199). Later popes had a first refusal on most new sculptures as they were excavated except when they ended up in the collections of papal families such as the Farnese. The present semi-octagonal courtyard of the Belvedere was rebuilt behind the original Belvedere in c. 1775 (Pietrangeli 1985; Macadam 2000).

The unique set of steps that Bramante had designed for the colossal niche he used to buttress the Belvedere consisted entirely of concentric circles, but the steps in front of the niche appeared to be project forward, and the steps within the niche appeared to recede (Pietrangeli 1985: fig. 12). In 1551 to provide a place at the front of the niche for the sculpted base of a triumphal column, Michelangelo replaced the curving steps of Bramante with a pair of straight steps flanking the column base. Considering that in 1555 Michelangelo used oval stairs for the vestibule of the Laurentian Library, he is likely to have adapted one feature of Bramante's set of steps, which spread outward at their base (Michelangelo 1963: II, 157).

The closest parallels in ancient architecture to the spiral ramp Bramante in tower adjacent to the Belvedere are the spiral staircases of Trajan's Column and Marcus Aurelius' Column, but they have no open space in the middle and are poorly lighted. His adaptation of Niccola Pisani's spiral stairs with an open center had great influence on similar staircases later designed by Raphael for the Villa Madama, by Antonio Sangallo the Younger for the well at Orvieto, by Borromini for the Palazzo Barberini, and by Palladio for the Carità (Vasari 1568: II, 42).

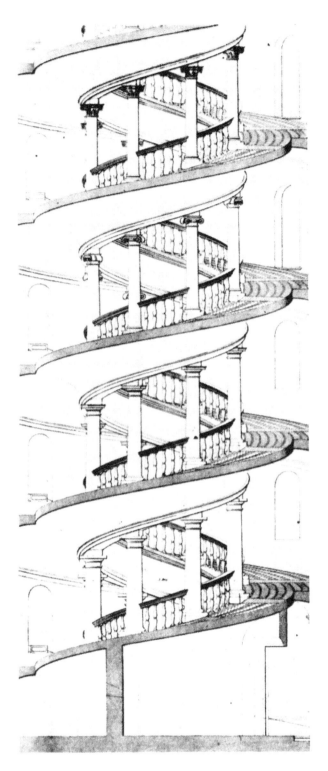

Spiral ramp for the Belvedere (Letarouilly)

Vatican Palace

The Vatican Palace was largely constructed during the Renaissance, and it consists principally of three separately constructed blocks of buildings that are interconnected: (1) the Sistine Chapel, (2) the Stanzas, and (3) the palace of Sixtus V. When viewed from the piazza in front of St. Peter's, these three blocks of buildings are seen from left to right or basically from west to east; it needs to be kept in mind that St. Peter's is unusual in having its front face east rather than in having its apse face east.

(1) The Sistine Chapel is parallel to the nave of St. Peter's, and it was built by Sixtus IV della Rovere (1471-1484), the uncle of Julius II (1503-1513), who had Michelangelo paint its ceiling. In between the Sistine Chapel and St. Peter's is the Scala Regia or royal entrance to the upper level of the Vatican Palace, the existing stairs of which were rebuilt by Bernini.

(2) The most important rooms of the stanza block were built by Nicholas V Parentucelli (1447-1455) and were painted primarily by Raphael, but this central block had been begun much in the 12th Century by Eugenius III Paganelli (1145-1148) and Innocent III dei Conti di Segni (1198-1216), and it had been substantially enlarged in the 13th Century by Nicholas III Orsini (1277-1280). When completed by Nicholas V da Corvara (1328-1330), it consisted basically of a cubical block with a small courtyard in the middle. A tower was added the northwest corner by Alexander VI Borgia (1492-1503), who resided on the lower floor of this block.

(3) The block to the right of the center is the main part of the present papal palace. Most of it was built Sixtus V Peretti (1485-1590). Having been built largely at one time, it was the most coherently designed part of the Vatican Palace, and it can be more readily perceived as a cube. It is almost ornamented entirely by window enframements and a cornice, and it too has a central courtyard like most Renaissance palaces.

In between the central block and the block to the right of it is a large courtyard with round-headed and glazed windows on three floors. This large courtyard, the Cortile di San Damaso, is a residual space between the two main blocks of the Vatican Palace rather than a separate building. The left-hand side of it was built by Julius II, and its upper floor has the Loggias of Raphael. The loggias were extended across two other sides of the courtyard Gregory XIII Boncompagni (1572-1585) to create the appearance of a coherent building, and he also added a wing to the north side of the palace created for Sixtus V.

In addition to the three main blocks of buildings closest to St. Peter's, the Vatican Palace includes two other separately constructed, but adjacent blocks of buildings: (4) the Belvedere and (5) the Belvedere Corridors that connect the Belvedere to the rest of the Vatican Palace.

(4) The Belvedere was begun as a villa by Innocenzo VIII, was enlarged by Julius II, and rebuilt and expanded from 1771-1793 as the Musei Pio-Clementino. It includes a semi-octagonal courtyard to display the most famous sculptures in the Vatican Museum, and it was constructed during the reigns of Clement XIV Ganganelli (1769-1774) and Pius VI Braschi (1775-1799).

(5) The Belvedere Courtyard was formed by corridors that were begun in 1505 by Julius II, who completed a substantial part of the east and north sides of the corridors. The west corridor was completed by Sixtus V and Pius IV de' Medici (1559-1565). This immense courtyard was eventually divided into three courtyards by the insertion of two wings in the middle: The wing for the Vatican Library was designed by Domenico Fontana and was built for Sixtus V from 1587-1589 (Hobson 1970: 81). The Braccio Nuovo was added in 1822 by Pius VII Chiaramonti (1800-1823) to display many of the finest ancient sculptures of the Vatican Museum. The courtyard to south of the library continued to be called the Cortile del Belvedere, and the courtyard to the north of the Braccio Nuovo was named the Cortile della Pigna (for the bronze pine cone that is displayed in the immense niche adjacent to the Belvedere).

This information on the history of the Vatican palace and museum is largely from a first-rate guidebook that is essential for understanding the development of the palace and how the museum relates to the palace: *Guida ai Musei e alla Città del Vaticano* (Monumenti, Musei e Gallerie Pontificie, 1986). This guidebook also has basic information on every major work of art on display and shows its location. The parts of the Vatican Palace that are most significance architecturally and artistically are the Sistine Chapel, the Stanzas, the corridors of the courtyard, and the Braccio Nuova, and only these three parts need to be illustrated and considered in further detail as part of an architectural history.

Cortile di San Damaso of the Vatican Palace with Bramante's additons on the left side (Specchi)

Loggia of Raphael (no. 982)

Santa Maria della Consolazione, Todi (begun 1508)

As Arnaldo Bruschi pointed out about various workmen who have been considered to have designed Santa Maria della Consolazione in Todi,

> given that the finished house of worship is the fruit of a range of contributions from many different master craftsmen, stonemasons, and consultants, the "author" of this design is not exactly the same as the "author" of the church as it stands today. It is worth affirming at this point that no one of the various *masetri* that appear in the archives (leaving aside the occasional consults and those involved in the dome) is a true "creative" architect as such. They are all in their own way executors of antoher person's design. In the first, decisive phase of construction (ca. 1508-14), Cola da Caprarola, as made plain by his anagraphical data (Bentivoglio 1982), worked here as elsewhere as a building contractor; he was active in the province, but from the time of Pope Alexander VI worked in the shadow of Anatonio da Sangallo the Elder, Bramante and their desciples. The man known as Giovanpietro or "Il Cione" is no more than a stonecutter, though, like Cola, not without some notions of architecture. ...Despite each craftsmans specialized contribution to the execution of the building, but not one was a true architect, capable of ideating and drafting the overall project for S. Maria della Consolazione [Bruschi 1994: 518].

Bruschi concluded that this church was certainly designed by an architect even though he could not be positively identified and that Bramante was a possibility. Considering that Bramante worked at nearby Loretto around the same time and that his initial design for St. Peter's was so similar, the possibility that he was the architect is greater than than any well documented workman was the architect. It would also be a mistake to consider every major building to have been designed by a major architect, but when there are close similarities and the architect was present and likely to have been involved, the greater probality should be accepted unless better evidence becomes available. To attribute undocumented skills to workmen is more likely to be a mistake.

Santa Maria delle Consolazione, Todi (Anderson in Heydenreich and Lotz)

MICHELANGELO

Michelangelo apprenticed with a painter and studied with a sculptor, and he later taught himself to be an architect. Although he began as a painter, he wrote "...it seems to me that painting may be held to be good in the degree in which it approximates to relief, and relief to be bad to in the degree in which it approximates to painting," but he acknowledged that both might be made equally good (Michelangelo 1963: 75). His approach to architecture was similarly sculptural with unified compositions, sculpted space, and sculptural details. He continually insisted his profession was sculpture even after having painted the Sistine ceiling, and he continued throughout his life to sculpt on a regular basis for exercise and because he liked to sculpt, but he ceased entirely to accept commissions as a sculptor when he was commissioned to compete St. Peter's in 1547, and for the last 17 years of his life, his profession was architecture. This account is about how he became capable of designing St. Peter's and why he was permitted to do so.

When he was 14 years old in 1488, Michelangelo was apprenticed for three years to Domenico and David di Tommaso di Currado (Ghirlandaio), and he then learned to paint frescoes. A 1485 fresco by Ghirlandaio provides a good indication of how much Michelangelo learned about painting frescoes, how differently his own style became, and what a Renaissance interior looked like by those who could afford to furnish them with ornamented architectural elements, sculpture, painting, and intarsia.

Fresco by Ghirlandaio of the birth of the Virgin Mary

In 1489 Michelangelo also began to learn how to sculpt and to cast bronzes by studying with Bertoldo di Giovanni, who had been a pupil of Donatello and who was employed by Lorenzo the Magnificent to teach promising Florentine youths (Vasari 1568 [1971]: 18). By the time Michelangelo was 25, he had completed the Pietà, and "through it he acquired great fame and reputation so much that already in the opinion of the world, he had not only far surpassed any other any of his time, and of the time before him, but he even rivaled the ancients" (Condivi 1553: 27). His fame was further augmented when he sculpted the David from 1501-1504 and painted the ceiling of the Sistine Chapel from 1508-1512, and he was then considered as great a painter as a sculptor (Ramsden in Michelangelo 1963: lviii-lxi).

Although Michelangelo never apprenticed under an architect, he no doubt learned a great deal about architecture and engineering from Lorenzo de' Medici and Guiliano da Sangallo during the years he lived in the Palazzo Medici and while Lorenzo's villas were under construction. Knowledge he surely acquired in his youth was ready for use when he designed better scaffolding for the Sistine Chapel than Bramante had proposed and when he designed fortifications for the city of Florence. It was to Giuliano that Michelangelo justified abandoning work on the tomb of Julius II and from Giuliano that he learned how to correct faults in the application of stucco for the Sistine Ceiling. Giuliano had recommended that Michelangelo paint the ceiling when Julius refused to permit the tomb to be completed during his lifetime. The important relationship with Giuliano no doubt began in Florence, continued in Rome, and provided sound introduction to structural requirements that Michelangelo drew upon as he gradually taught himself how to design buildings.

Michelangelo's first work of architecture to be largely designed by him that was constructed was the Medici Chapel (1520-1534), but it was built on existing foundations and was required to be have the same plan as Brunelleschi's Old Sacristy and also to have a dome; this was largely a sculptural commission, but the architectural part of it was completed.

The commission for the Laurentian Library provided Michelangelo with the first opportunity to show what he was capable of doing as an architect, but it was an addition on top of an existing building (1524-1534); it was completed several decades later.

Before redesigning St. Peter's Michelangelo's principal architectural commission was the Capitol in Rome in 1539-1564), but the project consisted of adding fronts to two exiting buildings and redesigning the piazza; the only entirely new building was constructed after his death, and it lartely duplicated the front of the flanking building opposite it. The only other significant commission before St. Peter's was to compete the Palazzo Farnese (1546-15490), which had been designed and largely constructed by another architect.

In 1547 when Michelangelo was nearly 72 years old and was put in charge of the construction of St. Peter's, its plan and scale had established by Bramante several decades earlier, and enough of it had been vaulted that its interior design had mainly to be followed, and when he was appointed, he had produced no comprehensive set of designs himself yet he was permitted to completely redesign the exterior and to make major changes in the interior (1547-1564). The best parts of the greatest building of the Renaissance are the ones he designed, and his designs for St. Peter's made him one of the greatest and most influential architects of all time.

How Michelangelo taught himself to be an architect is worth considering in some detail, and I have focused on this aspect of his life. To reconstruct his final intentions, I have relied very largely on primary sources: on the buildings themselves and his letters, drawings, and models. Secondarily, I have relied on the two main biographies written about him by writers who knew him well. The best evidence more than suffices to provide an outline of how Michelangelo taught himself to become an architect and came to be trusted with the most important commission since the end of the Ancient World.

Although I have checked my conclusions against a number of secondary sources, I have not attempted to deal with the innumerable uncertainties and controversies about Michelangelo's architectural designs. Instead, I have tried to bring together the most certain evidence about how he became an architect and how he approached architectural design and construction.

Three additional projects also deserve to be considered in some detail: Michelangelo's architectural design for the tomb of Julius II (1505-1545) and his architectural framework for the Sistine ceiling (1508-1512). He was hired for the tomb as a sculptor and for the ceiling as a painter, but he needed a setting for his sculpture and painted figures, and they are as important to consider as the sculptural settings for the front of San Lorenzo and for the interior of the Medici Chapel. The tomb and the ceiling were his introduction to architectural design. They were minor architectural commissions, but they were important for his development as an architect. A church for the Florentines in Rome (1559) was to have been a completely new building, but it was not constructed.

Tomb of Julius II

A reconstruction of the free-standing Tomb of Julius II (Panofsky 1937 in Argan and Contardi)

Work on a tomb for Julius II della Rovere continued intermittently for four decades from 1505-1545. During most of his adult life, Michelangelo was plagued by what Condivi referred to as "the tragedy of the tomb" (Condivi 1553 [1976]: 77; translated by Wohl). The tomb is important to consider in a book about architecture because it represents Michelangelo's first architectural design and because, according to Condivi, the initial enthusiasm that Julius had for the initial design for the tomb caused him to decide to rebuilt St. Peter's Basilica to have a more suitable place for his tomb. Michelangelo was 29 years old in 1504 when he completed the colossal statue of David, and "through it, he acquired great fame and reputation, so much that, already in the opinion of the world, he not only far surpassed any other man of his time, and of the time before him, but he even rivaled the ancients" (27). Although the colossal statues of Castor and Pollux in Rome were equivalent in size, Michelangelo's statue showed a far greater knowledge of anatomy. In 1505 the architect Giuliano da Sangallo persuaded Julius to require Michelangelo to come to Rome, which

Michelangelo did not want to do because he was under contract to sculpt a statue of a disciple (Matthew) for the Duomo in Florence and to paint a large fresco of the Battle of Càscina for the council chamber of the city (in competition with Leonardo, who was painting another fresco dealing with the Pisan War (Vasari 1568: II, 268). Julius II

> ...sent for the artist, who was then about twenty-nine, to make his tomb, paying him one hundred crowns for the journey. After reaching Rome, it was many months before he did anything. At last he settled on a design for the tomb, surpassing in beauty and richness of ornament all ancient and imperial tombs, affording the best evidence of his genius. Stimulated by this, Julius decided to rebuild S. Pietro in order to hold the tomb, as related elsewhere [Vasari 1568: IV, 119].

Michelangelo later recalled that "after many designs for his Tomb, one of them pleased him, on the basis of which we made a bargain" (Michelangelo 1963: I, 191; translated by Ramsden). Although a specific design was then selected, nothing is known about what the tomb would initially have looked like or even where it would have been located. In 1506, while still working on the tomb, he wrote that the tomb was to have been "...set up in St. Peter's, wherever he chooses, and that it shall be a work of art such as I have promised; for I am certain that if it is carried out, there will be nothing to equal it the world over" (I, 15).

In 1505, Michelangelo had spent from six to eight months quarrying marble at Carrara and having it transported to Rome, where he began work on the tomb in the Castle Sant'Angelo (Hadrian's Tomb). "I went and brought both marbles and men to Rome and I began to work on the frame and the figures.... But at the end of eight or nine months the Pope changed his mind and did not want to go on with it..." (191). "As very often happens at court, the many great favors thus conferred gave rise to envy and, after envy, endless persecutions. Thus the architect Bramante, who was loved by the pope, made him change his plans by quoting what common people say, that it is bad luck for anyone to build his tomb during his lifetime, and other stories" (Condivi 1553: 30). Since Michelangelo had designed a free-standing tomb by 1505 and since Bramante's Santa Casa at Loreto was begun in 1509, the overall resemblance in form and size between the two projects should be attributed to Michelangelo's influence on Bramante rather than the other way around.

Michelangelo wrote in 1506, "I immediately left Rome in a rage. ... After about seven or eight months which I spent practically in hiding through fear for the Pope was furious with me, I was forced, not being able to remain in Florence, to go and sue to him for mercy to Bologna. That was the first time he went there [on a military campaign], where he kept me for about two years to execute his statue in bronze..." (Michelangelo 1963: 191-192). Although the statue was completed for the front of the cathedral of Bologna, it was soon destroyed, and the bronze was recast as a canon to be used against Julius.

Julius next required Michelangelo to spend three additional years from 1509-1512 painting the ceiling of the Sistine Chapel, which had been constructed by his uncle Sixtus IV, and that work will be discussed later for its architectural significance. Finally, a few months before Julius died, Michelangelo made new designs for the tomb in November 1512, and two days before his death in February 1513, Julius willed that 10,000 ducats be spent to construct a tomb for him in the older Sistine or Giulia Chapel, where Sixtus had been buried (Ramsden in Michelangelo 1563: I, 250; II, 253). The amount was ten times what Julius had spent in 1505 on the marble for his tomb.

There is uncertainty about what designs Julius approved, but after his death four contracts survive between the executors of his estate (the Cardinal of Quattro Santi Coronati [Lorenzo Pucci] and Cardinal Aginense [Leonardo Gross della Rovere]). In March of 1513, the executors wanted an even grander tomb and agreed to pay Michelangelo 16,500 ducts or half again more to complete a tomb with 40 figures larger than life, and the contract stipulated that the tomb was to be completed within seven years and that during this time he was to work on nothing else. From 1513 to 1516 he worked happily on the tomb and completed at least the two bound captives that are now in the Louvre and almost certainly the statue of Moses as well. Condivi described what the architecture and sculpture of the tomb with 40 figures would have been like, and this tomb on the larger scale they had stipulated was unquestionably a free-standing structure designed by Michelangelo himself:

> And to give some idea of it, I will say briefly that this tomb was to have had four faces: two were to have been eighteen *braccia* long to serve as the sides, and two of twelve *braccia* as head and foot, so that it came to a square and a half [that is, 36 by 24 feet in plan with the proportions of 3:2]. All around he exterior there were niches for statues and between each niche and the next there were terms [herms] to which other statues [in front of them] were bound like captives, upon certain cubical bases which rose from the ground and projected outward. These represented the liberal arts, such as painting, sculpture, and architecture, each with its attributes so that it could easily be recognized for what it was, signifying thereby that all the artistic virtues were prisoners of death together with Pope Julius, as they would never find another to favor and foster them as he did. Above these statues ran a cornice which bound the whole work together on which level there were four large statues, one of which namely the *Moses*, appears in S. Pietro in Vincoli; and this will be discussed in its proper place. Continuing upward [on a second story], the work terminated in a surface upon which there were two angels, supporting a sarcophagus; one of them seemed to smile as if rejoicing that the soul of the pope had been received among the blessed spirits, the other to weep as if grieving that the world should be stripped of such a man. Through one end [of the tomb], the one which was at the upper side, one entered into a small chamber within the tomb resembling a *tempietto*, in the center of which was a marble chest where the body of the pope was to be placed; everything was executed with marvelous artistry. In short, the whole work involved more than forty statues, not counting the narrative scenes in bronze in *mezzo-relievo*, all pertinent to the subject, in which the deeds of this great pope were to be seen [Condivi 1553 (1976): 33-34; with footnotes and figure numbers omitted].

The second edition of Vasari has a similar description for the tomb with 40 figures, but with more specific information about the figures, their placement on the tomb, and their eventual dispersion:

> Of this work Michelangelo executed during the lifetime and after the death of Julius four statues completed and eight which were only blocked out, as I shall describe. Since the design of the tomb illustrates Michelangelo's extraordinary powers of invention, we shall describe here the plan that he followed. To give a sense of grandeur he intended the tomb to be free-standing so as to be seen from all four sides. The sides measured twenty-four feet in one direction and thirty-six in the other, the dimensions therefore being a square and a half. All round the outer side of the tomb were a range of niches, divided one from the other by terminal figures ([resembling herms] clothed from the middle upwards) which supported the first cornice with their heads [resembling caryatids]; and each of these figures had fettered to it, in a strange and curious attitude, a nude captive standing on a projection of the base [a pedestal projecting from the podium]. These captives were meant to represent all the provinces subjected by the Pope and made obedient to the Apostolic Church; and there were various other statues, also fettered, of all the liberal arts and sciences, which were thus shown to be subject to death no less than the pontiff himself, who employed them so honourably. On the corners of the first cornice were to go four large figures, representing [1] the Active and

[2] the Contemplative Life, [3] St Paul, and [4] Moses. The tomb rose above the cornice in gradually diminishing steps, with a decorated bronze frieze, and with other figures, putti, and ornaments all around; and at the summit, completing the structure, were two figures, one of which was Heaven, smiling and supporting a bier on her shoulder, and the other, Cybele, the goddess of the Earth, who appeared to be grief-stricken to having to remain in a world robbed of all virtue through the death of such a great man, in contrast to Heaven who is shown rejoicing that his soul had passed to celestial glory. The tomb was arranged so that one might enter and come out between the niches at the ends of the quadrangle; and the interior was in the shape of an oval, curving like a temple. The sarcophagus to take the Pope's dead body was to go in the middle. Finally, the tomb was to have forty marble statues, not to mention the other scenes, putti, and ornamentation, and the richly carved cornices and other architectural elements. To hurry the work on, Michelangelo arranged that some of the marble should be taken to Florence, where he intended at times to pass the summer in order to void the malaria of Rome; and there he executed one side of the work in several sections down to the last detail. With his own hand he finished in Rome two of the captives which were truly inspired, and other statues which have never been surpassed. And they were never used for the tomb, these captives were given by Michelangelo to Roberto Strozzi, when he happened to be lying ill in his house. Subsequently they were sent as a gift to King of France, and they are now at Ecouen in France [in the Louvre]. In Rome he also blocked out eight statues, and in Florence another five [four of which that were in the Boboli Gardens are now in the Accademia and the fifth is in the Casa Buonarroti], along with a Victory surmounting the figures of a captive, which are now in the possession of Duke Cosimo, to whom they were given by Michelangelo's nephew, Leonardo. His excellency has put the Victory in the Great Hall of his palace [the Palazzo Vecchio], which was painted by Vasari. Michelangelo also finished the Moses, a beautiful statute in marble ten feet high. With this no other modern work will ever bear comparison (nor indeed do the statues of the ancient world [Vasari 1553 (1971): 34-36]

As this description indicates, the bound captives symbolized the provinces captured by Julius while leading his armies, and the figures in niches represented "the liberal arts and sciences" (as was to be indicated by various emblems or implements).

When Vasari's description is compared to Condivi's description, it is evident that the free-standing tomb with 40 large sculptures was to have two niches in front and back and three niches on each side. Since the tomb was to be half-again larger on its sides than on the front and back, there were to be 10 niches with standing statues somewhat larger than life to represent the arts and sciences. Flanking these niches were to be pairs of nude captives for a total of 20 additional figures that were also to be somewhat larger than life, and Vasari accounts for 15 of the 20 nude or nearly nude statues. On the second level were to be four seated figures about twice the size of life (like the Moses), and on the third level was to be three smaller figures (Julius with two angels or victories). This accounts for 37 of the 40 large figures that were planned for the free-standing tomb. No information is available to account for the other three statues, but two additional seated statues twice the size of life are shown in the drawing reproduced as being on the sides on the second level (no doubt in the middle above the central niches on the sides). Presumably the statue of "Victory" (the male nude with his knee on an old man who appears to be Michelangelo) would have been inside the tomb since there was no room left for it on the outside. Vasari is explicit that the two statures in the niches for the front of the tomb of Julius II "...were to have contained the Victories. Instead of the Victories, however, in one of the niches [of the cenotaph] he placed a figure of Leah, the daughter of Laban, to represent the Active Life... In the other niche he placed a figure of Leah's sister, Rachel, representing the Contemplative Life.... Michelangelo executed these statues himself in less than a year" in order to complete the cenotaph without the two nude men who had been competed previously and were to have gone on either side of a single niche (Vasari 1568: 70). A copy of an early design for the tomb seems to show two female winged-victories in the front niches of the lower story standing in front of small reclining figures, and those standing statues must have had attributes to indicate that they represented the arts or sciences. Other than Moses, Paul, and possibly two angels (or more victories), the statue was essentially pagan. For symmetry, the statues he had planned to represent the Active and Contemplative Life on the free-standing tomb on the same level as the statues of Moses would have needed to be colossal and seated.

From when Julius II died in November of 1512 until the middle of 1515, Michelangelo worked intensively on the tomb. In June of 1515 he wrote, "...I must make a great effort here this summer to finish the work as soon as possible, because afterwards I anticipate having to enter the Pope's service. And for this I've bought some twenty-thousand weight of copper, in order to cast certain figures" (Michelangelo 1963: 90). This does not mean he was nearly through, but that he had been advanced enough money to proceed with the work more rapidly. In August of 1515 he wrote, "since I returned from Florence I have done no work at all; I have devoted my attention to making models and to preparing the work, in such a way that I can make one great effort with a host of workmen to finish the work in two or three years" (94). These were evidently full-sized models to be used by *scarpellini* to rough out the marble statues. He had a scarpellino working for him as early as 1506, and he had hired a different one by 1508 (Ramsden in Michelangelo 1963: 11-12, n. 12; 46-47, n. 2). With assistance, he was confident that he could complete the tomb by 1518 and then be free to work of Leo X on any commission that might be required of him.

The year 1516 was also the same year in which Leo asked Michelangelo to work on the church of San Lorenzo, which the Medici took over, and the same year in which the heirs of Julius decided to pay the same price of 16,500 ducats for only 22 figures rather than the 40 Michelangelo had agreed to provide, and they paid him 3,000 ducats for work already completed and allowed two additional years for the completion of the tomb. Though they stipulated that Michelangelo was to do no other work that would prevent him for completing the tomb in a total of the nine years starting in 1513, Leo X told Michelangelo he would deal with the heirs. The two heirs were both cardinals and were in even less of a position to disagree with Leo than the deposed Duke of Urbino.

Michelangelo prided himself on his fairness as, for example, in dealing with workmen, but he also put his family above his own well being, and before he was well known, when he needed money for his father and brothers, he passed off two sculptures of his own as antique statues to get a higher price for them. In 1509, he wrote to his father, "...for twelve years now I have gone about all over Italy, leading a miserable life; I have borne every kind of humiliation, suffered every kind of hardship, worn myself to the bone with every kind of labour, risked my life in a thousand dangers solely to help my family..." (Michelangelo 1963: 52). In 1512 he added, "...I live wearied by stupendous labours and beset by a thousand anxieties. And thus have I lived for some fifteen years now and never had an hour's happiness have I had, and all this have I done in order to help you..." (75). He continued to help his relations for the rest of his life.

The projects Michelangelo worked on for the Medici will be considered later, but to complete the history of the tomb, it should be noted here that in 1520 Leo cancelled his contract with Michelangelo for the front of San Lorenzo and required him to create the Medici Chapel instead. Leo died in 1521, and the next pope, Adrian VI, restored the Duke of Urbino. The heirs of Julius then wanted the tomb completed or to be repaid part of the 8,500 ducats they had already advanced rather than paying the remaining amount that had been agreed. The circumstances changed again in 1523 when Clement VII de' Medici succeeded Adrian, and in 1524 Clement added to

Michelangelo's assignments the creation of the Laurentian Library.

In 1525 Michelangelo took action to prevent a lawsuit over the tomb and to free him to work solely for the Pope:

> ...I don't want to go to law. They can't go to law if I admit that I'm in the wrong. I'll assume that I've been to law and have lost and must pay up. This I'm prepared to do. Therefore, if the Pope will help me in this matter, which would be a great favour, seeing that, whether through old age or ill health, I cannot finish the said Tomb, he, as an intermediary, can make it known that he wishes me to return what I've receive for its execution, so that I can be quit of this burden; and the relatives of the said Pope, having obtained restitution, can have it done to their satisfaction by someone else. ...I'll make restitution and be able to give my mind to the Pope's concerns and get on with the work, since it is I do not live life at all, much less do I work. There is no course that could be taken that would be safer for me, nor more acceptable to me, nor a greater relief to my mind, and it could be done amicably and without going to law [Michelangelo 1963: I, 159].

The executors of Julius's estate were unwilling to release Michelangelo, and negotiations continued until 1532 before a new contract was agreed to. In August 1525, he wrote, "...the said Tomb is more than half finished and of the six figures mentioned in the contract four are done [and] ...in my house in Rome" (161). In September, he wrote, as to executing the said Tomb of Julius as a wall tomb, like those of Pius ["The Tombs of Pius II and of Pius III."], I am agreeable to the method, which is quicker than any other" (162). Around the same time, he decided to make wall tombs in the Medici Chapel rather than free-standing tombs as he had initially planned for Julius II and for the Medici tombs.

> Clement descried an excellent opportunity to extract Michelangelo and to be free to employ him as he wished, so he sent for him and said, "Come now, you say that you want to build this tomb but that you want to know who is to pay you for the rest of it." Michelangelo, who knew what the pope wanted, that he would have liked to employ him in his own service answered, "And if someone can be found to pay me? To which Pope Clement said, "You are quite mad if you imagine that anyone is about to come forward who would offer you a penny." Thus, when Messer Tommaso, his attorney, appeared in court and made a proposal to this effect to the duke's agents, they began to look each other in the face and they concluded together that he should at least build a tomb for the amount he had received. As Michelangelo felt that a good settlement had been reached, he willingly agreed.... The agreement was this: that Michelangelo was to build a tomb with a single façade and that he was to use those marbles which had already been worked on for the rectangular tomb, adapting them as best he could. And thus he as under obligation to provide six statues by his own hand [Condivi 1553: 72].

This compromise finally resulted in a new contract in 1532 in which Michelangelo would make a wall tomb similar to two tombs in Old St. Peter's, and a third contract was signed, but before he was able to make a new design and get it approved, the duke's agent became seriously ill, Rome was sacked, and Florence was besieged. In 1531 Michelangelo again proposed to execute a free-standing tomb with 22 figures if the remaining 8,000 ducats of the earlier contract were paid in advance, but as Clement had predicted, the Duke of Urbino agreed to accept a wall tomb with six statues by Michelangelo for the 8,500 ducats that the heirs had already paid. In a new contract Michelangelo was given three additional years in which to construct the wall tomb (Ramsden in Michelangelo 1963: I, 255-258).

Mainly through having to work on papal projects, Michelangelo was unable to complete even a tomb with six statues. In 1531 Clement had forbid Michelangelo to work on projects for anyone else in order to complete the work on the Medici Chapel and Laurentian Library as quickly as possible, and in 1534 he ordered him to paint the Last Judgment in the Sistine Chapel. Michelangelo arrived in Rome two days before the death of Clement, but remained in Rome for the remainder of his life. The next pope, Paul III Farnese insisted that Michelangelo paint the Last Judgment, which was painted from 1535-1541; and afterwards Paul III insisted that he paint the Pauline Chapel from 1542-1545.

In the meanwhile, in 1536 Paul annulled the penalties that the third contract had imposed for non-fulfillment, and in 1538 the Duke of Urbino died, and his son and successor, the proverbially courteous Guidobaldo, wrote that Michelangelo should have as much time as he needed.

A petition by a representative of Michelangelo asked Paul III to intervene stated that he "...being an old man, and desiring to serve his Holiness with all his powers; being also constrained and compelled by him in the matter and being unable to do so, unless he is first released entirely from this work of Pope Julius, which keeps him in a state of physical and mental suspense..." (II, 21). Yet another contract was agreed to in 1542, and only three statues by Michelangelo himself rather than six were to be used for the tomb, and three additional statues that has been roughed out to his design were to be completed by Raffaello da Montelupo. Michelangelo was to be fully released from all obligations as soon as he personally completed work on the statue of Moses and allegorical statues of the Active and Contemplative Life (Ramsden in Michelangelo 1963: II, 19-22, 251-253; see pp. 244-250). By 1534 Michelangelo had completed the statue of Moses except for the final finish (Condivi 1553: 77). He had also completed the two nude captives that are now in the Louvre, but he agreed to complete two clothed females instead to go in the niches that flank Moses.

Michelangelo was still working on the three statues for the tomb in November 1542, but distracted by Paul's insistence that he execute two large frescoes for the Pauline Chapel (Michelangelo 1963: II, 32). To complete the tomb of Julius, two assistants augmented "the architectural frame and ornament," and they were supposed to work alternately, but they disagreed so much that he did much of the work himself to keep them from fighting or killing one another. "I have lost a month of my time on the said work, owing to their bestial ineptitude..." (Michelangelo 1963: II, 16). A reference to a "crowning pediment" presumably refers to the lunette with a coat of arms and four candelabra (21).

Michelangelo planned to finish only the Moses (Michelangelo 1963: II, 252). Da Montelupo was to have been paid

> ...for finishing five marble statues, begun and blocked out by me..., that is, Our Lady with the Child in her arms, a Sibyl, a Prophet, and Active Life and a Contemplative Life.... Of these five statues, Our Lord having at my entreaty and in order to gratify me granted me a little time, I finished two myself, that is the Contemplative Life and the Active, for the same price for which the said Raffaello was to do them, and out of the same money he would have had. And afterwards the said Raffaello finished the other three and built them into the said Tomb, as may be seen [45-46].

De Montelupo got sick and "...has had the work done by others" (44-45). Michelangelo was so dissatisfied with the results that he subsequently refused to recommend him for another commission. The awkwardly placed statue of Julius was added later and was probably made by Maso del Bosco.

The cenotaph was finally completed in 1545 (Michelangelo 1963: II, 21, 46). Condivi wrote, "today it may be seen in S. Pietro in Vincoli, not conforming to the first design of four façades, but with one façade which is one of the shorter sides, not detached all around but standing against a wall..." (Condivi 1553: 77). Of the 40 statues that were to have been executed by Michelangelo, only three were fully executed by him, and the others are greatly inferior. Since little work on the new St. Peter's had been completed by 1545, the tomb of Julius design became a cenotaph that was put in his titular church of San Pietro in Vincoli in a place where the light was good. About a year later, on January 1, 1547, Paul III put Michelangelo in charge of completing St. Peter's, where Julius was buried.

Condivi concluded about the tomb that "...patched up and reworked as it is, it is still the most meritorious tomb to be found in Rome and perhaps elsewhere, if for no other reason, at least by virtue of the three statues there which are by the hand of the master" (Condivi 1553: 77).

What is considered to be the earliest designs for Julius' tomb had columns rather on the lower story rather than bound captives. The upper story large statues at each of its corners, and one of the four was Moses, the centerpiece of the final version of the tomb. The structure stepped back, and the statures rested on the upper surface of the first story. In the center of the second story was a cenotaph or symbolic sarcophagus. Although the exact form of the monument is uncertain at any given stage, the surviving drawings indicate that it would have utilized a substantial number of classical architectural elements. Julius' sarcophagus would have been in an oval room in the ground floor of his tomb.

Upon being persuaded by Bramante that it was unlucky to construct a tomb during his lifetime, Julius had Michelangelo work instead on a seated bronze stature that was placed on the front of San Petronio in Bologna, a project which took two years. This statue was soon melted down to create a canon to use against Julius.

Early alternative designs for the tomb of Julius II (De Tolnay)

Design for a wall tomb for Julius II (anon. copy; Grimm)

Final design for the cenotaph of Julius II (Alinari)

Sistine Chapel Ceiling

Sistine Chapel (albumen by Anderson)

Composition of the Sistine Ceiling (detail; Symonds)

Sixtus IV, the uncle of Julius II, commissioned the creation of the Sistine Chapel as a palace chapel. Although it is in between the papal palace and St. Peter's, it was attached to the palace and was not accessible from the basilica.

The chapel is a large and well constructed building designed in the Romanesque style, and it was made as secure as if it were intended to serve also as a fortress, which it resembles and is closer to the palace than Castel St. Angelo (Hadrian's Tomb). The only windows in the chapel are in the uppermost part of its walls, and the only elaboration of the exterior is a row of crenellations. Its nearly featureless, but well lighted interior was embellished until it became the world's greatest art gallery. The interior dimensions are 40.5 m. long, 13.2 m. wide, and 20.7 m. high, and every square inch of its walls and ceiling were eventually covered with frescoes. Since soon after it was constructed, it has also served as the place where most popes have been elected.

Vasari attributed the design of the chapel and of numerous other buildings to Baccio Pontelli (1449-c. 1500). He wrote that

...there lived in Rome, under Pope Sixtus IV, one Baccio Pintelli [or "Pontelli"], a Florentine, who was deservedly employed by the Pope for every construction undertaken by him, on account of his skill in architecture. Thus it was from his design that the church and convent of S. Maria del Popolo were constructed ["1477-80"], and some chapels there with much ornamentation.... The same Pope constructed a palace in the Borgo Vecchio from Baccio's design, which was then considered a fine and well-planned edifice. The Pope also made the large library under the apartment of Niccola and the so-called Sistine chapel in the palace which is adorned with fine paintings ["carried out in 1473 by Giovanni de' Dolci" (d. 1486)]. He further rebuilt the new hospital of S. Spirito in Sassia.... He also made the Ponte Sisto called after him [Sixtus].... Similarly in the year of jubilee, 1475, he erected a number of small churches in Rome, to be recognized by the arms of Pope Sixtus, notably S. Apostolo, S. Pietro in Vincula, and S. Sisto. For the Cardinal Guglielmo, bishop of Ostia he made the model of his church and of the façade and staircases in their present form. Many affirm that the design of the church of S Pietro a Montorio at Rome was also by Braccio, but I cannot truthfully say that I have found this to be so. ... The worth of Baccio was so highly valued by the Pope that he would never undertake any building without his advice [Vasari 1568: II, 10].

Pontelli was unquestionably a highly skilled architect and engineer, and his bridge has survived intact even though an ancient Roman bridge in the same vicinity was pushed over in a flood. The Sistine Chapel is essentially intact, but buttresses have been added. The chapel had been constructed by Giovannino de' Dolci from 1473-1484.

Architectural historians had argued that Pontelli is unlikely to have designed all of the buildings Vasari attributed to him, yet have attributed other buildings to him that Vasari did not mention (Heydenreich and Lotz 1974: 62-79 *passim*; Frommel 2007: 91-97). In any case, Pontelli was the principal architect in Rome during the reign of Sixtus from 1471 (the year before Alberti died) to 1484 and also the architect also of many buildings subsequently constructed until 1500 (the year in which Bramante is said to have moved permanently to Rome and the approximate year of Pontelli's death).

When Michelangelo began to paint the ceiling of the chapel, the ceiling was painted blue with golden stars. The walls of the chapel had with 16 large panels that had been painted by some of the most famous artists in Italy and by some who were even then were less well known (Vasari 1568: I, 54). Of the 16, three have been destroyed (two to make room for Michelangelo's Last Judgment and one accidentally). Above the 16 panels and in between the windows of the clearstory are 28 standing figures of early popes that were part of the original painting project, and the lower part of the wall was painted to resemble curtains.

The 16 panels on the walls were frescoes painted from 1481 to 1483 by about a dozen artists and their assistants. There are six scenes on each of the longer sides of the chapel, and there were two scenes at each end. Looking from the altar, the eight paintings on the left half of the chapel were scenes from the life of Moses, and the eight paintings on the right half of the chapel were scenes from the life of Jesus. Each scene was chosen to correspond in at least some respect, and some panels depict multiple events in different parts of a single scene. This complex program had obviously been worked out in advance by a theologian and possibly by Bartolomeo della Gatta, the Abbot of San Clemente at Arezzo. He was responsible for painting one of the panels of the chapel, but "...in conjunction with Luca of Cortona and Pietro Perugino..." (Vasari 1568: II, 62). He was best known as an illuminator, and he had previously made a missal for presentation to Sixtus IV (61). He is the only painter involved in the project who was also a cleric. In any case, many theologians must previously have pointed out ways in which the lives of Moses and Jesus could be made to seem similar despite their fundamental differences.

Sandro Botticelli painted three panels, and was already so highly regarded that "...that Pope Sixtus IV entrusted him with the direction of the painting of the chapel which he was building in his palace at Rome" (Vasari 1568: II, 86-87). The only other artist responsible for three panels was Cosimo Rosselli, who was not considered one of the best painters in Italy, but who nonetheless won the competition for having painted the best panel (53-55). Domenico Ghirlandaio (Michelangelo's painting teacher) painted two scenes. Pietro Perugino (Raphael's first painting teacher) painted two scenes, but had assistance with both; "Pietro's fame being spread abroad throughout Italy he was to his great glory, invited to Rome by Pope Sixtus IV to work in the chapel with other famous artists..." (130), but because he repeated himself so often, "…he richly deserved Michelagnolo's [Michelangelo's] publicly-uttered description of him as a blockhead in art, as well as other rough words from the artists" (132). Luca Signorelli, who influenced Michelangelo, painted a scene by himself and assisted Perugino with another scene; "being summoned by Pope Sixtus to work in the chapel of the palace with other painters, he did two scenes..., which are reckoned among the best..." (148). "Luca's works were always highly praised by Michelagnolo, who in his divine Last Judgment in the chapel partly borrowed from Luca such things as angels, demons, the arrangement of the heavens, and other things in which Michelagnolo imitated Luca's treatment as all may see" (147). Thus, in addition to being compared to what Raphael was then creating in the Stanzas, Michelangelo knew he would be compared to the artists already represented in the chapel. Moreover, with the assistance of il Fattore (Giovanni Francesco Penni), Raphael later designed a set of tapestries to cover the lower walls of the chapel on special occasions, and the comparison with Raphael was made even more intentional and direct (300).

Cosimo Rosselli, "...although not a very rare or excellent painter, produced some very meritorious works." He was not highly regarded by the other artists (Vasari 1568: II, 53).

> It is said that the Pope had offered a prize to the painter who in his judgment should acquit himself the best. When the scenes were finished His Holiness went to see them and judge how far the painters had striven to earn the reward and honour Conscious of his weakness in invention and design, Cosimo had endeavoured to cover these defects by using the finest ultramarine and other bright colours, illuminating the whole with a quantity of gold, so that there was not a tree, a blade, a garment or a cloud which was not illuminated, in order that the Pope who knew very little of art, might be convinced that he ought to award the prize to him. When the day came for uncovering all the works the artists laughed at Cosimo and chaffed him, making jokes at his expense instead of pitying him. But the event proved that they were deceived, for, as Cosimo had expected, the Pope, being ignorant of such matters, though he took great

delight in them, judged that Cosimo had done much better than all the rest. Accordingly he received the prize, while the pope directed the other to cover their pictures with the best ultramarine which they could find, and touch them up with gold so as to make them resemble that of Cosimo in richness and colouring [54-55].

Botticelli probably thought he would win since he had been acknowledged to be the best painter by being put in charge of the execution of the project, and he had increased his chance to win by depicting the hospital of Sixtus as the centerpiece of one panel as if it were of equivalent importance to the Arch of Constantine that he included as the centerpiece of another panel. Notably, Perugino included a centrally designed church flanked by two triumphal arches in one of his panels. Cosimo won the competition with another essentially architectural composition as a setting for the Last Supper: in a semi-octagonal alcove, he placed a semi-octagonal table with the 12 Disciples on the farther side and with Jesus in the foreground, and by emphasizing his skills at perspective and foreshortening and by applying gorgeous colors, he managed to win despite his inadequacies. Despite adding pets and gold and silver containers in the foreground to fill vacant spaces, he very effectively created the illusion of a room, and he cleverly used pilasters similar to those that separate one panel from the next to create what appears to be a clearstory through which other events are foreshadowed. His painting has merit, but he was definitely not the best painter.

Each of the 16 scenes in the chapel was separated from the next by thick pilasters that have recesses with ancient Roman ornaments. On the upper level, pilasters also separate the pairs of popes in between each clearstory window; and on the lower level, pilasters were used to subdivide the curtains into panels. Four of the standing figures representing popes were destroyed to create the Last Judgment, and of the remainder, 11 were painted by Botticelli.

On each the three levels, the pilasters are aligned to create an overall architectural enframement for the walls. The lower and middle levels of the walls have Corinthian pilasters, and the upper level has Doric pilasters. Superimposition of the orders was well known, but ignored and did not matter in this case since their shafts have the same width and since these pilasters are not structural elements. However, the aligned pilasters on three levels appear to support the base or pendentive of each part of the vault that extended downward between each window.

For Michelangelo the most important consideration initially was where to put the 12 Apostles that Julius wanted to be painted on the ceiling, and since there are 12 pendentives, the obvious place to put them was at the top of the 12 rows of pilasters that enframe the walls. However, he was not satisfied with simply adding 12 impoverished figures to the ceiling, and when he objected to his assignment, the impetuous Julius told him to do whatever he wanted.

Michelangelo's first decision on how to organize painting for the ceiling was probably to substitute 12 prophets and sibyls in place of the 12 Apostles on the 12 pendentives. By choosing prophets and sibyls, he could at least give them elaborate clothing equivalent to the clothing depicted in the 16 panels of the walls. By depicting them as seated, he could have left the center of the ceiling blue with gold stars, and would probably have been the case if he had painted only 12 Apostles as his contract had stipulated. Although that would have sufficed, he was still not satisfied with what the effect would be, and he considered subdividing the center of the ceiling into geometric panels of various sizes, but he decided instead create an additional series of panels perpendicular to the panels of the walls so that they could be viewed sequentially from the altar of the chapel, and for the subject of his panels, he chose the creation of the world and the fall of Man and consequently the need for redemption that was predicted to become available by the male prophets and female sibyls, all of which are well clothed.

Michelangelo initially considered placing large figures in the spandrels and dividing the rest of the ceiling into a geometric pattern with circles and square. He soon decided to put the center of the ceiling to better use.

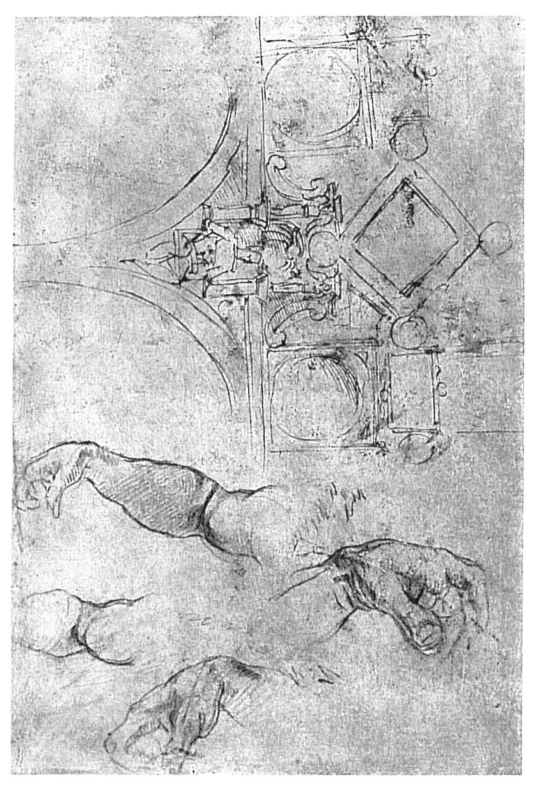

Preliminary designs for the Sistine ceiling (Grimm)

The next problem that needed to be solved was how to arrange panels on the ceiling in relation to the 12 seated figures on the pendentives, and the irregular corners of the vaulting did not allow for an entirely regular arrangement of design elements. Since there are five large seated figures on each side, he decided to create 5 smaller panels in between them and for larger panels in between the seated figures and above the "lunettes." A lunette is ordinarily a term for a semi-circular window, but in this case, it is a term that has been used for convenience to designate the parts of the vaults above the four windows in the center of each side; only these four windows have lunettes. Although each side has six windows, the windows at each end of the side walls have a larger pendentive above the corner windows instead of a pair of adjacent lunettes. Although there was room in the center of the ceiling for nine large panels, to have placed nine panels of equal size above four pairs of windows alternating with five large seated figures made less sense visually than to alternate large and small panels. By using five smaller panels in between four large panels, Michelangelo created room for four seated nudes at the corners of each of the five smaller panels.

To create an architectural enframement that would provide a clear separation between the principal groups of figures that differ greatly in size, Michelangelo had to ignore the arrangement of pilasters and instead to enframe each of 12 largest figures of all within an apparent niche or aedicule flanked by pedestals, and each pedestal supports a pair of nude male putti who provide visual support for the center of the ceiling. The putti support what resembles an attic story with the larger male nudes seated on corner blocks of the attic, and each pair of nude males pretends to be holding cloth that holds a gold shield or rondel in place in between them. Connecting the attic blocks and running from side to side in the center of the ceiling are broad bands that appear to be the ribs of barrel vaults, and the large male nudes are in front of them. Thus, these prominent ribs of the center of the ceiling run down to the pedestals on which the nudes are seated and then continue down to the putti and the pedestals on which they are standing and flank the prophets and sibyls, whose feet rest on shelves supported by brackets. Although the pedestals that support the putti rest on nothing at all, the whole arrangement seems to make visual sense even though it has no connection with the arrangement of the pilasters on the walls. Michelangelo also used the residual spaces in between the putti and the apex of the lunettes as places to put more nude males.

It was the vaulting of the corners of the ceiling that required compromise, and Michelangelo chose to ignore the architectural framework of the walls and to create an entirely separate framework based on the four pair of lunettes and the five pendentives on each of the longer sides. This is how the chapel came to have different architectural enframents to organize its separate programs of paintings: the enframents of the walls are based on providing visual support for the pendentives, and the enframements of the ceiling re based on creating large panels that correspond to the lunettes. The three panels in the center of the ceiling were reserved for the creation of the first man and woman and for the Original Sin. When Michelangelo later created the Last Judgment, he decided to do without an architectural enframement and to create a single scene for a simultaneous event with Heaven above and Hell below. He thus dealt with the creation of the world and the origin of sin on the ceiling, with the prediction of salvation in between the lunettes, and with the end of the world on the wall behind the altar, where the sacrament and repentance provides the opportunity for salvation. The controlling theme for all that he painted in the chapel was the inherent sinfulness of Man, but the possibility of redemption.

> Saint Catherine, whose revelations strongly influence the late trecento papacy and a significant group of the Forentine ruling elite, claimed that God Himself explained to her that the sin of Adam had opened a deep gulf between earth and heaven, filled by the turbulent waters of mortal life, but that He had thrown a bridge across these waters— the crucified Christ [Kent 2000: 443].

The Sistine ceiling can be considered to have been Michelangelo's second architectural project with his designs for the tomb Julius as his first. In both cases an architectural setting provided the enframents for the individual design elements that Michelangelo was most interested in creating and enabled the separate elements to be arranged coherently.

Michelangelo painted the ceiling of the Sistine Chapel between May 10, 1508 and October 31, 1512. "He finished this entire work in twenty months, without any help whatever, not even someone to grind his colors for him" (Condivi 1553 [1976]: 57-58). Although he objected that he was not a painter, he had previously painted a greatly admired tondo for Agnolo Doni (28). In October 1504 the city of Florence commissioned to paint a major fresco of the Battle of Càscina for the Palazzo Vecchio, and he had completed a full-sized drawing for the fresco before Julius summoned him to Rome in March 1505. Michelangelo considered the cartoon to represent half the work involved, but because the work was not completed, he was paid nothing (Michelangelo 1963, I, 148). These two works had established his reputation as a painter of the highest rank, but he continued throughout most of his life to consider sculpture to be his profession.

> When I had set up the figure [the seated bronze statue of Julius II] and returned to Rome, Pope Julius still did not want me to do the Tomb, and set me to paint the vault of Sixtus, and we made a bargain for three thousand ducats. The first design for the said work was for twelve Apostles [Disciples] in the lunettes and the usual ornamentations to fill the remaining area.
>
> After the work was begun it seemed to me that it would turn out to a poor affair, and I told the Pope that if the Apostles alone were put there it seemed to me that it would turn out a poor affair. He asked me why. I said, "because they themselves were poor. Then he gave me a new commission to do what I liked, and said he would content me and that I should paint down to the Histories below [Michelangelo 1963: I, 149].

According to Vasari, the architect Giuliano da San Gallo recommended Michelangelo to paint the ceiling: "Giuliano, seeing that the Pope was delighted with pictures, and that he wished to have the vaulting of the chapel of his uncle Sixtus painted, suggested Michelagnolo to him, saying that he had already done the bronze statue at Bologna. The idea pleased the Pope, who sent for Michelagnolo, and on his arrival the vaulting was allotted to him" (Vasari 1568: II, 218).

Although Michelangelo objected to working on the Sistine ceiling because he wanted to complete the tomb, but once he began to paint the ceiling, he was determined to complete the project better than anyone else could have done. When the ceiling was nearly complete in 1512, he wrote, I work harder than anyone who has ever live" (Michelangelo 1963: 70). Condivi briefly summarized the circumstances that led to the commission for the ceiling and the way in which Michelangelo chose to organize the composition within an overall architectural framework:

> ...Bramante and other rivals of Michelangelo put it into the pope's head that he should have Michelangelo paint the vault of the chapel.... And they were doing this service with malice in order to distract the pope from projects of sculpture, and because they took it for certain that either he would turn the pope against him by not accepting such an undertaking or if he accepted it, he would prove considerably inferior to Raphael of Urbino, whom they plied with every favor out of hatred of Michelangelo.... Michelangelo, who had not yet used colors and who realized that it was difficult to paint a vault, made every effort to get out of it, proposing Raphael and pleading that his was not his art and that he would not succeed; and he went on refusing to such an extent that the pope almost lost his temper. But, when he saw that the pope was determined, he embarked on that work which is seen today in the papal palace to the admiration and amazement of the world, which brought him so great a reputation that it set him above all envy. Of this work I shall give a brief account.
>
> The form of the vault is what is commonly called a barrel vault and its supports are lunettes, which are six along the length and two along the

breadth, so that the whole vault amounts to two and a half squares. In this space Michelangelo painted principally the Creation of the world, but he went on to embrace almost all of the Old Testament. And he divided this work in the following manner: starting from the brackets which support the horns of the lunettes, up to about a third of the arch of the vault, a flat wall is simulated; rising to the top of it are some pilasters and bases simulating marble, which project outward from a plane resembling a parapet, with its corbels below and with other little pilasters above against the same plane, on which Prophets and Sibyls are seated. Springing from the arches of the lunettes, these first pilasters flank the brackets, excluding, however, a segment of the arches of the lunettes which is greater than the space contained between them. On the said based are imitation figures of little nude children in various poses which like terms [caryatids], support a cornice which surrounds the whole work, leaving the middle of the vault from head to foot like an open sky. This opening is divided into nine bands, because there are certain arches with moldings which rise from the cornice over the pilasters, traverse the highest part of the vault, and rejoin the cornice on the opposite side, leaving between the arches nines spaces, terminating large and small. In each of the small ones there are two strips of imitation marble which cross the space, so placed that the center comprises two parts to one part at each side where the medallions are situated, as will be mentioned in the proper place. And this he did to avoid the sense of surfeit which comes from sameness [39, 42; notes omitted].

The most direct source for the subjects of the use of panels and for the subjects of the panels of the Sistine Ceiling was Jacopo della Quercia's marble reliefs on marble pilasters flanking the main entrance to the Basilica of San Petronio in Bologna (1425-1438). Michelangelo sent the years 1506-1508 working on the bronze statue of Julius II that was placed on the front of San Petronio and then spent 1508-1512 painting the Sistine Ceiling. He saw Della Quercia's reliefs frequently and undoubtedly had them in mind because the range of subjects is nearly the same, and the composition for the creation of Adam is closely similar, and Della Quercia also emphasized the initial nakedness of Adam and his later knowledge of his nakedness, and he featured the nakedness of Noah in four of his ten panels. Della Quercia's male nudes are conspicuously positioned, well proportioned, and well built. Della Quercia was the first sculptor "...to inspire others with courage and the belief that it would be possible to equal her [Nature] in some sort" (Vasari 1568: I, 210). As noted, Signorelli "...showed the way to represent nude figures in painting so as to make them appear alive..." (II, 145).

For his reliefs, Della Quercia chose Old Testaments subjects from the creation of Adam to the sacrifice of Isaac. Michelangelo added the creation of the universe for the first three of his nine panels and omitted the sacrifice of Isaac at the end of the series, but otherwise most of the same subjects are included are treated similarly and usually with a few figures in each panel. The composition of Della Quercia's creation of Eve and the temptation are also similar to Michelangelo's composition, but Della Quercia used two panels for these subjects, and Michelangelo combined them into one panel. Michelangelo omitted the subject of living by the sweat of his brow that Della Quercia included in a separate panel. The only large scene in Michelangelo's panels is the flood, which Della Quercia represented in a panel mainly by the faces of animals that had been in Noah's ark. Michelangelo included the sacrifices of Cain and Abel, but omitted the murder of Abel. There are differences in every composition such as having God and angels in the sky in several of Michelangelo's panels rather than on the earth, but in Michelangelo's the creation of Eve, God stands on the earth. Most of the differences can be attributed to the smaller size and vertical composition of Della Quercia's panels, which are roughly 3-feet high and 2-feet wide.

Birth of Eve by Della Quercia (Grimm)

Birth of Eve by Michelangelo (Richter, no. 11)

To a lesser extent, both Della Quercia and Michelangelo were successively influenced by Ghiberti's two sets of bronze doors on the Florentine Baptistery. Della Quercia had competed for the commission to design the main pair of doors of the Baptistery along with Ghiberti and Brunelleschi in 1401, and although his entry is not known to have survived, it was for the sacrifice of Isaac and is likely to have been similar to the panel he sculpted for San Petronio. In any case, Isaac is nude in the surviving entries that were submitted by Ghiberti and Brunelleschi. Michelangelo admired Ghiberti's second pair of doors so much that he said, "they are so beautiful that they could stand at the entrance of Paradise" (Vasari 1568: 130).

Ghiberti's first set of doors for the Baptistery have 28 smaller panels with 20 scenes from the life of Christ and 8 scenes with evangelists and doctors of the Catholic Church (1403-1424; Goldscheider 1949). These smaller panels generally contain only a few figures and consequently are ore similar to Michelangelo's compositions that consist mainly of a few figures. Ghiberti's main doors have 10 large panels that include scenes from the creation of Adam to Solomon (1425-1452). In these larger panels, Ghiberti sometimes used the Medieval convention of including multiple scenes as Michelangelo did with his creation and temptation panels. In his first panel at the top left, he included the creation of the earth, the creation of Adam, the creation of Eve, the temptation, and the expulsion (five subjects that Michelangelo dealt with in six panels (including two double scenes). In his second panel on the top right, Ghiberti included the sacrifices of Cain and Abel and the murder of Abel as well as man working by the sweat of his brow. In the third panel (the second on the left side), Ghiberti included Noah's ark, the sacrifice of Noah, and Noah's nakedness. Thus, in three panels Ghiberti included all of the subjects that Michelangelo devoted nine panels... In addition, Ghiberti "...was the first to begin to imitate the masterpieces of the ancient romans, studying them very carefully, as everyone should who wished to become a good craftsman" (Vasari 1568: 246; Pisano had done so less systematically and less successfully, but had set an important precedent with the first set of doors for the Baptistery). Moreover, some of the figures on both sets of Ghiberti's doors were intended to represent prophets and sibyls who foretold the coming of the Messiah (243,249).

It is readily apparent that Ghiberti influenced both Della Quercia and Michelangelo directly and also had an indirect influence on Michelangelo through Della Quercia. In all three examples, the same Old Testament scenes are treated similarly in panels within an architectural framework.

By comparison with Michelangelo's composition for the Sistine Ceiling, in 1517 Raphael dealt with the long and narrow space of the loggia of the Villa Farnesina (Chigi) by creating an illusion that two long and narrow tapestries were suspended from the ceiling; he ignored the decorative lunettes on three sides of the room (Chapter 16 herein). Earlier, Michelangelo had chosen to create a larger number of smaller panels to align with the lunettes on the sides of the Sistine Chapel and to correspond in shape to the series of panels previously painted by other artists below the main cornice of the chapel. When the work was half completed, the scaffolding was removed and the public was admitted.

> Raphael, who was excellent in imitating, at once changed his style after seeing it, and to show his skill did the prophets and sibyls in la Pace, while Bramante tried to have the other half of the chapel given to Raphael. On hearing this Michelagnolo became incensed against Bramante, and pointed out to the Pope without mincing matters many faults in his life and works, the latter of which he afterwards corrected in the building of S. Pietro [Vasari 1568: IV, 125).

Raphael had also been greatly impressed by Michelangelo's cartoon for the Battle of Càscina (II, 223, 225, 244). In Rome, he also made an intensive study of ancient Roman architecture and sculpture, and he developed a distinctive style of his own, but his figures continued to owe much to Michelangelo (231). "He thus formed a single style out of many, which was always considered his own, and was, and will always be, most highly esteemed by artists" (246).

In 1542 Michelangelo was still angry when he wrote that "all the discords that arose between Pope Julius and me were owing to the envy of Bramante and Raphael of Urbino; and this is the reason why he did not proceed with the Tomb in his lifetime, in order to ruin me. And Raphael had good reason to be envious, since what he knew of art he learnt from me" (Michelangelo 1963: II, 31). Raphael acknowledged his admiration of Michelangelo by adding him to the foreground of the School of Athens by putting Michelangelo (probably around 1511 when the Stanzas were completed). While in Florence, Raphael had studied Michelangelo's cartoon for the Battle of Càscina, and the impact of the Sistine ceiling is manifest. Raphael had been recognized as a highly accomplished painter before coming to Rome, but his style of painting did change dramatically after he studied Michelangelo's work. Raphael was an accomplished architect before Michelangelo began to consider architecture in terms of space and light rather than primarily as a setting for sculpture.

Although it is the architectural enframement of the Sistine Ceiling that is most relevant for this study, it should be noted that initially, Julius stipulated that the ceiling of the Sistine was to have the 12 Disciples (presumably seated between the lunettes), but Michelangelo objected that since they were poor, they would make a poor showing, and Julius told him "do what I liked" (Michelangelo 1963: 149). Before leaving Florence, among the projects Michelangelo worked on from 1503 to 1505 were statues of the 12 standing figures of Disciples for the Duomo in Florence, and he only partially completed a statue of St. Matthew, he was not paid for this work either. No Disciples were included in his ceiling, and since its subject he chose was the Old Testament rather than the New Testament, Michelangelo filled the larger spaces between the lunettes with prophets and sibyls who had prophesied the coming of the Messiah, and he painted the ancestor of Jesus in smaller spaces within the lunettes except at the corners of the room, which he reserved for stories about the salvation of the Hebrews by individuals.

The theme Michelangelo chose was Man's inherent disobedience and need for redemption. Consequently, even though the main panels were devoted to events in the first nine chapters of Genesis, the largest figures by far on the Sistine ceiling are the prophets and sybils who predicted the coming of Christ with the exception of Jonah, who is most prominently featured for having resurrected and prefigured the resurection of Christ. The corners of the ceiling were devoted to the salvation of the Hebrews by Moses, David, Judith, and Ahasuerus (with a dramatically foreshortened crucifixion substituted for the hanging of Haman; Vasari 1568: 52). Except for the scenes on shield-like rondels in between the nudes that are the smallest on the ceiling, nearly all subjects chosen for the ceiling except for the decorative nudes were relevant to the need for salvation. The theology is idiosyncratic enough to indicate that Michelangelo did not ask for advice from theologians (as in showing Adam and Eve still nude when they leave the Garden of Eden and Noah still nude even though the point in both myths was the sinfulness of nakedness). Overall the composition succeeds through the roughly equal spacing of the largest figures and largest panels and the chronological sequence for the central area of the ceiling. The architectural framework serves to separate and organize the events and figures rather than to unify them, but it is a more effective compositional device than the separate clusters of figures for the Last Judgment, an earlier compositon by Michelangelo would have been much more dramatic and successful (Grimm n. d.: pl. 140). The otherwise separate incidents and figures bear little relation to one another except in terms of the theme as a whole, but many of the figures are among the most memorable ever created.

What Michelangelo most preferred was to sculpt and to paint was the male nude, which he had sculpted in his earliest surviving relief of the Battle of the Centaurs and with the David and others of his earliest sculptures. When he was not permitted to sculpt nudes for the tomb of Julius, he found a way to add nudes to the ceiling of the Sistine and eventually into the Last Judgment on the end wall of the chapel. As noted, he planned for 20 of the large sculptures of the tomb to be nudes (the bound captives), ad this would have been half of the 40 large sculptures of the tomb. It is unlikely to be a coincidence that he included 20 large nudes so prominently on the ceiling of the chapel. This is not to say that he put the tomb on the ceiling; the subjects for the 40-statue tomb were entirely secular except incidentally for the two angels supporting a statue of Julius, and none of the figures were from the Bible. As Condivi noted, the subjects for the ceiling related entirely to the Old Testament with the exception of the large seated nudes and the nude putti:

> But no less marvelous than this is that part which does not appertain to the narrative. These are certain *ignudi* which, seated on bases over the aforesaid cornice, support at either side the medallions already mentioned, which simulate metal, on which, in the manner of reverses, various subject are depicted, all related, however to the principal narrative. In all these things, in the beauty of the compartments in the diversity of poses, in the contradiction of the contours of the vault, Michelangelo displayed consummate art [Condivi 1553: 48].

The subject most important to him was the human form in as great a variety of poses as possible, and tightly fitting clothing often reveals the form underneath that he had carefully considered beforehand in nude drawings, and in some cases male nudes were clothed as females. As he later wrote, "...painting may be held good to the degree which it approximates to relief..." (Michelangelo 1963: II, 75), and he generally chose to portray well built males in a great variety of dramatic and momentary poses. The ceiling is primarily a work of art in which in which individual figures are by far the most important subjects, and the actual subject matter is distinctly secondary, and this is still more the case with the Last Judgment in which nudity is still more prominently featured.

For the nine central panels of the ceiling, Michelangelo chose Biblical subjects that included nudity in five out of the nine: the creation of Adam, the creation of Eve, the expulsion from the Garden of Eden, the Flood, and the nakedness of Noah. All nine of the episodes Michelangelo chose were from the first nine chapters of Genesis. Emphasizing the nakedness of Noah in the concluding scene is intentionally ironic and otherwise irrelevant since his nakedness was considered sinful. Neither Julius II for his tomb and ceiling nor Paul III for the Last Judgment considered nudity sinful, but a more literal interpretation of the Bible was later required by the Council of Trent to counter the Reformation by conforming superficially without giving up any claims for the authority of the Church. Many of Michelangelo's nudes in the Last Judgment eventually became victims of prudery, but his ceiling was left intact.

Thus, the ribs that divide the center of the ceiling into panels extend from the niches that surround the 12 largest figures of the ceiling rather than from the pilasters of the walls of the chapel. Michelangelo designed the ceiling on the basis of his initial assignment, which was to paint 12 figures on the ceiling, and even after he changed the subjects to be able to paint 12 gorgeously clothed figures instead of 12 poorly clothed Apostles, he made the prophets and sibyls by far the largest figures on the ceiling even after they had ceased to be the most important figures. To work out the design for the rest of the ceiling, he started with the 12 largest figures and the niches in which he enframed them and extend the enframements to create the ribs, which divided the center of the ceiling into nine panels, and consequently, the central panels bear no relationship to the pilasters that enframe the wall panels. Michelangelo could have extended the pilasters to the base of the shelves on which the 12 largest figures sit, but instead, he separated the framework of the ceiling entirely from the framework of the walls by placing standing figures in between the top of the pilasters and the bottom of the shelves. Since he made no attempt to relate the niches for the largest figures to the lunettes, it is also evident that he did not use the lunettes to plan the enframement of the ceiling, and it is a coincidence that the four largest panels of the ceiling align with the four windows of the side walls. There can be no doubt that Michelangelo purposely ignored the architectural framework of the walls to create an entirely different framework that centers on the largest, but least important figures he placed in the prominent position in between the windows.

In Medieval art, the most important figures were invariably the largest. Michelangelo retained this and some other Medieval conventions including depicting multiple events in one panel, but he also made the seated figures farthest from main entrance the largest of all so they would appear to be the same size as the others. He was more concerned with the overall visual impact than with conforming to one set of rules; he knew the rules and generally observed them, but did not hesitate to break them when there was reason to do so. Frequently, he made seated figures as tall as nearby standing figures as if the seated figures were closer to the eye, and on the Sistine Ceiling they were. Although he understood the rules of perspective, he generally made no attempt to position his figures within a space constructed using one-point perspective. Everything is usually part of a foreground rather than a background.

The largest seated figures were among the most difficult to paint because of they had to be adjusted to fit the curving walls. The relatively flat panels in the center of the ceiling presented minimal difficulties, and the only spaces that presented more difficulties were the corners of the ceiling, where Michelangelo proved he could have placed small standing figures between the lunettes, but preferred large seated ones. Even he probably could not have painted large standing figures between the lunettes in a way that would make them seem undistorted.

Michelangelo had a decided preference for seated figures in sculpture and painting. Although his most famous sculpture is his David, he other two best known works are the seated Pietà and the seated Moses. The Moses was to have been one or the four or six largest figures on the freestanding tomb of Julius II, and the prominence given to the largest seated figures on the Sistine Ceiling was surely influenced in part by the largest and most elaborately clothed figures he had sketched in his designs for the tomb. These figures are also equivalent to the Madonna he painted for the Doni tondo and for the Madonnas he had sculpted in two tondos. The round shape could be better filled by a larger seated figure than by a smaller standing figure and the same was true of the triangular spaces between the lunettes. The figures within the lunettes were also seated to fit triangular spaces.

In art and architecture, Michelangelo had a decided preference for the massiveness of the most compact geometric forms: the square, the circle, and the equilateral triangle. His buildings and his figures are most often arranged to be as compact and monumental as possible, and compactness increases the sense of monumentality. His clothed figures are pyramids of folds of gorgeously colored cloth that must have had great appeal for the cloth manufacturers, merchants, and voluminously clothed people of Renaissance Florence. This is not to belittle him or them, but to point out why so many of his figures are so gorgeously colored and so elaborately clothed and why he had objected to painting poorly clothed Apostles. He grew up among people who made a great deal of money by manufacturing and trading in cloth and who spent a great deal on clothing themselves. Michelangelo, Leonardo, and many other Florentine artist went to as incredible lengths to depict drapery as realistically as they did to depict anatomy correctly, and they were careful to indicate that anatomy determined the shape of clothing instead of concealing anatomy within clothing. Michelangelo was not content to paint or sculpt only clothed figures. He could not depict most Biblical figures nude, but when he could as with Adam and Noah, he did, and when there were residual spaces, he generally filled them with nudes. When viewed form the main entrance, the entire room pivots on the clothed figure of Jonah, who was believed to have resurrected and prefigured the Resurrection.

Whether standing or seated, clothed or not, Michelangelo's most characteristic figures were seated, muscular, and pensive. Similarly, his buildings have the massiveness of his figures. Massiveness was the single most important characteristic of his work throughout his lifetime.

Designs for the Front of San Lorenzo, Florence (1516-1520)

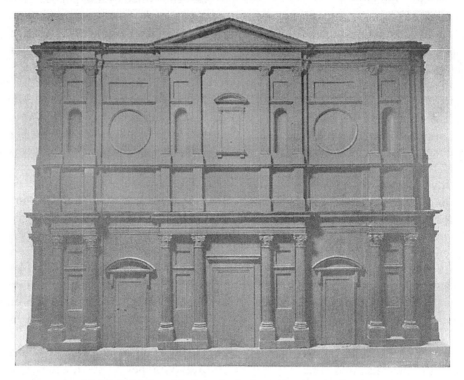

Model of Michelangelo's design for the front of San Lorenzo (Mariani)

Print showing sculpture planned by Michelangelo for San Lorenzo (G. B. Nelli in Schiavo)

Alternative design by Michelangelo for the front of San Lorenzo (De Tolnay, *Corpus* no. 497)

In 1515 with funding assured, Michelangelo fully intended to complete the tomb of Julius as well and as quickly as possible before starting another project, but Pope Leo X (Giovanni de' Medici) had other ideas. He wanted the neighborhood church of his family to have a magnificent front instead of rough blocks of stone, and when he asked for designs, many architects and sculptors from throughout Italy responded with designs, but not Michelangelo, who had good reasons to continue working on the tomb and no reason to set it aside for a possibility that might or might not materialize.

Most of the designs submitted approached the problem of dealing with the front of a Christian basilica much as Alberti had done when he added a front to Santa Maria Novella in Florence. He treated the lower story as a triumphal arch with an attic story extending from side to side to hide the sloping roofs of the side aisles, and he put a temple front on top of his attic. Instead, though, of placing gigantic scrolls on either side of the temple front as Alberti did, most participants in the competition put niches for sculpture at each end of the attic story (or "mezzanine" as it is sometimes referred to, but without rooms behind it or windows). Vasari noted that "designs were made by Baccio d'Agnolo, Antonio da Sangallo, Andrea and Jacopo Sansovino, and the gracias Raphael of Urbino, who was afterwards called to Florence for that purpose" in 1515 (Vasari 1568: 55). A number of designs have been assigned to the project though some may have been for Loreto, and there has been much disagreement about attributions and the design development (Millon in Millon and Smyth 1988: 1-89).

Leo X and Cardinal Giulio de' Medici (his first cousin and later Pope Clement VII) were not entirely satisfied with any of the designs submitted, and in the fall of 1516, they instructed Baccio d'Agniolo and Michelangelo to collaborate on a design. At the time, Bartolomeo (Baccio) d'Agnolo Baglioni was an architect and woodcarver in charge of the architecture of the Duomo in Florence. Michelangelo resisted, but Leo insisted that he provide at least some of the sculpture. When Michelangelo was asked to come to Rome to discuss the project, he declined saying that only the architect Baccio needed to go to Rome. He was then told to come to Rome, and he went in December. While there, he sketched how he thought the front could be improved, and Baccio was instructed to prepare a wooden model on the basis of Michelangelo's sketch (Millon and Smyth 1988: 8-9).

On February 2, 1517 Michelangelo was sent instruction about who was to be represented in wax figures that he was to make for the wooden model and on where the figures were to be placed on the model: four on a lower story, four in the attic story and two on an upper story (Ackerman 1964: 5). This indicates that the lower story and mezzanine-like story were still to be the full width of the church and that the upper story was to be only the width of the clearstory, and it also indicates that no consideration had yet been given to putting an addition on the front that would require additional statues on its sides.

Early in 1517, Michelangelo had gone back to Carrara to continue quarrying stone for the tomb of Julius and to make contacts for marble for the foundation and some architectural elements that would be needed for San Lorenzo; the foundations needed to be put in before winter to enable further work to begin in the spring. In Florence, Baccio began working on the wooden model that was supposed to be based on Michelangelo's sketch. In March, the model was finished, but when Michelangelo saw it, he wrote in disgust "...that it is a mere toy" (Michelangelo 1963: I, 104).

Disgusted, Michelangelo returned to Carrara, and by April with the help of a *scarpellino* named Della Grassa, he made "a small model" of unfired clay "for my own use here," and in the process of making this model, he came up with an entirely new concept for the front of San Lorenzo. Although his clay model got twisted, he decided nonetheless to sent it to Rome to show what he had in mind (Michelangelo 1963: I, 104-105).

Michelangelo now proposed a separate addition to the front of the church rather than simply a facade, and he wanted this new concept approved before having another wooden model made. That this clay model illustrated an entirely new concept is indicated a great increase in the estimated cost and by his sudden enthusiasm for the project. On May 2, 1517, he wrote to Buoninsegni (Cardinal Giulio de' Medici's treasurer) that the proposed changes would cost at least 35,000 gold ducats (worth about $55 each or around $440,000 in 1976 dollars; Hellmut Wohl in Condivi 1553 [1976]: 147), The budget previously approved for the project was 25,000 scudi (of about $50 each ; Ackerrman1964: 6). If approved, the larger project could be completed in six years. Michelangelo wrote, "...I feel myself able to execute this project of the façade of San Lorenzo in such a manner that it will be, both architecturally and sculpturally, the mirror of Italy, but the Pope and the Cardinal would have to make up their minds quickly as to whether they wish me to do it or not" (Michelangelo 1963: I, 106). The Pope and the Cardinal preferred Michelangelo's new concept and instructed him to have an entirely new wooden model made immediately.

Michelangelo agreed to go to Florence and spend "...the whole of August, in order to make the model of San Lorenzo to send to Rome, as I've promised" (Michelangelo 1963: 107). The new wooden model was completed on December 22, 1517, and Pietro Urbano da Pistoia, Michelangelo's assistant who helped construct it, then took it to Rome. The Pope and Cardinal quickly accepted new model as definitive and called Michelangelo to Rome to sign a contract for both the architecture and the sculpture on January 19, 1518.

The contract (Milanesi 1875, 671), based on the wood model, called for twelve standing figures [of marble] (six [standing figures] on the first level to be five *braccia* [10 feet or very nearly two feet per *braccia* of 58.36 cm.] tall, six [standing figures] on the upper level to be five and one-half *braccia* tall), and six seated figures in bronze at the mezzanine level four and one-half *braccia* tall. Four of each [of the standing and seated figures] were to be on the facade, the others [one on each level on each side] on the flanks. The contract specified an additional seven reliefs: five rectangular (four of them eight *braccia* wide and one about nine *braccia* wide) and two round marble reliefs (six or seven *braccia* in diameter). Also cited in the contract were the dimensions of some of the architectural members (eight fluted columns about eleven *braccia* high at the first level, and in the mezzanine, pilasters [piers] about six or seven *braccia* tall [Millon and Smyth 1988: 12].

For the bronze reliefs, "the figures are to be of life size or greater and the reliefs to be as deep as is necessary to make them 'evident.'" A pediment was also to be in the center (Ackerman 1964: 13-14).

The contract indicates that the planned front of five bays had been given side facades of one bay that were also to have sculpture. The size and number of statues specified also indicates that Michelangelo had proposed that this block be essentially a rectangle tall enough (with a pediment stipulated) to conceal Brunelleschi's entire front rather than to reflect its staggered profile. As shown in sections reproduced in Chapter 15, Brunelleschi had put a separate shed roof over each of his side aisles and another separate shed roof over each row of chapels that open into the side aisles. Consequently, each side of the church has clearstories on two levels, and the front of the church steps down twice on each side. This presented the main difficulty in for putting a classical front on an unusual form of a medieval basilica, and most of the surviving solutions for this problem put a temple front on the higher clearstory and an attic on the lower clearstories and frequently continued the attic across the middle of the front as if it were a mezzanine.

What Michelangelo now proposed to do was to continue the temple front across the entire width of the church on top of an attic story. To have done this simply as a false front would have looked like a stage set from the side so he proposed applying his design to a slab-like addition to the front of the church, thus giving the entire front the overall form of a triumphal arch, but with the attic story in the middle rather than on top.

Previously, medieval architects in northern Europe had dealt with the problem of a single clearstory by adding a pair of towers in front of the aisles. Alberti had dealt with the problem at Santa Maria Nuova by adding giant brackets in between the clearstory and roofs of the aisles, and this had become the standard Renaissance and Baroque solution.

Like some other architects who submitted designs for San Lorenzo, Baccio continued the attic entirely across the lower story with the result looking like a temple on top of the attic of a small triumphal arch surrounding the entrance. A vestige of a mezzanine also disunified all of Michelangelo's subsequent designs. The various designs by other architects and Michelangelo's own design process for the church have been considered very fully by De Tolnay, Ackerman, Millon, and other architectural historians without reaching agreement on who designed what and when. There has even been disagreement about whether the large wooden model in the Casa Buonarroti was commissioned by Michelangelo and when, and although there is now general agreement that he did, Carbon-14 dating would probably settle this controversy objectively.

I will attempt to determine how much existed when Michelangelo began his various architectural projects, the main problems that had to be solved, his unprecedented solutions, how he used design sources, and his final intentions. I have not attempted to reconstruct the entire design process for this or any other of his projects.

Although Baccio d'Agniolo was paid for the unacceptable model he had made, he was no longer part of the project. Although the sculptor Jacopo Sansovino understood he was to involve in the project, he too was dropped, and he wrote accusing Michelangelo of having stolen the project. Although Vasari wrote that Michelangelo was incapable of collaborating, this was untrue; he had been willing to collaborate with Baccio until he proved incompetent, and it was his incompetence that resulted in Michelangelo's preparing an entirely new design.

Since this was his first primarily architectural commission, it deserves to be considered in some detail to show how much his development as an architect progressed while he worked on this project for more than three years from 1516 to 1520. The adopted design showed that Michelangelo knew very little about ancient r Renaissance architecture at this point in his life. It was a serious mistake to extend the mezzanine entirely across the width of the church in a way that completely separated the upper story from the lower story and that disunified the design and that made it impossible for the upper story to have columns or pilasters of similar size to those of the lower story. The mezzanine had been inserted into a number of designs by Michelangelo and other architects to conceal the sloping roofs of the side aisles, and it was to be utilized for reliefs alternating with seated statues, but what it did visually was to add a level equivalent to the attic of triumphal arch into the middle of the design rather than across the top of the entire front. In any case, putting an attic story on the top would have been a better solution than putting one in the middle except that the life-sized sculptures of the reliefs could not have been seen so well.

What Michelangelo had done was to use classical design elements to conceal a medieval front. He knew the elements well enough, but so far he had little understanding of the principles of classical design including how attics were to be used and how the orders needed to be superimposed in a set sequence for structural reasons because each order had different proportions. He did consider omitting the mezzanine in the middle and having the upper order rest directly on the lower order as Alberti and Bramante had done in palace designs (without a pediment), but the 1518 contract specified the mezzanine was to be used for sculpture. The ancient Roman solutions would have been either superimposing arcades as for most basilicas and theatres or using a monumental order as for triumphal arches. Brunelleschi had, after all, used arcades in his nave, and Alberti had adapted both arcades and triumphal arches for his church fronts. Michelangelo inherited a bad design and used it for the placement of sculpture, but did little to improve upon the architecture. His sculpture would have helped to unify the design as a whole, but not enough to make it a good design by either ancient or contemporary standards.

Only a few years later in 1520 when Michelangelo designed the interior of the Medici Chapel, he had learned a great deal more about ancient Roman buildings, and in 1524 when he designed the Laurentian Library, he had mastered design principles so thoroughly that he adapted them successfully (as Vasari noted; Ackerman 1986: 74). In 1518, though, Michelangelo was still a sculptor and was beginning to become an architect, and his solution for the design of the front of the church had more to do with sculpture than architecture. His most fully developed drawing for the front is, in fact, the most incoherent with a divided mezzanine, and his largest model was only slightly less so. In his designs for the interior of the Medici Chapel, he did adapt the design of a triumphal arch successfully to enframe statues of seated men wearing Roman military costumes.

Pope Leo X, Michelangelo, and projects for San Lorenzo (1611 painting in the Casa Buonarroti; Millon and Smyth)

Design by Michelangelo for the front of San Lorenzo (Millon and Smyth)

Some surviving evidence does not fit any attempts to reconstruct what the front of San Lorenzo would have looked like, and this has been acknowledged, but not explained. Most importantly, a highly finished drawing of a niche with a rectangular shape rather than a rounded top does not correspond to any drawing or model of the entire front. Having finished this drawing so carefully, Michelangelo must have prepared it for presentation and if approved to guide the execution of the design. This is by far the most finished drawing that survives for the entire project, and it needs to be explained.

Other evidence also has not been explained includes a 1611 painting of Michelangelo presenting a wooden model of the San Lorenzo front to Leo that is much smaller than the model in the Casa Buonarroti and that differs from it in important respects. Although only the corner of the model is shown, that is enough to indicate that it had an attic story across the top of the building (as a triumphal arch invariably did) and that the mezzanine story had been made inconspicuous. One supposed problem with the painting is that the order of the pilaster on the upper story appear to be Ionic, but the most finished drawing by Michelangelo for the project make it likely that they were Composite, which would have been superimposed above the Corinthian order of the lower story. Since this painting of an event that took place nearly a century earlier has been dismissed as insignificant, but it was commissioned by his great nephew and namesake for the Casa Buonarroti to represent one of the principal events of Michelangelo's life. At the time it was painted, at least two wooden models of the front still existed, and a smaller one with most of its wax models was displayed in the vestibule of the Laurentian Library in the 17th Century; it was similar in most respects to the architecture of the larger model now in the Casa Buonarroti (Millon and Smyth 1988: 63-69). These two are in addition the rejected wooden model by Baccio d'Agniolo (that was, incidentally, paid for by the papacy at the same time the approved wooden model by Michelangelo was accepted). There was evidently a fourth wooden model that has also not survived. In my opinion, the better design depicted in this painting cannot be dismissed as imaginary any more than the model of St. Peter's that is depicted in the same series of paintings in the Casa Buonarroti and that includes lunettes known to have been built by Michelangelo in the attic of St. Peter's had been concealed before the painting was made. Most significantly, the model of San Lorenzo in the painting depicts a niche in the upper story with a rectangular shape rather than a round head like the most highly finished drawing by Michelangelo for the church. These paintings must be considered to have been based on good evidence unless it can be proven otherwise.

In addition, Michelangelo is known to have made some changes in the design for San Lorenzo after the large wooden model was completed. De Tolnay identified a set of drawings that were to be used to quarry marble bocks for the front of the church and published them in 1954, and in 1964 Ackerman compared the dimensions given for the blocks with dimensions computed from measurements of the large model. These sketches "...provide sufficient information for a fairly accurate reconstruction of the lower two orders [the lower story and the mezzanine] of the final façade design" (Ackerman 1964: 15). For the lower story, "the width of the column dadoes and of the side and central portals is increased. This may be due in part to the fact that the blocks were measured before final carving and polishing [or were trimmed at the quarry to correspond to the drawings]. Note, however, that the width of the central portal has grown substantially..." (17). The evidence for the mezzanine was less certain, and no blocks are known to have been drawn for the upper story.

The block sketches give no evidence of changes in the design accepted in the contract of 1518. They are incomplete, probably because the upper Order was not quarried at the time the project was abandoned, but for the lower story they are sufficiently detailed to permit an accurate reconstruction (Fig. 1). The uncertain factors in Fig. 1 are (1) bay and portal widths on the lower order; (2) the degree to which the bocks would have been reduced in size by carving; and (3) the handling of the wall surfaces as distinct from the members [Ackerman 1964: 17].

This evidence more than suffices to indicate that the model in the Casa Buonarroti had been at least planned if not built before stone began to be quarried for the church, but does not preclude still further changes. It seems to me likely that when Michelangelo learned he had made mistakes that he had them corrected while still hoping that the front would be constructed.

Although it has often been stated that the contract for the front was cancelled, "...action is sporadically considered in the next few years" (Ackerman 1964: 7). In the meanwhile, the Pope and Cardinal wanted Michelangelo to give priority to the design and construction of the Medici Chapel.

As to why the front was not completed, Michelangelo himself was given no explanation. By May of 1519 Michelangelo was able to commission two scarpellini to quarry the nine statues needed for the lower story and mezzanine (indicating that the statues on the mezzanine were to be of marble rather than bronze as stipulated in the contract; Michelangelo 1963: 125-126, n. 2). In 1520, he summarized the history of the project to account for the money he had received and his expenses:

> When I was in Carrara on business of my own, that is to say, obtaining marbles to transport to Rome for the tomb of Pope Julius, in fifteen hundred and sixteen, Pope Leo sent for me with reference to the façade of San Lorenzo, which he wished me to execute in Florence. I therefore left Carrara on the fifth day of December and went to Rome, and there I did a design for the said façade, and on the basis of which the said Pope Leo commissioned me to arrange for the quarrying of the marble at Carrara for the said work. ...
>
> Then, the following August [1517], having received instruction from the Pope foresaid bout the model of the said work, I came to Florence from Carrara to execute it. I accordingly made it to scale in wood, with the figures in wax, and sent it to Rome. As soon as he saw it he ordered me to go there. So I went and undertook the said façade on contract as appears from the covenant with Hi Holiness, which I have. And as, in order to serve His Holiness, I had to transport the marbles I needed in Rome for the Tomb of Pope Julius to Florence, as I have done, and then to transport them, when they had been worked, back to Rome, he promised to indemnify me for all the expenses....
>
> On the sixth day of February fifteen hundred and seventeen, I returned to Florence from Rome, and as I had undertaken the façade of San Lorenzo foresaid on contract.... [I] went to Carrara. But as they had not fulfilled the contracts and previous orders f the marbles for the said work, and as the Carrarese were bent upon balking me, I went to have the said marbles quarried at Seravezza, a mountain near Pietra Santa in Florentine territory. And then, when I had already blocked out six columns, each eleven and a half braccia, and many other marbles, and had there begun the workings that are to-day established, for no quarrying had ever been done there before, I went to Florence on the twentieth day of March, fifteen hundred and eighteen.... Afterwards, in the same year, the Cardinal, by order of the Pope, told me not to proceed further with the work aforesaid, because they said they wished to relieve me of the trouble of transporting the marbles, and that they wished to supply me with the in Florence themselves, and to make a new contract. And thus the matter stands, from that day to this. ...
>
> ...I was very upset, because neither the Cardinal nor the Commissioners were empowered to interfere in my affairs until I had first terminated the agreement with the Pope. And the said ["*façade*"] of San Lorenzo having been abandoned in agreement with the pope.... I am not charging to his [the Cardinal's] account, over and above the space of three years I have lost over this; I am not charging to his

account the fact that I have been ruined over the said work for San Lorenzo; I am not charging to his account the enormous insult of having been brought here to execute the said work and then of having it taken away from me; and I still do not know why [Michelangelo 1963: 129-131; notes omitted]

In any case, this account states explicitly that temporarily switching from Carrara to Pietra Santa was Michelangelo's decision, and Condivi got this part wrong (Condivi 1553: 61).

The main reason why Michelangelo was not paid to continue working on San Lorenzo evidently had entirely to do with papal finances. Leo was involved in a war in northern Italy as Julius had been earlier in central Italy, and he must have had no money to spare as had been the case with Julius. That there was no dissatisfaction with Michelangelo as an artist or architect is indicated by his being commissioned by Julius to make a colossal statue of himself and by his being commissioned by Leo to create the Medici Chapel when papal finances improved, but not enough to pay for two major projects at the same time. Another consideration may well have been, though, that Leo found out that Michelangelo was using 1,000 ducats (about $50,000) provided for the façade to obtain marble from Carrara for the tomb of Julius (Michelangelo 1963: II, 29-30; cf. I, 128; Condivi 1553: 60-61; and Vasari 1568: 55-56; Michelangelo refused to indicate what the funds were needed for and refused to sign a receipt). Although Michelangelo later admitted to having done wrong, at the time he must have considered himself justified since Leo had promised about 800 ducats to have the marble that had been sent to Rome for Julius's tomb transported to Florence at his expense, but did not (Michelangelo 1963: I, 128).

When Leo died in 1521, funds from the papacy were no longer available to the Medici until Giulio became Clement VII in 1523. Both Leo and Clement became successively more interested in the chapel and library than in the front of San Lorenzo, and nothing further was done to create a front for the church.

In the meanwhile, Michelangelo resumed working on the tomb of Julius II (Michelangelo 1963: 135). "Now, when he had returned to Florence and found that, as we have already said, Pope Leo had completely lost interest, Michelangelo sorrowfully remained a long time without doing anything, after wasting much of his time up to then on first one thing and then another, to his great regret. Nonetheless, with certain marbles which he had [procured largely at Leo's expense], he begun to proceed with the tomb in his own house" (Condivi 1553: 63).

Cardinal Giulio de' Medici later found funds himself for Michelangelo to continue working on the Medici Chapel. Around June of 1521, Michelangelo wrote, "they are quarrying hard at Pietra Santa for the work at San Lorenzo, and I am finding the Carrarese more submissive than they use to be, I have also placed an order for the quarrying of large amount of marble there..." (Michelangelo 1963: 136). There was again enough work to keep Michelangelo and both quarries busy. In or around 1523, the Cardinal told Michelangelo "...that if he survived, he would also do the façade and that he was leaving orders to Domenico Buoninsegni [his treasurer] to arrange about all the money required" (142).

In 1542, he confessed that he had reimbursed himself without authorization for what it had cost him to send the marble for the tomb of Julius from Rome to Florence and for what it would cost to send them back to Rome:

While I was in Florence for the façade of San Lorenzo, as I hadn't marble there for the Tomb of Julius, I returned to Carrara and stayed there thirteen months, and transported all the marbles for the said Tomb to Florence, and built a workshop in which to execute them, and began working. At this time Aginensis [one of the executors] send Messer Francesco Palavicini, who is to-day the Bishop of Aleria to urge me on, and he saw the workshop and all the said marbles and the figures blocked out for the said tomb, which are still there to-day. Seeing this, that is to say that I was working for the said Tomb, Medici, who afterwards became Pope Clement, who was living in Florence, did not permit me to proceed, and I continued to be impeded in this way until Medici became Clement [Michelangelo 1963: II, 29].

Thus, he finally confessed two decades later that he had spent 1,000 *scudi* (about $55,000 in 1974) from Leo X and had misled him about what the money was used for: "But I want to confess to Your Lordship—that is, that while I was at Carrara, where I stayed there thirteen months for the said Tomb [of Julius II], being in need of money, I spent a thousand *scudi* on marbles for the said work, which Pope Leo had sent me for the façade of San Lorenzo, or rather to keep me occupied, and I made him excuses, pretending there were difficulties" (Michelangelo 1963: II, 29-30). This letter in which he made this confession is addressed only "to Monsignore," and it is undated, and it is a copy made by someone other than Michelangelo, but it contains information that only Michelangelo could have known, and there is no reason to doubt it authenticity, yet his confession has been ignored. That he did receive this amount and spent it for another purpose is confirmed by a statement published by Vasari in 1568:

> Michelangelo, who was going to Carrara, had an order authorizing Jacopo Salviati [Leo's agent in Florence] to pay him a thousand crowns. However, when he arrived, finding Jacopo transacting business in his room with some other citizens, he refused to wait for an interview, left without saying a work, and made his way to Carrara. Meanwhile, having heard of Michelangelo's arrival but not finding him in Florence, Jacopo sent him the thousand crowns to Carrara. The courier demanded a receipt for the money, only to be told by Michelangelo that it was for the expenses of the Pope and no business of his, that he was not in the habit of writing out receipts or acknowledgements on behalf of other people, and that he could take the money back; and so in a panic the courier went back to Jacopo without a receipt. While Michelangelo was at Carrara and, thinking that he could finish it, was having marbles quarried or the tomb as well as for the facade... [Vasari 1568 (1971): 55-56].

In other words, Michelangelo had refused to say how the money would be spent or even to acknowledge having received it, but he had not been reimbursed for the marbles shipped from Rome to Florence so he would continue to work there on the Tomb of Julius II.

Michelangelo admitted that opening a quarry at Pietra Santa had been his idea, not a requirement imposed on him by Leo, and that he stood to benefit by having a monopoly during his lifetime on all stone quarried from Pietra Santa. He admitted nothing about spending 13 months at Carrara after having begun the contract and pretended that he had spent this time making a road to Pietra Santa and opening the quarry there.

In or about 1542, Michelangelo wrote that he could not devote his full attention to painting frescoes for Pauline Chapel until he was fully released from his obligations to complete the tomb of Julius II, and he reviewed the history of the project for a cleric who he hoped would persuade Paul III to get Guidobaldo, Duke of Urbino, to ratify the final contract:

> Your Lordship send to tell me that I should paint and not worry about anything else. I reply that one paints with the head and not with the hands, and if one cannot concentrate, one brings disgrace upon oneself. Therefore, until my affair is settled, I can do no good work. The ratification of the last contract hasn't come.... I maintain, with a clear conscience that the heirs of Pope Julius owe me five thousand *scudi*. ...I lost the whole of my youth, chained to this Tomb, contending, as far as I was able, against the demands of Pope Leo and Clement. An excessive honesty, which went unrecognized, has been my ruin. ...Pope Leo, who did not want me to execute the said Tomb, pretended that he wished to execute the façade of San Lorenzo in Florence and asked Aginensis for my services. He has therefore perforce to give me leave, with the proviso that I should do the said Tomb of Julius in Florence. While I was in Florence for

the said façade of San Lorenzo, as I hadn't marble there for the Tomb of Julius [the marble previously sent to Rome for this purpose being unavailable], I returned to Carrara and stayed there thirteen months, and transported all the marbles for the said Tomb to Florence, and built a workshop in which to execute them, and began working. At this time Aginensis sent Messer Francesco Palavicini, who is to-day the Bishop of Aleria, to urge me on, and he saw the workshop and all the said marbles and the figures blocked out for the said Tomb, which are still there to-day. Seeing this, that is to say that I was working for the said Tomb, Medici, who afterwards become Pope Clement, who was living in Florence, did not permit me to proceed, and I continued to be impeded in this way until Medici became Clement. Then in his presence the last contract up to now for the said Tomb was afterwards drawn up, in which it was stated that I had received the eight thousand ducts, which they say I lent at interest. But I want to confess a wrong-doing to Your Lordship—that is, that while I was in Carrara, when I stayed there thirteen months for the said Tomb, being in need of money, I spent a thousand *scudi* on marbles for the said work, which Pope Leo had sent me for the façade of San Lorenzo or rather to keep me occupied, and I made him excuses, pretending there were difficulties. This I did for the love I bore the said work.... I' not a thieving usurer but a Florentine citizen of noble family, the son of an honest man.... And those who have robbed me of my youth, my honour and my possessions, call me a thief! [Michelangelo 1963: II, 26-31].

Ramsden identified the recipient of this letter as Cardinal Alessandro Farnese, the grandson of Paul III, and although in 1542 he was only 22 years old, he had been a cardinal since he was 14, and in 1542 he did write to the Bishop of Sinigaglia asking him to persuade Guidobaldo, Duke of Urbino, to ratify the final contract, but Guidobaldo wanted the minimal terms of the final contract to be fulfilled before releasing Michelangelo from the previous contract (261). Considering that none of the three previous contracts had been fulfilled, this was a reasonable precaution against further papal interference rather than against Michelangelo.

To return to the question of why work ceased on the front of San Lorenzo, Ackerman summarized the relevant events that took place in 1520:

> Sometime after his arrival in Florence on 13 February 1520, Cardinal Giulio, who want some of the newly quarried marble for the Cathedral, demands reckoning from Michelangelo of his expenses at Carrara. Michelangelo, in an enraged letter to Rome, asks that the Pope issue a Breve absolving him of any debt arising from disbursements for quarrying (*Lettere*, pp. 415-416; *Aufzeichnungen*, pp. 53 ff.). On 10 March he is released from his responsibilities in procuring marble and the Pope declares the financial accounts balanced. Michelangelo claims in his notebook (*Lettere*, p. 581) that the purpose was "forse per fare più presto la sopra detta facciata" [work on the front might start again soon]. Though it is not the purpose of this agreement to cancel the project, little more is done for the façade. Columns are mentioned in the correspondence of December 1520 (Tolnay 1948, pp. 225226), and action is sporadically considered in the next few years (*Aufzeichnungen*, pp. 64-65; *Lettere*, p. 421; see the remarks on the façade interior, p. 32). I can offer no good reason for the abandonment of the façades. If, as Tolnay proposed (1948, . 7, the funds were used up on military operations, it would not have been possible to start the equally costly Medici chapel at the same time [Ackerman 1964: 7].

A few largely undated letters by Michelangelo have been assigned to the period from 1520-1523, and these few letters indicate nothing definite about what he was working on at the time (Michelangelo 1963: I, 135-149). Condivi's account of this period is brief and inconclusive (Condivi 1553: 63-64). Vasari indicates only that Michelangelo "...wasted a great deal of time now on one thing and now on another" (57), and he added,

> Michelangelo devoted many years of his life to quarrying marble, although it is true that while the blocks were being excavated he also made wax models and other things for the façade. But the project was delayed so long that the money the Pope assigned to it was spent on the war in Lombardy, and when Leo died the work was left unfinished, nothing having been accomplished save the laying of a foundation in front to support the façade and the transportation of a large column of marble from Carrara to the Piazza di San Lorenzo [Vasari 1568: 57].

Michelangelo told Condivi and Vasari very little about this period of his life.

Sometime in 1520 or 1521 Michelangelo prepared designs for the Medici Chapel, and since began to arrange to have marble quarried for the chapel, the designs had been approved, but Clement vacillated, and little was accomplished. Around April 1523 Michelangelo wrote at some point during the time of Adrian VI, "it is now about two years since I returned for placing orders in Carrara for quarrying the marbles for the Cardinal's Tombs...," but he had been given no specific instructions since placing the orders. He added significantly, "...and if, as you tell me, the Cardinal de' Medici now once again wishes me to execute the tombs at San Lorenzo, you see that I cannot do so, unless he releases me from this affair in Rome. And if he releases me, I promise to work for him without any return for the rest of my life" (Michelangelo 1963: I, 143).

Michelangelo's Study of Ancient Roman Architecture

Michelangelo eventually read Vitruvius with great care, and in a letter about the faults of Sangallo's design for the cornice of the Palazzo Farnese, Michelangelo demolishes the design as incompetent by paraphrasing Vitruvius and by citing him twice. Another important clue was the statement he made when he was asked why he was going to the Colosseum during inclement weather, and he replied, "I'm still going to school to learn" (Clements 1968: 21). Vitruvius and ruins were the chief sources available to all Renaissance architects to learn how about Roman architecture, and Michelangelo was well able to determine for himself how Roman architects designed. Evidence of careful study of Roman ruins is reflected in a number of reconstructions of the classical orders that he made beginning at least as early as c. 1515.

Michelangelo studied the Pantheon and concluded that it "...was built by three architects, the first carrying it up to the cornice above the columns, the second doing from the cornice upwards, containing the more slender windows, because this second portion differs from the lower part, the vaulting not corresponding with the lines of the divisions. The third is believed to have done the beautiful portico" (Vasari 1568: II, 276).

The main inspiration for the tomb celebrating the triumphs of Julius II was have come from the Triumphal Arch of Constantine, which has bound though clothed captives in front of its attic and a similar composition with a strong center. One of Michelangelo's surviving drawings is of the Arch of Constantine, and another drawing is of adaptations of a triumphal arch. Since triumphal arches generally incorporated sculpture, they were a design source that Michelangelo had undoubtedly studied carefully. He later made obvious use of the design elements of triumphal arches for the walls of his Medici Chapel.

Most importantly, the Arch of Constantine provided an early Christian precedent for compact buildings and for treating facades as settings for sculpture. More specifically, it also provided three architectural elements that recur frequently in Michelangelo's architectural designs: (1) sculpted reliefs, (2) paired columns, (3) attic story, and (4) pedestals. To show the impact the Roman triumphal arch had on the architecture of Michelangelo, I have listed the projects in which he used the principal design elements:

(1) sculpted reliefs: Tomb of Julius II, and San Lorenzo front (particularly sculpted rondels); also sculpted rondels are depicted in the frescoes of the Sistine ceiling.

(2) paired columns: Julius II initial design, San Lorenzo front, Medici Chapel, Laurentian Library, St. Peter's, San Giovanni de' Fiorentini design, and Porta Pia.

(3) attic story: San Lorenzo front, Medici Chapel, Campidoglio (adapted as a Renaissance balustrade), St. Peter's, San Giovanni de' Fiorentini design, and Porta Pia.

(4) pedestals (adapted from the podium of temples): Tomb of Julius II (for bound captives in the early designs), San Lorenzo front, Medici Chapel, Campidoglio, St. Peter's, San Giovanni de' Fiorentini design, and Porta Pia.

The use of all four of these design elements for the front of San Lorenzo clear indicate their source was a triumphal arch, and developmental drawings confirm this. Moreover, the final design for San Lorenzo is a block placed in front of and hiding the irregular profile of the clearstoried front of the church. Michelangelo's surviving sketch of the Arch of Constantine and its Christian association make it all but certain to have been the most influential source for these elements, and it was surely the source for the bound captives that were added to the of the tomb of Julius II, which was initially designed as a triumphal arch. The use of the first three design elements in the Medici Chapel make the importance of the triumphal arch still more evident. Consequently, there is good reason to think that for St. Peter's the use of paired columns on a running pedestal with an attic were also ultimately and knowingly derived from the design of a triumphal arch and specifically the arch of the first Christian emperor. Moreover, in choosing the name Julius and in leading armies personally, Julius identified himself with Julius Caesar as the first and greatest of Roman emperors. It was thus fitting for the Tomb of Julius II to feature bound captives and nude figures and for the Sistine Chapel to have decorative nudes as part of the revival of ancient Roman art, which Julius II collected for the Vatican Museum.

In addition, the Arch of Constantine provided Christian precedents for (5) bound captives; (6) crowded figures in action; (7) nude figures; and (8) sculpted and symmetrically placed pairs of rondels. These less frequently used design elements that occur on the Arch of Constantine were used by Michelangelo for the following projects:

(5) bound captives: Tomb of Julius II.

(6) sculpted friezes with figures in action: Although no building of Michelangelo has monumental reliefs equivalent to those incorporated in the Arch of Constantine, the twisting figures in motion of the great frieze seems likely to have been one of the principal influences of Michelangelo's style as a sculptor and painter. He is more likely to have gotten the idea for crowded reliefs with nudes from ancient Roman sarcophaguses reused or adapted by early Christians (especially for his Battle of Centaurs), but a more general influence on Michelangelo's art was compositions consisting largely or entirely of figures (without backgrounds either natural or architectural). He correctly considered this to be a classical convention, and he usually considered settings for his figures to be unneeded. In addition, the Arch of Constantine provided a classical precedent for the use of separate scenes with figures at various scales (even though in this case, it was the result of having combined figures from many sources).

(7) nude figures for architecture: Tomb of Julius II and Sistine Chapel ceiling.

(8) pairs of sculpted rondels: San Lorenzo front. Depicted on the Sistine ceiling. Rondels without sculpture had been frequently used by Bramante, and sculpted rondels had been frequently used by Della Robbia.

Other design elements that Michelangelo so frequently used that they became characteristic of his architecture were (9) segmental arched pediments (which he probably adopted from the Pantheon's aedicules) and (10) friezes of grotesque faces (Arch of Septimius Severus).

(9) segmental arched pediments: San Lorenzo front, Laurentian Library, and St. Peter's.

(10) friezes of grotesque faces: Medici Chapel.

Thus, for most of his design elements, Michelangelo adapted ancient Roman elements, which also included brackets, but mainly as modillions. Although Alberti had enlarged brackets monumentally for his church in Florence, Michelangelo seems to have been first to have regularly used relatively large brackets for architectural designs including under the windows he created for the Medici Palace, to provide visual support for columns in the vestibule of the Laurentian Library, and on the cenotaph of Julius II in place of captives. According to Vasari, Michelangelo invented the use of monumental brackets as a decorative feature.

Michelangelo's sketch of the Arch of Constantine (detail; De Tolnay, *Corpus* no. 512)

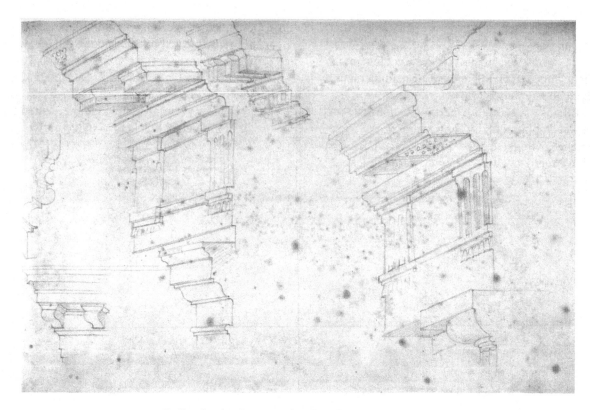

Studies of ancient Roman cornices (De Tolnay, *Corpus* no. 519r)

Medici Chapel, Florence (1522-1534)

Rather than constructing a new front for San Giovanni, Pope Leo X and his cousin Cardinal Giulio de' Medici (the future Clement VII) decided to give priority to the creation of a funerary chapel for their fathers and to one of Leo's brothers and nephews. Symonds noted that

> ...we first hear something definite about them in a *Ricordo* which extends from April 9 to August 19 1521.... Michelangelo says that on the former of these dates he received money from the Cardinal de' Medici for a journey to Carrara, whither he went and stayed about three weeks, ordering marbles for "the tombs which are to be placed in the new sacristy at S. Lorenzo. And there I made out drawing to scale, and measured models in clay for the said tombs." He left his assistant Scipione of Settignano at Carrara as overseer of the work, and returned to Florence. On the 20th of July following he went again to Carrara, and stayed nine days. On the 16th of August the contractors for the blocks, all of which were excavated from the old Roman quarry of Polvaccio, came to Florence and were paid for on account. Scipione returned on the 19thof August [Symonds 1901: I, 357].

This "New Sacristy" was to be closely similar in size and form to Brunelleschi's Old Sacristy, where other Medici ancestors had been buried, and it was to be placed symmetrically on the opposite side of San Lorenzo. The main difference in the space as a whole is that Michelangelo added an attic story. The main difference in the overall effect is that the sculpture predominates rather than being ornament, and the architecture is a background for the sculpture.

Even more than Michelangelo's previous architectural designs, this one owes an obvious debt the triumphal arch. Each of the four walls has a monumental arch in its center. Each wall is divided into three parts though the used of pilasters, creating a composition with a central block and flanking wings. At the same level as the heads of the arches, cornices above and below them create the effect of an attic. A dome with coffers adapted from the Pantheon's dome, but supported on pendentives.

In 1520, Michelangelo was 45 years old, and he had become an accomplished architect as well as the leading sculptor and painter by the midpoint of his life. His innumerable alternative designs for the Medici Chapel and the results of his work there demonstrate that he had fully developed his distinctive style. Most of the design employs conventional forms of the Corinthian order, enframements, and domes. Closely similar grotesque faces can be found on the Arch of Septimius Severus. However, the enframements above the doors could not have been designed by anyone earlier. He cut through the horizontal cornice of a segmental arched pediment to inserted first a recess with projecting corners, and within it he inserted a smaller rectangular recess. He made the cornice of the curving pediment break forward. He supported this enframement with his oversized brackets. Enframents within enframements was characteristic of his designs from this point on and was widely emulated.

Medici Chapel (albumen by Anderson)

Medici Chapel (Grimm)

Cenotaph for Lorenzo de\ Medici (Grimm)

Cenotraph for Giuliano de' Medici (Grimm)

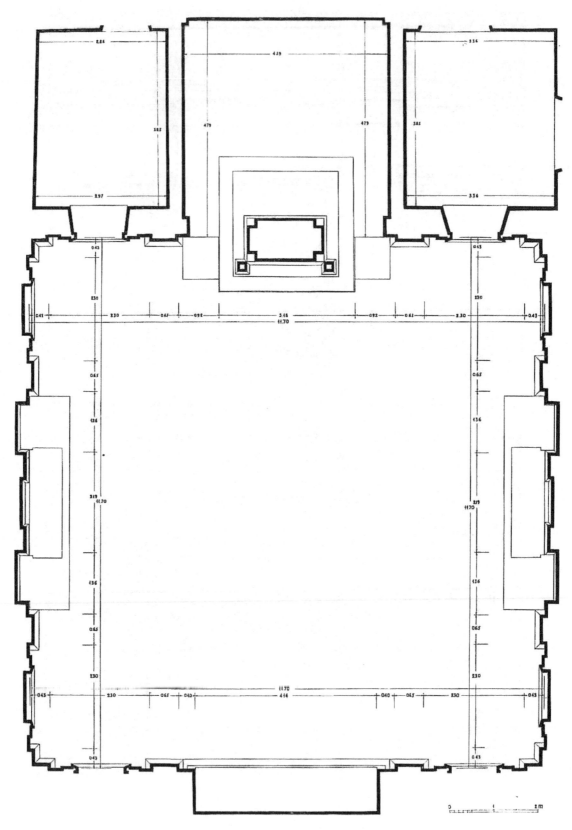

Medici Chapel (Facoltà Arch. Univ. Firenze in Schiavo)

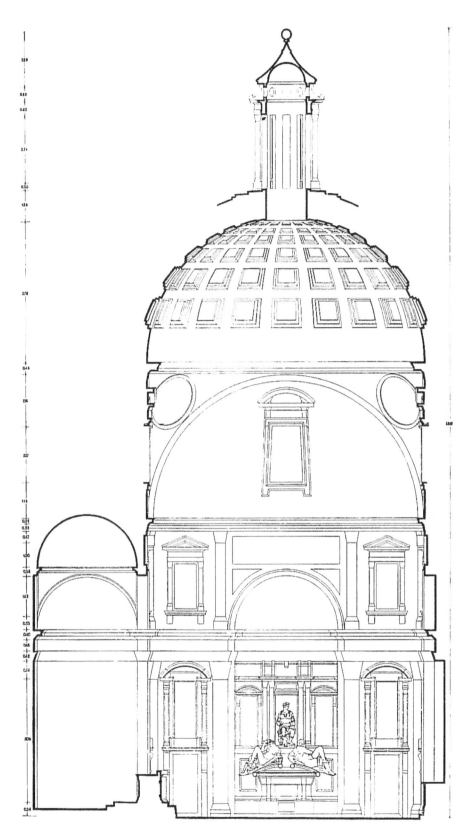

Section through the Medici Chapel (Facoltà Arch. Univ. Firenze; Schiavo)

Dome of the Medici Chapel (2015)

In April of 1523 Michelangelo proposed to Cardinal Giulio de' Medici completing the Medici Chapel by hiring numerous assistants to help him carry out the needed work:

> It is now about two years since I returned form placing orders in Carrara for quarrying the marbles for the Cardinal's Tombs [the Medici Chapel] and when I went to discuss them with him he told me to find some sound solution for doing the said Tombs ...I offered to make the models in wood to the full size that the Tombs are to be, and to put in all the figures in clay and shearings to the full size, and finished exactly as they are to be, and I pointed out that this would be a quick and inexpensive way to do them. ... He told me to expedite the marbles and to get the men and to do everything I could, so that he might see something completed without my consulting him further; and that he survived, he would also do the façade [of San Lorenzo] and that he was leaving orders to Domenico Buoninsegni to arrange about all the money required. ... [Later] he said to me, "For these Tombs we should require at least one good piece, that is to say something by your own hand." He did not say that he wanted me to execute them [immediately]. I left, and said that I would return to discuss them with him when the marbles arrived [Michelangelo 1963: I, 142-143; notes omitted].

Thus, between 1520-1523 little had been accomplished on the Medici Chapel even though Leo X and Cardinal Giuliano had agreed on a tentative design in 1520. During these two or more years, Michelangelo spent much of is time redesigning the Chapel, and consequently a large number of alternative designs exist for this project, but that was due more to Clement than Michelangelo. Clement prevented him from working either on the chapel or on the tomb of Julius II. Since Condivi stated that the new sacristy was "built for the purpose" of four Medici tombs, Michelangelo must have built it, and he must have spent much of the two years building most if not all of it; he certainly built the upper story, dome, and lantern.

The situation changed entirely when in November 1523 the Cardinal became Pope Clement VII. Michelangelo then wrote from Florence to a sculptor, "you will have heard that Medici is made Pope, which I think will rejoice everyone. I expect, for this reason, that as far as art is concerned many things will be executed here" (Michelangelo 1963: I, 146). In January 1524 Michelangelo requested payment for 15 gold ducats for "...the models of the Tombs for the Sacristy of San Lorenzo, which I'm doing for Pope Clement" (Michelangelo 1963: I, 150); this has to have been for the interior, and the lantern has been completed in or about January 1524 (Michelangelo 1963: I, 151). In addition, he was commissioned to design the Laurentian Library in January 1524, but even by July 1524 no one in Florence had authority to disburse funds for either the chapel or the library, and he wrote Clement, "...since I have no authority here, I do not think I should have the blame either. If Your Holiness wishes me to accomplish anything, I beg You not to have authorities set over me in my own trade, but to have faith in me and give me a free hand" (151 cf. 155).

The chapel was to be the burial place of four members of the Medici family: (1) the father of Leo X (Lorenzo the Magnificent, who had taken Michelangelo into his household and had him trained as a sculptor); (2) the father of the future Clement VII (Giuliano de' Medici, a brother of Lorenzo the Magnificent who had been assassinated in the Pazzi conspiracy in 1478); (3) a nephew of Leo X (Lorenzo, "Duke of Urbino," who had been given a duchy by Leo X and who was the father of Catherine de' Medici); and (4) a brother of Leo X (Giuliano, Duke of Nemours [Ramsden in Michelangelo 1963: I, App. 2]). Thus, the tombs were primarily for the father, a brother, and a nephew of Leo X and secondarily for the father of his first cousin, the future Clement VII. Buried in the chapel or "New Sacristy" are two Medici named Lorenzo and two named Giuliano. Buried in the Old Sacristy by Brunelleschi that was the model for the New Sacristy were ancestors of the four Medici buried in the New Sacristy (Medici Chapel). Although the church of San Lorenzo had been built with contributions by many of the families in the neighborhood, the church and the adjacent monastery became increasingly considered by the Medici to be their church.

To put some related events in context, the former Duke of Urbino (Francesco Maria della Rovere) was a nephew of Julius, who was also a Della Rovere, and in 1516 Leo X had excommunicated him and given his duchy to his own nephew (Ramsden in Michelangelo 1963: I, 251). Leo had also in 1516 pressured the two cardinals who were executors of the estate of Julius II to agree to pay Michelangelo the same price for about half as many sculptures for the tomb of Julius II, reducing the number of sculptures from 40 to 22. Since 1516 was the also the year in which Michelangelo was given the contract for the architecture and sculpture of the Medici's funerary chapel, it becomes clear that these events were not unrelated. However, in 1519 the putative "Duke of Urbino" died; in 1521, Leo died; and in 1523, Pope Adrian VI restored the Duke of Urbino, who by this time had become an executor of the estate of Julius II as well as being one of his nephews and who pressured Michelangelo to complete the tomb, but not for long (255). Consequently, little work progress was made on the Medici Chapel from December 1521 when Leo died and November 1523 when Clement VII became pope, but once another Medici was pope, he too applied pressure on the Della Rovere executors to enable Michelangelo to devote most of his attention the Medici Chapel. In 1524, Clement added the Laurentian Library to Michelangelo's commissions, and iIn1525, the executors agreed to accept a greatly reduced tomb for Julius II that would consist of a wall tomb with six sculptures by Michelangelo rather than the 40 sculptures agreed upon n 1513 or the 22 sculptures agreed upon in 1516. Although work resumed on the Medici chapel and library in 1524, it largely stopped again from 1527 to 1530 when the Florentine Republic was temporarily revived.

Leo X and Clement VII abused their positions as head of the Church for the benefit of the Medici family, to utilize Michelangelo increasingly, and to waste his talent and time. It was no exaggeration when Condivi wrote about Michelangelo that "...it had been some fifteen years since he had touched his tools..." as a sculptor (from 1516 to 1530; Condivi 1553: 67). It was no exaggeration when Vasari wrote about changes in the design of the tomb of Julius II that "...subsequently, of the four sides, one of the shorter sides was erected in San Pietro in Vincoli" (Vasari 1568: 37). Michelangelo had little control over what he was able to accomplish from 1516 to 1530, and he was not exaggerating when he wrote in 1526 about the tomb of Julius II, "...I desire to be rid of this obligation more than to live" (Michelangelo 1963: I, 169). As with the Sistine ceiling, he became increasingly interested in the Medici Chapel until his interest was all consuming, and it too provided his first opportunity to show what he was capable of producing as an architect. Condivi concluded about Clement VII that "...if in his lifetime he had done nothing else that was praiseworthy, whereas indeed he did much, this would suffice to cancel his every fault since, through him the world has so noble a work" (Condivi 1553: 67).

So little documentation relating to the Medici Chapel survives from 1520-1523 that is even uncertain if Michelangelo supervised the construction of the New Sacristy in which the new Medici tombs were to be placed. However, Condivi is explicit that the tombs were "...placed in a sacristy built for the purpose..." (Condivi 1553: 67). Although Condivi made mistakes, no one who wrote about Michelangelo had better access to him, and what he wrote must be accepted unless it can be disproven. Without indicating sources in this rare instance, Ramsden was explicit that "...the building (which was on a Quattrocento foundation) was well advanced, having been under construction since the March of that year [1520]... and by November 1529 Michelangelo was already in communication with Cardinal Giulio de' Medici bout the design for the tombs" (Michelangelo 1963: I, 275). Ackerman reviewed the available evidence and concluded that it could not be reconciled, but he noted that a c. 1502 sketch by Leonardo indicated the new sacristy did not then exist and that "according to the contemporary chronicler, Giovanni Cambri, a building program was initiated shortly before March 1520. On 1 March, the Chapter allotted funds for the programme" (Ackerman 1964: 23). He concluded that "the chapel entrance wall must have been constructed especially to accommodate a deep tomb niche after the final designs of 1521. Its peculiar plan and angled doorway may be explained by the tomb." Considering that arched recesses in the walls had to be provided for in a structurally sound way capable of supporting an added clearstory, it is all but certain that Michelangelo adapted the plan of the Old Sacristy by Brunelleschi for the plan of the New Sacristy and supervised its construction or at least its completion in ways that would make it suitable for wall tombs. He was definitely responsible for the design of the interior walls, clearstory, dome, and lantern as well as for the design of all the sculpture, and the Medici was his first architectural design to be constructed. As a sculptor Michelangelo made special provision for the lighting of his sculpture.

The basic architectural work had been completed by around the time the Cardinal became pope in November 1523. In January 1524, Michelangelo wrote Clement VII that even the lantern of the dome had been completed:

> Now I see that this is going to be a long business and I do not know how it wall proceed. Therefore, should matters turn out to be displeasing to Your Holiness, I desire to be exonerated; since I have no authority here, I do not think I should have the blame either. If your Holiness wishes me to accomplish anything, I beg You not to have authorities set over me in my own trade, but to have faith in me and give me a free hand. Your Holiness will see what I shall accomplish and the account I shall give of myself.
>
> Stefano [di Tomaso Lunetti, and illuminator and clerk of the works] had finished the lantern of the chapel of the said San Lorenzo here and has uncovered it. It is universally admired

by everyone, as I hope it will be by Your Holiness, when You see it. We are having the ball which surmounts it made about a *braccia* in diameter and, in order to vary it from the others, I decided to have it made with [72] facets, and this is being done [Michelangelo 1963: I, 151; with some notes added within brackets].

Michelangelo needed someone to supervise construction when he was not present, and he hired Stefano to do this as a favor to him, but he proved to be an "ingrate" and was soon fired (153). Although Michelangelo was ready to work on the chapel and tomb, in July 1524, he was still waiting for the arrival of more marble, and since no one in Florence had been authorized to make payments for either project, little had been done (155).

Michelangelo was also distracted by threats of a lawsuit over the tomb of Julius II, but in 1525 a tentative agreement was reached for a wall tomb with six figures by Michelangelo subject to the approval of a final design, but his responsibilities to Clement and political events prevented another contract from being signed until 1532. He wrote in 1525, ...if I'm given my salary, I'll always go on working for Pope Clement with such powers as I have, which are slight, as I'm an old man—with this proviso, that the taunts, to which I see I am being subjected [about the tomb] cease, because they very much upset me and have prevented me from doing the work I want to do for several months now. For one cannot work at one thing with the hands and at another with the head, particularly in the case of marble" (163).

The design development for the interior architectural elements and sculpture was long and complicated, and it is too poorly documented to reconstruct with certainty, but it is known that initially Michelangelo planned to put a free-standing tomb in the center with sculpture on four sides similar to the initial plan for the tomb of Julius II, that he early on decided to create three wall tombs, and that he briefly considered adding a fourth wall tomb for Leo X and Clement VII (Ackerman 1964: 22-30). "In April of 1521 Michelangelo went to Carrara to supervise the quarrying of blocks for the tomb figures, which indicates the acceptance of a final design both for the tombs and for the architecture" (24). Most of the surviving drawings are for the wall tombs of the four Medici who are buried in the funerary chapel, and only what was constructed will be considered here in some detail.

On July 17, 1526, Michelangelo gave a progress report to his friend and financial advisor Giovan Francesco Fattucci on the work that was being done on the Medici Chapel:

This coming week I shall have the figures that are blocked out in the Sacristy covered up, because I want to leave the Sacristy free for the *scarpellini* working on the marble, as I want them to begin building in the other Tomb opposite the one that is built in, which is aligned, or very nearly. And while they are building it in I thought the vault might be done [painted] and supposed that, with enough men, it could be done in two or three months, but I don't know. At the end of next week Our Lord can send [the decorative arts painter] Messer Giovanni da Undine whenever he wises, if he thinks the vault should be done now, as I shall be ready.

As to the recess, four columns have been built in this week—one of them was built in before. The tabernacles [enframements] will be a little behindhand; however, I think it will be finished in four months from today. The framework of the floor should be begun by now, but the limes [for cement] are not yet seasoned; we'll hasten the drying process as much as possible.

I'm working as hard as I can, and in a fortnight' time I shall get the other "Captain" started [the other seated figure for a Duke's tomb]; then of the important things, I shall have only the four "Rivers" [allegorical river gods] left. The four figures on the coffers [two on top of each sarcophagus], the four figures on the ground, which are the "Rivers," the two "Captains," and "Our Lady" which is going into the tomb at the top end [the Madonna and Child for the double tomb of the fathers of the two popes], are the figures I want to do myself. And of these [13 figures including the captains], six are begun. I feel confident about doing them within a reasonable time and having the others [SS. Cosmas and Damian], which are not so important, done in part [Michelangelo 1963: I, 165-166; notes omitted].

As this quotation indicates, Michelangelo planned to add pairs of additional river gods on the floor to each side of the sarcophaguses (which would have made a total of eight). His final intention seems to have been to create a number of triangular compositons resembling pediments/ His scroll-like pediments on top of the sarcophaguses are further indications of this evident plan to create a series of pediments within pediments as above doors in the reading room of Laurentian library and on the Porta Pia. The figures on top of the sarcophagusess are massive, and they lean on their elbows symmetrically just as the river gods would have done on the floor and as they do on the Capitol. The figures on the sarcophaguses are primarily river gods despite the allegorical interpretations that were assigned to them. The masssiveness and monumentality of river gods seems to have appealed to him greatly, but he also liked triangular compositions generally and placing design elements within design elements.

Giovanni da Undine had previously painted decorations similar to ancient Roman designs for the loggia Raphael designed for Clement that was later called the Villa Madama (named for Margaret, the daughter of Charles V and widow of Clement's son Alessandro). The paintings add greatly to the overall effect of the loggia, and Clement is likely to have stipulated that Udine paint the dome of the Medici Chapel. When his delicate paintings were for the chapel were completed, they proved to be less effective because of the height of its dome, and they were whitewashed. Michelangelo had used similar designs for the tomb of Julius, but not for the tombs of the dukes.

About four months later, by November 1526 the political situation had deteriorated so much that Michelangelo was asked to reduce expenses, and in December, he wrote, "...the times are unfavourable to this art of mine; I do not know whether I have any further expectation of my salary" (170).

...the struggle between France and the Empire for possession of Milan and for domination in Italy was soon renewed, the pope inclining first to one side and then to the other, as seemed the more politic or as best suited his ambitions.... As usual [and had also been the case under Julius II], alliance followed alliance in bewildering succession. But following the formation of the so-called Holy League against him, the Emperor Charles [who was also King of Spain] determined to punish Clement for his duplicity and in September 1526 incited the powerful Colonna family, who were Spanish in sympathy, to attack the Vatican. Clement wa forced to take refuge in the Castel Sant' Angelo and even the sacristy of St. Peter's was pillaged" [Ramsden in Michelangelo 1963: I, 285].

In May of 1527, Rome began to occupied for seven months by a pillaging an army of Spanish troops composed mainly of Protestant mercenaries.

While Rome was occupied, Florence restored its republic, and Ramsden summarized the situation there from 1527-1530: "In 1527 the city was thrown into a state of commotion by the advance of the Imperial troops and by the subsequent sack of Rome; in the same year and again in 1528, the work was further interrupted by an outbreak of plague, to which Buonarroto, Michelangelo's favourite brother succumbed during the second epidemic; while in 1529 the work had to be abandoned altogether when Michelangelo was appointed Procurator-General for the fortifications in anticipation of the Pope's attack on the city" (Ramsden in Michelangelo 1963: I, 275).

Most work on the Medici Chapel was done between 1531 and 1534. When Clement VII called Michelangelo to Rome to paint the Last Judgment, the chapel had been largely completed, but he had intended to do more. In October 15, 1533 he wrote "...by tomorrow night I shall have finish the two small models I'm making for Tribolo..." (Michelangelo 1963: I,

186). Il Tribolo was the sculptor Niccolò di Raffaello de' Pericoli, and Ramsden noted that he "...was commissioned to execute the flanking figures, "Heaven" and Earth," for the Tomb of Giuliano, Duke of Nemours, after the model supplied by Michelangelo, but he fell ill, and on the death of Clement VII, the work was abandoned... (Vasari, VI, p. 66)" (186-187, n. 1). Thus, if the Medici Chapel had been completed as Michelangelo intended, it would have had additional sculpture that he designed, but that others executed. Ramsden also summarized the extent to which work had been completed on the chapel by 1534:

> Having been resumed in the autumn of 1530, the work continued without undue interruption for the next four years, but when Michelangelo left Florence for good in September 1534, only the two ideal figures representing the Dukes (referred to by Michelangelo as the *Capitani*) had been completed and set in place. Of the other figures mentioned in the letter to Fattucci (No. 177 [quoted earlier]) the Madonna and Child, intended for the niche above the double tomb at the top end" of the Chapel, and the four symbolical figures for the sarcophagi, that is to say, *Day* and *Night*, *Dawn* and *Twilight*, were in varying stages of completion, but the four River Gods, designed to support [to flank] the symbolical figures, were not even begun. Two large-scale models for these had been made, however, and are mentioned by Doni (pt. iii, p. 24) as being in the chapel in the mid-sixteenth century, but only the one now preserved in the Accademia in Florence has survived [moved to the Casa Buonarroti]. The two less important figures to which Michelangelo also refers in his letter, namely the patron saints of the Medici family, *SS. Cosmas* and *Damian*, which were begun under his supervision, were afterwards completed by the sculptors to whom he had assigned them, the *S. Cosmas* being executed by Fra Giovanni Montorsoli (507-1563) and the *S. Damian* by Raffaello da Montelupo (c. 1505-1566)
>
> [Ramsden in Michelangelo 1963: I, 275].

An equivalent architectural setting had been planned for the double tomb of the fathers of the two popes, and it was to have had two sarcophagi side by side with the Madonna and Child above them and flanked by the saints, but eventually the Madonna and saints were place above a marble podium that serves also as the double tomb.

Much like the tomb of Julius II, none of the figures on the dukes' tombs had anything to do with religion. The dukes were depicted as Roman military officers rather than represented by portraits in contemporary costumes (as Leo X had been in the seated bronze statue that Michelangelo created of him). The four figures placed on top of a classical sarcophagus resembled statues of Roman river gods, and four additional river gods were intended to be added. The composition of the dukes' tombs was based on a triumphal arch, and it was placed within another adaptation of a triumphal arch (with an arch flanked by paired columns and an attic story). The pattern of coffers for the dome was adapted from the Pantheon rather than duplicating the gored dome of the Old Sacristy. Condivi discussed what Michelangelo had intended to convey by the statues:

> The tombs are four, placed in a sacristy built for the purpose in the left side of the church, across from the Old Sacristy. And although there was one conception and one form of them all, nevertheless the figures are all different and in different poses and attitudes. The tombs are placed in certain chapels [recesses] and on their covers recline two great figures more than life-size, a man and a woman, representing *Day* and *Night* and, collectively time which consumes all. And, in order for his intent to be better understood, he gave to *Night*, which is made in the form of a woman of wondrous beauty, the owl and other pertinent symbols, and to *Day* his symbols likewise. And to signify Time, he meant to carve a mouse, for which he left a little bit of marble on the work, but then he was prevented and did not do it; because this little creature is forever

gnawing on consuming just as time devours all things. Then there are other statues which represent those for which the tombs were built; and all of them, in conclusions, are more divine than human, but especially a Madonna with her little Son astride her thigh, about which I deem it better to be silent than to say little, so I shall forbear [Condivi 1553: 67].

The Madonna and two saints were placed opposite the chapel, and the dukes' tombs were entirely unrelated in subject matter, but all three walls with tombs would have had similar architectural designs. In addition to his other talents, Michelangelo wrote poetry and took a scholarly interest in Italian literature, and he often used classical allusions and literary conventions in his art. He made good use, for example, of Dante for the design of the Last Judgment (Condivi 1553: 84); "he was especially fond of Dante, whom he greatly admired, and whom he followed in his ideas and inventions..." (Vasari 1568: 125).

Michelangelo was much indebted to Luca Signorelli. "...Luca's works were always highly praised by Michelagnolo, who in his divine Last Judgment in the chapel partly borrowed from Luca such things as angels, demons, the arrangement of the heavens, and other things in which Michelagnolo imitated Luca's treatment, as all may see" (Vasari 1568: II, 147). Luca's "...works were more highly valued than almost any other master's, no matter of what period, because he showed the way to represent nude figures in painting so as to make them appear alive..." (145). "Luca being the one who by his ground-work of design, and especially of nudes, by his grace of invention and the grouping of his scenes, paved the way for the final perfection of art..." (149).

The four figures on top of the sarcophagi were decorative nudes equivalent to the captives for the tomb of Julius II and the seated nudes on the ceiling of the Sistine Chapel, but their pose and placement were entirely different. For the tomb, the captives were to all standing, and for the ceiling, the decorative nudes were all seated. The four nudes for the Medici chapel recline on an elbow and rest on top of tombs. By contrast, Medieval tombs often had fully reclining statues of the deceased lying in state. A representation of a living person rather than a corpse was a classical convention, and on Etruscan tombs, the individuals often reclined on an elbow, but this pose is more likely to have been based on the usual pose for Roman river gods like the ones Michelangelo intended to place beside the sarcophagi. Although the designs of the sarcophagi are based on ancient Roman examples, their covers are broken pediments with segmental arches. This explains why these four figures looks as if they were about to slide off the tops of the sarcophagi. If the four river gods that Michelangelo also intended to execute himself had been created, the base of each of the dukes' tombs would have had a triangular composition that would have been more effective visually.

Briefly, consideration was given to creating a single wall tomb for Leo X and Clement VII in the Medici Chapel, and Michelangelo made a design for two wall tombs to face one another on opposite sides of the choir of the church of San Lorenzo. Eventually, Leo and Clement were buried in Santa Maria sopra Minerva in Rome in large, but undistinguished wall tombs facing one another on opposite sides of the choir. Their tombs were designed by Antonio Sangallo the Younger (who Michelangelo succeeded as architect of St Peter's), and colossal seated statues of the popes were made by Raffaello da Montelupo (Michelangelo's inept assistant) and Nanni da Baccio Bigio (who created the greatly inferior colossal statue beside a copy of Michelangelo's David in front of the Palazzo Vecchio in Florence).

While completing as much of the chapel as possible before being called to Rome by Clement, Michelangelo "...lived in extreme fear, because he was deeply hated by Duke Alessandro, a fierce and vengeful young man, as everybody knows. And there is no doubt that, if it had not been for the respect shown by the pope, he would have gotten rid of Michelangelo. All the more so since, when the duke of Florence wanted to build that fortress which he built and had Signor Alessandro summon Michelangelo to ride with him to see where it could conveniently be built, Michelangelo would not go, answering that he had no such orders from Pope Clement. This made the duke very angry; so that, both for this new reason and on account of the old ill will and the natural disposition of the duke, Michelangelo was justified in being afraid..." (Condivi 1553: 70). Alessandro was assassinated in 1537, but Michelangelo never returned to Florence during the last three decades of his life, and the chapel and library remained incomplete, but were eventually finished.

Preliminary design for a single tomb in the Medici Chapel (De Tolnay, *Corpus* no. 185r)

Preliminary design for a double tomb in the Medici Chapel (De Tolnay, *Corpus* no. 180r)

Laurentian Library, Florence (1524-1534)

Reading room of the Laurentian Library (2014)

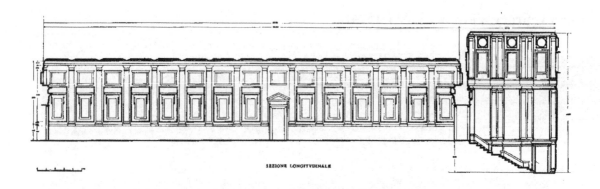

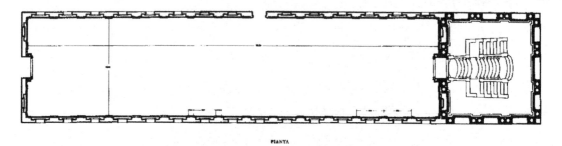

Section and plan of the Laurentian Library (Facoltà Arch. Univ Firenze; Schiavo)

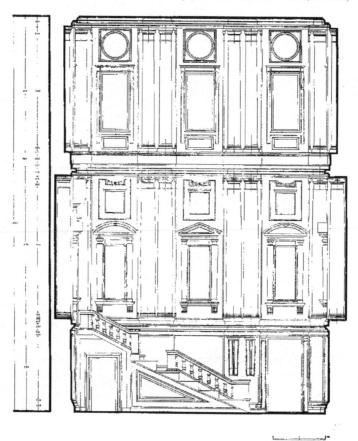

Side elevation of the vestibule of the Laurentian Library (Facoltà Arch. Univ Firenze; Schiavo)

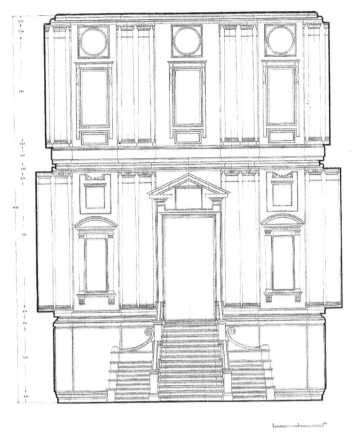

Entrance elevation of the vestibule of the Laurentian Library (Facoltà Arch. Univ. Firenze; Schiavo)

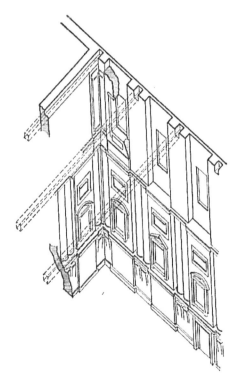

Structural diagram of the vestibule of the Laurentian Library (Ackerman)

Vestibule of the Laurentian Library (2014)

Preliminary study of an enframement for the Laurenziana Library (De Tolnay, *Corpus*, no. 551)

Laurentian Library vestibule (2015)

"Later Michelangelo sought to make known and to demonstrate his new ideas to even better effect in the library of San Lorenzo: namely, in the beautiful distribution of the windows, the pattern of the ceiling, and the marvellous entrance of the vestibule. Nor was there ever seen such resolute grace, both in detail and overall effect, as in the consoles, tabernacles, and cornices, nor any stairway more commodious. And in this stairway, he made such strange breaks in the design of the steps, and he departed in so many detail and so widely from normal practice, that everyone was astonished" (Vasari 1568 [1971]: 59).

In December 1523, Michelangelo learned "...that His Holiness Our Lord [Clement VII] wishes the design for the Library to be by my hand. I have no information about it nor do I know where he wants to build it. ... [I] will do what I can, although it's not my profession" (architecture; Michelangelo 1963: I, 150; Ackerman 1964: 33). This is the earliest mention of Clement's intention to have a library constructed as part of the monastery of San Lorenzo to house the great Medici collection of manuscripts.

John Addington Symonds briefly summarized how the collection was put together and why a new library was needed to house it:

> The books which Clement lodged there were the priceless manuscripts brought together by Cosimo de' Medici in the first enthusiasm of the Revival, at that critical moment when the decay of the Eastern Empire transferred the wrecks of Greek literature from Constantinople to Italy. Cosimo built a room [designed by Michelozzo] to hold them in the convent of S. Marco, which Flavio Biondo styled the first library opened for the use of scholars. Lorenzo the Magnificent

enriched the collection with treasures acquired during his lifetime, buying autograph [manuscripts of books in the handwriting of the authors] whenever it was possible to find them, and causing copies to be made. In the year 1508 the friar of S. Marco sold this inestimable store of literary documents, in order to discharge the debts contracted by them during their ill-considered interference in the state affairs of the Republic. It was purchased for the sum of 2652 ducats by the Cardinal Giovanni de' Medici, second son of Lorenzo the Magnificent, and afterwards Pope Leo X. He transferred them to his Roman villa, where the collection was still further enlarged by all the rarities which a prince passionate for literature and reckless in expenditure could there assemble. Leo's cousin and executor, Giulio de Medici, Pope Cement VII., fulfilled his last wishes by transferring them to Florence, and providing the stately receptacle in which they still repose [Symonds 1900: II, 3-4].

The Medici collected only manuscripts rather than printed books, and when possible, they acquired the oldest manuscripts with the best calligraphy and illustrations. Their collection was intended primarily to help establish accurate texts and to preserve books as works of art. Although Cosimo de' Medici had made his collection publicly available, it was again at risk of being dispersed. Julio trusted the friars of San Lorenzo most, and insisted that the new library be made an integral part of their monastery.

Several possible locations were considered before he decided to have the library placed on top of one side of the monastery's cloister. This required reinforcing the walls on the side chosen and creating a vestibule for stairs that would connect the existing second story with what was to become the third story.

No provision were made to pay for work on the chapel or library until the summer of 1524, and the earliest record of work on the library was in August, when three ducats (about $150) needed to be paid "...for the building stone... for the Library of San Lorenzo" (Michelangelo 1963: I, 157). As with the Medici Chapel, work was interrupted from 1527 to 1531 and then resumed from 1531 to 1534. By then the library room had been completed to Michelangelo's designs, and the vestibule had been competed except for the stairs that were needed to connect the two levels, but with the death of Clement VII, all work on both projects ceased for two decades until Cosimo I had the work completed.

Michelangelo especially hated being having to wait on others to make decisions that affected his work. For example, in 1518, he wrote, "...I'm being worn away here by suspense" (Michelangelo 1963: I, 112). In 1524, he wrote to Clement, "if Your Holiness wishes me to accomplish anything, I beg You not to have authorities set over me in my own trade, but to have faith in me and give me a free hand" (151). Instead of giving Michelangelo a free hand, Clement continually put off making decisions, changed his mind frequently, and required Michelangelo to submit every detail of the project for his personal approval. Nonetheless, he did have the good judgment hire him and to accept most of his recommendations. Since so many decisions required correspondence, the project for the library is unusually well documented, and it was nearly as frustrating as the tomb of Julius and took nearly as long to complete.

Clement did know what was required for the use and preservation of manuscripts, and he was determined to have the Medici collection permanently preserved and available for scholarly use. He insisted that the library be placed in or near San Lorenzo where its monks could care for it. He eventually decided that the location would be above the monastery itself to protect the books from damp, to enable good light to be required, and to provide good security against fire and theft, but these requirements previously met by Michelozzo at San Marco in a room that is wholly fireproof. On the other hand, Clement insisted that a minimum of space be taken from the rooms used by the monks of San Lorenzo and that vaulting be added only to prevent a fire from spreading from the monks' quarters to the library. Although he insisted on some provisions for fireproofing, he wanted a wooden ceiling; he did not want deep coffering;

and he changed his mind about the type of wood to be used. He was indecisive about having small rooms for rare books in each corner of the reading room, a separate room at the end of the reading room, or later adding a room off the middle of the reading room. He chose a location that made access difficult, and he refused to allow a skylight to be built to light the vestibule that was required to connect two levels. He created many difficulties that Michelangelo had to deal with, and unusual requirements produced unusual solutions that a less able architect could not have dealt with successfully. Ackerman summarized the detailed study of the available documentation made by Rudolf Wittkower in 1934 (Ackerman 1964: 33-36).

The vestibule was intended to be a two-storied space with its roof in line with the one-storied reading room, and a third story was added during a 20th Century renovation. Michelangelo had gone to a great deal of trouble to reduce the weight to be carried by the existing wing of the monastery and hence had constructed a vestibule with only two stories with walls of minimal thickness, and he had inserted stone columns into the walls as load bearing elements. Ackerman discussed in detail the structural problems Michelangelo needed to solve and the well he solved them:

> The isometric projection (Fig. 6) shows that the wall behind the columns is a fragile screen that could support nothing without their aid, so that the function as a substitute for the wall-mass. But they are more than a substitute; being monolithic stone shafts, they are stronger in compression than the brick masonry of the walls, and Michelangelo capitalized on this property by making the columns the chief support of the roof. Before the clerestory got its deceptive facing, one could see that the columns support heavy piers which sustain the roof, while over the tabernacles the walls recede to a thin plane that accommodates the windows (Fig. 6). In the final design, then, the structural function of column and wall are exactly the opposite of their visual effects. Michelangelo disguised his technical ingenuity because he was chiefly concerned with form, which partly justifies the failure of modern critics to detect the nature of the structure. Like many engineering discoveries, the recessed column device started as an expressive motive; in Pl. 19b the stresses are concentrated on the flanking pilasters rather than on the columns, and contemporary tomb designs (Pl. 13b) by Michelangelo used the recessed columns for sculptural effect. But even where it was not a conductor of major force, the recessed column remained an efficient substitute for the wall, and in this respect was more utilitarian than its projecting cousins. ...
>
> Though Michelangelo's drawings for the vestibule are all elevations of one wall—the west—this conventional device did not commit him to working in line and plane: shading and the indication of projection and recession give them sculptural mass. This consciousness of the third dimensions is what made the design uniquely successful spatially, for the room is not an assemblage of four walls but an organic unit: at the corners the elevations can be described as mating rather than meeting. Furthermore, motifs conceived for the west wall serve a different purpose on the north and south; at the entrance to the reading-room the recessed columns may be read as a monumental framework for the door, and on the wall opposite the door the central bay remains blank, without a tabernacle. Though the four walls of this remarkably confined space have three different elevations, unity is enforced by the power of the insistent and continuous alternation of receding and projecting elements [Ackerman 1961: 40-41].

Since the reading room was a story above the floor of the vestibule, Michelangelo treated the lower level of the vestibule as if it were the podium of a temple. He added the usual moldings for a podium at the floor level of the reading room, and consequently, the stairs of the vestibule had to be freestanding so as not to cut across the architectural elements of the walls. This led to the creation the unique staircase that would connect the two levels without leaving the vestibule looking empty. Several different arrangements were considered, and initially a pair of stairs was approved, but later a single flight substituted. Michelangelo later had the opportunity to design the existing solution. He made a clay model in 1533, but no one understood how the stones piled in the vestibule should be assembled and finished.

Duke Cosimo de' Medici, whose reign began in 1537, attempted repeatedly to persuade Michelangelo to return to Florence to complete the Medici Chapel and Laurentian Library. Failing to do so, he sent Tribolo (Niccolò Pericoli), a sculptor who had worked on the chapel, to ask "...about the stairway for the library of San Lorenzo, for which Michelangelo had caused many stones to be prepared although there was no model nor any certainty as to its exact form; there were some marks on a pavement and some rough designs in clay, but the true and final plan could not be found. However, despite all the entreaties made by Tribolo, who invoked the name of the duke, all Michelangelo would say was that he did not remember them" (Vasari 1568 [1971]: 94-95). In 1553, Condivi wrote that "...the books are still in strongboxes..." (Condivi 1553: 12).

In 1555, Vasari tried again, and this time he was able to persuaded Michelangelo to provide enough details for the stairs to be built:

> Concerning the stairway for the library that I've been asked about so much, believe me if I could remember how I planned it I would not need to be asked. A certain staircase comes to my mind just like a dream, but I don't think it can be the same as the one I had in mind originally since it seems so awkward. However, I'll describe it for you: first, it is as if you took a number of oval boxes, each about a span [*palmo*] deep but not of the same length or width, and paced the largest down on the paving further from or nearer to the wall with the door, depending on the gradient wanted for the stairs. Then it is as if you placed another box on top of the first, smaller than the first and leaving all round enough space for the foot to ascent; and so on, diminishing and drawing back the steps towards the door always with enough space to climb; and the last step should be the same size as the opening of the door. And this oval stairway should have two wings, one on either side, following the centre steps but straight instead of oval. The central flight from the beginning of the stairs to half-way up should be reserved for the aster. The ends of the two wings should face the walls and, with the entire staircase, come about three spans from the walls leaving the lower part of each wall of the ante-room completely unobstructed. I m writing nonsense, but i know you will find something here to your purpose [Vasari 1568 (1971): 95-96; cf. Michelangelo 1963: II, 157, 159].

In a separate note, Michelangelo wrote that "the middle oval section I intend for the master, the side sections for the servants going to see the library. The returns of the said wings from half-way up to the landing of the staircase are attached to the wall. From the middle down to the paved floor the said staircase is detached from the wall by about four *palmi*, so that the entrance of the vestibule is not encroached upon and allows free passage" (Michelangelo 1963: 213).

Florentine units of measure were different from Roman, and that created further difficulties. Ramsden noted that "the staircase, as finally constructed, is in fact separated from the side walls by about three 'braccia,' and a measurement of only three 'palmi,' which is only some 22 ½ inches, would in fact have been insufficient to allow for the effect Michelangelo apparently had in mind" (159, n. 2); however, Ramsden considered a palmo to be "about 7 ½ inches" while Hellmut Wohl considered it to be 29.18 cm. or about 12 inches and a braccia to be 58.36 cm. or twice as long (Condivi 1553 [1976]: 147). In any case, the information Michelangelo provided to Vasari and the material on site enabled the vestibule to be "...completed by Bartolommeo Ammanati, on designs sent by Michelangelo from Rome, in 1559" (126, n. 16).

By December 16, 1558, Michelangelo had made "...rather roughly, a little sketch of sorts for it in clay, as I think it might be done," and he had "the small model of the staircase for the Library" hand-carried in a box to Ammanato on January 13, 1559 (Michelangelo 1963: II, 184-185). He wrote Ammanati January 14,

> "..I have not been able to do more than give you an idea, remembering that what I formerly proposed was free-standing and only abutted on the door of the Library. I've contrived to maintain the same method; I do not want the stair side to have balusters at the ends, like the main flight, but a seat between every two steps, as indicated by the embellishments. There is no need for me to tell you anything about the bases, fillets for these plinths and other ornaments, because you re resourceful, and being on the spot wills see what is needed much better than I can.
>
> As to the height and length, take up as little space as you can by narrowing the extremity as you think fit.
>
> It is my opinion that if the said staircase were made in wood that is to say in a fine walnut—it would be better than in stone, and more in keeping with the desks, the ceiling and the door [186].

Ammanati constructed the stairs using the more expensive dark *pietra serena* that Michelangelo had quarried initially for the stairs as well as for the columns and trim of the vestibule and for the Medici Chapel.

The end result of all the care that went into designing and constructing the library is an entrance unlike any other and a reading room that is well lighted from both sides, that has a floor of tile designed with different shades of terracotta and a wooden ceiling with a matching design, and that has desks he designed for books to be readily consulted and used.

Michelangelo's first fully architectural project was a unparalleled success. Some chapels had been designed including the Medici Chapel as coherent wholes, but never so fully ans successfully. All elements of the reading room are carefully interrelated on the walls, floor, and ceiling in ways that were widely admired and influential particularly through the Neoclassical designs for rooms by Robert Adam.

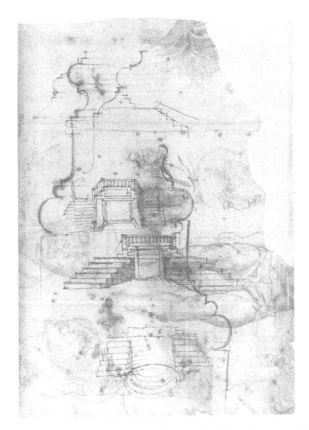

Alternative stair designs for the Laurentian Library (De Tolnay, *Corpus* no. 525 v & r)

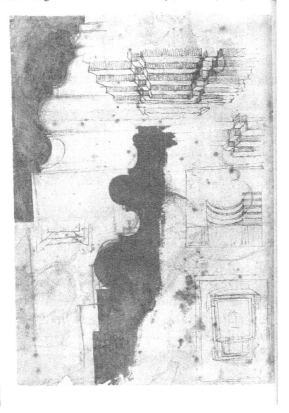

Patronage of Leo X and Clement VII

Despite his influence and great wealth, Lorenzo was concerned about the relative status of his family, and in 1473 he noted that the great amount it had provided for public projects since 1434 had been money "…well spent… having greatly enhanced our status…" (Kent 2004: 78). In 1472 he lamented, "'how long it has been our family's desire to have a cardinal in its ranks.' … Many years later, after much effort and expense, an extremely youthful Giovanni di Lorenzo attained the purple causing his father to call it 'the greatest achievement ever our house…'" (72). The pope at the time was Innocent VIII, and "in 1487 he married his elder son Franceschetto Cybo (d. 1519) to Maddalena de' Medici (1473–1528), the daughter of Lorenzo di'Medici, who in return obtained the cardinal's hat for his thirteen-year-old son Giovanni, later Pope Leo X" (Pope Leo X. https://en.wikipedia.org/wiki/Pope_Innocent_VIII). Giovanni was initially a cardinal-deacon and was admitted to full membership in the College of Cardinals three years later. Although large land holding enhanced the status of the family further, international renown eventually came to the family only through access to the influence and funds of the papacy. If Leo X and Clement VII had not become popes, the Medici family's political influence and patronate would have been primarily confined to Florence.

With hindsight, it is easy to exaggerate the importance of the Medici family on the history of Europe and the patronage of art. Pope Clement VII de' Medici arranged for Lorenzo's eldest grandson to marry into the French royal family, and that marriage produced Catherine de' Medici, who in turn married the second son of Francis I, a prince who was not expected to become king, but on the death of his elder brother became King Henry II of France. Catherine's children inadvertently included three French kings and a Spanish queen.

After the Sack of Rome by troops hired by Charles V, Clement VII formed an alliance with him to besiege Florence, destroy its republic, and to replace it with a hereditary monarchy. The distantly related Cosimo I founded the dynasty of the Grand Dukes of Tuscany.

A daughter of Catherine de'Medici married Henry IV of France, but produced no heir, and being in debt to a later grand duke of Florence, Henry IV married Marie de' Medici, a descendant of Lorenzo through a female line, and she became the mother of Louis XIII and an ancestor of Louis XIV and of Charles II of England.

In these ways, the Medici went from being the first citizens of a republic to becoming ancestors of numerous kings and queens. However, among the disasters that resulted from Lorenzo's intrigues to elevate his family, the most direct ones were the Reformation, the Sack of Rome, and the siege of Florence and destruction of its republican government.

Leo X greatly increased the prestige of the family, but the extravagance of the Vatican and Leo's abuse of the existing practice of indulgences was among the principal causes of the Protestant Reformation. After a brief interval, Leo X was followed in the papacy by Clement VII, a Medici cousin whose duplicity resulted in the Sack of Rome in 1527 and the Siege of Florence in 1529-1530. Considering that the Aragonese controlled southern Italy, that the mercenaries of the Emperor Charles V (who was also King of Spain) sacked Rome, that Spanish troops gave the Medici absolute control of Florence, and that Spain conquered Milan, it is no exaggeration that Spain "destroyed Italy" (Burckhardt 1944: 36); "...those who had called in the barbarians all came to a bad end" (59). Spain conquered most of Italy with the full cooperation of the Papacy, which also gave Spain title nearly all of the Americas. In 1860 Burckhardt concluded that the Papacy was "...the soruce of all foreign intervention and of all the divisions of Italy" (72), and by 1870 all Italy was in agreement on this point and on the need to end the secular authority of the Papacy.

It is relevant to note that Clement VII was one of a number of illegitate, but nonetheless influential Medici. Although Canon Law required priests to be of legitimate birth, Italy was unusual in Europe in innumerable ways including "…the public indifference to legitimate birth, which to foreigners… appeared so remarkable" (Burckhardt 1944: 12). In Rome alone in 1490, a census counted 6,800 prostitutes, but "...conjugal infedility has by no means so disastrous an influence on family life in Italy as in the North, so long ast least as certain limties are not overstepped" (242-243).

In monarchies, legitimacy of birth is considered an essential support for the divine right of kings, but popes were elected, and whether they were illegitimate or had illegitimate children was of little concern to most cardinals. For example, Alexander VI Borgia (1492-1502) had earlier made his illegitimate son Caesare Borgia a cardinal at the age of 18 and later allowed him to resign as a cardinal to become commander of papal troops and a duke. Paul III Farnese (1534-1549) later created duchies for his two illegitmate sons. In the case of the Medici, Leo X excommunicated the Duke of Urbino in order to make his legitimate nephew Lorenzo a duke, and the phoney title enabled Lorenzo to marry Madeleine de la Tour d'Auvergne and to father Catherine de' Medici, who married Henry II of France. The illegitimate Clement VII besieged Florence in order to make his illegitimate son Alessandro the Duke of Florence and eligible to marry the illegitimate daughter of Charles V, who actually besieged Florence as he had Rome a few years earlier. Thus, the illegitimate as well as the legitimate Medici were elevated and married off to create the kind of dynasty that Cosimo never attempted. Throughout Italy, "…there no longer existed a princely house where, een in the direct line of descent, bastards were not patienty tolerated" (12).

As a result of unscrupulous, unethical, and eventually illegal means, the Medici gradually came to have immense influence, but much the same kind of influence that many other papal families came to have. With the death of Cosimo, the Medici ceased to be papal bankers, and their bank ceased to provide their main source of income. They later became another papal family scheming to increase the status of of their families and descendants at the expense of the Church, and this kind of corruption contributed directly to the Reformation, to the withdrawal of half of Europe from the Church., and to the conservatism and repression that followed with the Counter-Reformation.

Nonetheless, three members of the Medici family were among the greatest patrons of art of all time, and they deserve full credit for their good judgment in art and the impact they had on what great architects and artists were able to accomplish. Cosimo had a great impact on the careers of Brunelleschi, Michelozzo, and Donatello. Lorenzo and Clement VII had a great impact on the career of Michelangelo.

Capitol, Rome (1539-1654)

Michelangelo's Capitol (albumen)

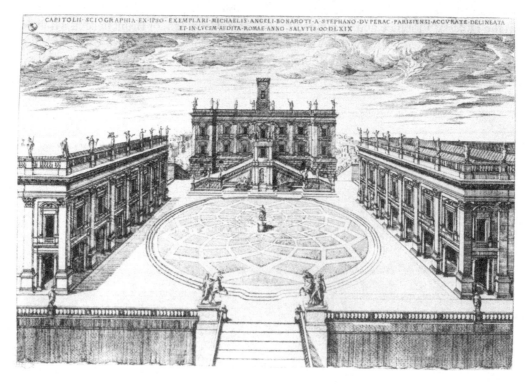

Michelangelo's design for the Capitol (Dupérac, 1569)

Campidoglio before and after being redesigned by Michelangelo (above, H. Cock, c. 1547; below, Letarouilly)

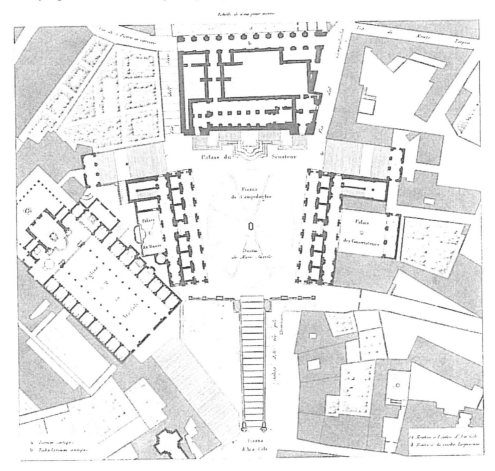

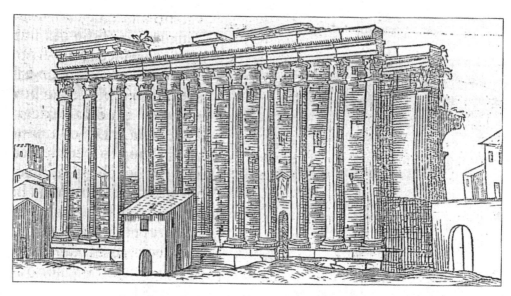

Ruins of the Temple of Hadrian in 1565 (Gamucci)

In 1534 Michelangelo returned to Rome, where Clement VII Medici commissioned him to paint the Last Judgment. Clement died the same, and although his successor Paul III Farnese was eager to employ Michelangelo, he agreed that the painting should be completed first. In the meanwhile, he persuaded the heirs of Julius II to agree to accept three statues that Michelangelo had already completed and to have others complete a cenotaph for San Pietro in Vincoli, the titular church of Julius before he became pope (Vasari). When the Last Judgment was nearly complete in 1537, Paul III assigned Michelangelo the task of creating the Capitol (Campidoglio) out of an existing group of ancient and medieval buildings, and Michelangelo worked intermittently on this project until his death in 1564.

Rome's Senate House had been built behind the Tabularium, the archival building of ancient Rome that faces the Forum. To the right of the Senate House was another medieval building that was used in part as headquarters for the city's builds. Michelangelo's main tasks were to put new fronts of these two existing buildings, to add another flanking building to enframe the piazza, to give some unity to the group of buildings, and to create an imposing Capitol. Vasari outlined the history and scope of the project:

> The people of Rome with the consent of Pope Paul, were anxious to give some useful, commodious, and beautiful form to the Capitol, and in order to embellish the district, to furnish it with colonnades with ascents, with inclined approaches and with and without steps, and also with the ancient and beautiful statues that were already there. For this purpose they sought advice from Michelangelo, who made for them a very rich and beautiful design in which on the side of the Senators' Palace (n the east) he arranged a façade of travertine and flight of steps ascending from the two sides to meet on a level space giving access to the centre of the palace hall, with ornate curving wings adorned with balusters serving as supports and parapets. Then to improve the effect he mounted on pedestals in front of the steps the two ancient figures of recumbent river gods, one representing the Tiber and the other the Nile. Between these two rare statues, each eighteen feet long, it is intended to have a niche containing a statue of Jupiter.) On the southern side, to bring the Conservators' Palace into line he designed for it a richly adorned façade, with a portico [loggia] at the foot filled with columns and niches for many ancient statues; and all around are various adornments of doors and

windows, some of which are already in place. Then on the opposite side, towards the north, below the Araceli, there is to be another similar façade, and in front of this, on the west, is to be an almost level ascent of shallow steps with a balustrade. And here will be the principal entrance to the piazza with a colonnade and various bases on which will be placed the collection of ancient statues with which the Capitol is now so richly furnished. In the middle of the piazza, on an oval base, has been erected the famous bronze horse bearing the figure of Marcus Aurelius, which Pope Paul had moved from the Piazza di Laterano, where it had been put by Sixtus IV. Today work on this whole enterprise is yielding such beautiful results that it is worthy of being numbered among Michelangelo's finest achievements; and under the supervision of Tommaso de' Cavalieri (a Roman gentleman, one of the greatest friends Michelangelo ever had it is now being brought to completion [Vasari 1568: 82-83].

The solution Michelangelo decided upon was essentially to design the fronts of all three buildings for the Capitol to resemble the sides of a Roman peristyle temple. He had used an equivalent solution for the side walls of the reading room of the Laurentian Library by placing a row of identical pilasters above a pedestal the entire length of the room, and in between the pilasters, he had created the appearance of a two-storied building by placing square enframements above the row of windows. The suitability of this design for a multistoried building may well have been suggested by the surviving colonnade of the Temple of Hadrian, which had been incorporated into the front of a building by constructing walls between the columns. In any case, Alberti had previously used the giant pilasters for a number of his buildings, most notably pairs of Corinthian pilasters for Sant'Andrea in Mantua in c. 1570 and Bramante had used giant pilasters in the transept he added to Santa Maria della Grazie in Milan beginning in 1403 and had used them against the piers he built for St. Peter's.

Both the Senate House and the Conservators' building were three storied, but the Senate House was somewhat taller. To make the building relate to one another as a main building with flanking wings, Michelangelo treated the ground floor of the Senate House as a podium on which the giant order stands. For the flanking buildings, the pilasters rest on low pedestals. Both building were given balustraded attic stories to hide the roofs, and statues were placed on pedestals in between the balusters to align with the pilasters. He enhanced the dignity of the Senate House by turning its end towers into matching pair of projections and by adding a double set of steps to the entrance. For the flanking buildings, he retained the open passage on the lower story of the Conservators' building, but replaced the medieval arcade with sections of a secondary entablature that is supported on one-storied columns.

In 1537 Paul III began the renovation of the Capitol by moving the bronze equestrian statue of Marcus Aurelius from the Lateran to the center of the open space in front of the Senate House and by having Michelangelo design a new base for it. By making it the centerpiece for the project an equestrian statue, Paul is likely to have been influence by the nearly adjacent Forum of Trajan, which was known from the historian Ammianus Marcellinus to have had an equestrian statue of Trajan in the center of its courtyard. In all respects and particularly in the various functions it served and its location, the Capitol had more in common with a forum than with a piazza, and Michelangelo gave its buildings the monumentality characteristic of fora, but created a matching set of building fronts. In 1538, one of his first designs was to enhance the equestrian statue by surrounding it with oval that has a convex surface and steps around it perimeter. The elliptical shape was probably suggested by the Colosseum, which Michelangelo is known to have studied, and the convexity was probably based on the floor of the Pantheon, a building he said was designed by angels rather than men. As Ackerman noted, the oval reinforced the axis and fit well in the irregular space (Ackerman 1986: 153).

Ackerman pointed out that although the trapezoidal courtyard of Pienza resembles the trapezoidal courtyard Michelangelo created for the Capitol, the resemblance is probably coincidental. At Pienza, the surrounding buildings do not form a coherent whole, but were simply built alongside two existing streets (Ackerman 1986: 137-138, fig. 59). Similarly, the Conservatori building was existing and had been built at an angle of less than 90° in relation the Senate house. "In accepting the existing conditions, Michelangelo had to rationalize the accidental orientation of the two palaces, the axes of which formed an 80° angle. An irregularity that might have defeated a less imaginative designer became the catalyst that led Michelangelo to use a trapezoidal plan and to develop from this figure other features of his scheme; he so masterfully controlled this potential disadvantage that it appears quite purposeful" (147).

Michelangelo had a clear conception from the start that the Capitol needed to be made to seem symmetrical and that an additional flanking building was needed opposite the Conservatori building for another of his earliest efforts was to create additional space for the entirely new building. To do this, he had to buttress the hillside that the church sits on so that he could place the new building in front of it. He was only able to create a triangular site that allowed for two bays to be built on the end wall facing the main entrance to the area but that sufficed to make the buildings appear to match one another.

Although the Senate house was given a new front after the Conservators' building, all three buildings had to have been planned as matching set before any construction began. Since its main room was on the piano nobile, Michelangelo undoubtedly intended from the start to have monumental pilasters and a podium for the front of his Senate house and to give it a rectangular outline like the block of a triumphal arch. In place of an attic story, he used balustrades (which Bramante had first used for the Tempietto) with pedestals for statues. The steps Michelangelo designed were suggested by the existing flight with a river god in front; he replaced these steps with a symmetrical set of flanking steps and added another river god (creating an arrangement that resembles a pediment with sculpture). Antique sculpture was thus available in abundance for the center, at the base, and on the balustrades of the buildings he planned.

The front Michelangelo designed for the Conservators' building was similar conceptually with the addition he planned for the front of San Lorenzo. Ackerman emphasized that structurally, the addition for the Conservatori building had nothing in common with the façade added to the Senate House. Michelangelo used two-storied piers with integral pilasters that actually provide support for the entablature. In between each pair of piers, he added segments of a smaller entablature that are supported by one-storied columns to support the floor above the open loggia, and above the loggia the rooms are fronted by infill walls that are strong enough to augment the rigidity of the entire front (Ackerman 1986: 155-159). Notably, the back of the portico of the Pantheon is supported by equivalent piers. Yet again, Michelangelo demonstrated that he had already gained a profound knowledge of structural requirements that enabled him to produce innovative solutions to unique problems.

Construction for this complex of buildings took from 1539 to 1654 (Heydenreich and Lotz 1974: 249-250). Michelangelo began by building a retaining wall prevent the collapse of Santa Maria in Aracoeli, which is located adjacent to the site on which the flanking building on the left side was eventually to be built. Michelangelo constructed a staircase from the piazza to the church with a loggia at the top of the staircase in 1544, and to maintain symmetry, Michelangelo added another staircase and loggia on the opposite side of the Senate House in 1550-1553. In the interval between building these two staircases, he added the baroque staircase to the Senate House. Work progressed so slowly in large part because Michelangelo was placed in charge of St. Peter's and the Palazzo Farnese when Antonio da Sangallo died in 1546. Construction did not begin on a new front for the Conservators' building until 1563, the year before Michelangelo died, but Tomaso dei Cavalieri, a friend of Michelangelo, was placed in charge to see that it was executed "'in accordance with Michelangelo' instructions'" (250). Initially, the architect Guidetto Guidetti worked under

Cavalieri's supervision, and the Conservators' building was finally completed in 1584 by Giacomo della Porta, who constructed the dome of St. Peters from 1588-1591 and who completed the Senate house in 1600. The flanking building on the left, the Palazzo Nuova or Capitoline Museum, was constructed from 1603-1654.

To see that Michelangelo's wishes were carried out, Cavalieri undoubtedly received detailed, measured drawings for the building; moreover, Michelangelo is known to have given Cavalieri many of his finest drawings, and many of the details such as the recessed columns of the Conservators' building and the capitals were obviously designed by Michelangelo. Dupérac must also have been given access to the drawings and probably a model as well that Cavalieri needed to fulfill his duty to his friend and that Dupérac needed to produce perspective drawings of a project for which so little had been completed.

Dupérac produced two editions of his print showing Michelangelo's design for the Campidoglio, and they are nearly identical except for the omission of coats of arms and a change in the title block in the version dated 1568 (De Tolnay 1975: fig. 286); the second edition differs in some details and is dated 1569 produced better prints (De Tolnay 1975: 157; Ackerman 1967: fig. 37). For example, a tower on axis was depicted as part of Michelangelo's design even though the asymmetrically placed tower existed until it was stuck by lightning in 1577 and was rebuilt in 1583. Dupérac had produced a site plan dated 1567 (Ackerman 1967: fig. 30B), and the plan shows that Michelangelo intended for the piazza to be trapezoidal rather than rectangular (like Rossellino's piazza for Piacenza). These prints are also significant for indicating a possible source of the plan of St. Peter's by Dupérac that is dated 1569 and for the undated elevation and section of St. Peter's that are all measured drawings produced in the same format and that were all probably produced from 1567-1569. It may well be that Michelangelo gave drawings to Cavalieri for work that had already been accomplished on St. Peter's or drawings that were out of date. This would help to explain why so few drawings have survived for the Capitol and for St. Peter's while so many have survived for other projects.

Palazzo Senatorio drawn by Dosio in c. 1559-1563 (Bedon)

Palazzo Senatorio (albumen by Alinari)

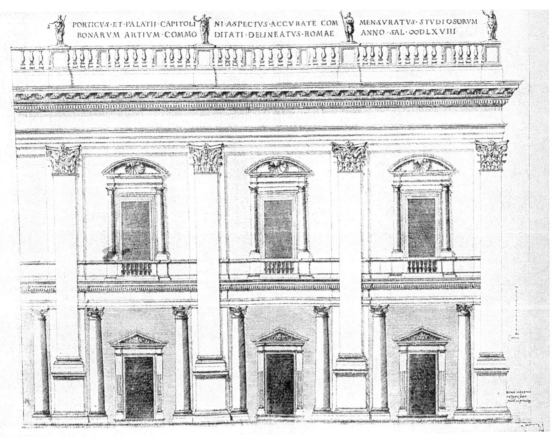

Palazzo dei Conservatori; 1568 elevation (Bedon)

Palazzo Nuovo; Capitoline Museum (Magni)

Piazza di Conservatori (Magni)

Michelangelo's Working Methods

The most important thing to bear in mind about Michelangelo's work is that there was no complete distinction between painting, sculpture, and architecture. His projects often included two or more of these types of work combined inextricably, and he used similar methods to create all three. "...by the middle of the sixteenth century, *disegno* ["drawing or design"] was considered the common foundation of the three arts of painting, sculpture, and architecture, and the phrase *arti del disegno* referred to the visual arts in general" (Hellmut Wohl in Condivi 1553 [1976]: 147).

The ideal of the Renaissance man had been accepted at least by the beginning of the the 1400s with men who like Brunelleschi were sculptors as well as architects, and Alberti and Bramante were artists a well as architects. As Condivi noted, Michelangelo was nonetheless considered exceptional for how equally he excelled in art, architecture and literature; he was "...a noble and lofty genius, destined to succeed universally in any undertaking, but principally in those arts which delight the senses, such as painting, sculpture and architecture" (6). In 1553, Michelangelo was "...the only one to handle the chisel and the brush both equally well..." (94), and before his death in 1564, he proved that he designed architecture equally well.

Vasari also considered Michelangelo pre-eminent and "equally skilled" in sculpture, painting, and architecture in that he attained "...perfection in design (by correct drawing and by the use of contour and light and shadows so as to obtain relief in painting and how to use right judgement in sculpture and, in architecture, create buildings which would be comfortable and secure, healthy, pleasant to look at, well-proportioned, and richly ornamented" (Vasari 1568 [1971]: 15). By creating shadows on buildings, he enhanced their form and gave them vitality. By sculpting space and form, he made buildings more usable and more "pleasant to look at." He designed buildings as coherent, three-dimensional objects rather than as two-dimensional planes.

How Michelangelo went about creating designs is amply indicated by his statements and drawings. For all types of art and architecture, his most consistently important design principles were unity, symmetry, and variety. It is irrelevant to discuss the finished designs in terms of symbolism and psychology because he did not think in those terms when he was creating an individual form or a composition. He was concerned about the effects of light on the visibility of his sculpture, and he took into consideration what would be appropriate for his allegorical sculptures, but rarely did more than include anything that would suffice to identify a subject. He did not position sculpture in architecture in any way except as separate design elements that needed unity as separate objects and as parts of a composition, that needed to be arranged symmetrically, and that needed to be varied in term of design and materials. The overall effect is what concerned him most rather than subject matter.

For example, every figure on the of the Sistine Chapel has a different pose, but the poses are almost invariably compact. Their relative sizes depended most on the overall composition. The largest figures by far are the prophets and sibyls who predicted the coming of a savior, and they are larger and more prominently positioned even than God Himself, who is much smaller and less prominently positioned than the adjacent Noah. Large and small panels alternate entirely for the sake of variety. Large nudes are included primarily for the sake of variety and to fill the residual space alongside the smaller panels.

In the case of sculptures of the Medici Chapel, the statues of the two dukes are as large as the statue of the Madonna because all three were intended to be central figures flanked symmetrically by smaller figures. The sculptures for the tomb of Julius II were also arranged symmetrically and were given a variety of poses in all designs made for this project for four decades.

In the case of St. Peter's, the overall form of the building is compact and well unified. Although the planes of the exterior walls vary continually, the use of a monumental order, the same materials, and a small number of design elements created a largely uniform and unified design.

Paintings, sculpture, and architecture planned using drawings and afterwards often either models or full-scale mock-ups were prepared to judge what the overall effect was likely to be in terms of space, light, and interrelationships. Michelangelo made much use of assistants to help him create art and architecture. He prepared designs and models, and his assistants generally prepared wall surfaces for frescoes, assisted in quarrying stone, roughed out blocks of marble using his models, made larger wooden models of buildings using his clay models and drawings, and so forth. This had been standard practice during the Medieval Period when training was through apprenticeship, and it continued to be standard practice during the Renaissance.

Design: Michelangelo wrote about the need for symmetry in architecture as for the human body though centerpieces exceptional:
> When a plan has diverse parts all those that are of the same character and dimension must be decorated in the same way and in the same manner; and their counterparts likewise. But when a plan changes its form entirely it is not only permissible, but necessary to vary the ornament also and ["that of"] their counterparts likewise. The central features are always as independent as one chooses—just as the nose, being in the middle of the face, is related neither to one eye nor to the other, though one hand is certainly related to the other and one eye to the other, owing to their being at the sides and having counterparts.
>
> It is therefor indisputable that the limbs of architecture are derived from the limbs of man. No-one who had not been or is not good master of the human figure, particularly of anatomy, can comprehend this [Michelangelo 1963: II, 129].

As Ramsden noted, "the whole argument of this letter is based upon the principles of Vitruvius, notably those discussed in the Third Book of *De Architectura*, his treatise on architecture" (130, n. 2): "'...the planning of temples depends upon symmetry... for without symmetry and proportion no temple can have a regular plan; that is to say it must have an exact proportion worked out after the fashion of a finely-shaped human body' (Vitruvius, Bk, III, p. 59 et seq.)" (290). Vitruvius wrote at the beginning of his first book that "similarly, in the members of a temple there ought to be the greatest harmony in the symmetrical relations of the different parts to the general magnitude of the whole. ...since nature has designed the human body so that its members are duly proportioned to the frame as a whole, it appears that the ancients had good reason for their rule, that in perfect buildings the different members must be in exact symmetrical relations to the whole general scheme" (Vitruvius I, i, 3-4; 1914: 72-73). Moreover, in addition to having developed for most types of organisms for functional reasons, symmetry has been used for most types of architecture including Egyptian, Greek, Roman, and Chinese temples and for Gothic churches so that foundations will not crack and roofs will not pull apart through uneven settlement.

Michelangelo learned much from a careful study of Vitruvius, but in architecture as in sculpture attempted to go beyond him in handling the elements of architecture rather than to be limited by him: "...he departed a great deal from the kind of architecture regulated by proportion, order, and rule which other artists did according to common usage and following Vitruvius and the works of antiquity but from which Michelangelo wanted to break away" (Vasari 1568: 59); "...in everything he did he was in no need of architectural rules, either ancient or modern, being an artist with the power to invent varied and original things as beautiful as those of the past" (92). Vitruvius had codified the rules of classical architecture, and Michelangelo created new rules that no one could use as well as he could. He created new styles of art and architecture rather than entirely different rules. He adapted classical design elements rather than creating new elements. As in writing sonnets, he wrote in Italian and used the formula for the sonnet so in architecture he worked entirely within the classical tradition, but in distinctive ways and with supreme skill.

Vasari wrote that Michelangelo preferred to create compositions using the human body and considered this preferable to adding landscapes. Even in his latest painting for the Pauline Chapel, "...Michelangelo concentrated his energies on achieving absolute perfection in what he could do best, so there are no landscapes to be seen in these scenes, nor any trees, buildings, or other embellishments and variations; for he never spent time on such things..." (Vasari 1568: 78). The Tree of Life could not be omitted from the Garden of Eden, and a tree was added to the Great Flood, but despite his love of nature, he preferred human beings.

His preference for depicting male nudes was evident in his early relief sculpture and painting in which a few bodies tightly fill the space. In the case of his earliest surviving work, lapiths and centaurs fill the space entirely, and in the case of the Doni tondo, the margins are filled with nude men (as Signorelli had done in an earlier tondo). For the Sistine ceiling, "...he accommodated the various compartments to the figures, rather than his figures to the compartments, for he was resolved to execute both the draped figures and the nudes so that they should demonstrate the perfect quality of his draftsmanship" (Vasari 1568: 46). As a few of his drawings show, he understood perfectly well the principle of one-point perspective, but made little use of it because his subject in sculpture and painting was nearly always the human body, and when possible, he embellished his architecture with sculpture (as for the front of San Lorenzo, in the Medici Chapel, on the balustrade of the Capitol, and around the base of the dome of St. Peter's).

Use of Models: As noted, in a 1523 proposal to complete the tomb of Julius II in 1523, Michelangelo "...offered to make the models [of the architecture] in wood to the full size that the tombs are to be, and to put all the figures in clay and shearings to the full size, and finished exactly as they were to be, and I pointed out that this would be a quick and inexpensive way to do them" (Michelangelo 1963: 142; notes omitted). As Ramsden pointed out, "this was in fact the method ultimately adopted. If the full-size models were made, the work could be more swiftly and accurately carried out by a large body of assistants working under Michelangelo's supervision" (143, n 1).

His models were prepared on the basis of measured drawings. As Vasari noted about preparing a model of San Giovanni de' Fiorentini, "Tiberio was then given the plan to produce a fair copy, with interior and exterior elevations, as well as a clay model which Michelangelo advised him how to set up" (Vasari 1568: 116). His assistant, the sculptor Tiberio Calcagni, then produced a larger clay model and finally a wooden model.

Michelangelo used models to enable large numbers of assistants to help create architecture and groups of sculpture, and he mastered coordinating large numbers of artists and artisans with the projects for San Lorenzo (Wallace 1994). As Vasari wrote about Clement VII,

> the Pope gave him instructions to return to Florence and finish the library and sacristy of San Lorenzo and to save time, considerable number of statues that were to be included were allocated to various other sculptors. Michelangelo allocated two of them to Tribolo, one to Raffaello da Montelupo, and one to Fra Giovanni Angelo of the Servites; and he assisted these sculptors in the work, making for them the rough clay models. They all set to with will, and meanwhile Michelangelo had the library itself attended to. The ceiling was finished with carved woodwork, executed from Michelangelo's models by the Florentines Carota and Tasso, who were excellent carpenters and masters of wood-carving; and similarly the bookshelves were designed by Michelangelo and executed by Battista del Cinque and his friend Ciappino who were skilled in that kind of work. To enhance the work still more there was brought to Florence the inspired artist Giovanni da Udine, who with some of his own assistants and various Florentine craftsmen decorated the tribune with stucco. So with great solicitude everyone worked hard to

bring the project to completion [Vasari 1568: 66-67].

All of these artists and artisans were needed to carry out his designs; none produced equivalent work on their own. Michelangelo also generously prepared designs for painters such as Sebastian del Piombo and Condivi to carry out for their own commissions that were far better than anything they could have produced on their own. He collaborated with popes as difficult as Julius II and as hard to please as Clement VII, but the credit for the excellence of the work belongs entirely to Michelangelo. This is not to belittle the skill that was required to assist him, but their skills would have been put to less good use for executing the work of any other artist or architect.

When Michelangelo was too old to go to St. Peter's on a regular basis, he depended increasingly on models to guide his workmen, and they usually sufficed, but did not in the case of the vault for the apse of the south arm of St. Peter's (the "Chapel of the King of France"). This will be discussed in the next chapter.

The sculptor Benvenuto Cellini noted about Michelangelo use of models that

> he wishing to show his stonecutters certain windows, made them in clay before he came to other measurements by drawing. I shall not mention the columns, arches, or other beautiful work of his which one sees, which were all made first in this way. The other artists who have followed and follow the profession of architecture take their works from small sketch made on paper, and from that they make the model. Therefore, their works are much less satisfying than those of this angel ["Michelangelo"] [Holt 1982: 36].

Cellini added that "today one recognizes Michelangelo to be the greatest painter ever known among either ancient or modern ["artists"], only because all that he knows of painting he derived from carefully studied methods of sculpture" (35).

Quarrying Stone: Michelangelo personally went to quarries to select stone for statue and buildings. He preferred Carrara marble for its whiteness and uniformity, and marble from this area had been widely used by the Romans from around the time of Augustus, and it was close enough to the Mediterranean that large blocks of stone could be transported by sea. If stone were not carefully selected, a discolored seam or inclusion could turn up and make it necessary to start a piece of sculpture all over again, and sometimes it was impossible to tell what a large block of stone might include.

Before going to a quarry, Michelangelo made at least small wax or clay models of sculpture or determined the size of the blocks he would need for the facing of a building made largely of brick and mortar. Each block had to be more than large enough for its intended purpose and to removed any parts damaged while being transported, and it was necessary before hand to prepare sketches with accurate measurements. In other words, a sculpture or building had to be carefully planned before any stone was quarried.

The actual quarrying could take many months or even years, and he had to supervise the quarrying to ensure that the material selected likely to be uniform and without flaws, to ensure that the blocks were cut the right size and shape for the intended use of each block (with an adequate provision being made for possible damage to the surfaces of the blocks during transportation). He also had to arrange for transportation, storage, and places to work the blocks, and he used his considerable administrative skills to plan all such work carefully so that it would not need to be one again (Wallace 1994).

Michelangelo took from six to eight months to quarry stone for the tomb of Julius II and had the carefully measured blocks of stone brought to Rome, but Julius decided not to have the tomb constructed during his lifetime, and "...in one way or another they [the blocks] came to grief" (Michelangelo 1963: I, 148). Some were stolen and others used for other projects while he was in Florence and Bologna, and additional blocks had be quarried for the tomb after Julius's death to replaced those missing and to provide additional material for a tomb that was then planned to be larger. He spent most of two years quarrying stone for the front of San Lorenzo, and much of the stone was used instead to pave the interior of the Duomo in Florence.

Additional stone had to be quarried for the Medici chapel and library.

Blocking Out: A *scarpellino* was a "...stone-mason, employed to do the initial blocking out of a figure under a sculptor's instructions" (Ramsden in Michelangelo 1963: 12). At least as early as 1506 when Michelangelo was working on the tomb of Julius II, he had a scarpellino working for him, and he had hired a different one in 1508 (11-12, n. 12; 46-47, n. 2).

Michelangelo had ceased to accept new commission for sculpture by 1534 when he returned to Rome and began painting the Last Judgment and Pauline Chapel and the began work on St. Peter's and other architectural projects. He resumed sculpting for about a year to complete the tomb of Julius II in c. 1544, and for the last two decades of his life sculpted only for pleasure and exercise (Vasari 1568: 99-101). He sometimes changed the design of these sculptures while working on them and purposely broke them into pieces. These unfinished sculptures are not in the same category as the unfinished sculptures that were partly blocked out by assistants on the basis of full-scale models. Vasari wrote that

> ...the statue of Victory with a captive beneath, ten feet in height, an four other captives in the rough... serve to teach us how to carve figures out of marble b a method which leaves no chance of spoiling the stone. This method is as follows: one must take a figure of wax or some other firm material and lay it horizontally in a vessel of water; then, as the water is, of course, flat and level, when the figure is raised little by little above the surface [as the water level is lowered,] the more salient parts are revealed first while the lower parts (on the underside of the figure) remain submerged, until eventually it all comes into view. In the same way figures must be carved out of marble by the chisel; the parts in highest relief must be revealed first and then little by little the lower parts. And this method can be seen to have been followed by Michelangelo in the statues of the prisoners mentioned above, which his Excellency [Duke Cosimo de' Medici] wants to be used as models by his academicians [Vasari 1568: 123-124].

Bronzes: In 1515 for bronze reliefs that were to be enframed on the tomb of Julius II, Michelangelo "...bought some twenty thousandweight of copper, in order to cast certain figures" (Michelangelo 1963: 90). He also planned to include bronze reliefs on the front of San Lorenzo.

Earlier in 1507 for the seated bronze statue of Julius that was placed on the front of Bologna's cathedral, Michelangelo ordered 720 pounds of wax (25). This statue was twice the size of life. He later made full-sized models in wax at least for the river gods that were to be part of the Medici Chapel, and the torso of one of these models has survived.

Bronzes were usually cast by specialists, but Julius insisted that Michelangelo cast the statue of him despite his protests. The statue had to be cast twice before he succeeded with the assistance of two specialists, one of whom cast ordnance (32, n. 2). In 1507 Michelangelo wrote that he had "...finished the wax of my figure. The coming week I shall begin to make the outer mold ["The third stage in the direct method of *cire perdue* bronze casting"; this was the "lost wax" process that had been widely used in the Ancient World.] and I think this will be completed in twenty or twenty-five days. Then I shall give the order for casting..." (33). The first casting "...turned out in such a way that I firmly believe I shall have to re-do it. ...Maestro Bernardino either through ignorance or by accident, did not melt the stuff properly.... it is not that he is not a good craftsman, nor that he did not put his heart into it. But he who tries may fail...." (35-36). Trying again, "...the further I uncovered my figure the better I found it had turned out, and I see that it is not as bad as I had expected, and considering what might have happened it seems to me I have come off well. So we must thank God. As far as I can see, the business of cleaning it up will certainly take six weeks" (37). Although Michelangelo admired Donatello, he criticized him because he "...lacked patience in polishing his works, so that, thought they were admirably successful from a distance, they lost their reputation when seen from nearby..." (Condivi 1563 [1976]: 28). This statue was installed in 1508, but destroyed to make a canon in 1511 (Ramsden in Michelangelo 1963: 42, n. 1).

Frescoes: Preliminary sketches were made for paintings on an architectural scale as for separate painting to determine the composition; then individual figures were sketched, sometimes in great detail; and finally, for frescoes cartoons were prepared that were full sized on heavy paper so that minute holes could be punched through the paper and chalk dust could be rubbed through onto the wet plaster to provide an accurate outline. This was especially necessary in the case of figures that were larger than life and still more so when painting figures on curved surfaces.

Before painting the Sistine ceiling, Michelangelo had mastered the making of cartoons so well that the cartoon he prepared to paint the monumental fresco of the Battle of Cascina in the Palazzo Vecchio in Florence in competition with Leonardo was considered to be a great work of art in its own right and was carefully preserved the Sala del Papa (where the pope stayed when in Florence), and it was copied by other artists before it was cut up for souvenirs (Michelangelo 1963: 45-46). He wrote, "...I had undertaken to execute half the Sala del Consiglio of Florence, that is to ay to paint it, for which I was getting three thousand ducats; and I had already done the cartoon, as is known to all Florence, so that the money seemed to me half earned" (148). However, because Julius called him to Rome, he had to abandon this project, and "I got nothing...."

Although Michelangelo had apprenticed with the painter Ghirlandaio for three years, he had probably worked only on wall paintings, and he did not know how to paint a curved ceiling or how to prepare the final layers of plaster correctly. "Michelangelo, who had not yet used colors and who realized that it was difficult to paint a vault, made every effort to get out of it..." (Condivi 1563: 39).

Michelangelo wanted to work on the tomb of Julius II and did not want to paint even a dozen Disciples on the ceiling of the Sistine Chapel, but when Julius insisted, he "...was anxious to show that his paintings would surpass the art done there earlier, and he was determined to show modern artists how to draw and paint. Indeed, the circumstances of this undertaking encouraged Michelangelo to aim very high, for the sake both of his own reputation and of the art of painting..." (Vasari 1568: 43). As later with the sculpture and architecture of the front of San Lorenzo and inside the Medici Chapel, Michelangelo wanted to create work that would be exemplary. Despite being distracted from doing work he preferred and despite the great labor that was required, "...every day the work moved him to greater enthusiasm, and he was so spurred on by his own progress and improvements that he felt no fatigue and ignored all the discomfort" (46).

He also used only the finest materials. For the Sistine ceiling, he was dissatisfied even with the way that his assistants ground colors, and he ground them himself. He decided to used concrete, and he chose "...the roman lime, which is white in colour and made of travertine, does not dry very quickly and when mixed with pozzolana, which is a brownish colour, forms a dark mixture which is very watery before it sets; then after the wall has been thoroughly soaked, it often effloresces when it is drying" (Vasari 1568: 44). Vitruvius had given the formula, and this seems to have been the earliest use of concrete since Antiquity. When mold formed, Giuliano da Sangallo "...explained how to remove the moulds and encouraged him to continue." Since concrete sets up quickly through a chemical reaction and was relatively dark, it must have been used as the undercoat for plaster made from travertine.

Highlights in a fresco are achieved as with watercolors, and a stucco is a watercolor: the white of the plaster or paper is allowed to show through a thin and translucent payer of paint. After frescoes were competed, they were sometimes touched up. In the case of the Sistine ceiling, "what was lacking was the retouching of the work *a secco* [when dry] with ultramarine and in a few places with gold, to give it a richer appearance. Julius, when the heat of his enthusiasm had subsided [after insisting that the scaffolding be taken down], really wanted Michelangelo to finish these touches; but when Michelangelo thought about the trouble it would gave him to reassemble the scaffolding, he answered that what was lacking, was nothing of importance. 'It really ought to be retouched with gold,' answered the pope, to whom Michelangelo responded with the familiarity which was his way with His Holiness, 'I do not see that men wear gold." The pope said It will look poor." Michelangelo rejoined, 'Those who are depicted here, they were poor too.' So he remarked in jest, and so the work has remained..." (Condivi 1563: 58).

"The ceiling has proved a veritable beacon to our art, of inestimable benefit to all painters, restoring light to a work that for centuries had been plunged into darkness" (Vasari 1568: 47).

Foreshortening: Sculpture in the round requires no foreshortening, but reliefs like painting can make good use of foreshortening to create the illusion of depth. Michelangelo had mastered foreshortening so fully that by the time he painted the Sistine ceiling, he was able to use it effectively where the surface curved on the sides of the ceiling (with the seated prophets and sibyls) and even in the corners of the ceiling where the surface was doubly curved. In the case of the figure of Jonah that is directly above the altar, "...the torso which is foreshortened backward is in the part nearest the eye, and the legs which project forward ar in he part which is farthest. Stupendous work, and one which proclaims the magnitude of this man's knowledge, in his handling of lines, in foreshortening, and in perspective" (Condivi 1563: 48). Foreshortening on a flat surface is relatively simple for artists who paint what they see rather than what they think they see. Michelangelo's distoritons prevented things from appearing to be distorted.

Even for the panels of the Sistine ceiling, "for the foreshortenings in these compartments he used no consistent rue of perspective, nor is there any fixed point of view" (Vasari 1568: 46). "Haman himself was depicted in an extraordinary example of foreshortening, for Michelangelo painted the trunk that supports his persons and the arm thrust forward so that the seen in living relief, the same effect being seen in the leg that Haman stretches out and the other parts of the body that bend inwards. Of all the beautiful and difficult figures executed by Michelangelo this is certainly the most beautiful and the most difficult" (52).

Best All Round: For Renaissance artists, nothing was more characteristic that attempting to be as good as possible in a wide range of endeavours. This was what being a Renaissance man was all about. They were exceptionally well educated and informed as well as well trained in multiple fields of endeavor. They were ambitious and diligent. They developed good judgment on the basis of wide-ranging knowledge of the best efforts of earlier artists and architects and of their own contemporaries and sought to surpass them all in at east one field and if possible in more than one. They had a broad background to draw upon, and they carefully considered various approaches and carefully selected the subject, pose, composition they would use. They often considered many possibilities as Michelangelo did in developing plans for San Giovanni dei Fiorentini. Most of all, they carefully thought through what they intended to do and carefully planned how the would do it taking into consideration as many different aspects of every problem as they could. As Vasari wrote about Leonardo, "...men of genius really are doing most when they work least, as they are thinking out ideas and perfecting the conceptions, which they subsequently carry out with their hands" (Vasari 1568: II, 161).

Vitality in Architecture: A most important principal of design in architecture and art is to impart a sense of vitality, and this is done by using similar means. For example, the earliest Greek sculptures looked like they had rigor mortis. They initially had human forms, symmetry, proportions, and a third dimension but lacked vitality. They were increasingly made to resemble living beings by being given more relaxed poses, by being depicted in arrested motion, by being give accurate anatomies, and by being given individuality. All of these characteristics must also be given to buildings to make them seem to have vitality and none at the expense of others.

Michelangelo carried vitality to its limits in sculpture, painting, and architecture. The lack of vitality in Medieval art was quickly superseded during the Renaissance as more and better examples of Ancient art were found and became more widely known. Artists continued to depict the same subjects, but with increasing vitality, and no one copied less good artists for long. Giotto had many followers, but as soon as better methods of representation were introduced, he ceased to be copied. Giotto had made progress by copying Nature rather than his Medieval predecessors, but he was a transitional painter of the late Medieval Period rather than a Renaissance artist.

Andrea Pisano's sculpture had more vitality than Giotto's paintings to extent that shadows were cast and their three-dimensionality was enhanced. Pisano advanced farther than Giotto by copying Nature as Giotto had done, but also by learning from the conventions of the better examples of ancient sculpture that were available to him while Giotto had no examples of ancient painting to learn from, but had observed and depicted Nature more accurately than his immediate predecessors. Painters such as Giotto had to learn how to create a sense of three-dimensionality by making better use of shadows, through the use of perspective, and by learning other artistic conventions. Copying natural outlines accurately was not enough to convey a sense of three dimensionality much less vitality. Similarly, in architecture, means were found to create a sense of three dimensionality and structural sufficiency by emulating the principles of organisms and the conventions that were used to achieve a sense vitality.

There is a fine line between an original and a copy. An exact copy of nature is a snapshot unless good judgment is used in selecting a subject and limiting the amount of information that a picture contains to what is coherent. In general, even the best copies of works of art lack the vitality of originals because of the hesitancy of the copyist as opposed to the self-assurance and clear sense of purpose of a great artist or architect. Even highly skilled apprentices were usually unable to convey the same sense of vitality than an original design could have and were hesitant rather than fluent.

Copies of copies got continually worse. Copying is a good way to learn, but a bad way to create works of art unless a copyist is better than the original creator.

In the case of copying Nature, it is by selecting the best parts of multiple figures and combining them that Greek artists went beyond Nature. All organisms are complex, but their pars are interrelated, and this is what is meant by the principle that a work of art cannot be better if nothing can be added or subtracted without injury to the whole.

Essentially the same thing is true of literature. A paraphrase of Shakespeare will almost invariably be a poor copy and will lack the vitality he gave to characters he adapted from Plutarch and Holinshed. However, any work of art that requires an explanation is a failure.

Incoherent architecture is as incomprehensible as incoherent speech. The parts of speech must be well selected and well arranged to achieve an intended effect consistently and well. The same statement translated into a wholly different language will usually be incomprehensible, but in architecture, structural, aesthetic, and other functional requirements have produce more nearly equivalent results worldwide.

The Classic Orders are a visual language comparable to a sign language, and they usually have some structural as well as aesthetic significance. For example, an engaged column or pilaster thickens a wall like a pier buttress and allows the rest of the wall to be thinner and less expensive, but rigid and secure. Although a buttress would suffice, it would not look as good to anyone accustomed to the the Orders. Also, exposed rafter ends might suffice, but would be less permanent than a well stuccoed cornice.

In architecture, a flat and featureless wall lacks vitality and interest. A featureless wall can be sufficient structurally and for security, but needs at least texture if not niches, windows, alcoves, sculpture, or plant life to be visually satisfying and to be other than oppressive. A wall cannot extend indefinitely and have the coherence of an organism. A building can be made to seem more like an organism by being relatively compact and symmetrical and less like a wall. It can be given vitality by being made to appear more three-dimensional. This is not to argue that buildings should copy organisms, but that they will have more visual appeal if they seem to have vitality.

As with all other principles, imparting vitality to art and architecture needs to be applied with moderation. There is a wide range for moderation, but is not unlimited, and all parts of a work or art or architecture must form a visually coherent whole. The architects before Michelangelo could often have done better by giving their designs more vitality, and the architects after Michelangelo could have done better with more moderation. The greatest mastery is required to exceed the usual limits of any principle successfully. Like Michelangelo, Palladio considered principles important yet his buildings vary greatly from one another without departing significantly from his principles.

With the Sistine ceiling, Michelangelo often exaggerated features to create a sense of monumentality from a distance, and he sometimes exaggerated too much. He generally failed to create an overall sense of coherence for his compositions as a whole, but individually his figures whether sculpted or painted are easily among the finest ever created. With St. Peter's, he achieved as great a sense of vitality as possible in architecture without becoming incoherent. His shortcomings are insignificant compared to his achievements, but his few shortcomings were more easily imitated.

Secular Renaissance

The Renaissance was most characterized by the desire to equal or surpass the ancients in everything. The most celebrated example came with nearly equaling the span of ancient buildings. Other attempts to equal and surpass ancient knowledge included the fields of medicine, literature, geography, zoology, botany, astronomy, mathematics, and art. These were all secular concerns, and scholarship increasingly became more concerned with such subjects as these rather than religion.
The superiority of ancient knowledge became more and more obvious as more classical texts were recovered and particularly the texts of Aristotle and Pliny and the great historians of Antiquity. The superiority of ancient literature and the use of language was obviously better than any Christian writings, and classical Latin and later classical Greek began to be mastered in Italy during the Renaissance.

Classic Texts

One of the principal concerns of the Renaissance was to recover as much ancient knowledge as possible, and great efforts were made to locate, copy, and disseminate classical texts to ensure their availability for study and their permanent survival. This was an entirely different point of view from the occasional copies that were made of individual ancient writings in Latin and the general neglect of ancient knowledge for religious subject matter. It was a secular concern to recover ancient knowledge systematically rather than for a few individuals to copy works for practical purposes such as Vitruvius on architecture or from personal interest. The concerted and well coordinated efforts by the Medici and others to rescue and revive classical writings was a new and secular concern that was essentially different from the occasional and uncoordinated Medieval efforts to preserve a small part of ancient Latin writings. "...with the fifteenth century began the long list of new discoveries, the systematic creation of libraries by means of copies, and the rapid multiplication of translations from the Greek" (Burckhardt 1944: 114).

The best evidence of the relative lack of interest in ancient Latin writings during the Medieval Period is how little of its survived intact relative to the largely complete survival of the principal writing of ancient Greek writers. Although Latin continued to be the official language of the Catholic Church, it deteriorated so greatly that it was obvious to the Latin scholar Lorenzo Valla that the supposed "Donation of Constantine" to of territories in the West the Papacy was a medieval fake. By contrast, ancient Greek continued to be taught in the schools of Byzantium despite its pagan content and to be used for the administration of government. Greek also deteriorated in common use, but its standards were maintained in scholarship, and the greatest Greek historians, philosophers, and dramatists continued to be appreciated and regularly copied.

> Had it not been for the enthusiasm of a few collectors of that age, who shrank from no effort or privation in their researches, we should certainly possess only a small part of the literature, especially that of the Greeks, which is now in our hands. Pope Nicholas V, when only a simple monk, ran deeply into debt through buying manuscripts or having them copied. Even then he made no secret of his passion for the two great interests of the Renaissance, books and buildings. As Pope he kept his word. Copyists wrote and spies searched for him through half the world. Perotto received 500 ducats for the Latin translation of Polybius; Guarino, 1,000 gold florins for that of Strabo.... Nicholas left a collection of 5,000 or, according to another way of calculating, of 9,000 volumes, for the use of the members of the Curia, which became the foundation of the library of the Vatican [Burckhardt 1944: 115].

By contrast, Pope Paul II (1458-1464) "...called the huanists heretics one and all" (47, n. 11).

The other great collection that was the foundation of the Vatican Library was from Urbino. Federigo da Montefeltro began to collect manuscripts while still a youth, and

> ...in after years he kept thirty or forth 'scrittori' employed in various places, and spent in the course of time no less than 30,000 ducats on the collection. It was systematically extended and completed, chiefly by the help of Vespasiano.... It was noted with pride that in richness and completeness none could rival Urbino. Theology and the Middle Ages were perhaps most fully represented. There was a complete Thomas Aquinas, a complete Albertus Magnus, a complete Bonaventura. The collection, however was a many-sided one, and included every great work on medicine which was then to be had. Among the "moderns" the great writers of the fourteenth century—Dante and Boccaccio, with their complete works—occupied the first place. Then followed twenty-five select humanists, invariably with both their Latin and Italian writings with their translation. Among the Greek manuscripts the Fathers of the Church far outnumbered the rest; yet in the list of the classics we find all the works of Sophocles, all of Pindar, and all of Menander [Burckhardt 1944: 146].

Considering that Leo designated a Medici nephew as duke of Urbino and confiscated the palace library, he probably intended to add Montefeltro's collection to the Laurentian Library.

The first great collection of books created in Florence was the one that formed the basis for the first public library of the Renaissance:

> The Florentine Niccolò Niccoli, a member of that accomplished circle of friends which surrounded the elder Cosimo de' Medici, spent his whole fortune in buying books. At last, when his money was all gone, the Medici put their purse at his disposal for any sum which his purpose might require. We owe to him the completion of Ammianus Marcellinus, of the 'De Oratore' of Cicero, and other works; he persuaded Cosimo to buy the best manuscript of Pliny from a monastery at Lubeck. ... His collection of 300 volumes, valued at 6,000 gold florins, passed after his death, through Cosimo's intervention, to the monastery of San Marco, on condition that it should be accessible to the public [in the influential library building created for it by Michelozzo; Burckhardt 1944: 115].

"Niccoli's will of 1430... entrusted his legendary library to Cosimo and eleven other executors.... It was probably not too difficult for Cosimo to persuade such a group to fulfil Niccoli's wish to put his library at the public disposal by making it the nucleus of the collection he himself bestowed upon San Marco. Niccoli's books were supplemented by gifts from Cosimo's own library and other manuscripts commissioned from [copied by] Vespasiano" (Kent 2000: 25). The gift was formally accepted with 1441.

Cosimo "...came to maturity surrounded by the early enthusiasts of the recovery of classical learning: Niccoli, Poggio, Bruni, and Traversari. He was an intimate of this circle and in some ways its focal point.... He subsidized and participated in the early discoveries of ancient manuscripts by the humanists Niccoli and Poggio..." (Kent 2000: 23).

> Of the two great book-finders, Guarino [da Verona] and Poggio [Bracciolini], the latter on the occasion of the Council of Constance and acting partly as the agent of Niccoli, searched industriously among the abbeys of South Germany. He there discovered six orations of Cicero, and the first complete Quintilian, that of St. Gall, now at Zurich; in thirty-two days he is said to have copied the whole of it in a beautiful handwriting. He was able to make important additions to Silius Italicus, Manilius, Lucretius, Valerius, Flaccus, Asconius Pendianus, Columella, Celsus, Aulus Gellius, Statius, and others; and with the help of Leonardo Aretino he unearthed the last twelve comedies of Plautus as well as the Verrine orations [Burckhardt 1944: 115].

In 1418 Poggio found a copy of Lucretius's *De Rerum Natura*, and Cosimo soon had a copy (Kent 2000: 284).

San Marco was the first monastery constructed at Cosimo's expense, and the last monastery he funded was at Badia near Fiesole:

> ...he sent for Vespasiano, and received from him the advice to give up all thought of purchasing books, since those which were worth getting could not be had easily, but rather to make use of the copyist; whereupon Cosimo bargained to pay him so much a day, and Vespasiano, with forty-five writers under him delivered 200 volumes in twenty-two months. The catalogue of the works to be copied was sent to Cosimo by Nicholas V, who wrote it with his own hand. Ecclesiastical literature and the books needed for the choral services naturally held the chief place in the list [Burckhardt 1944: 177].

Cosimo himself began collecting manuscripts as a youth, and by 1417/18 when he was nearly 30 years old, his collection included approximately 70 volumes (Kent 2000: 35). "Cosimo owned most of the classical works in general currency in the early years of the quattrocento..." including a volume of Tacitus in Monte Casino and copies of the volumes of Quintilian and Cicero made by Poggio. He later contributed some of his manuscripts to San Marco, but at the time of his death in 1464 he still had copies of "Terence, Virgil, Plutus, Martial, and Juvenal, all of whom were already in Cosimo's library in 1418, as well as his schoolbook copy of Ovid's *Epistolae*" (Kent 2000: 35).

> Among the volumes that passed to his son only after his death were the *Decades* of Livy, Plutarch's *Lives*, Bruni's *History of Florence*, and the Diogenes Laertius he had commissioned Traversari to translate in the early thirties. Cosimo has also kept the Christian classics he owned already in 1418: Jerome, Augustine, Cassian, Cyprian, Lactantius, and several bibles, psalters, and books of offices. Also in Cosimo's study at the time of his death were volumes of vernacular literature: Dante, Petrarch, and Boccaccio's *Genealogy of the Gods*, and the *Lives* of Saints Cosmas and Damian [36].

Cosimo's two sons, Piero and Giovanni; his grandson Lorenzo; and his great-grandsons Leo X and Clement VII added to the Medici family collection that Michelangelo designed the Laurentian Library to house.

> Any selection of the Library's treasures would have to include: the Codex Mediceus of Virgil (5th century), which bears the subscription of Asterius, consul in AD 494; the Syriac Gospels copied by monk Rabbula in 586, a magnificent example of early Byzantine illumination; the earliest witness of the *Corpus Iuris Civilis*, the body of civil law compiled under Emperor Justinian, copied shortly after its promulgation

(534); the most important manuscript of the first ten books of Livy, produced in Verona between 932 and 968 at the behest of Bishop Ratherius; Plutei 68.1-2, which have preserved books 1-6 and 11-16 of the *Annals* and the *Histories* of Tacitus (the former, written in the 9th century in the German abbey of Fulda and later transferred to Corvey, surfaced in 1508 in the hands of Cardinal Giovanni de' Medici; the latter, written at Montecassino in the 11th century, came into the possession of Niccolò Niccoli); the only complete Carolingian manuscript of Cicero's letters *ad familiares*, of which Coluccio Salutati received a copy in 1392 (he was actually searching for Cicero's *Letters to Atticus*, which he obtained the following year); Pluteo 32.9 (10th century), containing all the surviving tragedies of Aeschylus and Sophocles and the *Argonautica* of Apollonius Rhodius…; manuscripts crucial to the textual tradition of Herodotus, Thucydides, Demosthenes, Pliny and Quintilian; the Codex Etruscus of Seneca's *Tragedies* (11th century), studied by Politian; valuable Byzantine manuscripts…; a manuscript of Varro and Cicero from Montecassino (11th century) acquired by Giovanni Boccaccio, who in 1355 copied it for Petrarch in his own hand; a complete collection of Plato's *Dialogues*, in Greek, given to Marsilio Ficino by Cosimo the Elder for translation. The Codex Amiantius (679-716) deserves special mention, arguably the most celebrated manuscript of the Latin Vulgate, it was written at Wearmouth-Jarrow, in northe-east England….
Not only were many of the manuscript written, copied or owned by prominent humanists—they also contain some of the finest illuminations ever produced.
…

The Library… has some 11,000 manuscripts… [quoted from "Biblioteca Medicea Laurenziana," a brochure produced by the Library]

Relatively few Italians could read ancient Greek until there was an influx of Greek refugees following the fall of Constantinople to the Turks in 1453. Cardinal Bessarion collected at least 500 volumes in Greek and donated them to the city of Venice in 1468 (Reynolds and Wilson 2013: 150); he "…collected, at a great sacrifice, 600 manuscripts of pagan and Christian authors. …The Venetian government declared itself ready to erect a suitable building, and to this day the Biblioteca Marcia [by Sansovino] retains a part of these treasures" (Burckhardt 1944: 116). Greek manuscripts had begun, though, to reach Italy in large quantities as early as 1423 when Giovanni Aurispa acquired 238 volumes of "pagan" Greek texts (Reynolds and Wilson 2013: 149). Some of Aurispa's volumes became part of the Laurentian Library, and his book collecting in Germany with Tommaso Parentucelli (later Pope Nicholas V) contributed to the basis for the Vatican Library (Hobson 1970: 77). As late as 1492 Lorenzo de' Medici sent "…the learned Greek Janos Lascaris to search for [Greek classics] in the Lavant… for scholarly use, and particularly for his enthusiastic young friends Poliziano and Pico della Mirandola" (Hobson 1970: 89).

Translating: Early efforts were made to translate the principle classical Greek texts into Latin, and the humanist Pope Nicholas V Parentucelli, who reigned from 1447-1455, "…commissioned versions of Thucydides, Herodotus, Xenophon, Plato, Aristotle, Theophrastus, Ptolemy, and Strabo" (Reynolds and Wilson 2103: 149). As noted, from Nicholas V, "Perotto received 500 ducats for the Latin translation of Polybius; Guarino, 1,000 gold florins for that of Strabo…." An example of the immense interest in secular Greek writings is that the Latin translation of the works of Plato by Marsilio Ficino that was published in 1484 was printed in an edition of 1,025 copies, and after it sold out within six years, it was reprinted (Reynolds and Wilson 2013: 156).

Federigo da Urbino "…was the most learned in the whole court" (Burckhardt 1944: 135). "It was to him and for Nicholas V that most of the translations from the Greek, and a number of the best commentaries and other such works, were written…."

Classical antiquity, indeed, only formed a part of his culture. An accomplished ruler, captain, and gentleman, he had mastered the greater part of the science of his day, and this with a view to its practical application. As a theologian, he was able to compare Scotus with Aquinas, and was familiar with the writings of the old fathers of the Eastern and Western Churches, the former in Latin translations. In philosophy, he seems to have left Plato altogether to his contemporary Cosimo, but he knew thoroughly not only the "Ethics" and "Politics" of Aristotle but the "Physics" and some other works. The rest of his reading lay chiefly among the ancient historians, all of whom he possessed; these, and not the poets, he was always reading and having read to him [Burckhardt 1944: 135].

As noted, his library (including the translations he had made) also became part of the Vatican Library.

Printing: When it became possible to ensure the permanent preservation of ancient Greek writings through the use of printing, accurate copies of complete sets of the most important Greek texts were readily available. The individual who deserves the greatest credit for preserving ancient Greek writings was Aldus Manutius, who printed nearly all of the Greek Classics in Greek in Venice from 1494 to 1515. On philosophy, he first printed the complete works of Aristotle and Theophrastus in five folio volumes from 1495-1498 and the complete works of Plato in 1513. On history, he first printed the works of Herodotus and Thucydides. On literature, he first printed the surviving plays of Sophocles and Euripides. "Nearly all Aldine books were classical texts; Christian writers only occasionally appeared" (Reynolds and Wilson 2013: 158). In other words, this was a systematic attempt to preserve ancient Greek knowledge. Exceptionally, the most important Roman history that was written in Greek by Polybius was not published until 1582 and was then printed in Rome (Reynolds 1983: 169/ Renaissance printing is discussed further in Appemdix IV hereins).

Sources of Latin Manuscripts: Most surviving Latin texts were initially published before 1500 in various places at various times. As noted, Vitruvius was first printed in Latin in Rome in c. 1486 (Vitruvius 2003: 26). Although it was largely complete in one volume, its text was corrupt, and its illustrations had not been copied. Also in Rome, the first edition of Caesar's *Gaelic Wars* had been published in 1469 and the first edition of Tacitus in 1515. Tacitus, another of the greatest of Roman historians, is an example of the general neglect of subjects as important and useful as ancient history during the Medieval Period. Cosimo de' Medici had acquired a copy of Tacitus's *Annales 11-16* as early as 1418 that was based on the unique manuscript at Montecasino, and this portion of Tacitus's history was published in Venice in 1472-1473. A unique surviving copy of Tacitus's *Annales 1-6* had been made in Germany in c. 850 and was in German monastery at Corvey. By c. 1508 Leo X had acquired it and added it to the Laurentian Library, and this part was published in Rome in 1515 (Reynolds 1983: 407). A copy of Tacitus's *Annales 7-10* has never been found. When he granted permission for publication, Leo said "…that the great writers were a rule of life and a consolation in misfortune; that helping learned men and obtaining excellent books had ever been one of his highest aims; and that he now thanked heaven that he could benefit the human race by furthering the publication of this book" (Burckhardt 1944: 133).

Cicero never ceased to be appreciated for the quality of his writing, and he was, for example, one of Cosimo de' Medici's favorite authors. However, the unique surviving manuscript of Cicero's *De. Re publica* is fragmentary. It was "Cicero's answer to Plato's *Republic*…. A fine copy of all six books of [Cicero's] Republic did outlive the collapse of the Roman world and found a refuge in the monastery of Bobbio [in northern Italy], but here in the seventh century the text of Cicero was washed off to make way for Augustine's commentary on the Psalms" (Reynolds 1983: 131-132). The parchment was so thoroughly cleaned that no one noticed faint traces of Cicero's work until 1819. Less than half of it survived because the original book was dismantled, and only a portion of the pages were reused for a religious commentary. What survives was published in Rome in 1822.

The monastery of Bobbio was notorious for erasing and reusing "palimpsests," but was not the only one. With improved forensic techniques, more examples should be found in addition the seven treatises by Archimedes that were recently discovered beneath the text of a Byzantine book of prayers that was competed in 1229 (http://archimedespalimpsest.org/about/). No copy of an ancient Greek or Latin book is known to have been erased and reused for religious writings during the Renaissance. (The trnsmission of Latin Classics is discussed further in Appendix III herein and the transmission of Greek Classics in Appendix IV.)

Humanists: The first three great humanists were Dante (1265-1321), Petrarch (1304-1374), and Boccaccio (1313-1375), all three of who had a profound knowledge of ancient Rome and wrote about it in admiration in both Latin and Italian, but from a Christian point of view of everything reflecting the will of God. They and their successors added further to the deeply held conviction that the Italian states and particularly Florence were the inheritors of ancient Rome. "No conviction was more firmly rooted in the popular mind than that antiquity was the highest title to glory which Italy possessed" (Burckhardt 1944: 123).

"In his *Divine Comedy*, written in the early 14th century, the poet Dante Alighieri wrote, 'Ahi, Costantin, di quanto mal fu matre, / non la tua conversion, ma quella dote / che da te prese il primo ricco patre!' ('Ah, Constantine, how much evil was born, / not from your conversion, but from that donation / that the first wealthy Pope received from you!' ["Dante Alighieri. *Inferno*. Canto 19, lines 115–117."])." Dante had considered the document genuine and had regretted that the supposed donation was made (https://en.wikipedia.org/wiki/Donation_of_Constantine). Although Dante "…was and remained the man who first thrust antiquity into the foreground of national culture…," further advances in scholarship were made by later humanists such as Lorenzo Valla, who established that the document was a fake (Burckhardt 1944: 121); "…Vlla concluded his famous declamation against the gift of Constantine, with the wish for the speedy secularization of the States of the Church" (66). By contrast, in the 'Divine Comedy' he [Dante] treats the ancient and the Christian worlds, not indeed as of equal authority, but as parallel to one another. Just as, at an earlier period of the Middle Ages types and antitypes were sought in the history of the Old and New Testaments, so does Dante consistently bring together a Christian and a pagan illustration of the same fact" (121-122).

[Petrarch]…lives in the memory of most people nowadays chiefly as a great Italian poet, owing his fame among his contemporaries far rather to the fact that he was a kind of living representative of antiquity, that he imitated all styles of Latin poetry, endeavoured by his voluminous historical and philosophical writings not to supplant but to make known the works the ancients, and wrote letters that, as treatises on matters of antiquarian interest, obtained a reputation which to us is unintelligible, but which was natural enough in an age without handbooks.

It was the same with Boccaccio. For two centuries, when but little was known of the "Decameron" north of the Alps, he was famous all over Europe simply on account of his Latin compilations on mythology, geography and biography [Burckhardt 1944: 122].

As noted, the Laurentian Library contains "…a manuscript of Varro and Cicero from Montecassino (11th century) acquired by Giovanni Boccaccio, who in 1355 copied it for Petrarch in his own hand…."

Education: In the 1400s most school teachers and university lecturers were humanists regardless of their religious beliefs. "There were Latin schools in every town of the least importance, not by any means merely as preparatory to higher education, but because next to reading, writing, and arithmetic, the knowledge of Latin was a necessity; after Latin came logic. It is to be noted particularly that these schools did not depend on the Church, but on the municipality; some of them, too, were merely private enterprises" (Burckhardt 1944: 127). Some wealthier men such as Cosimo de' Medici hired a tutor for their sons, and he lived in the Palazzo Medici as a member of the family (teaching Michelangelo as well).

The first university in Europe was at Bologna, which "…is said to have sometimes devoted the half of its public income (20,000 ducats) to the university" (Burckhardt 1944: 125). The principal subjects taught there were law and medicine. "Few of the Italian universities show themselves in their full vigour till the thirteenth and fourteenth centuries, where the increase of wealth rendered a more systemic care of education possible. At first there were generally three sorts of professorships—one for civil law, another for canonical law, the third for medicine; in course of time professorships of rhetoric, of philosophy, and of astronomy were added, the last commonly, though not always, identical with astrology" (125). "…most of the humanists of their day deserved small praise in the matter or morals or religion" (128).

By around 1300, "there was then, we are told, nobody in Florence who could not read; even the donkey-men sang the verses of Dante; the best Italian manuscripts which we possess belonged originally to Florentine artisans; the publication of a popular encyclopædia, like the 'Tesoro' of Brunetto Latini, was then possible; and all this was founded on a strength and soundness of character due to the universal participation in public affairs [of the republic], to commerce and travel, and the systematic reprobation of idleness" (121). By early in the 1400s, "…humanism first showed itself practically as an indispensable element in daily life" (128). For example, Niccolò Niccoli, one of the first great collectors of manuscripts, persuaded Piero de' Pazzi, the son of Andrea, to study Latin despite being rich and handsome:

> When he asked further what his pursuit was, Piero replied, as young people are wont to do, "I enjoy myself" ("attendo a darmi buon tempo"). Niccolò said to him, "As son of such a father, and so fair to look upon, it is a shame that thou knowest nothing of the Latin language, which would be so great an ornament to thee. If thou learnest it not, thou wilt be good for nothing, and as, soon as the flower of youth is over, wilt be a man of no consequence (*virtù*). When Piero heard this he straightway perceived that it was true… [129]

Niccoli found a teacher for him, and Pazzi "…became a friend of all learned men and a noble-minded statesman.

Principalities were partly perpetuated by the superior education that the children to princes and dukes received, and this was particularly the case in Mantua, where the Gonzaga accepted the children of aristocrats from other states, but also "the gifted poor" (Burckhardt 1944: 127). In Ferrara, the D'Este also helped fund the education of poor, but outstanding scholars. "Not only in these two courts, but generally throughout Italy, the education of the princely families was in part and for certain years in the hands of the humanists, who thereby mounted a step higher in the aristocratic world. The writing of treatises on the education of princes, formerly the business of theologians, fell now within their province" (128). Michelangelo received the rudiments of a humanist education while living with the family of Lorenzo de' Medici.

Burckhardt acknowledge that humanism later degenerated into pedantry and inhibited creativity more than it stimulate it (121). The same was true, though, of the teaching of art when the objective was to require a student to be like his master. Burckhardt also felt that the demands of humanists to conform to ancient precedents eventually led to an excessive "obedience to authority" that facilitated the creation of despotic states. However, humility was not a virtue taught by humanists, and most humanists admired Cicero more than Caesar. Burckhardt included the Papacy among Italy's despotic states and noted that "the sack of Rome in the year 1527 scattered the scholars no less than the artists in every direction…" (134). Other places derived more benefit than harm by the availability of these scholars and artists, and the Papacy lost further credibility.

Classic Nudes

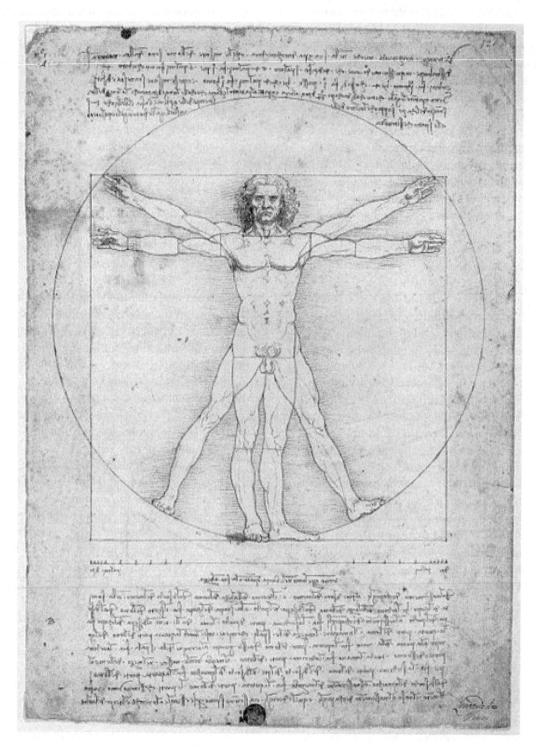

Vitruvian man by Leonardo da Vinci

The analogy that Vitruvius made between human proportions and architectural proportions resulted in numerous attempts during the Renaissance to determine more precisely what he meant in the unillustratied copies of his treatise that survived. He is explicit that he meant only an analogy that the parts of a building need to be interrelated in some coherent way just as the parts of the human body are. In his chapter "On Symmetry: in Temples and in the Human Body," Vitruvius wrote,

1. The design of a temple depends on symmetry, the principles of which must be most carefully observed by the architect. They are due to proportion, in Greek αναλογία [analogy]. Proportion is a correspondence among the measures of the members of an entire work, and of the whole to a certain part selected as standard. From this result the principles of symmetry. Without symmetry and proportion there can be no principles in the design of any temple; that is, if there is no precise relation between its members, as in the case of those of a well shaped man.

2. For the human body is so designed by nature that the face, from the chin to the top of the forehead and the lowest roots of the hair, is a tenth part of the whole height; the open hand from the wrist to the tip of the middle finger is just the same; the head from the chin to the crown is an eighth, and the neck and shoulder from the top of the breast to the lowest roots of the hair is a sixth; from the middle of the breast to the summit of the crown is a fourth. If we take the height of the face itself, the distance from the bottom of the chin to the under side of the nostrils is one third of it; the nose from the underside of the nostrils to a line between the eyebrows is the same; from there to the lowest roots of the hair is also a third, comprising the forehead. The length of the foot is one sixth of the height of the body; of the forearm one fourth; and the breadth of the breast is also one fourth.

The other members, too have their own symmetrical proportions, and it was by employing them that the famous painters and sculptors of antiquity attained to great and endless renown.

3. Similarly, in the members of a temple there ought to be the greatest harmony in the symmetrical relations of the different parts to the general magnitude of the whole. Then again, int the human body the central point is naturally the navel. For if a man be placed flat on his back, with his hands and feet extended, and a pair of compasses centered at his navel, the fingers and toes of his two hands and feet will touch the circumference of a circle described therefrom. And just as the human body yields a circular outline, so too a squre figure may be found from it. For if we measure the distance from the soles of the feet to the top of the head, and then apply that measure to the outstretched arms, the breadth will be found to be the same as the height as in the case of plane surfaces which are perfectly square.

4. Therefore, since nature hsa designed the human body so that its members are duly proportioned to the frame as a whole, it appears that the ancients had good reason for their rule, that in perfect buildings the different members must be in exact symmetrical reelations to the whole general scheme. Hence, while transmitting to us the proper arrangements for buildings of all kinds, they were particualrly careful to do so in the case of temples of the gods, buildings in which merits and faults usually last forever [Vitruvius III, i, 1-4; Vitruvius 1914: 72-73; Morgan translation].

Regardless of what he meant by some of the technical terms he used or their translation, what Vitruvius meant overall is clear: that the human body as it was created through a natural process is the best guide for architects to emulate. This passage from his *Ten Books on Archtiecture* had great impact in principle on the art and architecture of the Renaissance for interrelating the parts of the human body and of buildings proportionately despite varying interpretations of its meaning.

Moveover, the nude body was often depicted by Michelangelo, Leonardo, and other artists to achieve lasting aesthetic results in preference to depicting fashions that were short lived. As Cicero wrote of Caesar's writings, "his *Commentaries* [*on the Gallic War*] are quite admirable. They are like nude figures, straight and attractive, stripped of all adornment of style, like models that have lost their finery" (Cicero quoted in Manutius 2017: 107).

Also, the study of human anatomy resulted in great improvements in medicine and in the accuracy with which nature could be emulated in art. For example, one of the ways that medicine was improved was the ability to perform surgery safely, and the dissection of corpses was necessary to learn internal anatomy. Artists took advantage of the same knowledge and opportunities to learn in order to surpass the ancients in the depiction of surface anatomy.

The advances in Renaissance art and architecture were made possible by a more secular approach to design rather than by a more religious approach. Although the subject matter of art continued to be largely Biblical, the form and purpose of art and architecture became increasingly secular.

Donatello's erotic statue of David was a private commission for a house, and Michelangelo's statue of David was a public commission for a public space (Kent 2000: 284-285). These were secular commissions of statues with pagan nudes, and they were intended to represent the defiance of Republican Florence to superior foes rather than to increase the religious veneration of King David. No nude statues of David had been previously created for a church. It was incidental that David was a Biblical king and more important that he be depicted nude.

The purposes of both of these statues were thus primarily secular in that they were aesthetic and political statements rather than religious depictions. David was undoubtedly not nude when he killed the giant Goliath, and he was not a giant.

To assume that these statues were in any way religious is contrary to their form and locations. To assume that Renaissance art developed out of Medieval art rather than out of the study of nature as Classical art did also is an often taught absurdity.

In 1400 the artists who were chosen to complete for the second set of bronze doors were required to produce equivalent designs to enable a fair comparison to be made: "It was determined that the scene represented should be the sacrifice of Isaac by Abraham, which was considered to be a good subject in which the masters could grapple with the difficulties of art, because it comprises a landscape, figures both nude and draped, and animals, while the figures in the foreground might be made in full relief, those in the middle distance in half-relief, and those in the background in bas-relief" (Vasari 1568: I, 241). Although only two of the six or seven designs submitted a year later have survived, both the one by Ghiberti and the one by Brunelleschi depict Isaac as being nude and has having classical proportions. The Bible does not mention that Isaac was nude or that he had classical proportions. Nudity must have been stipulated as Vasari stated. Since the subject chosen for this set of doors was the New Testament, the sacrifice of Isaac was not included, but since the subject of the main doors was the Old Testament, Isaac was then depicted nude. Also on the main doors, in the panel depicting the creation and fall of man, Adam is depicted nude while being created and while Eve is being created, but when they are being driven out of the Garden of Eden, their nudity is concealed. In the panel depicting the story of Noah, Noah is show nude with no attempt to cover his nudity.

Della Quercia also submitted an entry in the competition for the second set of Baptistery doors, and although his entry does not survive, the stone reliefs he created to surround the doors of San Petronio in Bologna provide a good indication of what he could have created for Florence.

The work of Michelangelo provides the best example of the changing attitudes towards nudity during the Renaissance and most of all his tomb for Julius II. In 1505 the tomb was to be surrounded by nudes, but when it was completed in 1545 there were no nudes. Notably, when Michelangelo depicted the creation of Eve and the expulsion from the Garden of Eden on the Sistine Ceiling, both Adam and Eve are show nude while Eve was being created as well as while they were being driven out. Masaccio had also depicted both Adam and Eve as nude while they were being driven out of the Garden of Eden in his frescoes for the Brancacci Chapel (paintings that Michelangelo had studied and sketched at least in part). In the drunkenness of Noah, Michelangelo shows Noah nude with one of his sons about to conceal his nudity rather than having done so. Any excuse to depict nudity was often taken during the 1400s and early 1500s, and Michelangelo needed no excuse to include decorate nudes on the tomb planned for Julius II or on the Sistine Ceiling. As Michelangelo wrote in a sonnet, "...nor hath God deigned to show Himself elsewhere/ more clearly than in human forms sublime; /which, since they image Him, alone I love" (Michelangelo 1967: 135). "So God created man in his *own* image, in the image of God created he him" (Gen. 1: 27; King James Version).

The best evidence for the essentially secular basis for Renaissance art and architecture is what popes and cardinals commissioned and collected. The nudes created for the tomb of Julius II, for the Sistine Ceiling, and for the Medici Chapel were unprecedented in Medieval art except when nudity was being condemned as with Adam and Eve's expulsion. Renaissance popes and cardinals did not collect or commission Medieval art, and except for a work by Giotto, nearly all of the Medieval art of Old St. Peter's was destroyed. Instead, they collected Classical sculpture and built classically inspired rather than Gothic buildings. To argue that the Renaissance was essentially a continuation of a religious traditions is to ignore its primarily pagan basis and the main interests of its principal artists and patrons.

Provincial cities continued longer than Florence or Rome to prefer religious scenes painted in traditional ways, and uneducated people continued to think as they were told to by ignorant priests until styles and techniques gradually improved throughout Italy and eventually throughout Europe on the basis of the revival of classical styles. Everywhere, Gothic architecture was replaced until it too was eventually revived during a period of eclecticism for largely nationalistic rather than religious reasons. In the meanwhile, there was a Catholic retrenchment in reaction to the Protestant Reformation, but that has nothing to do with the Renaissance, which must be considered separately for what it was rather than what preceded it and what it turned into.

A clear distinction needs to be made between the Renaissance and the period of the Renaissance. By definition, the Renaissance was a revival of pagan civilization in preference to Christian civilization. Pagan history, literature, art, and architecture began again to be recognized as superior to Christian civilization. As Vasari argued throughout his *Lives of the Painters, Sculptors and Architects*, Renaissance art and architecture did not develop out of Medieval art and architecture, but replaced Byzantine art and Gothic architecture gradually and entirely. The preference for Classical art and literature began to take place in Italy during the 1300s, began to predominate in the 1400s, culminated in the 1500s, and declined in the 1600s. The Renaissance was most fully complete during the lifetime of Michelangelo, who created sculpture, painting, and architecture that equaled the finest works that had been created during Antiquity. Considering that Michelangelo was the greatest sculptor, painter, and architect of the Renaissance, it is not arbitrary to consider the Renaissance as having culminated during his lifetime. The two other greatest artists of the Renaissance worked almost entirely during his lifetime: Leonardo (1452-1519) and Raphael (1483-1520).

Although Vasari began his *Lives* with Cimabue (1240-1302), he considered Giotto (1266-1337) to be the first painter of the Renaissance; Cimabue continued to be more of a Byzantine painter than a Renaissance painter. Although the second life he included was of Arnolfo di Lapo (1232-1302), he considered Brunelleschi (1377-1446) to be the first Renaissance architect; Arnolfo continued to be more of a Gothic architect. Although he praised Andrea Pisano (1270-1348) for having benefitted by studying classical sculpture, he considered Jacopo della Quercia (?1371-1438) to be the first Renaissance sculptor; Pisano continued to be primarily a Medieval sculptor. He makes very clear that the work of Giotto, Brunelleschi, and Della Quercia was fundamentally different from the work of Medieval artists and architects rather than a continuation of Medieval practices. He also makes clear that Classical influences were not the only difference between Medieval art and architecture and Renaissance art and architecture, but that the study of Classical art and architecture had by far the greatest impact and that the new period deserved to be considered a rebirth rather than either a continuation or a new development. He also credited the direct study of Nature by Giotto and others as a major influence as well as the discovery of one-point perspective by Brunelleschi.

This is not to say that Renaissance was in all respects different from the Medieval Period for the subject matter continued to be largely the same, but even so nude statues of David were unprecedented, and they had a different meaning than simply illustrating a Biblical story. It is to say that during the lifetime of Michelangelo and very substantially through is efforts, Classical art and architecture were equaled in in some respects surpassed until the Council of Trent insisted on a literal interpretation of Biblical stories and forbid nudity except when it was an integral part of a story. It is to say that although the Renaissance can be considered to have begun by around 1400, it flourished most fully while the Papacy was most secular from 1503 through 1549. The diagnostic trait of the Renaissance was the use of male nudes as decorative elements, and four popes commissioned Michelangelo to create designs with decorative nudes:

(1) Julius II della Rovere (1503-1513), who commissioned Michelangelo to create a tomb that was to be surrounded by nude captives and to paint the Sistine Ceiling with decorative nudes;
(2) Leo X de' Medici (1513-1521), who commissioned Michelangelo to design the Medici Chapel with decorative nudes;
(3) Clement VII de' Medici (1523-1534), who commissioned Michelangelo to complete the Medici Chapel and to paint the "Last Judgment";
(4) Paul III Farnese (1534-1549), who commissioned Michelangelo to complete the "Last Judgment" and to paint the Pauline Chapel

Michelangelo was not the first artist of the Renaissance to depict the male nude. Ghiberti and Brunelleschi both depicted Isaac nude even though nudity is not part of the Biblical story. As noted, Donatello had no better reason to depict David nude than Michelangelo had. Masaccio depicted Adam and Even still nude as they were driven from the Garden of Eden, and their nudity was later covered over as for Michelangelo's "Last Judgment" and paintings in the Pauline Chapel. Subject were often chosen by artists for the opportunity to introduce nudity including the resurrection of the dead and the last judgment by Signorelli, who took for granted that nudity was appropriate for the chapel of a church. Even after clothing was required, St. Sebastian continued to be a popular subject for painting in order to depict him as if he were an all but nude classical statue. Atypically, Leonardo often drew nude men, but mainly in studies of anatomy or proportion, and Raphael preferred nude females; Leonardo had little interest in ancient architecture, but Raphael made a careful study of ancient Roman architecture. On the Sistine ceiling, "in the nudes, Michelangelo displayed complete mastery: they are truly astonishing in their perfect foreshortenings, their wonderfully rotund contours, their grace slenderness, and proportion. And to show the vast scope of his art he made them of all ages, some slim and some full-bodied, with varied expressions and attitudes, sitting, turning, holding festoons of oak leaves and acorns (to represent the emblem of Pope Julius and the fact that his reign marked the golden age of Italy...)" in art and architecture (Vasari 1568: 47).

It is enough for us to understand that this extraordinary man chose always to refuse to paint anything save the human body in its most beautifully proportioned and perfect forms and in the greatest variety of attitudes, and thereby to express the wide range of the soul's emotions and joys. He was content to prove himself in the field in which he was superior to all his fellow craftsmen, painting his nudes in the grand manner and displaying his great understanding of the problems of design. Thus he has demonstrated how painting can achieve facility in its chief province: namely, the reproduction of the human form [72].

It needs to be kept in mind that during the Renaissance, Christians believed God had created Man in his own image and had also created every kind of animal. Consequently, studying the form of Man and of every kind of animal was a study of God's creations. Condivi wrote that

> from boyhood Michelangelo has been a very hard worker, and to his natural gifts he has added learning, which he was determined to acquire not through the efforts and industry of others but from nature herself, which he set before himself as a true example. Thus there is no animal whose anatomy he would not dissect, and he worked on so many human anatomies that those who have spent their lives at it and made it their profession hardly know as much as he does. I am speaking of the knowledge which is necessary to the art of painting and sculpture and not of the other minutiae which anatomists observe. And that this is so is demonstrated by his figures, in which there is such a concentration of art and learning that they are almost impossible for any painter whatever to imitate [Condivi 1553: 90, 93; cf. 97, 99].

As Vasari also noted, among Michelangelo's goals was to depict the full range of possible poses that the human body was capable of assuming, and he came close to doing so in the Sistine Chapel:

> And in order to achieve perfection he made endless anatomical studies, dissecting corpses in order to discover the principles of their construction and the concatenation of the bones, muscles, nerves, and veins, and all the various movements and postures of the human body. He studied not only men, but animals as well, and especially horses, which he lived to own. Of all these he was anxious to learn the anatomical principles and laws in so far as they concerned his art; and in his works he demonstrated this knowledge so well that those who study nothing except anatomy achieve no more. As a result everything he made, whether with the brush or the chisel, defies imitation, and (as has been said) imbued with such art, grace, and distinctive vitality that, if this can be said without offence, he surpassed and vanquished the ancients, for the facility with which he achieved difficult effects so great that they seem to have been created without effort, although anyone who tries to copy his work finds a great deal of effort is needed [Vasari 1568 [1971]: 120-121].

In a passage well known during the Renaissance, the orator Qunitilian indicated the need for variety in speech by noting how effectively it was used in art:

> It is often expedient and sometimes also becoming to make some change in the traditional arrangement, in the same way as in statues and paintings we see variation in dress, expression and attitude. For when the body is held bolt upright it has little grace, the face looks straight forward, the arms hang down, the feet are together and the work is stiff from head to toe. The familiar curve and, if I may call it such, movement, gives a certain effect of action and animation. For the same reason the hand are not always disposed in the same way, and there are a thousand different kinds of expression for the face…. Rhetorical figures, whether of thought or of speech, produce the same effect of grace and charm. For they introduce a certain variation of the straight line and have the virtue of departing from ordinary usage [Quintilian, *Istitutio Oratoria*, II, xiii, 8-11; quoted in Kent 2000: 434, n. 17].

Vasari also noted that Michelangelo "…used to make his figures the sum of nine, ten, and even twelve 'heads' [tall]; in putting them together he strove only to achieve a certain overall harmony of grace, which nature des not present; and he said that one should have compasses in one's eyes, not in one's hands, because the hands execute but it is the eye which judges. He also used this method in architecture" (121-122). In other words, he also depicted the full range of human proportions in addition to his ideals. What looked right (as in using foreshortening) was his goal when seeking to achieve monumentality.

Condivi added that Michelangelo "...loved not only human beauty but everything beautiful in general: a beautiful horse, a beautiful dog, a beautiful landscape, a beautiful plant, a beautiful mountain, a beautiful forest, and every place and thing which is beautiful and rare of its kind, admiring them all with marveling love and selecting beauty from nature as bees gather honey from flowers who use it later in his works" (105). Michelangelo himself wrote, "...peace is not really to be found save in the woods" (Michelangelo 1963: II, 169). He liked being in the mountains selecting stone to be quarried for sculpture and architecture, and he sometimes went to a mountain retreat to rest and recover. That he could paint horses well in motion is evident from some of his work, but he ordinarily did not include animals or plants for decoration or compositional purposes. In a sonnet Michelangelo wrote in praise of Vasari's *Lives* and paintings, he stated, "...you have shown how art/ Can equal nature. ... When men have tried in other centuries/ To vie with nature in the power to make,/ Always they had to yield to her at last" (Vasari 1586: 88).

He preferred depicting male nudes to all other subjects for sculpture and painting. His sculpture of lapiths and centaurs first demonstrated his potential as a sculptor. His cartoon for a painting of the Battle of Cassena established him as the peer of Leonardo, and "he filled it with naked men who are bathing because of the heat in the River Arno when suddenly upon an attack by the enemy the alarm is raised in the camp. . [They were] drawn in various unusual attitudes: some upright, some kneeling or leaning forward, or half-way between one position and another, all exhibiting the most difficult foreshortenings" (Vasari 1568: 33). His designs in sculpture and painting were already characterized by nude men, knowledge of anatomy, proportion, variety, figures in motion and skill in foreshortening.

Condivi recorded that as a young man, Michelangelo

> ...was very intimate with the prior [of Santo Spirito in Florence], from whom he received much kindness and who provided him both with room and with corpses for the study of anatomy, than which nothing could have given him greater pleasure. This was the first time that he applied himself t this study, and he pursued it as long as he had an opportunity [17].

Drawings and models by Michelangelo have survived and indicate his profound knowledge of anatomy including, for example, detailed anatomical models of muscles for the legs of his statue of David (Symonds 1901: I, opp. 100; cf. De Tolnay 1975: I, 105-116).

As had often been the case with the ancient Roman architecture that was being revived, nudes were part of the projects for sculpture, painting, and architecture. Ancient Greek athletes practiced and competed nude. Nudity was part of the daily life of the ancient Romans, who regularly bathed and exercised nude in public baths. Emperors were regularly depicted as nude athletes.

Male nudes were an obsession with Michelangelo as they had been for many Renaissance artists for at least a century, and they became increasingly so as more and better ancient Roman stature were discovered. In art as well as in architecture and literature, the ancients were the ones who needed to be emulated and equaled if not surpassed. The whole point of the Renaissance or "rebirth" was to begin again where Antiquity had left off rather than to continue or develop further the Medieval tradition, which had been more concerned with an afterlife than with life. Often Biblical subjects had previously been often chosen that allowed for male nudes to be included. For example, in 1401 both Ghiberti and Brunelleschi included a nude figure of Isaac in their competition models for the second bronze door of the Florentine. Michelangelo later referred to these Ghiberti's main doors as "...so beautiful that they could stand at the entrance of Paradise" fit to be the gates of Paradise (Vasari 1568 [1971]: 130). Donatello had depicted David nude before Michelangelo, and Michelangelo admired Donatello though he criticized him for neglecting to finish his work well. Many hundreds of other examples of Renaissance nudes made during the 1400s could be readily cited. Nudity was an accepted subject for painting and sculpture. The most direct influence on the use of muscular male nudes in paintings of Biblical subjects was the frescoes that Luca Signorelli painted from 1499-1502 for the Duomo in Orvieto, which is half-way between Rome and Florence and which was one of the places Clement VII took refuge after the Sack of Rome. As in ancient art, nudity was a standard subject for Renaissance art. It had become standard in Italy long before Michelangelo chose the male nude as his main subject for the Battle of Cassena, and he chose the male nude as one of the principal subjects of the Sistine Ceiling and of the Last Judgment. After being accepted for a century and a half, nudity ceased to be regularly depicted in Italy with the Counter-Reformation.

By the beginning of the 16th Century, nude figures were taken for granted and particularly as increasing numbers of ancient nude statues were excavated in Rome. Julius II purchased the Apollo Belvedere and the Laocoön for display in the Vatican, and the Laocoön was restored with the advice of Michelangelo, who also particularly admired the Belvedere Torso. When the Sistine ceiling was unveiled, few persons are likely to have been surprised that Michelangelo had included nude figures so prominently and least of all Julius, who wanted nudes on his tomb.

One reason Michelangelo alternated four large panels with five smaller ones was for variety, but the main reason was to have a place to include 20 large nudes in the center of the ceiling. They were, though, seated rather than standing as on the tomb, and they were not captives. They were included primarily because he liked to depict the nude male.

Michelangelo copied nature for the positions of muscles, but preferred to depict only the well developed muscles of men whose work involved lifting heavy loads such as workers in quarries and stevedores who had physiques equivalent to those of the ancient statues he most admired and particularly the Belvedere Torso, a Hellenistic work signed by the sculptor Apollonios. As a sculptor, he himself "...is well built..." (Condivi 1553: 108). Although the faces of the nudes on the Sistine ceiling are of individuals and vary greatly, the faces on his sculpture were usually more idealized like the statues of ancient athletes.

> In order to create a *Venus*, the ancient master was not content to consider a single maiden, but he wanted to contemplate many, and from each he took her most beautiful and perfect feature to use in his *Venus*. And in truth, anyone who thinks to arrive at some level in this art without this means (whereby true knowledge of theory can be acquired is greatly deceiving himself [Condivi 1553 (1976): 105; notes omitted]

The Greek writer Xenophon recorded that Socrates, who was by profession a sculptor, asked Cleitos if this was not how he created sculptures, and this almost certainly referred to Polycleitos' Canon of proportions (Waddell 1991). The editor of Condivi noted that the Roman writer Pliny recorded a similar story about the Greek painter Zeuxis (Michelangelo 1963: 145, n. 124). "He greatly loved human beauty for its use in art; only by copying the human form, and by selecting from what was beautiful, the most beautiful, could he achieve perfection" (Vasari 1568: 125). Vasari wrote that Renaissance artists since Giotto had used essentially the same method of selecting and combining the best parts of the best examples they could find.

Michelangelo's approach to architecture was similar in that once he became capable of doing so, he stopped copying the works of others, but sometimes adapted and changed them greatly, and he did not copy his own work. "Michelangelo has a most retentive memory, so that, although he has painted all the thousands of figures that are to be seen, he has never made two alike or in the same pose. Indeed, I have heard him say that he never draws a line without remembering whether he has ever drawn it before and erasing it if it appears in public. He also has the most powerful faculty of imagination, which gives rise in the first place to the fact that he has not been very satisfied with his works and has always belittled them, feeling that his hand did not approach the idea which he formed in his mind" (Condivi 1553: 107).

Michelangelo sometimes adapted drawings of men to serve as women on the Sistine ceiling, but this was obviously not the case with the female nudes in the Medici Chapel. He preferred strong men and women rather than the delicate women in Raphael's early paintings. According to Condivi, "Raphael, of Urbino, however anxious he might be to compete with Michelangelo, often had occasion to say that he thanked god that he was born in Michelangelo's time, as he copied from him a style which was quite different from the one he learned from his father, who was a painter or from his master Perugino" (94; notes omitted). He praised Raphael and said Raphael "...did not come by his art naturally, but through long study" (106).

To put the influence of the Reformation on art and architecture in a broader context, Martin Luther wrote while visiting Rome that the funds of the Church should not have been spent to acquire the Apollo Belvedere, and he objected strongly to cardinals living like princes. Later, he opposed the sale of indulgences, a practice that was partly intended to provide funds for the construction of the new St. Peter's. As a priest, Luther wanted to reform the Catholic Church from within until Leo X excommunicated him, which freed him to refer to the pope as the Anti-Christ, the whore of Babylon, and the devil incarnate. Luther made effective use of art in his pamphlet war against the abuses of the Church, and his translations of the Bible were illustrated; he was no iconoclast. Some of his followers became fundamentalists and intolerant and broke away to form other denominations. To try to deal with the popularity of Luther's teachings, Paul sided with the Emperor Charles V in his wars against various German states. In 1538 he excommunicated Henry VIII of England; in 1540 he recognized the Jesuit Order; in 1542 he revived the Inquisition; and in 1545, he convened the Council of Trent. In its final decree in 1563,

> the holy council commands all bishops and others... all superstition shall be removed, all filthy quest for gain eliminated and all lasciviousness avoided so that images shall not be painted and adorned with a seductive charm.... nothing may appear that is disorderly or unbecoming and confusedly arranged, nothing that is profane, nothing disrespectful, since holiness becometh the house of God [quoted in Holt 1982: 62]

In 1573 when Paolo Veronese had to defend himself to an Inquisition tribunal for having included "buffoons, drunkards, Germans, dwarfs and similar vulgarities" in a famous painting of the Last Supper ("Feast in the House of Simon"), he referred to the inclusion of nudity in Michelangelo's Last Judgment as an example of poetic license without intending to be irreligious. He managed to avoid prosecution by changing the title of his painting to "the Feast in the House of Levi" (Holt 1982: 62-70).

Michelangelo had painted the Last Judgement with innumerable nudes, and when it was largely complete, the Paul's master of ceremonies said it was

> ...no work for a papal chapel but rather for the public baths and taverns. Angered by this comment, Michelangelo determined he would have his revenge; and as soon as Biagio had left he drew his portrait from memory in the figure of Minos [with the ears of an ass], shown with great serpent curled round his legs [biting and concealing his genitals], among a heap of devil in hell; nor for all his pleading with the Pope and Michelangelo could Biagio have the figure removed... [Vasari 1568: 73].

To the request to have himself painted out, Paul III is said to have replied that if only he were in Purgatory, a pope could do something about it. However, Paul IV (1555-1559) objected to the nudity in the Last Judgment, saying that "the figures there revealed their nakedness too shamelessly. When he heard this, Michelangelo commented: 'Tell the Pope that this is a trivial matter and can be easily be arranged; let him set about putting the world to rights for pictures are soon put right'" (Vasari 1568: 97).

Athens, Rome, and Florence

Greek civilization culminated in Athens, Roman in Rome, and Renaissance in Florence. A comparison of all three places reveals that they had much in common and helps to determine why they developed as the principal centers for Greek, Roman and Renaissance architecture.

In the increasinglysophisticated humanistic climate of the early fifteenth century, Florentines had made ever more elaborate use of classical symbols and parallels between their own society and that of Greece and Rome seeing Florence, like Ahtens and Rome before it, as the bastion of republican civilization [Kent 2000: 283-284].

All three were near the Mediterranean Sea, but inland at fording places on relatively minor rivers. They locations facilitated travel by land across the fords and by water to the sea, but they were far enough inland to have access to better agricultural land that on the coast and to be relatively safe from raids. Their trade depended mainly on the sea, but their source of food was mainly agricultural. Athens and Florence depended more on livestock and Rome more on planting. The produce of the land was enhanced by the presence of minerals in volcanic soil, but their geology was more favorable to trade than agriculture.

Athens traded mainly olive oil and wine and developed a ceramic industry to provide containers to transport these products by sea in return for wood and metals. Rome had a more favorable climate than Athens or Florence and was able to grow its own food while it remained small, but as it grew larger, it had to import increasing amounts of food and to bring water from great distances through aqueducts. Rather than trade, it conquered to supply its needs. Florence was too far north for grape vines to flourish except in sheltered areas, but its location was ideal for raising livestock, and its trade in wool was profitable.

All three locations had long been occupied by relatively primitive cultures and were sparsely settled until they began to grow and urbanize. All three had to defend themselves initially, and they were not always successful. Athens began to flourish most when in league with Greek cities it was able to defeat two attempts by the Persians to invade it. It flourished most after expelling its tyrants and created a democracy. Rome began to flourish when it expelled the Etruscan kings that had conquered it and when it began, in its turn, to conquer its neighbors, but to extend to them the rights of citizenship in a republic. Florence flourished moderately as an Etruscan and Roman city in relative isolation, but its access to the sea was controlled by Pisa until early in the 1400s, when it conquered Pisa and began to conquer most of the rest of Tuscany. Its increasing trade made manufactures of all kinds more worthwhile, and the guilds that produced good largely controlled its republican form of government.

All three places had good building materials close at hand and made good use of them. In Athens, it was primarily marble, in Rome primarily brick and tufa, and in Florence primarily brick and sandstone. Most of these materials were ultimately of volcanic origin. Brick is made from clay that consists of deteriorated granite; tuff is a volcanic stone; and concrete is produced by mixing volcanic sand, lime and water to produce an artificial stone that sets up through a chemical reaction and is much harder than mortar than dries out. The limestone near Rome had settled out of water from springs originating in volcanic areas rather than the shellstone that was used to create early temples in many Greek colonies.

All three cities began to flourish through agriculture and trade, but as they grew they incited envy and had to defend themselves. Initially, the military prowess of Athens and Rome grew for defense, but when it was no longer needed for defense, it was used for offence and other purposes. Athens formed the Delian League to keep the Persians out of the Mediterranean, but the league gradually truned into an empire, and in times of peace, Athens spend its contributions increasingly on public works rather than defense; the Parthenon was financed by funds from the Delian League. Polybius describes in detail how Rome's defense of itself led to the continual expansion of its territory until it was invaded by Carthage and Macedon and took to the sea to defend itself further until it successively unified Greece and the Mediterranean. Florence was wealthy enough to hire mercenary soldiers to defend it against most attacks, but fewer mercenaries that their enemies could hire.

Thus, Athens, Rome, and Florence grew despite disadvantaged and because they needed to trade and defend themselves. All three flourished as republics that controlled others, but for their mutual benefit more often than not. Trade promoted specializations, professionalism, and individuality and was the primary source of wealth in Athens and Florence, but taxation in kind was the primary source of wealth in Rome. All three places had slavery, but their prosperity depended much less on slavery than on trade and taxation. Rome generally allowed local rulers to remain in office so long as taxes were paid. All three places reached their culmination intellectually as republics and in most respects began to decline to the extent that one or a few individuals limited their options or involved them in wars.

The disunity of the Greek states led to continual wars among them. Thucydides recorded that architecture flourished most under the leadership of Pericles and direction of Phidias, but that the execution of Phidias for blasphemy precipitated the Peloponnesian War. Democracy facilitated mob rule and led to the execution of Socrates for blasphemy. Greece settled down when Macedon conquered all of it as well as the eastern Mediterranean and Egypt.

Rome was highly tolerant of religions until religious became intolerant of one another tolerant of individuality so long as it did not threaten the government, and architecture flourished even more through the Pax Roman than it had previously and Greek architects and artists were able to work in Rome and to influence its development. Rome flourished most intellectually from the time of Lucretius to Cicero, and Caesar and Vitruvius were products of the Republic. The use of concrete had begun during the republic, but climaxed with imperial baths and the Pantheon.

Florence built its best buildings while it was a republic until it was conquered by allies of the Vatican, and as the taste of its rulers declined, its architecture did also. The dome of the Duomo, the Medici Palace, and the Laurentian Library were built during the republic. Its greatest artists were trained during the republic, but some of their greatest accomplishments were made possible by making use of the resources of the Papal States as well as its subject cities. It is true that the principal commissions often came from philosopher-kings or individuals who thought of themselves in this way.

When any place becomes prosperous enough, it is likely to attract the best architects and artists from elsewhere, and commissions are less likely to go to local architects and artists. The result is that the opportunities for local talent to develop become restricted. During the Renaissance, for example, the only artist or architect of any renown who was of Roman origin was Giulio Romano. On the other hand, localities tend to lose their best talent to places that offer more opportunity as Urbino lost Bramante and Raphael, and Bramante brought Raphael to Rome. Florence lost Michelangelo and Leonardo. Similarly, Athens had attracted Phidias from the Peloponnese, and Rome had attracted Apollodorus from the Greek East.

It is important to bear in mind too that the greatest advances in architecture coincided with advances in the fields of art, history, geography, literature, and science. As architects and artists were attracted by greater opportunities, so were philosophers and writers either to work, study, or both. Athens, Rome, and Florence became places where all intellectual endeavors flourished primarily to the extent that they continued to attract the greatest talent, helped it develop, and kept it provided with challenging commissions. On the other hand, decreasing opportunities and interference with intellectual development led inevitably to decline. The Sack of Rome in 1527 led to the Counter-Reformation and largely successful attempts to censor and persecute dissent. The siege of Florence in 1530 was the beginning of the end of its Renaissance.

How did Greece and Rome accomplish so much without Catholicism? Why did Italy accomplish so much during the Renaissance and so little during the Counter-Reformation?

19. Michelangelo's Design for St. Peter's

St. Peter's Dome, Rome (Magni)

Not until Julius II (Della Rovere) did anyone begin to tear down the church built over the grave of the Apostle Peter by the Emperor Constantine around 12 centuries earlier. Vasari summarized the history of the various designs for St. Peter's from Bramante to Michelangelo:

> Bramante's spirit being thus grown great, and seeing the Pope's wish corresponded with his own desire to pull down the church of S. Pietro and build it anew, he made a great number of designs one being especially admirable, displaying his wonderful skill. It has two campaniles, one on either side of the façade, as we see on the coins of Julius II and Leo X, designed by Caradosso, an excellent goldsmith, unequalled for his dies, and by the little medal of Bramante himself. The Pope then decided to undertake the stupendous task of building S. Pietro, and caused a half to be pulled won, intending that in beauty, invention, order, size, and richness and decoration it should surpass all the buildings ever erected in that city by the power of the republic and by the art and genius of so many able masters. Bramante laid the foundation with his accustomed speed, and before the Pope's death the walls were raised as high as the cornice, where the arches to all four pilasters are, and he vaulted these with the utmost rapidity and great art. He also vaulted the principal chapel where the niche is, and proposed to push forward the chapel called after the King of France [the south apse]. ... Since his death many architects have meddled with this work, so that, excepting the four outside arches bearing the tribune, there is nothing of his left. Raphael of Urbino and Giuliano da S. Gallo, who had charge of the work after the death of Julius II, together with Giocondo of Verona, began to change it. After their death Baldassare Peruzzi made the alterations in building the chapel of the King of France in the crossing towards the Camposanto while under Paul III, Antonio da S. Gallo changed everything; and finally Michelagnolo Buonarroti did away with their various ideas and useless expenditure, and brought it to a unified whole of great beauty and perfection, feeling himself, as he has frequently told me, the executor of the plan and design of Bramante, an idea which had never entered the heads of the others, who only though of their own designs and judgment, although those who began construction of an edifice are its real author. Bramante's conception of this work seemed limitless; he initiated a great building, and if he had begun this magnificent church on a lesser plan it would not have been possible for S. Gallo and the others, no, not even for Michelagnolo, to increase it, indeed they diminished the size, for Bramante conceived something larger [Vasari 1568: II, 188-189].

Michelangelo's version of how Julius came to decide to replace Old St. Peter's is told by Ascanio Condivi, a former pupil of Michelangelo who had lived and worked with him in Rome. Condivi is explicit that Julius decided to rebuilt St. Peter's primarily because he wanted a grander setting for the free-standing tomb he had commissioned Michelangelo to create. By 1503, when Michelangelo was about 29 years old, he had created his Pietà and statue of David and was the most famous sculptor in Italy. "Through it [the David], he acquired great fame and reputation so much that, already in the opinion of the world, he not only far surpassed any other man of his time, and of the time before him, but he even rivaled the ancients" (Condivi 1563 [1976]: 27). In 1503 Julius summoned Michelangelo to Rome without having decided what he wanted him to do there:

> After he came to Rome, then, many months passed before Julius II could decide in what way to employ him. At last it entered his mind to have him make his tomb. And, when he saw he design, he liked it so much that he sent him at once to Carrara to quarry the amount of marble required for the project, and he had Alemannno Salviati in Florence pay him a thousand ducats

for this purpose. He remained in those mountains for more than eight months, with two helpers and a horse and no provisions other than food. ...

So great was the quantity of the blocks of marble that, when they were spread out in the piazza, they made other people marvel and rejoiced the pope, who conferred such great and boundless favors on Michelangelo.... As very often happens at court, the many great favors thus conferred gave rise to envy and, after envy, endless persecutions. Thus the architect Bramante, who was loved by the pope, made him change his plans by quoting what common people say, that it is bad luck for anyone to build his tomb during his lifetime and other stories. Apart from envy, Bramante was prompted by the fear he had of the judgment of Michelangelo, who kept discovering many of Bramante's blunders. Because Bramante, who was as everyone knows a great spendthrift and given to every sort of pleasure, so that the funds provided him by the pope, however ample, did not suffice, tried to gain advantage in his buildings by making the walls of poor materials and inadequately strong and secure for their size and extensiveness. This is obvious for everyone to see in the buildings of St. Peter's in the Vatican, in the Belvedere Corridor, in the monastery of S. Pietro in Vincoli, and in his other buildings, all of which have required new foundations and reinforcement with buttresses and retaining walls, as if they were falling or would shortly have fallen down. Now, because he did not doubt that Michelangelo recognized these misdeeds of his he constantly sought to remove him from Rome, or at least to deprive him of the pope's favor and of the glory and reward he might acquire by his industry. This happened to him in the case of this tomb; if it had been built according to his first design (be it said without envy), there is no doubt that in his art he would have prevailed over any other artist, however highly regarded, as he had ample scope in which to show his worth. ... In short, the whole work involve more than forty statues, not counting the narrative scenes in bronze in *mezzo-relievo*, all pertinent to the subject, in which the deeds of this great pope were to be seen.

When the pope had seen this design, he sent Michelangelo to St Peter's to see where it could suitably be placed. The form of the church then was that of a cross, at the head of which Pope Nicholas V had begun to rebuild the choir, and it had already reached a height of three *braccia* aboveground when he died. It seemed to Michelangelo that this was a very appropriate place and, returning to the pope, he presented his opinion, adding that, if His Holiness though so too, it was going to be necessary to raise the structure and roof it over. ...After sending San Gallo, the architect, and Bramante to see the place, in the course of these arrangements the pope as inspired to build the whole church anew. Various designs were ordered, and Bramante's was accepted as more attractive and better conceived than the others.... Thus it was because of Michelangelo that the part of the building that was already begun was finished because, if this had not happened, perhaps it would still be s it was, and also that the pope conceived the desire to renovate the rest according toa new and more beautiful and magnificent design [Condivi 1563 (1976): 29-34; notes omitted].

The design and construction of the new St. Peter's took more than a century, and Ramsden provided a summary:

> The corner stone was laid by Julius II on Sunday April 18th 1506: the dome was completed in 1590 under Sixtus V and the lantern in 1592 under Gregory XIV. ... But it was not until 1607 when Paul V commissioned the nave and narthex, which were completed in 1614, that the last remains of the old Basilica, which

373

had been founded in the fourth century by the Emperor Constantine during the pontificate of Sylvester I, were finally swept away [Ramsden in Michelangelo 1963: II, 303].

Then, instead of completing the front to Michelangelo's design, the plan was changed from a Greek cross to a Latin cross, and an entirely different front was completed in 1626 and dedicated by Urban VIII (316).

Initial Stages of Design and Construction

By far the most important stages in the design and construction of St. Peter's were the initial design phase by Bramante and the redesign and principal phase of construction by Michelangelo, and these two stages will be considered in this chapter in most detail. Additions to the building will be considered in the next chapter. Although little will be included in either chapter on design that were not used, some of the more significant designs by Giulio da Sangallo, Raphael, Peruzzi, and Antonio da Sangallo will be briefly noted.

From Bramante through Michelangelo, there were six main stages of design and construction:

(1) Bramante's initial design for a basilica with a Greek-cross plan with corner towers that included sacristies was accepted by Julius II della Rovere in 1505.

(2) Giuliano da Sangallo persuaded Julius II to add ambulatories.

(3) Julius II decided to add a nave, but at the time of his death in 1513 construction had been limited to the creation of the four central piers of the transcept and the arches that joined them, and Bramante died in 1514. As much as Julius has successively approved, he realistically insisted that Bramante complete the choir that had been begun by Rossellini in c. 1450 rather than replace it.

(4) From 1513 to 1546 construction progressed less than it had previously because of lack of funds and structural deficiencies that had to be corrected. Innumerable designs produced by Raphael, Peruzzi, and Antonio da Sangallo had little effect on the final appearance of St. Peter's. Leo X Medici (1513-1521) wanted all of the added features that Bramante had been forced to accept and also wanted an impressive portico, but although Julius II left the Vatican with 700,000 ducats in its treasury, Leo X was mainly intent on enjoying the papacy (Burckhardt 1944: 74). Clement VII Medici (1523-1534) accomplished little because of the Sack of Rome in 1527 and the attack on Florence to impose Medici rule, and Raphael and Peruzzi later produced plans to reduce the intended size of St. Peter's.

(5) Paul III Farnese (1534-1549) wanted even more than Leo X, but had funding for little more than to pay for an immense model by Antonio da Sangallo that would have attached an immense benediction loggia in front of a Greek-cross plan with ambulatories, to add some vaulting, and to begin the construction of ambulatories.

(6) After Sangallo's death in 1546, Paul III eventually persuaded Michelangelo to accept the task of designing a more coherent and affordable building and agreed to allow him to remove any parts of the building that had already been constructed. Michelangelo adapted Bramante's first plan, but eliminated the corner towers, redesigned the entire exterior of the building, and planned to add a monumental portico.

In brief, both Bramanate and Michelangelo wanted St. Peter's to have the plan of a Greek cross; Bramante fixed its dimensions, and Michelangelo constructed an entire wing that was to have been duplicated and the drum for the dome, and he planned a portico suitable for the scale of the building. Michelangelo further reinforced Bramante's piers, eliminated the corner towers that had been part of most plans from 1505-1546, tore down the ambulatories that had been begun by Antonio da Sangallo, competed enough of the building that the body of it is largely based on his designs, and designed a structurally sound dome. If St. Peter's had been completed to his design, there would have been no nave, and his dome would have been fully visible from the front of the building.

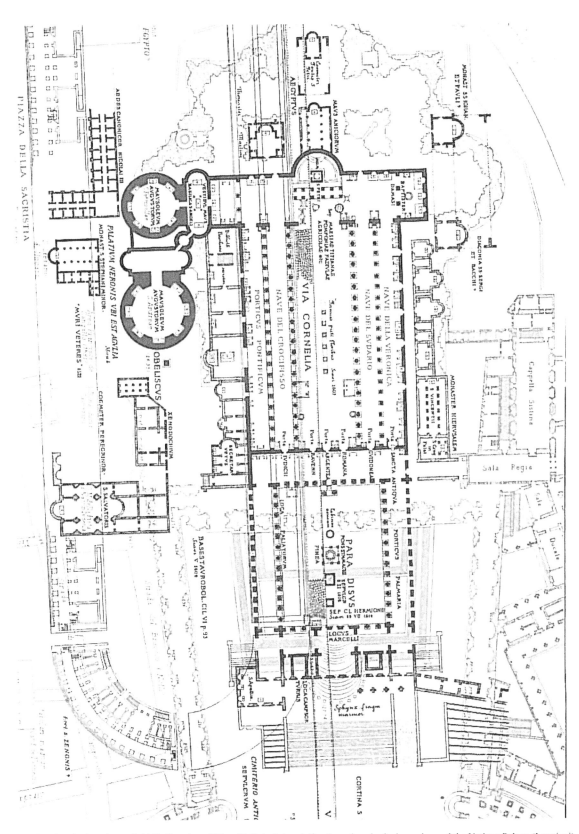

Map showing the locations of old St. Peter's and New St. Peter's in relation to archaeological remains and the Vatican Palace (Lanciani)

Bramante's Designs for St. Peter's (1505-1514)

Bramante designed a building that would have been considerably large than Old St. Peter's in area though with aisles of similar width and that would have had a Greek-cross plan rather than its Latin-cross plan. The initial plan that is recorded on parchment is a finished presentation drawing for a somewhat simpler design, and it was soon followed by a more elaborate design drawing that shows how Bramante took advantage of the foundations of the older building, how he greatly enlarged his initial design for central piers, and how he used graph paper to work out his plan with precision.

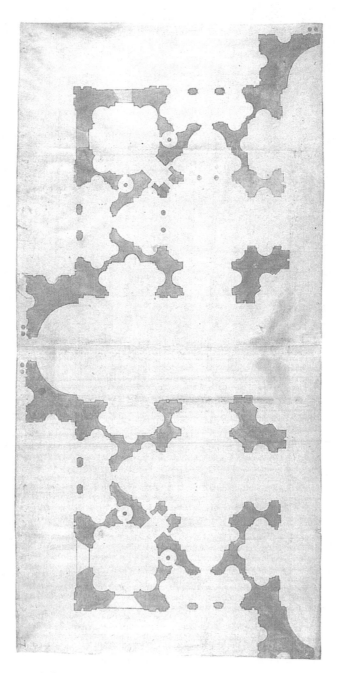

Bramante's first plan for St. Peter's on parchment, 1505 (Millon and Lampugnani)

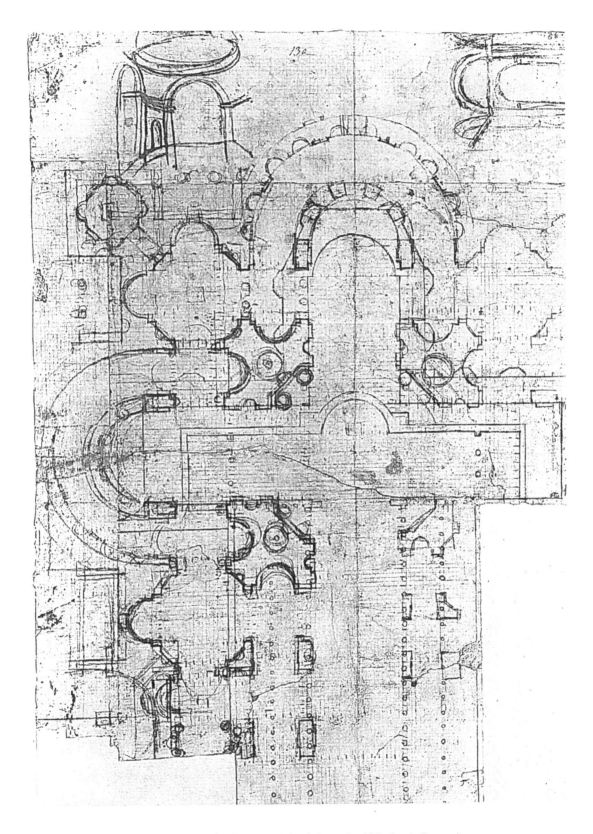

Bramante's third plan for St. Peter's in relation to the old St. Peter's (Spagnesi)

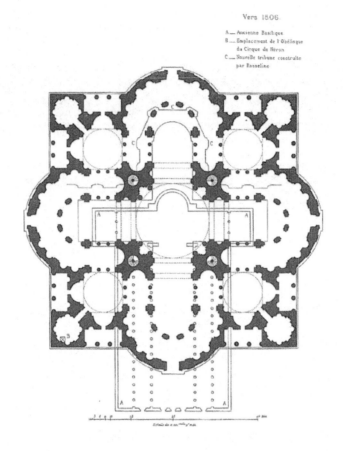

Bramante's plan superimposed on Old St Peter's with "Rossellino's choir" indicated in outline (Letarouilly)

Foundation medal with Bramante's elevation for St. Peter's, 1505 (Bruschi)

AN_1506

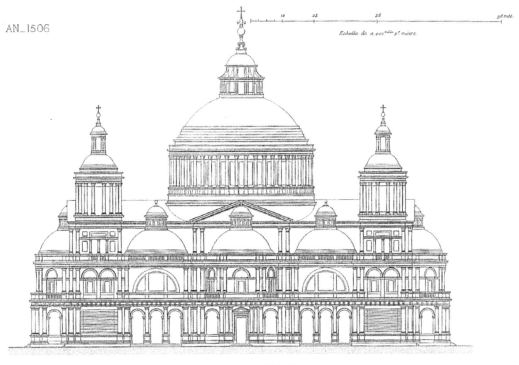

Façade projetée, d'après la Médaille ci-dessous

Coupe longitudinale d'après le plan (Pl.18) et la façade ci-dessus

Reconstructions of Bramante's initial design for St. Peter's (Letarouilly)

Bramante's plan was based on the plan of Old St. Peter's. His nave was the same width as the nave of Old St. Peter's, and the length of his crossing was the length of the crossing of Old St. Peter's with apsidal ends added. The four equal arms of Bramante's plan were essentially the size and shape of the choir that Rossellino had added to the transept of Old St. Peter's. The principal differences in Bramante's designs were in creating a central space twice the width of the nave of Old St. Peter's and in adding chapels and towers in the corners of his Greek cross plan. Over a crossing with diagonal piers and pendentives, Bramante designed a dome nearly as large as the Pantheon's, and the dome was to sit on a tall drum that would serve as a clearstory. In this way, the central space was made as wide s the nave and inner aisles of Old St. Peter's. In between the four equal arms of the plan, Bramante placed four large chapels with cupolas. At the four corners of the plan, he intended four bell towers to enframe the domes and to have additional chapels in their bases. These elements show in his earliest surviving plans and persisted as he redesigned the building. Except for the towers, most of these features were constructed, but redesigned.

The medal Bramante had cast in 1505 provides the best indication of how the four fronts of the building would have looked if the original plan had been followed. Since this medal was reissued in 1506 with the portrait of Julius and again in c. 1513 with a portrait of Leo X, Bramante's elevations continued to be more of less the same even after ambulatories were added to the plan (Million and Lampugnani 1994: 325; cf. Lees-Milne 1967: 1145 and Letarouilly 1953: figs. 18-19).

Bramante planned to construct a dome with a single shell and with steprings like the Pantheon, but he hoped to put it on top of a drum that would have consisted of piers with columns as many as three deep in its openings. "The crossing piers were completed and joined in 1510-11 by great coffered arches. Bramante also completed Rossellino's mid-fifteenth-century choir, and built a temporary Doric altar-house [fig "104"]" (Ackerman 1986: 317). Before his death in 1514, his piers and the four arches that connect them to one another had been completed, and the scale he set for the building both vertically and horizontally had been permanently fixed. The aisles remained the same width and height. The pattern of coffers had been established on the underside of the arches between the piers.

Bramante's fully cross-axial plan eventually lost three of its entrances. Michelangelo later planned four smaller dome, but two were built. Bernini designed two bell towers for the front, but after structural difficulties, the only one that was partially built was removed. The piers Bramante designed to support his dome were later considered inadequate and were enlarged still further. His two-storied exterior with engaged Roman Doric columns was partly built, but was destroyed and replaced by smaller apses with monumental columns similar to those he had designed for the interior. Surprisingly, his own design for a dome bears less resemblance to his Tempietto than Michelangelo's design.

The sources for the design of St. Peter's are much debated. They range from a Carolingian church in Milan to a Roman tomb, both of which had similar plans and may have suggested a Greek-cross plan, but after the fall of Constantinople in 1453, Rome had large numbers of Greek refuges who knew the plans of Byzantine churches well enough to have promoted their plans. Another likely influence are Roman baths, and a drawing by Bramante of the Baths of Diocletian has a small sketch of a square building with four apsidal ends.

Essentially Bramante put the Pantheon's dome on top of a Greek tholos. He supported his dome and clearstoried drum on pendentives used in Roman architecture, but perfected in Byzantine churches such as Hagia Sophia so that a dome could be supported over a square crossing on four piers (as in a drawing by Ciriaco d'Ancona copied by Giuliano da Sangallo in Millon and Lampugnani 1994: 271; cf. the vault of Bramante's crypt in Pavia Cathedral in Frommel 2007: 83). For St. Peter's, Bramante chose barrel vaults to stabilize the piers rather than cross vaults with domed chapels in the corners to prevent the barrel vaults from spreading laterally rather than cross vaults, which could have provided better light for a large space, but that would have resembled a Roman bath rather than a Romanesque church.

The two principal versions of Bramante's plans differ mainly in the addition of an ambulatory, which Frommel pointed out is likely to have been suggested by either Julius II or Giuliano da Sangallo. Whole Alexander VI Borgia was pope, Cardinal Giuliano della Rovere left Italy and travelled in France, and Sangallo accompanied him. While there, they undoubtedly saw many examples of French Gothic cathedrals with ambulatories that provided a good way to accommodate large numbers of pilgrims. Notably, S. Front in Periguex has a similar ambulatory and a Greek-cross plan with five domes, but does not have an overall square plan with four apsidal wings.

In a surviving plan, Giuliano da Sangallo proposed a square church with a large cruciform plan in the center and with small cruciform plans in each corner. On the back of Sangallo's drawing, Bramante made a sketch showing how ambulatories could be added to his initial plan without changing the overall cruciform shape of the building, and evidently Julius II accepted Bramante's compromise (Frommel in Millon and Lampugnani 1994: 603-604, entry 287).

Consequently, Bramante's second plan with the addition of a separate ambulatory around the perimeter of the cruciform center determined the most basic features of all accepted designs for St. Peter's from around 1505 to 1547, when Michelangelo was given full charge, tore down the what little had been built of the ambulatory as well as the choir, and began to adapt Bramante's first plan as the basis for his design of St. Peter's.

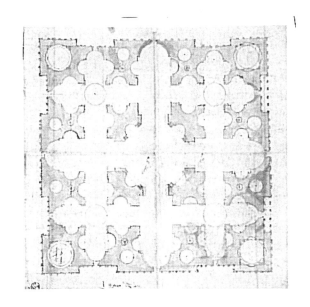

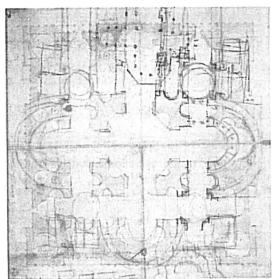

Plans for St Peter's: above, by Giuliano da Sangallo; below, by Bramante; c. 1505 (Uffizi 8A; Frommel in Millon and Lampugnani)

Bramante deserves great credit for having convinced Julius II that a far greater building than Old St. Peter's was feasible, for having established the scale of the New St. Peter's, and for having constructed the framework of the transept that fixed the scale and principal design element of the new building. He can be blamed for having created deficient structural elements and for having added corner towers that would have resembled the minarets that were added to Hagia Sophia. He cannot be blamed for the choir he was required to complete or for the ambulatories and nave that he was required to incorporate in his designs, but his design for Rossellini's choir provides a good indication of what the interior and exterior of St. Peter's would have been like if it had been completed to Bramante's designs. The interior would have had Corinthian columns on pedestals while the exterior would have had slender Doric columns with disks on their necks. The interior would have had relatively primitive detailing similar to what he had designed for Santa Maria delle Grazie in Milan including arches with oculi and over-scaled decorative elements such as the giant shell in the half-dome of the choir. The compromised he was required to accept and the provincial design elements he preferred would have resulted in a far less well designed building than Michelangelo deserves the most credit for having created. Bramante also deserves great credit for having designed the Tempietto, which Michelangelo had the good judgment to adapt for St. Peter's, but his design for St. Peter's would have been greatly inferior to his design of the Tempietto, which he would have done well to adapt himself. Bramante was a great architect, but less great than Michelangelo, who learned from him and who surpassed him.

Bramante's design for Rossellini's choir (detail of a drawing by Giuliano da Sangallo in Frommel *et al.*)

How much Bramante and his successors completed during the 16th Century is best indicated by drawings made by Marten van Heemskerck in c. 1532 (Holt 1981: 346). Heemskerck (1498-1574) remained in Rome at least until 1536, but he is likely to have drawn St. Peter's soon after arriving (Vasari1568: IV, 16). His drawings and later drawings and paintings provide a good indication of what Raphael, Antonio da Sangallo the Younger, and Michelangelo accomplished at various stages in the construction of St. Peter's

Stages of Construction for St. Peter's from c. 1532-c. 1569

Two views of the north side of Bramante's crossing for St. Peter's in c. 1532 (Heemskerck in Dunbar)

North side of St. Peter's in c. 1532 with "Rossellino's choir" as completed by Bramante (Heemskerk in Dunbar)

South side of new and old St. Peter's (Heemskerck in Dunbar)

Western end of St. Peter's in c. 1532 showing Bramante's additions with part of Old St. Peter's in the foreground (Heemskerck in Spagnesi)

Flanking pier buttress with Raphael's cornices (Heemskerck in Dunbar)

South side of St. Peter's in c. 1532 with the beginning of Sangallo's ambulatory (Heemskerck in Baldrati)

Paul III approving Sangallo's additions to the souths ide of St. Peter's (1546 fresco by Vasari; detail from Lees-Milne)

South side of St. Peter's in c. 1556 with the nearly completed wing by Michelangelo and the earlier choir (Anon. in Dunbar)

North side of St Peter's in c. 1556 with the beginning of Michelangelo's wing (Anon. in Dunbar)

St. Peter's in c. 1569 with the apse of Old St. Peter's, Bramante's crossing, Sangallo's base, and Michelangelo's drum (Dosio in Spagnesi)

Bramante's Intended Dome

The plans, elevations, and section that Serlio published of Bramante's final design indicate that Bramante intended to have an ambulatory around the top of the drum of the dome equivalent to the ambulatory he planned for the perimeter of the interior, but no access to the lantern. Although Serlio's woodcuts are not detailed, they provide sufficient information to determine more or less how the dome would have been constructed.

Bramante's elevation and plan for the dome of St. Peter's (Serlio)

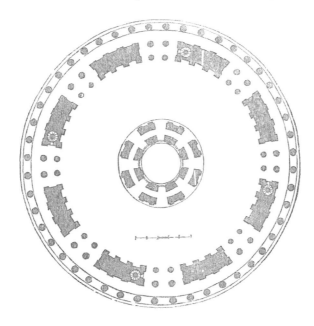

A solid dome with steprings of similar size to the dome of the Pantheon leave no doubt that Bramante believed he could construct a solid dome above the crossing of St. Peter's. He intended to support his dome above a drum that would also have been constructed similarly to the largely hollow walls of the Pantheon.

Bramante's plan of the dome shows that he intended to carry most of the weight of the dome directly downward onto a ring of masonry supported by four pendentives. Four of the eight large openings would have aligned with the centers of the four barrel vaults and the other four large opening with the centers of the pendentives in order to lighten the load at these eight critical points.

In this way four pairs of wide and thick walls would have been carried more by the sides of the pendentives than by their centers and would have transferred the weight of the drum and dome downward more safely than if the large openings had been where the sections of wall were to be located, and the foundation ring for the drum would have been less likely to fail.

The eight sections of walls of the drum would probably have been constructed of brick and faced with stone to reduce the weight to be carried but the columns with pedestals would have been constructed of stone for the same reason that the columns of the interior were of stone: to have greater compressive strength and so enable the opening between the walls of the drum to be as wide as possible. Since neither the walls nor the columns were arranged in a way that would have effectively buttressed the base of the dome, Bramante must have been fully convinced that the solid dome would contain its thrust like the dome of his Tempietto, which is similar in many respects though on a much smaller scale.

In my opinion, Bramante must have recognized that the steprings of the Pantheon indicaed that its dome was constructed one ring at a time and allowed to solidify before another ring was added. Presumably, his dome would have been constructed of brick and mortar rather than concrete, which was known through Vitruvius, but had not been used on a large scale in the Renaissance. In any case, constructing each ring of the dome separately would have been equivalent to constructing the foundation ring for the drum above the pendentives in terms of the compressive strength that was needed to carry the weight of the dome directly downward. By successively cantilevering each ring inward, Bramante could have reduced the space to be spanned by a relatively small saucer dome with a large oculus as for the Pantheon's dome.

Bramante's lantern would have served only to let light in through the oculus while keeping rain out. It was not needed to direct the weight of the dome downward or to serve as a compression ring. As the woodcut shows, the rim of the oculus was thickened to prevent the collapse of the saucer dome while it hardened. There is no indication that the lantern would have been accessible to the public, and it would have been dangerous to have weakened a solid dome by tunneling through it. The four spiral stairs of the piers and the four spiral stairs in the walls of the drum would not have endangered elements that were not expected to carry any thrust, but tunnels throught an otherwise solid dome would have created weak places like scratches on a pane of glass.

When Michelangelo took over the construction of St. Peter's, the younger Sangallo had completed the pendentive and the foundation ring for the drum. Michelangelo distrusted Bramante's plan to have a small number of large opening in the drum and instead constructed a drum with a continuous wall with numerous small windows. He knew that a solid hemispherical dome could be constructed similar to the dome of the Pantheon, and he initially planned to have a basically hemispherical dome, but to lighten its weight by using ribs and hollow spaces between the ribs. Michelangelo's large wooden model indictes that he wanted to have an inner dome similar in shape to the hemispherical intrados of the Pantheon, but he largely completed the construction of the drum before making a final decision on what shape the outer dome would have and how it would be constructed.

Bramante's Apprentices

Between Bramante and Michelangelo, little was accomplished towards the completion of St. Peter's. During nearly all of the more than three decades from 1514 to 1546, confusion reigned, and even if it had not, there was little money available for construction. The extravagances of Leo X, the lack of interest by Adrian VI, the duplicity of Clement VII, the Sack of Rome, the Medici's determination to rule Florence as well as the Papal States, and the plague were followed by the Reformation.

When Bramante died in 1514, Leo X appointed Fra Giovanni Giocondo and Raphael as co-architect of St. Peter's, but Giocondo was paid one-third more than Raphael and their assistant Giuliano da Sangallo was paid the same as Raphael. Giocondo, who had been born in 1433 died in 1515. Giocondo had been hired as an accomplished engineer who had worked in Paris and Venice, an architect who had worked in Naples, and as the editor of two editions of Vitruvius published in 1511 and 1513. He was able to begin to correct some of the structural faults of Bramante's work on St. Peter's. (Heydenreich and Lotz 1974: 164; 194; 355-356, n. 42; 365, n. 28).

When Giocondo died, Raphael was put in charge, and Giuliano returned in disgust to Florence in 1515. Raphael was in charge until his death in 1520. Antonio da Sangallo the Younger was hired as Raphael's assistant in 1516, and at least by 1520, he owned a copy of Giocondo's Vitruvius. Sangallo was in charge of St. Peter's from 1520-1546, and Baldassare Peruzzi was an associate architect from around 1520 until 1527.

Having worked with Bramante and having designed important commissions on their own, Raphael and Antonio da Sangallo were well qualified to carry out Bramante's intentions, but Leo X and Paul III wanted a larger basilica even than the second design Bramante had made for Julius II. Different popes and different architects had many different ideas, but very little money to carry them out. Leo's sale of indulgences to help provide for the construction of St. Peter's was one of the reasons for the Reformation. Conflicts between republics and monarchs; between Spain, France, and Italy; between the Roman Catholic Church and the Holy Roman Empire, between Catholicism and the Reformation very largely took precedence over the patronage of art and architecture.

The three decades between Bramante and Michelangelo were characterized by indecision and inaction. Innumerable alternatives were proposed at various times by a number of architects, and a large number of drawings survive, but none of these alternatives were adopted by Michelangelo, and what had been begun in the interval was largely demolished by him and consequently had no impact on the final design of St. Peter's. The importance of these designs for the study of Raphael, Peruzzi, and Antonio da Sangallo have been considered in detail in various monographs, and the great amount of scholarship hat has been devoted to the individual drawings has been summarized in detail by Christoph Luitpold Frommel, Christof Thoenes, and other architectural historians (Millon and Lampugnani 1994: 598-672).

Wolfgang Lotz summarized the numerous variants that were considered even during the period from 1514 to 1520:

>...an unusually large number of drawings has survived from this stage of building, and their attribution and dating has ever since been one of the most fascinating and difficult problems in art history....

What is common to all these plans is Bramante's piers for the dome, whether it is the centre of a centrally planned building or the crossing of a basilica. The point at issue was the kind of building—a Greek or a Latin cross—and the shape of the arms. Four solutions were put forward for the latter:

>[1] (a) Plain apses between the subsidiary domes as shown in the parchment plan, but the west choir begun by Rossellino and completed by Bramante to be retained.

>(b) Ambulatories to be carried round the apses of the transepts, but

Rossellino's choir to remain in its original form without an ambulatory.

(c) The Rossellino choir, like the transepts, were later to be provided with an ambulatory, but the latter not to be opened towards the interior by the arrangement of columns and piers.

(d) All the arms of the cross to have identical ambulatories, which would entail the demolition and rebuilding of the west choir. ...

[2] Apart from the shape of the arms of the cross, the purely central designs are mainly distinguished by their exteriors. The following variants occur:

(a) Square plan with slightly projecting towers at the corners.

(b) The towers and the apses provided with ambulatories to stand out boldly.

(c) The apse of the arms of the cross, but not the towers, to project from the square of the ground plan. .

[3] The largest number of variants is to be found in the plans for the nave:

(a) The nave and the inner aisles of old St. Peter's to remain as the nave of the new building.

(b) A new, double-aisled, seven-bay nave; tunnel-vault on plan, square piers.

(c) Double-aisled nave of seven bays, the supports with niches on the model of the piers of the dome.

(d) Double-aisled nave, five bays.

(e) Triple aisles, five bays with a simplified form or pier.

(f) Single aisles, five bays, chapels instead of outer aisles.

(g) Single aisles, five bays, with the nave groin-vaulted after the manner of the Basilica of Maxentius.

(h) Single aisles, three bays; a dome over the middle bay of the nave and tunnel-vaults with penetrations in the first and third bays, i. e. a nave on the triumphal arch principle. ...

[4] The façades of the basilican plans have a portico as wide as the nave with all the aisles, with or without flanking towers; some of the plans provide for a deep vestibule. The exterior view of the purely central design recalls that of the foundation medal.

This list, which could be increased by several variants, is certainly not very entertaining. It reflects not only the bewilderment of Bramante's successors, bu also the more theoretical than practical frame of mind of the architects at work. Peruzzi and Giuliano da Sangallo made perpetually new combinations of all the variants mentioned [Heydenreich and Lotz 1974: 164-165; see also, 365-366, notes 31-33)].

Raphael (from 1514-1520)

Design by Raphael for St. Peter's (Heydenreich and Lotz)

Raphael's plan for St. Peter's (Serlio)

Bramante persuaded Raphael to come to Rome in 1508. Both were from Urbino, and Vasari stated that "Bramante, who was in the service of Julius II, wrote to him on account of a slight relationship, and because they were of the same country, saying that he had induced the Pope to have certain apartments done, and that Raphael might have a chance of showing his powers there" (Vasari 1568: II, 226). Bramante "…sketched for hi the buildings which he afterwards drew in perspective in the Pope's chamber, representing Mount Parnassus [the School of Athens]. Here Raphael drew Bramante measuring with a sextant" (187).

Bramante "…instructed Raphael of Urbino in many points of architecture" (187), and Raphael eventually became his most trusted assistant, and in addition to his great skill as a painter, he became highly skilled as an architect, proving himself by designing the Church of Sant'Eligio degli Orefici and the Chigi Chapel in S. Maria del Popolo while he was painting the stanza and later designing the Villa Madama. Fra Giocondo was an accomplished architect, and his expertise in bridge building enabled him to improve Bramante's structural provisions, but Giocondo was 79 at the time of his appointment, and when he died in 1515, Raphael replaced him. Raphael had assistants who, like himself, had been trained by Bramante. In 1516 Antonio da Sangallo, a nephew of Giuliano da Sangallo.

Raphael's principal surviving plan was for a basilica with a Latin cross rather than a Greek cross. Bramante had also considered the Latin cross in an earlier attempt to satisfy the Vatican, and Peruzzi later produced a similar plan.

Structurally, the four pairs of pairs flanking the four main piers that support the dome were the by far the most important change in the plan of St. Peter's that was made while Raphael was in charge. Bramante had planned to support his dome on four piers that he had reduced in size by cutting away their inside corners to widen the span and by further reducing the size of these essentially triangular piers by inserting three large niches into their main remaining faces, and he had initially relied only on the four arms of his Greek-cross plan to buttress the dome and its supporting piers. The ambulatories he later added would have provided additional buttressing, but they are open-ended for circulation. When Bramante added a nave, his plan ceased to provide even support on all four sides, but his four towers would have continued to have evenly supported the four corners of the building. Almost certainly upon Giocondo's advice, Raphael closed off the ends of the ambulatories with three pairs of flanking piers to provide better buttressing for the dome and its supporting piers, but retained the nave.

Raphael was a great architect but a greater artist. His Villa Madama is one of the great villas even though only a portion of it was completed, and he designed a number of influential palaces and apartment buildings (Frommel et al. 1984). His Chigi Chapel is superbly proportioned and detailed (Bentivoglio 1984). His Sant'Eligio is a fine small church, but it was a minor commission that owes much to Brunelleschi's Pazzi Chapel and Giuliano da Sangallo's Santa Maria della Carceri in Prato (Valtieri 1984).

No doubt Raphael would have accomplished even greater buildings if he had lived longer. In 1520 he was bled to death by an incompetent physician for a minor illness. In 1521 when Leo X died and a pope with little interest in architecture succeeded him, all work on St. Peter's stopped, and political instability and the Reformation prevented substantial progress on the construction of St. Peter's for nearly two decades.

Stanza della Segnatura with frescoes by Raphael (Letarouilly)

School of Athens; fresco by Raphael (with Michelangelo near the center in the foreground; albumen)

Raphael's Chigi Chapel (drawn by Dosio; Bentivoglio)

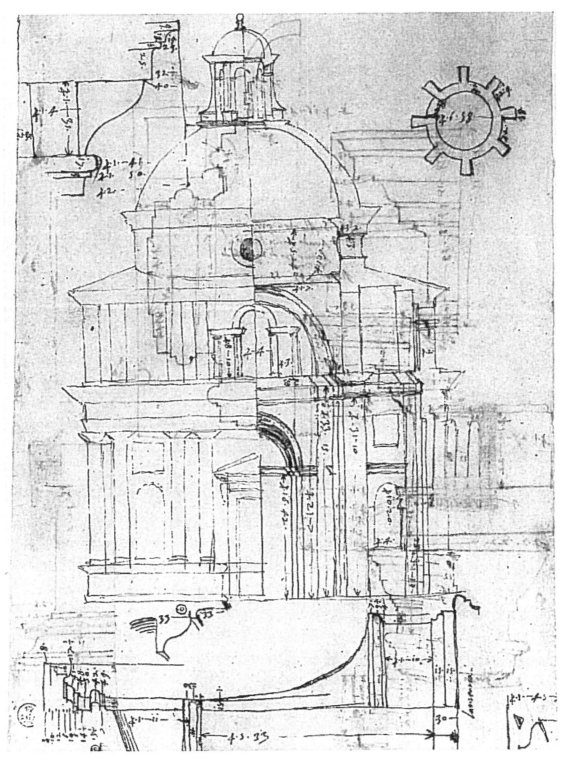

Rapahel's Sant'Eligio degli Orefici (rawn byu Peruzzi; Valtieri)

Peruzzi (from 1520-1527)

When Raphael died in 1520, Leo appointed the brilliant Peruzzi and highly competent Antonio da Sangallo the Younger co-architects of St. Peter's, but little money was available then and none following the Sack of Rome in 1527. Peruzzi planned to restore Bramante's Greek cross plan (as Serlio indicated in a plan he published in 1540). He also produced alternative designs for a basilica with the plan of a Latin cross, but his most detailed proposal was for a Greek-cross with a portico.

Alternative designs by Peruzzi for St. Peter's (above: Serlio; below, Kent)

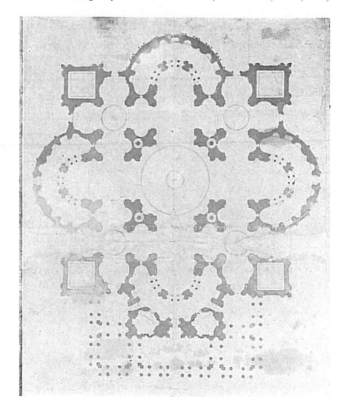

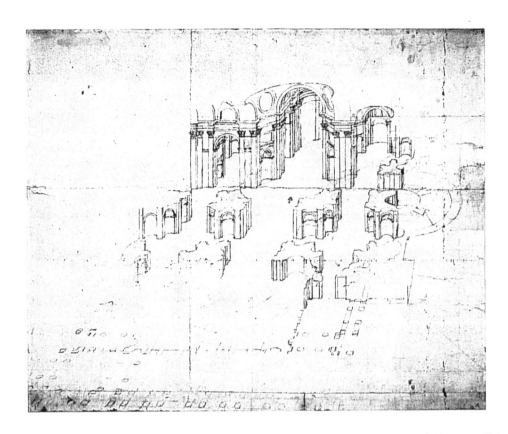

Design by Peruzzi for St. Peter's (above, Heydenreich and Lotz; below, with construction lines added by Letarouilly)

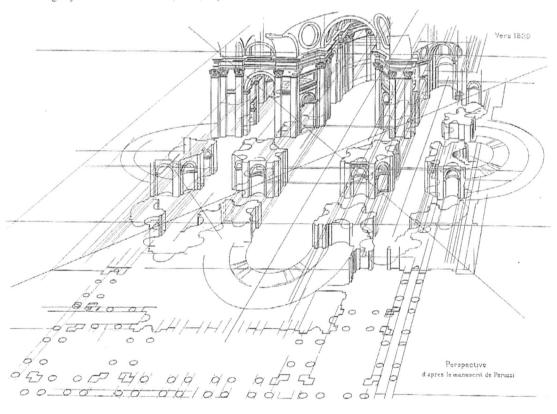

Sangallo (from 1520-1546)

From 1520 through 1546, work slowly continued on the walls and vaulting, but relatively little was accomplished, and part of what was built was later demolished by Michelangelo. As noted in Chapter 16, Antonio da Sangallo the Younger had worked with Bramante on St. Peter's as a draftsman and had been trained by him as an architect (Vasari 1568: III, 87). Afterwards, he worked for decades on the Palazzo Farnese, and when Paul III (Farnese) became pope, he placed Sangallo in charge of St. Peter's.

In general, Sangallo followed Bramante's Greek-cross plan with ambulatories, but he attached to the front an immense benediction loggia flanked by a pair of towers. This largely separate structure was connected to the rest of the building by vaulting, but the atrium in between was an outdoor space open at each end. The main difference was less in overall form than in covering most of the exterior with patterns of fornices that are small in relation to its overall size. Although some major examples of ancient Roman basilicas had been covered by fornices, applying them to rounded surfaces created more the appearance of the Colosseum than of the Basilica Nova (renamed the Basilica of Constantine). Despite the use of a large number of one-storied columns that Sangallo planned to use, the core of the design retained a coherent overall form, but Bramante's symmetrical arrangement of four towers became an asymmetrical arrangement that more closely resembled a Gothic cathedral than a classical basilica or early Christian church.

Sangallo spent seven years from 1539-1546 designing every detail for an immense wooden model of what the church could have looked like, but it had no influence on the final design. Vasari painted a fresco in the Cancelleria, and a detail shows Paul III inspecting the work that had been completed and that was later demolished. "He thickened the pilasters [piers] of S. Pietro to bear the weight of the tribune and filled the foundations with solid materials, making it so strong that it could not move as it had done in Bramante's time. If that masterpiece were above ground instead of being hidden beneath, it would dismay the most formidable intelligence, and for it this admirable artist must always retain a place among the rarest intellects" (Vasari 1568: III, 95).

Benvenuto Cellini's gibe that Sangallo's buildings lacked greatness and distinction because he was neither a sculptor nor a painter, but only a master carpenter, ... renders precisely, and in the idiom of the time, what distinguished Sangallo from Bramante, Raphael, and Peruzzi. His buildings and designs are practical and made to last, but what they lack is architectural imagination. ... His method of representation is that of the expert; he consistently keeps in mind the distinction between plan, section, and elevation first recommended by Raphael for architectural drawings. Yet no drawing of his could stand as an independent work of art, as so many of Peruzzi's can [Heydenreich and Lotz 1974: 205].

Nonetheless, Sangallo accomplished a substantial amount of construction, and Ackerman summarized his permanent accomplishments:

Work began, in accordance with the model, in walling up the niches in the four principal piers and in closing off the ambulatories around the hemicycles. From 1543 to 1546 building went on busily on the vaults of the east and south arms, the walls of the eastern hemicycle and the pendentives f the central dome. The following summary indicates what portions of the Basilica had been established definitely by 1547 that Michelangelo was constrained to accept them with only superficial changes ["90, 91"].

The four piers of the main crossing, the arches connecting them; and the pendentives defining the base of the drum.

The four main arms of the church with their barrel vaults, and the easternmost of their terminal hemicycles (although only two of the arms had been built, there could be no question in central-plan church of a different design for the remaining two).

The barrel-vaulted transverse aisles between the crossing piers and the buttressing piers (four of the eight vaults planned were completed).

The side aisles of the eastern arm, up to the narrow doorway alongside the hemicycle [Ackerman 1986: 317-318].

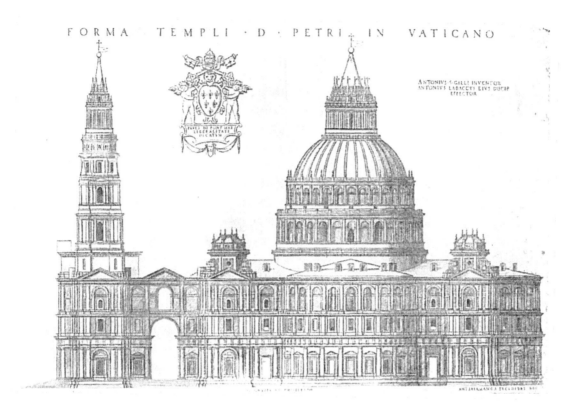

Above: Sangallo's model for St. Peter's (Salamanca); below, plan (Letarouilly)

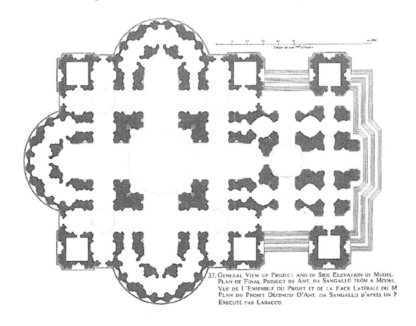

Sangallo's model for St. Peter's (Alinari; above, in Mariani; below, in Grimm)

Michelangelo's Designs for St. Peter's

In 1547 Michelangelo proposed destroying everything Sangallo had built that went beyond what Bramante had begun:

> One cannot deny that Bramante was as skilled in architecture as anyone since the time of the ancients. He it was who laid down the first plan of St. Peter's, not full of confusion, but clear, simple, luminous and detached in such a way that it in no wise impinged upon the Palace. It was held to be a beautiful design, and manifestly still is, so that anyone who has departed from Bramante's arrangement, as Sangallo has done, has departed from the true course; and that this is so can be seen be anyone who looks at his model with unprejudiced eyes.
>
> He, with that outer ambulatory of his, in the first place takes away all the light from Bramante's plan and not only this, but does so when it has no light of its own, and so many dark lurking places above and below that they afford ample opportunity for innumerable rascalities, such as the hiding of exiles, the coining of base money, the raping of nuns and other rascalities, so that at night, when the said church closes, it would need twenty-five men to see out those who remained hidden inside, whom it would be a job to find. Then, there would be this other drawback—that by surrounding the said composition of Bramante's with the addition shown in the model, the Pauline Chapel, the offices of the Piombo, the Ruota and many other buildings would have to be demolished; nor do I think that the Sistine Chapel would survive intact. As regards the part of the outer ambulatory that has been built, which they say cost a hundred thousand *scudi*, this is not true, because it could be done for sixteen thousand, and little would be lost if it were pulled won, because the dressed stones and the foundations could not come in more useful and the fabric would be two hundred thousand *scudi* to the good in cost and three hundred years in time. This is s I see it and without prejudice—because to gain my point would be greatly to my detriment. And if you are able to persuade the pope of this, you will be doing me a favour... [Michelangelo 1963: II 69 with notes omitted].

The recipient of this proposal has been identified as Bartolomeo Ferratini, a deputy of the fabric of St. Peter's, and the proposal had the desired effect (273-274)..

Vasari wrote similarly in his biography of Michelangelo:

> It happened that in 1546 Antonio da Sangallo died; and since there was no one supervising the building of St Peter's various suggestions were made by the superintendents to the Pope as to who should take over. At length (inspired I feel sure by God) his holiness resolved to send for Michelangelo; but when he was asked to take Sangallo's place Michelangelo refused saying, to excuse himself, that architecture was not his vocation. In the end, entreaties being of no avail, the Pope commanded him to accept. So to his intense dismay and completely against his will Michelangelo was to embark on this enterprise. Then one day or other he made his way to St Peter's to have a look at the model in wood that Sangallo had made and to study the building himself. ...afterwards he used to say openly that Sangallo's model was deficient in lights, that on the exterior Sangallo had made too many rows of columns one above another, and that with all its projections, spires, and subdivision of members it derived more from the German manner than from either the sound method of the ancient world or the graceful and lovely style followed by modern artists As well as this, he would add, fifty years of time and over three hundred thousand crowns of money could be saved on the building

which could also be executed with more majesty, grandeur, and facility, better ordered design, and greater beauty and convenience. Subsequently, Michelangelo convincingly demonstrated the truth of his words with a model he made himself, which showed the building completed on the lines we can see today. This model cost him twenty-five crowns and it was made in a fortnight. In contrast, Sangallo's (as I said earlier) cost four thousand and took many years. ... Finally, the Pope issued a *motu proprio* putting Michelangelo in charge of the building, with full authority, and giving him power to do or undo whatever he chose, and to add, remove, or vary anything just as he wished; the Pope also commanded that all the officials employed there should take their orders from him [Vasari 1568 [1971]: 79-81 with notes omitted].

In January 1, 1547, Paul III put Michelangelo in charge. Nearly three years later, after having approved a wooden model Michelangelo had prepared, on October 11, 1549 Paul III issued a *motu proprio* that specified the extent of Michelangelo's authority fully and clearly:

> Of our sure knowledge and in the fullness of our Apostolic power, we hereby approve and confirm the aforementioned new design and alteration, and all and several demolitions and constructions of whatever kind are caused to be done in the said fabric by the same Michel Angelo and on his order, and whatever else he may do there, even if these things shall have been caused to be done at considerable expense and with damage to and destruction of the fabric; and these conditions, together with the model or plan for or in respect of the said fabric, drawn up and submitted by the same Michael Angelo, are to be observed and carried out in perpetuity, so that they may not be changed, re-fashioned, or altered....
>
> And, moreover, trusting in the good faith, experience and earnest care of Michael Angelo himself, but above all trusting in God, we appoint him te prefect, overseer ["*operarius*"] and architect of the building and fabric of the aforementioned Basilica on behalf of ourselves and of the Apostolic See for as long as he shall live. And we grant him full, free and compete permission and authority to change, re-fashion, enlarge and contract the model and plan and the construction of the building as shall seem best to him; to choose and commission all and several helpers and prefects and other men needed to work in the said building, and to arrange their due and customary wages and fees; and to release, dismiss and withdraw at will those same men,, and others chosen previously, and his deputies; and to provide others as shall seem best to him to do and perform all and several other things which shall be necessary, or in any way appropriate for the aforesaid work, without seeking permission from the Deputies of that fabric who shall be in office at that time, or from anyone else whatsoever. Moreover, in order that Michael Angelo himself shall be able more freely to direct the work of the said building, we entirely and completely release and free him and his assistants and deputies from the power, jurisdiction and authority of the Deputies of the same fabric [Paul III in Michelangelo 1963: II, 308].

In 1551, the Deputies of the fabric tried unsuccessfully to get Julius III to limit Michelangelo's authority, and the informed him,

> as regards the progress and the designs and the prospects of the basilica, the deputies know nothing whatever, Michelangelo despising them worse than if they were outsiders. They must, however, make the following declaration to ease their conscience: they highly disapprove Michelangelo's methods, especially in demolishing and destroying the work of his predecessors. This mania for pulling to pieces what has already been erected at such enormous cost is criticized by

everybody; however, if the Pope is pleased with it, we have nothing to say [Michelangelo 1963: II, 310]. "...just before the beginning of 1551, when the Sangallo clique in a plot against Michelangelo persuaded the Pope to summon to a meeting in St Peter's all the builders and overseers, hoping to convince his holiness by slanderous accusations that Michelangelo had ruined the building" (Michelangelo 1568: 91) Their ringleader, a cardinal Michelangelo referred to as "the busybody" claimed Michelangelo had made no provisions to light the south transept, and he replied that three windows were being added in the vault. "'But you never told us that,' the cardinal remarked.' And then Michelangelo announced: 'I'm not and I don't intend to be obliged to discuss with your Eminence or anyone else what I ought to or intend to do. Your duty is to collect the money and guard it against thieves and you must leave the task of designing the building to me" (Vasari 1568: 91). Julius III reaffirmed the absolute authority of Michelangelo, "'...not allowing you to be disturbed or hindered, or disquieted in any way...'" (Michelangelo 1963: 311). Every successive pope also gave Michelangelo a free hand until his death in February 1564 (Vasari 1568: 111, 119).

Michelangelo made many bitter and vindictive enemies throughout his life by exposing ignorance, incompetence, and pretension. Although he admired Bramante as an architect, he exposed his incompetence as an engineer; and although he respected the younger Sangallo as an engineer, he did not admire him as an architect. He had special contempt for meddlesome usurpers and clergymen accustomed to being flattered and to getting their own way regardless and for suppliers of inferior materials at inflated prices and builders who gave bribes. Since there are always plenty of such people, those who oppose them will always be much hated. Although he often made enemies, he also had many loyal friends, apprentices, and assistants, but outlived many of them. It was true, though, that people sought him more than he sought them.

No one should think it strange that Michelangelo loved solitude for he was deeply in love with his art, which claims a man with all his thoughts for itself alone. Anyone who wants to devote himself to the study of art must shun the society of others. In fact, a man who gives his time to the problems of art is never alone and never lacks food for thought and those who attribute an artist's love of solitude to outlandishness and eccentricity are mistaken, seeing that anyone who wants to do good work must rid himself of all cares and burdens: the artist must have time and opportunity for reflection and solitude and concentration. Although all this is true, Michelangelo valued and kept the friendship of many great men and of many talented and learned people, when it was appropriate [122].

"Michelangelo rightly scorned those who injured him; but he was never known to harbour a grudge. On the contrary, he was a very patient man, modest in behaviour and prudent and judicious in all he said. His remarks were usually profound, but he was also capable of shrewd and witty pleasantries" (128). For example, "told that he ought to resent the way Nanni di Baccio Bigio was always trying to compete with him, Michelangelo said: 'Anyone who fights with a good-for-nothing gains nothing'" (131).

Towards the end of Michelangelo's life, Vasari "...suggested that the Pope [Pius IV; 1559-1565] should make arrangements so that, in the event of his having an accident, as old men often do, all his clothes, his drawings, cartoons, models, money and other possessions should be set down in an inventory and placed in safe-keeping for the sake of the work on St Peter's. In this way, if there were anything there concerning St Peter's or the sacristy [Medici Chapel], library, and façade of San Lorenzo, no one would make off with it, as frequently happens in such cases. In the event, these precautions proved well worth while" (119-120). Unfortunately, "...he has often destroyed his work, and I know for a fact that shortly before he died he burned a large number of his own drawings, sketches, and cartoons so that no one should see the labours he endured and the ways he tested his genius, and lest he should appear less than perfect" (121). "...to Antonio Mini, his disciple, he gave drawings, cartoons, the picture of the Leda, and all the models in wax and clay that he ever made, which, s explained, have been left in France" (127).

After Michelangelo's death in 1564, Vasari met with Pius V (1566-1572), who

> ...talked only of how to make sure that Michelangelo's designs were followed. Then to avoid any confusion his holiness commanded Vasari to go with his private treasurer, Guglielmo Sangalletti, and on his authority to tell Bishop Ferratino, who was supervising the builders, to pay strict attention to all the important memoranda and records that Vasari would give him, so that the words of malignant and presumptuous men would have no power to upset the arrangements or details left to posterity by Michelangelo's genius. Giovanbattista Altoviti, a friend of Vasari and of the arts, was present on this occasion; and after Ferratino had heard what Vasari had to say, he eagerly accepted every available record and promised that everyone, including himself, would without fail observe all Michelangelo's arrangements and designs in the building he would, he said, protect, safeguard, and maintain the work of the great Michelangelo [Vasari 1568: 119].

During the period of 17 years that he had worked on St. Peters, Michelangelo largely redesigned the building and managed, as he set out to do, to complete enough of it to ensure that his designs would be followed in all major respects until a committee of cardinals preferred a Latin cross in place of a Greek one.

Michelangelo's Plans

Michelangelo opened the interior of the church to light and simplified the complex plans by the simple expedient of eliminating all of the smaller spaces that had been planned around the edges of the building. He built completely new outside walls on what had been foundations for interior walls, and he used the monumental Corinthian order throughout as Bramante had begun to do on the interior rather than superimposing multiple orders as Sangallo planned to do. The exterior walls of the back and both sides of St. Peter's were completed wholly to his designs.

Michelangelo reduced the area to be covered by St. Peter's. Bramante's plan would have covered 24,000 square meters of space, and Michelangelo's covered about 14,500 (Lees-Milne 1967: 143). In other words, Michelangelo's plan was 60 percent of the size of Bramante's, and the adoption of his plan represented a potentially large savings by omitting aisles, remote chapels, and towers, and he retained all principal spaces.

With a free hand and generous funding, Michelangelo accomplished far more than any of his predecessor. The main concern of the successive popes who trusted him completely was that he was 72 when he took charge of the work in 1546, and there was increasing concern that he might die before revealing all parts of his design.

As with other commissions that he was forced to take throughout his life by a succession of popes, once he began each of them, he wanted to complete it to his full satisfaction. By 1554, he was determined to build enough of the basilica that his design would have to be carried out rather than superseded as he had done with Sangallo's design, and he wrote Vasari, who urged him to return to Florence, "...if I were to leave here now, it would be the utter ruin of the fabric of St. Peter's, a great disgrace and a greater sin. ... But when the structure has been completely taken shape, so that it cannot be altered, I hope to do as you suggest, unless of course it be a sin to keep a few sharks waiting who anticipate my early departure" (Michelangelo 1963: II, 146-147). In 1555 he reiterated to Vasari that the work was at a critical stage, and even though he had begun his 81st year, he could not retire: "I was forced to undertake the work on the fabric of St. Peter's, and for about eight year I have served not only for nothing, but at great cost and trouble to myself, but now that the work is advanced, that there is money to spend on it, and that I am almost ready to vault the dome, it would be the ruin of the said fabric if I were to depart..." (Michelangelo 1963: II, 153; cf. 154-155, 174; cf. Vasari 1568: 96). He wrote similarly about the dome in 1557, insisting that he could not retire and return to Florence until he had prepared a detailed model of the dome to ensure that it could be executed as he intended (Michelangelo 1963: II, 171). Unhappily, in 1555, when Paul IV became pope, Michelangelo wrote, "...for lack of money the work has been continually delayed and it is now being held back just as the construction has reached the most exhausting and difficult part. ...he continued working on various parts of St Peter's, with the object of making it impossible to change what was done" (Vasari 1568: 96).

Structurally, Michelangelo retained the four pairs of flanking piers that had been added to the ends of the ambulatories during Raphael's tenure. In a comparison made by Vanvitelli, these flanking piers are shown as being added to Bramante's plan, which is true, but misleading in that three of the four pair had been part of the final plan for St. Peter's since the time of Raphael, and all four pair had been included in Peruzzi's Greek-cross plan. As Vanvitelli's comparison shows, Michelangelo eliminated the ambulatories and strengthened the new exterior walls by infilling the opening that would have provided access to them and into the chapels that were planned for the areas in between the ambulatories and cornier towers, and he took advantage of the opportunity to insert large spiral staircases to facilitate construction. He strengthened Bramante's piers by infilling two of the three large niches Bramante had hollowed out of the piers. He added back the pair of piers that had been replaced by plans for a nave. He strengthened the four corners of the building by infilling the openings that would have let to the sacristies in Bramante's corner towers. His plan was far more sound structurally as well as less expensive, and his interior would have been much more coherent visually. Thus, Bramante's initial plan and Michelangelo's adaptation of it were conceptually more sound in principle as well as having other major advantages, but the clergy's preference for a more complex plan was repeatedly adopted. As Thoenes noted, "...the clergy's vested inters tint he basilica and in having available the utmost possible number of altars, confessionals, nooks and crannies for worship—all of which were amply catered for in Sangallo's complex" determined what the final results would be, and the unity of both the interior and exterior were destroyed, and most of Michelangelo's exterior was concealed by the nave and widened front (Thoenes 1994: 635).

Ackerman summarized Michelangelo's accomplishments on the basis of payment records:

The chronology of the construction of the Basilica under Michelangelo can be established fairly accurately by analyzing the documents of the papal treasury (K. Frey, 1916, pp. 22-135), contemporary views and perspective plans, and Vasari's *Lives.* Here only a summary can be given of the condition of St. Peter's at Michelangelo's death in February 1564: the bulk of this work was executed in the years 1549-58.

Façade arm and crossing apparently left as finished by Sangallo [fig. "91"]. Southern arm and Capella del Re: complete both inside (the Capella vault being of finished travertine without decoration) and out (the attic remaining unadorned as in [fig. "103"]). (Millon and Smyth 1969, p. 491f").

Western arm: the Rossellino-Bramante apse still untouched [fig. "104"].

Northern arm and Cappella del Imperatore: vaulting of the arm not started; chapel vault half constructed. The existing attic, department from Michelangelo's design for the southern arm, was begun here by Pirro Ligorio immediately after Michelangelo's death.

Drum: largely completed up to the level of pilaster- and buttress-capitals; imposts and entablatures executed on the eastern but not the western half [fig. "104"].

Corner chapels: foundations begun on the north side.

Models of the dome: a clay model complete by July 1557 (K. Frey, 1916, 81); the wood model, which till survives, altered by della Porta [fig. "96"], made November 1558-November 1561 (K. Frey, 1909, p. 177ff.; 1916, pp. 81ff., 87) [Ackerman 1986: 319].

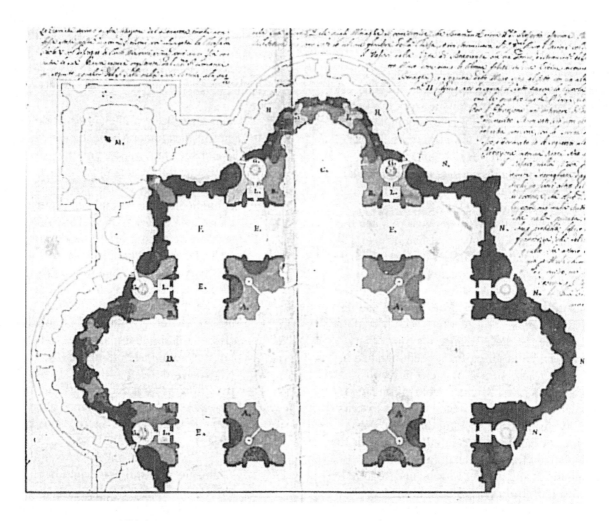

Michelangelo's plan (dark) compared with Bramante's plan (light; Vanvitelli; Di Stefano)

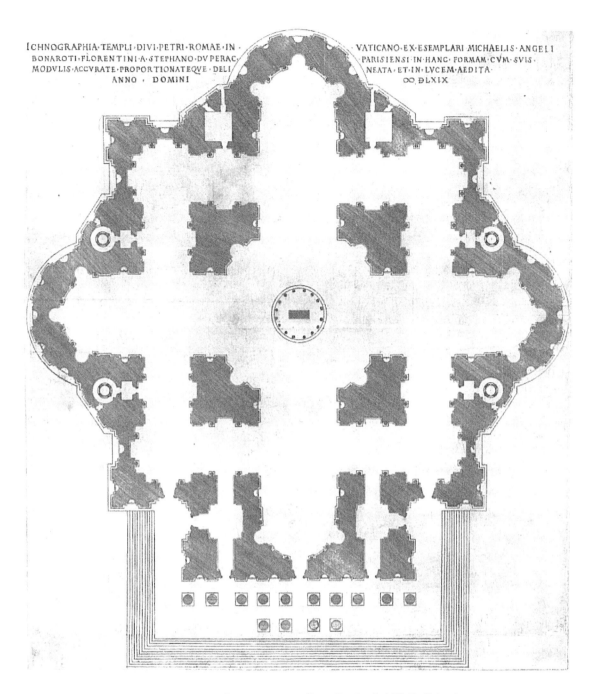

Michelangelo's plan for St. Peter's according to Dupérac in 1569 (De Tolnay)

Michelangelo's Dome

In July 1547 Michelangelo asked his nephew to obtain information about the size of the lantern of the Duomo in Florence from one of its priests: "I want you to get, through Messer Giovan Francesco the height of the cupola of Santa Maria del Fiore from where the lantern begins to the ground, and then the overall height of the lantern, and to send it to me. Also send me in the letter the measured length of third of a Florentine *braccio*" (Michelangelo 1963: II, 78). He was already thinking of designing a different lantern from Bramante's and a taller dome. No doubt included a dome in the first model he built of his new design for St. Peter's, but the model has not survived, and the few drawings by him for the dome and copies by others are undated. What he intended at any given time is disputed.

In 1557, Michelangelo's friends persuaded him to made a model for the dome, and a model in clay was used to construct a large wooden model (Vasari 1568 [1971]: 105). He wrote on February 1557,

> ...I am obliged to make a large model in wood, including the cupola and the lantern, in order to leave it completed as it is to be, finished in every detail. This I have been begged to do by the whole of Rome, and particularly by the Most Reverend Cardinal di Capri so that I think it will be necessary for me to stay here for at least a year in order to do this. ...if the form of the said fabric were changes, as envy is seeking to do, I might as well have done nothing up till now [Michelangelo 1963: II, 171].

Ramsden noted that the model was completed in 1561 and that "Cardinal Ridolfo Pio di Carpi (1499-1564), [was] archpriest of the Basilica, a diplomat, and a very eminent and cultured man. He was at the time a Deputy of the fabric" (17, n. 3). In the fall of the previous year little work had been done because of the threat of a Spanish invasion, but by this time, "...there are still sixty men working here, counting scarpellini bricklayers and labourers, and doing so with the expectation of continuing" (171).

When Michelangelo died in 1564, the drum for the dome had been largely completed, but the dome had not yet been begun. He had designed a double dome similar in structure to Brunelleschi's dome for the Florentine Duomo, but with a drum similar to Bramante's Tempietto. It has ribs and a drum surrounded by columns, but the drum is circular rather than octagonal and has pairs of columns rather than single columns. Bramante had planned to construct a single, solid dome like that of the Pantheon and his Tempietto, but Michelangelo decided that an outer shell was needed to keep the hemispherical inner shell from speading.

Every subsequent pope and architect wanted to leave his mark on St. Peter's, and most of them did. Consequently, Michelangelo's intentions are difficult to reconstruct, and they were not always carried out.

After a thorough review of scholarly opinion about Michelangelo's intentions for the dome of St. Peter's, Henry A. Million and Craig Hugh Smyth noted that "scholars have been concerned above all with two main problems: 1) whether the finished model in its original state had a hemispherical or an elevated dome and 2) whether the dome as built by Giacomo della Porta with an elevated profile represents Michelangelo's final wishes or not. Many scholars now believe that the models as it is today is not in its original condition" (Millon and Smyth 1994: 656). There is no question that the large model that Michelangelo prepared of the dome has been altered, but there is much disagreement about how much it has been altered. In actual fact, as Million and Smyth point out, there is no contemporary "archival documentation" to indicate Della Porta altered Michelangelo's model; to have done so would have been time consuming and expensive, and the Vatican's payment records are unusually complete (656). The only definite evidence of changes to the model are indications that Luigi Vanvitelli made in the 18th Century of the location of cracks that had developed in the dome and of reinforcements that he proposed to prevent a major structural failure. Nonetheless. some highly reputable scholars have argued that "...the entire exterior dome and lantern of the model were built in the mid-eighteenth century by Vanvitelli..." rather than two centuries earlier (656). Although most unlikely, this could be easily disproven either by radiocarbon dating or dendrochronology. Uncertainties have been caused mainly by Dupérac's 1569 prints and by the Vatican archivist Grimaldi's statement that during the reign of Sixtus V (1585-1590) some models that were probably by Michelangelo had a lower dome than the one constructed and that Giacomo della Porta was then believed to have redesigned during construction (656). Della Porta definitely made minor changes, but it is more likely that the large model of the dome represents Michelangelo's final intentions for the size, shape and structure of the dome, and the evidence that this was the case deserves to be discussed in some detail.

The evidence that has been given the most weight are the engraved prints that Dupérac published about five years after Michelangelo's death, but these magnificent illustrations are composites based partly on what had been constructed and on what was believed at the time to have been intended. There is good evidence, though, that Michelangelo did not intend for the attic to have the design that Pirro Ligorio added after his death. There is general agreement that the inner dome of the large model was designed by Michelangelo yet Dupérac omitted it. The evidence Dupérac provided is not definitive, and it too must be reconsidered.

All of the available evidence about the design and construction of one of the most important buildings of all time has been discussed by numerous architectural historians without reaching a consensus. Recently, all known drawings, prints, and models have been reproduced and summarized by Million and Smyth in 1988 and 1994 and by Christoph Luitpold Frommel and Christof Thoenes in 1994, and all contemporary statements and scholarly opinions have been discussed by them. Their exemplary studies deserve the most careful consideration, but I have been unable to agree with some of their conclusions about how Michelangelo intended for the dome, portico. and attic of St. Peter's to look at the time of his death in 1564.

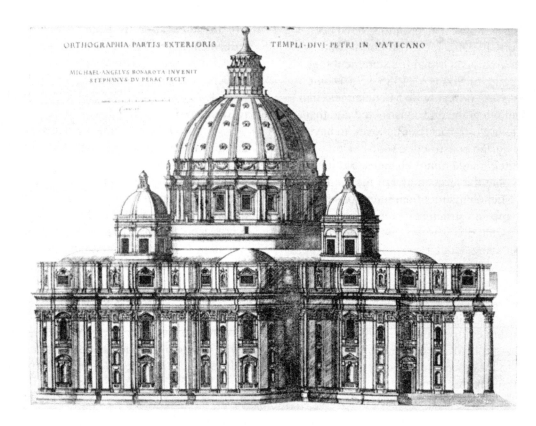

Dupérac's 1569 prints reconstructing Michelangelo's design for St. Peter's (Millon and Smyth)

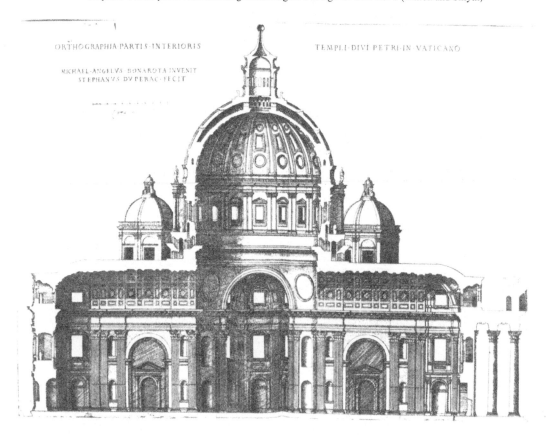

In 1568 (one year before Dupérac's prints were published), Vasari express grave concern that there might be plans to change Michelangelo's design for the dome of St. Peter's.

As briefly as possible, therefore, I shall give straight-forward account, so that if it should ever happen (which God forbid) that this work was impeded now that Michelangelo is dead by the envy and ill-will of presumptuous men (as it has been hitherto), these pages of mine, such as they are, may be able to benefit those faithful men who will execute the wishes of this rare artists, and also restrain the ambition of those evil men who might wish to change them. And so this account my please and benefit and at the same time enlighten those men of distinction who are patron and friends of architecture. ...

Michelangelo had brought the building thus far and it remains for us only to make a start on vaulting the cupola; and since the model for this exists we shall continue to explain the detail left for its construction. He designed the curve of the dome as a three-centered arch in this way:

A.   B.
C.

Point C, which is the lowest, is the point from which he drew the curves of the inner shell of the cupola, so determining the form, height, and width of this vault, which he instructed should be built entirely of herring-bone brickwork very well baked. He made this shell four and a half spans thick, the same thickness as the base as at the top, and he left a space in the middle (four and a half spans at the foot) which is to serve for the stairway climbing to the lantern, leading from the level of the cornice where the balustrade is. The curve for the interior profile of the outer shell which must be wider at the foot and narrow at the top) is turned using the point marked B, giving the four and half pans to the space of the outer shell. And the final curve for the exterior of the outer shell (which broadens at the base and narrows at the top) had to be turned from point A. With this arch turned, the void between the shells increases as it goes upwards, taking the stairway which is eight spans high and allows one to walk upright. The thickness of the outer shell gradually diminishes, so that from being, as was said, four and a half spans at the base it becomes three and a half spans at the top. The outer shell is joined to the inner shell with ties and steps in such a way that the one sustains the other. And of the eight sections into which the cupola divides at its base, four resting on the arch are hollow, to reduce the load, while the other four are bound and secured with ties to the piers, so that the structure can last forever [Vasari 1568 (1971): 105, 108-109].

Even the herringbone pattern of the brick work and the ribs of Brunelleschi's faceted dome were to be emulated.

Brunelleschi, Bramante, and Michelangelo had studied the Pantheon, but without being able to determine how to make concrete or how to use it to create a permanent dome. Vitruvius had explained how to make concrete, but no one seemed to know where to obtain the needed type of volcanic material that was the key ingredient.

When Michelangelo made the surviving drawing that shows most clearly what his intentions were, he made the upper dome pointed and a nearly adjacent lower dome circular. That much is readily apparent.

The large wooden model of the dome is quite different mainly in including an entirely separate inner dome that is well below the lower surface of the upper dome. Three separate and distinct curves are present in the model rather than the two curves of the drawing: two layers in the upper dome and one layer in the lower dome.

The lower dome appears in photographs to be hemispherical, but is not. Photographs taken close to and near the base of the model, which is 5.3 meters tall, provide a false perspective, as is evident from the fact that the oculus is seen from below. The space between the upper and lower domes is also exaggerated. The architect Beltrami made a measured drawing of the model in which the oculus is depicted correctly as horizontal, and he omitted the infill between the two layers of the upper dome so that the true curves for all three elements are clearly shown. Also notably, the panels for the decoration of the dome are on the underside of the lowest dome rather than on the lowest surface of the upper dome.

Most significantly, Beltrami's drawing shows that the lower dome was flattened and ovoid rather than hemispherical. It was essentially U-shaped rather than a circular. Michelangelo had previously designed a U-shaped ceiling for the uppermost hall of the Farnese Palace. This kind of flattened curve was standard for the coved ceiling of Renaissance palazzi including the loggia of the Villa Farnesina that Raphael painted. It was also standard for Renaissance bridges, and Michelangelo was well aware that a bridge required abutments to contain its thrust.

Bramante had planned to use rings of masonry to contain the thrust of a solid masonry with a hemispherical upper and lower surface. This solution had worked well for the Pantheon for 1,400 years. Brunelleschi had simply found a better way to build the kind of Gothic "dome" like that of the Florentine Baptistery that was a complex vault rather than a dome; it avoided the problem of thrust by using pointed sections of vaulting to lean together and buttress each other. Michelangelo intended to use a wholly different structural solution than the ones Bramante had used for the Tempietto and that Brunelleschi had used for the Duomo. He planned to use a wholly separate pointed dome to provide the needed weight to contain the thrust of a flattened dome below it.

What Della Porta did was simply to omit the lower dome and to use Michelangelo's decorative panels for the inner surface of the upper dome. In other words, Della Porta constructed another Gothic dome rather than the Renaissance dome that Michelangelo had designed and that was later used by Wren for St. Paul's Cathedral in London and by Soufflot for the Panthéon in Paris.

The differences between Michelangelo's clearest drawing for the construction of the dome and his model required explanation. Della Porta has been assumed to have removed the upper dome and to have replaced it with a similarly designed upper dome with a taller profile, but if he did reuse Michelangelo's model to show what he intended, why did he not remove the lower dome as well as the upper dome? The flattened lower dome makes no structural sense unless it was designed for its thrust to be contained by a taller upper dome.

Consequently, the flattened lower dome is definite evidence that Dupérac was incorrect that Michelangelo intended for his lower dome to be hemispherical, and it is good evidence that he was wrong that Michelangelo intended for the exterior surface of his upper dome to be hemispherical. In brief, Dupérac's measured drawing cannot represent Michelangelo's final intentions.

There has been much debate about how much of the large wooden model for St. Peter's dome was designed by Michelangelo and how much by Della Porta or still later by Vanvitelli. Dendrochronology and Carbon-14 dating can probably determine the relative dates of the parts that have been assigned to other architects. In my opinion, the entire model represents Michelangelo's final intentions except for the metal reinforcements that Vanvitelli is documented as having added.

A large number of 16th Century drawings exist for the dome of St. Peter's though few are by Michelangelo. The attributions, dates, and purposes of the drawings by others has been much debated, and this evidence has been discussed in detail by Millon and Smyth (1988: 91-187). For example, a design drawings for a 16-sided dome that is unquestionably by Michelangelo shows uncertainty about whether the outer dome should be hemispherical or pointed (p. 145; *Corpus*, no. 595). A drawing with variant designs for the lantern that is certainly by Michelangelo definitely shows a pointed upper dome, and although it too is undated, it is undoubtedly earlier because it is for a 8-sided dome (p. 178; fig. 32; *Corpus*, no.596).

Since one of the first things Michelangelo did on becoming the architect of St. Peter's was to ask for measurement of the dome of the Duomo in Florence and since he followed its ribbed pattern and brick pattern, it would need to be explained why he departed from its profile. Michelangelo was very cautious about structure as in strengthening the piers considered sufficient by Bramante before adding weight to them. It does not make sense to me that he would have taken a chance about so crucially important a structural problem when the only basis he had for making such decisions what had worked in the past. To believe otherwise, it would be necessary to point out a precedent for a large outer dome of brick and stone that was hemispherical and that had proven to be structurally sound for an extended period of time, and I know of no such example.

The large wooden model definitely shows that the lower dome was intended by Michelangelo to be ovoid rather than hemispherical. Although it has been repeatedly referred to as hemispherical, this is an optical illusion produced by the usual angle of view that is corrected in Beltrami's measured drawing. While Michelangelo was designing St. Peter's, he designed a church for Florentines in Rome that also was to have an ovoid dome. This is further evidence that the lower dome that Della Porta omitted during construction was designed by Michelangelo, and it is further evidence that Dupérac was wrong that Michelangelo planned to have a hemispherical outer dome over a hemispherical inner dome. In brief, Dupérac's design cannot be considered the best evidence for what Michelangelo intended to construct at the time of his death.

Although Dupérac's engravings have been assumed to represent Michelangelo's final intentions, Ackerman noted that they "...apparently were made without knowledge of Michelangelo's drawings, by combining the dome of the model with the drum as executed by Michelangelo. ... The only drawings that survive, however, are for a dome of elevated profile. ... In short, the concept of an elevated dome was originally Michelangelo's, and appear in the earliest sketches, but probably he had decided that the hemisphere of the model was the final solution [Ackerman 1986: 323-324].

It would be convincing that Della Porta rebuilt Michelangelo's large model for the dome if financial records indicated that, but in the absence of such records or drawings, it is only an assumption that he made any changes in the model. The copies of drawings for a lower dome could equally well have been made from drawings initially prepared for the model and later rejected; only one set of payment records exist for the model, and they indicate that it took years to build. Della Porta did not have years, and since was required to produce a full-scale drawing of how he intended to construct the dome, he had no need of a partially rebuilt model that includes a lower dome that was not built and that does not show in Dupérac's engravings. The ovoid lower dome has to be explained, and in my opinion, there can be no doubt that it was designed by Michelangelo and that a thin ovoid dome required a taller outer dome to prevent it from spreading.

My conclusion is that Dupérac worked from existing conditions including the drum and Ligorio's attic and from out-of-date drawings for the model that had been given to Cavalieri. The large wooden model of the dome represents Michelangelo's final intentions except for the metal reinforcements that were added in the 18th Century by Vanvitelli.

Michelangelo's designs for an 8-part dome (De Tolnay, *Corpus* no. 596r)

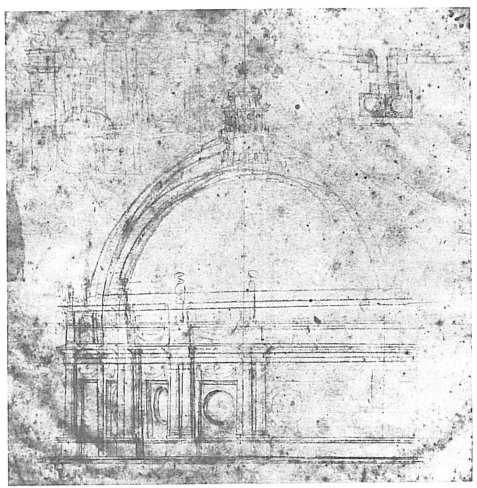

Michelangelo's design for a 16-part dome (*Corpus*, no. 595r)

A wooden model prepared for Michelangelo with pointed profiles for the outer dome (Millon and Lampugnani)

Section of the Duomo, Florence (Letarouilly)

Michelangelo's model with the drum and U-shaped inner dome he planned for St. Peter's (Beltrami)

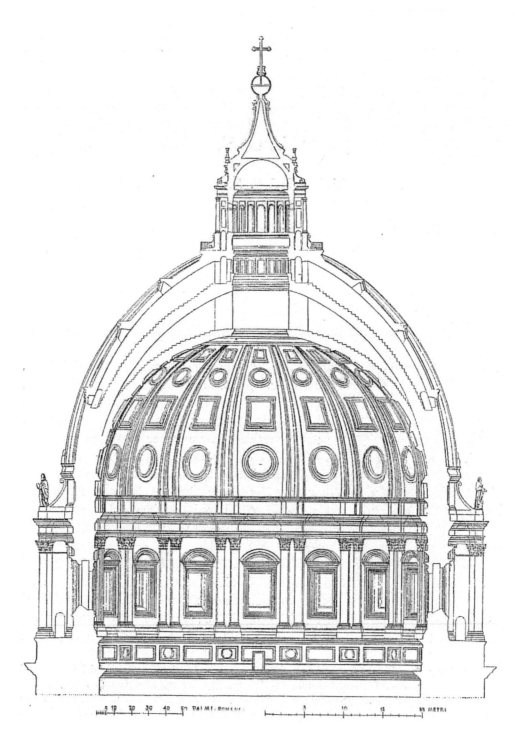

Measured drawing of Michelangelo's model for the drum and dome (Beltrami)

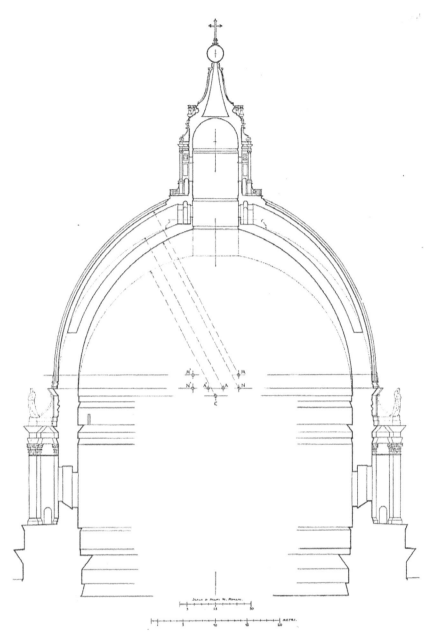

Sections of St. Peter's upper dome as completed (Beltrami)

Beltrami reconstructed the curves Vasari stated Michelangelo intended for the dome of St. Peter's to have (drawing from points A, A^t [Vasari's B] and C, but that they were drawn from the top of an elevated base for the dome. He shows the points that were used on either side of the points recorded by Vasari and the effect the additional points had on the height and curvature of the dome (Beltrami 1927: 60, pl. 14). He concluded that these minimal differences did not significantly change the amount of thrust at the base of the dome (80; pl. 20).

An undated design drawing by Michelangelo with alternatives for lanterns has an upper dome that is pointed and a lower dome that is hemispherical. De Tolnay noted that the lanterns indicate that the dome would have had eight sides like the Duomo in Florence (De Tolnay 1980: 144, fig. 348 [rather than 349]).

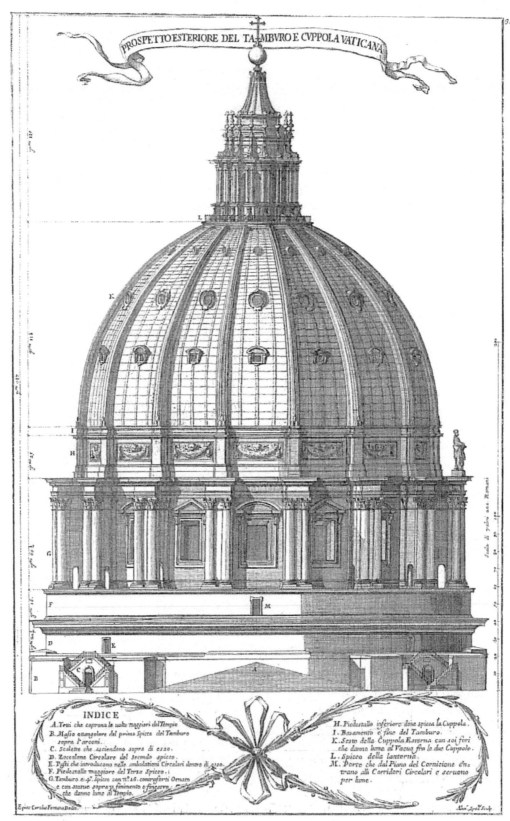

St. Peter's dome as built (Carlo Fontana)

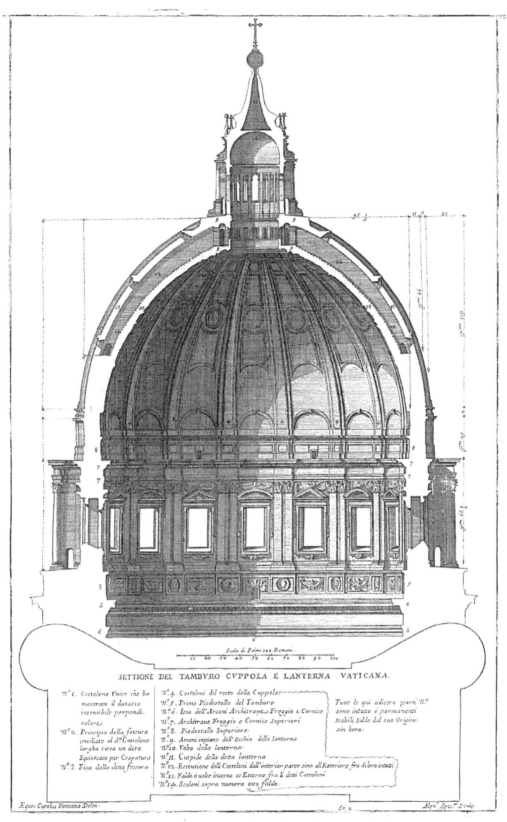

St. Peter's dome as built (Carlo Fontana)

Michelangelo's Intentions

As De Tolnay noted, the drawing with alternatives for lanterns was for a dome with eight sides, and the drawing with the drum included has a dome with 16 sides (De Tolnay 1975: 144). Since Michelangelo began constructing the drum with sixteen pairs of columns, the 16-sided dome represents his final intentions, and the design with eight sides that resembles the design for the octagonal cross of the Duomo in Florence is undoubtedly earlier. This is made all the more likely by Michelangelo's request for measurements of the dome and lantern of the Duomo when he was put in charge of St. Peter's in 1547 (Michelangelo 1963: II, 78).

According to Lees-Milne, Della Porta make a full-scale drawing to illustrate changes he proposed making in the dome of St. Peter's, and "it was spread out on the nave floor of St Paul's Outside the Walls, which was the largest covered space available in Rome, and duly examined by the pope [Sixtus V] from the gallery above. Thus was Della Porta's raised profile for the dome approved" (Lees-Milne 1967: 211). With a full-sized working drawing to guide construction, why would it have been necessary to change the model Michelangelo commissioned of the dome and drum? If Michelangelo's model had been altered by Della Porta either earlier to gain approval or later to guide construction, why would he not have omitted the lower dome and had the model-maker apply the needed decoration directly to the intrados of the upper dome?

Almost everyone writing about St. Peter's has assumed that the large wooden model of the dome and drum was made taller by Della Porta because they assumed that Dupérac correctly represented Michelangelo's intentions at his death, but there is not good evidence for either of these assumptions. Although De Tolnay studied Michelangelo's work intensively from 1925-1975, he could find no documentation that would substantiate either that Della Porta increased the height of the dome in the late 16th Century or that Vanvitelli increased the height in the mid-18th Century (De Tolnay 1975: 145). For a total of 24 years from 1564 when Michelangelo died until 1588 when Della Porta resumed construction, no work was done on the dome (Di Stefano 1963: 6). Various drawings by others dating from the 16th Century have been assumed to provide conclusive evidence that the model originally had a lower dome, and the conflicting evidence continues to cause disagreement. No doubt Michelangelo did plan at one point to construct a lower dome and had detailed drawings produced for a large model with a lower done, but in my opinion, the existing large model represents his final intentions, and the surviving drawings for a model with a lower profile are copies of drawings rather than being based on an earlier version of the large model. The measurements indicated are so precise that they appear to have been calculated rather than actually measured from a model.

In his *Corpus dei Disegni di Michelangelo*, De Tolnay identified only 13 drawings out of the 633 he reproduced as relating to St. Peter's, and they are mostly undated (De Tolnay 1980: nos. 591-603). In a half century of study, he found documentation that Michelangelo created only two models for St. Peter's: (1) one model for the entire building (with a terracotta version in 1546 and a wooden version in 1546-1547) and a model for the dome and drum (with terracotta version in 1557 and a wooden version in 1558-1561). Only one of the four versions of these models is known to exist, and its significance is disputed. Michelangelo's letters and other records (*recordi*) and Vasari's explicit statements are also important primary sources. With so little evidence by Michelangelo for what his intentions were at any given time, it might seem that there was little on which speculation could be based, but, instead, the absence of evidence has provided more opportunities for speculation.

Considering how few drawings for St. Peter's have survived and that none of them are working drawings, De Tolnay concluded that Dupérac's 1569 prints must have been derived from the wooden model of the building that was completed in 1547 (De Tolnay 1975: 142). This approved model must have been the basis for the overall conception of the exterior and interior of the building, which was largely completed by 1564 when Michelangelo died, and any changes that Michelangelo made between 1547 and 1564 could have been readily measured from the building itself.

Michelangelo had also designed a ovoid dome for the chapel of the King of France in the south transept, and it had not been built properly despite his having prepared a model. Vasari noted that this chapel was "...the hemicycle of the king of France (where the three chapels are with the three upper windows" (Vasari 1568: 91). In 1557 Michelangelo wrote, "...I am in a state of greater anxiety and difficulty over the affairs of the said fabric than I have ever been. This is because, owing to my being old and unable to go there often enough, a mistake has arisen over the vault of the chapel of the King of France, which is unusual and cunningly conceived, and I shall have to take down a great part of what has been done..." (Michelangelo 1963: II, 174). He was so embarrassed by this mistake that he fired the mason and had the travertine vault taken down and rebuilt (173).

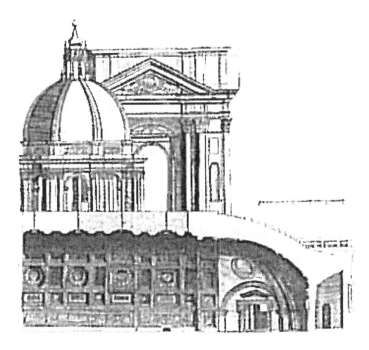

Elliptical profile of an apsisal wing of St. Peter's (Ferrabosco in Millon and Lampugnani)

Michelangelo explained in detail in two drawings and in two letters to Vasari what he had designed and what had been done incorrectly, and Vasari wrote, "what happened was that the master builder shaped the whole vault on one curve, struck from a single center instead of from several" (Vasari 1568: 103). The two letters and drawings survive, and Vasari included the most relevant parts of what Michelangelo wrote in his biography of him. The first letter with a drawing was dated July 1, 1557:

> The curve marked on the drawing in red was taken by the master builder as the shape of the whole vault so that when it became a semi-circle at the apex of the vault he realized he had made an error in the shape of the curve as a whole, as is shown here in the drawing in black. With this error, the vault has progressed to the point where it is necessary to remove a large number of stones since it is built of travertine instead of brocks. The diameter of the arch, including the surrounding cornice, is twenty-two spans. The mistake arose (even though I made an exact model, as I always do) because in my old age I have not been able to go there all that often. So whereas I expected that the vault would be finished by now, it will take all winter. If people could die of shame and grief I would be dead by now. Please explain to the duke why I

am not in Florence. ["Then on another of the drawings, showing the plan of the building, Michelangelo wrote:" on August 17]

So that you can understand the problem of the vaulting better, note the way it rises from ground level and was of necessity divided into three [segments] over the lower windows, separated by pilasters, as you see; and they go up pyramidally in the centre, towards the apex of the vault, as do the ends and sides of it. It has to be struck from an infinite number of centres, which keep changing and alter from point to point so that it is impossible to lay down a fixed rule, and the circles and rectangles created by the movement of the planes towards the centre have to be increased and diminished in so many directions at once that it is difficult to find the right way of doing it. All the same they had the model (which I always make) and they ought not to have committed so gross an error as to try and make one single curve of vaulting do for all three vault shells. This is why, to our great shame and loss, it has to be reconstructed, and a great number of stones have been removed. The vault with its ornaments and sections is entirely of travertine, like the lower part of the chapel, and this is something rarely seen in Rome [Vasari 1568: 103-104; cf. Michelangelo 1963: II, 178-182].

He hoped to persuade Vasari to come to Rome to help him supervise the work (180). As a sculptor, Michelangelo could easily make the most complex curves accurately, and as these drawings indicate, he could represent what the curves would be at any given point, but the first builder was unable to reproduce the "exact" model he had made. The second builder succeeded.

On September 12, 1560, Michelangelo was told that the Cardinal di Capri had said "...the fabric of St. Peter's could not be going worse than it is." Believing that a principal ally had lost confidence in him, he wrote Capri on September 13 that he himself had believed "...it could not be proceeding better. But since I may perhaps be easily deceived by self-interest and old age and, contrary to my intention, may in consequence be the cause of damage and loss to the aforesaid fabric, I intend, as soon as I can, to ask his Holiness Our Lord for my release" (Michelangelo 1963: II, 197). His resignation was not accepted, and he continued to be in charge of the design and construction of the basilica until his death in 1564. Dupérac's 1569 section of St. Peter's shows that the apsidal half-dome of the south wing has an elliptical rather than semi-circular profile, and this is shown in more detail in record drawings published by Martino Ferrabosco in 1620 (Millon and Lampugnani 1994: 655, no. 383).

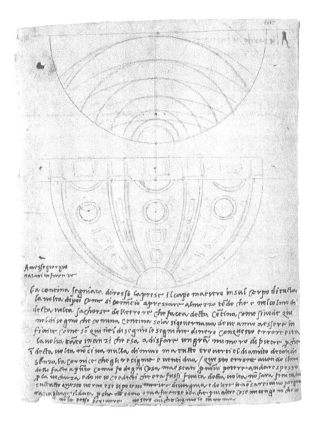

Diagram for the vaulting of the south transept (De Tolnay, Corpus n. 593 and 594)

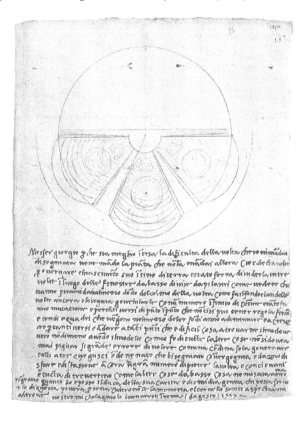

De Tolnay wrote that

> when Michelangelo died, the south arm of the transept with its apse (the Capella del Re di Francia) was built, the north [arm] had got as far as the vaulting, and a large part of the drum was already finished while the west apse was hardly begun. ...
>
> There never existed a definitive plan by Michelangelo for the facade of St Peter's. But we know from a sketch in the Codex Vaticanus 3211, folio 92, and from the drawings attributed to Dupérac in the Feltrinelli Collection, Milan, that he first thought of a portico like that of the Pantheon with six columns supporting a triangular pediment (see Tolnay, *Cod. Vat.*, pp. 160f.; Thoenes, *Festschrift H. Kauffmann*, Berlin, 1968, pp. 333ff.) [148].

There is good reason to believe that Dupérac did not produce a front elevation to go with the plan, side elevation, and longitudinal section because none existed; notably, when a painting was made by Passignano in 1619, the presentation model of the entire building is shown without a front.

If the date 1575 is correct for the view of the building attributed to Dupérac, the artist who drew the view somehow had access to information that must not have been known to Dupérac in 1569 or to the painter of the model in 1619, but that was known to the creator of a medal showing the front that was issued during the reign of Gregory XIII from 1572-1585, but between 1564 and 1590, it was generally thought that Michelangelo planned a portico with four columns rather than six, a lower dome, and an attic with lunettes rather than rectilinear enframements. In any case, it needs to be kept in mind that no work on the dome much less the front was done between 1564 and 1588.

The view of St. Peter's attributed to Dupérac or his circle in c. 1575 and the medal issued during the reign of Gregory XIII from 1572-1585 are definitely better evidence than the Vatican drawing cited because it is a very "rough sketch" of a portico with only five columns across the front (De Tolnay 1975: fig. 347; the columns show clearly in the *Corpus*, IV, no. 592r). This portico is in front of a tri-lobed plan that bears a much closer resemblance to designs for San Giovanni de' Fiorentini than for any design of St. Peter's.

San Giovanni de' Fiorentini (1550-1559)

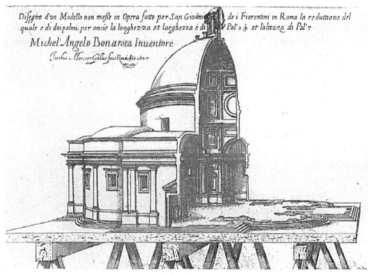

Michelangelo's model for San Giovanni de' Fiorentini (Le Mercier, 1607)y

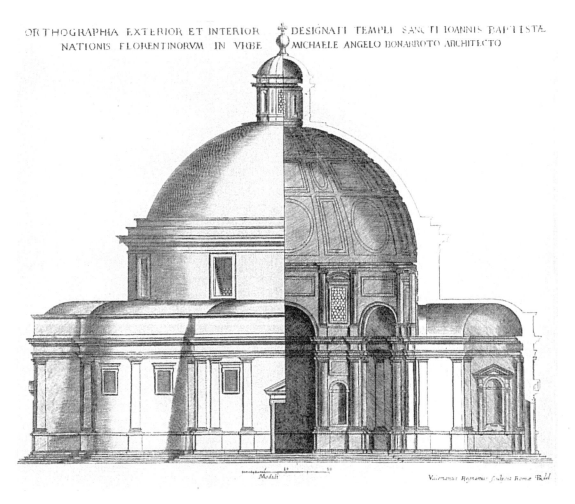

Elevation and section combined for Michelangelo's model of San Giovanni de' Fiorentini (Régnard, 1683)

During the reign of Leo X (1513-1521), a church for Florentines in Rome had been designed by Jacopo Sansovino, and foundation had been completed alongside the Tiber at great expense. Vasari summarized the subsequent history of this project in his biography of Michelangelo:

> Several times the Florentines living in Rome discussed how best to make a start on the church of San Giovanni in the Strada Giulia, and at one of their meetings the heads of the wealthiest families among them each promised to contribute to the building according to his means, and a good sum of money was collected. Then, after they had argued whether they should follow the original plans or to try to do something better, it was decided to raise a new edifice on the old foundations; and eventually they put three people in charge of the project, namely, Francesco Bandini, Umberto Ubaldini, and Tommaso de' Bardi. They in turn asked Michelangelo for a design, pleading that it was a shame that the Florentines had spent so much money in vain, and adding that if his genius did not avail to finish the work then there was nothing they themselves could do. Michelangelo promised that he would do what they wanted as devotedly as he had ever done anything, both because in his old age he was glad to be occupied with sacred things, redounding to the honour of God, and then because of his love for his country, which had never left him [Vasari 1568 (1971): 115].

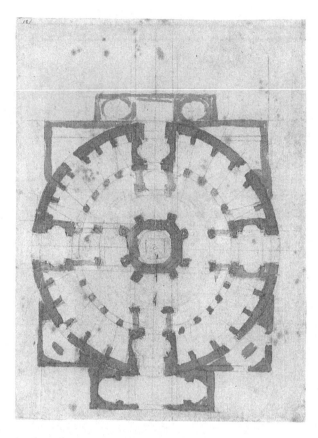

Alternative plans for San Giovanni de' Fiorentini (De Tolnay's *Corpus;* above, no. 609r; below, no. 612r)

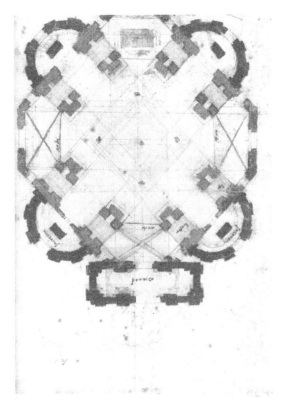

Alternative plans for San Giovanni de' Fiorentini (De Tolnay's *Corpus* ; above 610r; below, a design redrawn by Calcagni)

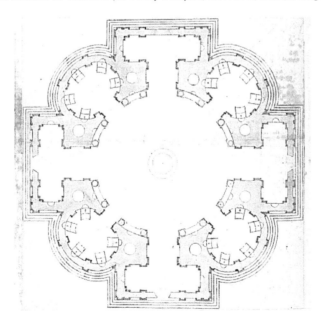

When Michelangelo initially produced designs for San Giovanni is uncertain, but it was at least by 1550 and probably earlier. On August 1, 1550, Michelangelo had written to Vasari that following his suggestion, the Florentine consul, Bindo Altoviti, had persuaded Pope Julius III to pay for one of the seven funerary chapels to be built in the church as a place for his Del Monte relations rather than in San Pietro in Montorio, but he wrote again on October 13 that the Pope had changed his mind again and decided to have build a chapel in Montorio (88-90). "Anyhow, I think we have to forget all about the church of the Florentines" (90). Later attempts to build a church to Michelangelo's design for the Florentines also failed.

Nonetheless, San Giovanni deserves further consideration for a number of reasons. Most importantly, it shows Michelangelo's unquestionable mastery of dome construction. He planned to prevent a very thin and low dome from thrusting outward by having it spring from a thick attic story that functions as a containing ring and by having steprings at mid-level similar to those of the Pantheon and in Bramante's design for the dome of St. Peter's. He also planned to use the lantern as a keystone and compression ring to rest thrust (as opposed to containing it). Della Porta was wrong if he said as reported that Michelangelo's "...ideas were conceived by intuition rather than technical experience" (Lees-Milne 1967: 211).

Vasari later described in some detail the great amount of effort that had gone into designing San Giovanni:

> So for his architectural work, since his old age meant that he could no longer draw clear lines, Michelangelo made use of Tiberio [Calcagni], who was a modest and well-mannered young man. He wanted to use his services for the church of San Giovanni and he asked him to take [measure] the ground-plan of the original foundations. This was brought to him as soon as it was ready; and then, through Tiberio, Michelangelo informed the commissioners (who had not expected him to have anything ready) that he had been working for them; and finally, he showed them the drawings for five beautiful churches which left them amazed. They were reluctant to choose one of themselves, as Michelangelo suggested, and they preferred to rely on his judgment; but he insisted that they should make up their own minds and they, unanimously, they picked out the richest. After the choice had been made, Michelangelo told them that if they put the design into execution the would produce a work superior to anything done by either the Greeks or the Romans: words unlike any ever use by him, before or after, for he was very modest man. At length it was resolved that Michelangelo should supervise the work and that it should be executed by Tiberio; Michelangelo promised to serve them well, and with this arrangement the commissioners were fully content. Tiberio was then given the plan to produce a fair copy, with interior and exterior elevations, as well as a clay model which Michelangelo advised him how to set up. In ten days Tiberio finished a model of eight spans, which pleased the Florentine colony so much that they then had him make a wooden model which is now in the consulate: here is a building as rare in its ornate variety as any church every seen. But after work had been started and five thousand crowns had been spent, the funds failed, much to Michelangelo's annoyance, and the project has remained suspended ever since.
>
> Michelangelo also procured for Tiberio the commission to finish under his director a chapel for Cardinal Santa Fiore in San Giorgio Maggiore; but this remained unfinished because of the unhappy death of Tiberio himself as well as of the cardinal and Michelangelo [Vasari 1568: 116].

In 1559, Michelangelo was asked by Duke Cosimo of Florence to provide a new design for a church for Florentines in Rome, and his hopes were renewed. He wrote the Duke on November 1, 1559, "I have already done several designs suited to the site for the building, which the above-mentioned Deputies have shown me. They, being men of great judgment and discretion, have selected one of them, which I frankly think is the most imposing" (Michelangelo 1963: II, 191; cf. Heydenreich and Lotz 1974: 257-258, fig 84).

The three presentation drawings by Michelangelo are undated, but are likely to date from before 1547, when Serlio published several similar designs in the first edition of his fifth book (folios 1-10); all of these designs of Serlio have centralized plans though none is identical, and none of the domes has a drum. Conceptually, all of the plans are based on the Greek Cross with corner chapels and in these respects resemble Bramante's plan for St. Peter's, but were developed very differently. That Michelangelo had a Greek cross in mind is evident from a small sketch he made on a drawing for San Giovanni that simply consists of a plus-sign with circles in each corner (De Tolnay *Corpus* no. 601v; cf. 610v). The next to last design (no. 612) was slightly modified and redrawn by Michelangelo's draftsman Calcagni (Ackerman 1986: 227, fig. 112), and it was the basis for the model. The earlier designs that show how the alternatives were laid out and that indicate the shaky hand of an old man and are undoubtedly by Michelangelo himself. Vasari and Michelangelo could have worked from Bramante as a common source, but it is more likely that Michelangelo had been consulted at intervals during the last three decades of his life in Rome, and his designs were widely used in attempts to raise funds for the project (even being taken to Florence to show to Duke Cosimo).

Inside and out, this would have been Michelangelo's most sculptural building. Insufficient funds prevented it from being constructed to Michelangelo's designs, and when it was finally begun in 1588, a more traditional design by Giacomo della Porta was preferred. Della Porta was a very good architect and a great administrator, but he was no Michelangelo. As De Tolnay noted, "...the other cupolas of Giacomo della Porta, those of Santa Maria ai Monti and of the Gesu, are static octagons with a low, flattened form. The idea of raising the cupola [of St. Peter's] was not, therefore part of Della Porta's esthetic thinking or that of his generation, which preferred the shallow cupola" (De Tolnay 1975: 147). Santa Maria ai Monti is one of the finest churches of moderate size in Rome, but San Giovanni de' Fiorentini would have been finer. The best Baroque architects including Bernini for Sant'Andrea al Quirinale and Borromini for St. Ivo emulated Michelangelo.

Why did Michelangelo think that with his design for San Giovanni de' Fiorentini he had surpassed the Greeks and Romans? The ancient Roman building he admired most was the Pantheon, the dome of which he emulated in his designs for the dome of the Medici Chapel and for the dome of San Giovanni. Bramante had set as his main goal for St. Peter's to equal the dome of the Pantheon in size and had planned to do so by using the Pantheon's steprings as Michelangelo had planned to do for the dome of San Giovanni. Moreover, in his design for San Giovanni, Michelangelo adapted the two-storied interior elevation of the Pantheon and the use of eight alcoves that enabled its entire interior to be unified. It is evident that he had the Pantheon in mind as the ancient Roman building to be surpassed.

Michelangelo had found a way to provide more space and better light for each of his eight alcoves than was possible for the alcoves of the Pantheon, which were limited in size and shape by the thickness of its walls and which were given no windows. To have more regularly shaped and better lighted chapels, Michelangelo designed them to extend well beyond the walls of his central space and to be separate from one another to enable more windows to be used. When considered in terms of a cross section, San Giovanni would have resembled the cross-section of a basilican church more than the Pantheon. He also intended to provide light into the central space through the use of windows in the drum of the dome that sloped downward to a lower level in the interior (a solution he used for windows in the vaults of the apsidal wings of St. Peter's). Michelangelo sculpted space with light. Overall, his space would have been better unified and lighted even than the Pantheon, and although the span would have been considerably smaller, the elliptical dome could have been made proportionately much thinner.

San Giovanni would have been most like the form of the "temple" of Minerva Medica, which has a dome with steprings, a central space that is taller than it is wide, and apses that project beyond its walls. It is also similar in size to the foundations that already existed for San Giovanni. As noted, the Minerva had been previously adapted for the transept of Santissima Annunziata in Florence. Although ten-sided rather than eight, the Minerva Medica was probably the building Michelangelo set out to surpass. Possibly, the Domus Aurea had some influence on Michelangelo, but less than on Raphael (Lanciani 1897: 361-365).

No other ancient Greek or Roman building was more comparable to Michelangelo's design for San Giovanni than the Minerva Medica, but several others were similar. In Rome, Santa Constanza, the tomb of the daughter of the first Christian emperor, has a centralized plan, but has a clearstoried central space, a lower ambulatory space, and circular outer walls. San Stefano Rotunda in Rome was generally considered to be an ancient Roman building, but its plan is closely based on that of Santa Constanza. Octagonal churches such as San Giovanni in Florence (converted into a baptistery) and San Vitale in Ravenna and octagonal baptisteries such as the baptistery believed to have been built by Constantine were probably more influential than these circular buildings considering that the church in in honor of St. John the Baptist. Early Christian churches varied a great deal more in plan than later ones.

During the Renaissance, little more was known about ancient Greek architecture than could be inferred from Vitruvius. He certainly knew that most Greek temples had peristyles and pediments, and he certainly was not thinking of their exterior when he said he had surpassed the Greeks, but he may have concluded that the two-storied internal elevation of the Pantheon was in emulation of the two-storied interiors of most Greek Doric temples. Since he had not been to Sicily, he had probably never seen an ancient Greek temple, and Paestum had not yet been rediscovered.

What Michelangelo meant by Greek architecture probably refers to Byzantine architecture, and San Giovanni resembles a Greek Orthodox Church more than a Greek temple. In 1529 he went to Venice and saw St. Mark's, the central dome of which is only 42-feet in diameter. Although the Greek-cross plan of San Marco may well have influenced Bramante and Michelangelo, the Duomo in Florence had a more direct influence on the form and scale of St. Peter's, and Bramante's plan for St. Peter's undoubtedly had a more direct influence on the intended church for Florentines in Rome than any Byzantine church. On the way to or from Venice Michelangelo could well have visited Ravenna also and seen San Vitale, which has separate alcoves extending beyond its octagonal central space and which, as Ackerman pointed out, has a vestibule similar to the three that Michelangelo designed for San Giovanni, but not close enough to be considered a direct influence.

Where Michelangelo went beyond the Greeks and Romans was in devising a structural arrangement that was capable of buttressing even an oval dome with minimal use of masonry, by adding separately usable spaces without loosing the unity of the interior, and by providing for better lighted spaces round the perimeter of his building. In one design, he solved problems of structure, spacial unity, and lighting in ways that could not be matched by any ancient Greek or Roman building.

Michelangelo was extremely disappointed that in Duke Cosimo's support for the project. When Cellini conveyed the Duke's request that Michelangelo return to Florence, "upon this he looked me hard in the face and said with sarcastic smile: 'And you! To what extent are you satisfied with him?' Although I replied that I was extremely contented and was very well treated by his Excellency, he showed that he was acquainted with the greater part of my annoyances, and gave as his final answer that it would be difficult for him to leave Rome" (Cellini c. 1566 [1923]: 392).

Cupolas for St. Peter's

Michelangelo planned four cupolas near the corners of the large dome to serve as lanterns to admit light into large chapels at the corners of the building (rather than the four spires planned by Bramante for sacristies that were not built). Only the two cupolas in front were eventually built, and they were redesigned and rebuilt twice by Della Porta but the overall form and placement of the cupolas was based on Michelangelo's design as represented by Dupérac or his circle.

Bramante designed cupolas similar to the ones shown in Dupérac's engravings (Ackerman 1961: fig. 51b). The ones Dupérac illustrated do not resemble a surviving design by Vignola, who was in charge of St. Peter's in the interval between Michelangelo and Della Porta. The dome for Vignola's Gesù was designed by Della Porta and resembles Della Porta's design for Santa Maria dei Monte. The two cupolas that now exist on St. Peter's seem to me to resemble Michelangelo's designs more than either Vignola's or Della Porta's designs. Leonardo had also designed a church with a cruciform plan, a large central dome on a drum, and four cupolas, but the dates of his drawings are less than certain (Heydenreich and Lotz 1974: pls. 146-147), and whether or not they had any influence on Bramante's designs or vice versa is disputed. There seems to have been no influence by Leonardo on Bramante's designs in Milan, and it was necessary structurally to add chapels in the corners of cruciform plans to buttress large domes. The closer resemblance of Leonardo's drawings of centralized churches to Michelangelo's final design than to Bramante's original design is probably coincidental.

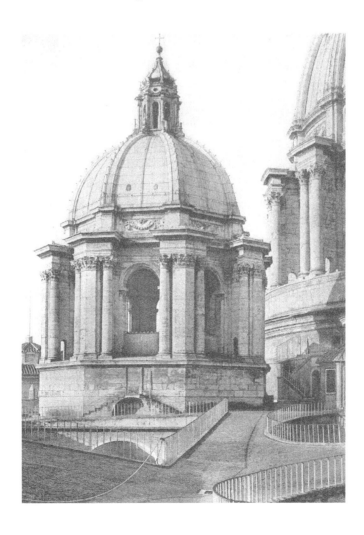

Redesigned cupola by Della Porta (Magni)

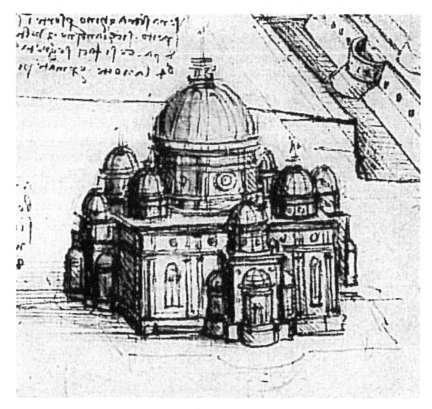

Designs by Leonardo for a centrally planned church (details; Heydenreich and Lotz)

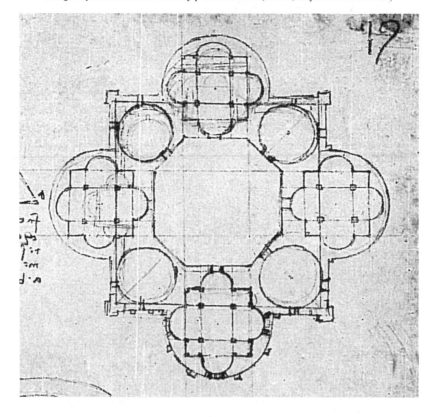

Michelangelo's Design for the Front
In my opinion, the front that Michelangelo designed for St. Peter's was probably best recorded in a drawing attributed to Dupérac and in a medal issued in c. 1590 or around the time the dome was begun. The drawing has been dated by various writers from 1558-1575, and the attribution is uncertain, but as Millon and Smyth concluded, "with a date of 1574-1575 and the author's explicit statement of intention to represent the building as he understood it was to be completed , the manuscript presents evidence, in its picture of St. Peter's that ten years after the death of Michelangelo a knowledgeable author (if not Dupérac, as Wittkower though, then perhaps someone in his circle) believed that St. Peter's was still to be built 'following the design of Buonarroti' with a hemispherical exterior dome" (Millon and Smyth 1988: 131). Presumably, the free-hand sketch is based on Michelangelo's lost model referred to by Vasari.

None of Michelangelo's front had been constructed because much of the nave of Old St. Peter's still survived and continued to be uses while New St. Peter's was under being constructed. Later, when all of the old church was destroyed, another Latin plan was adopted with a much longer nave and a redesigned front.

In 1538 a wall was erected in between the new building and the old building, and until 1606 the surviving nave of the old building prevented the construction of a front for the new building (Lees-Milne 1967: 233-234). Thus, during the entire time Michelangelo was in charge from 1546-1564 he was unable to begin construction on a front for his building. Likewise, none of Michelangelo's successors were able to begin construction of a front for the new building until about 42 years after his death.

During this period from 1564-1606, ten different popes reigned, and it was not until 1607 that a decision was made to extend the nave (235). Although there was general agreement among popes following Michelangelo's death that his designs were to be followed, there was evident disagreement about which of his designs should be followed, and there is good evidence that he had not made a final decision about the front at the time of his death: In 1569, the dated plan by Dupérac indicated that he was convinced Michelangelo intended for his front to have a portico with four columns, and in 1590 a print of the front with the relocated obelisk indicated that Domenico Fontana was still convinced St. Peter's was to have a portico with four columns. A fresco at the entrance to the Biblioteca Apostolica that was dated 1556 by Letarouilly also has a four-columned portico, but it wa not made during Michelangelo's lifetime; it was painted by Paris Nogari in or around 1587, and the enormous square was never intended (Spagnesi 1997: 198; Zöllner 2010: 327).

Design for a four-columned portico depicted in a fresco in the Vatican, c. 1587 (Alinari in Mariani)

Model of the four-columned portico (Di Carlo in Mariani)

Design for a four-columned portico, 1590 (Domenico Fontana)

As noted, during the reign of Pope Gregory XIII from 1572-1585, a metal was issued showing a six-columned portico. At some point in between 1558 and 1575, either Dupérac or another "knowledgeable author" drew a six-columned portico and stated explicitly that it represented Michelangelo's intentions (Millon and Smyth 1988: 131).

A drawing in a manuscript volume of drawings attributed to Dupérac that includes the view said to represent Michelangelo's final intentions for the exterior of St. Peter's. "The drawing has been dated 1558-1564 by Ackerman (1961, II,9 9); before 1565 by Wittkower (1963, 15-33); and 1565 by Thoenes (1965, 10-20). Evidence internal to the manuscript text and illustrations indicates that they were written and drawn in 1574-1575, for presentation as a gift during the Holy Year of 1575 (see Smith 1970, 265; for an extended treatment see Millon and Smyth, forthcoming [1994])" (Millon and Smyth 1988: 131). If the drawing dated from before Michelangelo's death in 1564, it would be better evidence than if it were made a decade or so after his death. Moreover, it is difficult to accept that the same person could have created such precise measured drawings several years before he is thought to have created such a disproportionate drawing. Whoever created it and when, it does correspond in important respects to other good evidence for what had already been constructed and for what Michelangelo's intentions are known to have been.

In my opinion, the available evidence can be better accounted for by accepting that Michelangelo's final choice was for a 6-columned portico as well as the taller dome depicted in the large wooden model, but with the ovoid lower dome that Della Porta omitted.

Regardless of the number of columns the portico had, the front Michelangelo designed would have stepped back again, and pilasters on each side of the body of the building would also have been visible.

Design for St. Peter's (with Gregory XIII on the obverse; (Lees-Milne)

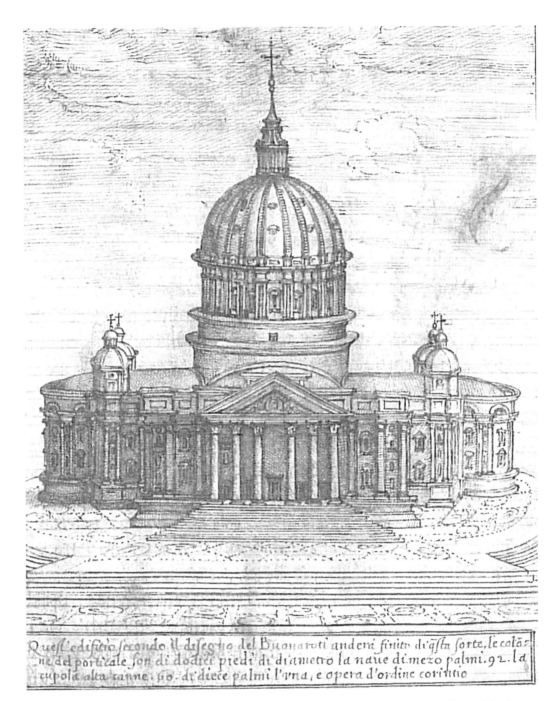

Drawing attributed to Dupérac claiming to depict Michelangelo's final design, c. 1575 (detail: Millon and Smyth)

Quest'edificio secondo il disegno del Buonaroti anderà finito di q[ue]sta sorte, le colo[n]ne del porticale son di dodici piedi di diametro la nave di mezo palmi .92. la cupola alta canne .60. di diece palmi l'una, e opera d'ordine corintio.

This building according to the design of Buonaroti will be finished in this way: the columns of the portico are twelve feet in diameter, the central nave 92 palmi, the dome 60 canne of ten palmi each in height, and the work [is] of the Corinthian order [transcribed and translated by Patricia Waddy].

Carlo Fontana meticulously computed the dimensions of St. Peter's as it was completed, and he wrote that its overall height from the floor to the top of the cross on the dome is 593 Roman palmi. Irrespective of the dimension of the palmi in use at the time, the actual dimension of 593 palmi given by Fontana is 99 percent the same as the 600 palmi height that was intended in c. 1575 according to the inscription on the drawing by Dupérac or a member of his circle. This is further evidence that Michelangelo final intention was to construct a dome the height of the one that was built (Fontana 1694 [2003]: 378 [194]).

When it is taken into consideration that this sketch depicts the lunettes that Michelangelo constructed for part of the attic and that were changed to rectangular windows by Ligorio soon after Michelangelo's death, there can be no doubt that the artist who drew the sketch and who presumably wrote the caption had good sources of information about how Michelangelo intended for St. Peter's to look (allowing for the inability of the artists to indicate perspective correctly). The lunettes and the overall height in turn lend credibility to the depiction of a portico with six columns rather than four, and the metal that Gregory XIII produced during his reign from 1572-1585 is further evidence that the sketch got the number of columns for the portico right.

Millon and Smyth argued that a set of five dimensioned drawings attributed to Dosio were based on measurements taken from the great model of the dome and drum before it was altered (Millon and Smyth 1988: 158-172). However, the very precise dimensions on these drawings indicate that they are more likely to have been based on computations than on measurements of a model (particularly the drawing on p. 169) They are more likely to be drawings or copies of drawings that were produced to build a model with a lower dome and that were not used when a decision was made to create a higher dome with a U-shaped inner dome inserted within in.

The U-shaped inner dome was unquestionably designed by Michelangelo and was retained in the great model yet it does not show in the drawings and prints that are assumed to have been based on the final version of Michelangelo's model. It is not credible that Della Porta added a U-shaped inner dome to to Michelangelo's model or that an inner dome would have been needed unless Michelangelo himself had decided to made the outer dome taller. The U-shaped inner dome that was omitted by Della Porta cannot be attributed to anyone but Michelangelo, and attempts to explain the design development of St. Peter's and Michelangelo's final intentions that do not account for the presence of the inner dome cannot be correct. Judging by all of the available evidence, the rough sketch has more value for determining Michelangelo's final intentions than the scale drawings published by Dupérac.

In addition, the sketch provides some further indication of how the basilica would have related to a piazza. It shows the ground terraced to enable the basilica to sit on an immense circular platform with steps projecting in front and continuing around the perimeter. In front of the basilica would have been paving with a pattern similar to the interior of the Pantheon. This is more likely to represent Michelangelo's intentions than the c. 1587 fresco that shows a similar pattern of paving, but no circular terrace around the perimeter of the building, and that seems to show a later plan to construct an immense plaza that would have been similar to the one Bramante had planned for the Tempietto, but since this would have required the destruction of the Vatican palace including the Sistine Chapel and Michelangelo's ceiling and Last Judgment, it surely cannot represent Michelangelo's intentions. Domenico Fontana's 1590 view of the obelisk in front of Michelangelo's basilica show a piazza that was to be at the same level as the obelisk with a row of fornices across the front of a higher terrace on which the basilica would then have been located. All three illustrations show that some kind of piazza would have had a rectilinear pattern for its paving and that a portico was intended, but there was considerable disagreement about the level at which the piazza should be located as well as about the number of columns for the portico, and lack of funds largely prevented any major changes for several more decades..

Attic Story

As Ackerman noted, "the existing attic, departing from Michelangelo's design for the southern arm, was begun here [on the northern arm] by Pirro Ligorio immediately after Michelangelo's death" (Ackerman 1986: 319). Millon and Smyth concluded "…that there is no secure evidence that Michelangelo changed his mind after he completed the attic on the south apse…" (Millon and Smyth 1994: 649). Nonetheless, Ligorio's design for the attic was later applied to the entire building including the part that Michelangelo had completed.

Although the lunettes in the attic were also depicted in the drawing attributed to Dupérac, the 1569 side elevation in the print that is definitely by Dupérac shows rectangular openings that were eventually built decades later. Prints dating for the 1580s show that Michelangelo's lunettes spanned between the pairs of pilasters and helped to interrelate them visually into a more coherent design. The arches were required for the windows to provide support at the base of the vaults of the apses.

The pointed dome shown in the painting has been consistently attributed to Della Porta and assumed to have been added to the model. This is one assumption piled on top of the assumption that the dome model was altered, but there no documentation such as financial evidence has been produced to support this assumption. It is also based on the assumption that the Dupérac prints accurately represent Michelangelo's final intentions, but the four-columned portico he depicted in plan, and the attic he depicted had not been built and was an inferior design.

St. Peter's in 1580-1581 with lunettes in the attic story (Millon and Smyth)

St. Peter's with lunettes in the attic story in or before 1586 (Carlo Fontana)

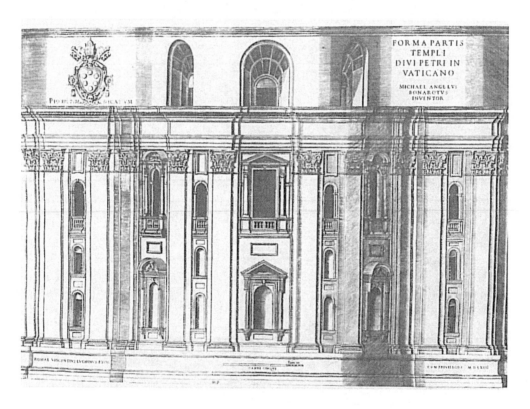

Elevation of southern arm of St. Peter's dated 1564 (Ackerman)

Around 1619, Michelangelo the Younger commissioned Passignano to create a painting for the Casa Buonarroti that purports to show Michelangelo presenting a model of the church for approval to Paul IV (1555-1559), and notably the front of the basilica was omitted and at least by 1555 must not have been decided upon either by Michelangelo or by the pope. That a wooden model of the church was built and was approved is documented and that it was used for the painting is likely since semi-circular windows are shown in the attic, but the dome as built was substituted by the artist Millon and Lampugani 1994: 665-666). Although there are a number of problems with this painting, it can be taken as evidence that by 1559, no design for the front had been adopted. Michelangelo no doubt did design a front before his death, and he probably produced more than one alternative design.

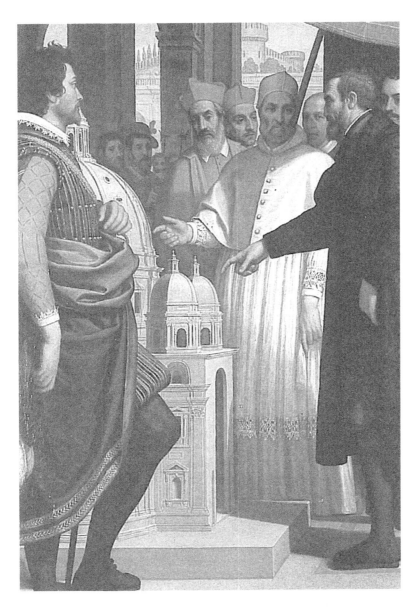

Presentation model of St. Peter's except for its front detail from an imagined painting by Passignano, 1619)

Apse of St. Peter's (Alinari in Mariani)

Michelangelo's design for St. Peter's (albumen in Schiavo)

Summary on the Design of St. Peter's

Michelangelo's front would probably have consisted of a free-standing, pedimented portico with six monumental columns (rather than four) and an intermediate block with a stepped semi-dome over the apse-ended west arm of the building. The pediment would have been the width of the nave, and the portico would have projected from of a row of 10 monumental columns. As the shading of the drawing attributed to Dupérac shows, the effect would have been of a 10-columned portico with the pedimented portico projecting from it. The attic story would have been lower, and on the sides and back of the building, lunettes like those already constructed on one side would have spanned between pairs of columns.

Essentially, Michelangelo put Brunelleschi's dome on top of Bramante's Tempietto rather than the Pantheon's rounded and solid dome that Bramante had intended for St. Peter's. Michelangelo intended for the inner profile of the inner dome and for the outer profile of the outer dome to be hemispherical, but for the outer dome to taper and to rise from a higher point than the inner dome. There is no other way to account for the insertion of the lower U-shaped dome in the large model of the dome; it would be pointless unless Michelangelo had decided to increase the height of the dome.

With overlapping brickwork, with ties, and with monumental statues to prevent the base of the dome from expanding laterally, Michelangelo's solution was sound even though Della Porta later thought it would be safer to have a more pointed dome like the Duomo for the outer shell. The cracks that eventually developed can be attributed to Della Porta's solution rather than to Michelangelo's design. Despite the relatively small amount by which the dome was heightened, its form is nonetheless almost entirely as Michelangelo designed it.

Nothing further was done about the construction of the dome until the reign of Gregory XIII, who in 1573 appointed Giacomo della Porta as chief architect and commissioned him to complete the dome, and it was finally completed in 1590 under Sixtus V, who gave Della Porta all the help he needed to bring the work to a rapid conclusion during his papacy. As completed, it lacks either the colossal statures planned to go around the base of the dome or oversized brackets that were an alternative plan, and one or the other would have helped to stabilize the dome. The dome survived nearly intact for about a century and a half, and there was general agreement that it could have survived indefinitely, but some substantial cracks did develop that seem likely to have been caused by too rapid construction, insufficient compression at the base of the dome, and the absence of flanking buttresses where the nave was later built. Strikes by lightning probably caused some cracks, but they were anticipated and adequately provided for (and the problem was finally eliminated when Franklin invented the lightning rod and the Vatican was eventually persuaded to install one on top of St. Peter's). In the 18th Century, further reinforcements were added to be on the safe side desspite disagreement about the need for them.

Of the many architects who worked on St. Peter's, Michelangelo deserves by far the most credit for the final form of the building. Bramante's concepts were utilized, and by constructing and connecting the piers, he established the plan and scale, but the piers had begun to crack even before the drum was added and so had to be enlarged. Little of the building resembles his designs besides the plan. Michelangelo demolished the exterior walls that had been constructed before 1547, and he followed through with his conception of a unified whole with a well scaled entrance. What Michelangelo contributed to St. Peter's entitled him to be considered as great an architect as a sculptor.

CONCLUSION

Those who argue that the Renaissance was a continuation of the Medieval Period ignore the fact that before and after the Renaissance, Italy was repressed by Catholicism. Humility and submission were considered virtues. Everyone was a sinner, and every sinner deserved to be eternally tortured in Hell. Information even about religion was strictly censored.

> The century which escaped from the influence of the Middle Ages felt the need of something to mediate between itself and antiquity in many questions of morals and philosophy; and this need was met by the writer[s] of treatises and dialogues. Much which appears to us as mere commonplace in their writings, was for them and their contemporaries a new and hardly-won view of things upon which mankind had been silent since the days of antiquity [Burckhardt 1944: 144].

It was a revived concern with this World rather than with the consequences in a presumed afterlife that made all the difference in how much progress could again be made in the increase of knowledge. Catholicism suppressed the human spirit and kept the mind ignorant of everything contrary to the interests of the Church.

> These modern men, the representatives of the cuture of Italy, were born with the same religious instincts as other mediæval Europeans. But their powerful individuality made them in religion, as in other matters, altogether subjective, and the intense charm which the discovery of the inner and otuer universe exercised upon them rendered them markedly worldly. ...
>
> Further, the close and frequent relations of Italy with Byzantium and the Mohammedan peoples had produced a dispassionate toleration which weakened the ethnographical conception of a privileged Christendom. And when classical antiquity with it men and institutions became an ideal of life as well as the greatest historical memories, ancient speculation and scepticism obtained in many cases a complete mastery over the minds of Italians. ...
>
> Finally, these intellectual giants, these representatives of the Renaissance, show, in respect to religion, a quality which is common in youthful natures. Distinguishing keenly between good and evil, they yet are conscious of no sin. Every disturbance of their inward harmony they feel themselves able to make good out of the plastic resources of their own nature, and therefore they feel no repentance. The need of salavation thus become felt more and more dimly, while the ambitions and the intellectual activity of the present either shut out altogether every thought of a world to come, or else caused it to assume a poetic instead of a dogmatic form. ...
>
> That religion should again become an affair of the individual and of his own personal feeling was inevitable when the Chruch beoame corrupt in doctrine and tyrannous in practice, and is proof that the European mind was still alive. ...The worldliness, through which the Renaissance seems to offer so striking a contrast to the Middle Ages, owed it first origin to the flood of new thoughts, purposes, and views, which transformed the mediæval conception of nature and man [Burckhardt 1944 (1860): 303-304].

"In Italy, and especially in Florence, it was possible to live as an open and notorious unbeliever, if a man only refrained from direct acts of hostility against the Church" (335).

During the Renaissance, the extent to which Italy surpassed the rest of Europe depended on its becoming increasingly secular. After the Renaissance, the extent to which Italy fell behind the rest of Europe depended on how much Catholicism was able to control thought. Much great architecture and art was created with the Catholic Church as a patron, but chiefly while the Papacy itself was least religious.

Italian humanists revived the knowledge, architecture, and art of Antiquity and did most to preserve and disseminate pagan knowledge in place of Christian beliefs. In particular, every aspect of science had been almost completely neglected: "...the Italian investigators of this period, chiefly through their rediscovery of the results attained by antiquity..., mark a new epoch..." rather than a continuation of the Medieval Period in science as well as in art by the recovery of what knowledge had survived and by again directly studying nature rather than the Bible to learn about the World (Burckhardt 1944: 148). In Italy during the Medieval Period, the Latin Classics were widely scattered and neglected while in Byzantium the Greek Classics were being carefully copied and taught.

Italians equaled and in many cases surpassed the Ancients and began to generate new knowledge about the entire World. Marco Polo revealed Asia to Europe; Columbus revealed the Americas to Europe, and the Americas were named for the Italian who mapped them and proved they were a new world not mentioned in the Bible. Galileo demonstrated the value of the scientific method, but was put under house arrest for insisting the Bible was wrong that the Sun rotated around the Earth. "We must insist upon it, as one of the chief propositions of this book, that it was not the revival of antiquity alone, but its union with the genius of the Italian people, which achieved the conquest of the western world" (Burckhardt 1944: 104). However, after the Renaissance, the rest of Europe benefitted more than Italy, and everywhere missionaries went, knowledge was replaced by beliefs; and independence was replaced with dependence as had been the case during the Medieval Period throughout Europe.

The Renaissance ceased to flourish in Italy when the Counter-Reformation and Inquisition attempted to control all knowledge with unparalleled success. The Renaissance provides the best documented example that thought flourishes most when religion and government are least able to control it.

Michelangelo was not humble, and he had little interest in poverty. If he had been chaste, he would probably have been less in fear of being tortured for all eternity. He was the supreme Renaissance man in every respect and the best in every art. Nonetheless, he had been indoctrinated from his youth that he was a sinner, that he deserved to be punished, and that he could expect to be tortured forever unless the Church intervened for him. Throughout his life he was tortured with doubt, and at the end of his life he hoped that by devoting himself fully to the rebuilding of St. Peter's to save his soul, but only on his own terms.

APPENDICES

Appendix I

Outline of Italian Architecture from Julius II to Alexander VII

major events	popes	major buildings
	1503-13 Julius II (della Rovere)	1504 Tempietto, Bramante
		1505-06 St. Peter's Bramante
1508 Palladio born		1505-11 Villa Farnesina, Peruzzi
1514 Bramante dies	1513-22 Leo X (de' Medici)	1518 Villa Madama, Raphael
1517 Luther's 95 Theses		
1520 Raphael dies		1520-34 Medici Chapel, Michelangelo
1527 Sack of Rome	1523-34 Clement VII (de' Medici)	1524 Laurentian Library, Michelangelo
1537 Serlio's *Five Books*	1534-50 Paul III (Farnese)	1539-45 Capitol, Michelangelo
1541-49 Palladio makes five trips to Rome		
1545 Council of Trent begins		1547-64 St. Peter's Michelangelo
	1550-55 Julius III (del Monte)	1551 Villa Giulia
	1555-59 Paul IV (Caraffa)	1558 Villa Foscari, Palladio
1563 Council of Trent ends	1559-66 Pius IV (Medici)	1565 Palazzo Valmarana, Palladio
1564 Michelangelo dies		

1570 Palladio's *Four Books*	1566-72 Pius V (Ghislieri)	1566-69 Villa Rotunda Palladio
1580 Palladio dies	1572-85 Gregory XIII (Boncompagni)	1576-80 Il Redentore, Palladio
1585 St. Peter's Dome resumed	1585-90 Sixtus V (Peretti)	1585-90 Plan of Rome
1598 Bernini born	1592-1605 Clement VIII (Aldobrandini)	
1606 Old St. Peter's demolished	1605-21 Paul V (Borghese)	1607 St. Peter's Latin Cross adopted
	1623-44 Urban VIII (Barberini)	1623-33 St. Peter's Baldacchino; Bernini 1642-60 St. Ivo Borromini
1648 End 30 Year's War	1644-55 Innocent X (Pamfili)	1648-51 Four Rivers, Bernini 1653-55 St. Agnes, Boromini
	1655-67 Alexander VII (Chigi)	1656-66 Throne St. Peter, Bernini 1656-67 Colonnade, Bernini 1658-70 St. Andrea, Bernini

1667 Boromini dies
1680 Bernini dies

Note: The impact of the Papacy on Italian architecture was greatest from 1503-1680. I omitted the 14 popes of the 15th Century because their impact on architecture was minimal compared to the popes beginning with Julius II and ending with Alexander VII.

Appendix II

Vasari's Art History

Part 1: "Preface to the Lives"

[Vasari 1568: I, 1-19; quoted in full; paragraphs added]

[*Origin of Art*]

I am aware that it is commonly held as a fact by most writers that sculpture, as well as painting, was naturally discovered originally by the people of Egypt, and also that there are others who attribute to the Chaldeans the first rough carvings of statues and the first reliefs. In like manner there are those who credit the Greeks with the invention of the brush and of colouring. But it is my opinion that design, which is the foundation of both arts, and the very soul which conceives and nourishes in itself every part of the intelligence, come into full existence at the time of the origin of all things, when the Most High after creating the world and adorning the heavens with shining lights, descended through the limpid air to the solid earth, and by shaping man, disclosed the first form of sculpture and painting in the charming invention of things.

Who will deny that from this man, as from a living example, the ideas of statues and culture, and the question of pose and of outline, first took form; and from the first pictures, whatever they may have been, arose the first ideas of grace, unity, and the discordant concords made by the play of lights and shadows? Thus the first model from which the first image of man arose was a clod of earth and not without reasons, for the Divine Architect of time and of nature, being all perfection, wished to demonstrate, in the imperfections of His materials, what could be done to improve them, just as good sculptors and painters are in the habit of doing, when by adding additional touches and removing blemishes, they bring their imperfect sketches to such a state of completion and of perfection s they desire. God also endowed man with bright flesh colour, and the same shades may be drawn from the earth, which supplies materials to counterfeit everything which occurs in painting.

It is indeed true that it is impossible to feel absolutely certain as to what steps men took for the imitation of the beautiful works of Nature in these arts before the flood, although it appears most probable that even then they practised all manner of painting and sculpture; for Belus, son of [p. 2] the proud Nimrod, about 200 years after the flood, and a statue made, from which idolatry afterwards arose; and his celebrated daughter-in-law, Semiramis, queen of Babylon, in the building of that city, introduced among the ornaments there coloured representations from life of divers kinds of animals, as well as of herself and of her husband Ninus, with bronze statues of her father, her mother-in-law, and her grandmother, as Diodorus relates, calling them Jove, Juno, and Ops, Greek names, which did not then exist. It was, perhaps from these statues that the Chaldeans learned to make the images of their gods. It is recorded in Genesis how 150 years after, when Rachel was fleeing from Mesopotamia with her husband Jacob, she stole the idols of her father Laban.

Nor were the Chaldeans singular in making statues and paintings, for the Egyptians also had theirs, devoting great pains to those arts is shown by the marvellous tomb of that king of remote antiquity, Osymandyas, described at length by Diodorus, and as the severe command of Moses proves, when, on leaving Egypt, he gave orders that no images should, be made upon pain of death. Moses also, after having ascended the Mount, and having found a golden calf manufactured and adored by his people, was greatly troubled at seeing diving honours accorded to the image of a beast; so that he not only broke it to powder, but, in the punishment of so great a fault, caused the Levites to put to death many thousands of the false Israelites who had committed this idolatry.

But as the sin consisted in adoring idols and not in making them, it is written in Exodus that the art of design and of making statues, not only in marble but in all kinds of metal, was given by the mouth of God himself to Bezaleel of the tribe of Judah, and to Aholiab, of the tribe of Dan, who made the two cherubim of gold, the candlesticks, the veil, and the borders of the sacerdotal vestments, together with a number of other beautiful things in the tabernacle, for no other purpose than to induce people to contemplate and adore them.

From the things seen before the flood, the pride of man found the means to make statues of those whose fame they designed to remain immortal in the world; and the Greeks, who assign a different origin to this, say that the Ethiopians invented the first statues, according to Diodorus, the Egyptians imitated these, while the Greeks followed the Egyptians. From this time until Homer's day it is clear that sculpture and painting were perfect as we may see from the description of Achilles' shield by that divine poet, [3] who represents it with such skill that the image of its is presented to our minds as clear as if we had seen the thing itself. Lactantius Firmianus attributes the credit of the invention to Prometheus, who like God fashioned the human form out of clay. But according to Pliny this art was introduced into Egypt by Gyges of Lydia, who, on seeing his shadow cast by the fire, at once drew an outline of himself on the wall with piece of coal. For some time after that it was the custom to draw in outline only, without any colouring, Pliny again being our authority. Colour was afterwards introduced by Philocles of Egypt with considerable pains, and also by Cleanthes and Ardices of Corinth and by Telephanes of Sicyon. Cleophantes of Corinth wa the first of the 8Greeks to use colours, and Apollodorus was the first to introduce the brush. Polygnotus of Thasos, Zeuxis and Timagoras of Chalcis, Pytheus and Aglaophon followed them, all most celebrated, and after them came the renowned Apelles who was so highly esteemed and honoured for his skill by Alexander the Great, for his wonderful delineation of Calumny and Favour, as Lucian relates.

Almost all the painters and sculptors were of high excellence being frequently endowed by heaven, not only with the additional gift of poetry as we read in Pacuvius, but also with that of philosophy. Metrodorus is an instance in point for he was equally skilled as a philosopher and as a painter, and when Apelles was sent by the Athenians to Paulus Æmilius to adorn his triumph he remained to teach philosophy to the general's sons. Sculpture was thus generally practised in Greece where there flourished a number of excellent artists, among them being Phidias of Athens, Praxiteles and Polycletus, very great masters, Lysippus and Pyrgoteles who were of considerable skill in engraving, and Pygmalion in ivory carving in relief, it being recorded of him that he obtained life by his prayers for the figure of a maid carved by him. The ancient Greeks and Romans also honoured and rewarded painting, since they granted the citizenship and very great honours to those who excelled in this art.

Painting flourished in Rome to such an extent that Fabius gave a name to his family, subscribing himself in the beautiful things he did in the Temple of Safety as Fabius the Painter. By public decree slaves were prohibited from practising painting, and so much honour was continually accorded by the people to the art and to artists that rare works were sent to Rome among the spoils to appear in their triumphs; excellent artists who were slaves obtained their liberty and received notable rewards from the [4] republic. The Romans bore such a reverence for the art, that when the city of Syracuse was sacked Marcellus gave orders that his men should treat with resect a famous artist there, and also that they should be careful not to set fire to a quarter in which there was a very fine picture. This was afterwards carried to Rome to adorn his triumphs. To that city in the course of time almost al the spoils of the world were brought, and the artists themselves gathered there beside their excellent works. By such means Rome became an exceedingly beautiful city, more richly adorned by the statues of foreign artists than those made by natives.

It is known that in the little island city of Rhodes there were more than 30,000 statues, in bronze and marble, nor did the Athenians possess less while those of Olympus and Delphi were even more numerous, and those of Corinth were without number, all being most beautiful and of great price. Does not everyone know how Nicomedes, king of Lycia, expended almost all the wealth of his people owing to his passion for a Venus by the hand of Praxiteles? Did not Attalus do the same? Who without an afterthought expended more than 6000 sesterces to have a picture of Bacchus painted by Aristides. The picture was placed by Lucius Mummius with great pomp in the temple of Ceres, as an ornament to Rome.

But although the nobility of this art was so highly valued it is uncertain to whom it owes its origins. As I have already said, it is found in very ancient times among the Chaldeans, some attribute the honour to the Ethiopians, while the Greeks claim it for themselves. Besides this there is good reason for supposing that the Tuscans may have had it earlier, as our own Leon Battista Alberti asserts, and weighty evidence in favour of this view is supplied by the marvellous tomb of Porsena at Chiusi, where not long ago some tiles of terracotta were found under the ground, between the walls of the Labyrinth, containing some figures in half-relief, so excellent and so delicately fashioned that it is easy to see that art was not in its infancy at that time, for to judge by the perfection of these specimens at that time, it was nearer its zenith than its origin. Evidence to the same purpose is supplied every day by the quantity of pieces of red and black Aretine vases, made about the same time, to judge by the style, with light carving and small figures and scenes in bas-relief, and a quantity of small round masks, cleverly made by the masters of that age, and which prove the men of the time to have been most skillful and accomplished in that art. Further evidence is afforded by the statues found at Viterbo [5] at the beginning of the pontificate of Alexander VI, showing that sculpture was valued and had advanced to no small state of perfection in Tuscany. Although the time when they were made is not exactly known, yet from the style of the figures and front the manner of the tombs and of the buildings, no less than by the inscriptions in Tuscan letters, it may be conjectured with great reasons that they are of great antiquity and that they were made at a time when such things were highly valued. But what clearer evidence can be desired than the discovery made in our own day in the year 1554 of a bronze figure representing the Chimera of Bellerophon, during the excavations form the fortifications and walls of Arezzo. This figure shows to what perfection the art had arrived among the Tuscans, in this Etruscan style. Some small letters carved on a paw are presumed, in the absence of a knowledge of the Etruscan language, to give the master' name, and perhaps the date. This figure, on account of its beauty and antiquity, has been paced by Duke Cosimo in a chamber in his palace in the new suite of rooms where I painted the deeds of Pope Leo X. The Duke also posses a number of small bronze figure of similar character which were found in the same place.

[Nature as the Source of Art]
But as to the antiquity of the works of the Greeks, Ethiopians, Chaldeans, and Tuscans is equally doubtful, like our own or even more so, and because it is necessary in such matters to base one's opinions on conjectures, although these are not so ill founded that one is in danger of going very far astray, yet I think that anyone who will take the trouble to consider the matter carefully will arrive at the same conclusion as I have, that art owes its origin to Nature herself, that this beautiful creation the world supplied the first model, while the original teacher was the divine intelligence which ahs not only made us superior to the other animals, but like God Himself., if I may venture to say it. In our time it has been seen, as I hope to show quite shortly, that simple children, roughly brought up in the wilderness, have begun to draw by themselves, impelled by their own natural genius, instructed solely by the example of these beautiful paintings and sculptures of Nature. Much more then is it probable that the first men, being less removed from their divine origin, were more perfect, possessing a brighter intelligence, and that with Nature as a guide, a pure intellect for master, and the lovely world s a model, they originated these noble arts, and by gradually

improving them brought them at length, [6] from small beginnings, to perfection.

    I do not deny that there must have been an originator, since I know quite well that there must have been a beginning at some time, due to some individual. Neither will I deny that it is impossible for one person to help another, and to teach and open the way to design, colour, and relief, because I know that our art consists entirely of imitation, first of Nature, and then, as it cannot rise so high of itself, of those things which are produced from the masters with the greatest reputation. But I will say that to declare absolutely it was one man or antoher is a very dangerous and perhaps unnecessary task, since we have seen the true and original root of all. The works which constitute the life and fame of artists decay one after the other by the ravages of time. Thus, the artists themselves are unknown, as there was no one to write about them and could not be, so that his sources of knowledge was not granted to posterity. But when writers began to commemorate things made before their time, they were unable to speak of those of which they had seen no notice, so that those who came nearest to these were the last of whom no memorial remains. Thus, Homer is by common consent admitted to be the first of the poets, not because there were none before him, for there were, although they ere not so excellent, and in his own works this is clearly shown but because all knowledge of these, such as they were, has been lost two thousand years before. But we will now pass over these matters, which are too vague on account of their antiquity, and we will proceed to deal with clear questions, namely, the rise of the arts to perfection, their decline and their restoration or rather renaissance, and there we stand on much firmer ground

[*Decline of Ancient Roman Art*]
    The practice of the arts began late in Rome, if the first figures were, as reported, the images of Ceres made of the metal of the possessions of Spurius Cassius, who was condemned to death without remorse by his own father, because he was plotting to make himself king. But although the arts of painting and sculpture continued to flourish until the death of the last of the twelve Cæsars yet they did not maintain that perfection and excellence which had characterized them before, as we see by the buildings of the time under successive emperors. The arts declined steadily from day to day, until at length by a gradual process thy entirely lost a perfection of design. Clear testimony to this is afforded by the works in sculpture and architecture produced in Rome in the time of Constantine, notably in the triumphal arch made [7] for him by the Roman people at the Colosseum, where we see that for lack of good masters not only did they make use of marble reliefs carved in the time of Trajan, but also of spoils brought to Rome from various places. Those who recognise the excellence of these bas-reliefs, statues, the columns, the cornices and other ornaments which belong to another epoch will perceive how rude are the portions done to fill up gaps by sculptors of the day. Very rude also are some scenes of small figures in marble below the reliefs and the pediment, representing victories, while between the said arches there are some rivers, also very crude, and so poor that they leave one firmly under the impression that the art of sculpture had begun to decline even before the coming of the Goths and other barbarous and foreign nations who combined to destroy all the superior arts as well as Italy.

    It is true that architecture suffered less at that time than the other arts of design. The bath [baptistery] erected by Constantine at the entrance of the principal portico of the Lateran contains, in addition to it porphyry columns, capitals carved in marble and beautifully carved double bases taken from elsewhere, the whole composition of the building being very well conceived. On the other hand, the stucco, the mosaic and some incrustations of the walls made by the masters of the time are not equal to those which had been taken away for the most part from the temples of the gods of the heathen, and which Constantine caused to be placed in the same building. Constantine observed the same method, according to report with the garden of Æquitius in building the temple which he afterwards endowed and gave to Christian priests. In like manner the magnificent church of S. Giovanni Lateran, built by the same emperor, may serve as evidence of the same fact, namely, that sculpture had already greatly declined in this time, because the figures of the

Saviour and of the twelve apostles in silver, which he caused to be made, were very base works, executed without art and with very little design. In addition to this, it is only necessary to examine the metals of this emperor, and other statues made by the sculptors of his day, which are now at the capitol to perceive clearly how far removed they are from the perfection of the medals and statues of the other emperors there. All these things prove that sculpture had greatly declined long before the coming of the Goths to Italy. Architecture, as I have said, maintained its excellence at a higher though not at the highest level.

[*Quarrying Ancient Buildings*]

Nor is this a matter for surprise, since large buildings were almost entirely constructed of spoils, so that [8] it was easy for the architects in great measure to imitate the old in making the new, since they had the former continually before their eyes. This was an easier task for them than for the sculptors, as the art of imitating the good figures of the ancients had declined. A good illustration of the truth of this statement is afforded by the church of the chief of the apostles in the Vatican, which is rich in columns, bases, capitals, architraves, cornices, doors and other incrustations and ornaments which were all taken from various places and buildings, erected before that time in very magnificent style. The same remarks apply to S. Croce at Jerusalem, which Constantine erected at the entreaty of his mother, Helena; to S. Lorenzo outside the walls, and to S. Agnese, built by the same emperor at the request of his daughter Constance. Who also is not aware that the font which served for the baptism of the latter and of one of her sisters, was ornamented with fragments of much greater antiquity? Such as the porphyry pillar carved with beautiful figures and some marble candelabra exquisitely carved with leaves, and children in bas-relief of extraordinary beauty? In short, by these and many other signs, it is clear to what an extent sculpture had declined in the time of Constantine, and with it the other superior arts. If anything was required to complete their ruin it was supplied by the departure of Constantine from Rome when he transferred the seat of government to Byzantium, as he took with him to Greece not only all the best sculptors and other artists of the age, such as they were, but also a quantity of statues and other beautiful works of sculpture.

After the departure of Constantine, the Cæsars whom he left in Italy were continually building in Rome and elsewhere, endeavouring to make their works as good as possible, but as we see, sculpture, painting and architecture were steadily going from bad to worse. This arose perhaps from the fact that when human affairs begin to decline, they grow steadily wore until the time comes when thy can no longer deteriorate any further. In the time of Pope Liberius, the architects of the day took considerable pains to produce masterpiece which they built S. Maria Maggiore, but they were not very happy in the result because although the building, which is mostly constructed of spoils, is of very fair proportions, it cannot be denied that, not to speak of other defects, the spaces running round the church above the columns, decorated with stucco and painting, are of very poor design, and that many other things to be seen there leave no doubt as to the imperfection of the arts. Many [9] years later, when the Christians were suffering persecution under Julian the Apostate, a church was erected on the Celian Hill to SS. John and Paul, the martyrs, in so inferior a style [built partly by reusing the walls of apartment blocks] to the others mentioned above that it is quite clear that at that time, art had all but entirely disappeared.

The edifices erected in Tuscany at the same time bear out this view to the fullest extent. To take one example among many: the church outside the walls of Arezzo, built to St. Donato, bishop of that city, who suffered martyrdom with Hilarion the monk, under the same Julian the Apostate, is in no way superior to those mentioned above. It cannot be contended that such a state of affairs was due to anything but the lack of good architects, since the church in question, which is still standing ["...destroyed in 1561..."], has eight sides, and was built of the spoils of the theatre, colosseums and other buildings erected in Arezzo before it was converted to the Christian faith. No expense was spared, and it was adorned with columns of granite, porphyry and variegated marble taken from ancient buildings. For my own part, I have no doubt, seeing the expense incurred, that if the Aretines had possessed better architects they would have produced something marvelous, since what they actually accomplished proves that they spared nothing in order to make this building as magnificence and compete as possible. But as architecture had lost less of its excellence than the other arts, as I have so often said before, some good things may be seen there. At the same period the church of S. Maria in Grado was enlarged in honour of St. Hilarion, who had lived in the city a long time before he accompanied Donato to receive the palm of martyrdom.

But as Fortune when she has brought men to the top of the wheel, either, for amusement or because she repents usually turns them to the bottom, it came to pass after these things that almost all the barbarian nations rose in diverse parts of the world against the Romans, the result being the speedy fall of that great empire, and the destruction of everything, notably of Rome herself. That fall involved the compete destruction of the most excellent artists, sculptors, painters and architects, burying them and their arts under the debris and ruin of that most celebrated city. The first to go were painting and sculpture, as being arts which served rather for pleasure than for utility, the other arts, namely architecture, being necessary and useful, for the welfare of the [10] body, continued in use, but not in its perfection and purity. The very memory of painting and sculpture would have speedily disappeared had they not represented before the eyes of the rising generations the distinguished men of another age who had been honoured thereby. Some of these were commemorated by effigies and by inscriptions placed on public and private buildings such as amphitheatres, theatres, baths, aqueducts, temples, obelisks, colosseums, pyramids, arches, reservoirs and treasuries, yes, and even on the very tombs. The majority of these were destroyed and obliterated by the savage barbarians, who had nothing human about them but their shape and name. Among the many others there were the Visigoths, who having made Alaric their king, invaded Italy and twice sacked Rome without respecting anything. The Vandals who cam from Africa with Genseric their king, did the like. But he, not content with his plunder and booty, to their infinite woe, and with them Eudoxia the wife of the Emperor Valentinian, who had only recently been assassinated by his own soldiers. These men had greatly degenerated from the ancient Roman valour, because a great while before, the best of them had all gone to Constantinople with the Emperor Constantine, and those left behind were dissolute and abandoned. Thus, true men an every sort of virtue perished at the same time; laws, habits, names and tongues suffered change, and these varied misfortunes, collectively and singly, debased and degraded very fine spirit and every lofty soul.

[*Christian Intolerance*]

But the most harmful and destructive force which operated against these fine arts was the fervent zeal of the new Christian religion, which, after long and sanguinary strife, had at length vanquished and abolished the old faith of the heathen, by means of a number of miracles and by the sincerity of its acts. Every effort was put forth to remove and utterly extirpate the smallest things from which errors might arise, and thus not only were the marvellous statues, sculptures, paintings, mosaics and ornaments of the false pagan gods destroyed and thrown down, but also the memorials and honours of countless excellent persons, to whose distinguished merits statues and other memorials had been set up in public by a most virtuous antiquity. Besides all this, in order to build churches for the use of the Christians, not only were the most honoured temples of the idols destroyed, but in order to ennoble and decorate S. Pietro with more ornaments than it then possessed, they took away the stone columns from the mole [tomb; 11] of Hadrian, now the castle of S. Angelo, as well as many other things which we now see in ruins. Now, although, the Christian religion did not act thus from any hatred for talent, but only in order to condemn and overthrow the heathen gods, yet the utter ruin of these honourable professions, which entirely lost their form, was none the less entirely due to this burning zeal.

That nothing might be wanting to these grave disasters there followed the rage of Totila against Rome, who destroyed the walls, ruined all the most magnificent and noble buildings with fire and sword, burned it from one end to another, and having stripped it of every living creature left it a prey to the flames, so that for the space of eighteen days not a living soul could be found there. He utterly destroyed the marvellous statues, paintings, mosaics and stuccos, so that he left Rome not only stripped of very trace of her former majesty, but destitute of shape and life. The ground floors of the palaces and other buildings had been adorned with painting, stuccos and statues, and these were burned under the debris, so that many good things have come to light in our own day. Those who came after, judging everything to be ruined, planted vineyards over them so that these ruined chambers remained entirely underground, and the moderns have called them grottos and the paintings found there grotesques.

[*Disorder*]

The Ostrogoths being exterminated by Narses, the runs of Rome were inhabited in a wretched fashion when after an interval of a hundred years there came the Emperor Constans II of Constantinople, who was received in a friendly manner by the Romans. However, he dissipated, plundered and carried away everything that had been left in the wretched city of Rome, abandoned rather by chance than by the deliberate purpose of those who had laid it waste. It is true that he was not able to enjoy this booty, for being driven to Sicily by a storm at sea, he was killed by his followers, a fate he richly deserved, and thus lost his spoils, his kingdom and his life. But as if the troubles of Rome had not been sufficient, for the thing which had been take away could never return, there came an army of Saracens to ravage that island, who carried away the property of the Sicilians, and the spoils of Rome to Alexandria, to the infinite shame and loss of Italy and of all Christendom. Thus, what the popes had not destroyed, notably St. Gregory, who is said to have put under the ban all that remained of the statues and of the spoils of the buildings, perished finally through the instrumentality of this traitorous Greek.

Not a trace or vestige of any good thing [12] remained, so that the generations which followed being rude and coarse particularly in painting and sculpture, yet feeling themselves impelled by nature and inspired by the atmosphere of the place, set themselves to produce things, not indeed according to the rules of art, for they had none, but as they were instructed by their own intelligence. The arts of design having arrived at this pitch, both before and during the time that the Lombards ruled Italy, they subsequently grew gradually worse and worse, until at length they reached the lowest depths of baseness. An instance of their utter tastelessness and crudity may be seen in some figures in the Byzantine style over the door in the portico of S. Pietro at Rome, in memory of some holy fathers who had disputed for Holy Church in certain council. Further evidence is supplied by a number of examples in the same style in the church in the whole of the Exarchate of Ravenna, notably some in S. Maria Rotonda outside that city ["Known to-day as the Mausoleum of Theoderic."], which were made shorty after the Lombards were driven from Italy. I will not deny that there is one very notable and marvellous thing in this church, and that is the vaulting or cupola which covers it which is ten braccia [c. 20 feet] across and serves as the roof of the building and yet is of a single piece and so large that it appears impossible that a stone of its description, weighing more than 200,000 pounds, could be placed so high up. But to return to our point, the masters of that day produced nothing but shapeless and clumsy things which may still be seen to-day. It was the same with architecture, so it was necessary to build, and as form and good methods were lost by the death of good artists and the destruction of good buildings, those who devoted themselves to this profession built erections devoid of order or measure, and totally deficient in grace, proportion or principle. Then new architects arose who created that style of building, from their barbarous nations, which we call Gothic, and produced some works which are ridiculous to our modern eyes, but appeared admirable to theirs.

This lasted until a better form somewhat similar to the good antique manner was discovered by better artists, as is shown by the oldest churches in Italy which are not antique, which were built by them, and by the palaces erected for Theoderic King of Italy, at Ravenna

Pavia, and Modena, though the style is barbarous and rather [13] rich and grand than well-conceived or really good. The same may be said of S. Stefano at Rimini and of S. Martino at Ravenna, of the church of S. Giovanni Evangelista in the same city built by Galla Pacidia about the year of grace 438 of S. Vitale which was built in the year 547, and of the abbey of Classi di fuori and indeed of any other monasteries and churches built after the time of the Lombards. All these buildings as I have said are great and magnificent, but the architecture is very rude.

Among these are many new abbeys in France built to St Benedict and the church and monastery of Monte Cassino, the church of S. Giovanni Battista at Monza built by that Theodelinda, Queen of the Goths, to whom St. Gregory the Pope wrote his dialogues. In this place that queen caused the history of the Lombards to be painted. We thus see that they shaved the backs of their heads, wore their hair thick in front and were dyed to the chin. Their clothes were of linen like those worn by the Angles and Saxons, and they wore a mantel of divers colours; their shoes were open to the toes and bound above with small leather straps.

Similar to the churches enumerated above were the church of S. Giovanni, Pavia, built by Gundeberga, daughter of Theodelinda, and the church of S. Salvatore in the same city, built by Aribert, the brother of the same queen, who succeed Rodoald, husband of Gundeberga, in the government; the church of S. Ambrogio at Pavia, built by Grimoald, King of the Lombards, who drove from the kingdom Aripert's son Pentharit. This Pentharit being restored to his throne after Grimoald's death built a nunnery at Pavia called the Monasterio Nuovo, in honour of our Lady and of St. Agatha, and the queen built another dedicated to the Virgin Mary in Pertica outside the walls. Cunipert, Pentharit's son, likewise built a monastery and church to St George called di Coronate in a similar style, on the spot where he had won a great victory over Alachis. Not unlike these was the church which the Lombard king Luitprand, who lived in the time of King Pepin, the father of Charlemagne, built at Pavia, called S. Pietro, in Cieldauro, or that which Desiderius, who succeeded Astolf, built to S. Piero Clivate in the diocese of Milan; or the monastery of S. Vincenzo at Milan, or that of S. Giulia at Brescia, because all of them were exceedingly costly, but in almost ugly and characterless style.

In Florence the style of architecture improved slightly somewhat later, the church of S. Apostolo built by Charlemagne, although small, being very beautiful, because the shafts of the columns, although [14] made up of pieces are very graceful and beautifully formed, and the capitals and the arches for the vaulting of the side aisles show that some good architecture wa left in Tuscany, or had arisen there. In fine the architecture of this church is such that Pippo di Ser Brunellesco did not distain to make use of it as his model in designing the churches of S. Spirito and S Lorenzo in the me city

The same progress may be noticed in the church of S. Marco at Venice, not to speak of that of S. Giorgio Maggiore erected by Giovanni Morosini in the year 978. S. Marco's was begun under the Doge Giustiniano and Gionvanni Particiaco near to S. Tedosio, when the body of the Evangelist was brought from Alexandria to Venice. After the Doge's palace and the church had suffered severely from series of fires, it w rebuilt upon the same foundations in the Byzantine style as it stands to-day, at a great cost and with the assistance of many architects, in the time of the Doge Domenico Selvo, in the year 973, the columns being brought from the place where they could be obtained. The construction continued until the year 1140., M. Piero Polani being then Doge, from the plans of several masters who were all Greeks, as I have said. Erected at the same time, and also in the Byzantine style, were the seven abbeys built in Tuscany by Count Hugh, Marquis of Brandenburg, such as the Badia of Florence, the abbey of Settimo, and the others. All these structures and the vestiges of others which are not standing bear witness to the fact that architecture maintained its footing though in a very bastard form far removed from the good antique style. Further evidence is afforded by a number of old palaces erected in Florence of Tuscan work after the destruction of Fiesole, but the measurements of the very elongated doors and the windows and the sharp pointed arches after the manner of the foreign architects of the day, denote some amount of barbarism.

[Influence of Pisa]

Subsequently, in 1013, the art appears to have received an access of vigour in the rebuilding of the beautiful church of S. Miniato on the Mount in the time of M. Alibrando, citizen and bishop of Florence, for in addition to the marble ornamentation both within and without, the façade shows that the Tuscan architects were making efforts to imitate, so far as they were able, the good ancient order in the door, windows columns, arches and cornices, which they perceived in part in [15] the ancient church of S. Giovanni [later the Baptistery] in their city. At the same period, pictorial art, which had all but disappeared, seems to have made some progress, as is shown by a mosaic in the principal chapel of the same church of S. Miniato.

From such beginnings design and a general improvement in the arts began to make headway in Tuscany, as in the year 1016 when the Pisans began to erect their Duomo. For at that time it was a considerable undertaking to build such a church, with its five aisles and almost entirely constructed of marble both inside and out. The church was built from the plans and under the direction of Buschetto, a Greek from Dulichium and a most remarkable architect for his time, was erected and adorned by the Pisans when at the zenith of their power with an endless quantity of spoils brought by sea from various distant parts, as the columns, bases, capitals, cornices and other stones there of every description, amply demonstrate. Now since all these things were of all sizes great, medium, and small, Buschetto displayed great judgment and skill in adapting them to their places, so that the whole building is excellently devised in every part, both within and without. Amongst other things he devised the façade very cleverly, which is made up of a series of stages gradually diminishing toward the top and consisting of a great number of columns, adorning it with other carved columns and antique statues. He carried out the principal doors of that façade in the same style, beside one of which, that of the Carroccio, he afterwards received honourable burial, with three epitphs, one being in Latin verse, not unlike other things of the time: *Quod vix mille boum possent juga juncta movere,/ Et quod vi x potuit per mare ferre ratis/ Buschetti nisu, quod erat mirabile visu/ Dena puellarum turba levavit onus.* As I have mentioned the church of S. Apostolo at Florence above I will here give an inscription which may be read on a marble slab on one of the sides of the high altar, which runs: *VIII. v. Die vi. Aprilis in resurrectione Domini Karolus Francorum Rex a Roma revertens ingressus Florentiam cum magno gaudio et tripudio succeptus, civium copiam torqueis aureis decoravit. Ecclesia Sanctorum Apostolorum in altari inclusa est lamina plumbea, in qua descripta apparent praefata fundatio et consecratio facta per Archiepiscopum Turpinum, testibus Rolando et Uliverio.*

The edifice of the Duomo at Pisa gave a new impulse to the minds of many men in all Italy, and especially in Tuscany, and [16] led to the foundation in the city of Pistoia in 1032 of the church of S. Paolo, in the presence of St. Atto, the bishop there, as a contemporary deed relates, and indeed of many other buildings, a mere mention of which would occupy too much space.

I must not forget t mention either, how in the course of time the round church of S. Giovanni was erected at Pisa in the year 1060, opposite the Duomo and n the same piazza. A marvellous and almost incredible statement in connection with this church is that of an ancient record in a book of the Opera of the Duomo, that the columns, pillars and vaulting were erected and completed in fifteen days and no more. The same book which may be examines by anyone relates that an impost of a penny a hearth was exacted for the building of the temple, but does not state whether this was to be of gold or of base metal. The same book states that there were 34,000 hearths in Pisa at that time. It is certain that the work wa very costly and presented formidable difficulties, especially the vaulting of the tribune, which is pear-shaped and covered outside with lead. The interior is full of columns, craving, scenes, and the middle part of the frieze of the doorway contains figures of Christ and the twelve apostles in half relief and in the Byzantine style.

About the same time, namely in 1061, the Lucchese, in emulation of the Pisans, began the church of S. Martino at Lucca, from the designs of some pupils of Buschetto, there being no other artists then in Tuscany. The façade has a marble portico in front of it containing many ornaments and carvings in honour of Pope Alexander II, who had been bishop of the city just before he was raised to the pontificate. Nine lines in Latin related the whole history of the building and of the Pope, repeated in some antique letters carved in marble between the doors of the portico. The façade also contains some figures and a number of scenes in half-relief under the portico relating to the life of St. Martin executed in marble and in the Byzantine style.

[*Continuing Byzantine Influence with Later Exceptions*]

But the best things there over one of the doors, were done by Niccola Pisano, 170 years later, and completed in 1233 as well be related in the proper place, Abellanato and Aliprando being the craftsmen at the beginning, as some letter carved in marble in the same place fully relate. The [17] figures by Niccola Pisano show to what an extent sculpture was improved by him. Most of the building erected in Italy from this time until the year 1250 were similar in character to these, for architecture made little or no apparent progress in all these years, but remained stationary, the same rude style being retained. Many examples of this may be seen to-day, but I will not now enumerate them, because I shall refer to them again as the occasion presents itself.

The admirable sculptures and painting buried in the ruins of Italy remained hidden or unknown to the men of this time who were engrossed in the rude productions of their own age, in which they used no sculpture or paintings except such as were produced by the old [Byzantine] artists of Greece, who still survived making images or clay or stone or painting grotesque figures and only colouring the general outline. These artists were invited to Italy for they were the best and indeed the only representative of their profession. With them they brought the mosaic sculpture, and painting as they understood them, and thus they taught their own rough and clumsy style to the Italians, who practised the art in this fashion up to a certain time, as I shall relate.

As the men of the age were not accustomed to see any excellence or greater perfection than the things thus produced they greatly admired them, and considered them to be the type of perfection, barbarous as they were. Yet some rising spirits aided by the quality of the air of certain places, so far purged themselves of this crude style that in 1250 Heaven took compassion on the fine minds that the Tuscan soil was producing every day, and directed them to the original forms. For although the preceding generation had before them the remains of arches, colossi, statues, pillars or carved stone columns which were left after the plunder ruin and fire which Rome had passed through yet they could neer make use of them or derive any profit from them until the period named. Those who came after were able to distinguish the good from the bad, and abandoning the old style they began to copy the ancients with all ardour and industry That the distinction I have made between old and ancient may be better understood, I will explain that I call ancient the things produced before Constantine at Corinth, Athens Rome and other renowned cities, until the days of Nero, Vespasian, Trajan, Hadrian and Antoninus; the old works were those which are due to the surviving Greeks from the days of S. Silvester whose art consisted rather of tinting than [18] of painting. For the original artists of excellence had perished in the wars as I have said and the surviving Greeks of the old and not the ancient manner, could only trace profiles on a ground of colour. Countless mosaics done by these Greeks in every part of Italy bear testimony to this and every old church of Italy possesses examples, notably the Duomo of Pisa, S. Marco at Venice and yet other places. Thus they produced a constant stream of figures in this style, with frightened eyes, outstretched hands and on the tips of their toes, as in S. Miniato outside Florence between the door of the sacristy and that of the convent, and in S. Spirito in the same city, all the sides of the cloister towards the church, and in Arezzo in S. Giuliano and S. Bartolommeo and other churches, and at Rome in old S. Pietro in the scenes about the windows all of which are more like monsters than the representation of anything existing.

They also produced countless sculptures, such as those in bas-relief still over the door of S. Michele on the piazza Pandella at Florence, in the Ognissanti, and in many places, in tombs and ornaments for the doors of churches, where there are some figures acting as corbels to carry the roof, of rude and coarse, so grossly made, and in such a rough style, that it is impossible to imagine worse.

Up to the present, I have discoursed upon the origin of sculpture and painting, perhaps more at length than was necessary at this stage. I have done so, not so much because I have been carried away by my love for the arts, as because I wish to be of service to the artists of our day, by showing them how a small beginning leads to the highest elevation, and how from so noble a situation it is possible to fall to uppermost ruin, and consequently how these arts resemble nature as shown in our human bodies; and have their birth, growth, age, and death, and I hope by this means they will be enabled more easily to recognise the progress of the renaissance of the arts and the perfection to which they have attained in our own time. And again, if ever it happens, which God forbid, that the arts should once more fall to a like ruin and disorder through the negligence of man, the malignity of the age, or the decree of Heaven, which does not appear to wish that the things of the world should remain stationary, these labours of mine, such as they are (if they are worthy of a happier fate), by means of the things discussed before, and by those which remain to be said, may maintain the arts in life, or, at any rate, encourage the better spirits to provide them with every [19] assistance, so that, by my good will and the labors of such men, they may have an abundance of those aids and embellishments which, if I may speak the truth freely, they have lacked until now.

[*Revival of the Ancient Approach*]

But it is now time to come to the life of Gionvanni Cimabue, who originated the new method of design and painting, so that it is right that this should be the first of the Lives. And here I may remark that I shall follow the schools rather than a chronological order. And in describing the appearance and the features of the artists, I shall be brief, because their portraits which I have collected at great expense, and with much labour and diligence, will show what manner of men they were to look at much better than any description could ever do. IF some portraits are missing, that is not my fault, but because they are not to be found anywhere. If it chance that some of the portraits do not appear to be exactly like the others which are extant, it is necessary to reflect that a portrait of a man of eighteen or twenty years can never be like one made fifteen or twenty years later, and, in addition to this, portraits in black and white are never so good s those which are coloured, besides which the engravers, who do not know design, always take something from the form, because they are never able to reproduce those small details which constitute the excellence of a work, or to copy that perfection which is rarely, if ever, to be found in wood engravings. To conclude, the reader will be able to appreciate the amount of labour, expense, and care which I have bestowed upon this matter when he sees that I have got the best that I could.

Introduction to Part II

(Translated by A. B. Hinds, 1927; reprinted in Vasari 1568: 201-209; divided into paragraphs)

When I first undertook to write these *Lives* I did not propose to make a mere list of the artists with an inventory, so to speak, of their works. I should not considerer it a worthy end of all my labours, which, if not distinguished, have certainly been long and tedious, merely to find out their numbers, their names and countries, and to relate in what cities or places their paintings, sculptures or buildings may now be found. This I could have done by a mere table without introducing my own criticisms anywhere. But I have remarked that those historians who are proclaimed by common consent to have written with the best judgment have not been contented with confining themselves to a bare narration of facts, but with all diligence and the utmost curiosity they have investigated the motives, the methods, and the lives of the worthies of old in the management of their affairs, have taken pains to point out their errors, their fine strokes, their expedients, and the prudent course sometimes taken in the management of affairs, and, in short, all that they have done, wisely or negligently, with prudence, reverence, or generosity. Such are the methods of those who regard history as the mirror of human life, not merely to write down a dry record of the events which happen to a prince or to a republic, but to set forth the opinions, counsels, decisions and plans of men, the causes which lead to successful or unsuccessful action. This is the true spirit of a history that really teaches men how to live, and renders them prudent; and this, next to the pleasure derived from seeing things both past and present, is the true end of history. For these reasons I have undertaken to write the history of the finest artists, in order, first, to assist the arts to the utmost of my power, and next, to honour them, so that so far as I am able I have adopted this method in imitation of the great historians. Thus, I have endeavoured not only to relate what the artists have done, but I have tried to distinguish the good from the better, and the best from the medium work, to note somewhat carefully the methods, manners, processes, behaviour and ideas of the painters and sculptors [201], investigating into the causes and roots of things, and of the improvement and decline of the arts which took place t divers times and in divers persons for the benefit of those who cannot do so for themselves.

At the beginning of these Lives I spoke of the nobility and antiquity of these arts, as was suitable at that stage, passing by many things of Pliny and other authors of which I might have made use, if I had not been anxious, perhaps against the judgment of many, to leave everyone free to see for himself the fancies of others in their proper setting. It now appears to me that the present opportunity is a fitting one to do what I could not do then, if I wished to avoid tediousness and length fatal to the attention I desire, namely, to disclose my purpose and intention more carefully, and to show to what end I have divided the body of these Lives into three parts. It is very true that some excel in the arts by diligence, some by study, some by imitation, and others again by a knowledge of the sciences, which are all useful aids, while some unite all these attributes or the greater number of them; but here I will deal only in generalities, because in the individual Lives I have said enough of the methods, arts, manners, and the causes of good, superior and pre-eminent workmanship, and I will review the matter generally, considering rather the nature of the times than the persons, whom I have divided into three parts, or ages if you will, in order not to push the investigation too far, from the renaissance of the arts until the century in which we live, differing from each other in a very marked manner.

[Development of Renaissance Art]
[A1] Thus, in the first and earliest period the three arts are seen to be very far from perfection and though they possess some amount

of excellence, yet this is accompanied by such imperfections that they certainly do not merit extravagant praise. But since they prepared the way and formed the style for the better work which followed, it is not possible to say anything but good of them, and I must give them rather more glory than their works deserved in themselves, and than if it was necessary to judge them by the perfect rules of the art.

[A2] In the second part there is a manifest improvement both in the inventions and in the execution, with more design, a better style and greater finish, the roughness of the old style being both rid of, and that rudeness and want of proportions which the grossness of the time had brought in its train.

[A3] But who will venture to say that anyone perfect in everything was found in this [second] period, who produced things equal to the present state of invention, design and colouring? Who has observed in them the soft shading away of the figures with the dark [202] coloring, the light being left on the prominent parts only, and who has seen there the perforation and fine finishing of the marble statues which are done to-day? This praise certainly belongs alone to the third period, of which I may safely say that art has done everything that is permitted to an imitator of Nature, and that it has risen so high that its decline must now be feared rather than any further progress expected.

Turning these things over carefully in my mind, I conclude that it is a property and peculiarity of these arts that from a humble beginning they gradually improve and attain the summit of perfection. I am led to believe this by an observation of the same phenomena in the other liberal arts, and the fact that there is a species of relationship between them in an argument of its truth. The fate of painting and sculpture in the ancient times must have been so similar that with a change of names their cases would be exactly alike.

[Development of Ancient Sculpture]

[B1] If we may credit those who live near those times, and who were able to see and judge the labours of the ancients, the statues of Canachus were very hard and without any vivacity or movement, and withal considerably removed from the truth; the same is said of those of Calamides, although they were somewhat smoother.

[B2] Myron followed, and although he did not precisely imitate the truth of Nature, yet he endowed his works with such excellent proportion and grace that they might, without exaggeration, be termed beautiful.

[B3] In the third degree of succession came Polycletus and the other renowned men who are said to have attained absolute perfection, as were are bound to believe.

[Development of Ancient Painting]

[C1] The same progress, again, must have taken place in painting, because it is said that the works of those who painted in a single colour, and who were called Mono-chromatists, did not attain to a high state of perfection, and we may readily believe this.

[C2] In the succeeding works of Zeuxis, Polygnotus, Timanthes, and the rest, who only employed four colours, the lineaments, outlines and forms are unreservedly praised, though doubtless they left something to be desired.

[C3] But in the productions of Erione, Nicomachus, Protogenes and Apelles everything is so perfect and beautiful that one can perceive nothing better, for they not only painted the form and gestures of the body with the highest excellence, but the emotions and passions in addition. But I pass these by, for we are forced to estimate them by the opinions of others, who frequently do not agree, the very dates being uncertain, although in this matter I have followed the best authors.

We now come to out [203] own day, I which the eye is a considerably better guide and judge than the ear.

[A1a. Precursors of Renaissance Architecture]

To take one subject, is it not manifest what improvements and advances have been made in architecture from the time of Buschetto the Greek to that of Arnolfo the German and of Giotto [as an architect]? The buildings of the day show this, in the churches, pilasters, columns, bases, capitals, and all the cornices with their formless members, such as those of S. Maria del Fiore at Florence, the incrustation of the exterior of S. Giovanni, S. Miniato, the

Vescovado of Fiesole, the Duomo of Milan, S. Vitale of Ravenna, S. Maria Maggiore at Rome, and the old Duomo outside Arezzo, where apart from some good remnants of antique fragments, there is nothing well ordered or executed. But those two men [Arnolfo and Giotto] introduced improvements, so that the art made no little progress under them, for their improved the proportions, and not only made the buildings stable and strong, but also in some measure ornate, though to be sure their ornaments are confused and very imperfect, and, if I may say so, not very decorative. For in their columns they did not observe the measurements and proportions required by the art, nor did they distinguish the orders, so that there were not distinctively Doric, Corinthian, Ionic, or Tuscan, but mixed after a rule of their own which consisted of absence of rule. They made them very thick or very slender, as it happened to suit their purpose. Their invention proceeded in part from their own brains and in part from remnants of antiquity which they had seen. Their plans were partly borrowed from good sources and partly the accretions of their own fancies, so that when the walls were erected they had a different form. Yet anyone who compares these things with those which preceded them will remark an improvement in every particular and will observe certain things which are somewhat out of favour in our day, such as some small examples of brick covered with stucco at S. Giovanni Lateran at Rome

[A1b. Precursors of Renaissance Sculpture]
I make the same observations with regard to sculpture, which in the first age of its renaissance had some excellences, for it had shaken off the rude Byzantine style which wa so rough that it smacked far more of the quarry than of the talent of the artist, the statues being utterly devoid of folds, pose, or movement, and hardly worthy to be called statues. Afterwards, when designs had been improved by Giotto, marble and stone figures were also greatly improved by such men as Andrea Pisano, his son Nino, and his other pupils, who were far better than their predecessors. They endowed their statues with more 204] flexibility and set them in considerably improved postures, as did the two Sienese, Agostino and Agnolo, who, as I have said, made the tomb of Guido, bishop of Arezzo, and also those Germans who made the façade of Orvieto. Thus, sculpture manifestly made some progress at this time, the figures receiving a better form and a better arrangement of folds and draperies, some of the heads a better carriage, while the attitudes were less stiff, so that, in short there is a sign of an attempt to reach the good. But nevertheless they fell far short of it, because the art of design was not then very perfect, and there was no great number of good works for the to imitate. Accordingly, the masters of that day, whom I have put in the first part, merit praise and esteem for their production, because it must be remembered that they, as well as the architects and painters of the time, had no assistance from their predecessors, and were obliged to find a way for themselves; and a beginning, however poor, is always worthy of praise by no means poor.

[A1c. Precursors of Renaissance Painting]
Painting enjoyed little better fortune at this time, except that it was more practised owing to its popularity with the people, so that it had more professors who thus made more evident progress than was perceived in the other two arts. Thus, we see that the original Byzantine style was entirely abandoned, at first through the efforts of Cimabue and then by the help of Giotto. From it arose a new style which I like to call Giotto's, because it was introduced by him and his pupils, and was afterwards universally admired and imitated. In this the profile surrounding the whole figure is abandoned, as well as the lustreless eyes, the tip-toed feet, the attenuated hands, the absence of shadow, and all the other Byzantine absurdities, which were replaced by graceful heads and beautiful colouring. Giotto in particular improved the attitudes of the figures, and began to give a measure of vivacity to the heads and folds to the draperies, which made a closer approach to nature than is seen in the work of his predecessors, while he partially discovered the art of foreshortening figures. He also was the first to express the emotions, so that fear, hope, rage and love may be recognised. He rendered his style smooth where it was originally uneven and rugged, and if he did not in giving his eyes the beautiful expression of

life, or the right expressions to his weeping figures, or make his hair pretty, his beards downy, his hands knotty and muscular, or his nudes like the reality, he must be excused on account of the difficulty of the art, and because he had not seen any painters better than himself. Amid the general [205] poverty of art everyone can grasp the excellence of his judgment displayed in his works, his observation of expression and his ready following of Nature, for his figures naturally perform what they have to do and prove that his judgment, if not perfect, was very good. The same qualities appear subsequently in the others, as in the colouring of Taddeo Gaddi, which is softer and more forceful, has better flesh-tints and better coloured draperies, while the movements of the figures are more powerful. Simon of Siena excelled in the composition of scenes, Stefano Scimmia... and Tommaso introduced great improvements in design, in new ideas in perspective, and in shading and harmonizing the colours, while adhering steadily to Giotto's style. A like amount of skill and dexterity was exhibited by Spinello of Arezzo, Parri his son, Jacopo di Casentino, Antonio of Venice, Lippi, and Gherardo Starnini, and the other painters who laboured after Giotto, following his expressions, lineaments, colouring and style, making some improvements it is true, but not to such an extent as to make it appear that they wished to introduce another method.

[A1. Conclusions on the Precursors of the Renaissance]

Thus, anyone who had followed my argument will see that the three arts were, so to speak, merely sketched up to this point, and that they lacked much of the perfections which belongs to them, and if there had been no improvement to follow, the advances they made would have been of little service, and would not have been worthy of much esteem. I hope that no one will believe me to be so gross or of so little judgment as not to be aware that the things of Giotto, of Andrea Pisano, of Nino, or all the rest, whom I have put together in the first part on account of their resemblance in style would deserve more than a moderate amount of praise if they were to be compared with the works produced after their time. I was well aware of this when I praised them. But those who take into consideration the nature of their age, the scarcity of artists, the difficulty of obtaining good assistance, will consider them not merely beautiful, as I have said, but miraculous, and will take infinite pleasure in noticing the first efforts and those sparks of excellence which begin to appear in their paintings and sculpture. The victory of L. Marcius in Spain was not of such great importance as many of the triumphs of the Romans, but considering the time, the place, the circumstances, the persons, and the numbers, it was considered stupendous and worthy to this day of praises which [206] are lavishly bestowed upon it by the historians. For all these reasons I have considered that these artists deserve not only a careful account from me, but all the praise which I have so readily and sincerely bestowed upon them. It seemed to me that it would not be displeasing to artists to hear these Lives and to examine the methods and styles of those men, and possibly they may draw no small advantage from them. If so, I shall be greatly delighted, and shall consider it a rich reward for this labour, in which it has been my sole object to serve and please them to the extent of my powers.

[A2. Early Renaissance]

Having now, if I may say so, taken these three arts from the nurse, and having passed the age of childhood, there follows the second period in which a notable improvement may be remarked in everything. The inventions are more lavish with figures, richer in ornament, design is more firmly grounded and more natural and life-like, while even in the works executed with less skill there is purpose and thought expressed with diligence, the style is lighter, the colours more charming, so that little is wanting of complete perfection, and the truth of Nature is exactly imitated.

[A2a. Early Renaissance Architecture]

In the first place, by means of the study and diligence of the great Filippo Brunelleschi, architecture once again discovered the measurements and proportions of the ancients, as well in the round columns as in the square pilasters and in the rough and the polished corners; order is distinguished from order, the difference between the being made apparent, matters are arranged to proceed according to rule with more order, things are partitioned out by measure, design shows increased power and method, gracefulness pervades everything and exhibits the excellence of the art, the beauty and variety of capitals and cornices are rediscovered, so that the plans of churches and other buildings are well conceived, the buildings themselves being ornate, magnificent and in proportion,

An example is afforded by the stupendous cupola of S. Maria del Fiore at Florence, in the beauty and grace of its lantern, in the varied and gracefully decorated church of S. Spirito, in the no less beautiful S. Lorenzo, in the curious invention of the octagonal church of the Angioli, in the airy church and convent of the abbey at Fiesole, and in the magnificent and grandiose commencement of the palace of the Pitti, not to speak of the convenient and commodious erection due to Francesco di Giorgio of the palace and church of the Duomo of Urbino...., the rich an powerful castle of Naples, the impregnable [207] castle of Milan, and many other notable buildings of that time. These works may safely be called beautiful and good, although they do not yet possess that fitness and a certain exquisite grace and finish of the cornices, with delicate and light methods of marking leaves, and in making the extremities of foliage, and other perfections which came afterwards, and will be seen in the third part, which will contain those who surpassed the other architects of old in perfection, grace, finish, fertility and dexterity.

I cannot call it perfect at this [second] state, although certainly beautiful and good, became improvements were afterwards made in it so I think I may reasonably assert that something was still lacking. Certainly, there were some things truly miraculous which have not been excellent even in our own day, and perhaps never will be; such, for example, as the lantern of the cupola of S. Maria del Fiore, and the cupola itself as regards its size, where Filippo not only dared to equal the ancients in the body of the building, but to surpass them in the height of the walls. Nevertheless, as we are dealing in generalities, the perfection and excellence of a single thing must not be advanced to prove the excellence of all.

[A2. Early Renaissance Art]
The same applies to painting and to sculpture also, in which we may see to-day works of rare excellence by masters of this second period, such as those of Masaccio in the Carmine, who painted a naked man shivering with cold, produced other vigourous and spirited works, but as a general rule they did not attain to the state of perfection of the third age, of which I shall speak when the time comes. Here I must confine myself to the men of the second period.

[A2b. Early Renaissance Sculpture]
To speak in the first place of the sculptors who made such great advances on the early style that they left little for the third period to complete. They introduced so much more grace, nature, order, design and proportion into their works that their statues begin to appear almost like living persons and not mere statues as the first ones were. This will be seen in the second part, where the figures of Jacopo dalla Quercia of Siena possess more movement, grace, design and diligence, those of Filippo [Brunelleschi] a better knowledge of the muscles, better proportions and more judgment, and those of their pupils exhibit the same qualities. But Lorenzo Ghiberti added yet more in his production of the doors of S. Giovanni [the Baptistery] in which he displayed his invention, order, style and design, so that his figures seem to move and breathe. Although Donato [Donatello] lived at the same time, I am uncertain whether I ought not to place him in the third period, since his works are up to the level of [208] the good antiques; placed in the second period, I may call him the standard of the others, because he combined in his person all the qualities which were distributed among many others, for he imparted to his figures a movement, life and reality which make them worthy to rank with modern works, and even with those of antiquity, as I have said.

[A2c. Early Renaissance Painting]
At this time also, painting made equal advances, and in this art Masaccio entirely freed himself from Giotto's style, his heads, draperies, buildings, nudes, colouring and foreshortening being in a new manner, introducing that modern

style which has been adopted by all our artists from that time to our own day, embellished and enriched from time to time with additional graces, invention and ornaments. This will be seen when we are are dealing with the separate Lives, where we shall meet with new method of colouring, of foreshortening, natural attitudes, a much better expression of the emotions of the e spirit and of the gestures of the body, joined to a constant endeavour to get nearer to the truth of Nature in design, while the faces are exactly like those of men as they were seen and known by the artists. Thus, they sought to reproduce what they saw in Nature and no more, and thus they came to considerer more closely and understand more fully. This encouraged them to make rules for perspective, and to get their foreshortening in the exact form of natural relief, proceeding to the observation of shadows and lights, shading and other difficulties, composing their scenes with greater regard for probability, attempting to make their landscapes more like reality, as well as the trees, grass, flowers, air, clouds and other natural phenomena, so that it may be said without fear of contradiction that the arts were not only improved, but have reached the flower of their youth, giving promise of fruit in the future, that they would soon attain to their age of perfection.

And now with Gods help I shall begin the Life of Jacopo dalla Quercia of Siena, to be followed by those of other architects and sculptors until we come to Masaccio, who was the first to improve design in painting, when we shall see what a debt is due to him for his new discovery. I have chosen Jacopo as a worthy beginning for this second part, and shall follow the order of styles, showing in each life the difficulties presented by their beautiful, difficult and most honourable arts [209].

Introduction to Part III

(Translated by A. B. Hinds, 1927; reprinted in Vasari 1568: II, 151-155; divided into paragraphs)

Those masters whose Lives we have written in the second part made substantial additions to the arts of architecture, painting and sculpture, improving on those of the first art in [1] rule, [2] order, [3] proportion, [4] design and [5] style. If they were not altogether perfect, they came so near the truth, that the third category of whom we are now to speak, profited by the light they shed and attained the summit of perfection, producing the more valuable and renowned modern works. But in order that the nature of these improvements may be better appreciated, I will describe in a few words the five points already enumerated and relate succinctly the source of that excellence which, by surpassing the achievements of the ancients, has rendered the modern age so glorious.

[1.] Rule in architecture is the measurement of antique, following the plans of ancient buildings in making modern ones.

[2.] Order is the differentiation of one kind from another so that everybody shall have its characteristic parts, and that the Doric, Ionic, Corinthian and Tuscan shall no longer be mingled indiscriminately.

[3.] Proportion in sculpture, as in architecture, is the making of the bodies of figures upright, the members being properly arranged, and the same in painting.

[4.] Design is the imitation of the most beautiful things in nature in all figures whether painted or chiseled, and this requires a hand and genius to transfer everything which the eye sees, exactly and correctly, whether it be in drawing, on paper, panel, or other surface, both in relief and sculpture.

[5.] Style is improved by frequently copying the most beautiful things, and by combining the finest members whether hands, heads, bodies or legs, to produce a perfect figure, which, being introduced in every work and in every figure, form what is known as a fine style.

[Period I: Late Medieval:] Giotto and the early artists did not do this, although they had discovered the principles of every difficulty and superficially treated them, as, for example, in [152] drawing more correctly than had been done before and in approaching nature more nearly in blending colours, in the composition of figures in scenes, and many other things, of which enough has been said.

[Period II: Early Renaissance:] But although the artists of the second period made great additions to the arts in all these particulars, yet they did not attain to the final stage of perfection, for they lacked a freedom, which, while outside the rules, was guided by them, and which was not incompatible with order and correctness. This demanded a prolific invention and the beauty of the smallest details. In proportion they lacked good judgment which, without measure in the dimensions chosen. They did not attain to the zenith of design because, although they made their arms round and their legs straight, they were not skilled in the muscles, and lacked that graceful and sweet ease which is partly seen and partly felt in matters of flesh and living things, but they were crude and stunted, their eyes being difficult and their style hard. Moreover, they did not possess that lightness of touch in making all their figures slender and graceful, especially the women and infants, who should be rendered as truthfully as the men, while avoiding coarseness so that they may not be clumsy, as in nature, but refined by design and good judgment. Their draperies lacked beauty, their fancies variety, their coloring charm, their buildings diversity and their landscapes distance and variety. Although many of them, like Andrea Verrocchio, Antonio del Pollajuolo and others of more recent date endeavoured to improve the design of their figures by more study while approaching nature more closely, yet they were not quite sure of their ground. However, their work would bear comparison with the antique, as we see by

Verrocchio's restoration of the marble legs and arms of the Marsyas of the Casa Medici at Florence. They also lacked finish and perfection in feet, hands, hair, beards, and did not make all the members correspond to the antique with their proper proportions. If they had possessed this finish, which is the perfection and flower of the arts, they would have also possessed a resolute boldness in their work, and would have obtained a lightness, polish and grace to which they did not attain, despite all their efforts which gave the supreme result of art to fine figures, whether in relief or painted. That finish and assurance which they lacked they could not readily attain by study, which has a tendency to render the style dry when it becomes an end in itself. The other were able [153] to attain it after they had seen some of the finest works mentioned by Pliny dug out of the earth: the Laocoon, the Hercules, the great torso of Belvedere, the Venus, the Cleopatra, the Apollo, and endless others, which are copied in their softness and in their hardness from the best living examples, with actions which do not distort them, but give them motion and display the utmost grace. This removed a certain dryness and crudeness caused by overmuch study, observable in Piero della Francesca, Lazzaro Vasari, Alesso Baldovinetti, Andrea del Castagno, Pesello, Ercole Ferrarese, Giovan. Bellini, Cosimo Rosselli, the abbot of S. Clemente, Domenico del Ghirlandajo, Sandro Botticello, Andrea Mantegna, Filippo ["Lippi"] and Luca Signorelli. All of these endeavoured to attain the impossible by their labours, especially in foreshortening and unpleasant objects, but the effort of producing that was too apparent in the result. Thus, although most were well designed and flawless, vigour was invariably absent from them, and they lacked a soft blending of colour, first observable in Francia of Bologna and Pietro Perugino. The people, when they beheld the new and living beauty, ran madly to see it, thinking that it would never be possible to improve upon it.

[Period III: Late Reniassance:] But the works of Lionardo da Vinci clearly proved how much they erred, for he began the third style, which I will call modern, notable for boldness of design, the subtlest imitation of Nature in trifling details, good rule, better order, correct proportion, perfect design and divine grace, prolific and diving to the depths of art, endowing his figures with motion and breadth. Somewhat later followed Giorgione da Castel Franco, who gave tone to his pictures and endowed his things with tremendous life by means of the well-managed depth of the shadows. No less skillful in imparting to his works force, relief, sweetness and grace was Fra Bartolommeo of S. Marco, but the most graceful of all was Raphael of Urbino, who, studying the labours of both the ancient and the modern masters, selected the best from each, and out of his garner enriched the art of painting with that absolute perfection which the figures of Apelles and Zeuxis anciently possessed, and even more, if I may say so. Nature herself was vanquished by his colours, and his invention was facile and appropriate, as anyone may judge who has seen his works, which are like writings, showing us the sites and the buildings, and the ways and habits of native and foreign peoples just as he desired. Besides the grace of his heads, whether young or old, men or women, he represented the modest [154] with modesty, the bold as bold, and his infants sometimes with mischievous and sometime with playful eyes. His draperies are neither too simple nor too involved, but simply natural. Andrea del Sarto followed him in this manner, but with softer and less bold colouring, and it may be said that he was a rare artist because his works are faultless. It is impossible to describe the delicate vivacity which characterizes the work of Antonio da Correggio. He depicted hair in a manner unknown before, for it had previously been made hard and dry, while his was soft and downy, the separate hairs polished so that they seemed of gold and more beautiful than natural ones, which were surpassed by his colouring. Francesco Mazola Parmigiano did the like, surpassing him in many respects in grace, ornament and fine style, as many of his painting show, the faces laughing, the eyes speaking, the very pulses seeming to beat, just as his brush pleased. An examination of the wall-paintings of Polidoro and Maturino will show how marvellous are their figures, and the beholder will wonder how they have been able to produce those stupendous works, not by speech, which is easy, but with the brush, as they have done in their skillful representations of the deeds of the Romans.

How many are there among the dead whose colours have endowed their figures with such life as is imparted by Il Rosso, Fra Sebastiano, Giulio Romano, Perino del Vaga, not to speak of the many celebrated living men. But the important fact is that art has been brought to such perfection to-day, design, invention and colouring coming easily to those who posses them, that where the first masters took six years to paint one picture, our masters to-day would only take one year to paint six, as I am firmly convinced both from observation and experience; and many more are now completed than the masters of former days produced.

But the man who bears the palm of all ages, transcending and eclipsing all the rest, is the divine Michelagnolo Buonarroti, who is supreme not in one art only but in all three at once. He surpasses not only all those who have, as it were surpassed Nature, but the most famous ancients also, who undoubtedly surpassed her. He has proceeded from conquest to conquest never finding a difficulty which he cannot easily overcome by force of his divine genus, by his industry, design, art, judgment and grace, and this not only in painting and in colours, comprising all forms and bodies, straight and not straight palpable and impalpable, visible and invisible, but in the extreme rotundity of his statues. [155] With the point of his chisel and by his fruitful labours he has spread his branches far, and filled the world with more delicious fruit than the three noble arts had produced before, in such marvellous perfection that it may well and safely be said that his statues are in every respect much finer than the ancient ones, as he knew how to select the most perfect members, arms, hands, heads, feet, form them into a perfect whole, with the most complete grace and absolute perfection, the very difficulties appearing easy in his style, so that it is impossible ever to see better. If by chance other were any works of the most renowned Greeks and Romans which might be brought forward for comparison, his sculptures would only gain in value and renown as their manifest superiority to those of the ancients became more apparent.

But if we so greatly admire those who devoted their lives to their work, when induced by extraordinary rewards and great happiness, what must we say of the men who produced such precious fruit not only without regard but in miserable poverty? It is believed that if there were just rewards in our age we should become undoubtedly greater and better than the ancients ever were. But the necessity of fighting against famine rather than for fame crushes men of genius and prevents the from becoming known, which is a shame and disgrace to those who could improve their condition and will not. Let this suffice; it is now time to turn to the Lives and treat separately all those who have produced celebrated woks in this third style. The first of these was Lionardo aa Vinci, with whom we now being.

Appendix III

Latin Literature and the Latin Church: the Survival of Knowledge During the Medieval Period

The first seven hundred years of the history of Roman civilization were discussed in the history written by Livy, who began with the founding of Rome and continued down to 9 B. C. Altogether, Livy wrote 142 books (scrolls), and if his entire history had survived, it would have filled about 50 printed volumes. Three-fourths of it did not survive. Altogether, only 35 of Livy's 142 books survived the Middle Ages. Of this total of 35 books, 10 continued to exist in a single manuscript that had been written before the end of the Antiquity and that was not discovered until 1527. An additional 10 books were erased so that the parchment they had been written on could be reused for religious writings. The almost completely obliterated text of those 10 books was not made legible until chemical reagents were used in the 19th Century.

There is no evidence that any of Livy's work was recopied from the end of Antiquity until the Carolingian Renaissance. When the portion of his history that had survived the Dark Ages--the period from the 5th through the 8th Centuries--began to be recopied, the ancient manuscripts were discarded, erased, or reused for rebinding books and lining shelves and boxes.[1]

Although Livy's work was exceptionally long, it was also exceptionally important. There were few Latin writings that would be more useful for the modern world to have. His accomplishment was admired as long as the Roman Empire existed, and it has been admired since the Renaissance, but it was so unappreciated during the Middle Ages that little was done to help preserve it. What was preserved is a random selection.

Shorter works by other Latin historians fared little better. Tacitus began his histories of the Roman Empire where Livy left off, and altogether he wrote 30 books (scrolls), of which about 17 survived. Of his *Histories,* somewhat less than five books survived in a single late Medieval manuscript. Of his *Annales,* 12 books survived, six in a single Carolingian manuscript and six in the unique late Medieval manuscript that contains the *Histories*. Had those two manuscripts been destroyed, almost nothing of the work of Tacitus would have survived.[2]

Some historians who wrote in Latin survived more nearly intact, such as Caesar and Suetonius, but most did not. By contrast, most historians who wrote in Greek fared better. We have essentially intact histories by Herodotus, Thucydides, Xenophon, and Arrian, and an immense amount of history was preserved in the monumental biography of Plutarch, which survived despite its large size. These Greek works survived in the Byzantine Empire, where the political situation was not only more stable, but was less controlled by religion. In the West, where the Latin Church increasingly exercised both secular and religious powers, including control over most education, much Latin literature did not survive as a direct result. The Latin Church had little interest in pagan history and less interest in every other aspect of pagan civilization, and there was no reason, considering its purpose, why it should have taken an interest. What did survive of Latin literature survived largely despite the indifference or hostility of the Church.

Ancient Manuscripts
Parchment was used to copy most of the manuscripts that have survived from late

Antiquity, and it is an unusually permanent material. Unlike papyrus or paper, parchment does not burn readily, and it is resistant to water damage.[3]

A parchment manuscript had a good chance of surviving indefinitely so long as it had minimal protection from insects, rodents, and monks. Insects and rodents might consume it and monks erase it. Many parchment pages show evidence of having been partly eaten away, but the codex form of books helped to protect all but the margins. Many more books show evidence of having been intentionally erased so that the parchment could be reused, and when it was reused, it was nearly always for religious texts.[4]

Of the two dozen or so major Latin authors, we would have about one-fourth of their most important works if we had to rely solely on what survived without having been copied after Antiquity. We would have, for example, substantial portions of the writings of Cicero, Livy, Plautus, Pliny the Elder, Terence, and Virgil.[5] It is evident from this list that the authors which survived more or less on their own were the ones that were most widely read and most extensively copied during Antiquity, and consequently, from the many copies that were made, at least a few survived every kind of accidental or intentional damage. There was, though, a large element of randomness in what survived. Of Cicero's works, for example, his more important *De Republica* survived in only one incomplete copy that was almost entirely erased while his less important *Letters to Atticus* also survived in an essentially intact copy.[6]

Nearly three-fourths of the major works of Latin writers would survive through copies made during the Carolingian Age. Since virtually no copying was done during the 6th through the 8th Centuries, it is all but certain that these 9th Century copies were made directly from ancient copies. The ancient copies might well have survived if they had not been recopied and then discarded.[7] Authors whose major works survive in copies made during the 9th Century are Caesar, Horace, Juvenal, Lucan, Lucretius, Martial, Ovid, Petronius, Pliny the Younger, Quintilian, Sallust, Statius, Valerius, Maximus, and Vitruvius.[8]

During the 4th and 5th Centuries, much pagan literature continued to be studied and copied, and pagan schools were probably responsible. Secular education continued in Rome at least until the 6th Century. St. Gregory (Pope Gregory the Great) wrote that St. Benedict of Nursia (founder of the Benedictine Order) abandoned his secular studies in Rome in c. 500:

> ...when he saw that many of the students rushed headlong into vice, he withdrew from the world he had just entered, lest, in acquiring worldly knowledge, he might also fall down the same terrific precipice. Despising, therefore, the study of letters, he desired only to please God by a hold life. Accordingly, he departed from Rome skillfully ignorant and wisely unlearned.[9]

Around the middle of the 6th Century, Cassiodorus noted that not only were the classics still being taught in Rome, they were being taught effectively:

> When I saw the great longing to study profane letters, so great that many men thought of attaining the wisdom of the world by them, I admit I was quite saddened to see that the Divine Scriptures were not publicly taught, whereas brilliant teaching made the profane authors celebrated.[10]

St. Gregory himself in letters written during his pontificate (590-604) refers to "'worldly wisdom' that was being taught to children for a price."[11]

Elsewhere in about the middle of the 6th Century, public education also continued to exist. Instruction in grammar, rhetoric, and law was being offered in Ravenna. Classical literature was being taught in Marsailles.[12] Secular instruction continued in Gaul at least until the beginning of the 7th Century, and to a limited degree it continued in Italy throughout the Middle Ages.[13] Some persons from the West had access to the classics while visiting or residing in Byzantium. St. Gregory resided there for some years, but he is unlikely to have taken advantage of this opportunity.

Even some new work was produced by writers during the early years of the 6th Century. Boethius (c. 480-524), who was consul in 510, wrote original treatises on a wide variety of subjects, and his translations of Plato and Aristotle were almost all of these writer's works available to the West during the Middle Ages. At least eight manuscripts of Virgil and 14 of Cicero were copied during the 5th Century and then were probably not recopied for three centuries.[14] Latin literature continued to be edited to combine the readings of many manuscripts to produce a version as close as possible to the author's intentions. For example, a copy of Virgil contains corrections by Turcius Rufius Apronianius Asterius, who was consul in 494.[15] There was thus a break in the creation of new work, in the copying of literature, and in editing the classics that lasted throughout the Medieval Period.

It is clear, then, that two periods were crucial for the transmission of Latin literature: the end of antiquity (the 4th and 5th Centuries) and to a lesser degree the Carolingian Renaissance (particularly during the 9th Century), and the later copies were made largely, if not entirely, from ancient manuscripts. Had no manuscripts survived other than the ones copied during these two periods, the most important Latin literature would still exist.

If no copies had been made after the 9th Century, only about one-tenth of the surviving works by the most important classical writers would have been lost. Catullus probably survived in an ancient copy until the 14th Century, when his poems are first known to have been recopied, and afterwards, the ancient version disappeared. Seneca the Younger and Tibullus were copied later than the 9th Century, as well as important portions of Tacitus and some other authors. The latest copying of secular works was largely of authors who would probably have survived anyway. Relatively little of the works of major writers was preserved solely as a result of the copying done during the later Middle Ages.

Medieval Period

From c. 550 to c. 750, not only were Livy, Virgil, and Cicero no longer copied, but all Latin classics "virtually ceased being copied.[16] From the 8th Century, not a single fragment of Latin literature or history has been identified that would indicate any copying of Latin pagan literature was being done in Italy. From the 7th Century, only one fragment survives, a small part of Lucan, to show any interest in the preservation of Latin literature. From the 6th Century, fragments survive of only three other authors: Juvenal, Pliny the Elder, and Pliny the Younger.[17] Thus, from the 6th through the 8th Centuries--from the end of antiquity to the Carolingian Renaissance--only four classical authors are known to have been copied. Since some pagan schools remained open and since professional scribes continued to work throughout the Middle Ages, these four manuscripts are far more likely to have been copied for secular purposes than for the Church.[18]

The very small number of manuscripts that were copied during these three centuries suggests that some copying was being done despite the Church, rather than because of it. If the Church had begun to take any interest in pagan literature, the number of copies would have increased, rather than decreased during the 7th Century and then stopped altogether during the 8th Century. Books did not cease to be copied, but the copying that was done was almost wholly religious.

Since E. A. Lowe has summarized the information on all surviving manuscripts known to have been created before about A. D. 800, it is possible to determine with a high degree of probability what was taking place between the end of Antiquity and the beginning of the Carolingian Renaissance.[19] Analysing Lowe's data on the more than 1600 early manuscripts that have survived above ground, only 10 percent of the total was secular, and these were largely grammars and other treatises with practical application.[20] The actual number of secular manuscripts copied from the 5th through the 8th Century was small, and it changed little from century to century. On the other hand, the number of religious manuscripts increased continually and substantially.[21]

Analysing Lowe's data by century, the proportion of secular works being copied declined continually in relation the number of religious manuscripts. Although the number of manuscripts that date from the 4th Century is very small, the 70 percent that it represents for secular subject matter may well be correct for the end of Antiquity. The percentages for the far larger number of manuscripts that survive from the 5th through the 8th Centuries show an unchanging and indisputable trend: During the 5th Century, 36 percent was secular; during the 6th Century, 16 percent; during the 7th Century, 8 percent; and during the 8th Century, 6 percent.[22] In other words, during the Dark Ages, the percentage of secular works copied decreased by one half from the 5th to the 6th Century and decreased again by one half from the 6th to the 7th Century. The Dark Ages were getting progressively darker.

The evidence of manuscripts exactly reflects what is known from historical evidence. The Church considered pagan literature, history, and philosophy dangerous to doctrine and morals, and these categories of writing were the first to cease being copied. The Church had to rely on pagan grammar, law, and medicine, and such writings continued to be copied, but even those were copied in continually declining percentages. The practically oriented subjects were copied not because the Church had any interest in secular writings, but because the information they contained could be put to use without endangering Church teachings.[23] From the 1st through the 8th Century, the sole interest of the Church's hierarchy was in religion, including what could be placed in the service of religion, and pagan literature was treated as either superfluous or dangerous.

How, then, did any Latin literature survive the Dark Ages? Where were the ancient copies physically located? Many, but far from all, were located in monasteries, where classics are known to have been erased by monks during this period. How did they get there and how did any survive?

It was by no means true that a manuscript in the Church's possession was safer than one in private possession. Church property is known to have been a frequent target of raids, and secular property was often better defended. Political authority was fragmented during the Dark Ages, but sufficiently well organized to make war and to raise defences.

A considerable number of manuscripts remained in private possession throughout the Dark Ages, but this is better documented for Byzantium than for Italy. Many towns and castles were continuously occupied, and not all privately owned books were given to the Catholic Church like increasing amounts of land. The contents of some secular libraries were enumerated in surviving wills, and there are references to privately owned libraries in various parts of Europe.[24] Lists of donations to monasteries indicate that books continued to be contributed and consequently, until they were contributed, had been preserved in places such as castles and the few walled towns that survived. One specialist on Medieval bookmaking concluded, "library collections in monasteries grew with donations coupled with the practice of requiring members to assign all their worldly possessions, especially books, to the order." Another specialist in Medieval libraries wrote, "purchases and exchanges of books were of little importance when compared with the number of gifts and bequests from pious donors."[25] Although much copying was done by monks, it was most often copying of religious books. The surviving works of secular literature, history, and philosophy that monasteries are known to have possessed during the Dark Ages were ancient manuscripts; they were gifts, not copies made by monks.

Numerous books found their way into the Church's possession in the same way that land and other property did, and they were undoubtedly given with the understanding that they would be used to further the purposes of the Church. Since the purposes did not include the preservation of pagan literature and since during the Dark Ages secular manuscripts were frequently erased, but rarely if ever copied, the only conclusion consistent with the evidence is that pagan works were being accepted by the Church with the intention of destroying them and reusing the materials on which they were written.

It is an understatement "...that Christians of this period were predominately hostile to pagan literature."[26] Another author concluded similarly that "the Church's attitude towards classical culture during the fourth, fifth, and sixth centuries was not merely one of indifference; it was one of hostility."[27] The official position of the Church had not changed from the time of its early fathers. It is given in detail in the *Didascalia Apostolorum*, a work which dates at least from Antiquity and which claims to have been prepared by the disciples of Jesus with the assistance of Paul and a brother of Jesus. The instructions for leading a Christian life included the following rule and explanation:

> Avoid all books of the heathen. For what has thou to do with strange sayings or laws or lying prophecies, which also turn away from the faith them that are young? What is lacking to thee in the word of God, that thou shouldest cast thyself on these fables of the heathen? If thou wouldest read historical narratives, thou hast the *Book of Kings*; if philosophers and wise men, thou hast the prophets, wherein thou shall find wisdom and understanding more than that of the wise men and the philosophers. And, if thou wish for songs, thou hast the *Psalms* of David; if thou wouldst read of the beginning of the world, thou hast the Genesis of the great Moses; and if laws and commandments, thou hast the glorious Law of the Lord God. All strange writing therefore which are contrary to these wholly eschew.[28]

The first major theologian of the Church, Tertulian (c. 160-c. 230), was a convert who perhaps because he had received too thorough a pagan education later rejected it. He wrote that it gave him "joy" and "exultation" to think of pagan philosophers and poets in hell.[29] Although influential, Tertulian eventually became a heretic. If there is only one true church, his exultation may well be diminished.

By far the most influential theologian of the Roman period and a "doctor" of the Church, St. Augustine (354-430), wrote, "Burn all those parchments, with their splendid bindings in adorned hide, so that nothing superfluous will burden you, and your God, bound in servitude to the Codex, will be freed."[30] Augustine also wrote that "gold and silver" could be extracted from pagan literature for the use of the Church, but otherwise, he advised that "...all branches of heathen learning, have not only false and superstitious fancies and heavy burdens of unnecessary toil, which every one of us, when we go out under the leadership of Christ from the fellowship of the heathen, ought to avoid."[31]

Another "doctor" of the Church, St. Jerome (c. 347-420?), dreamed "that he would be tortured until he agreed not to read the works of the Gentiles." He wrote, "I could not bring myself to forgo the library I had formed for myself at Rome with great care and toil." By comparison with Cicero, he found the style of the prophets "rude and repellent, and in his dream, he was "dragged before the seat of the Judge.... Asked who and what I was I replied: 'I am a Christian.' But he who presided said: 'You lie; you are a Ciceronian and not a Christian.'" In his commentary on the book of Daniel, Jerome wrote, "'and if we are sometimes obliged to refer to secular literature and to quote from it—something we gave up long ago—it is not of our own volition but, as I may say, from direst necessity.'"[32]

The last of the four principal "doctors" of the Church, St. Gregory (the Great, c. 540-604), was outraged by the conduct of a bishop in Gaul named Desiderius, and he wrote to him, a report has reach me, a report I cannot mention without a blush, that you are lecturing on profane literature to certain friends, whereat I am filled with such grief and vehement disgust that my former opinion of you has been turned to mourning and sorrow. For the same mouth cannot sing the praises of Jupiter and the praises of Christ. Consider yourself how offensive, how abominable a thing it is for a bishop to recite verses which are unfit to be recited by even a religious layman....[33]

One of the most widely read Medieval authors, St. Isidore of Saville (c. 560-636), wrote,

> In themselves the profane authors are harmful. The study of them inclines men to despise the simplicity of Scripture and leads to intellectual arrogance, while the fragments of ancient poetry are actually incentives to lust. To the monks they are to be forbidden absolutely.

There were some dissenting voices, but their

very dissent indicates that they were going against the position of the leadership, as well as of the position of most members of the Church. For example, the theologian St. Gregory of Nazianzen (c. 325-c. 389) urged reconsideration for "that pagan culture which many Christians spit upon, as treacherous and dangerous, and keeping us afar from God."[34] As Reynolds and Wilson concluded, "...there can be little doubt that the major reason for the loss of classical texts is that most Christians were not interested in reading them...."[35]

During the Church's ascendancy from the 5th through the 8th Centuries, when its help was needed the most to ensure the survival of classical contributions to human knowledge, it did the least. From the statements that have been quoted, from the amount of copying that was done during the Dark Ages, and especially from the large number of manuscripts that were erased, it is clean that the Church deserves no credit for preserving classical literature before the 9th Century at the earliest. Evidence will be presented to show that its position did not change until the Italian Renaissance, when its leadership went to men with predominantly secular interests.

Palimpsests

The practice of erasing manuscripts (palimpsesting) was so common during the 6th Century that the St. Gregory who was Bishop of Tours felt it necessary to end his *History of the Franks* with a curse on any of his successors who allowed his writings to be damaged or altered:

> ...I conjure you all...that you never permit these books to be destroyed, or to be rewritten, or to be reproduced in part only with sections omitted, for otherwise when you emerge in confusion from this Judgement Day you will be condemned with the Devil. Keep them in your possession, intact, with no amendments and just as I have left them with you.[36]

During the Dark Ages, when parchment was needed for copying, an existing text might well be erased, and when it was, it was usually destroyed as completely as possible to make room for a religious text.

A number of scholars, particularly Charles Henry Beeson, have argued that the erasure of manuscripts was not an indication of hostility to secular writings because religious writing were also erased.[37] Although religious writings were frequently erased, they were largely, if not entirely, superseded translations, duplicate texts, apocryphal works, and heretical writings.[38] Almost no religious writings were erased so their parchment could be reused for pagan works of literature, history, or philosophy and none whatever during the Dark Ages.[39] The evidence indicated that any secular work might be singled out for erasure while only unneeded religious works were erased.

One writer has gone so far as to assert that palimpsesting "has sometimes been of great benefit in preserving works or fragments that would otherwise have been lost forever."[40] But many palimpsests even now are partly or entirely unreadable, and none was intended to be read. Most of the ancient texts supposedly preserved in this way are incomplete. To credit the Church for preserving palimpsests is to credit its failure to destroy what it intended to. As Reynolds and Wilson noted, when monks helped to preserve manuscripts, it was "often in spite of themselves."[41]

Beeson in writing about Bobbio, the monastery where more palimpsesting was done than any other, argues that the monks erased classical texts without malice: "To characterize their activity as vandalism is unjust. Hostility to the Classics was not a factor."[42] Discussing a manuscript of Plautus that is generally agreed to have been palimpsested at Bobbio, Beeson wrote,

> ...this does not mean that a Classical MS was wantonly destroyed to make a biblical text. The monks would scarcely be interested in the original and undoubtedly would find it very difficult to read if they were. The MS had probably become defective and been thrown aside to be used as need arose.[43]

In this passage Beeson admits that monks were probably uninterested anyway, and even if they had been, were too ignorant to make much sense out of a pagan manuscript. Indifference or ignorance are supposed to preclude malice. The monks were not so ignorant of Latin as to let many pre-Jerome translations of the Bible escape or many heretical writings. Beeson admitted that the destruction of heretical texts "may" represent "some animus" inasmuch as "they were bent on destroying [them], but otherwise their attitude was impersonal."[44] Beeson argued that the manuscript of Platus was probably damaged before being erased and, assuming that it was, he was sure that no malice was involved. He believed that "the palimpsest themselves are monuments of their [the monks'] devotion to learning. They loved books but to get them they often had to use the debris of old MSS."

Beeson cited another example which probably explains what generally happened when parchment was being reused: A copy of the *Codex Theodosianus* was erased and reused in two different books.[45] Beeson allowed for the possibility, but then ignored the important fact than more than one scribe might be reusing the parchment from a single manuscript to create two or more new manuscripts.[46] Most monastic scriptoria had accommodations for from "three to twenty scribes, though twelve was the popular number."[47] The example Beeson cited and numerous other examples indicate that older manuscripts could find their way into as many new books as were being created at any particular time by three or more monks.[48]

It is easy to see how a manuscript might lose its beginning or its end, but it is next to impossible for the beginning and the end to survive intact and for the middle of a manuscript to be so damaged as to make the whole valueless. This is exactly what would have to be believed to explain why only the middle portion was missing from a palimpsest that contained the *Didascalia Apostolorum*.[49]

Beeson's example of the Platus is no more likely to have been damaged before being palimpsested. He mentioned that the original manuscript contained a total of 89 quires, and it would not be implausible, as he argued, that the first 14 quires could have been lost before the rest was erased--providing that the remainder represented a consecutive portion of the text, but it does not. An accident cannot explain why 24 quires "scattered throughout the whole text are entirely missing."[50] The manuscript had to have been taken apart quire by quire as parchment was needed by at least two monks who were working on two or more new texts at the same time. Since this was obviously the case, there is no reason to assume that the first 14 quires had been damaged before palimpsesting began. They too are likely to have been incorporated into another new manuscript, one that happened not to survive or that has not yet been identified.

When pages are missing at the beginning or end of a manuscript, there is another possible explanation aside from accidental damage. Boccaccio described how the monks of Monte Cassino "...were in the habit of cutting off sheets and making psalters, which they sold to boys. The margins too they manufactured into charms, and sold to women...."[51] And as has been mentioned, other portions of manuscripts were sometimes reused to line shelves and boxes, and even a manuscript of Livy that is known to have been complete when it was recopied was afterwards cut up and used for bindings.

No doubt some manuscripts were damaged before being palimpsested, and no doubt some of them had been damaged through neglect and some others purposefully damaged. But what convinced Beeson most of all that palimpsests represented no hostility towards classics was that "classical texts suffered less in palimpsested MSS than theological and technical writings." Before he made this assertion, it had been disproven.[52]

Two articles by E. A. Lowe summarize information on the format of "a very large proportion of the oldest MSS. extant" and on the format of "nearly all extant Latin MSS. of the fifth and sixth centuries."[53] Lowe's first list consisted of 47 manuscripts that were almost entirely written during late Antiquity. Summarizing his data, 23 were classical manuscripts, and 13 of them or 57 percent had been erased. Of the 24 religious texts, 8 or 33 percent were erased. Classical manuscripts were twice as likely to be erased, a proportion that increased substantially in the second group.[54]

Lowe's second list generally consisted of somewhat later manuscripts, and there was accordingly a much smaller percentage of classical manuscripts--with the total for the classics dropping from 49 percent to 17 percent. Again, summarizing his data, of the 103 items in this list, only 13 were classical, a situation which he noted was an indication of the "growing tendency to neglect the classics." The proportion of classical manuscripts that were erased remained about the same--53 percent as compared to 57 percent earlier. However, only 11 of the 90 religious manuscripts were erased-- about 12 percent compared with 33 percent earlier.[55] Thus, the classics soon became four times as likely to be erased as religious manuscripts even though the classics were far more likely to be unique.

Analysis of Lowe's subsequent study of all pre-800 manuscripts produces nearly identical results. Only about 10 percent of all of the earliest religious works were erased, but 40 percent of all of the earliest secular works were erased.[56] This trend is so well established and it so closely parallels the trends in the subject matter being copied and the trend in the use of palimpsests that there can be no doubt that the classics were being most abused during the period that was most crucial for their survival.

Lowe's separate study of palimpsests indicates that by far the greatest number of secular texts were erased during the 7th and 8th Centuries, but after the 8th Century, the erasure of early secular texts stopped almost completely. Secular texts began to be written over pre-800 religious texts in small numbers in the 8th Century and continued to be until the 12th. There was, though, a major difference between the secular texts that were erased and the ones that were copied: the ones erased were often rare literary texts, and the ones copied were nearly always more common, practical texts. During the Dark Ages, the evidence consistently indicates that the Church was destroying works it considered harmful to religion and copying only those works it could adapt for its own purposes.[57]

Lowe's study of palimpsests also shows that when a new text needed to be copied, the old text was usually erased at that time.[58] In more than half of his examples, a substantial part of an old text was converted into a single new text. In about one-fourth of his examples, parts of two old texts were reused for a single text. In less than one-tenth of the examples cited, a new manuscript was created from five to 13 old texts. Lowe argued that these large numbers of old manuscripts used for one new manuscript implied that the old ones had all been damaged. It is more likely that some monasteries dismantled and washed a number of complete manuscripts at one time, and the pages were reused randomly as needed. Since the original texts were not visible, the old parchment might be reused in any order or in any number of volumes that were being newly made. Erased religious texts and secular texts were not infrequently combined indiscriminately to provide enough material to copy a new religious text.

Further evidence that some monasteries accepted classical writings with the intention of erasing them is that there are no examples dating from the Dark Ages in which a Latin classic was recopied before being erased.[59] Since much pagan literature was written in large capital letters, space could have been saved by recopying them in smaller letters.[60] Nearly always, the space was saved, instead, for religious writings. During this period, even an uncontroversial author like Cicero was erased on eight occasions. Livy was erased three times. Neither author was recopied until later in the Middle Ages.[61]

It is significant that only a handful of surviving works were erased during the 5th or 6th Centuries, when the Church was establishing itself. Palimpsests became common during the 7th Century as monasteries became common. Although the practice of erasing and reusing manuscripts existed in ancient time, ancient manuscripts would then have been duplicates. Later, monks erased the classics without any regard for whether other copies existed or not. It is no coincidence that the greatest number of palimpsests survive from the 8th Century, the same century during which not a single work of classical literature is known to have been copied.[62]

How many religious texts were erased to copy classical texts? How many classical texts were erased to copy classical texts? The evidence is consistent and clear regardless of attempts to explain it away.

Writing about the Dark Ages, Lowe admitted that "...a historical interest in preserving the records of the past was not a noticeable characteristic of the period in question." Nonetheless, he attempted to defend monks by arguing that "if there had been a systematic campaign hardly any unpalimpsested classics would have survived."[63] Even though he took an extreme position, his argument is insupportable. There can be little doubt that at the beginning of the Dark Ages, if the Church had possessed the power to destroy all pagan writings, its few dissenting members would have been unable to prevent it. As much survived as did by staying out of the hands of clerics long enough, as F. W. Hall wrote, for the Church to "recover its senses and breed up men of the type of Cassiodorus in the place of the early fanatics."[64] From the 5th through the 8th Centuries, the Church showed no sign of reversing itself and taking an interest in secular literature. Since copying totally stopped in the 8th Century, there is no reason to suppose the Church would have changed what had developed into a policy not to copy secular literature. If the Carolingian Renaissance had not happened when it did and if continually more classical manuscripts were erased and none were recopied, we can be sure that in the West "hardly any unpalimpsested classics would have survived."[65]

Carolingian Renaissance

If nothing had been copied after the 9th Century, we would still have about 90 percent of the major Latin works that we do have. What was copied from the 10th through the 14th Centuries is important for variant readings, but this was mainly because so many of the individual copies were so carelessly made and because the originals were afterwards discarded. The copying done after the 9th Century was far less important than the copies made directly from ancient manuscripts during the Carolingian Renaissance.

There is no doubt that the "Carolingian court and the monasteries closely associated with it were the prime agents in the whole movement." Moreover, "the revival largely took place within the Carolingian sphere of influence."[66] The sponsorship was thus secular. In some monasteries, abbots were interested in classical literature, but their interest was unauthorized and was exceptional.

To see the accomplishment of the Carolingian Renaissance accurately, it is important to bear in mind that by the 8th Century, the Church had essentially achieved its goal of imposing a single system of thought, a system that demanded acceptance of the Bible and of Church doctrine as divinely inspired truth. Manuscripts provide an accurate reflection of how fully this goal had been accomplished. Very suddenly in the 9th Century, after the classics had ceased to be copied altogether, Latin literature, history, and philosophy began to be recopied. The Carolingian Renaissance thus represented a true rebirth of interest in all aspects of pagan culture and a renewed appreciation for literary excellence. It represented a decisive break with the past, a break with the whole point of view of the Dark Ages. The Church temporarily lost its nearly complete hold on thought. Although its hold was reimposed somewhat during the 10th Century, when far fewer classics were saved, there was afterwards an increasing interest in Antiquity that became so great by the 15th Century even the papacy began to collect Latin literature.

The copying of ancient texts reveals that the Carolingian Period is distinguishable from the Dark Ages in a way that was more important than any forms of political or economic difference.[67] The Carolingian Period represented the first major break in the barriers to a free exchange of thought in the West. Manuscripts show, too, that the period had a discernible end, but that its secularizing effects persisted and reasserted themselves. This rebirth of reason led directly and inevitably to the Italian Renaissance and the Reformation, and despite the Counter-Reformation, it led directly to the Modern World. The Church's efforts to control thought through the confessional, parochial schools, the Inquisition, imprimatur, excommunication, interdict, and the Index of Prohibited books represent a consistent counter current in opposition to the free exchange of ideas. If all these methods had been applied before the invention of printing, the secularizing effects of the Italian Renaissance might well have been suppressed even more fully than those of the Carolingian Renaissance, and even fewer classical texts would have survived.

In another important sense, the Carolingian age was more a rebirth than a revival. The creative spirit of Latin literature and art had long been dead. No major works had been created for centuries.

Increasing secularization is also demonstrated by the number of private libraries that are known to have existed. Inventories survive for many private libraries from the 9th through the 15th Centuries, and an early listing of them reflects minimal totals for each century: 9th--23; 10th--17; 11--43; 12--70; 13th--60; 14th--114; 15th--219. No doubt there were far more private libraries for which inventories were either never made or have not survived.[68]

During the 6th Century, the first monastic order was founded in Europe, and although for some centuries earlier individual monks and small communities of monks had copied religious manuscripts, few if any of the pagan manuscripts that had been copied before the end of Antiquity were copied by monks. Since many hundreds of religious manuscripts survive from the Dark Ages, but literally not more than a handful of secular manuscripts, it is so unlikely that monks before the 9th Century were copying secular manuscripts that the possibility can be ruled out. There is good reason to believe, then, that the Latin literature which survived to be recopied in the 9th Century had been copied in late Antiquity and had not been recopied since the end of the Roman Empire.

After being copied, the same thing happened to ancient manuscripts in the West as in the East: "the uncial book [with mainly upper-case lettering] was then discarded, and the minuscule book [with mainly lower-case lettering] became the source for all further copies." That the manuscripts were actually discarded in the West is indicated by Lowe's study of Pre-800 palimpsests: After the 9th Century, only a single early classical manuscript is known to have been erased.[70] The early architypes must, then, have been largely set aside as no longer needed and to have deteriorated through neglect, though some, such as parts of Livy, were cut into pieces to use for bindings and lining boxes.

During the 9th Century, agents of the Carolingian Empire brought together all the ancient manuscripts they could locate and had them recopied in the current style of lettering. These manuscripts were transliterated from texts that had been mainly written in in rustic, uncial, or half-uncial lettering to new copies that were written mainly in minuscule. As the ancient texts were being recopied, spaces between words and punctuation were often added for the first time.

The new minuscule copy had a number of advantages over the ancient copy in majuscule: It was more compact, and taking less space, it required less materials and so was less expensive. It was easier to read for anyone unaccustomed to the earlier styles of lettering, and it was made still easier through the insertion of spacing and punctuation. Consequently, the ancient manuscripts were rarely used again for recopying. That they were no longer used has been established by tracing errors incorporated into texts at the time they were translitereated.[71]

What happened to the ancient copies? In damp climates, papyrus self-destructed. Parchment copies could be destroyed or damaged by fire, water, and insects, but were more likely to survive indefinitely. Parchment manuscripts that had survived five hundred years or more, and much of the parchment they were written on has survived as palimpsests to the present so they could have continued to survive, as some did, if they had not been discarded. Had they been simply set aside, they might well have managed to survive despite neglect. Many were intentionally destroyed.

Most ancient manuscripts were lost because they were copied. The Carolingian Renaissance was crucial for the survival of most texts, but it was crucial because it usually destroyed what it copied. This statement of fact is not to blame the Carolingian Age more than the Dark Ages, when manuscripts were being erased without being copied. Copying usually resulted in the preservation of an entire text, even if it was somewhat garbled, while palimpsesting usually resulted in the preservation of only parts of texts.

Although copying was generally considered an adequate substitute for preserving an ancient text, it was not. Numerous errors crept in when a scribe was distracted by transliterating, by adding spaces, and by adding punctuation as he went along. Not infrequently, spaces were added in the wrong place and letters were miscopied, and these mistakes happened either because words had become archaic and so were not recognized or because of simple human error. Also, not infrequently, texts were expurgated or abstracted at the same time or ignorant guesses were made in an attempt to make copies more intelligible. These are among the reasons that the earliest possible copy would ordinarily be more valuable and why it would have been desirable for the ancient copies to have been preserved.

Insofar as the preservation of knowledge was concerned, the Carolingian Renaissance was a mixed blessing. Its results were beneficial mainly because the Church's neglect and hostility had been so harmful for so long. It was fortunate for the Modern World that it occurred when it did, but it took so long to happen that much had already been destroyed and much of what remained was less intelligible than it would have been earlier. Unfortunately, when it happened, a new script was in use, necessitating transliteration and causing the ancient manuscripts to be undervalued and discarded. But if it had happened any later, very little would have survived.

Assistance of the Church

The position of the Latin Church changed substantially during the thousand years of the Middle Ages. At the end of Antiquity, when the fear of paganism was greatest, the Church was able to do the least about the threat to its doctrines. It necessarily had to coexist with paganism during most of the 4th Century, but less so during the 5th Century as pagan temples and schools were permanently closed by secular authority. In late Antiquity the attitude of Church leaders such as Augustine was to take from paganism anything useful for the support of Church doctrine and to try to keep the faithful from being contaminated by the rest. During the Dark Ages, when paganism ceased to be a threat, the attitude of the Church was more often to ignore pagan literature. It was then that a Church leader such as Gregory the Great could praise Benedict for being "skillfully ignorant" of "worldly knowledge." Although there is no evidence of a concerted effort to destroy pagan literature, monasteries accepted copies of the classics with the intention of erasing them-- slowly supplanting concern for the past and the future with concern for an afterlife. During the later Middle Ages, the attitude of the Church unofficially reversed itself to a considerable degree in an effort to maintain its position of authority in an increasingly secular age. The challenges by university scholars could not be ignored, and attempts, most notably by Thomas Aquinas, were made to synthesize religious and secular learning. In doing so, the Church once again returned to the policy of making what use it could of pagan learning for its own purposes.

There is nothing surprising about the fact that far more religious literature was copied than pagan literature.[72] What is surprising is that so many apologists have tried to credit the Church with actively preserving pagan literature. We have as much as we do because the Church did not entirely succeed in imposing its view of the world.

During the Dark Ages, when there is no evidence that the Church took an active part in the preservation of Classical literature, history, or philosophy, many scholars have given great credit for saving the classics to two churchmen. The two who are supposed to have had the most influence, Cassiodorus and Benedict, can be shown to have had little or no influence.

During the 6th Century, Cassiodorus, the former Chancellor under Theodoric, retired from public life, and although he did not become a monk himself, he founded a monastery at Vivarium. He attempted to foster an interest in copying Christian and pagan writings, mainly medical writings and grammars. His monastery soon ceased to exist. There is not a single surviving manuscript of pagan literature that can be credited to him.[73] The most that can be said of him is that he had good intentions, yet Lowe wrote that Cassiodorus "is justly praised as the man whose zeal in the cause of letters has been largely responsible for the preservation of learning."[74] More recently, another scholar wrote,

> ...the chief credit for the physical preservation of the classics by continuous copying through the Middle Ages belongs to Cassiodorus Senator.... His provision that in the intervals of copying sacred texts the monks should copy secular works was of great importance, for the practice of Vivarium set an example for similar foundations elsewhere.[75]

However, there was no such "continuous copying" of pagan literature from the 5th through the 8th Century, and since there was none, neither Cassiodorus nor Benedict can be credited with having started such a tradition. Reynolds and Wilson were undoubtedly correct when they wrote, "...Cassiodorus seems to have had little or no effect on the transmission of classical texts."[76]

Benedict, the founder of the first monastic order in the West, is supposed to have directed the Benedictines to copy books. Benedict's rules survive, and they required that part of each day be spent reading. Benedict indicated that reading was intended to occupy the monks' minds fully when they were not doing manual labour or praying. He stated nothing whatever about copying, and it is only by implication that he is believed to have expected copying to have been done to supply material for reading. But as we have seen, most books came to monasteries as gifts, not by having been borrowed and copied by monks. Since Benedict created a monastic order to provide places for persons to withdraw from the world and since he was so "skillfully ignorant," it is an altogether unsupportable assumption that he intended for Benedictines to help preserve pagan literature. Several centuries later, when some Benedictines began to copy secular literature, they were betraying the ideals of their founder.

When the Dark Ages ended, the official attitude of the Church towards pagan literature was slow in changing, and it never entirely changed. In 1231, when Pope Gregory IX learned that Aristotle was being copied indiscriminately by secular booksellers in Paris, he wrote,

> Since the sciences ought to render service to the wisdom of holy writ, they are to be in so far embarrassed by the faithful as they are known to conform to the good pleasure of the Giver, so that anything virulent or otherwise vicious, by which the purity of the Faith might be derogated from, be quite excluded...[;] exclude what you shall find there erroneous or likely to give scandal or offense to readers....[77]

This might equally well have been later written about Galileo or any other scientist who offended an inquisitor by teaching any well established fact that contradicted the Bible, and it might equally well have been written about any writers whose works were placed on the Index of Prohibited Books from the 16th through the 20th Centuries. Even as late as the beginning of the 15th Century, the official position of the Church, the position defined in its Canon Law, forbad the study of pagan writings.[78] It does no credit to the Church to say that its position was increasingly ignored and impossible to enforce. This position was the only one the Church could take that was consistent with its claim of possessing revealed truth.

If the Latin Church had been interested in secular learning, it would have helped to preserve both Greek and Latin texts. Since only a handful of Greek manuscripts are known to have been copied in Western Europe from the 4th through the 13th Centuries, this was definitely not the case. Even though most, if not all, of the New Testament had been written in Greek and even though the Greek language continued to be spoken in south Italy and Sicily, there was no scholarly interest in studying the original text of the Greek New Testament. Jerome's Latin translation of the Bible was considered canonical for more than a thousand years. What interested the Church most was a uniformity of doctrine, and even the scholarly study of doctrine was discouraged or prohibited.

In the Byzantine Empire, education remained largely in secular hands, and many Greek classics survived intact because they continued to be used in secular schools. They continued to be read and to be copied accurately because ancient Greek continued to be used by the State for its official writings. In the East, the ability to write classical Greek prose was required for civil service, and although this requirement was deadly for creativity, it contributed importantly to the continued appreciation of ancient Greek.[79] In the West, ancient Latin developed into Church Latin and into the Romance languages, and a knowledge of it was largely lost.

The difference between the Eastern and Western Empires is reflected most dramatically in the correctness and completeness of texts, but it is also reflected in the quantities of literature that survived. Although only about 9 million words of Latin literature survived, over 57 million words of Greek literature survived--more than five times as much.[80]

This substantially better record in all respects is not because the Orthodox Church was officially more favourable to classical literature than the Latin Church. The better record is because, unlike the Pope, the patriarch of Constantinople had no secular power, not even the pretence that Constantine had donated secular authority. Although some secular authority continued to be exercised in the West, it was so localized during most of the Middle Ages that the Church gained the upper hand and was able to impose a more nearly theocratic form of government than was possible in the East.

Although there were exceptions such as Planudes, It cannot be said that the Greeks of the Byzantine state had a much greater interest in Latin literature than the Latin Church had in Greek literature. The ancient Greeks had little regard for Latin literature and translated little of it into Greek. The ancient Romans regarded Greek literature very highly and translated much of it into Latin, but the Church allowed nearly all of these translations to disappear. Even during the Byzantine period, few Latin works were translated into Greek, and as soon as Roman law was available in Greek, the Latin originals largely ceased to be consulted by lawyers. Nonetheless, "...the Byzantines have handed down without irretrievable loss the trust they received...."[81]

The Byzantines would have preserved even more if the Crusades had not been unleashed by the Latin Church. In the 9th Century, the Byzantine scholar Photius made notes on 280 Greek books he read. Of this total, 122 works were secular, including the writings of 33 historians. Twenty of the 33 historical works disappeared after the 1204 sack of Constantinople by Catholic Crusaders.[82] Photius also prepared a list of 470 authors available to an anthologist and of this total, not more than 40 have survived substantially intact.[83] What losses there have been to Greek literature has often been attributed to the Turkish capture of the city in 1453, but no major work is known to have survived after 1204 and to have disappeared after 1453. The Catholic Crusaders did irreparable damage to Greek literature while the infidel Turks did not.[84]

The credit for transmitting Greek literature to the West in the 14th and 15th Century belongs almost entirely to private individuals. Johannes Bessarion, a high official of the Orthodox Church who was made a Cardinal of the Latin Church, deserves much credit for collecting about 500 volumes of religious and secular Greek literature at his own expense. He collected these works with the specific intention of helping to ensure their survival, and significantly, he gave his collection to the city of Venice, not to the Church. His library contained 87 Greek works on philosophy, 54 on history, and 42 on literature--as well as 57 works on Latin philosophy. No monastic library in the West had such extensive holdings in these subjects, and few had any Greek works at all.[85] Much credit should also go to private individuals like Cosimo de' Medici, who commissioned agents to search out Greek as well as Latin works for him, something the Latin Church with all its connections and resources did not do until it had humanist popes that ignored its traditions.

The contribution of the Catholic Church to the survival of Latin literature during the 10th through the 14th Century has been greatly exaggerated. What was copied during this period was too little and too late to have had a major impact on what survived. Much had already been irretrievably lost through a thousand years of neglect. The most important works that had survived until the 10th Century had become sufficiently appreciated that the Church's help was no longer a crucial factor in their survival.

Some works did continue to survive in unique copies in monasteries, but that the copies were unique indicates they were not appreciated and not copied. Few monasteries knew what other monasteries had, and few persons outside monasteries had any way of knowing what was in them. When private individuals began to search for classical literature during the Italian Renaissance, they found shocking neglect. Boccaccio has already been quoted on manuscripts that were being cut up to make psalters and charms. When he visited Monte Cassino and asked a monk to show him the library,

The monk answered stiffly, pointing to a steep stair case, "Go up; it is open." Boccaccio went up gladly; but he found the place which held so great a treasure, was without door or key. He entered, and saw grass sprouting on the windows, and all the books and benches thick with dust. In his astonishment he began to open and turn the leaves of first one tome and then another, and found many and divers volumes of ancient and foreign works. Some of them had lost several sheets; others were snipped and pared all around the text, and mutilated in various ways. At length, lamenting that the toil and study of so many men should have passed into the hands of most abandoned wretches, he departed with tears and sighs.[86]

If this were the only such description of a monastic library, it would be suspect, but there are others that are equally convincing. In 1416, Poggio and two others who sought classic texts visited St. Gall, where they discovered the only known copy of Quintilian's book on rhetoric. Poggio recorded that this work and numerous other books "were not in the Library, as befitted their worth, but in a sort of foul and gloomy dungeon at the bottom of one of the towers, where not even men convicted of a capital offence would have been stuck away."[87] One of the men who accompanied Poggio wrote that on seeing "countless books were...neglected and infested with dust, worms, soot, and all the things associated with the destruction of books, we all burst into tears thinking this was the way in which the Latin language lost its greatest glory and distinction." Outraged, he added, "there were in that monastery an abbot and monks totally devoid of any knowledge of literature. What barbarous hostility to the Latin tongue! What damned dregs of humanity!"[88]

Judging by descriptions of monastic libraries, by the general hostility of the Catholic Church to pagan writings, and by the widely scattered distribution of rare copies of classic texts, it is evident that most monasteries did not actively seek pagan works in order to preserve them much less systematically attempted to aquired them. Instead, such works must have been largely unsolicited gifts and in some cases unwanted gifts or gifts sought only for the value of their materials. There were very notable exceptions among the leadership of monasteries, men such as Abbot Disiderius (later Pope Victor III) of Monte Cassino, but when he left, the monastery's interest in the classics soon died.[89] Other exceptions include Abbot Wiebald of Corvey, Abbot Lupus of Ferrières, and Archbishop Ado of Vienne, men notable for their attempts to collect what they could, but their love of the classics was not part of their duty to the Church.[90]

Numerous inventories of Church property, including inventories of books, survive for the Middle Ages, and they indicate that monastic libraries were small even by the standards of personal libraries at the beginning of the Italian Renaissance. They were infinitesimal compared to the major libraries of the ancient world, libraries such as the most famous ones at Alexandria, Pergamon, and Rome. For the period between the 9th through the 12th Centuries, ten libraries are known to have had from 171 to 666 books. The largest of these was at Bobbio. In the 9th Century, of the 666 volumes at Bobbio, only 124 were secular, and most of those were practical in content, and the number was continually declining through erasure.[91] Although this library did have an important collection of Latin literature, it was

485

the library that was most actively erasing the classics, including the unique copy of Cicero's *De Republica*. Small monasteries were more likely to have had "only a few dozen" books and medium-sized monasteries to have only "a few hundred," and their books were mostly or entirely religious.[92]

By contrast, during the first half of the 15th Century, one individual, Nicolaus de Niccolis, had personally collected 800 books, more than the largest monastic library accumulated in centuries.[93] Considering the resources of any one monastery (and disregarding the immense resources of the Church as a whole), a large monastery could have exceeded what any individual was capable of accomplishing if it had wished to do so. Cosimo de' Medici is known, for example, to have hired 45 copiest, who in only 22 months transcribed 200 volumes.[94] It could have borrowed manuscripts to copy them, sent its monks to other monasteries to make copies, or commissioned copies of classic texts scattered widely throughout Europe as many private individuals were then doing, and it could have done so earlier more easily yet no monastery in all of Europe took such the initiative to try to assemble as much classical writing as possible. This is what could have been done, but was not done by monasteries because it was never part of their purpose. Again, the evidence is consistent and clear that they accumulated books rather than making any systematic effort to collect them. The supposed early exception of Cassiodorus cannot be confirmed by the existence of a single manuscript from his monastery, and although it is not unlikely, it was uncharacteristic of the purpose of monasteries, which were created to get away from this world in order to prepare for the next.

Impact of the Codex and Minuscule

Another claim has been made in an attempt to credit the Church with a crucial role in the preservation of Latin literature: that Christians adopted the codex and thereby ensured that the more perishable scroll would be replaced. Until the 1st Century A. D., the papyrus scroll was the standard format for most books in the Ancient World, but before the end of the 5th Century, the codex had almost entirely replaced the scroll. The evidence for this change is presented in detail in *the Birth of the Codex* by Colin H. Roberts and T. C. Skeat.[95]

The codex must have been relatively new to the Romans during the late 1st Century A. D. because the word "codex" was still being used to designate a tablet of wood with a wax writing surface. In about the year 85 Martial mentioned that the works of Homer were available in a single, conveniently sized parchment tablet, one made up of "many-folded skins," and he was obviously referring to the present form of a book.[96] Somewhat earlier in the 1st Century A. D., the Roman jurist Cassius, who died in c. A. D. 69, argued that the definition of a book (scroll) should be expanded to included parchment notebooks. Such notebooks are known to have been used at least as early as the 1st Century B. C.,[97] and they represented what would constitute a quire in a modern book. The earliest surviving fragment of a codex preserves part of a pagan text that was written in c. A. D. 100.[98] During the early 2nd Century, the law notebooks of Neratius Pricius were praised for their superior ease of reference.[99] The codex form of book had become common enough by the time of Ulpian (d. 228) that he proposed defining a codex legally as any type of tablet, regardless of the material used for it, and he proposed reserving the word "liborum" for scrolls, again regardless of the material.[100] This evidence indicates that the Romans of the 1st and 2nd Centuries A. D. were well aware of the advantages of the codex and that the codex was well on its way to becoming common among pagans. To argue otherwise, it is necessary to discount this evidence and to believe that Christians somehow had the ability to recognize the obvious advantages of the codex over the scroll while the practically minded Romans did not.

The main evidence used to assign priority for the adoption of the codex to Christians is from Egypt. To believe that this evidence is convincing, it is necessary to accept that Egypt was typical for the whole of the Roman Empire. This can hardly have been the case for the Egyptians were new to the Empire and were notoriously conservative. Since the

Egyptians were so singularly conservative, it seems more likely that they would have been reticent to adopt a new form of book than that most Romans would have been unable to recognize the advantages of a codex.

The Egyptian evidence indicates an almost exclusive preference by Christians for the codex from the 2nd Century A. D. and a gradually increasingly preference by pagans that did not become as exclusive until the 5th Century.[101] However, there are a number of possible reasons why Christian codices would have been more common than pagan codices in Egypt: The Christian codices may well have been imported while the pagan ones were more likely to have been copied locally from scrolls, which had been the traditional form of book even among the Ptolemies. If some early Christian codices were written in Egypt, they may have been written either by a visiting missionary or by a recent convert who copied not only an imported text, but its format. Actually, pagan codices were equally common in Egypt during the 2nd Century, but they represented a small proportion of the total for pagan books. Some pagan codices are likely to have been imported also and to have been imported initially in a similarly small quantity.

Another assumption is required to credit Christians with having influenced the preservation of the classics: that the pagans would not have adopted the codex without Christian influence in time to recopy many classics in the 4th or 5th Centuries and so increase their chances for survival. Considering that Christianity was largely practiced in secret from the 1st through the 3rd Centuries, this is unlikely. The whole argument for the influence of Christians on the adoption of the codex is thus based on atypical evidence and unlikely assumptions.

The whole question of Christian priority might be relevant to the transmission of texts if the Ancient World had ended in the 2nd Century, but there is very little question that pagans, having used the codex from the 1st Century, would have adopted it more and more exclusively by the 4th Century, with or without Christian influence. The question need not be considered except for the claim that this was yet another important Christian influence.[102]

Until recently, it was also claimed that Christians influenced the adoption of parchment, but it is now recognized that the widespread use of parchment preceded the adoption of the codex. Moreover, since papyrus was generally used for early codices, the adoption of parchment was not directly related to the adoption of the codex. It is true that almost no scrolls have survived from Antiquity except in archaeological context.[103] The reason for this is that most scrolls were made of papyrus, and although papyrus is a tough and versatile material, it deteriorates more rapidly than parchment, particularly in a climate that is alternately wet and dry. Papyrus scrolls rarely lasted longer than two or three hundred years,[104] and consequently, it was necessary for them to be recopied at regular intervals.

When parchment began to be used for scrolls, at least as early as the 2nd Century B. C., recopying on a regular basis became less necessary, but even so, scrolls continued to be made largely of papyrus.[105] Little is known about the comparative prices of parchment and papyrus, but it seems reasonable that material and labour costs in Egypt would have been low. Perhaps more importantly, papyrus initially provided a better writing surface. Nearly all the ancient manuscripts that did survive in Europe were parchment codices, and this is the surest indication that neither scrolls nor papyrus were as well suited for permanence as codices and parchment.

Italian Renaissance

As long as classical texts remained inside monasteries, they had little effect on anyone, cleric or layman. It was only after they were physically removed from monasteries or were copied and began to circulate that their effect began to be felt. Monks made few, if any, major contributions to secular literature, history, philosophy, and science, and friars and other clerics did not make many more.[106] As Reynolds and Wilson noted, "humanism was fundamentally secular, and the thin but unbroken tradition of lay education in Italy had doubtless contributed to this."[107] For creative work to be done again that was even remotely comparable to the best of the Ancient World, Latin literature had to find its way back into the hands of a more appreciative, secular audience.

In some monasteries during the late Middle Ages, the classics were increasingly read and copied, but by the early 15th Century, they were being neglected even in the most well-established monasteries such as Monte Cassino and St. Gall. Persons with any secular interest were less likely to become monks, and even monasteries that once had important libraries were losing, rather than gaining books, and were neglecting what they had more than at any time since the Dark Ages.[108]

After the end of the Carolingian Renaissance, several more centuries were required for a major literary figure to emerge. Dante was the first in about nine hundred years, and he was notably a layman. As a wholly credulous Christian, Dante represented more the end of the Middle Ages than the beginning of the Renaissance, but even so, his writings owed much to Antiquity. Much of his education was secular, particularly his training in law and in the classics.[109] In his vision of an afterlife, Dante notably chose Virgil as a guide. Nonetheless, he placed one of his own teachers and numerous other scholars in Hell.

For a rebirth of learning, the recovery of ancient texts was indispensable. It was no coincidence that among the most ardent book hunters, collectors, and copiers of ancient books during the 14th and early 15th Century were the most important writers of the period, particularly Petrarch and Boccaccio. Both of these collectors generously shared what they can legitimately be said to have "rediscovered."

Although Francesco Petrarch (1304-1374) may well have taken minor orders in the Church, he obligated himself at most to minimal personal observances, and in return he became eligible for benefices.[110] He had professional training as a lawyer, but he chose, instead, to devote most of his time to collecting and studying Latin literature and to creating literary works of his own. He systematically sought out books and assembled, for example, the most complete manuscripts of the writings of Livy[111] and of Cicero[112] that had existed in any one place since Antiquity. He is generally credited with being the first humanist, and in most respects, he was the first person since Antiquity to transcend the intellectual limitations imposed by the Church. When he could, he employed up to six copiests,[113] and he undoubtedly owned far more than the 52 manuscripts that have survived from his library.[114]

Giovanni Boccaccio (1313-1375) had no official connection with the Church, and if he had, he would probably have been defrocked. In his *Decameron*, he consistently has his characters express contempt for the contemporary clergy. For example, he has one say,

> ...the priesthood consists for the most part of extremely stupid men, inscrutable in their ways, who consider themselves more worthy and knowledgeable than other people, whereas they are decidedly inferior. They resemble pigs, in fact, for they are too feeble-minded to earn a living like everybody else, and so they install themselves wherever they can fill their stomachs.

Early during the Reformation, Erasmus wrote "'that Luther had sinned in two points; he had touched the crown of the Pope and the bellies of the monks'..."[115]

At Monte Cassino, Boccaccio discovered unique manuscripts of parts of Tacitus's *Annals* and *Histories*, and he has been accused of having stolen a manuscript of Tacitus from Monte Cassino. Whether he stole it or not, he is not likely to have lied about the condition of the library at Monte Cassino since such conditions are too well attested otherwise, and it was never known to have been copied previously, but immediately afterwards began to be widely distributed and appreciated as some of the finest histories ever written.[116]

Giovanni Francesco Poggio Bracciolini (1380-1459) was "never in holy orders," and at the end of his life was Chancellor of Florence, but for most of his life he was a papal secretary (c. 1403-1418; 1423-1453). Even though Poggio was part of the papal court, he had no way of knowing what any particular monastic library held without visiting it; before Nicholas V became pope in 1447, the papacy itself was unaware of what Latin works had survived. If it had been interested, it could more easily have found out what survived than anyone else. Even though the papacy had ready access to copies through Poggio during the early years of the 15th Century, there was no interest in acquiring them until later.

Poggio acquired at least 95 books for his own use, sometimes copying them himself in his own version of Carolingian minuscule, but more often paying to have professional scribes copy them. When he found previously unknown manuscripts at St. Gall and Monte Cassino, he did not entrust the copying of them to monks. He remained at St. Gall long enough to do the most important work himself, and he arranged for a loan from Monte Cassino so a work could be copied by an employee of his in Rome. Since two of the most famous monasteries lacked competent copiests, it is unlikely that many other monasteries had them. During one of his trips to Germany in search of books, he took a professional scribe with him.[117]

Like Boccaccio, Poggio had contempt for monks, and when he learned that the nearly 300 volumes of Antonius Corbinellus' library had been bequeathed to a monastery in Florence, he wrote,

What a stupid thing to do, to thrust that treasure into a place where it will do no good. I cannot think what his purpose was to establish Greek books among those two-legged donkeys who do not even know a word of Latin.[118]

In England, Poggio searched long, but unsuccessfully for otherwise unknown manuscripts. He concluded, "Nearly all the monasteries of this island have been built within the last four hundred years [between the 10th and 13th Centuries] and that has not been an age which produced either learned men or the books which we seek; these books were already sunk without trace."[119]

Petrarch and Poggio not only copied ancient books, but they compared all the texts they could locate and combined the best readings to produce the most accurate possible version. Poggio edited them. He sought multiple copies to improve "both for the public good and for my own...."[120] When asking to borrow a manuscript, he wrote, "you will not only be doing me a kindness but you will also be doing a public service and helping that man's [the author's] reputation. For I make books not only for myself but for other people and even for posterity, which the wise always keep in mind."[121] His fellow humanist Leonardo Bruni wrote that Poggio would "deservedly be called the second author of all the works which were once lost and now returned to us by your integrity and diligence."[122] So long as manuscripts of the classics remained in monasteries, they were lost to scholars, and they were increasingly unlikely to survive. Many disappeared after having been copied by humanists.

Niccolò Niccoli was the recipient of most of Poggio's letters that have been quoted, and it was Niccoli who collected approximately 800 volumes, the largest private library of the early 15th Century. He inherited a substantial income, but exceeded his resources acquiring books:

> If anyone left Florence to go to Greece or France or some other place, Nicholaus gave him a memorandum of books that did not exist in Florence and with the help of Cosmus de Medicis who was in complete accord with him, he bought books from many sources.[123]

Niccoli collected with the intention of creating the first public library since the ancient world. In a funeral oration for Niccoli, Poggio said,

> he determined in his will that his more than eight hundred codices should become through his friends a public library, to be forever useful to men.... He wanted the extraordinary library to be brought to the common good, to the public service, to a place open to all, so that all eager for education might be able to harvest from it as from a fertile field the rich fruit of learning.[124]

Cosimo paid off a substantial debt, paid for a library designed by Michelozzo to house Nicolaus's books as part of the rebuilt monastery of San Marco, and later added substantially to the collection. Although Nicolaus's books went to a monastery, he stipulated that they were to be under the control of trustees to ensure that they were accessible to the public.[125] As noted, when monasteries were eventually secularized,

Niccoli's colletion of manuscripts joined Cosimo's in the Laurentian Library.

Conclusion

The contribution of individuals such as Plutarch, Boccaccio, Poggio, Nicolaus, and Cosimo were more public spirited than a thousand years of accumulation and hoarding by the Church. The Church's version of the history of the Middle Ages has been that barbarians destroyed most of Western civilization, and the clergy deserves credit for carefully preserving what remained. Most classical literature is supposed to have survived because monks diligently copied it from a love of learning and a desire to preserve knowledge. How, then, did many single individuals early in the Renaissance assemble larger and more complete collections than the largest monasteries assembled in centuries?

There is no way to determine accurately how many ancient Latin manuscripts survived war, fires, and natural disasters to be later lost through neglect. However, enough is known to justify a conclusion that the Church deserves little or no credit for most of the classics that did survive. Unquestionable, what survived from Antiquity to the Carolingian Renaissance did so despite the Church. Manuscripts dating from before the 10th Century usually exist in one or a few copies, many of which were erased by the Church. When it is considered how much the Church could have done and how little it did, its role was insignificant. The Latin Church had even less interest in preserving or in acquiring copies of Greek works that were available to it from the 6th through the 14th Centuries through Byzantium. What the Church did was consistently too little and too late to have had a significant effect on the transmission of texts, and if the neglect had not stopped with the Carolingian Renaissance, far less would have survived. When these demonstrable facts are taken into consideration, the inevitable conclusion is that the influence claimed for the Church was due to a small number of individuals who were acting on their own behalf and contrary to the most basic aims of the Church.

Praising the Church for preserving Latin literature is like crediting it with the preservation of Roman architecture. When one of Poggio's friends described the discovery of abandoned classics at St. Gall, he compared their fate to that of the art and architecture of Ancient Rome:

> Every day you see citizens (if indeed a man should be called a citizen who is so degraded by abominable deeds) demolishing the Amphitheatre or the Hippodrome or the Colosseum or statues or walls made with marvellous skill and marvellous stone and showing that old and almost divine power and dignity.... But if anyone asks these men why they are led to destroy marble statues, they answer that they abominate the images of false gods.[126]

In *the Destruction of Ancient Rome,* Lanciani assembled hundreds of examples that justified his conclusion: "More works of art have been destroyed in the last five centuries than in all the centuries of barbarian plundering."[127] It would be incorrect to say that the Church attempted to destroy all classical architecture, but it would also be incorrect to say the Church had as one of its purposes the preservation of ancient buildings. As with manuscripts, it preserved what it could adapt for its own use, and what survived is what it did not destroy.

Notes

1. L. D. Reynolds, "Livy," in L. D. Reynolds, ed., *Texts and Transmission; a Survey of Latin Classics* (Oxford: Oxford University Press, 1983), xxxiii-xxxiv, 205-214. Hereafter, Reynolds, *Texts.*

E. A. Lowe, "Codices Rescripti," reprinted in E. A. Lowe, *Palaeographical Papers, 1907-1965* (Oxford: Oxford University Press, 1972), 512, 514, 515 (items 169, 193, 202). Hereafter, Lowe, "Rescripti" or Lowe, *Papers.*

2. M. Winterbottom, "Tacitus," in Reynolds, *Texts,* 407-411.

Citing Haverfield, Lowe suggested that Tacitus may not have been as highly regarded in Antiquity as he has been since his rediscovery and, therefore, that most manuscripts of Tacitus did not survive Antiquity. He pointed out, for example, that when the Roman Emperor Tacitus decreed that copies of his ancestor's work should regularly be made, "...we can only infer that the works of Tacitus had fallen into neglect...." On the contrary, for the emperor to have claimed descent, we can also infer that Tacitus was highly regarded. Lowe also cited several Christian writers who attempted to refute Tacitus, and if Tacitus had not been highly regarded, he would not have needed refutation. E. A. Lowe, "The Unique Manuscript of Tacitus' *Histories*, Florence Laur. 68.2," in Lowe, *Papers,* 289, 290, 296. Hereafter, Lowe, "Tacitus' *Histories*." F. Haverfield, "Tacitus During the Late Roman Period and the Middle Ages," *the Journal of Roman Studies* 6 (1916), 196-201.

3. Colin H. Roberts and T. C. Skeat, *the Birth of the Codex* (London: British Academy by Oxford University Press, 1983), 13. Hereafter, Roberts and Skeat, *Codex*.
Richard Ronald Johnson, "The Role of Parchment in Greco-Roman Antiquity" (Los Angeles: University of California dissertation, 1968). Hereafter, Johnson, "Parchment." Also, Richard R. Johnson, "Ancient and Medieval Accounts of the 'Invention' of Parchment," *California Studies in Classical Antiquity* 3 (1970), 115-122.

4. E. A. Lowe, "Some Facts About Our Oldest Latin Manuscripts" and ""More Facts About our Oldest Latin Manuscripts," Classical Quarterly, XIX (1925), 197-208; XXII (1928), 43-62. Hereafter, Lowe, "Some Facts" and "More Facts."

Lowe, "Rescripti," 494-519

5. Reynolds, Text (in which all Latin authors for which any substantial writings have been preserved are considered in alphabetical order).

6. *Ibid.*, 131, 132, 135.

7. Reynolds, *Texts,* xvii. L. D. Reynolds and N. G. Wilson, *Scribes and Scholars; a Guide to the Transmission of Greek and Latin Literature* (London: Oxford University Press, 1968), 79-81. Hereafter, Reynolds and Wilson, *Scribes.*

8. Reynolds, *Texts* (arranged alphabetically by author).

9. F. Holmes Dudden, *Gregory the Great; His Place in History and Thought* (London: Longmans, Green, and Co., 1905), 287. Hereafter, Duden, *Gregory*.

10. Cassiodorus, *Institutiones*; quoted in Pierre Riché, *Education and Culture in the Barbarian West from the Sixth Through the Eighth Century* (Columbia: University of South Carolina Press, 1976), 133. Hereafter, Riché, *Education*.

11. *Ibid.*, 144.

12. *Ibid.*, 143-4, 187.

13. James Westfall Thompson, *the Literacy of the Laity in the Middle Ages* (Berkeley: University of California Press, 1939), 1, 7, 8, 11, 15. Hereafter, Thompson, *Literacy.*

14. Reynolds, *Texts,* xvi.

15. *Ibid.*, 434. Portions of single manuscripts survive for three of the four authors, and parts of two manuscripts survive for Pliny the Younger. Altogether, only five classical manuscripts are known to have been recopied from the 6th through the 8th Centuries in the whole of Western Europe.

16. Reynolds and Wilson, *Scribes,* 73.

17. *Ibid.*

18. In Italy at least, "professional copiest continued to function throughout the entire medieval period, [and] the commercial production of books [continued] as practiced in ancient times...." Karl Christ, *Handbook of Medieval Library History.* Revised by Anton Kern and translated by Theophil M. Otto (Metuchen, N. J.: Scarecrow Press, 1984), 28. Hereafter, Christ, *Handbook.*

A similar conclusion was reached by James Westfall Thompson, *the Medieval Library* (Chicago: University of Chicago Press, 1939), 132. Hereafter, Thompson, *Medieval Library.* For a diametrically opposed opinion about the continued existence of professional copiest, see E. A. Lowe, "Handwriting," in G. C. Crump and E. F. Jacob, eds., *The Legacy of the Middle Ages* (Oxford University Press, 1926), 202. Hereafter, Lowe, "Handwriting."

19. E. A. Lowe, *Codices Latini Antiquiores; a Paleographical Guide to Latin Manuscripts Prior to the Ninth Century.* 12 volumes (Oxford: Oxford University Press, 1934-1972). Hereafter, Lowe, *CLA.*

20. In the *CLA* Lowe listed 1811 items, 90 percent of which are included in the present

analysis. The remaining 10 percent were irrelevant to the present study for 8 percent consisted of archaeological finds (mostly papyrus manuscripts from Egypt) and 2 percent of fragments too small to be identified.

21. This information was compiled from Lowe's *CLA* data, which assigned dates that generally represent a consensus of opinion. When Low assigned either of two centuries as the time period during which a manuscript was likely to have been written, I have followed the practice of William H. Willis and assigned half of those manuscripts to the earlier century and half to the later (Roberts and Skeat, *Codex*, 36).

For comparative purposes, Lowe included a small number of manuscripts that can be dated to the 9th Century. Also, by using two centuries as a time period, he assigned about 400 manuscripts to either the 8th or the 9th Century. Thus around 200 manuscripts are likely to date from the 9th Century (after his cut-off date of A. D. 800). These 200 manuscripts are omitted from because they represent a small fraction of surviving 9th Century documents; if they had been included, they would have implied--very incorrectly--that copying of religious manuscripts declined during the 9th Century. Studies as comprehensive as Lowe's have not been made for later manuscripts, but there is no question that the quantities for both religious and secular manuscripts were higher in the 9th Century than in the 8th.

22. Again, the manuscripts assignable statistically to the 9th Century have been omitted. Secular manuscripts represented only 5 percent of the latest manuscripts selected by Lowe. However, if equivalent data were available for all surviving 9th Century manuscripts, the percentage would probably have been higher.

23. Reynolds, *Texts*, xvi.

24. Thompson, *Literacy*, 1. Riché, *Education*, 255 (citing the library of a Spanish count of the mid-7th Century).

25. Doris H. Banks, *Medieval Manuscript Bookmaking; a Bibliographic Guide* (Metuchen, N. J.: Scarecrow Press, Inc., 1989). Christ, *Handbook*, 29.

26. Reynolds and Wilson, *Scribes*, 69.

27. James Westfall Thompson, *Ancient Libraries* (Berkeley, University of California Press, 1940), 41.

28. *Didascalia Apostolorum*, 12. Quoted in William Barclay, *Educational Ideals in the Ancient World* (London: Collins, 1959), 230. Hereafter, Barclay, *Ideals*. This passage was reused in the *Apostolic Constitution*, I, 6 (J. Bass Mullinger, *the Schools of Charles the Great and the Restoration of Education in the Ninth Century* [London: Longmans, Green, and Co., 1877), 8).

29. *De Spectaculis*, 30. Quoted in Barclay, *Ideals*, 202-203.

30. *Contra Faustum*, xiii, 18. Quoted in Johnson, "Parchment," 90.

31. *De Doctrina Christiana*, 40. Quoted in Barclay, Ideals, 231.

32. *Epistle*, 50.5. Quoted in Barclay, *Ideals*, 212. The second quote is from *Aldus Manutius: the Greek Classics*, ed. and trans. by N. G. Wilson (London: the I Tatti Renaissance Library; Harvard University Press), 143.

33. *Epistle*, xi, 24. Quoted in Dudden, *Gregory*, 287.

About this passage, Dudden wrote, "it is impossible to explain away language such as this" (ibid., 288). At least one apologist has attempted to do so. Charles H. Beeson wrote that Gregory's outrage "may well have been caused, in part at least, by his concern that more important duties were being neglected" ("the Collectaneum of Hadoard," *Classical Philology*, XL, no. 4 [Oct., 1945], 209). However, Gregory's statement that pagan literature was "unfit to be recited by even a pious layman" indicates exactly what his concern was and what his attitude towards the classics was.

34. *The Panegyric on Basil*, 11. Quoted in Barclay, *Ideals,* 221. Barclay felt that churchmen such as Gregory of Nazianzen must have had considerable influence, but the almost complete lack of demonstrable interest in pagan literature during the Dark Ages argues otherwise.

35. *Scribes*, 41. 36. Gregory of Tours, the History of the Franks, X, 31; translated by Lewis Thorpe (Harmondsworth: Penguin Books, 1974), 603.

37. Charles Henry Beeson attempts to refute "the myth that palimpsests are evidence of this

hostility." "The Palimpsests of Bobbio," *Studi e Testi, 126: Miscellanea Giovanni Mercati, VI* (Città del Vaticano: Biblioteca Apostolica Vaticana, 1946), 162-184 (quote on 163). Hereafter, Beeson, "Bobbio."
38. Lowe, "Rescripti."
"Of the palimpsested lower texts the largest group [of religious writings] seems to have been condemned on the grounds of obsolescence." "After cases of obsolescence came those of duplication." Lowe, "Rescripti," 482, 483.
39. *Ibid.*, 483. Few methods the Church used to discourage an interest in classical literature can have been as effective as the study of grammar.
40. Giulia Bologna, *Illuminated Manuscripts; the Book Before Guttenberg* (New York: Weidenfeld & Nicholson, 1988), 19.
41. Reynolds and Wilson, *Scribes,* 73.
42. Beeson, "Bobbio," 183.
43. *Ibid.,* 170.
44. *Ibid.,* 182-184 and n. 54.
45. *Ibid.,* 176.
46. *Ibid.,* 182.
47. Florence Edler de Roover, "The Scriptorium," in Thompson, *Medieval Library,* 595.
48. Lowe, "Rescripti."
49. *The Didascalia Apostolorum in Syriac*, I (Chapters I-X), translated by Arthur Vööbus. Corpus Scriptorum Christianum Orientalium, vol. 402; Scriptores Syri, tomus, 176 (Louvain: Secrétariat du Corpus SCO, 1979), 28-29.
50. Beeson, "Bobbio," 170-171.
51. Quoted in John Addington Symonds, *Renaissance in Italy* (New York: Modern Library, 1935), I, 391. Hereafter, Symonds, *Renaissance*.
52. Beeson, "Bobbio," 164.
53. Lowe, "Some Facts"; "More Facts," 43.
54. Lowe, "Some Facts."
55. Lowe, "More Facts."
56. Lowe, "Rescripti." Lowe, *CLA*.
57. Lowe, "Rescripti."
58. Ibid.
59. Ibid.
60. Ibid., 497; Lowe's item 41 was a majuscule copy of a religious text that was erased and recopied in minuscule.
61. Ibid., 490-491.
62. Reynolds and Wilson, *Scribes,* 73.

63. Lowe, "Rescripti," 483.
64. F. W. Hall, review of C. E. Boyd, *Public Libraries and Literary Culture in Ancient Rome* in The Classical Review, XXXVI (1922), 32.
65. Only about 100 secular manuscripts of all types survived after c. A. D. 800 without being erased. Nearly all were practical in subject matter, and many survive in fragmentary condition. About 13 times as many religious manuscripts survived from the same period without any being erased except those that came to be considered heretical. Lowe, *CLA* with deductions from Lowe, "Rescripti."
66. Reynolds, *Texts,* xxv, lxxx.
67. Richard E. Sullivan argued that little happened after the 4th Century that would have an impact on the Modern World until around the year 1000, but the evidence of manuscripts indicates that this is incorrect ("The Carolingian Age: Reflections on Its Place in the History of the Middle Ages," *Speculum* 64 (1989), 267-306; quote from 281).

One of the most important aspects of the Carolingian Period was that it allowed people and ideas to travel more freely in Western Europe than at any time since the Roman Empire (even though both empires never lost their regional characteristics). There may have been no directly influential political or economic precedents, but this does not mean, as has been asserted, that the Carolingian Period was insignificantly different from the period that preceded it. For centuries, the Church had largely succeeded in closing minds through indoctrination. Seeking verifiable facts is not insignificantly different from accepting doctrine on the basis of faith. Surviving manuscripts indicate that Charlemagne and his successors had religious interests as well as secular ones, but that they strove to reopen minds to the intellectual contributions of the Ancient World.
68. Pearl Kibre, "The Intellectual Interests Reflected in Libraries of the Fourteenth and Fifteenth Centuries," *Journal of the History of Ideas,* VII, no. 3 (Jun. 1946), 257, fn. 2. Hereafter, Kibre, "Interests."

R. W. Southern made the point that a classical writing that was popular in the Middle Ages might well be popular for an entirely different reason during the Renaissance. He prepared a bar graph showing the surviving manuscripts of the *Timaeus* by the number of copies made during fifty-year intervals from 900 to 1550 (summarizing Waszink's data with some modifications). The graph shows two dramatic peaks, one for the second half of the 12th Century and the other for the second half of the 15th Century. Southern noted that the first peak was "a sign of a growing interest in natural science, which first needed and then outgrew the information in the *Timaeus*"; the second peak represented "a wider interest in Plato's writings as a whole" (*Platonism, Scholastic Method, and the School of Chartres* [Reading: University of Reading, 1979], 14-15).

The popularity of most classics during the later Middle Ages was to support theology or, where they went beyond sacred writings, as authorities in their own right. Their popularity during the Renaissance was more often as examples of excellence worthy of emulation and eventually as standards to surpass.

69. Reynolds and Wilson, *Scribes*, 52.
70. Lowe, "Rescripti."
71. Reynolds, *Texts*, xxv, lxxx.
72. There are, for example, around 8,000 manuscripts of the Vulgate New Testament and approximately 1,000 earlier versions and 4,000 Greek manuscripts or about 13,000 handwritten copies of the New Testament alone--compared to a single handwritten copy of some classical manuscripts of equivalent size such as a decade of Livy or the *Histories* of Tacitus. A. T. Robertson, *an Introduction to the Textual Criticism of the New Testament* (London: Hodder & Stoughton, 1925), 70.
73. Pierre Courcelle has shown with a high degree of probability that at least two religious works described by Cassiodorus did survive. By considering dates, pagination, and unusual combinations of titles bound together by Cassiodorus, Courelle was also able to "invalidate" the theory that Bobbio's collection of classical titles came from Vivarium. The fate of Cassiodorus's library is otherwise unknown (*Late Latin Writers and Their Greek Sources* [Cambridge, Mass.: Harvard University Press, 1969], 363, 386, 391).

On the Bobbio "hypothesis," Lowe had written previously that "the entire thesis, it seems to me, is built on the naïve assumption that Cassiodorus is the only man of late antiquity who could have possessed so large and varied a collection. Surely men like Ennodius, Boethius, and the Symmachi were equally well-read and had shelves full of books...." He concluded that the "theory rests on palaeographical misconceptions, and on literary and historical assumptions that border on the absurd." *CLA*, IV, xxvi, xxvii. See also, Lowe, "Some Facts," 197, for disproof of the assumption that capital letters at the head of each page were unique to manuscripts written at Vivarium.

The monastery at Vivarium lasted at least eight years after Cassiodorus's death, but no subsequent mention of it is known. Riché, *Education*, 169.

74. Lowe, "Handwriting," 203.
75. Moses Hadas, *Ancilla to Classical Reading* (New York: Columbia University Press, 1954), 30-31.
76. *Scribes*, 71.

In an essay entitled "The Influence of Cassiodorus on Medieval Culture" published in 1945, Leslie W. Jones asserted, "the manuscripts of Vivarium and of Cassiodorus preserved in sound form for generations to come both the Fathers of the Church and the ancient Latin authors; this two-fold culture might of course have survived somehow without the aid of Cassiodorus but, as it is, the credit should go primarily to him." So many scholars took issue with so many points of Jones's article that he amended it in 1947 with "Further Notes Concerning Cassiodorus' Influence on Medieval Culture." He then noted that "preserved" ought to have read "attempted to preserve." *Speculum* 20 (1945), 442; 22 (1947), 256.

77. Quoted in Lynn Thorndike, *University Records and Life in the Middle Ages* (New York: W. W. Norton & Co., Inc. 1975), 39.
78. When the humanist Coluccio Salutati asked a colleague to purchase a copy of Virgil, he was told that "it is forbidden by the canon law to concern oneself with books of that sort" (recorded in Salutati's response dated 1378). Quoted in James Bruce Ross and Mary Martin McLaughlin, eds., *the Portable Medieval Reader* (New York: the Viking Press, 1949), 614.
79. N. G. Wilson, *Scholars of Byzantium*

(Baltimore: Johns Hopkins University Press, 1983). Hereafter, Wilson, *Byzantium*. When a Greek scholar was reckless enough to derive heretical opinions from the classics, he could expect active opposition from the Greek Church, but otherwise, the classics were too much a part of Byzantine civilization to be supressed.

80. Luci Berkowitz and Karl A. Squitier, *Thesaurus Linguae Graecae; Canon of Greek Authors and Works*, 2nd ed. (New York: Oxford University Press, 1986), vii, xii. Most authors represented in the second edition of the *TLG* wrote before A. D. 400, and the total number of words entered in the computerized canon by 1985 was nearly 57 million. The total number for all Latin classical texts is around 9 million. Berkowitz and Squitierss noted that the preface to the 1925 edition of Liddell, Scott, and Jones's *Greek-English Lexicon* estimated that there was altogether "at least 10 times" as much early Greek as Latin writing--even though much Greek literature has also not survived.

81. F. W. Hall, *a Companion to Classical Texts* (Chicago: Argonaut, Inc., Publishers, 1970 reprint of 1913 edition), 25.

82. Wilson, *Byzantium*, 93. Reynolds and Wilson, *Scribes*, 54.

83. List compiled by Photius of authors used by John Stobaeus to compile his *Anthology*. Frederic G. Kenyon, *Books and Readers in Ancient Greece and Rome* (Oxford: Oxford University Press, 1932), 29. Hereafter, Kenyon, *Books*.

84. In 1204 "great damage was done, and there is little doubt that libraries suffered greatly. For the historian of literature this sack of the city was a greater disaster than the more famous one in 1453.... By the time that the city fell into the hands of the Turks little remained to be discovered by the collectors...." Reynolds and Wilson, *Scribes*, 62. These authors state that Diodorus Siculus's *Universal History* as "the only substantial and well-attested loss" in 1453, but an 11th Century copy survived in the Monastery of St. John on Patmos (Anthony Hobson, *Great Libraries* [New York: G. B. Putnam's Sons, 1970], 63).

After the fall of Constantinople, a collection of Greek books was assembled for the library of Mehmed the Conqueror. Mehmed also commissioned copies of Greek classics, including Homer's *Iliad*, Hesiod's *Theogony*, Pindar's *Olympiaka*, and Arrian's *Anabasis of Alexander*. In 1687, a Frenchman saw what remained of this library, and he recorded that it then numbered around 200 works. Julian Raby, "Mehmed the Conqueror's Greek Scriptorium," *Dumbarton Oaks Papers* 37 (1983), 15-34, figs. 1-43.

This evidence demonstrates that the Turks had a greater appreciation for Greek literature than the Crusaders; little in Greek reached the West as a result of their long occupation of Constantinople. Although 200 volumes is a modest number, it is more volumes than for Latin authors in the Leob Classical Library.

85. Kibre, "Interests," 278.

86. Symonds, *Renaissance*, I, 391.

87. Letter dated Dec. 15, 1416, in Phyllis Walter Goodhart Gordon, ed. and translator, *Two Renaissance Book Hunter; the Letters of Poggius Bracciolini to Nicolaus de Niccolis* (New York: Columbia University Press, 1974), 193. Hereafter, Gordon, *Poggius*.

88. Letter of Cincius Romanus of c. 1416 in *ibid.*, 188-189.

89. Reynolds and Wilson, *Scribes*, 93.

90. Thompson, *Medieval Library*, 93-100. James Stuart Beddie, "The Ancient Classics in the Medieval Libraries," *Speculum* 5 (1930), 9 (noting that Wibald assembled the largest collection of Cicero of the 12th Century).

91. *Ibid.*, 130, 159-163. The libraries at Alexandria held 132,800 titles (an estimated 400,000 to 700,000 scrolls). Pergamon had to surrender 200,000 scrolls to Mark Anthony. The single private library of the Villa of the Papyri at Herculaneum contained at least 1,700 scrolls, and its subject matter was so limited that the owner may well have had another library. Rodolfo Lanciani, *Ancient Rome in the Light of Recent Discoveries* (Boston: Houghton, Mifflin & Co., 1898), 181, 185.

92. Christ, *Handbook*, 14.

93. Gordan, *Poggius*, 334, n. 7.

94. Symonds, *Renaissance*, I, 409-410.

95. Roberts and Skeat, *Codex*. 96. Martial, *Epigrams*, XIV, 184. Translated by Walter C.

A. Ker (London: William Heinemann; New York: G. P. Putnam's Sons, 1930), II, 505. A scroll written on both sides in equally small letters would have been approximately the same size, but less convenient to consult. Both parchment and papyrus had to be treated for both writing surfaces to be equally usable. Ordinarily, scrolls were written on only one side, but Pliny the Elder, for example, is known to have used a small handwriting on both sides of scrolls (Roberts and Skeat, *Codex*, 12). A scroll could be rolled clockwise at one end and counter-clockwise at the other to enable either side to be read, though still less conveniently consulted than a codex. Kenyon, *Books*, 64.

97. Johnson, "Parchment," 74. Roberts and Skeat, *Codex*, 15-23.

98. Reynolds and Wilson, *Scribes*, 30.

99. Johnson, "Parchment," 83-84.

100. *Ibid.*, 74.

101. Roberts and Skeat, *Codex*, 35-37.

102. Kenyon, *Books*, 95: "It is therefore fair to attribute to the Christians a considerable share in the introduction of the codex form...." Reynolds and Wilson, *Scribes*, 30: "The impulse to change the format of the book must have come from the early Christians...."

103. Lowe lists a segment of a papyrus scroll that was cut out to serve as an individual page, and its plain reverse was used for a different text (*CLA* IX, 32; item 1349). Since papyrus could not be erased readily, most scrolls were presumably cut apart for use as scratch paper. Parchment scrolls must have been occasionally have been cut into segments and erased for reuse in codices. Both parchment scrolls and codices must have been dismantled at times for separate documents (for a palimpsest which appears to have been taken from a codex, see Albert Bruckner and Robert Marichael, eds., *Chartae Latinae Antiquiores; Facsimile-Edition of the Latin Charters Prior to the Ninth Century* [Olten & Lausanne: Urs Graf-Verlag, 1954], I, 42; item 42).

104. Three-hundred years was estimated by Galen (18 [2].630; cited by Reynolds and Wilson, *Scribes*, 30. Two-hundred years was considered a long time for a papyrus scroll to last by Pliny the Elder (xiii, 83; cited by George Haven Putnam, *Authors and Their Public in Ancient Times...*, 3rd ed. rev. (New York: Cooper Square Publishers, 1967 reprint).

105. Johnson, "Parchment," 54.

106. The Franciscan Roger Bacon (c. 1214-1294?) was a conspicuous and late exception who spent 14 years in prison for his impertinence. The Augustinian Gregor Johann Mendel (1822-1884) was another exception whose research was ignored during his lifetime. The secular studies of both men were the result of their own interests, not on behalf of the Church.

For medieval historians, see Eva Matthews Sanford, "The Study of History in the Middle Ages," *Journal of the History of Ideas* V, 1 (Jan. 1944), 21-43.

107. *Scribes*, 102.

108. "Through war, loans, fire, and theft in the later Middle Ages, the number of books in monasteries actually decreased. To these factors must be added the intellectual decline of the monasteries." For example, Bobbio's total of 666 volumes in c. 850 was reduced to approximately 336 in 1461. Thompson, *Medieval Library*, 130, 164.

109. The teacher was Brunetto Latini, whose secular teaching was marked "by a distinct advance in general culture and by a new enthusiasm for the ancient authors." Charles T. Davis, "Education in Dante's Florence," *Speculum* 40 (1965), 418-421. Davis cites Giovanni Villani that in 1339 about 10 percent of Florence's population was enrolled in secular schools *(ibid.*, 415).

110. "There is no evidence, however, that he took even the minor orders: theoretically only one who had taken those orders could hold benefices, but in Petrarch's time this requirement was not enforced. He certainly never took the major orders." Ernest H. Wilkins, "Petrarch's Ecclesiastical Career," *Speculum* 28 (1953), 754. Hereafter, Wilkins, "Career."

Petrarch lived most of his life in self-imposed seclusion. Despite many offers of employment in cities, he preferred the solitude of his country retreat. Petrarch, "Epistle to Posterity," in Morris Bishop, ed. and translator, *Letters from Petrarch* (Bloomington: Indiana University Press, 1966), 9.

111. G. Billanovich, "Petrarch and the Textual

Tradition of Livy," *Journal of the Warburg and Courtauld Institutes* 14 (1951), 150.

112. Reynolds and Wilson, *Scribes,* 108-109.

113. Wilkins, "Career," 773.

114. B. L. Ullman, *The Origin and Development of Humanistic Script* (Roma: Edizioni di Storia e Letteratura, 1960), 15-16.

115. Giovanni Boccaccio, *the Decameron,* translated by G. H. McWillam (Harmondsworth: Penguin Books, 1972), 247 (III, 3). Thomas M. Lindsay, *Luther and the German Reformation* (Edinburgh: T. & T. Clark, 1900), 109.

In the 14th Century, Boccaccio and Geoffrey Chaucer shared what seems to have been a widespread contempt for the hypocrisy of friars. Boccaccio mentions in his epilogue that he knew he was likely to be said to "have an evil and venomous tongue, because in certain places I write the truth about the friars. But who cares?" (*ibid.,* 832-833). "Whenever Chaucer has occasion to mention friars, we get the same characterization, on unextenuated hypocritical villainy." Arnold Williams, "Chaucer and the Friars," *Speculum* 28 (1953), 449. Williams concluded that since other clergy were extremely critical of friars, secular writers followed their lead, but Boccaccio and Chaucer were not followers. It is more likely that in writing for publication they could safely criticise only friars. Private correspondence such as that of Poggio contained similar opinions about monks.

116. Lowe suggests that Boccaccio misrepresented the conditions at Monte Cassino in order to place a theft in a better light, but there is no definite evidence of a theft, and Boccaccio was not likely to have been defending himself when he told the story to the student who recorded it. Lowe, "Tacitus' *Histories,*" 296.

117. Gordan, *Poggius,* 6 ("never in holy orders"); 334, n. 7 (number of books); 74 (copiest to Germany).

118. *Ibid.,* 99.

119. *Ibid.,* 46.

120. *Ibid.,* 92; cf. 113.

121. *Ibid.,* 135.

122. *Ibid.,* 191.

123. *Ibid.,* 305, n. 10.

124. Berthold L. Ullman and Philip A. Stadter, *the Public Library in Renaissance Florence; Niccolò Niccoli, Cosimo de' Medici and the Library of San Marco* (Padova: Eritrice Antenore, 1972), 9.

125. *Ibid.,* 10-12.

126. Gordan, *Poggius,* 189-190.

127. Rodolfo Lanciani, *the Destruction of Ancient Rome; a Sketch of the History of the Monuments* (New York: Benjamin Blom, 1967 reprint of 1901 edition), 102.

Palimpsest with Cicero's *De re Publica* restored (Vaticano Latino 5757, p. 148)

Appendix IV

Greek and Latin Classics Printed by Aldus Manutius

Aldus Manutius (c. 1451-1515) was one of the individuals who had the greatest impact on the Renaissance and on subsequent thought. He was the pivotal figure in attempts to preserve ancient Greek knowledge and to disseminate ancient Roman knowledge, and for these accomplishments, he deserves to be considered one of the greatest benefactors of humanity.

Aldus deserves much of the credit for ensuring the survival of ancient Greek knowledge. Within half a century of the use of movable type for printing in Germany, nearly all Latin Classics had been printed, and their continued existence was insured, but even though most Greek Classics had reached Italy before the invention of printing, very few were printed for another half century. Even then, there was initially almost no market for the sale of book in Greek, but Aldus nonetheless decided it was crucial to publish as many of the Greek Classics as quickly as possible, and over a period of about two decades he succeeded in producing editions that ensured their survival and that provided a crucially important basis for further corrections. In addition, Aldus produced small, affordable editions of the Latin Classics to make them more widely available in better editions and to help underwrite the higher costs of printing of the Greek Classics. With the essential assistance of a well established printer and an investor, Aldus produced large first editions of the works of Aristotle, Plato, and numerous other Greek authors.

"Aldus's earlier career had been as a tutor, initially perhaps in Rome, then in Ferrara and Capri" (Wilson in Manutius 2016: 326, n. 14). For example, he taught Alberto Pio, the Prince of Capri, for more than six years (Manutius 2017: 171). He relocated to Venice in 1489 or 1490, but "it is notable that the first Greek texts issued by his press did not appear until 1495, which suggests that the economic and technical difficulties he faced were probably much greater than he had foreseen" (Manutius 2016: xv). He was the publisher of the company he created, but the printing was done by the employees of Andrea Torresani, and most of the funding was provided by Pierfrancesco Barbarigo, their silent partner (Davies 1999: 13; except when noted otherwise, all page numbers in this introductory section are to Davies 1999). Aldus largely decided what would be printed and supervised the editing. He devoted the last 25 years of his life almost entirely to publishing approximately 100 volumes of Greek and Latin Classics (with some volumes containing the works of more than one author).

From the time that Jerome translated the New Testament into Latin in the late 4th and early 5th centuries, there was little interest in Greek texts in Italy for about a thousand years. Greek continued to be spoken widely in southern Italy, but few Greek classics were copied in Italy, and copies were extremely rare. Jerome's translation was eventually accepted as canonical, and no further translation was considered necessary or desirable by the Catholic Church from 1563-1979 (https://en.wikipedia.org/wiki/Vulgate). Even Biblical studies were no longer considered to require a knowledge of Greek. The Crusades to take back the Holy Land took back little of anything. Even though the Crusaders held Constantinople, they took few Greek texts back to Italy either sacred or profane unless they were considered works of art.

It was not until 1457, a few years after the fall of Constantinople in 1453 that "...John Gutemberg, a German discovered the use art of printing books..." (Vasari 1568: I, 347). Consequently, no Greek text was ever printed in Constantinople. The possibility of producing large numbers of Greek texts thus coincided with the transfer of large numbers of Greek manuscripts from Turkey to Italy along with large numbers of Greeks who learned Latin and Italian and began to teach Greek. There had been scattered attempts to teach Greek in Italy throughout the 1400s and a few attempts to publish individual titles in the late 1400s, but no systematic attempts. With Italian states frequently at war, Aldus decided to devote much of his life to the urgent need to preserve ancient Greek knowledge and the opportunity to make it widely available through printing.

From 1494-1515, Aldus and his partners printed approximately 120 separate editions of mostly Greek texts, and they made available first editions of the greater part of the Greek Classics (Davies 1999: 62). Most importantly, from 1495-1498 he published all available works of Aristotle in five volumes. Including related works by Theophrastus, the total number of folio pages was 3,700 (20, 32, 50). "The centrality of Aristotle in intellectual life of the time can hardly be overstressed. In Latin dress he lay at the heart of any university course in philosophy, as dominant at the end of the Quattrocento as in the preceding three hundred years" (20). Erasmus later used Aldus's edition of Aristotle to compare the printed text to manuscripts that were not available to Aldus and to produce a corrected and less expensive edition in 1531 (25), improving upon what Aldus had been able to do, but Aldus nonetheless deserves the credit for ensuring the survival of nearly all of Aristotle's works and for enabling manuscript copies to be compared. In 1502 Aldus published quarto editions of the Greek texts of Herodotus and Thucydides, which had previously been accessible in Italy only in a Latin translation by Lorenzo Valla (50).

In 1513, Aldo's great project to preserve and disseminate the Greek Classics culminated with the first edition of the works of Plato (30, 60). It could have been even better if Aldus had been able to use Bessarion's copy of Plato, but there is no definite evidence that Aldus had access to Bessarion's collection, which was stored in the Cathedral of San Marco until a library could be built to make it available (59).

In addition to publishing standard works of the Greek Classics in folio and quarto editions for scholars, Aldus made available many standard Latin authors in octavo editions that primarily for students "The Greek folios were once more buoyed up by a steady stream of quarto reprints of standard Latin authors, grammars in Greek and Latin, and octavo Classics in Latin and Italian" (62). For example, there had previously been no inexpensive edition of Lucretius, and he produced two increasingly accurate quarto editions (40, 43, 62). He began producing inexpensive octavo editions of Virgil and other standard Latin authors in 1501, and with two editions of Virgil, he printed and sold a combined total of around 6,000 copies (42, 46). Aldo also produced a more accurate printed versions of Dante and Petrarch than had been previously available. "These two editions marked a radical overhaul and purification of the text of the Tuscan poets. They were to prove of central importance for the development of Italian vernacular literature in the sixteenth century..." (46)

Before Aldus came to Venice, between 1470 and 1480 the city already had about 50 printers (8).

> From the mid-1470s the partners to a contract took on more and more the specialized roles of merchant backers, printers, publishers, distributors and booksellers, often with some degree of overlap. The efficient capitalist structure of the biggest firms and the constant competition both tended to drive down prices, so that for the first time in history, books were widely and cheaply available throughout Europe [8].

"...there was at Venice a highly developed printing trade which by 1490 had far eclipsed any other city of Europe in terms of production and organized distribution" (7). As a maritime city, its books were exported by sea throughout the Mediterranean and along the Atlantic coast of Europe, and geographically, Venice was well situated to export books by land to southern Germany and from there still farther north and east. Although the book trade was well established in Venice before Aldus began publishing, no one had appreciated the great opportunity that he recognized. "Very little Greek printing had been done at that stage anywhere in Italy, and none at all elsewhere in Europe" (9). "Before the Aldine press was set up the total number of volumes printed in Greek was scarcely more than a dozen" (Reynolds and Wilson 2013: 156).

The immense impact that Aldus had on ensuring the survival of Greek literature and on making it widely available had the overall effect of greatly increasing the appreciation for the influence of the Greeks on the Romans in all respects including architecture. Vitruvius had been printed in Rome in 1486 and so was already available when Aldus began publishing in 1494, and there was nothing else of comparable importance on architecture. Nearly all of Aldus's books were unillustrated except for decorative initials, but a major exception was the *Hypnerotomachia Polyphili* by Francesco Colona that Aldus published in Italian in 1499, and it set a new standard for incorporating excellent images into the body of printed texts:

> The great distinction of the *Hypnerotomachia*... lies in its blending of type, woodcut capitals and woodcut illustrations into a harmonious whole. The illustrations themselves closely follow the text.as Poliphilo moves through the dream landscape of ancient ruins and shattered inscriptions, arcane hieroglyphs and obelisks, triumphal processions of nymphs and satyrs. The great beauty of the classicizing style of these woodcuts has provoked many attempts to identify the artists with a known master, none of which has met with widespread favour ... The most that can be said with assurance is that the designer was familiar with the work of Andrea Mantegna and Giovanni Bellini and lies within that ambit of north Italian classicism which contributed so much to the hand-painted illumination of incunabula... [39-40].

The books published by Aldus were uniformly well designed and printed, and he had typefaces designed to enhance their appearance. Miniscule script had been adapted in 1465 for printing by Sweynheym and Pannartz at Subiaco, where the first printing in Italy had been done. Aldus refined it further with a Roman typeface named for Bembo, and he first printed books in an Italic font that he had designed in emulation of cursive handwriting.

The Greek front Aldus had designed was less easy to ready than his Roman fonts and more like his Italic font, but more complex and still harder to read. The font he commissioned became and remains standard, and he simplified how it could be printed. Earlier printed books in Greek had needed approximately 1,300 separate pieces to type to reproduce "...all possible forms and combinations of letters, breathings and accents..." (10). The Greek Classics had been composed using only a couple of dozen capital letters, but an attempt to transliterate miniscule back into uncials had failed: "...the Florentine model of [Janus] Lascaris's inscriptional capitals, beautiful and clear, but not easy to read over the long stretch, were not encouraging" (14). Aldus decided, instead, to develop a less expensive method of printing in which most diacritical marks could be inserted separately in between lines of lettering. This reduced the number of separate pieces of type from about 1,300 to about 330 (14), but it made Greek quotations within a Latin text so small as to be almost illegible (27, fig. 8).

Cursive writing can be great calligraphy when done by as great an artist as Michelangelo, but when communication is the main goal, a simpler and less obtrusive form of writing is needed, and Aldus was able to provide it for Latin minuscules, but not for Greek. Since the teaching Greek was one of Aldus's main goals, a simpler form of writing would have facilitated learning as well as reduced the cost of producing Greek editions.

"By the time of his death [in 1515] Aldus had transformed the face of learning in Europe..." (60). "When the protagonist of Thomas More's *Utopia* (1516) wants to teach the Utopians how to print, it is naturally the Greek books of Aldus that he shows them, symbols of the best that European literature and technology could offer. Contemporaries like More and Erasmus understood his greatness in securing the foundations and diffusion of classical studies..." (63). With the publication of his edition of Plato, Aldus noted that his friends had been too kind to claim "...that he had single-handedly done more to help literature than anyone for centuries" (60), but it was true, and he was later fully justified in making the claim himself. Overall, he did most to ensure the survival of the Greek Classics and most to disseminate Latin Classics, and he set new standards for every aspect of book production.

Greek Classics

The primary goal of Aldus was to publish all Greek Classics, and in 1495 the preface to his first publication in Greek (a grammar), he announced this goal: "...all the best books of the Greeks will be printed for scholars and men of learning. ...We have decided to devote our whole life to benefiting mankind" (all page numbers in this section on Greek Classics refer to Manutius 2016: 5, 7). He rightly considered Greece the "...mother of all intellectual and scientific life..." (197). "...with the aid of Greek literature, they [students] will easily become proficient in philosophy, the mother of all reputable arts, and equally in medicine" (69). "Not just in Italy, but also in Germany, France, Hungary, Britain, Spain, and in almost every place where the language of the Romans is read, there is great eagerness to study Greek, and not only among adolescents and young people, but also among the elderly" (91).

To the extent possible in order to meet this continually increasing demand, Aldus published the Greek Classics in roughly the following order: (1) Aristotle, (2) dramatists, (3) historians, (4) Homer, (5) Orators, and (6) Plato. His priorities are evident from the sequence in which he published the principal examples of these categories.

(1) Aldus's first priority was to publish the complete works of Aristotle, which he accomplished in five volumes from 1495-1498, and he published the zoological and botanical writings of Aristotle and Theophrastus in 1504. He published several commentaries on Aristotle from 1503-1514. He published all of Aristotle's surviving writings that were available to him, but did not have copies of several works. In 1499 the British humanist William Grocyn praised Aldus for printing Aristotle before Plato:

> Nor without the finest judgment ["could you have succeeded"] in choosing the authors whose works you wanted to print, even putting Aristotle ahead of Plato, despite the considered opinion of Cicero ["*Tusculan Disputations* 1.22"] (In this matter I too certainly take your view, since I feel that the difference between these two greatest of philosophers is simply—forgive me, everyone—the difference between a polymath and a "polymyth...") [285].

(2) Aldus's second main goal was to publish the Greek dramatists, and he published the available works of Aristophanes (9 plays), Sophocles (7 plays), and Euripides (17 plays) in three volumes from 1498-1503. He published Aristophanes immediately after completing his edition of Aristotle, and in the preface to Aristophanes, he wrote,

> for people wishing to learn Greek there is nothing more suitable, nothing better to read [than Aristophanes]. And that is not simply my opinion, but that of Theodore Gaza..., a man of much learning in all fields. When he was asked which Greek author should be read assiduously by people wishing to learn Greek he said: "Only Aristophanes," because he was very witty, rich, erudite and pure in his Attic language. John Chrysostom is said to have had such a high opinion of him that he always had twenty-eight comedies of Aristophanes to hand and used them as a pillow when sleeping; which is how he is said to have acquired the elegance and solemnity for which he was remarkable.... I think Greeks ought to read Aristophanes as assiduously as we read Terrence, whom Cicero termed a close friend because he was always reading him... [71, 73].

Gaza taught Greek at Ferrara and Rome, and he made Latin translations of Aristotle and Theophrastus (Manutius 2017: 338). John Chrysostom (A. D. 347-407) was Archbishop of Constantinople. In 1498, Aldus was able to find only nine complete plays by Aristophanes; two more were later found complete (Manutius 2016: 339, n. 177). In 1507, Aldus published Erasmus's Latin translation of Euripides and noted that "...there were surprisingly few who excelled in both languages". (in Latin as well as Greek well enough to produce readable as well as accurate translations; 301) Aldus was unable to publish Aeschylus.

(3) Aldus's third main goal was to publish the Greek historians, and he published Thucydides, Herodotus, and Xenophon in three volumes from 1502-1503. Aldus noted that Quintilian stated,

> many have written splendid histories, but no one doubts that two are to be placed far above the rest, their different qualities having brought them almost equal fame. Thucydides is dense, succinct and always pressing forward, Herodotus is charming, clear and discursive. One is superior in strong, the other in calm emotions; one in speeches, the other in conversations; one in forcefulness, the other in his will to please [2016: 111, 113].

Aldus noted that "Demosthenes wrote out the text [of Thucydides] eight times to increase his familiarity with it" (103; cf. 221). Aldus published several minor Greek historians in the same volume as Xenophon, whose *Hellenica* "...is said to be matter omitted by Thucydides" (123).

Aldus did not publish Polybius, whose history of the rise of Rome had been one of the books chosen by Pope Nicholas V to be translated into Latin from 1452-1454. Polybius was not printed until 1582 (Manutius 2017: 364, n. 45; Reynolds and Wilson 2013: 169).

(4) Homer was less of a priority that he would have been ordinarily because his works had been well edited and published in Greek in Florence in 1488-1489. Aldus published more affordable editions of the *Iliad* and *Odyssey* in two volumes in 1504 and noted that "it is agreed by almost all who have studied him closely that he is as it were a source of the Greek language, a model for human life, a kind of beacon to the other Greek and Latin poets, and a guide for literary education in general" (169, 170).

(5) Also in 1504, the Greek orator Demosthenes immediately followed Homer in print in a specially produced edition: "...of all the Latin or Greek books we have printed this [by Demosthenes] is the most beautiful issued to the public from our house..." (187).

In his preface, Aldus wrote at length about the life of Demosthenes "for along with much other advice the divine orator tells the Athenian state to be wary of tyrants because they are natural enemies of republics, as wolves are of sheep..." (187); "'every king and tyrant is an enemy of freedom and an opponent of law'" (quoting Demosthenes; 189). In 1498, Aldus contrasted the men who governed Venice with earlier and later rulers: "they are skilled not only in governing the state and ruling its subjects—in this respect to which they are so much to be admired that without any argument they must be judged superior to all rulers of states, both past and present—but also in rhetoric and in every possible branch of learning" (Manutius 2017: 183). Greek writings on politics were of great interest to them and to other Venetians as well as to Florentines.

In 1497, Aldus wrote, "...I hope there will soon come a time when men of our generation will be skilled in all the liberal arts and medicine itself; and all the best scholars, unless they let themselves down, will have the strength to challenge antiquity" (55), but in 1504 he wrote more pessimistically that "no one contests that among the Greeks, Demosthenes is foremost in oratory and Homer in poetry, just as among the Romans, Cicero is easily best for oratory and the poet of Mantua [Vergil] for poetry. This seems to me to be so clear that I think not only will there be no one in future to surpass or equal them, but no one even to come close" (171).

Their writings in Greek and Latin might well never be surpassed for the excellence of expression in those languages, but equivalent results could be achieved in other languages using similar means and could be made more vivid in other media. For example, the same stories in Plutarch were brought to life by Shakespeare, and Michelangelo made Dante more vivid. Moreover, evolution has continually demonstrated that new unities of form can be achieved using the same means to fit different circumstances. In any case, Aldus was wholly convinced that the Greek and Latin classics were the essential basis for a good education.

Lesser Greek rhetoricians and orators were published in three volumes from 1509-1513. Much of this material had been recently brought to Italy by Janus Lascaris.

(6) The publication of Plato's *Complete Works* in 1513 essentially marked the conclusion of the life work of Aldus, who died two years later. In his preface to Plato, Aldus wrote that Marcus Musurus, a Greek from Crete and "...a man of great judgment and great learning... has carefully edited these works of Plato, collating the oldest manuscripts... so that, in conjunction with myself, as always, he has conferred a great benefit on the Greeks and on our people" (2016: 243). Musurus also edited the editions of Aristophanes and Euripides for Aldus, and he successively taught Greek in Padua, Venice, and Rome (2017: 332, n. 76).

The delay in the printing of Plato's works is inexplicable considering that in 1493 Aldus referred to "...Plato, [as] easily the most learned of the Greeks, and his pupil, the great Aristotle..." (2017: 179). In 1497 he wrote in that he hoped that soon after completing Aristotle to follow him with "...the complete works of the divine Plato and all the commentaries on him" (2016: 45) Presumably, Aldus continually hoped to be to use Cardinal Bessarion's copy of Plato, but no definite evidence has been found that he ever had direct access to that copy (2016: xv). "It is important to bear in mind that, contrary to what was assumed for a long time, the wonderful collection of Greek and Latin manuscripts donated by Bessarion to Venice in 1468 was not ordinarily accessible to the public at this date. It is odd that Aldus was not influential enough to gain access" (331). In 1503 Aldus had published Bessarion's *In calminatorem Platonis*, reprinting a previous edition that had been "badly printed in Rome" in 1469 and adding a portion of the third book written "in Bessarion's own hand... to ensure that it is not lost I have had it printed in this volume" (297; 367, n. 42). Bessarion's invaluable collection of early Greek manuscripts seems to have been closed to everyone for decades, but a number of other copies of Plato had reached Italy during the 1400s including the copy owned by Petrarch and the copy acquired by the city of Florence before the fall of Constantinople, and a number of copies had to be compared to reconstruct the text rather than using the earliest available copy as the basis for editing.

From time to time, Aldus also published miscellaneous titles in Greek as they became available and were made ready for printing. He published numerous books on Greek grammar and several Greek dictionaries; in 1495, the first and fourth title he published in Greek were grammars. Grammars were obviously much needed for teaching, but they also helped to create a demand for the Greek Classics. He generally provided Latin translations of Greek grammars for beginners, but the translations were printed separately so that advanced students could omit them when their copies were bound (85, 87).

Greek poets published at various times by Aldus. They included Theocritus and Hesiod in 1496, the *Greek Anthology* in 1503, and Pindar and others in 1513 (in addition to Homer in 1504).

Among the other major titles Aldus published were *Greek Epistolographers* (letter writers) in two volumes in 1499, two treatises on pharmacology in one volume in 1499, and a bilingual edition of Aesop's *Fables* in 1505; although Aesop had been previously printed in Greek and often in Latin, Aldus noted that the previous Greek version was based on "a faulty exemplar," and therefore the previous translations into Latin "was quite unfaithful" (2016: 299). He also published Plutarch's massive *Moralia* (essays) in 1509, but did not publish Plutarch's *Lives*, which along with Polybius is one of the most important sources for ancient Roman as well as Greek history. He did publish Plutarch's life of Demosthenes to accompany Demosthenes's writings and made other use of his work and no doubt would have published the *Lives* if he had lived longer.

In 1497 Aldus wrote that he also hoped after completing Aristotle to "...offer Hippocrates, the whole of Galen and all the other eminent medical writers. After that we shall give you all the mathematicians. What else do you want? I will certainly make sure, if I live long enough, that there is no lack of good books for students of literature and the liberal arts" (2016: 44). His successors carried out many projects he began including Pausanias's guide to Greece, which was published in 1516, the year after Aldus's death (337, n. 147).

Overall, Aldus published the great majority of the Greek Classics. He published no major Christian writings in Greek or Latin; "nearly all the Aldine books were classical texts; Christian writers only occasionally appeared" (Reynolds and Wilson 2013: 158).

In 1513 in his preface to his edition of Plato, Aldus wrote what could have been used as his own epitaph in 1515: "...I do not give way in the face of any troubles or succumb in the face of any toil, and by my single-handed efforts have done more to help the world of letters than everyone else put together, however numerous they were over the course of many centuries" (2016: 241). At the same time, he also wrote, "...I want the books which I put into the hands of the educated to be very accurate and very beautiful."

Latin Classics

Aldus's approach to the Latin Classics was entirely different from his approach to the Greek Classics. Nearly all Latin Classics had already been published before he started the Aldine Press, and there was no pressing need to reprint them (Manutius 2017: xxii; except as noted, all page numbers in this section on the Latin Classics refer to Manutius 2017). However, better and more affordable editions were needed, and Aldus abundantly supplied these needs by printing huge editions of pocket editions with more accurate texts and easier to read fonts, and he made them available at a fraction of the cost of the same works in larger formats. His main goals in printing the Latin Classics were to make them more widely available and to provide funds to underwrite the costs of printing the less salable Greek Classics that were more expensive to produce. Far more people in Europe could read Latin than Greek.

The basic order in which he published Latin Classics also indicates a good deal about his priorities: (1) Lucretius, (2) standard authors, (3) Cicero, and (4) Caesar.

(1) Aldus was especially anxious to make available a better text of Lucretius, the first great Roman philosopher and poet. In 1500, the first ancient Latin author he published was Lucretius, and in 1515 the last ancient Latin author he published was Lucretius. In the preface of the 1500 edition, Aldus noted that

> ...the earlier printed texts of Lucretius that are in circulation are so full of errors and so disfigured by the loss of verses that our author can be understood in very few passages. This text of ours that is now available to the public is so free of mistakes and lacunae that very few passages require correction.
>
> In this respect we are deeply grateful to Girolamo Avanzi of Verona..., a man of extraordinary mastery of the Latin language and the liberal arts, for having worked so laboriously and carefully for many years in correcting Lucretius and restoring him to his original purity and for having emended Lucretius with the help of the author himself. For in Lucretius are to be found not only half-lines or complete verses but even many longer passages that are often repeated elsewhere, in Homeric fashion. Accordingly, since our dear Avanzi knows the poems of Lucretius as well as his fingers and nails..., he has emended hemistiches and verses with the greatest of ease by using other hemistiches and verses of the poet. He achieved the same results with the help of those verses that are cited in various places in other Latin writers [7, 9].

Avanzi himself wrote, "...as for the poem of Lucretius, I found so many passages that were mutilated, deformed and mangled that scarcely any part was free from corruption before my enjoyable labors." Avanzi correctly considered Lucretius "...the most knowledgeable of Latin poets and one whom the incomparable Vergil imitated to a very great extent in many places...." (237).

In the preface of the 1515 edition, Aldus noted that "now Lucretius is being issued from our printing house in a much more correct form than has often been the case in the past and for this we must thank especially our dear Andrea Navagero..., who has gone over the text with great care even though he has done so very rapidly because of his own obligations and the impatient demands of our printers. ...Lucretius can finally be read with understanding" (169).

(2) Aldus's second priority was to publish standard Latin Classics in small formats and in large editions. From 1501-1502, he published editions of Vergil, Horace, Catullus, and others, and from 1502-1503 he published three volumes of Ovid. In 1503, he also published a new edition of Vergil and yet another edition in 1514, and as noted, the total number of copies sold of Vergil exceeded 6,000 and helped greatly to underwrite the Greek Classics. In the interval, in 1509, he published Horace.

(3) Aldus's favorite Latin author was Cicero, and he published as much of the great body of Cicero's writings as he could. He published his *Letters to Friends* in 1504, his *Letter to Atticus, Brutus and His Brother Quintus* in 1513, and his *Rhetorical Works* in 1514. Atticus was Cicero's closest friend and publisher, and he kept him well informed about what he was doing and his reactions to current events (95); "'whoever reads these [letters to Atticus] does not miss much of the complete history of those times'" (quoting Cornelius Nepos; 99). These three massive publications were less salable than Latin poetry, but nonetheless sold well and were made affordable by being printed in octavo editions. Cicero's works were widely read as example of the finest Latin writing, for their philosophy, and for the history they contained.

> ...although all the works of Cicero are marvelously beneficial if they are read continually and carefully, this is especially true of his letters. For the writings of anyone who studies them closely will display richness, eloquence and, what I value most highly, fluency. ... Quintilian... writes: "He who takes delight in Cicero will know that he has made great progress" [27, 29].

In 1514 Aldus also published Quintilian.

Since Aldus was especially interested in publishing letter as examples of everyday use of Latin, he was immensely pleased when an exceptionally early manuscript of Pliny the Younger's letters turned up in France. He published the manuscript in 1508 with a lengthy, scholarly, and persuasive preface defending the authenticity of Pliny's letters to Trajan (71-83). He was able to include a number of previously unpublished letters by Pliny along with a much improved text.

(4) One of the most carefully edited texts that Aldus published was Caesar's *Commentaries on the Gallic War* and his other writings. Caesar's writings were restored by Giovanni Giocondo, who wrote in a letter to Giuliano de' Medici (the third son of Lorenzo) in April 1513,

> I sought out many manuscripts in the whole of France. Because many copies were regularly taken there from Italy and they were less exposed to pillage and wars, much superior manuscripts of every kind can be found in that country. I collated all of them and scrutinized them with great care. But I was not content to rely on my own judgment, and when I had gathered together many of these manuscripts from all sources, I brought together numerous scholars in Venice and put before them everything for their talents to pass judgment on. There was nothing that was not given careful assessment. The result was that very few passages are left that have not been restored to their original splendor. Eventually perhaps someone will wipe

away those remain blemishes. Let me be satisfied in having brought it about that very few of these now remain [259-261].

Aldus's first edition of Caesar's writings included a map of France and adjacent areas, and it is a watercolored woodcut showing the tribes and places mentioned in Gaul (Manutius 2017: 107-113; reproduced in Bonomelli 2016: 48). This edition was published in December 1513, the same year that Cardinal Giovanni de' Medici (the second son of Lorenzo) became Pope Leo X. In May 1514 Giocondo dedicated the volume he edited for Aldus on agriculture to Leo, and in August, Leo appointed Giocondo co-architect of St. Peter's along with Raphael (Heydenreich and Lotz 1974: 355-356, n. 42; 365, n. 28). Giocondo was also the editor of two editions of Vitruvius, the first published in Venice in 1511 and the second in Florence in 1513, but neither was published by Aldus (Manutius 2017: 343, n. 172).

Aldus's first publication by an ancient Latin author had been on astronomy. As in publishing Aristotle and Theophrastus as soon as possible, Aldus was eager to make ancient scientific knowledge available as well as books primarily of interest for their general knowledge, literary value, and practical application. In 1514 he published the four principal treatises on Roman agriculture by Cato, Varro, Columella, and Palladius that had been edited by Giocondo and that was also dedicated to Leo X (2017: 263, 265).

In addition, Aldus published Erasmus of Rotterdam's *Adages* in 1508, and the examples were selected from ancient writings and were edited while Erasmus resided with Aldus in Venice in 1507-1508 (2016: 368, n. 50). Aldus wrote, "...it is a work that can stand comparison with the products of antiquity. ...not only because of the huge number of adages that he has collected so consciously—indeed with much toil and assiduity—from very many authors, both Greek and Latin, but also because of the many passages in the authors of both languages that he has brilliantly corrected in passing or explained with such learning" (Manutius 2017: 215; 371-372, notes 100-104)

In addition to the Latin Classics, Aldus published a dozen books by contemporary humanists. Two were grammars he wrote himself, and the prefaces he wrote for his publications fill two volumes. The other works by humanists were relatively inconsequential except for the *Complete Works* of Angelo Poliziano and the *Land and Customs of the Zygians called Circassians* by Giorgio Interiano. Poliziano lectured in Greek and Latin at the Studio (university) in Florence and published a substantial body of writings before his death at the age of 40. "He made a great contribution to the practice of textual criticism, stressing the importance of the detailed study of manuscripts to establish their relationship and therefore their significance as witnessed to the text" (Manutius 2017: 362, n. 27). Interiano was from Genoa, and he served as governor of Corsica before travelling in the Middle East (367, n. 70). His ethnography is about "...the life and the customs of the Sarmatians, who are called Zygians by Strabo, Pliny and Stephanus..., and who live in the east beyond the river Don and the sea of Azov..." (205).

Except for Origen's *Homilies*, Aldus published almost no early Christian writings in Latin, but most were already in print in multiple editions. He planned to publish a polyglot Bible, but got no further than a prospectus. He did regularly include Christian examples of writing in grammars that were primarily for children, and in 1501 he published a volume of "Christian poets" including Prudentius:

>...my aim was to introduce young children of impressionable age to these poets instead of to the myths and works of pagans and to lead them to recognize what is really true and what is really false so that, in their adolescent years, they would not turn out to be morally corrupt and unfaithful to their religion, as very many are at the present time, but rather upright men and strict adherents of the Christian faith—"so important is habituation in one's tender years!" [11; ironically quoting a pagan source, Vergil's *Georgics* 2.272 [324, n. 17].

From the 1501 octavo edition of Vergil's works, Aldus purposely omitted Virgil's minor poems and erotic poems, but informed "students" that he had done so:

> You see with what an unblemished text and in what form we give you the *Eclogues*, the *Georgics* and the *Aeneid* of Publius Vergius Maro. We did not think that all the other poems that he composed to practice his skills and the obscene poems that are ascribed to him were worthy of this pocket-book size format...
>
> It is our intention to publish from now on all the best authors in the same format [17].

There were so many objections to these omissions that in his 1505 octavo edition of Vergil, Aldus relented and wrote,

> we have also included his short works, both those that he composed in his youth and those that are included with them. We did not think that the obscene poems... were worthy of our pocket-sized edition but since many persons have demanded them with constant clamor we ordered them to be added to the volume on condition that they could be detached separately if anyone so wished. You will readily see in what a corrupt and depraved state these short works have been circulating widely when you compare such copies with ours [69].

In other words, he added the excuse that at least his versions were more correct. In the 1514 edition of Virgil, there is no mention of the controversial poems.

Moreover, a few years before omitting Vergil's erotic verse, in 1499 Aldus had published the *Hypnerotomachia Poliphili* with erotic illustrations and an Italian text. The year after his first edition of Vergil, in 1502 he published a volume that included the erotic Latin poetry of Catullus and asked, "...what can be more delightful than Catullus' wit and charm?..." (25). Of this volume, he "printed about three thousand copies or more... in this very small format of ours. We hope that you [the person he dedicated the edition to] and everyone else will find them convenient to use and will continually pick them up, along with Catullus, to read time and time again" (25; see 237 for Avanzi's corrections; see 328, n. 44 for earlier editions by other publishers; and see 329, n. 48 for conformation of the size of the edition, one of the largest he ever published). "...we issue every month from our Academy a thousand and more copies of some good author" (2016: 115).

Aldus seems to have been sincerely religious, but more so later in life than earlier. He was continually insistent, though, that classical writers must be read to be well educated. For example in 1515, the years in which he died after a long and serious illness, he wrote about Lucretius,

> ...some people believe that he should not even be read by Christians, who adore, worship and venerate the true god. But since truth shines all the more brightly and becomes all the more revered the more it is searched for—as is the case with our Christian faith, which Jesus Christ, Lord God Almighty, proclaimed to mankind while he lived among mortals—I think that Lucretius and those who are very similar to him should be read, but only as falsifiers and liars, as they assuredly are [2017: 167].

This assertion is otherwise unparalleled in his prefaces. Nonetheless, he ended the preface by pointing out that "Lucretius can finally be read with understanding" (169).

Aldus considered his afflictions to be suffering he deserved and to be a test of his worthiness for salvation. In the 1515 preface to Lucretius, he indicated that he had hoped to improve it still further, but had been prevented by the "...ill health with which I have been afflicted, ever more severely, for some months now...." When a Catholic is reminded of his mortality, he is likely to recall his indoctrination and to reconsider the possibility of eternal tortures of a similar or worse kind (169). In 1514, the year before he died, he had written that "...God regularly tests the resolve of his servants, as we read of Job... and corrects and chastises those whom he loves. ... So when one trouble after another afflicts us, it is a sign of salvation and God's unsurpassed goodwill towards us" (2016: 249, 251, 253). "...in our own time... we see not just Italy but practically the whole world engaged in war because of human greed and avarice or, as I prefer to think, because of our faults and sins—God usually punishes human crimes mainly by these three evils, war, famine, and plague, and often together, since famine follows war and plague famine..." (223). In 1495 in the first preface to his first publication in Greek, he indicated a sense of urgency about "...the printing of Greek texts of all kinds..." for two reasons: because of "the number of people wishing to learn Greek..." and because of "...the current state of affairs, the great wars which now afflict the whole of Italy..., since God is angry at our misdeeds, and which look as if they will soon upset or indeed shatter the whole world, on account of the multifarious crimes of humanity, far more numerous and serious than those which were once the reason for an angry God to submerge and destroy in a flood the whole human race" (3).

Despite his faith, Aldus devoted his adult life to teaching, making available, and preserving the Greek and Latin Classics. In 1497, when he had published four of the five volumes of his edition of Aristotle, he wrote,
> the poet said, "fortunate is he who has been able to discover the cause of things" ["Vergil, *Georgics* 2.490"]. If this is true, students, you will surely be fortunate; for you now enjoy a greater supply of fine books than ever existed in the past. You are surrounded by the tools that will enable you to master the liberal arts. Already from us you have a large number of Greek works, both in dialectics and in philosophy..., so that if you realize your full potential you will easily turn out to be the most learned of men and be able to know the causes of things [Manutius 2017: 181; 361, notes 22-23].

Book Production

Editing: Aldus wrote in a preface, "if, learned master, you find errors, either here or in other books which I am printing for the general benefit of the educated public—and I do not deny that there are some—do not put it down to me but to the exemplars used. I do not undertake to correct the texts..., but I do undertake to make every effort to ensure that the printed texts are at least more correct than the exemplars. ...if it reaches the public there will be many people to correct it over a very long period" (2016: 25). He noted that "...each reader, finding a better copy, will be able to correct them [in this case, the names of medicines] for himself. We have provided what we could find" (77).

To prepare his edition of Aristotle, "...the best manuscripts were sought, several copies of the same text were collated and corrected.... It was not possible to ensure that nothing should be found wanting in these books. That is not my fault—I can truthfully say that whatever I take the trouble to print emerges from our house in far better and more correct form than it exhibited in the exemplars—it is the fault of earlier generations and the destructiveness of time..." (2016: 43).

Whenever possible, Aldus attempted to find and compare "...at least three copies..." of any text before printing it (2016: 103). In editing a commentary on Aristotle, he noted,
> since we found variation in the exemplars while printing, not venturing to add, delete or alter anything (that would be rash), we have marked with asterisks passages where variants were found; these are added at the end of the volume, so that everyone can exercise his own judgment about them. Having found an alternative exposition of the second book of the *Analytics*, we gave instruction to print both; my aim is not to omit anything that looks as if it will be useful to scholars [127].

His editions were works in progress intended to make further progress possible, but most of all to ensure that nothing he found would be lost.

To further facilitate the usefulness of his books, he regularly added indices: "It is my intention to make an index of all matters worth knowing that are found in these commentaries.... This we will do in all books to emerge from our house and reach the public..." (221).

Fonts: Ancient Greek as well as Latin had been written entirely in capital letters, and the first edition of the *Greek Anthology* that was printed by Janus Lascaris in 1494 in Florence restored the use of capital letters (uncials) in place of minuscules uncials without diacritical marks, ligatures, and other inessential additions that were subsequently made in handwritten Greek, but to same space Lascaris attempted to imitate miniscule handwriting for marginal notes (Manutius 2016: xiii-xiv). Miniscule letters had begun to be used for copying Greek manuscripts as early as A. D. 835 (Reynolds and Wilson 2013: 59). They greatly reduced the number of pages required, made copying faster, and made books less expensive. Latin minuscules had far fewer embellishments than Greek minuscules, and educated Greeks preferred what they were accustomed to writing and reading. Aldus found a way to make printing Greek minuscules with diacritical marks, ligatures, etc., more practical and enabled the unneeded marks to persist. However, his contemporaries thought this was wonderful and erudite; for example, the British humanist William Grocyn wrote Aldus in 1499, "you could not have devised without the highest degree of ingenuity that marvelous technique for printing Greek letters" (2016: 285).

Wilson wrote, "almost early Greek types, including the four used by Aldus, were made unnecessarily complex by the inclusion of many abbreviations, chiefly for the syllables that occur in grammatical inflections. Aldus' influence was so great that these annoying and aesthetically unpleasing conventions remained in use until the nineteenth century, whereas the simpler uppercase type devised by Janus Lascaris in Florence in the early 1450s was not adopted" (2016: 325, n. 11).

By contrast, the Latin miniscule text that Aldus perfected was eminently legible, required a small fraction of the number of letters, and was widely emulated. He also introduced an italic text that was closer to handwriting, but less easy to read, and in 1501 he used it to print his first edition of Vergil. The *Italic* "...font closely resembles the humanistic cursive as propounded and practiced by Pomponio Leto in Rome and reflected in Aldus' own hand" (2017: 326, n. 30).

The dies for casting Aldus's Greek, Latin, and Italic fonts were cut by Francesco Griffo of Bologna (2017: 17; 326, n. 32): "in addition to his Greek and italic fonts, the Roman front that he cut for Pietro Bembo's *De Aetna*, published by Aldus in 1496, was very influential" (and fonts based on it have continued to be called Bembo; 326, n. 32).

Format: As noted, the first edition of Vergil was also the first of the Latin classics to be issued in octavo (2017: 325, n. 27). Scipione Forteguerri, an appreciative purchaser of Aldine Classics, was among many who wrote thanking Aldus for making classic texts available in pocket editions: "...having given so much help to men with good taste in the acquisition of books, you have in addition found a way to facilitate their use, lest readers should be distracted from the contents of the text by the weight of the volumes being handled" (2016: 297, 299). "Aldus says that he got the idea from the small books (that is, manuscripts) in the library of Bernardo Bembo, the famous Venetian nobleman and bibliophile" (the father of Pietro Bembo; 2017: 324). Earlier pocket books in manuscript were for devotional use such as the prayer books that were sometimes extra illustrated and collected.

One reason Aldus produced books in small format, unbound, and as inexpensively as possible was so that personal copies could be annotated by their owners. He wrote, "I cannot easily describe how much it helps the memory to note in the margin details worth knowing and remembering..." (2016: 221).

"...we shall see to it that, with Jesus' support, we supply devotees of learning with portable libraries, so to speak, in both Latin and Greek" (2017: 27). "The pocket edition in small format for literary texts was one of Aldus's greatest contributions to publishing" (Wilson in Manutius 2016: 344, n. 228).

Sources of Manuscripts

Since manuscripts of Greek and Latin Classics had been copied and collected more or less systematically for about century before Aldus began publishing, most had already been found, but some continued to turn up in distant locations, and Aldus did all he could to acquire the earliest copies available for use in his editions. In 1502 he thanked the lender of several manuscripts and wrote, "I only wish that we had a great number of such benefactors of the republic of letters. And yet we hope to have very many of these soon, not only in Italy, but also in Germany and all parts of France and among 'the Britons, though cut off from the whole world...'" (Manutius 2017: 37). In 1508 when he had nearly given up hope of any major new finds, an extremely early copy of Pliny the Younger's *Letters* turned up in France; "...written on parchment and in a script so different from ours that one cannot read it without a great deal of practice.... This led me to have wonderful hopes that our age would witness the discovery of very many fine authors whom we believe to have perished. For the manuscript is not only very free of errors, but is so old that I think it was written in Pliny's lifetime. ... They also include many letters that were previously not known..." (71, 73; cf. 343, n. 171). He mentioned that a Polish humanist had "...promised to send someone as far as Romania to find manuscripts, and to do so at your own expense no matter how great it might be. For there is said to be a tower... there full of ancient manuscripts" (41). He literally tried to track down all manuscripts of Greek and Roman classics from Britain to Turkey.

Some early and rare copies even of Greek manuscripts continued to become available from isolated locations such monasteries at Mt. Athos and eventually from the island of Patmos. In general, Greek monasteries took better care of pagan manuscripts than Latin monasteries, but this was not invariably the case, and they too were sometimes willing to part with them.

In his preface to the 1513 edition of the *Greek Orators,* Aldus noted that it was based primarily on a unique manuscript that had been recently located:

> ...the speeches written by most of these orators have lain hidden and unknown for many centuries. But they were hidden [in the monastery] on Athos, a mountain in Thrace [then still part of Turkey]. They were brought back to Italy by Lascaris, a scholar and a man of great accomplishment... ["Janus Lascaris...; he traveled to Greece in 1491-92"]. The famous Lorenzo de Medici had sent him to Greece... to look for good books and buy them at any price; from there he returned to Florence with these very orations and other rare and precious volumes [Manutius 2016: 229; 369, n. 446].

Monasteries has a significant, but largely passive role in the transmission of Greek texts. For example, they were willing for monks to copy pagan literature when paid to do so. This was the case with Arethas (c. 860-c. 935), a cleric who for his own use "...commissioned books from professional scribes, in the main monks of monasteries, which accepted regular orders on a commercial basis..." (Reynolds and Wilson 2013: 65). He created a large library of copies in the newly introduced miniscule letters in Greek that made it cheaper to copy works on velum and that was almost invariably used rather than the uncial letters from the time it was introduced (60). He was later able to afford to add greatly to his library when he became an archbishop, but he commissions a copy of Plato, Euclid, and other Greek Classics while still a deacon. His copy of Plato later became part of the monastic library of St. John on the island of Patmos, where Edward Daniel Clark found it among a pile of books in 1801:

> We entered a small oblong chamber, having a vaulted stone roof, and found it to be nearly filled with books, of all sizes, in a most neglected state: some lying upon the floor, a prey to the damp and to worms; others standing upon shelves, but without any kind of order. The books upon the shelves were all printed volumes; for these, being more modern, were regarded as the more valuable, and had a better station assigned to them than the rest, many of which were considered only as so much rubbish. Some of the printed books were tolerably well bound, and in good condition. The Superior said they were his favourites; but when we took down one or two of them to examine their contents, we

discovered that neither the Superior nor his colleague were able to read. ...

At the extremity of this chamber, which is opposite to the window, a considerable number of old volumes of parchment, some with covers and some without, were heaped upon the floor in the utmost disorder: and there were evident proofs that these had been cast aside, and condemned to answer any purpose for which the parchment might be required. ...the whole of this contemned heap consisted entirely of Greek manuscripts, and some of them were of the highest antiquity [Hobson 1970: 64-65].

Among them was the copy that Arethas had commissioned in 895 of Plato's *Dialogues* (63). The monks agreed that any five of the manuscript volumes could be purchased "...provided the islanders did not see the books leave," and to avoid suspicion the volumes were smuggled out in a bread basket on the head of a monk (65). In 1809 Clarke sold these volumes to the Bodleian Library.

As Hobson indicates, the library at Patmos now deserves to be considered one of the world's great libraries and is highly valued and well maintained. It must have been generally well maintained at least from the 12th Century for so many books of great value to have survived, but it had reached a low point in the 18th Century similar to the library at Monte Cassino in the 1400s, and these were not unique cases.

The erasure of velum at Bobbio was the most notorious example of the total disregard for Latin Classics. Although in general, Greek Classics continued to be used in teaching and were always highly regarded in Byzantium, the Archimedes palimpsest indicates that there were at least some major exceptions in which Greek Classics of the highest importance were also erased so that the parchment could be reused for religious writings of little consequence, but this seems to have taken place in Southern Italy. "Attic style was the ideal to which most writers in Greek had aspired from the second century CE onward; this fashion for adhering as closely as possible to the vocabulary and syntax of the leading Athenian authors of the classical period lasted right up to the end of the Byzantine period" (Wilson in Manutius 2016: 328, n. 43). The point is that monks in particular were more concerned about the salvation of their souls than the transmission of pagan learning, and the credit that has been given to them has been greatly exaggerated.

The example of the works of Plato copied for Arethas is important evidence that at least some monks copied whatever they were paid to copy, and since monasteries had to be supported either by alms or to be self-supporting, this is not surprising. Considering the general indifference and frequent hostility of the Latin Church to classical learning during the Medieval period, the routine assumption that any handwriting that can be traced to a monastery means its monks copied it for their own use is unjustified. A more reasonable assumption is that someone with more reason to be interested in the Latin or Greek Classics had them copied for his own use and that they somehow ended up in a monastery, and the widely scattered distribution of copies, the miscellaneous contents of monastic libraries, and the complete absence of any Medieval attempt to create a collection of pagan writings systematically is good evidence of being uninterested.

Since this copy of Plato is dated 895 and the island of Patmos was granted for use as a monastery in 1091, it is certain that this volume was not copied by the monks of Patmos, but somehow ended up in their library (Hobson 1970: 61). This too is important evidence that every book found in a monastery was not copied there, but generally an assumption has been made that every manuscript was copied by monks and in the monastery where it was initially found by humanists. No such assumption is justifiable unless there is explicit evidence that a Classic work was copied at a specific monastery for use there. Nonetheless, a great deal of circular reasoning has been based on dubious assumptions to try to give credit to the Catholic Church credit for saving what it did not destroy.

Copying pagan writings is only known to have been part of the stated purpose of one monastery, which was founded by Cassiodorus around A. D. 540, but not a single manuscript can be traced to his monastery, and there is no reason to believe that it "...played any direct part in the transmission of classical texts. The monastery seems to have died with its founder..." (Reynolds and Wilson 2013: 84).

Without question, many important manuscripts were preserved at Monte Cassino, which was founded in c. 529 by Benedict of Nursia.

> ...by the promulgation of his rule, [Benedict] laid the foundation on which monastic life in the West was based for centuries to come. Apart from setting aside a period each day for reading—a spiritual rather than intellectual operation—the Benedictine Rule had nothing to say about intellectual pursuits, and the copying of books had no explicit part in the monastic ideal; but, in saying nothing, it left the way open for liberal influences when the time was ripe, and reading could in any case not be carried on without books [84-84].

The absence of evidence is not evidence. Instead, the available evidence is wholly contrary to the assumption that Benedict "...left the way open for liberal influences...." Chapter 33 of Benedict's rules on "Whether Monks Ought to Have Anything of Their Own" states that

> this vice is especially to be cut out of the monastery by the roots. Let no one presume to give or receive anything without the Abbot's leave, or to have anything as his own—anything whatever, whether book or tablets or pen or whatever it may be—since they are not permitted to have even their bodies or wills at their own disposal; but for all their necessities let them look to the Father of the monastery. ...if anyone is caught indulging in this most wicket vice, let him be admonished once and a second time. If he fails to amend, let him undergo punishment [Benedict c. 529 (1948): 52].

Those who repeatedly infringed rules were to "undergo corporal punishment" (44). Monks were not free to read or to write anything without being given permission to do so. Almost every minute of every day by Benedictine rules, monks were required to say specific prayers, to sing specific songs, or to do something else specific. Instead of being open to "liberal influences," "hostility to pagan literature is explicit in some of his [Benedict's] public pronouncements, and he was more at home in the neutral pages of the scholiast and compiler than in the classical authors themselves, whom with a few exceptions he quotes second hand; but his curiosity knew no barriers and he took for granted the independent value of profane culture" (85). Actually, Benedict's attitude towards pagan literature was characteristic of the attitude of the Catholic Church from the 5th through the 9th centuries and from the time of the Counter-Reformation for as long as the index of prohibited literature could be maintained.

The evidence as a whole indicates that copies of classic books accumulated in monasteries and were neglected rather than utilized or copied for use by monks. Monasteries were not bastions of learning, but prisons. The survival of the Latin Classics was despite them rather than because of them, and there is no reason to praise neglect when praise is so manifestly deserved by humanists and most of all for Aldus Manutius for the preservation and dissemination of ancient knowledge.

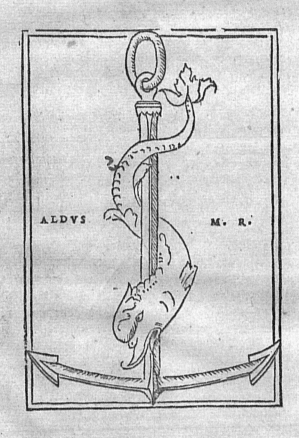

"Make haste slowly"; symbol of Aldus Manutius in his edition of Plato (Bonomelli)

Appendix V

Chronological List of Buildings

Renaissance buildings are characterized by rooms with classical proportions and cornices; palazzos; the use of the porticos on houses; numerous small piazzas; stucco or plaster walls subdivided by pilasters; relatively attenuated and flattened design elements; entablature blocks supporting arches; increased number and size of windows; classical window and door enframements; the incorporation of realistic frescoes with perspective.

c. 1418; 1421-1460—San Lorenzo, Florence; Filippo Brunelleschi, architect (the earliest major building of the Renaissance; adapted Roman Corinthian and the Roman basilica)

1419—Foundling Hospital (Ospedale degli Innocenti), Florence; Filippo Brunelleschi, architect (one of the earliest monuments of the Renaissance)

1420-1426—Dome of Santa Maria del Fiore (Duomo), Florence; Filippo Brunelleschi and Lorenzo Ghiberti, architects* (first attempt to surpass the span of the Pantheon, but with a pointed dome divided into segments rather than a hemispherical dome and not quite as large a span)

1444-1459—Palazzo Medici, Florence; Michelozzo di Bartolomeo, architect (enlarged using the same design; highly influential palazzo design based on the rusticated wall behind the Forum of Augustus)*

1450-1461—San Francisco, Rimini; Leone Battista Alberti, Archtiect

1470-1472—Sant'Andrea, Mantua; Leone Battista Alberti, architect (completed 1481)*

1465-1482—Palazzo Ducale, Urbino; Luciano Laurana (1465-1472), Francesco di Giorgio Martini, architect (1476-1482), et al. (major Renaissance palace; influential decorative details)

c. 1505?—Cancelleria, Rome; attributed to Bramante and others (one of the earliest and most influential Roman palazzos; incorporates a renovated Medieval church, San Lorenzo in Damaso; initial construction may have begin as early as c. 1485; door enframements added by Domenico Fontana in 1589)*

1504—Tempietto; San Piedro in Montorio, Rome; Donato Bramante, architect* (by Palladio's standards, the first building in the Renaissance to equal ancient Roman architecture; influence the dome of St. Peter's)

1504—Cloister of Santa Maria della Pace, Rome; Donato Bramante, architect (major early Renaissance attempt to solve the problems of designing a courtyard using a classical vocabulary)

1505-1511—Villa Farnesina, Rome; Baldassare Peruzzi, architect* (highly influential villa design; famous for its architectural use of frescoes that were designed principally by Raphael)

1505-1506—St. Peter's Basilica, Rome; Donato Bramante, architect of the initial plan used for foundations and overall form (but his design was greatly altered by Michelangelo)

1515?-1546—Palazzo Farnese, Rome; Antonio da Sangallo the Younger (barrel-vaulted entrance), Michelangelo Buonarotti, architects (upper story of courtyard), et al.

1518—Villa Madama, Rome; Raphael, architect (Raffaello Sanzio; partially completed; even the portion completed makes this the finest of Roman villas)*

1520-1534—Medici Chapel, Florence; Michelangelo Buonarotti, architect and sculptor (partially completed; one of the most integral uses of sculpture in architecture; dome based on the Pantheon)

1524-1534—Laurentian Library (Biblioteca Laurenziana), Florence; Michelangelo Buonarotti, architect (completed 1571; the principal Renaissance library building designed for the Medici's collection of manuscripts)*

1533-1536—Palazzo Massimi alle Colonne, Rome; Baldassare Peruzzi, architect (completed after 1536; Rome's finest Renaissance palazzo)*

1539-1564—Capitol (Campidoglio), Rome; Michelangelo Buonarotti, architect* (existing buildings entirely redesigned as a city hall for Rome and as the first public museum; highly influential design details)

1542-1558—Palazzo Thiene, Vicenza; Andrea Palladio, architect* (one of Palladio's most influential palazzo designs)

1546-1564—St. Peter's Basilica, Rome (Vatican); Michelangelo Buonarotti, architect (dome completed 1590; his façade was not built; one of the most influential building ever created)*

1547-1552—Palazzo Giuseppe Porto, Vicenza; Andrea Palladio, architect* (one of Palladio's most influential palazzo designs)

c. 1549-1553—Villa Foscari (Malcontenta), Gambarare; Andrea Palladio, architect* (one of Palladio's most influential villa designs, particularly for its monumental portico on a podium)

1552/53-1555—Villa Pisani, Montagnana; Andrea Palladio, architect *(one of Palladio's most influential villa designs)

1565/66-1569—Villa Rotonda (Almerico-Capra), Vicenza; Andrea Palladio, architect (completed after 1580; the most influential of Palladio's villa designs for its monumental porticoes and central dome)*

1565/66-1571—Palazzo Valmarana, Vicenza; Andrea Palladio, architect* (one of Palladio's most influential palazzo designs)

1559 (begun)—Palazzo Farnese, Caprarola; Antonio da Sangallo the Younger (fortress base of Castello Farnese, 1522-1527) and Vignola, architects (major example of a Renaissance palace)

1570—Publication of Palladio's *Four Books of Architecture (Quattri Libri d'Architettura;* the most influential designs in the history of architecture; provides the best record of many Roman buildings that survived until the Renaissance)

1576/77-1580—Church of the Redentore (Redeemer), Venice; Andrea Palladio, architect (completed 1591; Palladio's finest church)*

Appendix VI

Locations of Buildings

N. B.: Renaissance buildings are listed separately in alphabetical and then chronological order by the following locations in Italy: Caprarola, Finale di Aguglaro, Florence, Frescatti, Gambarare, Mantua, Milan, Montagnana, Piombino Dese, Ravenna, Rome, Tivoli, Todi, Urbino, Venice, and Vicenza.

Caprarola
1559 (begun)—Palazzo Farnese; Antonio da Sangallo the Younger (fortress
   base of Castello Farnese, 1522-1527) and Vignola, architects (major example of a
   Renaissance palace)

Finale di Agugliaro
1545—Villa Saraceno; Andrea Palladio, architect

Florence
c. 1418; 1421-1460—San Lorenzo; Filippo Brunelleschi, architect (the earliest
   major building of the Renaissance; adapted Roman Corinthian and the Roman basilica)
1419—Foundling Hospital (Ospedale degli Innocenti); Filippo Brunelleschi,
   architect (one of the earliest monuments of the Renaissance)
1420-1426—Dome of Santa Maria del Fiore (Duomo); Filippo Brunelleschi
   and Lorenzo Ghiberti, architects* (first attempt to surpass the span of the Pantheon, but
   with a pointed dome divided into segments rather than a hemispherical dome and not
   quite as large a span)
1444-1459—Palazzo Medici; Michelozzo di Bartolomeo, architect (enlarged
   using the same design; highly influential palazzo design)*
1520-1534—Medici Chapel (San Lorenzo); Michelangelo Buonarotti, architect and sculptor
   (partially completed; one of the most integral uses of sculpture in architecture; dome
   based on the Pantheon)
1524-1534—Laurentian Library (Biblioteca Laurenziana; San Lorenzo); Michelangelo
   Buonarotti, architect (completed 1571; the principal Renaissance library building
   designed for the Medici's collection of manuscripts)*

Gambarare (near Vencie)
1553—Villa Foscari (Malcontenta); Andrea Palladio, architect* (one of
   Palladio's most influential villa designs, particularly for its monumental portico on a
   podium)

Mantua
1470-1472—Sant'Andrea; Leone Battista Alberti, architect (completed 1481; influential plan based on the Basilica Nova)*

Milan
c. 1492—Santa Maria delle Grazie; addition by Donato Bramante, architect
c. 1495—Santa Maria presso San Satiro; additition by Donato Bramante, architect

Montagnana
1552/53-1555—Villa Pisani; Andrea Palladio, architect *(one of Palladio's most influential villa designs)

Piombino Dese
1552-1554—Villa Cornaro; Andrea Palladio, Architect

Rimini
1450-1461—San Francisco; Leone Battista Alberti, architect

Rome (see also, Frescatti, Ostia, and Tivoli)
c. 1505?—Cancelleria; attributed to Bramante and others (one of the earliest and most influential Roman palaces; incorporates a renovated Medieval church, San Lorenzo in Damaso; initial construction may have begin as early as c. 1485; door enframements added by Domenico Fontana in 1589)*
1504—Tempietto; San Piedro in Montorio; Donato Bramante, architect* (by Palladio's standards, the first building in the Renaissance to equal ancient Roman architecture; influence the dome of St. Peter's)
1504—Cloister of Santa Maria della Pace; Donato Bramante, architect (major early Renaissance attempt to solve the problems of designing a courtyard using a classical vocabulary)
1505-1511—Villa Farnesina; Baldassare Peruzzi, architect* (highly influential villa design; famous for its architectural use of frescoes that were designed principally by Raphael)
1505-1506—St. Peter's Basilica; Donato Bramante, architect of the initial plan used for foundations and overall form (but his design was greatly altered by Michelangelo)
1518—Villa Madama; Raphael, architect (Raffaello Sanzio; partially completed; even the portion completed makes this the finest of Roman villas)*
1530-1589—Palazzo Farnese; Antonio da Sangallo the Younger (barrel-vaulted entrance), Michelangelo Buonarotti, architects (upper story of courtyard), et al.
1533-1536—Palazzo Massimi alle Colonne; Baldassare Peruzzi, architect (completed after 1536; Rome's finest Renaissance palazzo)*
1539-1564—Capitol (Campidoglio); Michelangelo Buonarotti, architect* (existing buildings entirely redesigned as a city hall for Rome and as the first public museum; highly influential design details)
1546-1564—St. Peter's Basilica, Rome (Vatican); Michelangelo Buonarotti, architect

(dome completed 1590; his façade was not built; one of the most influential building ever created)*

Tivoli
1549-1572—Villa d'Este; Pierro Ligorio, Architect

Todi
c. 1508 (begun)—Santa Maria della Consolazioni; Donato Bramante, architect (attribution)

Urbino
1465-1482—Palazzo Ducale; Luciano Laurana (1465-1472), Francesco di
    Giorgio Martini, architect (1476-1482), et al. (major Renaissance palace; influential
    decorative details)

Venice
1537—Library of St. Mark; Jacopo Sansovino, architect
1561 (begun)—Carità; Andrea Palladio, architect
1576/77-1580—Church of the Redentore (Redeemer); Andrea Palladio, architect
    (completed 1591; Palladio's finest church)*

Vicenza
1542-1558—Palazzo Thiene; Andrea Palladio, architect* (one of Palladio's
    most influential palazzo designs)
1546-1549—Basilica (additions); Andrea Palladio, architect
1547-1552—Palazzo Giuseppe Porto; Andrea Palladio, architect* (one of
    Palladio's most influential palazzo designs)
1550—Palazzo Chiericati; Andrea Palladio, architect
1565/66-1569—Villa Rotonda (Villa Almerico-Capra); Andrea Palladio, architect
    (completed after 1580; the most influential of Palladio's villa designs for its monumental
    porticoes and central dome)*
1565/66-1571—Palazzo Valmarana; Andrea Palladio, architect* (one of
    Palladio's most influential palazzo designs)
1580—Teatro Olympico; Andrea Palladio, architect

Appendix VII

Glossary

abacus--the tile-like slab on top of the capitals of the columns of all orders (above an echinus). The Doric abacus is square and flat. The Ionic and Corinthian abacus has moldings, and the Corinthian abacus has concave sides.
acanthus--a plant with a deeply serrated leaf, which was stylized and applied in two rows around the lower part of Corinthian and Composite capitals.
acroteria--decorative elements at the apex and corners of pediments.
Adamesque--in the style of Robert Adam (characterized by attenuation, complex room shapes, unusual circulation, delicate and flattened classical ornament, and variety).
aggregate--relatively large additions added to concrete to provide material for the concrete mixture to adhere to. The aggregate used most frequently by the Romans was fist-sized pieces of tufa, but brick, volcanic ash, and other material were also used. Quartz pebbles is now commonly used as aggregate for concrete. Cf. temper.
agora--the open area in the public market in Greek cities usually with one or more stoa.
aisle--(1) spaces flanking a nave to enlarge the open area of a building without increasing the maximum distance that can be readily spanned (as in a basilica or churches; in both of these examples, the aisles are usually separated from the nave by rows of column) or (2) an open corridor separating sections of seats (as in a theatre).
amphiprostyle--a temple with porticoes in front and back (amphi- meaning both).
amphitheatre--an oval or elliptical theatre that resembles two semi-circular theatres joined together.
antae--the projecting side walls of a cella or the end walls of a small building such as the Treasury of Athens at Delphi; cf. in antis.
anthemion--a stylized flower that was often used as part of a decorative band alternating with palmettes or palm fronds (most notably on the neck of column of the Erechtheum).
apse--semi-circular niche with a half-dome (as at the end of the nave of a temple or church).
aqueduct--channel for conveying water from a spring or other distant source to a city. The channel is often underground for most of the distance, but carried on an arcade across ravines or when the level of the ground drops suddenly in order to maintain a slight slope so that water can flow downhill at an even rate.
arcade--a row of arches resting on piers or columns.
arch--The most effective form of an arch is semicircular, and each of its voussoir has sides that are angled towards a point at its center. Its base tends to thrust outward, and it needs to be held in place by weight at each side of the base or by superimposed weight. Lower types of arches such as elliptical arches have still greater thrusts. A taller or "pointed arch" is two segmental arches joined to reduce thrust rather than a true arch.
architrave--a horizontal piece of wood, stone, etc., spanning a space such as between

columns and piers. The Doric architrave was plain and equal in height to the frieze. The Ionic and Corinthian architrave was divided into three parts that together were narrower than their frieze, and a tri-part moulding around doors and windows was derived from it. A true architrave is a loadbearing element (cf. frieze and entablature).

arris--the sharp edge of Doric flutes.

ashlar--blocks of cut stone.

astrigal--a narrow convex band as at the base of the neck of a Tuscan capital.

atrium--a skylighted space near the front of Greek and Roman urban houses. A small atrium had beams spanning from side to side and front to back with an opening in the center. A large atrium might have a roof supported on four columns (rather than a colonnade as for the roof of a Roman courtyard).

attic--(1) the uppermost part of a triumphal arch or (2) the part of any building above its main cornice.

Attic base--the usual base for Ionic, Corinthian, and Composite columns with a smaller torus at the top, a scotia, a larger torus, and a plinth at the bottom. The earliest known use of this type of base was for the Propylea of the Athenian Acropolis (in Attica). Cf. Ionic base.

baluster--a bulbous element derived from the shape of a Renaissance candelabra that can be used in place of an attic or in place of pickets on a fence or stair railing.

balustrade--a row of balusters.

barrel vault--semicircular vault (shaped somewhat like half of a barrel cut through. lengthwise); the base of a barrel vault tend to thrust outward, and the thrust needs to be countered by a buttress, an adjacent barrel vault, a superimposed weight, or a medal rod (in tension).

base--the lowest part of an architectural element such as a column (which consists of a capital, shaft, and plinth or base except for the Doric column, which has no base).

basilica--an ancient Roman law court and exchange or a Christian aisled church (both having aisles and a clearstory to provide light for the nave). The Roman basilica differed from the form of a church in having aisles on all sides and recessed space for a tribunal.

blocking course--a row of stone blocks in place of a pediment; cf. ranked blocking course.

bracket--a vertical element cantilevered to support a cornice or other feature; it usually has the form of an S and can also called a console bracket (cf. modillion).

brick--a block of clay that has been sun dried (adobe) or fired. The Roman brick was usually fired and rectangular, and it resembled a tile and could also be used as a tile. The Romans also used triangular bricks with mortar as a protective facing for concrete, and the inner point of the brick bonded to the concrete.

buttress--(1) a pier buttress that consists of a thicker section of wall added for stability or (2) a flying buttress that connects a higher element to a lower one or to the ground for stability. The Romans preferred adequately thick walls without pier buttresses, but used flying buttresses to stabilize the clearstories of termae.

cantilever--the structural principle that enables a projection (such as a cornice, corbel, or bracket) to be held in held in place either by (1) being firmly attached (like a tree limb), (2) the greater part of its weight being in back of the point it projects from and counterbalancing the front, or (3) a greater weight being superimposed that the amount of weight of the projection.

carytid--a statue used as a supporting element (as on the Erecheum's Carytid Porch, where enslaved maidens support the roof).

centering--a usually temporary face for scaffolding that was used to erect arches and vaults. The scaffolding supported the weight until all voussoirs were put into place, and then the centering was struck so that the voussoirs could begin to function as a "living" arch (with its voussoirs held in place by compression rather than mortar). A concrete vault might have a permanent centering of tiles that became bonded to it when the concrete set up.

cella--the enclosed part of a Greek or Roman temple.

clearstory--an upper story rising above the body of a building and has windows that usually light a central space or nave flanked by aisles (cf. basilica).

coffer--square or nearly square recesses in the ceiling of a temple or surface of a vault or dome. Coffers were originally formed in between intersecting beams, and the recess was covered to provide a ceiling. They were later used widely as decorative elements.

colonnade--a long row or rows of columns as a pattern that can be repeated indefinitely and that is usually viewed in perspective (as opposed to a portico, which is usually seen from in front and is a unified design).

composite order--a Roman column similar to Corinthian, but with larger volutes and often with relief sculpture.

compression--a material resisting being compacted by an external weight or force; a lintel or entablature is ordinarily in compression. Cf. tension.

concrete--a chemical compound made of lime, sand, water with some form of alumina as an element essential for a chemical reaction to take place and with an aggregate for the mixture to adhere to. The ancient Romans added alumina through the use of volcanic sand or ground potsherds (fired clay). Since the 18th Century, clay has furnished the alumina in Portland Cement and similar types of concrete. Concrete sets up as a compound that has different properties from mortar that simply dries out. Cf. *opus incertum, opus reticulatum, opus testaceum,* shuttered concrete, and through-courses.

corbel--a stone in a false arch that is held in place by the structural principle of a cantilever.

corbelled arch--a false arch that consist of corbels (which are cantilevered from each side and held in place at each side); the shape of a corbelled arch is usually an inverted-V or a pointed.

Corinthian--the most elaborate Greek order and the preferred Roman order; characterized by two rows of acanthus leaves beneath corner volutes and an Attic-Ionic base (cf. Ionic).

cornice--moldings that are usually horizontal at the top of walls (where the uppermost part, the cyma, originally served as a gutter), but that can also be used on the top of pediments (raking cornices) or in other locations as decoration.

country house--a large primary residence in rural parts of England or its colonies; the owners of country houses usually had secondary residences in cities (vs. the villa, which was a secondary residence for the enjoyment of a rural setting).

courtyard--an open area within a building; characteristic of Roman urban houses and

Renaissance palazzi and widely used in Europe to provide light and ventilation to internal rooms.

crepidoma--the platform of a Doric temple; see krepis.

cross vault--two intersecting barrel vaults that appear to be X-shaped when seen from below; a correctly made cross vault contains the thrust of its semicircular elements.

cyma--a moulding that is the uppermost past of a cornice (shaped like a gutter and originally intended to serve that purpose with water spouts located over columns and frequently faced by lion's heads).

dentil--literally tooth-like elements that are part of an Ionic and Corinthian cornice (with block alternating with spaces).

detached house--a multistoried dwelling similar in form to a row house, but entirely separate rather than attached on one or both sides within a row; many country houses has the form of a detached double house.

diminution--the tapering of a column shaft.

dome--a hemisphere or part of a hemisphere (saucer dome) covering a space; when a dome covers a cubical or octagonal space rather than a cylinder, pendentives are needed at the corners for continuous support.

Doric--the simplest Greek order consisting of a shaft and capital without a base; the Doric cornice usually consists of triglyphs and metopes. Doric columns have the broadest proportions of any order (from 1:4 to 1:7 for ancient Greek columns and about 1:8 for Renaissance columns). The Romans generally preferred Tuscan in place of Doric columns.

double house--a house two rooms deep of any length (whether part of a row or detached).

drum--(1) a section of a column or (2) a cylindrical element such as the circular wall of a building or a cylindrical clearstory.

echinus--the part of a capitol that is rounded and located beneath the abacus.

enframement--moldings that surround a door, window, etc. When engaged columns or pilasters are applied to the pier in a fornix, they also function as a pier butress.

egg-and-dart moulding--a much used decorative band that consists of alternating eggs and darts (based on earlier bands of lotus buds and lotus flowers).

engaged column--half or two-thirds of a column that is part of a wall (rather than a freestanding column; cf. pilaster).

entablature--the lintel of a classical order that usually includes an architrave, frieze, and cornice.

entasis--curvilinear bulge of a column shaft; the curve usually extends the full height of a Doric shaft and the upper two-thirds of an Ionic or Corinthian shaft.

exedra--a relatively small recess usually containing a bench for discussion or the seat separately. Cf. hemicycle.

facing--a relatively thin front added to a wall to protect it and/or to improve its appearance. For example, an integral facing of brick was most often used for the exteriors of Roman buildings, and thin slabs of marble were often affixed to interior walls.

filet--the thin flat surface in between flutes of the Ionic, Corinthian, and Composite orders.

flutes--vertical elements of a column that are concave in section; Doric flutes come to a sharp point (arises) and Ionic and Corinthian have a narrow flat section in between each flute (filets). In section, they are usually segmental arcs (Doric) or semicircular, but can be elliptical (Ionic or Corinthian). Flutes are rarely spiral.

formwork--(1) Temporary formwork usually consists of boards within which concrete was placed in thin layers by the Romans and in which it is now poured; after the concrete sets up, this type of formwork is removed and is often reused. (2) Permanent formwork is a wall or facing that is built first for concrete to be laid up within, and when the concrete cures, it bonds the facing to itself as a protective facing.

fornices--the Roman design element with an arch flanked by columns supporting an entablature (as on basilicas and theatres).

forum--a place where a large part of the population of a Roman community could assemble in the open air to transact business, listen to speeches, etc.; usually partly or wholly surrounded by buildings and in some cases with buildings within the forum area (equivalent to a Greek agora; generally larger than an Italian piazza); a Roman forum usually included public buildings, particularly a temple and a basilica.

French windows--glazed double doors; on upper levels, they usually have grills or balconies. When open, they admit more light and air than sash windows and serve also as door openings.

frieze--the part of a classical entablature above the architrave and below the cornice; a frieze may or may not be load-bearing. The Doric frieze consists of alternating triglyphs and metopes, and the metopes (with or without sculpture). The Ionic and Corinthian frieze could be plain or sculpted with reliefs.

gabled roof--a tent-like roof with two symmetrical planes angled downward from a ridge (with or without a pediment). Greek and Roman temples have gabled roofs.

guttae--the drop-like elements beneath a triglyph (cylindrical pegs in Greek architecture and truncated pyramids in Roman architecture); rows of guttae were sometimes used decoratively.

gymnasium--a public athletic facility in ancient Greece where athletes exercised nude (gym-). A gymnasium usually included a track, a bath, and places for lectures, and it became the basis for educational institutions (most notably Plato's Academy and Aristotle's Lyseum). The Greek gymnasium was also the origin of the Roman termae. Cf. palestra.

hemicycle--a relatively large recess such as the extremely large curves in the walls of termae for use as lecture halls or seating for athletic contests. Cf. exedra.

hipped roof--a roof with four planes; two longer sections of roof angle downward from the ridge, and two shorter planes angle downward perpendicular to the ridge. Early English houses generally have hipped roofs.

hypocaust--an arrangement consisting of a floor raised on piers to provide space for hot air to circulate beneath the floor and for heat to radiate through the floor (as in a Roman bath); the hot air is drawn underneath the building by being able to escape only on its opposite side (through flues or chimneys).

Ionic--the second Greek order consisting of a relatively thin shaft with a capital. consisting of large volutes and an echinus and with a base. The Ionic order provided the basis for the Corinthian and Composite orders, which differ chiefly from it by having more elaborate capitals. Cf. Attic base and Ionic base.

Ionic base--one of the two principal types of bases for the Ionic order and for other orders based on it; usually consisting of pairs of small toruses separated by a scotias (characteristic of Ionia, where the Ionic order was created). Cf. Attic base.

in antis--columns placed between the ends of walls (as at the entrance to Greek cellas with or without a portico or peristyle); exs., the Athenian Treasury, Delphi, and the cella of the Parthenon.

insula--ancient Roman apartment block made of brick-faced concrete.

interaxial--the distance from the center of one column to the center of an adjacent column; used by the Greeks to determine a key proportional relationship for the design of temples (cf. intercolumniation).

intercolumniation--the distance in between adjacent columns; used by the Romans to determine a key proportional relationship for the design of temples (cf. interaxial).

krepis--the base of a Greek temple that ordinarily consisted of three large steps (referred to as a crepidoma by the Romans, who used the podium as the base for their temples).

limestone--sedimentary rock consisting wholly or primarily of calcium carbonate. Limestone has two basic forms: (1) rock created when dissolved lime settles in horizontal layers and is compressed as it is weighted down by added layers (such as travertine) and (2) rock that consists of compressed shells that were created by living marine organisms (shellstone). Early Greek temples were generally made of shellstone, which was covered with stucco to resemble limestone or marble.

lintel--the horizontal supporting element in the post-and-lintel structural system.

loadbearing--supporting weight (rather than appearing to; as a free-standing column that is loadbearing vs. a pilaster that is not).

Mansard roof--a double hipped roof popularized by François Mansart to provide more usable space in attic stories. The window in a Mansard roof are in dormers.

marble--crystalline rock that is formed under great pressure and that has the same chemical composition as limestone. Marble is harder and more difficult to carve than limestone, but weathers better and has luster and is translucent.

massive--appearing larger than it is; buildings with compact masses with minimal details (such as few windows) often seem larger.

metope--the slab of stone in between triglyphs in a Doric frieze; it can be plain, painted, or sculpted with reliefs. Some early metopes were made of fired clay slabs.

modillion--a horizontal element cantilevered to support a cornice or other feature; it frequently has the form of an S like a console bracket, but it can consist of blocks with an alternately concave and convex underside (as on the Pantheon's drum). Cf. bracket.

module--any measurement or element that is repeated so that the proportions of a building will all be related to it. The ancient Greeks most often used the triglyph as a module for peristyle temples, and the ancient Romans most often used the lower diameter of columns. A module can consist of a dimension such as two feet or five-feet, and all other dimensions can be divided by the module chosen (as for the shafts of column shafts of standard sizes).

monolith--literally, "one stone"; made of solid stone such as the shaft of a monolithic column.

mortar--usually referring to a wet mixture of lime, sand, and water; this mixture dries out and hardens into stone that has about one-third the strength of concrete, which has most of the same elements, but is a different compound (q. v.).

oculus--the opening in the center of a dome (as in the Pantheon).

opus incertum--concrete faced with a protective layer of irregular stones (resembling a wall of fieldstones, but with a concrete core).

opus reticulatum--concrete faced with a protective layer of truncated pyramids with the points inserted into the concrete and with the flat bases laid up in a pattern of diamond shapes resembling a net.

opus testacium--concrete faced with a protective layer of triangular bricks (initially broken pieces of roof tiles) laid up in mortar with the inner point of the triangle bonded to the concrete. Late in the 1st Century and throughout much of the 2nd century, *opus testacium* was divided into sections by through courses of bipedales.

orders--The classical orders consist of columns and entablatures. The two main orders of the Greeks were the Doric and Ionic (q. v.). The Greek Corinthian order was developed from the Ionic by adding a taller capitol with acanthus leaves and otherwise has similar elements. The Romans adapted the Tuscan Order of the Etruscans and adapted the Corinthian order of the Greeks by combining the larger Ionic volutes to create a Composite order. Most Greek and Roman versions of the orders are different from one another in at least some respect, but they generally observe similar relative proportions (with Doric the thickest and Composite the thinnest in terms of height divided by lower diameter). Usually, Roman columns of the same orders are thinner than Greek columns; Renaissance columns are thinner than Roman; and Adamesque columns are the thinnest of all.

monumental order--an order that is the height of two or more stories of a building (regardless of actual height; for example, the 60-foot column of a Roman temple is equivalent in height to a six-story building even though the temple is only one-story tall). The monumental order was developed during the Renaissance to unify and enhance buildings with windows on multiple floors, and it can consist of columns, piers, or pilasters. It is sometimes called the giant order, but that designation implies that it is exceptionally large.

open pediment--a gable with raking cornices, but without a horizontal cornice.

palazzo--palace (Italian; derived from the Palatine Hill).

palestra--a private wrestling school in ancient Greece; frequently a gathering place for philosophers who discussed a wide variety of subjects or sophists who lectured for a fee.

parapet--a low blocking course or attic; a parapet is generally added to conceal a roof and make a building seem to have a more compact form.

pedestal--a tall block on which a column rests (as opposed to a plinth, which is a slab of stone at the base of a column similar in form to an abacus). A pedestal usually has a cornice at its top and a moulding at its base.

pediment--the triangular element facing each end of the gabled roof of a temple or a similar element applied to a building. A pediment consists of a tympanum (the flat, triangular surface surrounded by moldings), a horizontal cornice (without a cyma), and raking cornices (with a cyma). It may or may not be filled with free-standing sculpture or reliefs. Cf. open pediment.

pendentive--the curving and essentially triangular elements in corners that enable the circular base of a dome to be supported over a square or polygonal space (also called a squinch). A pendentive utilizes the principle of the cantilever. Pendentives were used by the Romans, for example, in the "Temple" of Minerva Medica (a garden pavilion in

Rome). Pendentives became characteristic of Byzantine architecture (to support domes over square spaces).

peristyle--columns on all four sides or literally "columns around" the cella of a temple.

piano nobile--the noble or main floor of a building that is usually distinguished by being much the tallest; for example, Palladio usually raised his piano nobile on a lower podium and surmounted it with a lower attic (creating a vertical composition with a strong center).

piazza--a public square in Italy that often has a fountain.

pickets--thin boards, iron struts, etc., used as the vertical elements of a fence or railing.

pier--a structural support that is usually square or half square in cross section and that can be freestanding, but is more often attached; unlike a pilaster, but like a column, it is usually a loadbearing element (cf. pilaster).

pilaster--a columnar element in which the shaft is reduced to a flat strip with vertical sides with a corresponding capital and base; it is a decorative element that resembles a column, but provides little if any support (cf. column and pier).

piazza--a public square (Italian).

plaster--a gypsum-based coating for the interior of buildings; cf. stucco. Gypsum is softer than plaster and weathers poorly, but it is inexpensive, casts well, and takes a high sheen.

plinth--the tile-like part of the base of a column.

podium--the base on which an ancient Roman temple rested; a podium was usually a plain, tall foundation with moldings like a pedestal. Palladio adapted the podium for houses.

portico--the integral porch of a classical temple or the attached porch of a house with classical details; a portico consists of columns, entablature, and pediment. The Greek portico was relatively shallow or filled with columns, and the Roman portico usually consisted of a deep open space.

post-and-lintel--a structural system that consists of vertical elements (posts, piers, or columns) supporting horizontal elements (lintel or entablature); by contrast, the arch and vault provide support differently from the post-and-lintel system.

proportion--interrelated parts of a building divisible by a module; Greek and Roman buildings were given proportional relationships equivalent to those of the ideal human body, which was defined as having all of its parts divisible by a module (such as the relationship of the length of the foot to overall height).

prostyle--columns only in front of a temple (cf. amphiprostyle and peristyle).

raked blocking course--a horizontal block with an open gable and ordinarily without moldings on top. Ledoux developed the raked blocking course by omitting the moldings on a classical entablature and pediment (thus combining the two elements). This element was widely used in Greek Revival architecture.

raking cornice--the cornices along the top edges of a pediment (with cymas as opposed to the horizontal cornice at the bottom that lacks a cyma).

roof-tile--largely flat bricks that overlap to provide roofing. Greek and Roman tiles had flanges along their sides (pan-tiles) and were protected by cover-tiles overlapping the flanges. A later type of roof-tile was S-shaped, and its smaller curve was overlapped by its larger curve (without a separate cover tile). Unless broken, a well-fired roof-tile will last indefinitely, and they can be set into concrete to minimize or prevent breakage. Tiles of baked clay were sometimes imitated in marble.

rotunda--a domed building with a circular exterior wall like the Pantheon.

rowhouse--a multistoried dwelling attached to another dwelling on one side or in between two other dwellings. English and early American urban dwellings were often separately owned rowhouses, which the English call "terrace houses." French rows of houses generally consist of separately owned or rented flats.

rustication--blocks of stone with their exterior surfaces roughened to look as if they have not been dressed and to appear rustic or bold (vs. ashlar). The edges of rusticated stones were usually dressed, and the surface was made uniformly rough. Rusticated columns that were popular during the reign of Claudius and during the Renaissance were made to seem to consist of alternating blocks of stone with cylindrical drums in between.

sash windows--windows consisting usually of two sashes; usually the upper sash is fixed and the lower sash slides up to open, but both sash can slide in separate tracks, and more than two sash can be used for one window. A sash can be held in place by a window weight concealed within the window frame. This type of window was invented in England in the 17th Century and is in general use in the United States. Most European buildings use French windows (q. v.).

saucer dome--a low dome that usually has the profile of a segment of a circle; widely used in Regency and Greek Revival architecture.

scotia--the concave element in the base of an Ionic, Corinthian, or Composite column; cf. torus.

shaft--the main part of a column that can be plain or fluted and that can have a base or no base, but that always has a capital.

shuttered concrete--concrete laid up or poured into a formwork of boards.

stoa--a long market building in a Greek agora; the stoa contained shops, generally had two stories, and was faced by columns on each story.

strut--a rigid internal element of a truss that can either be in tension or compression as needed, but not both at the same time.

stucco--a lime-based coating for the exterior of a building; cf. plaster.

symmetry--corresponding visually. The principal type of symmetry is bilateral (in which one side is the mirror image of the other side as for the human body). Radial symmetry is when the rays or arms of an animal or building are like one another (as in a snowflake or rotunda). Nearly all major buildings are symmetrical and compact so that they will rest evenly on their foundations and be as permanent as possible.

temper--any material mixed with a substance to help bind it together particularly while drying; materials used include sand that is added to clay for bricks and hair or rope fibers that are added to plaster. Cf. aggregate.

temple--a religious building that in Antiquity housed cult statues and that consisted of a cella with one or more pedimented porticoes and with either columns in front (the prostyle temple of the Greeks, Etruscans, and Romans); with columns in front and back (Greek amphiprostyle); or with columns across the front, back, and sides (primarily Greek peristyle). The Greeks most often used Doric columns in Attica or Ionic columns in Ionia; the Etruscans used Tuscan; and the Romans preferred Corinthian.

tension--a material resisting being stretched by an external force; a metal rod holding a barrel vault together or the central strut in a truss are in tension. Cf. compression.

termae--large public baths of the ancient Romans (vs. small private baths, which were called balnea); the major imperial baths of Rome were created by the emperors Trajan, Caracalla, and Diocletian. An imperial bath was a civic center that included bathing facilities for thousands of people at a time, a swimming pool, athletic facilities, lecture halls, and a library. It was open to the public for a nominal fee.

termae windows--a type of window used for the clearstories of Roman termae; it is semicircular and is divided into three parts by two mullions (with the widest part in the center).

through-courses--layers of bipedales separating sections of concrete (incorrectly referred to as bonding courses). Their purpose was to prevent a section of concrete from drying out before it could cure.

tile--a flat brick most often used for paving, but the Roman brick and tile were indistinguishable and were used for wall facing and paving. Cf. roof tile.

torus--the convex elements in the base of an Ionic, Corinthian, and Composite column (usually with a smaller torus above a concave scotia and a larger torus below the scotia).

triglyph--three-part element of the Greek Doric frieze that flanks metopes.

triumphal arch--a rectangular building with a large arch in the middle and an attic; most buildings of this type commemorated a Roman triumph or military victory. Some triumphal arches also have smaller flanking arches (three arches rather than one). All have inscriptions, and most have relief sculptures. The proportions and elements of the triumphal arch were adapted by Palladio and widely influential (particularly a blockish front, a strong central element, and an attic).

truss--a usually triangular unit used for the support of a roof, bridge, etc. The simplest type of truss is a triangle of wood with pegged corners or metal straps to hold the corners together and with a vertical strut joined in the center. The sloping sides of the triangle are in compression, and the strut is in tension. The strut divides the dead weight of the horizontal beam in half and has the potential to as much as double the width that be spanned. More than one strut and internal triangular arrangements of additional struts can be used to further increase the distance that can be span. Trusses can also be made entirely of medal (such as the bronze trusses of the Pantheon) and can be rectangular (with struts arranged as triangles).

Tuscan--The order created by the Etruscans and adapted by the Romans; it consists of a plain shaft with a simple capital (an abacus and echinus) and simple base (one torus on a plinth). This is the most economical order in that its proportions are moderate, the shaft is unfluted, and decoration is minimal. The Romans preferred the more elaborate and expensive Corinthian, but Tuscan was widely used by Renaissance and later architects.

tympanum--the triangular element within a pediment that was often used as a background for sculpture.

unity--a visually coherent design that is usually compact with no separate elements detracting from the overall appearance.

vestibule--a relatively small space at the entrance to a building; in the Roman urban house, it was a short hall; in later buildings, it was usually a small separate room.

villa--a country house primarily or exclusively for relaxation or study; a secondary rather than primary residence. Roman villas were usually located in relatively isolated areas such as low mountains or beaches. A Renaissance villa might be in the country or suburbs, but is always a detached building.

volute--a spiraled element like a snail shell such as the spiraled ends of Ionic, Corinthian, and Composite capitals.

voussoir--the individual wedge-shaped stones of a true arch with sides tapering to the central point within the arch (q. v.)

Bibliography

Ackerman, James S.
    1961 *Architecture of Michelangelo.* 2 vols. New York: Viking Press.
    1964 *Architecture of Michelangelo; Catalogue.* London: A. Zwemmer Ltd.
    1986 *Architecture of Michelangelo.* 2nd ed. with a catalogue of Michelangelo's works by James S. Ackerman and John Newman. Chicago: University of Chicago Press.

Adam, Robert, and James Adam
    1778 [1980] *Works in Architecture of Robert & James Adam.* New York: Dover Publications.

Alberti, Leon Battista
    1966 *On Painting* [1435]. Trans. by John R. Spencer. New Haven: Yale University Press.
    1755 [1986] *The Ten Books of Architecture; the 1755 Leoni Edition.* New York: Dover Publications, Inc.
    1988 *On the Art of Building in Ten Books* [1452]. Trans. by Joseph Rykwert, Neil Leach, and Robert Tavernor. Cambridge, Mass.: MIT Press.

Anderson, William J.; Richard Phené Spiers, and Thomas Ashby
    1927 *The Architecture of Ancient Rome: an Account of Its Historic Development: Being the Second Part of the Architecture of Greece and Rome.* London: Batsford.

Angeleri, Gianfranco, and Cesare Columba
    1985 *Milan Centrale: Storia di Una Stazione.* Banca Nazionale della Comunicazioni. Rome Edizioni Abete.

Audiat, Jean
    1933 *Trésor des Athéniens.* 2 vols. Fouilles de Delphes. Paris: De Boccard.

Baggio, Elena (ed.)
    n. d. *Passeggiata in Villa.* Rome: Ente Nazionale Italiano per il Turismo.

Baines, F.
    1914 *Westminster Hall: Report to the First Commissioner of H.M. Works, &c., on the Condition of the Roof Timbers of Westminster Hall, with Suggestions for Maintaining the Stability of the Roof.* London: H.M.S.O.

Balanos, Nikolaos
    1938 *Monuments de l'Acropole; Relèvement et Conservation.* Paris: C. Massin.

Baldrati, Barbara
    2014 *La Cupola di San Pietro: Il Metodo Costruttivo e il Cantiere.* Rome: Edizioni Studium.

Bartoli, Alfonso
    1914-1922. *I Monumenti Antichi di Roma nei Disegni degli Uffizi di Firenze.* 6 vols. Roma: C. A. Bontempelli Editore.

Begley, W. E., and Ziyaud-Din A Desai
    1989 *Taj Mahal: the Illumined Tomb : an Anthology of Seventeenth-century Mughal and European Documentary.* Cambridge, Mass.: Aga Khan Program for Islamic Architecture (distributed by the University of Washington Press, Seattle).

Belluzzi, Amedeo; Caroline Elam; and Francesco Paolo Fiore (eds.)
    2017 *Giuliano da Sangallo.* Milan: Officina Libraria for Centro Internazionale di Studi di Architettura Andrea Palladio and for Kunsthistorisches Institut in Florenz—Max-Planck-Institut.

Beltrami, Luca
    1898 *Il Pantheon... coi Rilevi e Disegni dell'Architetto Pier Olinto Armanini.* Milan: Tipografia Umberto Allegretti.
    1929 *La Cupola Vaticana.* Vatican City: Tipografia Poliglotta Vaticana.

Benedict of Nursia
    c. 529 [1948] *St. Benedict's Rule for Monasteries.* Trans. by Leonard J. Doyle. Collegeville, Minn.: Liturgical Press.

Bentivoglio, Enzo
    1984 "La Cappella Chigi." In Frommel *et al.* 1984: 125-142.

Bertotti Scamozzi, Ottavio
    1968 *Le Fabbriche e i Disegni di Andrea Palladio.* New York: Architectural Book Pub. Co.

Berve, Helmut; Gottfried Gruben; and Max Hirmer
    n. d. *Greek Temples, Theatres, and Shrines.* New York: Harry N. Abrams, Inc.

Bevilacqua, Mario, and Andriana Capriotti
    2016 *Sant'Andrea al Quirinle; il Resturo della Decorzione dell Cupola e Nuovi Studi Berniniaini.* Rome: De Luca Editori d'Arte.

Blomfield, Regnald, ed.
    1919 *Architectural Water-Colours & Etchings of W. Walcot.* London: H. C. Dickens.

Bolton, Arthur T.

1922 *The Architecture of Robert & James Adam (1758-1794).* London: Country Life (reprinted 1984; [London]: Antique Collectors' Club).

Bonomelli, Marina
2016 *Aldo Manuzio, 1495-1515; le Aldine della Biblioteca Ambrosiana.* Milan: Biblioteca Ambrosiana.

Borsi, Franco
1986 *Leon Battista Alberti: the Complete Works.* New York: Electa/Rizzoli.

Branner, Robert
1960 *Burgundian Gothic Architecture.* London: A. Zwemmer.

Branner, Robert, and Shirley Prager Branner
1989 *The Cathedral of Bourges and Its Place in Gothic Architecture.* New York, N.Y.: Architectural History Foundation; Cambridge, Mass.: MIT Press.

Bruschi, Arnaldo.
1977 *Bramante.* London: Thames and Hudson.
1994 "The Central Plan: S. Maria della Consolazione." In Millon and Lampugnani 1994: 515-518.
2007 "Brunelleschi e la Nuova Architettura Fiorentina." In Fiore 2007: 38-113.

Burns, Howard
2007 "Leon Battista Alberti." In Fiore 2007: 114-165.

Butler, A. S. G.; George Stewart; and Christopher Hussey
1950 [1989] *Architecture of Sir Edwin Lutyens.* 3. vols. Woodbridge, Suffolk: Antique Collectors' Club

Cassanelli, Roberto; Massimiliano David; Emidio de Albentiis, and Annie Jacques
2002 *Ruins of Ancient Rome: the Drawings of French Architects Who Won the Prix de Rome, 1786-1924.* Trans. by Thomas M. Hartmann. Los Angeles: J. Paul Getty Museum.

Cellini, Benvenuto
c. 1566 [1923] *The Life of Benvenuto Cellini.* Trans. by John Addington Symonds. New York: Charles Scribner's Sons.

Cevese, Renato
1980 *Invito a Palladio.* Milan: Rusconi Immagini.

Choisy, Auguste
1873 *L'Art de Batir chez les Romains.* Paris: Ducher et Cie, Éditeurs.
1899 *Histoire de l'Architecture.* 2 vols. Paris: Gauthier-Villars.

Ciceronis, M Tvlli (Marcus Tullius Cicero)

1934 *De re pvblica: Libri e Codice Rescripto; Vaticano Latino 5757; Phototypice Expressi.* Vatican: Bibliotheca Apostolica Vaticana.

Claridge, Amanda
1998 *Rome: an Oxford Archeological Guide.* With contributions by Judith Toms and Tony Cubberley. Oxford: Oxford University Press.

Clarke, Georgia
2003 *Roman House—Renaissance Palaces: Inventing Antiquity in Fifteenth-Century Italy.* Cambridge: Cambridge University Press.

Clérisseau, Charles Louis, and J. G. LeGrand
1778 *Antiquités de la France*, [part] *I: Monuments de Nisme.* Paris: P. D. Pierres.

Conant, Kenneth John
1973 *Carolingian and Romanesque Architecture, 800-1200.* 3rd ed. Pelican History of Art. Harmondsworth: Penguin Books.

Condivi, Ascanio
1976 *Life of Michelangelo.* Baton Rouge: Louisiana State University Press.

Cook, Sir Theodore Andrea, and Frederick H. Evans
n. d. [c. 1915] *Twenty-five Great Houses of France.* London: Country Life.

Cooper, Frederick A., ed.
1996 *Temple of Apollo Bassitas.* 4 vols. Princeton: American School of Classical Studies at Athens.

Coulton, J. J.
1977 *Ancient Greek Architects at Work: Problems of Structure and Design.* Ithaca, N.Y.: Cornell University Press.

Creswell, K. A. C.
1958 *A Short Account of Early Muslim Architecture* (Harmondsworth: Penguin Books).

Crosby, Sumner McK., and Pamela Z. Blum
1987 *Royal Abbey of Saint-Denis: from Its Beginnings to the Death of Suger, 475-1151* (with a separate roll of drawings). New Haven: Yale University Press.

Curtius, Ernst; Friedrich Adler; Richard Borrmann; Karl Friedrich Wilhelm Dittenberger; Wilhelm Dörpfeld; Adolf Furtwängler; Friedrich Graeber; Paul Graef; Josef Partsch; Karl Purgold; Georg Treu; Rudolf Weil
1890-1897 *Olympia: die Ergebnisse der von dem Deutschen Reich*

Veranstalteten Ausgrabung, im Auftrage des Königlich Preussischen Ministers der Geistlicher, Unterrichts- und Medicinal-Angelegenheiten. 10 vols. Berlin: A. Asher & Co.

Davies, Paul; David Hemsoll; and Mark Wilson Jones
    1987 "The Pantheon: Triumph of Rome or Triumph of Compromise?" *Art History; Journal of the Association of Art Historians* 10, no. 2 (Jun. 1987): 133-153.

De Caro, Silvana Balbi
    1993 *Roma e la Moneta.* With photographs by Saskia van Stegeren. Milan: Banca d'Italia.

De Fusco, Rento
    1992 *L'Architettura dell'Ottocento.* Turin: Garzanti.

DeLaine, Janet
    1997 *Baths of Caracalla: a Study in the Design, Construction, and Economics of Large-scale Building Projects in Imperial Rome.* Journal of Roman Archaeology Supplementary Series Number 25. Portsmouth, RI: Journal of Roman Archaeology L. L. C.

Desgodetz, Antoine
    1682 *Ēdifices Antiques de Rome.* Paris: Iean Batiste Coignard (reprinted).

D'Espouy, H.
    1896; 1905 *Fragments d'Architecture Antique d'Après les Relevés & Restaurations des Anciens Pensionnaires.* 2 vols. Paris: Charles Schmid, Ēditeur.
    1906 *Monuments Antiques Relevés et Restaurés par les Architectes Pensionnaires de l'Académie de France à Rome.* 3 vols. Publication de l'Institut de France. Paris: Ch. Massin.

De Tolnay, Charles
    1975-1980 *Corpus dei Disegni di Michelangelo.* 4 vols. Novara: Istituto Geografico De Agostini.
    1975B *Michelangelo: Sculptor, Painter, Architect.* Princeton: Princeton University Press.

Dinsmoor, William Bell
    1950 [1975] *Architecture of Ancient Greece: an Account of Its Historic Development.* New York: Norton.

Donaldson, Thomas Leverton
    1996 *Architetura Numismatic: Ancient Architecture on Greek and Roman Coins and Medals.* Chicago: Argonaut Publishers.

Dörpfeld, Wilhelm
    1881 *Ausgrabungen zu Olympia.* Ed. by Ernst Curtius and Friedrich Adler;
        vol. 5 on the Temple of Zeus. Berlin: E. Wasmuth.

Di Stefano, Roberto
    1963 *La Cupola di San Pietro: Storia della Costruzione e dei Restauri.* Naples:
        Edizioni Scientifiche Italiane.

Donaldson, Thomas Leverton
    1966 *Architectura Numismatica: Ancient Architecture on Greek and Roman Coins and
        Medals.* Chicago: Argonaut Publishers.

D'Ossat, Guglielmo de Angelis, and Carlo Pietrangeli
    1965 *Il Campidoglio di Michelangelo.* With measured drawings by Enrico del Debbio
        and Giuseppe Perugini and photographs by Leonard von Matt. Milan: "Silvana"
        Editoriale d'Arte.

Dunbar, Frederic L.
    1943 *Rom: Sechschundert Bauwerke der Ewigen Stad.* With 76 drawings from the
        Roman sketchbook of Marten van Heemskerck. Berlin: Carl Habel Verlagsbuch
        Handlung.

Du Pérac, Étienne
    1575 [1963] *Disegni de le Ruine di Roma e come Anticamente Erono.*
        Introduction by Rudolf Wittkower. 2 vols. Milan: A. Pizzi.

École Francaise de Rome; École Nationale Supérieure des Beaux-Arts, Parigi; & Comune
        di Roma Assessorato alla Cultura
    1985 *Roma Antiqua.* Paris: L'Académie
        de France à Rome; l'École Française de Rome; l'École Nationale Supérieure des
        Beaux-Arts, Paris.
    1992 *Roma Antiqua: "Envois" degli Architetti Francesi (1786-1901): Grandi
        Edifici Pubblici.* Roma: Edizioni Carte Segrete.

Eiche, Sabine
    1994 "The Villa Madama." In Millon and Lampugnani 1994: 561-564.

Fabbri, Marcello; Antonella Greco; Paolo Marconi; Mario Pisani, Paolo Portoghesi; and Carlo
        Vallauri
    n. d. *Il Palazzo di Giustizia di Roma.* With photos by Augusto de Luca. Rome:
        Gangemi Editore.

Filippi, Elena
    1990 *Maarten van Heemskerck: Inventio Urbis.* Milan: Berenice.

Fiore, Francesco Paolo
    2007 *Storia dell'Architettura Italiana: il Quattrocento.* Milan: Electa.

Fitchen, John
    1961 *Construction of Gothic Cathedrals; a Study of Medieval Vault Erection.* Oxford, Clarendon Press,
    1986 *Building Construction Before Mechanization.* Cambridge, MA: MIT Press

Fleming, John [ed.]
    1962 *Robert Adam and His Circle, in Edinburgh & Rome.* London: J. Murray

Fletcher, Banister
    1921 *A History of Architecture on the Comparative Method.* 6th ed. London: B. T. Batsford.

Fontana, Carlo
    1694 [2003] *Il Tempio Vaticano e Sua Origine con gl'Edifitii più Cospicui Antichi, e Moderni fatti Dentro, e Fuori di Esso/It Tempio Vaticano 1694 Carlo Fontana.* Ed. by Giovanni Curcio. Milan: Electa.

Frassineti, P. Mario; Rosa Auletta Marrmuci; Sylvia Righini Ponticelli; and Germano Mulazzani
    1998 *Santa Maria delle Grazie.* Milan" Centrobanca/Gruppo Bancario Centrobanca.

Frommel, Christoph Luitpold
    1994 "The Endless Construction of St. Peter's: Bramante and Raphael." In Millon and Lampugnani 1994: 598-631.
    2007 *The Architecture of the Italian Renaissance.* Trans. by Peter Spring. London: Thames & Hudson.

Frommel, Christoph Luitpold; Stefano Ray; and Manfredo Tafuri
    1984 *Raffaello Architetto.* Milan: Electa.

Galdieri, Eugenio (ed.)
    1972-1984 *Isfahan: Masgid-i Gum'a ...* 3 vols. Roma: Instituto Italiano per il Medio ed Estremo.

Garnier, Charles
    1876-1880 *Nouvel Opèra de Paris.* Paris, Ducher et cie.

Ghiberti, Lorenzo
    c. 1445 "Ghiberti's Autobiography." In Goldscheider 1949: 19-21.

Gibbs, James
    1728 *Book of Architecture Containing Designs of Buildings and Ornaments.* London.

Godfrey, Paul, and David Hemsoll
    1986 "The Pantheon: Temple or Rotunda?" M. Henig and A. King, eds., *Pagan Gods and Shrines of the Roman Empire*, pp. 195-209. Monograph 8. Oxford: Oxford University Committee for Archeology.

Goldscheider, Ludwig
    1949 *Ghiberti*. London: Phaidon Publishers Inc.

Gorski, Gilbert J., and James E. Packer
    2015 *The Roman Forum: a Reconstruction and Architectural Guide*. New York: Cambridge University Press.

Grimm, Herman
    n. d. *Leben Michelangelos*. Wien: Phaidon-Verlag.

Griseri, Andreina, and Giovanni Romano
    1989 *Filippo Juvarra a Torino: Nuovi Progetti per la Città*. Turin: Cassadi Risparmio di Torino.

Graßhoff, Gerd; Michael Heinzelmann; Nikolaos Theocharis; and Markus Wäfler (eds.)
    2009 *The Pantheon in Rome: the Bern Digital Pantheon Project; Plates; Pantheon 2*. Zürich: LIT Verag.

Guadet, J.
    1905 *Éléments et Théorie de l'Architecture; Cours Professé à l'École Nationale et Spéciale des Beaux-arts*. 4 vols. Paris, Librarie de la Construction Moderne.

Günther, Hubertus
    1994 "A History of the Construction of S. Giovanni dei Fiorentini." In Millon and Lampugnani 1994: 550-560.

Gwilt, Joseph
    1903 *Encyclopedia of Architecture: Historical, Theoretical, & Practical*. Rev. by Wyatt Papworth. London: Longmans, Green, and Co.

Hamlin, Talbot
    1944 [1964] *Greek Revival Architecture in America: Being an Account of Important Trends in American Architecture and American Life Prior to the War Between the States*. New York: Dover Publications.
    1955 *Benjamin Henry Latrobe*. New York: Oxford University Press, 1955.

Harvey, John
    1972 *Mediæval Architect*. New York: St. Martin's Press.

Haselberger, Lothar

    1997 "Architectural Likenesses: Models and Plans of Architecture in Classical Antiquity." *JRA* 10: 77-94.

Haselberger, Lothar (ed.)
    1999 *Appearance and Essence; Refinements of Classical Architecture: Curvature. Proceeding of the Second Williams Symposium on Classical Architecture Held at the University of Pennsylvania. Philadelphia, April 2-4, 1993.* Symposium Series 10. Philadelphia: University Museum.

Hemsoll, David
    1989 "Reconstructing the Octagonal Dining Room of Nero's Golden House." *Architectural History: Journal of the Society of Architectural Historians of Great Britain* 32 (1989): 1-17.

Hermanin, Federico
    1927 *La Farnesina.* Bergamo: Istituto Italiano 'Arte Grafiche.

Heydenreich, Ludwig H., and Wolfgang Lotz
    1974 *Architecture in Italy, 1400-1600.* Trans by Mary Hottinger. Pelican History of Art. Harmondsworth: Penguin Books.

Holt, Elizabeth Gilmore (ed.)
    1981 *A Documentary History of Art; volume I: the Middle Ages and the Renaissance.* Rev. ed. Princeton: Princeton University Press.
    1982 *A Documentary History of Art; volume II: Michelangelo and the Mannerists, the Baroque, and the Eighteenth Century.* Rev. ed. Princeton: Princeton University Press.
    1986 *From the Classicists to the Impressionists: Art and Architecture in the 19th Century; volume III of a Documentary History of Art.* New Haven: Yale University Press.

Huppert, Ann C.
    2015 *Becoming an Architect in Renaissance Italy: Art, Science, in the Career of Baldassarre Peruzzi.* New Haven: Yale University Press.

Kähler, Heinz
    1950 *Hadrian und Sein Villa bei Tivoli.* Deutsches Archäologisches Institut. Berlin: Gebr. Mann.

Kalnein, Wend Graf, and Michael Levey
    1972 *Art and Architecture of the Eighteenth Century in France.* Kalnein's text trans. by J. R. Foster. Pelican History of Art. Harmondsworth: Penguin Books.

Kent, Dale
    2000 *Cosimo de' Medici and the Florentine Renaissance: the Patron's Oeuvre.* New Haven: Yale University Press.
    2009 *Friendship, Love, and Trust in Renaissance Florence.* Cambridge, Mass.: Harvard

University Press.

Kent, F. W.
    2004 *Lorenzo de' Medici and the Art of Magnificence.* Baltimore: the Johns Hopkins University Press.

Kent, William Winthrop
    1925 *The Life and Works of Baldassare Peruzzi of Siena.* New York: Architectural Book Publishing Co., Inc.

Kimball, Fiske
    1916 [1968] *Thomas Jefferson, Architect; Original Designs in the Coolidge Collection of the Massachusetts Historical Society, with an Essay and Notes.* Cambridge: Privately printed (reprinted New York: Da Capo Press).
    1922 [1966] *Domestic Architecture of the American Colonies and of the Early Republic.* New York: Dover Publications.

Koch, Ebba
    2006 *The Complete Taj Mahal and the Riverfront Gardens of Agra.* With drawings by Richard André Barraud. New Delhi: Bookwise (India) Pvt. Ltd.

Krafft, J. Ch.
    1801, 1812 [1992] *Plans, Coupes, Élévations de Plus Belles Maisons et des Hôtels Construits à Paris et dans les Environs (tome premier); Recueil d'Architecture Civile Contenant les Plans, Coupes et Élévations des Chateaux, Maisons de Campagne et Habitations Rurales, Jardins Anglais, Temples, Chaumieres Situés aux Environs de Paris et dans les Departments (tome second).* Paris: Auteur, Treutell et Wurtz (reprinted Nordlingen: Alfons Uhl.

Krautheimer, Richard
    1956 Lorenzo Ghiberti. In collaboration with Trude Krautheimer. Princeton: Princeton University Press.
    1979 *Rome, Profile of City, 312-1308.* Princeton: Princeton University Press.
    1985 *The Rome of Alexander VII, 1655-1667.* Princeton: Princeton University Press.

Kuran, Aptullah
    1978 *The Mosque in Early Ottoman Architecture.* Publications of the Center for Middle Eastern Studies, Number 2; William R. Polk, General Editor. Chicago: The University of Chicago Press.

Lafever, Minard.
    1833 [1969] *Modern Builder's Guide.* New York: Dover Publications.

Lancaster, Lynne
    1996 "Concrete Vaulted Construction: Developments in Rome from Nero to

Trajan." 2 vols. Thesis for a Ph. D. in Classical Archaeology, Wolfson College, University of Oxford.
1998 "Building Trajan's Markets. *AJA* 102: 283-308.
2000 "Building Trajan's Market 2: the Construction Process." *AJA* 104: 755-785.
2005 *Concrete Vaulted Construction in Imperial Rome: Innovations in Context.* Cambridge: Cambridge University Press.

Lanciani, Rodolfo
1893-1901 *Forma Vrbis Romae.* Rome: Edizioni Quasar.
1897 *Ruins and Excavations of Ancient Rome.* New York: Houghton Mifflin & Co.
1901 *Destruction of Ancient Rome; a Sketch of the History of the Monuments.* London: Macmillan and Co. Ltd.
1902-1913 *Storia degli Scavi di Roma e Notizie Intorno le Collezioni Romane di Anticità.* 4 vol. Rome: Ermanno Loescher & Co. (Bretschneider e Regenberg).

Latrobe, Benjamin Henry
1977-1994 *Papers of Benjamin Henry Latrobe.* Ed. by Edward C. Carter, II. New Haven: Yale University Press.

Laugier, Marc Antoine
1977 *Essay on Architecture.* Trans by Wolfgang Hermann. Los Angeles: Hennessey & Ingalls.

Ledoux, Claude Nicolas
1847 [1983] *Architecture de C.N. Ledoux: Premier Volume, Contenant des Plans, Élévations, Coupes, Vues Perspectives ... : Collection qui Rassemble Tous les Genres de Bâtiments Employés dans l'Ordresocial.* Princeton, N.J.: Princeton Architectural Press.

Lees-Milne, James
1967 *Saint Peter's: the Story of Saint Peter's Basilica in Rome.* Boston: Little, Brown and Company.

Letarouilly, Paul Marie
1840 [1984] *Édifices de Rome Moderne, ou, Recueil des Palais, Maisons, Églises, Couvents, et Autres Monuments Publics et Particuliers les Plus Remarkables de la Ville de Rome.* Princeton: Princeton Architectural Press. Rev. 2nd ed. 3 v. in 1.
1953 *Basilica of St. Peter/ La Basilique de Saint-Pierre.* London: A. Tiranti.

Licht, Kjeld de Fine
1966 *The Rotunda in Rome: a Study of Hadrian's Pantheon.* Jutland Archaeological Society Publications VIII. Copenhagen.

Loerke, William C.
 1990 "A Rereading of the Interior Elevation of Hadrian's Rotunda." *Journal of the Society of Architectural Historians* 49 (Mar. 1990): 22-43.

Macadam, Alta
 2000 *City Guide: Rome.* 7th ed. London: A. & C. Black

MacDonald, William L.
 1976 *The Pantheon: Design, Meaning, and Progeny.* Cambridge, Mass.: Harvard University Press.
 1982 *Architecture of the Roman Empire, 1: An Introductory Study.* Revised edition. New Haven: Yale University Press.

MacDonald, William L., and John A. Pinto
 1995 *Hadrian's Villa and Its Legacy.* New Haven: Yale University Press.

Magnuson, Torgil
 1958 *Studies in Roman Quattrocento Architecture.* Stockholm: Almqvist & Wiksell.

Mainstone, Rowland J.
 1975 *Developments in Structural Form.* Cambridge, MA: M. I. T. Press.
 1988 *Hagia Sophia: Architecture, Structure, and Liturgy of Justinian's Great Church.* New York: Thames and Hudson.

Major, Thomas
 1768 [1969] *Ruines de Paestum ou de Posidonie dans la Grande Grece.* London: Thomas Major (reprinted, London: Gregg International).

Marder, Tod A.
 1998 *Bernini and the Art of Architecture.* New York: Abbeville.

Marder, Tod A., and Mark Wilson Jones (eds.)
 2015 *The Pantheon from Antiquity to the Present.* New York: Cambridge University Press.

Mariani, Valerio
 1943 *Michelangelo e la Facciata di San Pietro.* Rome: Fratelli Palombi Editori.

McKim, Charles Follen; William R. Mead; and Stanford White
 1914-1915 [1973] *Monograph of the Works of McKim, Mead & White, 1879-1915.* 4 vols. in 1. With an essay by Leland Roth. New York: B. Blom.

Meeks, Carroll L. V.
 1966 *Italian Architecture, 1750-1914.* New Haven: Yale University Press.

Mertens, Dieter
 1984 *Temple von Segesta und die Dorische Tempelbaukunst des Griechischen Westens in Klassischerzeit.* Manz am Rein: P. von Zabern.

1993 *Alte Heratempel in Paestum und die Archaische Baukunst in Unteritalien.* Mainz am Rhein: P. von Zabern.

Michelangelo Buonarroti
    1963 *The Letters of Michelangelo.* 2 vols. Trans. by E. H Ramsden. Stanford: Stanford University Press.
    1967 *The Sonnets of Michelangelo.* Trans. by John Addington Symonds. London: Vision Press, Ltd.

Middleton, J. Henry
    1892 *Remains of Ancient Rome.* 2 vols. London: Adam and Charles Black.

Middleton, Robin, and David Watkin
    1980 *Neoclassical and 19th Century Architecture.* New York: Harry N. Abrams, Inc

Millon, Henry A. (ed.)
    1964 *Key Monuments of the History of Architecture.* Englewood Cliffs: Prentice-Hall.
    1994 "Michelangelo and the Facade of S. Lorenzo in Florence." In Millon and Lampugnani 1994: 565-572.

Millon, Henry A., and Craig Hugh Smyth
    1988 *Michelangelo Architect: the Facade of San Lorenzo and the Drum and Dome of St. Peter's.* Milan: Olivetti.
    1994A "Michelangelo's Apse Vault and Attic of the South Transept." In Millon and Lampugnani 1994: 649-655.
    1994B "The Design of the Drum and Dome of St. Peter's in Rome." In Millon and Lampugnani 1994: 655-657.
    1994C "The Dupérac Group of Drawings in the Metropolitan Museum of Art and Related Sheets in the National Museum in Stockholm." In Millon and Lampugnani 1994: 658-669.
    1994D "The Dosio Group of Drawings in the Uffizi." In Millon and Lampugnani 1994: 670-672.

Millon, Henry A., and Vittorio Magnago Lampugnani (eds.)
    1994 *The Renaissance from Brunelleschi to Michelangelo: the Representation of Architecture.* Milan: Bompiani.

Moore, David
    1995 *The Roman Pantheon: the Triumph of Concrete.* Big Piney, Wyoming: David Moore.

Morassi, Antonio
    1955 *G. B. Tiepolo.* London: Phaidon-Sansoni.

Morisani, Ottavio
    1951 *Michelozzo Architetto.* N. p.: Giulio Einaudi editore.

Mottini, G. Edoardo
    1943 *Storia dell'Arte Italiana.* With revisions on ancient art by Vincenzo Costantini. 18th ed. Verona: A. Mondadori.

Nash, Ernest
    1961 *Pictorial Dictionary of Ancient Rome.* 2 vols. Rome: Deutsches Archaeologisches Institut; London: A. Zwemmer Ltd.

Necipoğlu, Gülru
    2005 *The Age of Sinan: Architectural Culture in the Ottoman Empire.* With architectural drawings and photographs of Sinan's works by Arben N. Arapi and Reha Günay. Princeton: Princeton University Press.

Packer, James E.
    1971 *The Insulae of Imperial Ostia.* Rome: American Academy in Rome.
    1997 *The Forum of Trajan in Rome: a Study of the Monuments.* 3 vols. Berkeley: University of California Press.
    2001 *The Forum of Trajan in Rome: a Study of the Monuments in Brief.* Berkeley: University of Cliforni Press.

Palladio, Andrea, 1508-1580
    1570 *I Qvattro Libri dell'Architettvra, ne' Quali, Dopo un Breue Trattato de' Cinque Ordini, & di Quelli Auertimenti, Che Sono Piu Necessarii nel Fabricare.* Venice: D. de' Franceschi.
    1570 [1997] *Four Books on Architecture.* Trans. by Robert Tavernor and Richard Schofield. Cambridge, Mass.: MIT Press.

Papafava, Francesco (ed.)
    1986 *Guida ai Musei e Alla Città del Vaticano.* Vatican City: Monumenti, Musei e Gallerie Pontificie.

Pasini, Pier Giorgio
    2000 *Il Tempio Malatestiano: Splendore Cortese e Classicismo Umanistico.* Milan: Skira.

Paulin, Edmond
    1890 *Restaurations des Monuments Antique: Thermes de Dioclétien.* Paris: Firmin-Didot.

Pedretti, Carlo
    2007 *Leonardo Architetto.* Milan: Electa Architettura Paperback.

Penrose, F. C.
    1888 [1973] *Investigation of the Principles of Athenian Architecture; or, the*

  Results of a Survey Conducted Chiefly with Reference to the Optical Refinements Exhibited in the Construction of the Ancient Buildings at Athens. Washington: McGrath Pub. Co.

Pierson, William H., Jr.
  1970 *American Buildings and Their Architects: the Colonial and Neoclassical Styles.* Garden City, NY: Doubleday.

Pietrangeli, Carlo
  1985 *I Musei Vaticani: Cinque Secoli di Storia.* Roma: Edizioni Quasar.

Piranesi, Francesco
  1790 *Raccolta de'Tempj Antichi* [Pantheon]. Vol. 2. Rome: Presso l'Autore.

Piranesi, Giovanni Battista
  1748-1753 *Veduta di Roma.*
  1756 *Le Antichita Romane.* 4 vols. Rome: A. Rotilj.
  2000 *Giovanni Battista Piranesi: the Complete Etchings/ Gesamtkatalog der Kupferstiche/ Catalogue Raisonné des Eaux-fortes / Giovanni Battista Piranesi.* Köln: Taschen.
  2011 *Giovanni Battista Piranesi: Catalogo Completo delle Acqueforti/ Catálogo Completo de Grabados/ Catálogo Completo das Ágauas-fortes.* 2 vols. Ed. by Luigi Ficacci. Köln: Taschen.

Placzek, Adolf K. (ed.)
  1982 *Macmillan Encyclopedia of Architects.* 4 vols. London: Collier Macmillan.

Pugin, Augustus Charles; Augustus Welby Northmore Pugin; James Edward Willson, and T. L. Walker
  1850 *Examples of Gothic Architecture Selected from Various Ancient Edifices in England: Consisting of Plans, Elevations, Sections, and Parts at Large...Accompanied by Historical and Descriptive Accounts.* 3 vols. London: H. G. Bohn.

Pugin, Augustus Welby Northmore
  1841 [1969] *True Principles of Pointed or Christian Architecture: Set Forth in Two Lectures Delivered at St. Marie's Oscott.* London: Henry G. Bohn (reprinted, Oxford: St. Barnabas Press, from the 1853 ed.).
  1841 [1969] *Contrasts.* Leicester, Leicester University Press.

Raeder, Joachim
  1983 *Die Statuarische Ausstattung der Villa Hadriana bei Tivoli.* European University Studies 38: Archaeology vol. 4. Frankfurt am Main: Peter Lang.

Reynolds, L. D., and N. G. Wilson

2013 *Scribes and Scholars: a Guilde to the Transmission of Greek and Latin Literature.* Fourth edition. Oxford: Oxford University Press.

Rivoira, G. T.
    1925 *Roman Architecture and Its Principles of Construction Under the Empire with an Appendix on the Evolution of the Dome Up to the XVIIth Century.* Oxford: Oxford University Press.

Robertson, D. S.
    1964 *A Handbook of Greek & Roman Architecture.* 2nd ed. Cambridge: Cambridge University Press.

Sapori, Francesco
    1953 *Architettura in Roma, 1901-1950.* Rome: Angelo Belardetti Editore.

Schiavo, Armando
    1949 *Michelangelo Architetto/ Michelangelo as an Architect.* Rome: Libreria dello Stato.
    1990 *Michelangelo nel Complesso delle Sue Opere.* Rome: Istituto Poligrafico Zecca dello Stato; Liberia dello Stato.

Schinkel, Karl Friedrich, 1781-1841
    1829-1835 *Sammlung Architectonischer Entwürfe von Schinkel Enthaltend Theils Werke Welche Ausgeführt Sind, Theils Gegenstände Deren Ausführung Beabsichtigt Wurde Drei und Zwanzigstes Heft.* Berlin: Duncker und Humblot.
    1989 *Collection of Architectural Designs: Including Designs Which Have Been Executed and Objects Whose Execution Was Intended.* New York: Princeton Architectural Press.

Serlio, Sebastiano
    1996 *Sebastiano Serlio on Architecture: Books I-V of Tutte l'Opere d'Architettura et Prospetiva' by Sebastiano Serlio.* Trans. and annotated by Vaughan Hart and Peter Hicks. New Haven: Yale University Press.

Shearman, John
    1971 *The Vatican Stanze: Functions and Decorations.* London: Oxford University Press.

Sinan
    2006 *Sinan's Autobiographies: Five Sixteenth-Century Texts.* Introductory notes, critical editions, and translations by Howard Crane and Ezra Akin; edited with a preface by Gülru Necipoğlu. Studies and Sources in Islamic Art and Architecture: Supplements to *Muqarnas*, vol. XI. Leiden: Brill.

Sirén, Osvald
    1926 [1976] *Imperial Palaces of Peking: Two Hundred and Seventy-four Plates in*

Collotype After the Photographs of the Author. Twelve Architectural Drawings, and Two Maps with a Short Historical Account. Three parts reprinted in one volume. New York: AMS Press.

Smith, A. H.
1910 *Sculptures of the Parthenon.* London: British Museum.

Spagnesi, Gianfranco (ed.)
1997 *L'Architettura della Basilica di San Pietro: Storia e Costruzione; Atti del Convegno Internazionale di Studi; Roma, Castel S. Angelo, 7-10 Novembre 1995.* Rome: Bonsignori Editore.

Spiers, Phené
1895 "The Pantheon of Rome. M. Chedanne's Delineation and Restoration." *Journal of the Royal Institute of British Architects*, 3rd series, 2, Nov. 1894-Oct. 1895 (1895): 180-182.

Stoddard, Whitney S.
1966 *Monastery and Cathedral in France: Medieval Architecture, Sculpture, Stained Glass, Manuscripts, the Art of the Church Treasuries.* Middletown, CT: Wesleyan University Press.

Stuart, James; and Nicholas Revett
1762, 1787, 1794. *Antiquities of Athens.* London: John Haberkorn (vol. 1) and John Nichols (vols. 2 and 3). Reprinted 1980; New York: Arno Press.

Sullivan, Louis
1924 *Autobiography of an Idea.* New York: Press of the American Institute of Architects.

Summerson, John Newenham
1946 *Georgian London.* New York, C. Scribner's Sons.
1953 *Architecture in Britain, 1530 to 1830.* London: Penguin Books.
1966 *Inigo Jones.* Harmondsworth: Penguin.

Symonds, John Addington
1901 *The Life of Michelangelo Buonarroti; Based on Studies in the Archives of the Buonarroti Family at Florence.* 3rd ed. 2 vols. London: Macmillan and Co., Ltd.

Terenzio, Alberto
1932 "La Restauration du Panthéon de Rome." *Mouseion* 20 (1932): 52-57; pls. 10-11.

Thoenes, Christof
1994 "St. Peter's 1534-46: Projects by Antonio da Sangallo the Younger for Pope Paul

III." In Millon and Lampugnani 1994: 634-648

Traulos, Ioannes N.
    1971 *Pictorial Dictionary of Ancient Athens.* Deutsches Archäologisches Institut Publication. New York: Praeger.

Valtieri, Simonetta
    1984 "Sant'Eligio degli Orefici." In Frommel *et al.* 1984: 143-156.

Van Nice, Robert L.
    1966, 1987 *Santa Sophia in Istanbul: an Architectural Survey* (portfolio issued in two parts). Washington: Dumbarton Oaks Center for Byzantine Studies.

Van Rensselaer, Mrs. Schuyler
    1967 *Henry Hobson Richardson and His Works.* Park Forest, Ill.: Prairie School Press.

Vasari, Giorgio
    1568 [1971] *Life of Michelangelo Buonarroti.* Trans. By George Bull. London: Folio Society.
    1568 [1963] *The Lives of the Painters, Sculptors and Architects.* 4 vols. Trans. by A. B. Hinde; ed. by William Gaunt. London: Dent; Everyman's Library.

Viollet-le-Duc, M. [Eugène-Emmanuel].
    1858 *Dictionnaire Raisonné de l'Architecture Française du XIe au XVIe Siècle.* 10 vols. Paris: B. Bance, Éditéur.

Vitruvius
    c. 25 B. C. *De Architectura.*
    1486 *L. Victrvvii Pollionis ad Cesarem Avgvstvm de Architectvra.* Ed. by Io. [Giovanni] Svlpitivs [Sulpizio da Veroli]. [Rome: G. Herolt].
    1486 [2003] *Vitruvius: Ten Books on Architecture; the Corsini Incunabulum with the Annotations and Autograph Drawings of Giovanni Battita da Sangallo.* Ed. with an essay by Ingrid D. Rowland. Rome: Edizioni dell'Elefante.
    1567 *I Dieci Libri dell'Architettvra.* Trans. with a commentary by Daniel Barbaro. Illustrated by Andrea Palladio. Venice: Francesco de' Franceschi Senese & Giuanni Chrieger Alemano Compagni.
    1914 *Vitruvius: the Ten Books on Architecture.* Tran. By Morris Hicky Morgan. Illustrations by Herbert Langford Warren. Cambridge, Mass.: Harvard University Press (reprinted 1960: New York: Dover Publications, Inc.
    1999 *Ten Books of Architecture.* Trans. by Ingrid D. Rowland; commentary and illustrations by Thomas Noble Howe ; with additional material by Ingrid D. Rowland and Michael J. Dewar. New York: Cambridge University Press, 1999.

Volta, Valentino (ed.)

2008 *Rotonde d'Italia: Analisi Tipologica della Pianta Centrale.* Milan: Jaca Book.

Waddell, Gene
1987A "The First Monticello," *Journal of the Society of Architectural Historians*, 46-1 (Mar. 1987): 5-29.
1987B "Latrobe and the Beginning of Professionalism in American Architecture," *Design Book Review*, Issue 11 (winter 1987): 30-34.
1991 "The Greek Pentathlon." *Greek Vases in the J. Paul Getty Museum* 5: 99-106.
2002 "The Principal Design Methods for Greek Doric Temples and Their Modification for the Parthenon" *Architectural History: Journal of the Society of Architectural Historians of Great Britain*, 45: 1-31.
2003 *Charleston Architecture, 1670-1860.* Charleston: Wyrick and Co.
2008 *Creating the Pantheon: Design, Materials, and Construction.* Bibliotheca Archaeologica, 42. Rome: "L'ERMA" di Bretschneider.
2015 "Sources and Parallels for the Design and Construction of the Pantheon." Marder and Wilson Jones 2015: 132-159.

Waddy, Patricia
1990 *Seventeenth-century Roman Palaces: Use and the Art of the Plan.* New York: Architectural History Foundation.

Wallace, William E.
1994 *Michelangelo at San Lorenzo: the Genius as Entrepreneur.* Cambridge: Cambridge University Press.

Warren, Herbert Langford
1919 *The Foundations of Classic Architecture.* New York: Macmillan.

White, John
1993 *Art and Architecture in Italy, 1250-1400.* 3rd ed. Pelican History of At. New Haven: Yale University Press.

Wilson Jones, Mark
1988 "Palazzo Massimo and Baldassare Peruzzi's Approach to Architectural Design." *Architectural History* 31: 59-106.
2000 *Principles of Roman Architecture.* New Haven: Yale University Press.
2014 *Origins of Classical Architecture: Temples, Orders and Gifts to the Gods in Ancient Greece.* New Haven: Yale University Press.

Winckelmann, Johann Joachim
1969 *History of Ancient Art* [*Geschichte der Kunst des Altertums*]. 4 vols. in 2. New York: Ungar Publishing Co.

Wittkower, Rudolf
1964 *La Cupola di San Pietro di Michelangelo; Riesame Critico delle*

Testimonianze Contemporanee. Florence: Sansoni Editore.

Wright, Frank Lloyd
    1910 [1983] *Drawings and Plans of Frank Lloyd Wright: the Early Period (1893-1909)* [Wasmuth portfolio]. New York: Dover Publications.
    1911 [1982] *Early Work of Frank Lloyd Wright; the "Ausgeführte Bauten" of 1911*. New York: Dover Publications
    1977 *An Autobiography*. New York: Horizon Press.

Wurm, Heinrich
    1984 *Baldassarre Peruzzi Architekturzeichnungen*. Tübingen: Verlag Ernst Wasmuth.

Yegül, Fikret
    1992 *Baths and Bathing in Classical Antiquity*. New York: the Architectural History Foundation; Cambridge, Mass.: MIT Press.

Zorzi, Giangiorgio
    1959 *Disegni delle Antichità di Andrea Palladio*. Venice: N. Pozza.
    1965 *Opere Pubbliche i Palazzi Privati di Andrea Palladio*. [Venice]: N. Pozza.
    1967 *Chiese e i Ponti di Andrea Palladio*. [Venice]: N. Pozza.
    1969 *Ville e i Teatri di Andrea Palladio*. [Venice]: N. Pozza.

Zuccari, Alessandro, and Stefania Macioce (eds.)
    2001 *Innocenzo X Pamphilj: Arte e Potere a Roma nell'Età Barocca*. 2nd ed. Rome: Logart Press.

Topical Index

Alberti, Leone Battista (architect; Leonbattista): 77-104
    Choir of St. Peter's Basilica (c. 1451-1455; attributed), 104
    Documented churches, 86-90
        Sant'Andrea, Mantua (1465-1494), 90-91
        Santissima Annunziata, Florence (1470-1473), 92-93
        San Francisco, Rimini (1450-1461),
        San |Sebastiano, Mantua (1470-1472),
        Santa Maria Novella, Florence (dated 1470), 90
    Development of the unaisled church, 102
    On Painting, 82-86;
    Ten Books of Architecture, 77-82; architectural writings compared to Vitruvius, Serlio,
        and Palladio, 204
    Undocumented buildings in Rome attributed to Alberti, 95-104;
    Writings, 77-90;
Ancients; equaling the ancients, 38
Appendices, 451
Architectural problems, 29-30
Arnolfo di Lapo (Arnolfo di Cambio; architect), 43; model of the Florentine Duomo depicted, 46
Artists, self-taught, 36-37
Athens, Rome, and Florence compared, 369-370
Attributions based on classical details, 146
Basilica, Vicenza (1546-1549), 239
Bramante, Donato (architect):
    Apprentices, (from 1514-1546), 391
    Belvedere Courtyard, Rome (begun 1505), 257-261
    Cancelleria, Rome (1486-1498), 141-143, 146-147
    Designs for St. Peter's (from 1505-1514), 376;
    Early life, 242-249
    Early work in Rome, 250-263
    Santa Maria della Consolazione, Todi (begun c. 1508; attributed), 264
    Santa Maria della Grazia, Milan, 243-244, 248
    Santa Maria della Pace, Rome; courtyard (1500-1504), 251-254
    Santa Maria sopra San Spirito, Milan, 245, 248
Brunelleschi, Filippo de ser (architect), 46-61
    Dome of the Duomo, Florence (1420-1436), 46-53
    Foundling Hospital, Florence, 57
    Pazzi Chapel, Florence (1442-1461; at Santa Croce), 59
    San Spirito, Florence (begun 1432), 60
    Studies of ancient Roman architecture, 47-48;
Buonarroti: see Michelangelo

Capitol, Rome (1537-1654), 336
Caprarola, Italy, 519
Catholic Church: censorship, 473; see also, Churches
Chronologies: Chronological List of Principal Buildings, (Appendix V), ??; Outline for Italian
 Architecture of the 16th and 17th Centuries, (Appendix I), 451

Churches: Development of the Unaisled Church,102
 Church of the Osservanza, Siena, 140
 Duomo, Florence, 54
 Florence's Cathedrals, 39
 Il Redentore, Venice (1577-1592), 234
 Old St. Peter's Basilica, Rome, 104; choir, 103-104
 Pazzi Chapel, Florence (1442-1461; at Santa Croce), 59
 Saint Peter's Basilica (see also, Old St. Peter's Basilica):
  Benediction Loggia, 98
  Bramante: intended dome, 389;
  Michelangelo: designs for St. Peter's (from 1547-1564), 403-449; plans, 406-409;
   dome, 410-423; intentions, 424-426; cupolas for St. Peter's, 435-436;
   designs for the front, 437-442; attic story, 443-446; summary on the
   design of St. Peter's, 447-449
  Peruzzi, Baldassare: designs for St. Peter's (from 1520-1527), 398;
  Raphael of Urbino: designs for St. Peter's (from 1514-1520), 393;
  Sangallo, Antonio the Younger: designs for St. Peter's (from 1520-1546), 400;
  Stages of construction for St. Peter's (from c. 1532-c. 1569), 383;
  Summary on the design of St. Peter's, 447-449
 San Francesco, Rimini (1450-1461), 87-88
 San Giorgio Maggiore, Venice (1560-c. 1610), 230;
 San Giovanni de' Fiorentini, Rome (1550-1559), 427-434
 San Lorenzo, Florence: 54-56; Brunelleschi's designs for (1420-1426), 54; designs for
  the front (1517-1520), 292; Old Sacristy, 56; Medici Chapel (1522-1534), 307
 San Sebastiano, Mantua (1470-1472), 88-89
 San Spirito, Florence (begun 1432), 60
 Sant'Andrea, Mantua (1465-1494), 90-91
 Sant'Eligio degli Orefici, Rome, 397
 Santissima Annunziata, Florence (1470-1473), 992-93
 Santa Maria del Fiore, Florence, 54
 Santa Maria del Popolo, 98-99; Chigi Chapel, 396
 Santa Maria della Carceri, Prato (begun 1485), 174-175
 Santa Maria della Consolazione, Todi (begun c. 1508), 264-265
 Santa Maria della Grazia, Milan, 243-244, 248
 Santa Maria della Pace, Rome; courtyard (1500-1504), 251-254
 Santa Maria Novella, Florence (dated 1470), 90
 Santa Maria sopra San Spirito, Milan, 245, 248
 Tempietto, Rome (c. 1502-c. 1506; at San Pietro in Montorio), 241, 255-256

Classic defined, 7

Conclusion, 449
Della Francesca, Piero, 138
Della Robbia family
- Andrea della Robbia: sculpture for the Foundling Hospital, Florence, 57-58
- Luca della Robbia: sculpture for the Pazzi Chapel, Florence, 59

Donatello (Donato):
- accompanied Brunelleschi to Rome, 47;
- rondels for the Palazzo Medici, 113;
- sculpture for the Old Sacristy of San Lorenzo, Florence, 56;
- statue of David, 126

Early Renaissance architecture, 10
Elements, design: classical design elements used as a basis for attributions, 146
Finale di Aguglaro, Italy, 519
Florence: why the Renaissance began in Florence rather than elsewhere, 30-39; Florence's cathedrals, 39-53; Baptistery, 39-42; Duomo, 43-53; Florence compared to Athens and Rome, 369-370; major buildings listed, 519
Frescoes:
- Sistine Chapel Ceiling (1508-1512), 278

Gambarare, Italy, 519
Ghiberti, Lorenzo, 62-76; Gates of Paradise, 10, 62-71; possible design for the dome of the Florentine Duomo, 70.
Ghirlandaio, Domenico: Michelangelo apprenticed to, 266
Giotto, 19
Glossary (Appendix, VII), ??
Gozzoli, Benozzi, 109-111
Greek Classics, 500-515
Heemskerck, Marten van: views of St. Peter's under construction, 382-386
Huts, primitive, depicted by Ghiberti 69
Lapo family
- Arnolfo di Lapo (Arnolfo di Cambio, architect), 43
- Jacopo Lapo(architect), 43

Latin Classics, 500-515
Latin Literature and the Latin Church: the Survival of Knowledge During the Medieval Period (Appendix III), 473
Laurana, Luciano, 134

Libraries: Renaissance, 114
- Laurentian Library, Florence (1524-1534), 323
- Library of San Marco, Florence, 114-115
- Library of San Marco, Venice, 190

Locations of principal buildings, (Appendix VI), 519
Mantua, Italy, 520
Manutius, Aldus; Greek and Latin Classics published (Appendix IV), 500-515
Martini, Francesco di Giorgio (architect), 134-140
Medici family

    Cosimo de' Medici: Patronage, 116-126; book owned, 125-126
    Giovanni de' Medici (Leo X), 334-335
    Guilio de' Medici (Clement VII), 334-335
    Lorenzo de' Medici: villas, 164-175
Michelangelo Buonarroti (architect): 266-353, 371-448
    Capitol, Rome (1537-1654), 336-344
    Laurentian Library, Florence (1524-1534), 323-333
    Medici Chapel, Florence (1522-1534), 307-322
    Palazzo Farnese additions, 155-156, 160, 162-163
    Patronage of Leo X and Clement VII, 334-335
    Saint Peter's Basilica (from 1547-1564), 403; plans, 406-409; dome, 410-423; intentions, 424-426; cupolas for St. Peter's, 435-436; designs for the front, 437-442; attic story, 443-446; summary on the design of St. Peter's, 447-449
    San Giovanni de' Fiorentini, Rome (1550-1559), 427-434
    San Lorenzo, Florence (designs for the front; 1517-1520), 292-303
    Sistine Chapel Ceiling, Rome (1508-1512), 278-291
    Study of ancient Roman architecture, 303-306
    Tomb of Julius II, Rome (1505-1545), 268-277
    Working methods, 345-353
Michelozzi, Michelozzo (architect): 112 (see also Palazzo Medici and library of San Marco)
Milan, Italy, 520
Models:
    Duomo, Florence: wooden models of the dome by Brunelleschi, 53; model of the Duomo by Arnolfo depicted in a fresco, 46
    San Lorenzo, Florence: wooden model by Michelangelo, ??

Monasteries:
    Carità, Venice (begun c 1561), 227
    San Marco, Florence, 115, 122
    Santa Maria della Pace, Rome; courtyard (1500-c. 1504), 251

Montagnana, Italy, 520
Montefeltro, Federico da, 133-139

Monuments: Tempietto, Rome (c. 1502-c. 1506), 255; see also, tombs and cenotaphs

Naples: why the Renaissance did not begin in Naples, 32
Niccolini, Niccolò: public library created, 123-124
Orphanage: Foundling Hospital, Florence, 57

Palaces:
    Belvedere, Vatican (begun 1505), 257-263
    Cancelleria, Rome (1486-1498), 141-143, 146-147
    Ducal Palace, Urbino (1465-1482), 133-139
    Palazzo Caprini (House of Raphael), Rome (begun 1509), 148-149
    Palazzo Chiericati, Vicenza (1550), 226

Palazzo del Te, Mantua, 225
Palazzo Farnese, Rome (1530-1589), 155
Palazzo Massimo, Rome (1532-c. 1536), 151;
Palazzo Medici, Florence (1445-1460), 105, 108-113
Palazzo Pandolfini, Florence (c. 1518), 159
Palazzo Pitti, Florence (begun 1458), 129-131
Palazzo Porto, Vicenza (1547-1552), 219-221
Palazzo Rucellai, Florence (1446-1451), 132;
Palazzo Strozzi, Florence (1489-1538), 127-128
Palazzo Thiene, Vicenza (1542-1546), 224-225
Palazzo Valmarana (1565), 222-223
Palazzo Venezia, Rome (1455-1471), 1442-147
Vatican Palace, 99-101, 257-263, 395

Palaces and villas, 105; summary, 192-196
Palladio, Andrea (architect):
    Four Books on Architecture (1570), 203; contents compared to Vitruvius, Alberti, and Serlio, 204
    Churches and related buildings, 227;
        Carità, Venice (begun c 1561), 227-229
        San Giorgio Maggiore, Venice (1560-c. 1610), 230-233
        Il Redentore, Venice (1577-1592), 234-238
    Other building types, 29
        Basilica, Vicenza (1546-1549), 239
        Teatro Olympico, Vicenza (1580), 240
    Palaces, 219;
        Palazzo Porto, Vicenza (1547-1552), 200, 219-221
        Palazzo Valmarana (1565), 222-223
        Palazzo Thiene, Vicenza (1542-1546), 224-225
        Palazzo Chiericati, Vicenza (1550), 226
    Villas, 205
        Villa Barbaro, Masser, 218
        Villa Foscari, Gambarare (1558-1561), 205-209
        Villa Rotunda, Vicenza (1566-1567), 197, 210-211
        Villa Pisani, Montagnana (1552-1554), 212-213
        Villa Cornaro, Piombino Dese (1552-1554), 214-215
        Villa Saraceno, Finale di Agugliaro (1545), 216-217
Patronage: 38;
    Cosimo de' Medici, 116;
    Leo X de' Medici and Clement VII de' Medici, 334
Peruzzi, Baldassare (architect):
    Designs for St. Peter's (from 1520-1527), 398
    Palazzo Massimo (1532-c. 1536), 151-154
    Villa Farnesina (Chigi; 1505-1511), 176
Piombino Dese, Italy, 520
Popes of the 16th and 17th centuries, 450-451

Problems, architectural, 29-30
Raphael of Urbino (architect):
    Chigi Chapel in Santa Maria del Popolo, Rome, 396
    Designs for St. Peter's (from 1514-1520), 393
    Frescoes in the Vatican Palace, 395
    Palazzo Pandolfini, Florence (c. 1518), 159
    Sant'Eligio degli Orefici, Rome, 397
    Villa Madama, Rome (begun 1518), 181-184
Renaissance:
    Art history, 12;
    Design principles, 23;
    Secular, 353
Renaissance men, 15
Rimini, Italy, 520
Romano, Giulio (architect): Palazzo del Te, 225
Rome, Italy; buildings listed, 520
Rome, Athens, and Florence compared, 369-370
Sangallo family (Giamberti)
    Antonio da Sangallo the Younger (architect):
        Designs for St. Peter's (from 1520-1546), 400.
        Palazzo Farnese, 155-161
    Giuliano da San Gallo (architect)
        Medici Villa, Poggio a Caiano, 164
        Plan for St. Peter's, 381
        Santa Maria delle Carceri, Prato (begun 1485), 174-175
Sansovino, Jacopo (architect), 190
    Library of St. Mark's, Venice (1537), 191
    Palazzo Corner, Venice (1532), 191
    Villa Garzoni; near Venice (c. 1537), 190
Secular Renaissance, 353
Serlio, Sebastiano (architect): writings on architecture compared to books by Vitruvius, Alberti, and Palladio, 202-204
Sistine Chapel Ceiling (1508-1512), 278
Tempietto, Rome, 241, 255-256

Theatres: Teatro Olympico (1580), 240

Todi, Italy, 521

Tombs and cenotaphs: Tomb of Julius II (1505-1545), 268

Transmission of Classic texts, 473-515
Urbino, Italy, 521
Vasari, Giorgio (architect):
    Prefaces for the *Lives* (Appendix II), 453-472;
    Renaissance design principles, 23-29

Vaulting: Renaissance elliptical vaults, 137
Venice, Italy: why the Renaissance did not begin in Venice, 31-32; buildings listed, 521
Vicenza, Italy, 521
Vignola, Jacomo Barozzi da (architect)
    Palazzo Farnese, Caprarola (begun 1558), 187
    Villa Giulia, Rome (1551-1555), 188-189

Villas:
    Lorenzo de' Medici's Villas, 164;
    Palazzo Farnese, Caprarola (begun 1558), 187
    Villa Barbaro, Masser (218)
    Villa Cornaro, Piombino Dese (1552-1554), 214-215
    Villa d'Este, Tivoli (1549-1572), 185-186
    Villa Farnesina (Chigi), Rome (1505-1511), 176-180
    Villa Foscari, Gambarare (1558-1561), 205-209
    Villa Garzoni; near Venice (c. 1537), 190
    Villa Giulia, Rome (1551-1555), 188-189
    Villa Madama, Rome (begun 1518), 181-184
    Villa Medici, Poggio a Caiano (1486-1492), 164-165, 171-174
    Villa Pisani, Montagnana (1552-1554), 212-213
    Villa Rotunda, Vicenza (1566-1567), 210-211
    Villa Saraceno, Finale di Agugliaro (1545), 216-217
Villas and palaces, 105; summary, 192
Vitruvius (architect): principal source for Palladio, 198; writings compared with Alberti, Serlio, and Palladio, 204

Made in the USA
Monee, IL
10 June 2021